IN PRAISE OF LOVE

IN PRAISE OF LOVE

An Introduction to the Love-Poetry of the Renaissance

Maurice Valency

OCTAGON BOOKS

A DIVISION OF FARRAR, STRAUS AND GIROUX

New York 1975

Reprinted 1975
by special arrangement with Maurice Valency

OCTAGON BOOKS
A DIVISION OF FARRAR, STRAUS & GIROUX, INC.
19 Union Square West
New York, N.Y. 10003

Library of Congress Cataloging in Publication Data

Valency, Maurice Jacques, 1903-
In praise of love.

Reprint of the ed. published by Macmillan, New York.
Bibliography: p.
Includes index.
1. Love poetry—History and criticism. 2. Romance poetry—History and criticism. I. Title.

[PN810.L65V3 1975] 809.1 75-22423
ISBN 0-374-98067-5

Manufactured by Braun-Brumfield, Inc.
Ann Arbor, Michigan
Printed in the United States of America

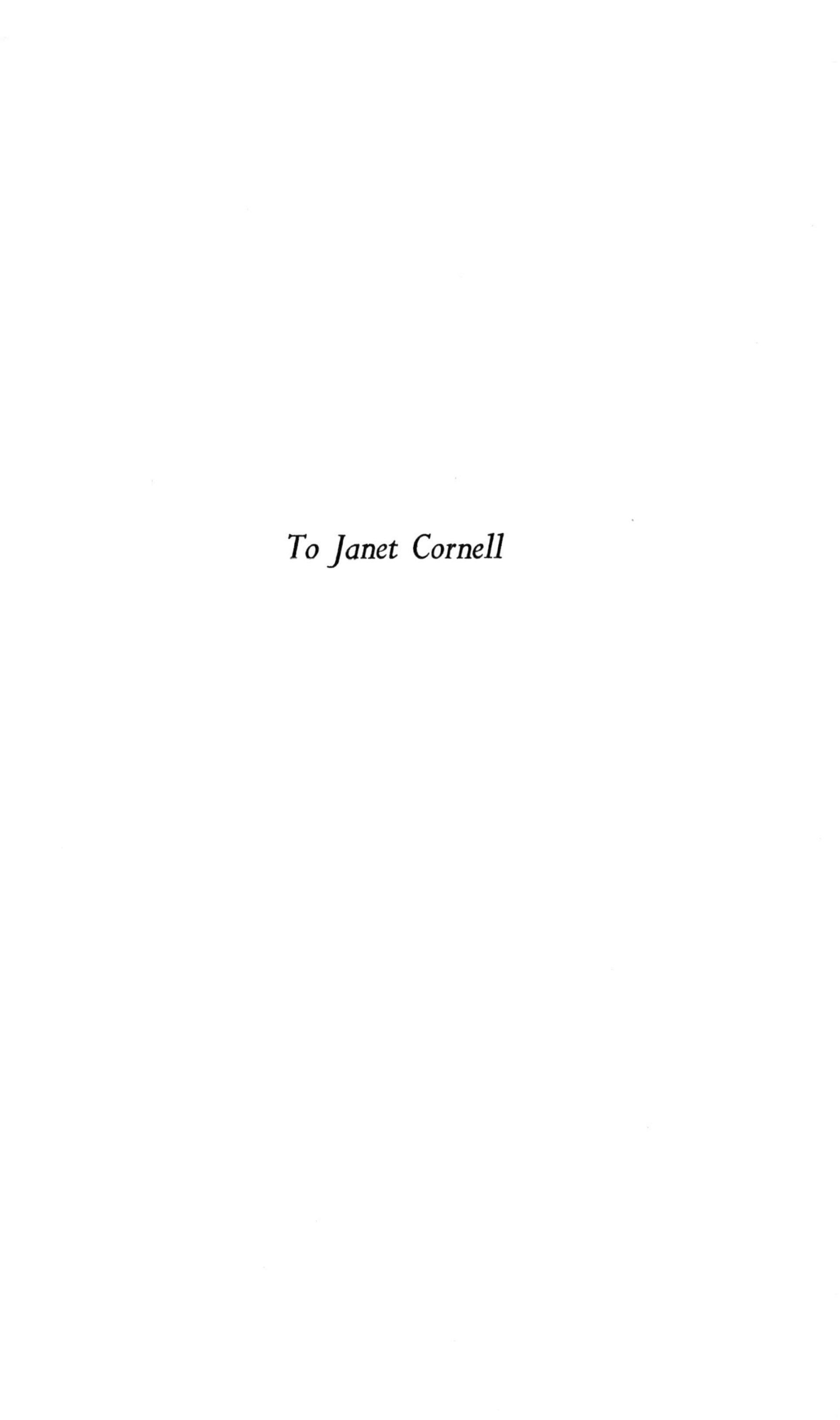

To Janet Cornell

PREFACE

I believe that the purpose of this essay will be apparent from the title and that it is necessary in this place to trouble the reader only with a word regarding its scope and method. It would doubtless be logical to carry a study of the development of the love-lyric in an unbroken line from the troubadours through the lyricists of the Italian *cinquecento* as far as Marino, through the French lyricists to Desportes, the English poets to Spenser, Shakespeare, and Donne, and the Spanish to Góngora. But there could obviously be no question of doing anything of this sort in a single volume, and for my purposes it seemed best to limit the discussion to the formative stages of the lyric tradition. I have accordingly stopped with Dante, considering that after Dante there is nothing that can really be called new, and that whoever understands Dante will have little trouble in understanding the lyric poets who came after him. A good part of this book is therefore concerned with the tradition which culminates in the *Vita Nuova*, that is, with the troubadours and their immediate successors in Italy.

In attempting to rationalize what is puzzling in this body of song—and there is much in it that remains puzzling—I have not hesitated to make some modest use of modern psychological methods in literary criticism. I am keenly aware of the dangers involved in the haphazard use of such techniques in literary studies, but even more aware of the danger of not using them at all. Some of the conclusions of psychology are doubtless still uncertain, yet not so uncertain as the conclusions of "common sense." In any case, these methods, in the hands of those who can control them, make it possible to comprehend in some measure what was formerly completely incomprehensible, and this must be their justification.

I have tried to bring to this study, as far as is possible, a fresh mind, and therefore I have concerned the reader chiefly with primary materials. Some of the notions that occurred to me in the course of my reading seemed to me original, at the time. But I have long since abandoned any pretense to originality. Most of the good things have been said before, and I am increasingly conscious of the heavy debt I owe to the many gifted scholars who have been over the ground since the time of Raynouard, Diez, and Fauriel. It would serve no purpose in a work of general nature to express in detail my obligations to the many sources from which, wittingly and unwittingly, I have drawn facts and ideas. Some of my obligations I have indicated in the text, but, I fear, not all. I must therefore take this opportunity of expressing my deep sense of gratitude to those from whom I learned without knowing that I was learning and to those I have followed without knowing that I was being led.

Because much of the source material of this subject is difficult to come by, I have tried to cite as frequently as possible from editions and anthologies which are in print or else readily available. It is safe to assume that a good many of those to whose interest a work of this sort may recommend itself will be able to read French and Italian without undue strain, but it would be too much to imagine that any considerable number of readers can cope with Provençal. I have therefore translated everything, or nearly everything, into English, and I have not scrupled to include explanations of a very elementary sort where it seemed that the matter might be unfamiliar to the non-specialist, whose needs I had in mind, most of all, in putting these chapters together.

In the nature of things, it is all but impossible to reproduce both the meaning and the form of Provençal poetry in English verse. I have therefore followed the usual practice of translating literally, or almost literally, into prose. This results, of course, in a complete betrayal of the original from the standpoint of those qualities which meant most to the troubadour. It is unfortunate, but it cannot be helped, and I can only solicit the reader's forgiveness. It may be that the infelicities of this sort of translation will drive him, in his exasperation, to the original. In that case, one purpose of this book, at least, will have been achieved, and by no means the least.

It remains only to write a word of thanks to my friends and colleagues, whose never-failing assistance and encouragement have contributed substantially to the pleasure I have had in writing this book. I am especially indebted to Dr. William Nelson, to Dr. Gustave Reese, and to Dr. Toby Lelyveld, who read the manuscript and made interesting suggestions; to Dr. Mark Van Doren; to Mr. Saxe Commins, who suggested the present title; to Dr. Edmund Bergler, whose brilliant mind has been a source of constant stimulation; to Miss Constance M. Winchell and Mr. John N. Waddell of the Columbia University Libraries, whose generous and expert assistance saved me much travail; finally, to Mr. Emile Capouya, whose kindness above and beyond the call of duty has greatly lightened the process of seeing this volume through the press. It was my teacher, the late Jefferson B. Fletcher, who first set me to wondering about the questions I have endeavored to treat in the following pages. That was many years ago, but it is impossible for me to forget the debt I owe him and I most gratefully acknowledge it.

M. J. V.

CONTENTS

LOVE

AND THE POETRY OF LOVE

To begin an essay on the poetry of love with the assertion that love was not an invention of the eleventh century, or perhaps the twelfth, might well serve as an amusing example of scholarly self-absorption. But for well over a hundred years the idea has gained ground that the period which contributed to our domestic well-being such essential items as the wheelbarrow, the candle, and the living-room chimney crowned its endeavors by the invention also of love. "*L'amour?*" says Charles Seignobos, "*une invention du douzième siècle.*" Mr. C. S. Lewis amplifies this view in the introductory chapter of his masterful survey of the medieval allegory:

> French poets in the eleventh century discovered or invented or were the first to express that romantic species of passion which English poets were still writing about in the nineteenth.[1]

Formulations of this sort are perhaps unduly stimulating. What is meant is simply that the system of love-poetry developed by the troubadours of the twelfth century differs in certain important aspects from those amatory patterns which we find reflected in the literature of antiquity. Unquestionably this is true. But the salt of the expression is in the implication that what the troubadours expressed represents, not merely a new literary fashion, but a psychic posture which had not before existed in the history of our culture. If this were true, we should indeed have to explain a psychological phenomenon of the first magnitude, something which would have "left no corner of our ethics, our imagination, or our daily life untouched," a revolution compared with which "the Renaissance is merely a ripple on the surface of literature." [2]

Apart from the troubadour poetry, there is, however, nothing to indicate that such a revolution took place. We look in vain to the economic, political, or social life of the Middle Ages for a sign that anything of unusual character was going on with regard to the relations of men and women during the period when the amatory poetry of the troubadours was taking shape. What we do become aware of in the history of the period 1050–1300 is the constant play of contradiction and paradox, the result of man's never-ending ambivalence with respect to the other sex. But of this ambivalence, the classic writings also make us abundantly aware.

The emergence of a body of poetry based on the worship of women should imply the existence in some degree of a matriarchal way of life. But the fact is, history has preserved no definite record of a time when women had other than a secondary status in our culture. In the twelfth century the normal assumption would be that woman was a misbegotten male, an inferior form of humanity, a mill-second, so to speak, in the biological process. This view Thomas Aquinas correctly referred to Aristotle. In St. Thomas' opinion also, woman—as regards the individual nature—is the result of defective procreation, since the "active power in the male seed tends to the production of a perfect likeness according to the masculine sex." Nevertheless, St. Thomas felt that since God created woman she must serve some necessary function in the natural order, and therefore, however imperfect she might be, she could not, with reason, be called "misbegotten" from the point of view of universal nature.[3]

Nothing is more familiar to the student of Renaissance literature than the swelling chorus of invective directed against women in the course of the age-long *querelle des femmes*. Three centuries after the time of St. Thomas, we find the jurist Tiraqueau holding forth in precisely the same vein as the Angelic Doctor, though with different authority: "Many believe that women are deprived of reason, for the divine Plato seems to hesitate whether he should place women in the category of reasonable creatures or of brutes." [4] Almost all the humanist writers of the Middle Ages, from Egidio Colonna to Gerson, took this position. Petrarch who attributed, both in Italian verse and in Latin prose, all his glory and all his wisdom to Laura, simultaneously and apparently with no sense of self-contradiction professed himself a fervent woman-hater, quite in the style of Tertullian or St. Jerome:

> Foemina . . . verus est diabolus, hostis pacis, fons impatientiae, materia jurgorum, quâ caruisse tranquillitas certa est.[5]

It would astonish us to find such dedicated lovers as Petrarch going on in this manner, were it not the most common thing in the world for medieval writers to exhibit contradictory views with regard to women. This strange dualism, observable everywhere, is amply illustrated in the twelfth century treatise on love of Andreas Capellanus, and even more fully in the thirteenth century *Breviari d'Amor* of the friar Matfré Ermengaud, whose absorbing interest in matters of love appears to have been matched only by his detestation of the sex. As for the Renaissance humanists, the only observable variation in their attitude toward women is one of style. The elegant classicist Aeneas Sylvius writes very much in Petrarch's vein:

> Quid est, oro, mulier nisi juventatis expilatrix, virorum rapina, senum mors, patrimonii devoratrix, honoris pernicies, pabulum diaboli, janua mortis, inferni supplementum? [6]

But the learned Alberti, first of the "universal men" of the Renaissance, observed shortly and without any recourse to rhetoric: "They are all crazy and full of fleas, the women." [7]

Such was the view which recommended itself generally to the Renaissance male, and behind this attitude were organized all the resources of medieval and classical learning. We begin, therefore, with an interesting paradox. The idea that women are nuisances and half-wits established itself most firmly in our cultural pattern during the very years in which there flowered most abundantly the poetry of woman-worship.

But while women in our culture seem at all times to have labored under the disadvantage of a bad, and even the worst possible, press, there has never been a time when we do not find them playing dominant roles in the events of the day. It is difficult indeed to generalize from the mass of conflicting evidence which has come down to us from the Middle Ages. What we know is that from the tenth to the fourteenth centuries there were women who held land, made war, signed treaties, dubbed knights, ruled principalities, and, in short, exercised all the rights of lordship quite as if they had been men, while at the same time and in the same countries other women of the same class were oppressed, maltreated, beaten, robbed, cast off, cloistered against their will, and denied even the most elementary human rights. We have a host of instances of women who were men for the time being, *hommes d'occasion.* Thus at the beginning of the twelfth century, Bertrand de Toulouse left his mother to rule his lands during his absence in the Holy Land. The mother of St. Louis ruled France during her son's minority. The Countess Ermengarde de Narbonne ruled her personal estates during the lifetime of both her husbands, from 1143 to 1192. In Tuscany, from a legal point of view the most rigorous of anti-feminist countries, the Countess Matilda not only ruled in her own right, but went so far as to expel her husband, Guelf, from her dominions on the ground that he was not man enough for her. The very gallant Eleanor of Aquitaine accompanied her husband Louis VII of France on the crusade, and, we are told, betrayed him often and with impunity, but the same lady was very sternly used by her second husband, Henry II of England. Doubtless the question of personality, then as always, was quite as important as the question of sex.

The more examples one adduces, the more confused one is likely to become as to the status of women in the Middle Ages. There is, of course, something organic about this confusion; it has the feel of life in it. But it does not help us to account for the seemingly spontaneous emergence in the twelfth century of a poetic attitude which exalted the lady far above her lover and based all his hope of earthly happiness upon her beauty and her wisdom. With regard to the social background, all that can be stated with confidence is that we know of nothing in the objective relationships of men and women in the Middle Ages which might conceivably motivate the strain of love-poetry which the troubadours developed in the Midi of France.

The types of vernacular poetry which were cultivated in the twelfth century in the regions north and south of the Loire were quite different, and very dissimilar also were the amatory patterns displayed in these genres; yet nothing definite can be said as to the cultural differences between these regions. But even if there were differences sufficient to account for the fundamental disparity of these poetic types—the pagan laxity of the south, the more military character of the north, the superior Roman culture of Provence or its closer proximity to Arab Spain—these differences would hardly help us to understand how it was that the woman-worship of the Midi spread like wildfire throughout the north once the northern courtiers became aware of it. If the southern poets invented love somewhere about the year 1100, the northerners certainly displayed exceptional aptitude once its possibilities were brought to their attention. Within fifty years of the emergence of love in Poitou, we find the northern *trouvères* practicing the love-song like masters, and by 1170 the poetry of love was already firmly established in Alsace, in Switzerland, in Germany, in Austria, Italy and Spain—in fact, everywhere in the Western world where a courtly art could conceivably take root.

The romantic passion which these poets popularized was not, properly speaking, a passion at all. It was, from the beginning, a sort of cult, a creed which based the well-being of man upon the love of woman and exalted this love accordingly. Beyond doubt, the rationalizations upon which this system was founded bear witness to the existence of psychic undercurrents of such power as would have resulted, had they been new, in a social upheaval of the first magnitude. Of that, or of anything of the sort, there is absolutely no trace. Indeed, the nature of these psychic forces is such that it is obviously impossible to assign any historical period to their resurgence. It seems therefore beside the point to trace these attitudes to Mozarabic Spain, although doubtless they existed there. They must have existed everywhere and always, a basic attribute of human nature. Even if we had no evidence that what we call romantic love existed in what we call classical culture, we should have to postulate its existence in that culture on the most fundamental psychological grounds.

But it is perfectly evident that the entire psychic and literary apparatus of romantic love was in existence among the ancients. Phaedrus in the *Symposium* furnishes a complete blueprint for the romantic passion just about as the troubadours conceived it—but the love he speaks of is homosexual. In the same dialogue Socrates elaborates the type of abstract longing which has perfection for its object; but it is obviously not with a woman that Socrates expects us to begin the spiritual ascent through love. For Plato the object of love is beauty. The most beautiful form in nature, its masterpiece, is the human form in its perfection, and that, in fifth century Athens, would be achieved only in the male. Since the aspiration of the lover of beauty is normally toward what is perfect, as we are told in *Phaedrus*, the natural choice leads us upward in the scale of forms. The love of an inferior form would then be unnatural and perverse, a sickness of the soul. It is therefore normal and healthy for women to love men, but not for men to love women. Physical union with women is, of course, unavoidable, and it need not be disagreeable; indeed, it may be the source of considerable pleasure. But love of woman can result only in pain and misfortune. For the ancients, in general, love of this sort was a disaster.

Behind these commonplaces, the facts are simple and clear. Greek culture in classical times was strongly patriarchal in its outlines. It was a resolutely masculine culture, from the more significant aspects of which women were excluded. What may be considered official in the literature and art of fifth century Athens was predominantly intended, therefore, to exhibit the beauty and the greatness of the Athenian male. Insofar as it was praiseworthy, love would be a spiritual relationship between males. Since women were considered intellectually on the plane of the more amenable animals, the only secure relationship a man could have with them would be on the animal plane. Aristotle, indeed, conceded the possibility of something like friendship between husband and wife, but the idea does not appear to have excited his enthusiasm, for it plays even a smaller role in the *Ethics* than the idea of the equality of sexes in the *Republic* of Plato. On the other hand, misogyny was not considered a reasonable attitude. It was, after all, a man's duty to serve God and society by procreating children, so we read in the *Laws*, and if he refused he should be subject to a fine.[8]

Marriage, from the classic viewpoint, was a serious business, a social obligation, not a source of pleasure. However unworthy woman might be of man's attention, she was nevertheless indispensable to him—there was no other convenient way of perpetuating the race. Hippolytus in Euripides' play felt indeed that Zeus might have thought of something better:

> Zeus! Why did you let women settle in this world of light, a curse and a snare to men? If you wished to propagate the human race you should have arranged it without women. Men might have deposited in your temples gold or iron or a weight of copper to purchase offspring, each to the value of the price he paid, and so lived in free houses, relieved of womankind. . . .[9]

But, as Euripides gives us to understand, Hippolytus, who prided himself upon his *sophrosyne*, had not enough *sophrosyne*. There was the madness of Aphrodite and the madness of Artemis. Both were destructive. Between the two there was that practical middle way so dear to the classic thinker, the way of sanity, and for the cultured Greek this would involve neither the love nor the hatred of woman, but a virile indifference to woman and her concerns. The lover of the golden mean assigned to woman her due, without passion, without aversion, and without poetry.

Attic culture thus did not encourage passionate involvements between the sexes. It took account of their possibility, of course, but its official literature regularly depicted this sort of love as an upsetting social influence, the cause of misfortune, domestic discord, and civil strife. Roman Venus, too, was most often depicted as a malevolent influence upon the affairs of men, and this tradition still clings to her name day. The reason is evident. Love of woman was a subversive influence in a man's world. Subject neither to law nor to reason, it received a heavy share of that awe and distrust with which the Greek male viewed whatever was not under the rational control of the male Greek. The good citizen was above all a reasonable citizen whose desires and appetites were firmly controlled by the sovereign intellect; emotionally he was oriented toward an ideal of Spartan imperturbability, which eventually was developed into a philosophical principle. For such a solid citizen, obviously, passionate love would be a dangerously unsettling experience; the sober joys of wedlock were vastly more suitable to his needs:

> Love may go too far and involve men in dishonor and disgrace. But if the goddess comes in just measure, there is none so rich in blessing. May you never launch at me, O Lady of Cyprus, your golden bow's passion-poisoned arrows, which no man can avoid.[10]

Except for love-stories that end in marriage—a strain of literature that owes much to the Greek romances—this view of the mischievous influence of love is characteristic also of our contemporary culture. Our interest in the courtship which leads to marriage amounts to an obsession; but we have not lost our classical distrust of love. The "romantic" view that love is a good in itself has never achieved orthodoxy. We incline more readily to the view that love is a catastrophe. In the culture of Europe, from first to last, the only official justification for love and marriage has been the procreation of the race; strictly speaking, all other passion is taboo.[11] But what is forbidden is not necessarily unfashionable—on the contrary. It is only when we consider how great a proportion of our literary activity has developed in the unsanctioned areas of our cultural structure that we are able to make a realistic approach to the culture of the ancients.

The Greeks of the classical age do not seem, in any case, to have shared our interest in stories of courtship and marriage. Bawdy stories amused them and stories of tragic love made them cry and shudder; but their tastes did not encourage the development of courtship as a literary theme. In the fifth century, marriage was considered a social rather than a private concern. Athenian girls were not usually given much voice in the choice of a husband, nor did young men commonly seek out their own wives. Judging by the evidence, passion seldom played a role in these arrangements.[12] The opposition of father and son with relation to the choice of a wife was a favorite subject for comedy, but young love was not often portrayed sentimentally in the Greek theater nor in the Roman, and the scene of romantic courtship which is the gainpenny of the modern dramatist was almost completely absent from the classic stage.

The epic hero wasted no more time in courtship than his counterpart on the stage. As for the Olympian,

> Short are god's ways, and soon they reach their aims . . .
> And they were wedded ere the evening hour.[13]

There were, of course, in early Greek literature descriptions of competitions for exceptionally desirable women, esteemed as valuable possessions, such as Helen or Alcestis, or of women who transmitted power and property, such as Penelope. But it is not really until the Alexandrian period that the traditional pattern of the love-story, Hollywood style, comes to light. Later still, in the Greek romances, we find for the first time the combination of elements from which are drawn the most familiar of our romantic stereotypes—young love, parental obstacles, rivalry, cruel separation, and after many hardships steadfastly endured, marriage, and happiness ever after.[14] In this application of epic principles and epic machinery to the field of love, love becomes for the first time an adventure worthy of a hero's interest.

Of the authorship of these stories we know very little, and we can only guess at the social levels to which they were directed. But it seems likely that these romances reflect older literary traditions, for the underlying plot patterns of Greek New Comedy are not different from these stories in basic structure, although the emphasis is in another place. There is, at any rate, no reason to connect romantic love with the third century of the Christian era because the *Aethiopica* is thought to have been written then, nor with the preceding century because of *Daphnis and Chloe* and *The Golden Ass*, nor with the sixth century because it was then apparently that one Musaeus wrote the delightfully tragic love-story of Hero and Leander. It seems rather more reasonable to conclude that in the literature of the ancients there are observable a number of different attitudes with regard to love, and that the pattern of "romantic" love had a somewhat later literary development than the others, though there could hardly have been a time at which it was not comprehensible. As for that love which might subsist between man and wife, undoubtedly Eros took a hand in that from time to time also, but the uxorious male was evidently considered even more ridiculous in the fifth century B.C. than he was in the Renaissance. The ancients have left us no love-stories of this type, and those Greek stories in which a man makes love to another man's wife can hardly be considered sentimental.

In classical times the function of an Athenian wife was to bear Athenian sons, as many and as quietly as possible. She was also expected to look after the house of her husband and to direct the household chores. For the rest, the social position of a respectable married woman differed only theoretically from that of the domestic slaves among whom she was destined to pass her life. It was in her domestic utility that her chief beauty resided and in these terms the Athenian gentleman instructed his wife, not without some obvious cynicism:

> I also said it was excellent exercise to mix flour and knead dough and to shake and fold cloaks and bedclothes; such exercise would give her a better appetite, improve her health and add a natural color to her cheeks. Besides, when a wife's looks outshine a maid's, and she is fresher and more becomingly dressed, they're a ravishing sight, especially when the wife is also willing to oblige, whereas the girl's services are compulsory.[15]

The Athenian girl passed without transition from the tutelage of the father to that of the husband. Brought up by her parents for a life of respectable drudgery, discouraged from following intellectual pursuits, and bound under heavy penalties to absolute sexual fidelity to a man whose sexual interests were predominantly extra-marital, she would not ordinarily be considered a subject of romantic interest. "We have courtesans for our pleasure," said the Athenian orator, "concubines for the daily needs of our bodies, and wives to keep our houses and to bear us legitimate children." [16]

As it was the courtesans who chiefly gave pleasure, it was normally in those circles that one made love. A good many of the amatory poems of the Greeks were obviously directed to courtesans, and the passions they express run the entire gamut of poetic possibility. The best of these versatile ladies were elegant by profession and accomplished by education. Such women might properly become, like men, the subject of poetry, but the good Greek wife, unlike her prototype in the heroic legends, did not often come into literature. "Hers is the greatest glory who has the least renown among men"—such was the Periclean formula.[17] It is a very far cry from the social attitude exemplified by the medieval knight whose boast it was that he would spread the renown of his lady to the farthest corners of the earth.

Far from creating a literature in praise of the beauty of women, the classical writers did what they could to mobilize the aggressions of society against the female component. Scorn was the keynote of their chorus, rather than the disgust of the patristic writers, but there is much in Greek literature to bear witness to the fear which underlay this scorn. Both in comedy and in tragedy, most official of the Greek genres, women were depicted as enemies of the rational order of society. In Clytemnestra, Medea, Phaedra, and Antigone we see nothing of the passive attitude considered suitable to the Athenian lady, and in fact none of these heroines is Athenian. Such women were traditionally depicted as passion's slaves; whoever loved them came to grief. They had in addition a dangerous sense of having been unjustly treated and they bore mankind a grudge. The Erinyes of Aeschylus in a sense speak for the entire sex,

> Who stand apart, a race by Zeus abhorred,
> Blood-boltered, held unworthy of the council
> And converse of heaven's lord.[18]

But while in Aeschylus' play the female Furies, disinherited by the younger gods, their powers usurped, their privileges taken away, were at last reconciled to the patriarchy through the mediation of the sexless Athena, there appears to have been no doubt in the Greek mind that the price of male supremacy was everlasting vigilance. It is inconceivable that the dangers of matriarchy would be vivid in the minds of the fifth century dramatists. Yet one is hard put to it to account in any other way for their intense preoccupation with the woman question.

The extremes to which Aeschylus went in minimizing the value of women to society would make one smile if one did not remember what an extraordinary development this attitude was to have in Western culture. In the contest to determine the relative worth of man and woman, as symbolized by the rival claims for vengeance of the slain Agamemnon and the slain Clytemnestra, Apollo—speaking, as he says, for Zeus—advances the remarkable proposition that the son is not related to his mother:

> The mother of what is called her child is not its parent, but only the nurse of the newly implanted germ. The begetter is the parent, whereas she, as a stranger for a stranger, doth but preserve the sprout. . . .

Then Apollo proceeds to cite the shining example of what the masculine imagination was able to conjure up as the triumph of sexual virtuosity:

> And I will give you a sure proof of what I say. There may be fatherhood without any mother. Here at hand is a witness, the child of Olympian Zeus, and not so much as nursed in the darkness of the womb, but such a bud as no goddess might bring forth.[19]

Athena, who sprang from the brow of Zeus, evidently represents the classical ideal of the perfect woman perfectly conceived. She was in all essential aspects a man, "in heart, as in birth, a father's child alone." Such was the ideal woman in a man's world. She set the pattern, undoubtedly, for the emancipated women described by Plato in the *Republic*, and she was the prototype of the Camillas, Clorindas, Marfisas, and even the Bradamantes of a later age. In the fifth book of the *Republic*, we are surprised to find that Plato hardly distinguishes between homosexual and heterosexual lovers in the warrior class. Remarkable as this may seem, it is a perfectly logical consequence of a system of thought in which women become proper objects of love in proportion as they approximate masculinity.

But while the Athenian dramatist, like the Athenian philosopher, went as far as he could to negate the importance of motherhood in the social frame, there are the strongest indications that Athenian culture was at all times shot through with mother-worship. Classic culture, as it is portrayed in the fragmentary literature that has come down to us, is neither simple to understand nor easy to interpret, but one thing about it, at least, is certain—it was not homogeneous. Like our own culture, it was a composite of sedimentary character in which the submerged levels remained dynamically effective long after they had disappeared from view. In Greece, after Homer, Zeus covered all; but beneath the smooth surface of the Olympian church the Greeks carried on vigorously the ancient cult of the Mother. In the bosom of the patriarchy, the Athenian women "kept the Thesmophoria as of old," [20] and a handful of legends such as that of the Argives Cleobis and Bito preserved the traditions of a maternalistic order which seems altogether alien to the Olympians. Ancient Greece therefore presents the interesting aspect of a society devoted to the worship of the Father, within whose cult the adoration of the Mother in her fatidic, mantic, and regenerative aspects played a chief part, while the Son had also his separate worship as creator and redeemer.[21]

In the complex of myth which Homer and Hesiod systematized in the service of the patriarchy, the female deities played, of course, secondary roles, but they were deeply troublesome, and the discord they brought about in heaven accounted in large measure for our troubles here on earth. In heaven as on earth, women were depicted as the chief obstacle to the sensible and ordered affairs of men. Such was the attitude which the ancients transmitted to the Christian Middle Ages and the Renaissance. Beyond any doubt a great deal of history underlies this attitude. But this history has not been, and very likely never will be, written, and nothing is more uncertain than the outlines of the primitive matriarchy, and the invasion and obliteration of the Golden Age before Zeus, that age of which mankind has lost the memory, but never the nostalgia.[22]

But while there is only the flimsiest evidence that the patriarchal culture which the Olympians symbolize supplanted a pre-existing matriarchal or matrilocal system common to the Mediterranean lands, it is entirely certain that there was in existence in Greece, in historic times, a matriarchal system which had the greatest possible influence upon Greek culture—that is to say, that matriarchy in which every human child necessarily lives during the first formative phase of his life, his infancy. In the nature of things, all children in our culture grow up under the absolute dominion of the mother, and the need, the rule, and the love of the mother underlie all other considerations in the infantile mind. Thus we hardly need to rationalize mythology in order to understand why Hera is more ancient than Zeus. Genetically the mother comes first, and it is to her that men look first of all for shelter, for nourishment, and for love. It is in her also that they find their first frustrations and disappointments. Toward her they direct their first hostility. The father is, for all his magnificence, a secondary figure in the psychic system. The initial equipment of aspirations, disappointments, aggressions and fears with which we enter upon life's career is developed with relation to the mother and the mother alone.

It is evidently to this fundamental complex of love, fear, and hostility that we must in the first place refer the ambivalent attitude toward women which characterizes our cultural pattern. It would seem that for the resentment which the mother unwittingly arouses in her infant, the entire female sex has had to pay in terms of social and economic enslavement: such is its reward for rearing the race of men. But, of course, the relation of child to mother is twofold. Underlying the child's first disappointments and his consequent aggressiveness, which, in accordance with the familiar pattern, he projects as fear, is his primal need to be loved and his love. This too has its manifestation in adult life, so that the enslaved and constantly denigrated sex is also, and at the same time, the object of adoration and extravagant honor. In this manner it becomes possible to understand the psychic import of the omnipotent lady, at once angel and tigress, who in time becomes the object of the romantic passion. "I learnt to know well what it is to be a woman," cries Phaedra in Euripides' play, "a thing the world detests."[23] But it was in terms of the Queen of Heaven that pagan and Christian in turn conceived their hope of salvation and eternal bliss.

There is no reason to suppose that we should have any difficulty in explaining to Aristotle, Virgil, or St. Paul that love is a noble and ennobling passion.[24] In one way or another, each of these worthies had said as much. But it would very likely have surprised them to discover that anyone in his senses would maintain seriously that a noble passion could be inspired by a woman, so completely were these men committed to a patriarchal way of thought. What seems novel therefore in the poetry of the troubadours is not their sense of the joy of love, nor the refining power of love, nor the inspiration of love, but only their idea of the proper object of love. The troubadours made a virtue of the love of woman. The ancients normally regarded it as a vice, and this view they passed on to the church fathers, who remained in this respect, as in so many others, stanch supporters of the classic tradition.

Curiously enough from our point of view, it is precisely what we call love that the Attic poets condemned, and not at all the normal inclination of man to woman, the animal appetite. This appetite might be inopportune or excessive, and it might have inconvenient consequences, but so long as passion remained on the animal plane it constituted no particular danger to the male personality. Zeus presents himself to the ladies who excite his interest as a bull, a swan, a cuckoo, an eagle, a husband, and in other interesting disguises which do not involve excessive conversation; but not often as a god. One would say that for all its resolutely patriarchal character, the culture which devised Zeus did not take the father-image with the greatest possible seriousness. Even aside from the treatment it accorded him on the comic stage, it found the Father an interesting subject for caricature. Greek mythology made of Zeus a somewhat preoccupied Don Juan, a philandering and hag-ridden husband, the apotheosis of the Greek traveling man. Nevertheless the Far-Darter represented a social ideal of the greatest significance.

Zeus was the divine aspect of the healthy male. An early prototype of the Machiavellian prince, he knew exactly what he wanted and set about efficiently to get it, without wasting time in introspection. His literature invariably celebrates his successes, never his failures. In consequence, his amatory exploits, while impressive, seem lacking in poetic content, for in our romantic view of the matter, poetry is the measure of man's capacity to feel, and the god is imperturbable. As the legatees of a romantic concept, we are likely to interest ourselves rather more in the victims than in the heroes of the amatory adventures of the gods. It is perhaps for this reason that Euripides seems so much closer to our time than his contemporaries of the Attic stage, and it is easy to understand why the patterns of Renaissance tragedy were derived from him and not from Sophocles. In Euripides the lyric strain was high. He was interested in suffering; therefore he was interested in women. In his hands, for example, the familiar scene of the rape of the country maid—the invariable theme of the medieval *pastourelle*—took on a dimension that is distinctly romantic, even though it was Apollo himself who was concerned in this most classic of situations:

> You came to me with the sunlight in your golden hair when I was gathering the yellow flowers in the folds of my robe, the flowers that shone like golden suns. You caught the white wrists of my hands and drew me screaming, "Mother, Mother" to the bed in that cave. Divine seducer, you drew me there and shamelessly you worked the pleasure of Cypris. And I bore you a son—O Misery!—and in fear of my mother I cast him upon your bed, upon the cruel couch where cruelly you ravished me, the hapless girl. Woe is me, woe! And now my boy is gone, fowls of the air have torn and devoured him,

my boy—and yours, cruel god. But you only play your lyre and sing songs of triumph.[25]

Between the passions of the god, or the godlike hero, and the type of love which without much precision we call romantic, the difference is measurable in terms of the aggressive component. Heroic love is a conquest: the lover attacks, the lady defends. Their relation is military, an encounter in which it is characteristic of the male to subdue and of the female to submit. When through superior force or cunning, the hero has mastered the more or less reluctant lady, he is at liberty to go about his business, leaving his lovely victim to care for the resulting demigod. Such is the stereotype of heroic love. Its symbol is Don Juan.

The romantic passion is of an entirely different nature. It involves not a succession of amatory exploits, but the fixation of the lover upon a single object of ideal character. The caricature is Don Quixote. Constancy is of its essence, and constancy means the surrender of the self-sufficiency of the individual. For the romantic lover, the beloved lady is unique. She is indispensable to his happiness and even to his health. His motility also suffers a transformation. He is no longer self-propelled in a line; love compels him to revolve in an orbit; he becomes a satellite. In this relation, naturally, he cannot sustain a heroic role and he takes on a measure of passivity. The emphasis of the love-story shifts significantly. It is no longer a tale of conquest. It centers upon courtship.

In the heroic tradition, the enamorment is a simple and straightforward affair. The hero comes upon the pretty lady, he feels the stirring of Eros, and he goes about the shortest way of satisfying his desire. The whole thing has about it the healthy zest of the primitive and uncomplicated. In a rustic setting, in the warm sun, the effect is precisely the same in thirteenth century France as in the high time of Greece:

Vers la touse m'avance,
Por oir s'acointance;
Je la vi bele et blanche,
De simple contenance:

Ne mist pas en oubliance
Ce que je li dis.
Maintenant sans demorance
S'amor le requis.[26]

The romantic situation, in comparison with the fresh outdoor quality of the *pastourelle,* seems somewhat wan and seedy. Where the heroic lover tightens his belt and gives chase, the romantic lover falls on his knees, trembling, pale, unstrung. Love fetches him such a buffet that his heart and soul die within him. He can only cry for mercy, and this is seldom forthcoming:

Davanti agli occhi miei veggio lo core
  e l'anima dolente che s'ancide,
  che mor d'un colpo che li diede Amore
  ed in quel punto che madonna vide.[27]

When the military conceit is used—and after the twelfth century nothing is more common—the lady has arrows and javelins and other warlike equipment constantly at her command. She looks like an angel; but this angel is in permanent ambush, there is a bent bow in her eyes, and woe to him who stops one of her glances. When the deed is done, the lady pursues her way in maiden meditation, fancy-free. The lover is left, more dead than alive, with the dart of love fixed and festering in his heart. The situation is by no means new in the Middle Ages—we find it, eye, dart, and all, in a choral ode in *Hippolytus* [28]—but from the twelfth century to the seventeenth it is indispensable to the romantic love-lyric.

The romantic lover thus offers the greatest possible contrast to the classic hero in his amatory aspect. In the classic view love is an appetite; in the romantic it is a thunderbolt. The heroic lover pleases himself; the romantic strives to please his beloved. The contrast is very striking in the epic narratives that have come under the one or the other influence. Achilles is served by his women. Troilus serves. When Agamemnon takes away Briseis, Achilles feels that he has been robbed, and he ponders his revenge. But when the medieval Troilus loses his mistress, he is brought to despair and death. Dido languishes and dies for love of Aeneas.

For his part, Aeneas languishes for no one; he has no time. He has work in hand, and when he marries the fair Lavinia it is in furtherance of his mission, not of his passion. But the medieval Lancelot has no mission and no destiny higher than his lady's wish.

Although there appears to have been no fundamental tradition in Christian doctrine with regard to the evils of sexuality as such, it was natural that whatever smacked of the romantic passion should be repugnant to its teachings. Almost from the beginning, the patristic writers manifested antagonism not only to love, but to marriage in any form. In the Scriptures the conflict between the love of woman and the love of God is explicit, but marriage is not flatly condemned. But by the end of the second century, Christian preachers were already stressing the importance of sexual purity, and by the fourth century chastity had taken a central place in the system of Christian virtues. For Athanasius the supreme message of Christ was the need for virginity. Nevertheless, five centuries after Christ, few teachers were prepared, like Tertullian and Ambrose, to face the issue squarely in preferring the extinction of mankind to its propagation through sin.[29]

When in the course of time it became necessary to define the permissible limits of sexuality, there developed an interesting divergence of clerical opinion. To Augustine, the sexual act appeared innocent, but the desire for it, evil. As he saw it, the laudable end, the propagation of the race, did not excuse the irrational appetite. In the state of innocence, in Eden, such a desire, he considered, would not have arisen. Offspring would have been begotten in calmness of soul and body, without concupiscence and with none but a rational incentive.[30] Such was the view which recommended itself also to Gregory the Great in the sixth century. The ideal compromise between concupiscence and abstinence would thus be found in cohabitation for utility and not for pleasure, and this doctrine effectively excluded passion from the good marriage. This was, in general, the position taken by most clerical writers on the subject in the Middle Ages. It was normally conceded that the sexual act was excusable and perhaps even necessary, but love was never condoned since in every case it drew the soul away from the proper object of its desire. To love a woman for her own sake was to be faithless to the Father.

With Albertus Magnus and Thomas Aquinas, the classical basis of this idea became yet clearer. Pleasure in itself, St. Thomas argued, is a good, and in Eden sexual pleasure would have been much more enjoyable than it is. But in the state of innocence man would not have been distracted from the First Good by sexual indulgence. The evil of the desire for the flesh is not in the pleasure which it affords, but in its irrational character, for passion distracts the mind, and sexuality submerges the reason. Paradise would include in its joys an endless renewal of the carnal relation, rationally motivated, intensely enjoyable, but passionless—that is to say, carnal pleasure without love.[31]

As to the position of woman in society, even the more moderate patristic writers agreed that while marriage itself was perhaps not an evil, woman was from first to last the principal tool of man's undoing. "Every woman," wrote Clement of Alexandria, "ought to be filled with shame at the thought that she is a woman." [32] It went without saying that the state of virginity was far preferable to the married state. "Virginity alone can make men equal to angels; it is as far above chastity as magnificence is above liberality." Those were St. Thomas' words, and such was the view finally established by the Council of Trent in the sixteenth century.[33]

Thus the woman question was ultimately resolved by the doctors of the church more or less along the lines long ago laid down by the Greek moralists. There were, of course, fundamental differences between the Christian and the pagan doctrines, but it was entirely possible, as St. Thomas demonstrated, to reconcile the two with respect to the relations between the sexes. The mystical components in these teachings offered, however, problems of a different nature. The influence of the Greek mystery-religions upon philosophical thought is very evident in the classic writers, especially in Plato. Through Philo, Porphyry, Plotinus, Origen, and the Pseudo-Dionysius, Platonic love-theory in its various forms exerted a profound influence upon the early Christian writers, the more readily as it afforded a means of organizing in a rational and more or less comprehensible system the vast complex of Eastern mysticism which pervaded the thought of the time.

Deus caritas est. Love was the basis of the Christian church. All human history—the creation, the fall, the redemption, even eternal damnation—was the fruit of love and of love alone. The movements of the universe, the cosmos itself, were intelligible in terms of love and only of love. The Holy Spirit was love, and this love the early Christians did not distinguish very clearly from Greek Eros, so that the charming story of Eros and Psyche, as Apuleius transmitted it, remained symbolically meaningful for centuries of early Christians. For the theologian as for the mystic, the cosmos was an amatory poem. God, who is Love, created the universe through love, and all His creation is moved by love of Him and aspires to ultimate union with Him. Thus a tide of love circulates unceasingly through the universe. It flows from the Father toward His creatures, and it flows back in the universal longing of the creatures for the Creator, the first and final cause.[34]

Physically this amatory cycle is perceptible in the revolution of the spheres, on which all earthly motion depends. The prime mover is that sphere which, in Dante's words, "has no other place than the divine soul in which is kindled the love which makes it turn and the influence which it transmits." [35] As Dante puts it, the reason why this sphere turns, carrying the entire cosmos with it, is that each of its parts wishes constantly to unite with each part of the tenth heaven, the abode of God, and it "turns toward this last with such desire that its velocity is almost incomprehensible." [36] The libidinous nature of this conceit is striking—like Augustine, Dante depicts the universe physically as a never ending act of love. In this universe, then, there is need of no other ordering principle, and Dante's credo is very acceptable when he defines it to St. Peter at the gates of heaven: "I believe in one God, sole and eternal, who, moveless, moves all the sky through love and desire." [37]

These are the formulations of a poet, of course, but the desire of the creature for the Creator of which the theologians wrote had never been thought of as merely an abstract principle. It had been expressed from the earliest times in language which left no doubt as to the nature of the underlying sentiment. "My soul thirsteth for thee, my flesh longeth for thee"—thus the Psalmist addressed his song of love to the Father.[38] Christ spoke of himself as the bridegroom of the church; Albertus explained the metaphor: "The church is called the spouse of Christ because she is coupled to the bridegroom by a spiritual love . . . also because, conceiving by him, she has brought forth many spiritual sons." [39] It was felt that the passionate language of the *Song of Songs* was entirely appropriate to this relation of Christ and the church, or of the soul and its God.

Endlessly commented on and elaborated by the church fathers, the *Song of Songs* formed the basis of a pious literature of astonishingly sensual character, for the mystical writers spared no pains to demonstrate how far superior in every way was the ecstasy of spiritual love over the hollow delights of the other. The greatest of the Latin hymnodists, St. Ambrose, who found the sexual relations of men and women utterly unworthy of the nature of man, spoke with fervor of the spiritual union of the soul and God:

> The soul, raising itself up from the region of the senses, and scorning the cares of the earth, aspires to the infusion of the Divine Word. And she bewails herself if he delays his coming; as if she were wounded by love, she can brook no delay and she says with impatience, Oh, that I might be kissed with a kiss of his mouth! and she asks not for one kiss but for many to appease all her desire. . . . The kiss of the Word signifies that she is illumined by the knowledge of God. And when she receives this proof of nuptial love, she exclaims in her joy, I have opened my mouth and I have breathed in his breath! . . . The soul clings to the Word with this kiss.[40]

In much the same way, St. Bernard spoke of the mystical union of the soul and God in language considerably more realistic than the analogous passages in the *Symposium* or the *Enneads:*

> A completely refined soul . . . has but a single and perfect desire, to be introduced by the King into his chamber, to be united with Him, to enjoy Him. . . .[41]

The difference between this good love of which the mystic dreamed and the bad love which the church rejected was ultimately a question of the degree of aspiration. In the highest love, the highest soul was concerned. "Charity," Thomas Aquinas wrote, "denotes in addition to love, a certain perfection of love, insofar as that which is loved is held to be of great price, as the word itself [*carus*] implies." [42] That love which stopped short of God would be in the Christian view no more than lust. "I mean by love [*caritas*]," wrote St. Augustine in an oft-quoted passage, "that affection of the mind which aims at the enjoyment of God for His own sake, and the enjoyment of oneself and one's neighbor in subordination to God; by lust [*cupiditas*] I mean that movement of the soul which aims at enjoying oneself and one's neighbor and other corporeal things without reference to God." [43]

It seems obvious that the romantic passion would in every case be in contradiction of the Christian moral order, for any love that turned aside from the adoration of the Father must be considered a deviation from the path of righteousness. To love the beauty of woman for itself was to lose one's way in a labyrinth that led nowhere, except perhaps to hell. "*Aut sistitur in pulchritudine creaturae, aut perillam tenditur in aliud. Si primo modo tunc est via deviationis.*" [44] But it was permissible to love the beauty of God in woman, and upon this idea the *stilnovisti* of the fourteenth century founded their school. Women, in the recurrent Augustinian phrase, were to be used, but not enjoyed. Accordingly, women were useful, but not enjoyable.

> . . . to enjoy a thing [*frui*] is to rest with satisfaction in it for its own sake. To use [*uti*], on the other hand, is to employ whatever means one has at hand to obtain what one desires. . . . If we wish to return to our Father's house, this world must be used, not enjoyed.[45]

Upon this basis rested the story of Dante and Beatrice and, in another way, the story of Petrarch and Laura, the fruit of a reconciliation which it took some centuries to achieve, and which was in any case not satisfactory to the church.[46]

In sum, the clerical writers were necessarily quite as inimical to the romantic passion as were the classical poets and for analogous reasons. The love of the good Christian, in his search for ecstasy and enlightenment and peace, would be ideally fixed upon an object higher than woman. The object of his desire, insofar as it was apprehensible by the human mind, would be divinely male. The human soul was a bride destined for himself by the celestial bridegroom; and for a bride, even though temporarily in male semblance, to consort in love with another woman was at best inappropriate. As for woman, who was *a fortiori* the destined spouse of God, it was permitted her to entertain the earthly husband only insofar as he represented the heavenly bridegroom in procreating the human race. Such passion as might go beyond what was strictly necessary for this purpose was construed as adulterous, even in wedlock, since the husband was lovable not in himself, but only as the agent of God.[47] Thus, if anything, Christianity was more directly oriented toward the Father, and more rigidly controlled in this direction, than any of the pagan patriarchies. And yet within this system, thus carefully controlled, there flowered magnificently the cult of the Blessed Mother.

The cult of the Mother was at first hardly favored by the church, and as we know, repeated efforts were made to put it down. But in 431 the Council of Ephesus declared the Virgin officially the Mother of God, *theotokos,* and she was henceforth represented royally clad, throned, and attended by saints and angels. By the twelfth century, her cult was strongly established in southern Europe, and a hundred years later, the Blessed Virgin had practically displaced the male Trinity in popular devotion, especially among the peoples of southern Europe. In her triune aspect as Maid, as Mother, and as Spouse of the Lord, the Great Goddess, as Albertus Magnus called her, became the subject of a vast literature of amatory character.

It is apparently impossible to find a date for the origin of this poetry. The celebrated hymn *Ave, maris stella* is first found in manuscripts dating from the eighth century, but it is doubtless older. By the time of the Confrérie de la Passion, established in the Midi of France in the thirteenth century, at the same time as the Inquisition, the development of religious poetry addressed to the Virgin was already impressive. Beyond doubt, the need for the gracious cult of the Mother was keenly felt by the religious in the years when the secular poetry of the troubadours was flowering everywhere in court circles. "The Virgin," wrote the Archdeacon of Bath, Peter of Blois, "is the only mediatrix between man and Christ. We were sinners and we were afraid to appeal to the Father because he is terrible; but we have the Virgin in whom there is no terror, for in her is the plenitude of grace and purity. . . . In fact, if Mary were excluded from heaven, there would be nothing left for humanity but the shadow of darkness." [48] It is in expressions of this sort that we find the psychic root of the amatory poetry of the period, whether in its religious or its secular aspect.[49]

Somewhere about the year 1100, we come upon the first vernacular love-poetry in a modern tongue. Its form is novel, its provenience uncertain, its substance strange—everything about it is mysterious. To the amatory attitudes which this poetry exemplifies, the term "romantic passion" most properly applies, but it would be a mistake to suppose that even here the epithct has any precise application. If the phrase has a certain usefulness, it is only because it enables one to allude in a general way to an undefined—and perhaps indefinable—area of erotic activity somewhere between the animal passion, on the one hand, and Christian charity on the other, the complex of erotic patterns which interested the courtly audiences of the Middle Ages, and which formed the basis of that body of literature which was written in the vernacular—*romanicè*—to suit their tastes.

It is sometimes said that the amatory patterns of this courtly class were codified by Andreas Capellanus, and that the rules of love in the eighth chapter of the second book of his treatise *De amore* furnish the blueprint for romantic love. But this work seems on the whole businesslike and practical, and it is written with a sense of humor that is unmistakably of the middle class. The amatory relationship which Andreas purported to interpret, however, was courtly and aristocratic, and its poetic expression is fervent in a way which appears to be completely foreign to Andreas or his Ovidian model. This fervor, indispensable to romance, is of the essence of *fin amor*, a term which is used with a good deal of precision in Provençal poetry. It is this poetic exaltation which gives to the love of the troubadours its pecular quality and color, and beguiles us into taking their stained-glass attitudes for a kind of religion.

The basis of *fin amor*, as we shall see in the sequel, was service. The True Lover, the *fin aman*, desired not to conquer and to dominate, but to serve and to adore. This adoration was in itself a joy, but not the ultimate joy of love. In return for true service the lover expected ultimately to receive his guerdon, his reward. But what, in general, the True Lover expected of his beloved was not a temporary physical appeasement; it was a perpetual benediction; he looked to his lady not for satisfaction but for blessedness. This blessedness proceeded from the unique psychic exchange which love brings about, that mutual acceptance which makes two hearts beat as one, puts two souls in one breast, and conjures up all the other psychophysical miracles of the romantic genre. The result would be that symbiotic relationship which is justly celebrated, along with wine, as among the greatest of human inventions, the joy of love.

It is readily comprehensible that in this extraordinary relationship, the beloved lady is not merely lovely and lovable, but the loveliest and most lovable of creatures to the utmost reach of the superlative. The high degree of perfection projected by the lover upon the lady is the very condition of this love. It involves not only the recognition of her worth, indispensable to the amatory relationship; it is also the measure of the lover's personal distinction. In the superlative worth of the lady, the lover finds the surest guarantee of his own pre-eminence, more particularly if his love is returned. The lover's compliments, like all self-flattery, are therefore utterly sincere. The lady, while he loves her, is for him really the loveliest and best of women, for it is in terms of his own self-love that he sees her, and we know what power to transfigure is residual in that.

Complex as this state of mind may seem when we try to understand it rationally, it appears never to have been a mystery to the intuition of the poet. The narcissistic nature of love is a commonplace of medieval literature. It is in the pool of Narcissus that the Dreamer in the *Romance of the Rose* first sees reflected the object of his desire.[50] Between the intricate psychic relations of

True Love and the heroic passion which is exemplified in the loves of Zeus the difference is immense. They have in common not much more than the sexual object, and even this they desire for different reasons. The psychological basis of heroic love, as we have seen, is the direct affirmation of virility in an act of physical domination. But the True Lover desires not so much to possess as to be accepted. The sexual reward, whatever its nature, is merely the seal of approval, the ultimate proof of his acceptance. As it is desired rather for the sake of the fantasy of which it is in some sense the realization than for itself alone, it may be postponed indefinitely, or even dispensed with altogether. Of this nature is the pure love of which Andreas speaks with enthusiasm in *De amore*, that love which consists "in the contemplation of the mind and the affection of the heart." [51]

This relationship, which we think of as essentially romantic and medieval, we do not find in Ovid, but it appears to have been well enough known to the ancients. It is described with surprising insight in the *Symposium*, in the famous speech which Plato attributes to Aristophanes:

> Each of us when separated is always looking for his other half; such a nature is prone to love and ready to return love. And when he finds his other half, the pair are lost in an amazement of love and friendship and intimacy, and one will not be out of the other's sight, as I may say, even for a moment; these are they who pass their lives with one another; yet they could not explain what they desire of one another. For the entire yearning which each of them has toward the other does not appear to be the desire of intercourse, but of something else which the soul desires and cannot tell, and of which she has only a dark and doubtful presentiment.[52]

In troubadour literature nothing is more common than the distinction between true love and false. That desire which is merely carnal and which, lacking the spiritual factor, may be gratified anywhere and by anyone, all the troubadours from Marcabru to Guiraut Riquier speak of with contempt. This love is not the subject of troubadour poetry. The troubadour Marcabru's tangled doctrine is nowhere clearer than in the distinction he draws between the kinds of love at the very dawn of the troubadour tradition:

> I shall nevermore sing in the strain of Messire Eblon, for he maintains a mad doctrine, contrary to reason. Aie! For my part I say, I have said, and will say that True Love and sensual love will never consent to go together—yes! And he is a bungler who blames True Love.[53]

Very likely, Marcabru had no idea of a love from which the carnal element was wholly absent. What he condemned as false love was adultery, and that, he maintained, leads to hell, while True Love, the source of all earthly good, is "happiness and joy, patience and measure,"

> benenanssa,
> as jois, sofrirs e mezura.[54]

Such love was not necessarily criminal. Adultery involved the commission of an illicit sexual act: the True Love of the troubadour, while it remained "pure," did not go so far. It was nonetheless an extremely sensual love that the troubadours celebrated. Although the True Lover might set a bound to his desire, this very fact involved a heightening of sensuality, since it brought about the concentration of enormous libidinous energy upon such casual contacts as ordinarily have no special erotic significance. In this manner, a glance, a touch of the hand, a word of greeting could be transformed into an event of crucial character, so that the relation of lovers whose contacts were purely visual could be more deeply sensual than the physical coupling of husband and wife.

There is certainly no lack of evidence among the troubadours of the desire for more complete satisfaction than pure love afforded. But it is in the shifting of emphasis to these minute and delicate contacts that the troubadours may be said to have invented something new in the way of love-making. By the concentration of erotic attention upon tiny areas of behavior they were able to transform the forthright joy of physical union, quickly attained and soon forgotten, into a love-affair of great duration adorned with a wealth of highly charged poetic detail. Thus courtship became an end in itself, an absorbing and arduous process which quite overshadowed the ostensible goal. The consequence was to transform the sexual pursuit from an athletic activity into a work of art requiring the greatest sensitivity and taste. Concomitantly, the hero became an artist and a gentleman. The art which he professed was called, appropriately, *cortesia.*

On the spiritual basis of the love which is the root of courtesy, were agreed not only the troubadours, but all those who developed the concept of *fin amor* through its many ramifications in the succeeding centuries. The other sort of love, we are repeatedly instructed, is folly, mischief, and lechery:

> N'est pas amurs, ainz est folie,
> Et mauveiste et lecerie.[55]

This distinction, axiomatic in the system of secular morality which we inherit from the Middle Ages, is hardly to be found in the writings of the ancients, since, as we have seen, there was little room in the classic concept for the sort of love which finds its joy in the adoration of women. Nevertheless, it is perfectly clear that the thing existed and, though it was never fashionable in philosophical circles, at last it found its way into song. In the late Greek poetry, especially, it is by no means uncommon to come upon strains that are unequivocally "romantic":

> Thou hast the beauty of Cypris, the mouth of Peitho, the form and freshness of the Spring Hours, the voice of Calliope, the wisdom and virtue of Themis, the skill of Athene. With thee, my beloved, the graces are four.[56]

The troubadour did not employ this type of classical compliment. It had too much learning for his taste or state of grace, but these were the things he too found worthy of praise in his lady—her form and freshness, her wisdom and virtue; she too was the epitome of godlike qualities. Rufinus perhaps had no idea of the labor of love through which the knightly poet strove to make himself worthy of so exalted an object, but we can hardly doubt that he considered the lady worthy of a certain respect to whom he sang in such terms. The love which he thus celebrated, without being especially spiritual, is certainly distinguishable from the simple sensual appetite, the plenitude of which found ample expression in the less idealistic poetry of his Greek and Latin contemporaries. His beloved was perhaps not, as in the troubadour conception, his leader and guide, but judging from his description of her, she was exceptional.

For the heroic lover no woman is unique. The hero's interest in the other sex is purely sporadic, and he is generally indifferent to the individual lady as such. He is therefore able to maintain a manly independence through the variety of his amatory experiences. What he desires, ideally, is pleasure without passion, as in the Eden imagined by St. Thomas. In this Eden, constancy would be in the nature of a serpent. And therefore he wryly protests in every age:

> I can love her and her and you and you,
> I can love any, so she be not true.

The romantic lover, as Aristophanes suggests, is psychically destined for a single mistress. She alone completes him, and nobody else in the world, as he thinks, will fit his preconceived ideal of perfection. He sings in quite another strain:

> From alle wymmen my love is lent
> And lyht on Alysoun.

He is thus in a state intermediate between the aggressive ardor of the hero and the submissive *latria* of the True Lover. He does not put himself in the posture of worship, but he abjures completely the bumptiousness of the conqueror, for what he requires of the lady cannot be forced: one can enforce compliance, not tenderness. Thus the romantic lover without necessarily entering into the complexities of *fin amor* yet assumes the posture of a suppliant, a child, one might say, at his mother's knee. The tableau can be charming, and it is not, of course, a troubadour invention. Centuries before the time of Guillaume IX, or of any of the Arab poets, we find Greek Rufinus writing in what is typically a Petrarchan mood:

> Finding Prodike happily alone, I besought her, and clasping her ambrosial knees, "Save," I said, "a man who is nearly lost and grant me the little breath that has not left me." When I said this, she wept, but wiped away the tears and with her tender hands, gently repulsed me.[57]

There is perhaps nothing ennobling in such a picture, but it has all the refinement and sweetness which charms us in the courtly poetry of a later age. This humility, which seemed effeminate to the Greek moralists and sinful to the Christian, was by no means foreign to the Roman poets. Catullus overwhelmed his faithless Lesbia with curses so impressive that they have served as models for future ages, but he wrote to her also in terms which might have been literally copied by any troubadour, and which were in fact copied from the celebrated ode of Sappho: [58]

> He appears to me to be the equal of a god, he appears to me, if it is possible, to surpass the gods, who seated over against you, can often look at you, gently smiling, and hear your voice,
>
> Such happiness I feel that it ravishes from my poor soul the use of all my senses, for no sooner do my eyes perceive you, Lesbia, than my voice dies in my mouth,
>
> My tongue is paralyzed, and a subtle fire flows through my limbs, an inward ringing sounds in my ears and a double night spreads over my eyes.[59]

The psychic state which Catullus describes in these familiar verses is in some degree typical of the entire tradition of romantic love wherever we encounter it. In all cases, the lover is touchingly helpless, like a child, weak, fainting, completely at the mercy of the goddess whom he adores. We find something of the sort in Ovid's comic description of the behavior proper to lovers; [60] the same state of mind is described carefully in the *risâla* of Ibn Hazm and in other Arabic *trattati d'amore* of the Middle Ages; after the time of the troubadours it becomes one of the most common stereotypes of European amatory literature.

If we ask what it is that ails the lover in this time-honored situation, since desire does not as a rule produce such desperate effects, the answer suggests itself readily—it is fear. Giraut de Bornelh in his day did not hesitate to identify his feelings in the presence of the lady with terror; after the twelfth century it became a matter of decorum to tremble with fear in the presence of beauty.[61] But in another tradition, fear was considered an emotion inappropriate to the male in any circumstances. The feelings which Catullus ascribed to himself as he sat looking at Lesbia were considered proper only to women in classical times; they were feelings suitable to Sappho. In the typical epic encounter of man and maid, it was invariably the maid who trembled as the resplendent male strode into her presence, magnificently self-possessed. So in the *Argonautica* of Apollonius even the powerful Medea was affected when Jason "appeared to her yearning eyes, stately striding,"

> Then it seemed as if her heart dropped out of her bosom; a dark mist came over her eyes, and the blushes were hot in her cheeks. She could stir neither backward nor forward, the strength was gone from her knees, and her feet seemed rooted to the ground.[62]

No classic hero was ever affected in this manner by the beauty of a woman. The reason is clear enough. The hero in all his erotic activity looks to fatherhood, and the affirmation of his latent paternity gives him manly pride and superiority. But the romantic lover applies for love in the role of the son and, unconsciously identifying the beloved with the mother, he is fearful and humble, and he asks for pity. Romantic love represents, therefore, a reversal of the traditional roles of man and maid in the classical conception of the love-story. Indeed, until this reversal became officially acceptable, no extensive development of the love-lyric was possible: the only important poetry of love in Greek before the Hellenistic period was written by a woman. Yet when Plato described poetically the moment of enamorment so dear to the lyricists of the romantic tradition, he did so in language which suggests that of the *stilnovisti* of the fourteenth century so significantly that one might imagine they had read him:

> But he whose initiation is recent, and who has been the spectator of many glories in the other world, is amazed when he sees anyone having a godlike face or form which is the expression or imitation of divine beauty; and at first a shudder runs through him, and some misgiving of a former world steals over him; then looking upon the face of his beloved as of a god, he reverences him, and if he were not afraid of being thought a downright madman, he would sacrifice to his beloved as to the image of a god; then as he gazes on him there is a sort of reaction, and the shudder naturally passes into an unusual heat and perspiration; for, as he receives the effluence of beauty through the eyes, the wing moistens and he warms. And this state is by men called love.[63]

The whole mechanism of romantic love is inherent in this passage pretty much as the Renaissance lyricists conceived it—it is quite the same, all but the gender of the pronouns. Among the troubadours, the love of woman became not only permissible but mandatory. Then, bit by bit, all the apparatus of the Platonic love-system was transferred to the service of woman. For the Renaissance it was chiefly in the eyes of a beautiful lady that the divine reflection was visible. In the Platonic love-scale as set forth by Bembo, woman occupied the first and, for all practical purposes, the principal place. Thus in the Platonism of the Renaissance, as in the philosophy of Dante, woman became the key to the highest love, the love of the Absolute.

The sort of love of which Catullus wrote had no such exalted flight as this. His love led nowhere; it had no moral outcome; his ladder had but a single rung. Insofar as this love was good, it was good in itself, a state to be desired for its own sake. Much in his poetry, as in that of his Syrian contemporary Meleager, and his followers Tibullus and Propertius, makes us think of the troubadours. As Scheludko has convincingly demonstrated, there is no evidence whatever that the troubadours knew any of these poets.[64]

Nevertheless, it is astonishing how many of the peculiarities of troubadour literature are foreshadowed in the Greek amatory epigrams. All the familiar paraphernalia of Love, as Ovid transmitted it—Love's lordship, his arrows, his mischievous nature, his injustices, the burning and chilling of love-sickness, the apostrophes to the eyes—all have their counterpart in the Hellenistic love-poetry. In the celebrated epigram, Ἤδη λευκόϊον θάλλει,[65] of Meleager, for example, or in the charming epistle of Agathias Scholasticus, Ἐνθάδε μὲν χλοάουσα,[66] we hear the very music of spring from which so much troubadour song takes its flight, quite as if it had been written in Provence:

> Here the land, clothing itself in greenery, has revealed the full beauty of the rich foliage, and here warble under shady cypresses the birds, now mothers of tender chicks. The goldfinches sing shrill, and the turtle dove moans from its home in the thorny thicket.[67]

We do not look for the *dramatis personae* of the troubadour lyric in fifth century Byzantium, but they are all there nonetheless—the lover, the jealous husband, the coy lady, even the ubiquitous talebearer who haunts the courtly poetry,[68] just as they are all in Ovid; and after all where are they not? Whether or not any of the medieval singers had access to the classics or any idea of the contents of the anthology which Constantine Cephalas compiled in the tenth century and Maximus Planudes revised in the twelfth, there is no reason to assume that the troubadours invented the joy of love. It is quite enough to say that in their day they discovered it.

After all, the joy of love and the pain of love, it seems superfluous to recall, are more than technical phrases in the history of poetry. These words sum up an experience which, judging from history at least, lovers have shared in all ages. It is also true that not everyone is capable of this experience; at all times, talented lovers have been rare. In certain periods love has tended to become a literary pose or a social fad; then, as the troubadours were at pains to point out, there are found many who pay lip service to the god without having the spiritual capacity to serve him truly. Upon the ability to love truly, the troubadours based an ideal of aristocracy which had never before explicitly existed, the aristocracy of the gentle heart. This was their invention, and upon it, strangely enough, was founded a new concept of manhood, the idea of the gentleman, the *courtois*.

All this seems sufficiently remarkable as an achievement; yet the contribution of these poets should not be overestimated. The troubadours did not develop the culture in which they lived. It developed them. As a class of more or less professional entertainers, they were hardly in a position to impose alien tastes upon the great lords and ladies at whose courts they practiced the precarious art of the minstrel. But they were in an excellent position to interpret and to express the needs of the society which supported them. That they succeeded in this, the magnitude of their literary achievement amply indicates; nevertheless it is not so much to them as to the culture that found voice in them that we must look for an explanation of their song and their mystery.

The eleventh century, then, did not invent the romantic passion; but it made it fashionable. The troubadours did not present the world with a new emotion; they established a literary genre. What we have to account for historically is not a psychic revolution or a social upheaval, but the emergence of a poetic mode. Yet a poetic mode which sweeps irresistibly over a continent can hardly be dismissed as a fad, a social pastime, or an aristocratic sport—it must be treated with the reverence due to a sociological phenomenon of importance. The wave of lyricism which, with seeming spontaneity, welled up at the end of the eleventh century must have served a fundamental human need. Arising in a society which was in its outward manifestations absolutely paternalistic, it realized in song a fantasy which rapidly revealed itself as dominant in a culture with the external realities of which it was completely at variance. Its extent measures the psychic reaction against the cult of paternalism upon which this culture was founded.

A priori one would say that the upper-class life of western Europe in the Middle Ages was no more appropriate to the cult of the gentle heart than that of Periclean Athens or Augustan Rome. Yet this cult gave direction to the most important literary trend of the period. It was the basis of a vast literary enterprise which involved not only the bulk of the lyrical poetry of five centuries, but also a great deal of what is most significant in the narrative and dramatic genres which were developed in those years.

How it came about that this wave of song arose at precisely this moment in the Middle Ages very likely we shall never completely understand. Granted the existence of cultural tensions which found expression in the new poetry, it is still in vain that we look for any immediate source or influence out of which the courtly lyric could have come. There was little in the classical tradition which the church kept alive to explain either the form or the substance of the new secular poetry. The medieval Latin lyric in its developed form might just as well have been its result as its cause. There may have been in existence a tradition of popular accentual poetry which stretched back to the time of the empire; but we are unable to trace its course. There may have existed important influences of Celtic origin. It is not possible to rule out absolutely the influence of native folk song on the courtly poets. Contacts may have been established during the crusades by means of which Western minstrels felt the influence of the late Greek poets. Finally—and it is by far the most probable theory—it may have been from Arab Spain that the first troubadours took their themes and their direction and, even more likely, their forms.[69]

The fact is that wherever we look in the literature of the period —in the Latin, the Greek, the Arabic, the Persian, even the Hebrew —we find analogies and parallels on every hand. The various hypotheses which have been adduced with regard to the origins of the Provençal lyric are not mutually exclusive. Most are in some degree acceptable; none is certain. What is certain is that when the Gallic civilization which arose upon the ruins of the Roman culture was willing and able to express itself in song, it employed neither the language nor the metric of the learned Latin writers. Quite spontaneously, as it seems, there appeared an elaborate and polished literary vernacular, and a well-developed system of prosody based on rime and accent. The substance was novel. If it was borrowed from the literature of Arab Spain, the debt was not acknowledged in any way. But the effect was immediate. After

1100 in the Midi of France, the courtly makers developed with startling rapidity a lyrical system the core of which was the adoration of woman and the ennoblement of man through love. Concomitantly, but quite independently, the cult of Our Lady established itself side by side with the cult of the Son as creator and redeemer, while, in the popular mind, the Father withdrew further and further into the mysteries of heaven and at last became ineffable.

The new poetry was not of general application. It was intended to express the ideals and the aspirations of an order of society which could not have come into being before the eighth century, and which barely survived the thirteenth. This poetry was knightly in character. Not all the troubadours were knights; but all the troubadours sang in the character of knights. The songs they sang, insofar as they had to do with love, were on the whole remarkably feminist in their orientation. Yet in these feminist songs, the lady remained as a rule vague and mysterious, while the knight bared his heart and his mind with all the intimacy of the confessional. The Provençal *chanson*, as we might expect in the poetry of a male society, directed itself to the female, but it focused interest unequivocally on the male. The song was in praise of the lady, but the voice, the heart, and the soul of the *chanson* were the voice, the heart, and soul of the knight.

It is therefore with the knight that we begin.

THE KNIGHTS

In the twelfth century, France and Provence—united under the French crown by Charles VIII in 1487—were distinct regions. The area north of the Loire, centered on Isle de France, together with Picardy, Champagne, and Normandy, had been settled by Salian Franks from the Low Countries. The warlike character of these tribes was encouraged by the Romans, who employed them as auxiliaries to repel further invasion. We hear little of these Franks before the time of Clovis, but after the establishment of the Frankish monarchy in the fifth century they play an increasingly important part in European history.

The country south of the Loire, and the valley of the Rhone south of Lyon, together with Aquitaine, made up the region which Dante called Provincia. Roman Provincia was not so extensive: its boundary had followed the line Bordeaux-Toulouse-Lyon-Geneva; it was bordered by Liguria on the east and by the Pyrenees on the west. This district had originally been conquered by Crassus. In the time of Augustus, it was again subjugated by Agrippa. Its Roman character, so early acquired, was never quite lost, for the Visigoths who colonized this region and held Septimania until the eighth century were among the least barbarous of the invading hordes and the least resistant to Roman culture. The public schools at Arles, Vienne, Toulouse, Lyon, and Bordeaux conserved the antique tradition until the end of the fifth century. In these regions the feudal structure never completely supplanted the Roman law and its organization.

On the other hand, the population of the Midi during the Dark Ages seems to have clung to its ignorance with the utmost resolution. After the fifth century few traces of learning of any sort, antique or Christian, are to be met with south of the Loire until relatively late times. It was in this area that the new vernacular poetry first flowered, in the courts of Poitou and Limousin first of all, then in Aquitaine and Languedoc, and lastly in Provence. The earliest examples we possess of the new lyric poetry belong to the very end of the eleventh century. There can be no doubt that the lyric tradition in the Middle Ages is older than that, but vernacular poetry can hardly have existed much before the year 1000.

The poetry which developed simultaneously north of the Loire in France was neither lyric nor amatory in character. It was narrative and warlike. By comparison with the intricate strophic forms which developed in the Midi, the northern *chanson de geste,* with its relentless beat and its bundles of lines tied together with assonance, seems rude and formless. Yet this metric was admirably adapted to the delivery of a narrative of impressive amplitude, and its best examples have wonderful epic movement.

The *chanson de geste* celebrated chiefly *prouesse,* and its hero was the man at arms, the *preux* or *prodom.* These stories were invariably set in the remote past, in the mythical age when knighthood was in flower, but the matter was of course grounded in the period of its composition, and the *preux* of the time of Charlemagne was therefore adorned with the very qualities which would endear a knight to his lord and his comrades in the time of the crusades. These qualities were courage and strength, loyalty, Christian zeal, and a burning desire for fame and glory—the very qualities with which the knight recommended himself to his lady in the southern love-lyrics. Insofar as the knight was concerned, the social matrix of these very different genres was precisely similar. The northern songs exhibited the knight as warrior; the southern depicted the knight in love. But the character of the knight in the two genres was significantly different.

Knighthood was a profession. In theory anyone might aspire to it, regardless of birth, but the presumption was that the order would sit badly on a churl since he would normally be lacking in the qualities requisite to a noble way of life. The knightly order tended therefore to form itself into a closed group, and those who conferred the honor—in the romances, at least—were usually careful to inquire into the lineage of the aspirant.

What actually made the knight was the *adoubement*. In early times this appears to have been a simple ceremony, the solemn presentation of weapons to the youth who was deemed properly qualified to receive them. The presentation was normally made by the father or the chief, so Tacitus tells us, but the chivalric relation was filial in itself, and whoever conferred arms upon the new knight acquired thereby some part of the parental authority. Accordingly, as feudalism developed, the dubbing of the knight was a function regularly assumed by the suzerain, who thus reinforced his authority as feudal lord with the authority of the patriarch. This authority was symbolized by a blow of the fist or stick, the *colée*, which often accompanied the dubbing, together with some words of admonition—"Be loyal," "Be brave," "Be brave and remember me." [1]

The investiture of a vassal with a vacant domain was similarly accomplished *par rain et par baston*, so that, in general, all ceremonies by which power was conferred or property transmitted were made to emphasize the patriarchal character of the chivalric order.[2] The force that flowed along the feudal lines and gave to each step in the hierarchy its appropriate strength and value was thus the power of the father. All feudal obligations were conceived of as filial in character, and in theory the king was the father of all, and the earthly representative of the Father in heaven.[3]

The system of military tenure had originated in the necessity for maintaining trained forces of heavy cavalry which could be put swiftly into the field against invading armies, particularly against the Arab horsemen. During the eighth century the Merovingian practice of granting benefices from the crown lands in payment for military service was adapted to the needs of the time, and a professional military class came into being which was supported by grants of land proportioned to the extent of the service contributed. The new vassals now held their lands not directly from the king, but from the great landholders whose interests they primarily defended. Thus, although the feudal authority theoretically descended from the apex of the feudal pyramid to the lowest vavasour, in reality, for most of these vassals power was resident in the immediate suzerain and hardly ascended further.[4]

As these grants of land for military service were not made in fee, the early chivalry retained for a time its character of a purely professional class. But the tendency in a paternalistic society to make all possession hereditary brought about the transformation of the equestrian class into a landholding aristocracy socially indistinguishable from the class which had created it. By the end of the ninth century the transformation appears to have been complete. The armed cavalry was now a hereditary nobility, and the relation of suzerain and vassal, with its bonds of mutual obligation, was sanctified as the traditional organization of upper-class society.

One hears very little about nobility prior to the twelfth century. The term itself seems to have marked chiefly an economic distinction. The hereditary landholders who were able to live on their lands in a noble manner—that is, without toil—were said to be noble. The bourgeois, as yet an anomalous urban class, and the free peasantry were not noble. The laboring serfs were classed as property, along with other captives, "*bêtes en parc, poissons en vivier et oiseaux en cages.*"[5] Aside from the landed gentry, all of the soldiers who followed a lord to battle, his servants and retainers, were classed as *sirvens,* regardless of their ancestry. The greater part of these retainers were in fact servile in origin, though some were impoverished descendants of the old equestrian class.

In the first years of the eleventh century, to meet the demands of the incessant petty wars of the period, the high nobility again found it necessary to expand its military forces, and grants of land began to be made in large numbers for military service. The new chivalric class appears to have been recruited chiefly from among the *ministeriales* of the manor, who already held posts of trust, and particularly from among those servants who were principally occupied as guards and watchmen and were therefore accustomed to the use of arms. These squires were dignified with knighthood and enfeoffed with lands from the seignoral domains. It was simply a matter of time before they too formed a hereditary nobility.

In a few generations this petty nobility constituted the bulk of the European upper class.[6]

It was, however, from first to last, a subsidiary aristocracy, and its members rarely succeeded in penetrating by conquest or marriage into the small and carefully guarded ranks of the superior nobility which had created it and which employed it. Its relations with this upper stratum were cordial. It mingled with it freely, attended its courts, and ministered to it in every way, while at the same time it remained absolutely distinct from it. As a privileged class, everywhere respected, the knights naturally aspired to the highest honors and distinctions their station could afford, but their aspirations were strictly defined and delimited. Service was the keynote of the knightly order. The knight was dedicated to the service of his lord, his country, his king, his faith, his church, and in time, his lady; he was not especially encouraged to serve himself. In theory, at least, he desired to own only his arms and his fame—he was, ideally, self-dedicated to a life of glorious poverty, and this ideal the courtly literature everywhere advanced.

Since the greater part of the noble troubadours and *trouvères* were drawn from this lesser nobility, it is reasonable to assume that the ideals of chivalry which they developed in the course of the next centuries would reflect the character of the knights themselves quite as much as the interests and tastes of the lords whom they served. The great nobles hardly needed other justification for their existence than their wealth and their traditional prestige. But the petty nobility could vaunt neither brilliant ancestry nor important possessions; it had to found its prestige upon less tangible assets—upon its prowess, its loyalty, its honor, upon the high standards of the class and the personal worth of the individual.

The ideals of chivalry did not have to be invented. In part they were dictated by the requirements of the profession; they reflected the traditional virtues of the fighting man. But when these values were elaborated from the point of view of the retainer, there emerged certain divergences of interest from the parent class, the usual disparity of interest of employer and employee. These found a speedy expression in literature.[7]

A consequence of the tension between the high nobility and the low was the age-long debate as to the nature of nobility and the worth of the individual. The high nobility, having been seized of the land for some centuries, felt that it had always owned it and was divinely appointed to rule. For this class, nobility—and its concomitants, privilege, virtue and wealth—were a matter of birth, transmissible only by heredity, and therefore the gift of the father. The upper class was to some extent encouraged in this conception by the teachings of the church, which saw in the established order the clearest evidence of the will of the Almighty. But as the new chivalric class was gradually ennobled, it became useful to distinguish between the nobility of birth and the nobility of personal merit, and it was normal for those who had not the former to insist on the unique importance of the latter.

The problem had been debated before. No less an authority than Boethius could be cited in support of the view that virtue is the only nobility,[8] and there was no lack of excellent saws to the same effect to be found in the handbooks and anthologies from which, in the Middle Ages, classical learning was chiefly culled. Seneca was often paraphrased:

> All men descend from the same original stock; no one is better born than another except insofar as his disposition is nobler and better suited to the performance of good actions.[9]

The fundamental difference between the poetic traditions which first manifested themselves in France north and south of the Loire related to the nature of the knight's personal nobility. The French *trouvères* based their idea of nobility upon the manly virtues, prowess, loyalty, and honor, those traits which would primarily recommend the fighting man to his lord. The southern troubadours grounded their concept of nobility not so much upon prowess as upon courtesy. In exemplifying these concepts, these poets developed two radically different types of poetry, the narrative of martial deeds and the song of love. Both in some sense involved the idea of the quest, but the goal on the one hand was fame, on the other it was love; one was a public and the other a private object, and the means of attaining these goals were not the same. To win the love of the lady one had to prove one's worth in long and patient service, and no one could serve properly unless he himself had true love in his heart to sustain him in the rigors of his servitude. For the troubadour, therefore, nobility was the capacity to love and to acquire worth through love. This was possible only to those who had a natural predisposition, and this disposition was the gentle heart. The gentle heart was not something one inherited. It was the gift of God. "The son," wrote the troubadour Arnaut de Marueill, "may receive from his father lands and a great inheritance, but merit he can hold from himself alone. High birth and great riches do not confer merit upon him who has not a noble heart, a noble heart well-disciplined." [10]

The troubadours debated everything; they formed indeed a sort of public debating society, but on this point all were agreed. Nobility came from the heart alone, and the noble heart was an individual characteristic, the outward sign of which was love. The possession of the gentle heart could not be deduced from one's ancestry, but the gentle heart conferred nobility regardless of ancestry:

gentil corage
fan los gentils e·ls ioios,
e·l gentilezza de nos
non val mais a eretage,
pos tut em d'una rasitz . . .
pos d'un paire son tut l'enfan.

> the gentle heart makes men gentle and joyous, and gentility owes nothing to heredity, since all come from one root . . . since all are children of one father.[11]

"We all come from one root, we are all children of one father" —upon this rock the troubadours founded their church. "When Adam delved and Eve span, who was then the gentleman?" The celebrated question in the *Roman de Rou* expressed an idea that found echoes everywhere in medieval literature and sometimes, as in the early fourteenth century *Roman de Fauvel,* with considerable resonance: "Nobility, as the sage says, comes solely from the heart graced with goodness. . . . Know that it comes not from the womb. . . . Did they issue from it on horseback?" [12] The question of nobility was however somewhat more complex than this. In an oft-quoted passage in *Politics* V, Aristotle had defined nobility in terms of personal excellence and inherited wealth, and it was noted that this sage had decided that no man could follow virtue who had to earn his livelihood, since trade was dishonest and toil was brutalizing. Juvenal furnished another commonplace: "*Nobilitas animi sola est atque unica virtus.*" It was argued therefore, very sensibly, that nobility had been the portion of those who in the beginning had manifested exceptional virtue, which they had passed along with their wealth to their progeny. "*De ce* [that is, *la vertu*]" wrote Brunetto Latini, "*nasqui premierement la noblete de gentil gent, non pas de ses ancestres.*"[13]

It was generally conceded that as between the two sorts of nobility, one's personal nobility—which Dante called *virtus*—and the nobility of one's ancestors, which was inherited, the former was the more important. Without personal excellence nobody could be called noble. The only question was whether one who was without noble ancestry could be considered capable of personal excellence. In time, this issue split along Guelf-Ghibelline lines. Dante, while he did not absolutely reject the idea of inherited nobility in the *Convivio* (IV, 3), put his chief emphasis on the nobility of the spirit, that is, upon the moral worth of the individual.[14] In the *canzone* which sets forth his views on the subject of nobility, he says flatly, "wherever virtue is, there is nobility":

> E gentilezza dovunque e vertute,
> ma non vertute ov'ella.[15]

Nevertheless, in *Monarchia* (II, 3) in discussing the nobility of Aeneas, the father of the Roman people, he lays the greatest stress upon the ancestry of this hero who transmitted to the Romans the nobility of three continents.[16]

The aristocratic view on this issue was that from one's ancestors one inherited not only one's station in life, but also the predisposition to noble and virtuous action which such station betokened. This inheritance, the result of God's will and providence, absolutely defined one's position in the cosmic structure; it foreclosed the status of each individual born into this world—it was his destiny. Thus Egidio Romano, himself a member of the high nobility, after summing up the four characteristics of noble natures,

> Primo enim sunt magnanimi, secundo magnifici, tercio dociles et industres, quarto sunt politici et affabiles,

goes on to tell us that these qualities are a sort of family heirloom. The nobleman is like that because his original ancestors were like that and

> cum filii sint quidam effectus parentum, naturale est filiis imitari parentes nobiles.

"Out of beasts come beasts, out of men come men, and out of the good and prudent are born the good and prudent." [17]

The troubadours founded their entire system on the social mobility of the individual, the perfectability of man through his own efforts, and they opposed vigorously the idea that each man's fate was determined by his ancestry. Heredity played a certain role in a man's character, Sordello admitted. It gave him his natural endowment. But one man can, through his desire to acquire merit, force his nature upward by taking on new and higher obligations, while another can force his nature down and cover himself with shame. A man of middle-class birth may become noble through his deeds and his love of honor; a gentleman may become ignoble because he does nothing worthy of praise. Therefore it cannot be said that nobility comes through good birth alone; but, he concluded, the gentle heart is always the source of noble deeds:

> Pero nobles cors e gentils
> Es de totz bos faiz segnorils.[18]

The continuator of the *Romance of the Rose*, Clopinel, developed this same position in a statement full of good sense. In the course of Nature's interminable harangue, she remarks that it is fortune alone who orders the social position of men:

> Through me they are all born equally naked, strong and weak, fat and thin. I put them all on the same footing as regards their humanity. It is Fortune who does the rest. If anyone, boasting of his nobility, dared to contradict me and pretended that gentlemen by birth are of better condition than those who till the soil or live by their labor, I should answer that nobody is noble unless he gives himself to the practice of virtue, and that none is a villain save for his vices, which make him odious. Nobility comes of natural generosity, and gentility of lineage is valueless when it lacks goodness of heart. That is why the noble must show in himself the qualities of his ancestors who attained to nobility by the greatness of their works. When they died they took all their virtues with them and left their heirs their wealth and nothing more; these succeed to their fortune, but not to their worth or nobility unless they try to distinguish themselves by their minds or their virtues.[19]

Evidently there was nothing new or startling in this idea when in the last third of the thirteenth century "the sage" Guido Guinizelli incorporated it, together with a great deal more of the troubadour love-theory, in the celebrated *canzone Al cor gentil,* with which, it is said, he inaugurated the "sweet new style" in Italy.[20] Through the vast influence not only of the *Romance of the Rose* but of troubadour doctrine in its many manifestations, these commonplaces took root everywhere.[21] Nevertheless the proposition continued to be put forward in chivalric literature for many centuries that unless a man was of noble ancestry he would have little capacity for virtue. The point was earnestly debated in the First Book of *The Courtier,* and in England both Shakespeare and Spenser found the Ghibelline view which Dante had developed in *Monarchia* most agreeable to the Elizabethan concept of a well-ordered kingdom. The doctrine that ancestry is a kind of destiny, so stimulating to the naturalistic novelists of the nineteenth century, was a stereotype of medieval epic. In the romances, whenever a young man of unknown origin distinguishes himself through some unusual feat, it normally turns out that he in fact is the son of a king, or at the least the bastard of some mighty champion.[22] It is therefore with some surprise that we first come upon what looks like an egalitarian principle in the love-poetry of the troubadours.

It has been said that the question of nobility of soul becomes important when people become indifferent to nobility of birth.[23] But in the Middle Ages nobody was indifferent to nobility of birth; least of all the bourgeois, whose besetting ambition it was to acquire lands and nobility as soon as might be. What seems on its face democratic and egalitarian in the doctrine of the troubadours was in reality the expression of a different and more rigidly exclusive ideal of aristocracy than the traditional concept; moreover, this was an ideal toward which a poor knight might aspire with some hope of success. The troubadours had no idea that all men were created equal. Even if all stemmed from one root, the differences were obvious. What the knightly poets had in mind was the formulation of a principle in terms of which an economically dependent class could assert its claim to the very highest nobility. To this end, they attacked the principle of inherited nobility with the sweeping assertion that nature puts all men on the same footing, while at the same time they insisted on the absolute superiority over all others of those favored few upon whom nature has bestowed the gentle heart.

Thus there emerged a new principle of nobility, individualistic in character, which could be deduced solely from a man's bearing and behavior. The net result was to minimize the role of the father in determining the worth of the individual, who thus became a self-contained entity of independent trajectory. In this view of the matter, nobility was transformed into a dynamic conception of moral and aesthetic nature, totally dissociated from questions of property and power. It ceased to be thought of as an inherited possession; it became an aptitude and a process, the ultimate aim of which was self-perfection through the love of beauty—that same principle which Burckhardt took to be cardinal in the Renaissance world-picture.

In this process the motivating force was not, however, an abstract longing for the beautiful in general, but specifically the love of a beautiful woman of whom the knight endeavored to make himself worthy. It was the high function of the lady, therefore, to guide the lover upward in worth and dignity to the utmost reach of his potentiality. This was the true justification of earthly love:

> And true love commands that neither count nor king be chosen, duke nor emperor, but a true lover, without a treacherous heart, frank and loyal, and who guards himself from falling into error.[24]

Thus in declaring himself independent of the determinism of the social system which had created him, the knight as lover submitted himself to another sort of servitude. Without ceasing to gravitate toward the lord who employed him, he assumed an orbital motion around the lady who fascinated him, his star. It was from this source that he acquired his worth and greatness; but the combination of forces necessarily gave his course a certain eccentricity.

In the epic tradition, on the other hand, love and the gentle heart were among the least of the knightly virtues. Courage and strength came first; after these, loyalty. In the chivalric stories the most odious of the knightly sins, after cowardice, was treason. It was also the most common. In this, no doubt, the storytellers reflected the untrustworthy nature of the vassal, whose loyalty outside the storybooks appears to have been as little as his material need was great. So fragile were the relations of lord and vassal in the Midi, in the thirteenth century, that the Counts of Toulouse generally found it more convenient to employ Navarrese and Aragonese mercenaries than to mobilize their own unruly chivalry.

In the primitive concept, the knight's honor, his worth or worship, was synonymous with his reputation, a fluctuating value which he labored to sustain. The knights of the romances were as avid of fame and noise as the modern athlete. They exerted themselves mightily to win praise; we find them weeping piteously when through some mishap they have suffered a loss in reputation.[25] In time, however, the concept of honor was developed to the point where it became a private matter depending on subtleties understandable only to knights. Bravery and loyalty were practical virtues useful in war, but the knight's honor became refined so that it was neither a rational nor a practical consideration. It was an artistic principle that shaped a gentleman's behavior, an aesthetic concept in which was rooted the *esprit de corps* of a class which sought to distinguish its customs as much as possible from the rationalistic practices of less dedicated people.

In the thirteenth century there was evidently still a certain confusion as to the style proper to the knight. The *chansons de geste* are full of incidents which reveal the development of an elaborate ideal of aesthetic behavior as between knight and knight, but it must be granted that these courtesies are sometimes strangely incongruous with the ferocity which these fictional champions display. In the *Covenant Vivien* the noble paladin Vivien cuts off the noses and lips of five hundred pagan prisoners; in the *Chanson d'Antioche* the Christian knights use the severed heads of their enemies as ammunition in their catapults; in *Raoul de Cambrai* the hero burns the Abbey of Origni with a hundred nuns locked up in it.

Judging by the chronicles, these imaginary barbarities did not come very far short of the facts of medieval life.[26] Richard Lion-Heart, the mirror of chivalry, a knight "ever motivated by inborn gentility and endowed with the valor of Hector"—so his chronicler tells us—is said to have put out the eyes of fifteen French knights. He had them led back to the French camp by one of their number whose right eye had been spared for the purpose, and his enemy, the most noble Philippe Auguste, in order "not to be thought inferior to Richard in prowess and valor," returned this compliment with fifteen English knights similarly mutilated.[27] With respect to these epic doings, as the chronicles report them, it is not at all easy to disentangle fact from fiction, or fiction from propaganda. The hero was supposed to inspire both admiration and terror. These were the components of medieval glamour. But there is little reason to doubt that the knights of the twelfth century demonstrated their brutality whenever they had occasion.[28] The Italian princes of the time of the Renaissance, if vastly more polished than their twelfth century prototypes, seem not a whit inferior to them in ferocity. The inconsistencies of behavior with which Richard Lion-Heart teases our comprehension are even more marked when we try to form an impression of the character of such polished noblemen as Filippo-Maria Visconti [29] or Sigismondo Malatesta,[30] in whom the barbarity of the savage and the delicacy of the courtier appear to have coexisted without merging in the least. In the same way, the epic and the lyric strains in romance poetry run side by side for centuries without losing their individual character as poetry of aggression and poetry of love.

What assimilated the one sort of poetry to the other was the generally developing sense of style. As the concept of chivalry was poetically elaborated, the knight's behavior, at least in fiction, became more and more subject to the aesthetic principle. Style was the obsession of the courtly maker in whatever genre he exerted himself and—he would have us believe—in life itself. The knight as hero and the knight as lover were poetic forms which grew out of the aspirations of the class that shaped them, and which in turn they helped to shape. Before Roland was imagined, there could have been no Bayard; before Amadis, no Philip Sidney. Knighthood originated, as we have seen, in a practical necessity. The knight was originally differentiated from other warriors chiefly by the nature of his equipment, and his superior utility in the field gave him social status. But his utility was ephemeral. In battle after battle from Crécy to Varna, it was amply demonstrated that the armed knight could not hold his own against the brigaded anonymous infantryman armed with the bow or pike. Yet knighthood did not die. Long after its practical value was lost, it retained its hold on the imagination. Its substance faded, but its style survived, and in this process of keeping alive what had never quite existed the poet was indispensable.

The *preux* of the *chansons de geste* and the *courtois* of the *chansons d'amour* were, after all, ideal fantasies, not creatures of flesh and blood. The stories of indomitable heroes who, after wading all day in seas of blood, at sunset lean moodily upon their swords and contemplate the vast field of the slain, came into being, it has been remarked, at precisely the time when battles were relatively bloodless scuffles. Similarly the humble posture which the knight assumes at his lady's feet in the troubadour love-song proceeded from the poet's imagination in an age when the social status of woman was in general not too far above that of the horse. The Age of Chivalry, like the Age of Faith, was in large part an artistic creation.

In sober fact, everything indicates that by the middle of the twelfth century the condition of the newly created class of petty nobles was already pitiable, and the chronicles of Ordericus Vitalis, Giraldus Cambrensis and Guibert de Nogent eloquently attest the greed and brutality of the higher aristocracy. It was not in imitation of reality, but in contrast to the social squalor of their time that the knightly poets concocted the tradition of chivalry, transforming the barbarism of the past into a golden age peopled with the paladins of Charlemagne and the knights of the Table Round.[31] The magnificent fantasies which these poets passed off as history had, needless to say, no relation whatever to the times described by Gregory of Tours, our chief source of information with regard to Merovingian times, nor to anything which can conceivably be regarded as a reliable record. The relation of these fantasies to the character of contemporary chivalry, as, for example, Peter of Blois described it in a letter to a friend, is more obvious.[32]

If the knightly poets set themselves the task of ennobling their order, it was doubtless not in any profoundly didactic spirit, but because the writer's profit has always arisen from showing people themselves as they would like to be. In any case, the poets elaborated a fantasy of knighthood which had decided social utility.[33] Their *chansons* were in a very special sense mirrors of knighthood, and they indicated at the same time for the benefit of their patrons what was fitting in a prince who desired to be properly served. In time, knighthood took on a religious color; the knights became the militia of the church and bravery was added to the Christian virtues. Flights of angels descended from the skies to fetch the souls of Roland and Oliver up to the throne of their heavenly Lord. To the formula of the *adoubement*, "*Sois preux*," was added the admonition "*Aime Dieu*." In spite of clerical opposition the *benedictio novi militis* found its way into the ritual of the church, and after the middle of the thirteenth century the sword was regularly bestowed in its service.[34]

In a system of chivalry based upon prowess, obviously, woman was of no great value. She might render occasional service of a more or less menial nature, but in general she was a nuisance, a distraction, and a source of trouble. Accordingly, in the *chansons de geste*, the knight does not serve the lady. She serves him.

It would be a mistake, however, to conclude from the cavalier treatment which the ladies of the epic tales receive that the knights were imagined as being devoid of sentiment. On the contrary, terrible as they showed themselves to their enemies, the knights were bound to their friends by bonds of the most exquisite tenderness. In story and in chronicle, they were depicted weeping together and kissing each other with a lack of restraint that seems astonishing in so warlike a context. Roland and Oliver weep for each other at Roncevaux; a hundred thousand knights weep for Thierri when he fights with Ganelon; Sir Palomides weeps piteously when Tristram defeats him. In the chronicles of Villehardouin, Joinville, Froissart, the knights are constantly shedding manly tears. The knights were not stoic in character. They were thought of as emotional people, warmhearted and generous; but their tenderness was mainly reserved for manly things. When Roland is about to die at Roncevaux, he thinks sadly of the beautiful world he is leaving; he thinks of his lord, his friend, his comrades, his sword. The thought of *la belle Aude*, his betrothed, never crosses his mind.

The epic knight evidently had no idea of wasting his time and his strength in dalliance with women. On the contrary, in these stories it was the women who were dazzled by the beauty of the men, and it was they who normally made the necessary advances. They were shameless. In *Raoul de Cambrai*, for example, the lady offers herself with such straightforward abandon as only a male author would readily conceive:

> Vees mon cors, com est amanervis:
> Mamele dure, blanc le col, cler le vis;
> Et car me baise, frans chevalier gentis,
> Si fais de moi trestot a ton devis.[35]

The *chansons de geste* represent, of course, a type of two-fisted, highly sexed fiction which has maintained its popularity in one form or another to the present day. It is characteristic of this sort of story that the women are often inclined to evil and always burning with desire, while the men are by nature temperate and businesslike. Whether in the epic or the lyric, the good knight's outstanding characteristic is *mesure.*

The ladies of the *chanson de geste,* in spite of the summary treatment they ordinarily receive, serve their knights indefatigably. They disarm them, bathe them and massage them after their warlike exertions,[36] and often they wait upon them in other ways, less consonant with honor. When the knight, after a good supper, retires to rest, it is not unusual for the fair lady of the house to appear at his bedside clad in a fur mantle only, or to slip quietly into bed beside him as he sleeps. In some cases the knight then proceeds to give the lady a lesson calculated to improve her morals. In *Ider,* when the hero wakes to find the lady of the house at his bedside, nude under her fur cloak, he sends her sprawling with a kick in the belly. King Arthur treats the lady with the golden hair in much the same way in the romance of *The Knight of the Parrot.* In *Morte d'Arthur* Sir Alisaunder declares he would rather cut off his hangers than give any pleasure to the lustful queen Morgan le Fay in whose castle he is being entertained.[37]

We must not, however, be deceived by the calmness with which the epic knight takes his amours. If the knight often seems indifferent to the charms of the lady in these tales, the audience certainly does not. Women play no significant part in *The Song of Roland,* but in many of the medieval narratives they occupy a considerable amount of text, for the poet reports with unflagging interest and satisfaction all the details of the encounter of the knight and the passionate lady. Evidently the knight's behavior in these passages was dictated by the conventions of the genre. The epic knight, like his modern counterpart, the cowboy of fiction, was more interested in deeds than in women. Moreover, French taste throughout the Middle Ages inclined pleasantly to the idea that love was the natural tribute which the female paid to the dazzling male, who, for his part, was accustomed to receive it with the carelessness of one who had no present need.

In these stories, of course, it is invariably the beauty and the strength of the knight which arouse the concupiscence of the lady. His intellectual or artistic qualities have no interest for her. When Iseult sees Tristan naked in the bath, she is greatly impressed with the noble proportions of his frame, and she runs over in her mind his possibilities as a warrior. As it happens, he is also a famous *jongleur*, but this is not the sort of attribute that would recommend him to *la belle Iseult*.[38] The usual rationalization is that in the unsettled times when these stories were written, the paramount need of a lady was for a man who could protect her, not for a lover who could amuse her, so that the indispensable attribute of a hero of romance would be prowess.[39] Perhaps this conclusion bears some relation to the fact, but the relation to the fantasy is more apparent. Women in our day stand in little need of the sort of protection which the knightly champion could afford them; they have the police. Yet the fictional qualifications of the romantic lover have not changed essentially since the time of the crusades. The audience for which the *chansons de geste* were designed was not much interested in the intellectual attributes of the epic hero. Intellect was an attribute of traitors and wizards. Love was for mollycoddles. The epic knight was a man among men.

The conventions which regulated the relations of knight and lady in the epic tales applied also to all the lyric modes which developed in France independent of the lyricism of the Midi. These early songs—the *chansons d'histoire, chansons de toile, chansons à personnages*—regularly depict the amorous lady as an enthusiastic person, not readily inhibited by her parents or her husband, while her lover is punctilious, patronizing, withdrawn, and proud. What underlay this convention was very likely the idea, characteristic of the epic, that concupiscence is primarily a female ailment to which the truly virile man is normally immune. In the *chansons de geste*, accordingly, the knight is made to move majestically along the road to glory through a host of admiring females whose hearts break like bubbles as he passes. In the *chansons de toile,* when we catch a glimpse of the shadowy lover, he is in much the same mood as his epic prototype. And when the hero occasionally gives the nod to one or another of the damsels who beset him, lured to her through fraud or sorcery, or out of pity, or through sheer excess of animal spirits, he seldom stays with her very long. Like Aeneas, he has other fish to fry.

These are by no means, however, the only traditions exemplified in the early romances. The Celtic heroes are often of another stripe, not only susceptible, but unpleasantly aggressive in their love-making. Gawain, for example, is a lady's man. In *Perceval le Gallois* he finds himself attracted by Gran de Lis; she refuses her favors, whereupon he ravishes her brutally in spite of her shrieks and her struggles.[40] In the *Lai de Graelent,* the wise and courteous hero, having exhausted his powers of persuasion on the recalcitrant lady he meets in the forest, at last drags her off into the bushes:

> Graelent la truve si fiere
> E ben entent que par proiiere
> Ne fera point de sun plaisir,
> N'il ne s'en veut ensi partir;
> En l'espese de la forest
> A fet de li ce que le plest.[41]

This unceremonious treatment of women is, as we have seen, a familiar aspect of the heroic nature, a necessary consequence of the fantasy of the aggressive male. It is natural that the contempt for the lady's feelings which the hero displays when he is not in the mood for love-making, he should exhibit also when he is. In any case his courtship is summary. The process, interesting but not protracted, by which the epic knight passed from flattery to persuasion and from persuasion to force became conventionalized quite early as a separate poetic genre, evidently of considerable popularity, the *pastourelle.*

The *pastourelle,* it is true, had nothing to do with ladies. It depicted the encounter of a knight with a *vilaine,* a farm girl or shepherdess. From the psychological point of view, of course, the class distinction is not the essential consideration; what is important is the behavior attributed to the knight. Nevertheless, the class distinction in these matters was conventionally considered of radical importance in dictating the behavior of the gentleman. This is apparent everywhere in the literature of love. As late as the last quarter of the eighteenth century, Goldsmith characterized his hero, Marlow, as a terrible swashbuckler with lower-class girls, but pitifully timid with ladies, and upon this comic combination of two separate literary traditions the plot hinges in *She Stoops to Conquer.*

The knights of the romances, moreover, did not scruple to take ladies by force when they had a mind to it. They won ladies as prizes in tourneys, they staked them as wagers in single combat, they relieved one another of their ladies on the highroad as a matter of routine. As for these ladies, it is by no means clear in the romances where they come from or where they go. They seem to have no regular means of support, but are led about by their knights, traded, exchanged, and abandoned rather like horses, and nobody troubles his head very much about them, least of all the poet. According to Chrétien de Troyes, in the golden age of chivalry it was considered dishonorable in a knight to force a defenseless lady or even a *vilaine,* but if one wrested a lady away from her knight by force of arms one was entitled to do with her as he pleased.[42] This idea, only partially borne out by the stories of "those times," appears to be based on the theory that it was not cricket for the knight to take what was undefended, but very sporting to take what was defended badly.

However that may be, the knights of these encounters give the impression of being untroubled hedonists who belong to a somewhat different tradition than the *prodom* of the *chansons de geste.* That worthy is, from the sexual point of view, the ancestor of Spenser's Sir Guyon or the Rinaldo of the *Gerusalemme Liberata,* for whom the delights of the Bower of Bliss constitute more of a menace than a temptation. Such heroes may be loved by women; but they are not characterized as lovers. Their bodies may flame briefly with desire, but the heart is not much involved. They are at the opposite extreme from the knight of the southern lyric.

As the epic narratives developed an ideal of the knight in the exercise of his profession, they necessarily insisted on his manly and aggressive character. In the southern lyric the knightly archetype was defined in its passive aspect. Here the knight was at peace, a courtier; and a different set of qualities was called into play. The two were opposite, but complementary characterizations; they reflected a normal polarity and emerged at about the same time, precisely as we should expect, though, as we have seen, in different places.

The southern poets, the troubadours, had evidently not much taste for the epic genres. They preferred shorter forms suitable to subjective expression. The song, the *canso,* which was their specialty celebrated one theme principally—not joy of battle and the pride of manhood, but joy of love and the beauty of woman. The characterization of the hero varied with the nature of the genre. The *preux* sought glory, moving athletically toward a noble death. The *courtois* did not exhibit any desire to die. On the contrary, he sought the joy of life in sensual and spiritual beauty and awaited in patience the rewards that beauty in time accords to the deserving. Roland was the ideal figure in the literature of prowess. In the literature of courtesy, the ideal of the knight, his leader and guide—*capdel et guitz*—was not a man. It was a woman.

THE LADIES

Whatever its origins, the state of perpetual wardship to which women were condemned in ancient Greece and in republican Rome was a matter of great economic importance, the result of which was to conserve the family property and to transmit it within the male line. In Greece the civil laws denied legal capacity to women as long as they lived. "The slave has no will," wrote Aristotle; "woman has, but it is powerless; the child has, but it is incomplete." As a woman was not considered to have sufficient mental or moral capacity, she was never *sui juris* and the law placed her under the tutelage of masters, *kyrioi*—her father, first, then her husband, her father's heirs, and, failing these, the state.[1]

In ancient Rome the *paterfamilias* was the sovereign of the household. None of its members had any legal rights with reference to him. He had the power to do as he pleased with his children. He could sell them if he wished, and he could give away his daughters in marriage without consulting their wishes. With regard to the inheritance of his property, nevertheless, the girls and boys stood on an equal footing, and it was only when the father died that the legal distinction between the sexes operated. In this case the boys, after they reached puberty, became legally independent. The girls were placed under the tutelage of a guardian and remained so all their lives.[2]

Normally, in ancient Rome, when a girl was married, her father gave her *in manum mariti*, and she had henceforth no family save her husband's. In this type of marriage, the husband acquired complete control of his wife's property, and only her dowry remained in her power. By the time of the XII. Tables, marriage with *manus* had become exceptional, and the original family retained control over the married woman's property; nevertheless when a girl was married she passed personally into her husband's *potestas*. He was expected to direct her and to chastise her; he could punish her, indeed, even with death—these rights were the common perquisites of marriage. Thus while the Roman *domina* was the respected mistress of her household, it was her tutors who controlled her property and her husband who controlled her person and, presumably, her mind.[3]

During the decline of the republic, and afterward during the empire, the *paterfamilias* lost much of his power to the state, and women were emancipated little by little both from *manus* and from tutelage. Under Augustus, wives who were mothers of several children were freed from wardship. Under Claudius, the tutelage of the agnates was suppressed. Under Justinian, a father could no longer force his daughter into marriage. Finally, an edict of Theodosius delivered all Roman women from tutelage. In this process the husband, like the father, lost a great deal of his authority, and eventually the civil judge took over the administration of domestic relations. Thus in the time of the Christian emperors, women were substantially the equals of men before the law. There remained, it is true, because of the *pudicitia* attributed to their sex, and the *fragilitas* of their nature, certain civil acts from which they were excluded, but these could hardly be considered serious disabilities.[4]

No such evolution is traceable in the history of German law, the other main influence upon the legal structure of the Middle Ages in France. German women spent their lives under constant tutelage, but the basis of their legal incapacity seems to have been rationalized not in terms of their moral or intellectual weakness but in terms of their physical shortcomings, their inability to maintain their rights by force of arms. German women were therefore, so to speak, in lifelong protective custody. A woman under the *mundium*, or right of wardship, could, in theory, do nothing without her guardian. He represented her at law, and he controlled her property.

The Lombard law was the extreme example of this system. Its influence persisted in many parts of Europe until a remarkably late date—in Tuscany, in the States of the Church, and in some of the German principalities it still regulated the position of women in the middle of the nineteenth century. Under this law, "*mulier semper sub potestate viri, aut potestate curtis regiae debeat permanere.*" [5] The *mundualdd*—father, husband, or brother—was legally responsible for the actions of his ward; it was he who suffered damage if she was injured by the act of a third party; in general it was he, and not she, who was seized of her property. When the *mundualdd* died, his male heirs inherited the *mundium*, so that their sisters or mother could not marry without their consent. Indeed, among the Lombards the *mundium* was a property right which could be sold like the Roman *manus*. The law of the Franks was more liberal. Frankish women were permitted to hold and to transmit property. By the time of Charlemagne, the *mundium* accrued to the state, not to the family; and while women had nothing like equality at law, their guardianship was generally administered for their protection rather than for the profit of their tutors.[6]

After the dissolution of the Carolingian Empire, the *mundium* devolved upon the individual suzerain, and the wardship of women took on specifically feudal character. Under feudal law the inheritance of land by a woman was considered an injury to her suzerain since she was unable to render military service. Once title was distinguished from possession, however, it was considered that an heiress was capable of acquiring the title even though she could not be permitted to enjoy the possession of the fief. Feudal wardship thus became a property right which was vested in the suzerain, and he could give it or sell it to a knight who would then "carry" the fief for the woman and act as her *advocatus* in civil matters. Out of this prerogative came the suzerain's right to choose a husband for a female vassal. Heiresses were, in consequence, frequently forced into marriage by their suzerain, so that wife and fief were bestowed together upon a deserving vassal. In this manner, we are told by the anonymous biographer, the troubadour Elias de Barjols and his *jongleur* Oliver were ennobled by Alfonso II of Aragon, who gave them as a reward for their service at his court in Provence, a wife and lands.[7]

When the system of military tenure became obsolete, the fief became a simple patrimony, and gradually the lord's rights of wardship were lost. Once a woman was allowed to possess her fief, she took over all the rights of a suzerain within the boundaries of her holding—the right of homage, the right of wardship, the power to make laws and treaties, raise troops and coin money. As far as the law was concerned, an unmarried woman in possession of a fief had all the rights and privileges of a man. It was thus not at all unusual for women of the nobility in France, in Provence, even in Italy, to administer important domains in their own right, or as regents during the absence of their husbands or the minority of their sons. Normally, however, a married woman was in the power of her husband as long as he could exert it. A maid might possess and rule her domains as long as she was single; the moment she married, in France, her husband took the investiture, and he became his wife's tutor, her *baillistre*. It was he who represented her henceforth in all civil actions; he carried her fief, and he had the usufruct of her property.

Under the customary law of the cities, codified in the charters which defined their rights, the legal position of women in the twelfth and thirteenth centuries in France did not differ materially from their situation under feudal law. As the basis of this law was Germanic, women were not considered inherently lacking in legal capacity; they were simply subordinated and made dependent on their husbands during the duration of their marriage. "The moment her baron is dead," wrote Beaumanoir, "the woman recovers her full will." [8]

The legal status of a married woman thus reflected, at least in theory, her relation to her husband in the home. In the domestic circle, presumably, the authority of the husband was paramount beyond dispute: the relation of man and wife was regulated by the Pauline dictum that "the head of every man is Christ and the head of the woman is the man." All the weight of church and state was massed behind this doctrine. A woman owed her husband the duty of unquestioning obedience. She had neither the capacity nor the right to form a separate opinion. "A wife should love what her husband loves," wrote Chiaro Davanzati, and without doubt such was the opinion, in general, of the thirteenth century husband. In view of woman's recalcitrant nature, a husband was accordingly considered both stupid and remiss in his duty to society if he did not correct her suitably, provided he did not willfully break her bones or mutilate her limbs.[9]

But in spite of the encouragement which law and custom gave the medieval husband in the enforcement of his authority, he does not appear to have been singularly successful in his efforts to control the medieval wife. The flood of misogynistic literature which rolls up from the thirteenth century in every country of Europe is truly impressive. From the huge and ill-assorted mass of material which we inherit from the Middle Ages, one fact, at least, emerges clearly—medieval man married for all sorts of reasons, but not often for love. Conditioned as we are, in our time, to regard marriage as the crowning event of a romantic courtship, it is difficult for us to realize that such a view is not only comparatively recent in point of time, but that in truth it is a concept which has never had much relation to the facts of life. In the Middle Ages, as in pagan times, marriage was primarily an economic arrangement which had no necessary connection with the tender passion. And even if the connubial arrangement resulted, as well it might, in a certain domestic affection, it was agreed on all hands that the quality of this feeling was very different from love.[10]

From the point of view of the church, Christian marriage was a sacrament, and therefore indissoluble. But in fact, marriage in the Middle Ages was normally an arrangement by which property was acquired, consolidated, and transmitted along predetermined familial lines: it was not so much people as lands which were joined in marriage. A bride not only brought property to her husband, but undertook to provide him with legitimate male children to carry on the family property in the future. In connection with this obligation she owed him the duty to make his marriage duties tolerable. Love was something very different from this. "A lady must honor her lover as a friend, not as a master," wrote the *trobairitz* Marie de Ventadour:

> E·il dompna deu a son drut far honor
> Cum ad amic, mas non cum a seignor.[11]

In the distinction that was regularly made between woman as mistress and woman as wife, freedom of choice naturally played an important part. It was not customary, in the Middle Ages, any more than in pagan times, to place weight on the preferences of young people in the choice of a spouse. Here, as elsewhere, father knew best, and courtship was normally an accord between elders. As the girl was from a legal viewpoint incapable of a rational choice, her enthusiasm with regard to the husband who was chosen for her was not an important consideration. Her consent to the marriage contract, of course, was indispensable, but as practically her sole alternative was the convent she did not often refuse what the gods provided. In the high nobility, especially, it was common practice to betroth a girl to a gentleman she had never seen, and, often enough, before she was nubile.[12] The results were not always happy. On the other hand, Eleanor of Aragon, for example, the daughter of Alfonso II, was betrothed to Raimon IV of Toulouse in 1200, when he was forty-seven. The girl was so young that the marriage had to be put off until she grew old enough. We have no reason to believe that the marriage was less successful than most: the lady turned out to be, in her day, one of the most widely celebrated of gallant women.

But while the medieval lady had little to say about the selection of a husband, generally speaking, she had complete freedom of choice with respect to a lover. Accordingly she was able to participate at the same time in two cultural patterns, each of which gave her a special status as a human being. While in the one system she was presumably an imbecile, of intellect insufficient to motivate a rational decision, in the other she was a goddess before whom strong men trembled, all-wise, all-beautiful, the object of adoration, the mirror of perfection, the guiding star of the knight.

What chiefly distinguished love from marriage was therefore

the voluntary element. What the lady bestowed upon her lover as a gift was essentially different from what she owed to her husband as a contractual obligation. In theory the two spheres of her activity were completely divorced. True love, so long as it remained pure, was a relationship in which a husband conceivably might acquiesce without dishonor, provided no breath of scandal touched his name. It might become adulterous, but it need not be so. The lover, too, had no cause for jealousy. Within the sphere of love an order of sexual intimacy was developed which had little to do with those straightforward passions which are normally directed to the enlargement of the family.

Marriage, indeed, offered the husband not even the pleasure of courtship. But this pleasure which marriage precluded could be enjoyed in the courtship of another man's wife, and the romantic exaltation which was alien to the home of a married man might well be found in the home of another married man—such, at least, was the rationale of the matter. Obviously, within the sanctity of his own home no husband could observe the laws of love even if he wished. The degree of spiritual absorption that was normal in a lover would be considered monstrous in the married state. Marriage imposed upon the husband the authority of the patriarch, whether he liked it or not, and in this august role it was chiefly a paternal affection that was appropriate to him. In marriage, the woman served; in love, it was the man. As between spouses the two attitudes could neither be reconciled nor alternated. The solution would have been perhaps to admit the equality of the sexes in marriage, but such an admission would have been, of course, inconceivable in the circumstances.

The medieval poets wisely kept the two orders of sexuality separate. There were the laws of marriage and the laws of love. They resulted in genres of fiction as widely different as the story of Griselda and the tale of Cabestaing. The list is short, in the literature of those times, of men who made mistresses of their wives, or wives of their mistresses.[13] The theory of marriage was based on the idea of the physical and mental superiority of the male, the fundamental dogma of a paternalistic culture. The theory of love was founded on the physical and spiritual prestige of woman. That two conceptions so widely opposed should coexist without contamination for centuries within the same historical frame may seem extraordinary; but such is the fact. Among the Provenceaux, a devoted lover was considered admirable; a uxorious husband, contemptible.[14]

In a *tenson* between Gui d'Ussel and his cousin Elias, Gui voices the orthodox doctrine of his day in this regard: "Through a mistress a man grows in worth, and through a wife he loses his prestige; for a man is esteemed for paying court to a mistress, but he is mocked for paying court to his wife":

> Per dompna vai bos pretz enan
> E per moiller pert hom valor,
> E per domnei de dompna es hom grasitz
> E per dompnei de moiller escarnitz.[15]

This view recommended itself fully to later ages. Four centuries after the time of Gui d'Ussel, Michel de Montaigne affirmed a very similar doctrine in terms most acceptable to his time:

> A good marriage—if such a thing exists—rejects the company and conditions of love. It endeavors to represent those of friendship. . . . Marriage has for its portion utility, justice, honor and constancy; a flat pleasure but of more universal nature. Love is founded upon pleasure only, and in truth its pleasure is more exciting, livelier and sharper, a pleasure inflamed by difficulty; it requires stinging and burning. It is no longer love when it is without arrows and without fire.[16]

Had marriages been arranged invariably with complete wisdom, it might perhaps have been more difficult to rationalize the extramarital relationship, but not impossible. Love and marriage were complementary not substitutive institutions. The poetry of *fin amor* expressed, among other things, the dissatisfaction of the upper classes with one aspect of the domestic arrangements they had made for themselves; but it did not reject marriage. It celebrated love, accepting marriage as a necessary evil. It is clear that this poetry was not the work of women, though they doubtless encouraged it. Nevertheless, the lyric tradition grew up about the person of the *mal mariée*, and in the stereotype of the unhappily married girl the poet found a bridge by means of which the opposed attitudes of the time might be connected in terms of common sympathy. Molière, in his day, sagely observed:

> Il est bien difficile enfin d'estre fidele
> A de certains maris faits d'un certain modelle,
> Et qui donne a sa fille un homme qu'elle hait
> Est responsable au Ciel des faites qu'elle fait.[17]

Behind the myth of the *mal mariée* was the widespread assumption that while sexual matters constitute a minor part of a man's business in life, they absorb all of a woman's existence. One meets everywhere in medieval literature the curious idea that women are inclined by nature to endless sexual indulgence, and that they derive from this activity much more pleasure than men. In the detailed analysis of the female character with which Andreas Capellanus embellished the third book of his treatise on Honest Love, the matter is set forth with characteristic vigor:

> Every woman in the world is likewise wanton, because no woman, no matter how famous and honored she may be, will refuse her embraces to any man, even the vilest and most abject, if she knows him to be powerful at the work of Venus; yet there is no man so strong at this work that he can satisfy the desires of any woman in any way.[18]

In his *Breviari d'Amor*, the earnest Franciscan Matfré Ermengaud elaborated yet more curiously upon this point:

> They spend their time walking the streets in order to get more gallants, and they make many men sin in this way by acting the courtesan with them, laughing too much and jesting with them, and speaking indecently . . . and through their evil instinct they wear very low-cut gowns, and show their breasts and their flesh in order to lure the sinner, to deceive him and to make him sin. The wretches do even worse; if they are married, they ruin the sanctity of the sacrament by desiring the company of their husband out of lechery

> and for vile carnal pleasure, and not in order to have children; and they cannot be satisfied in their vice, for they are constantly hanging about their husbands, and follow them day and night in order to make them surrender to their folly, and they will never say enough: in this manner they kill the most vigorous. And their husbands do not suffice for these traitresses; they will carry on their adulteries with the lowest actors, and nobody will ever be able to catch them at it once their skirts are down again.[19]

The tradition that women were not sufficiently endowed with reason to restrain their natural concupiscence found ample support in the classic writings which the fifteenth century humanists brought to light. The Renaissance writings on the subject of marriage regularly pointed out that the husband must explain to his wife that the object of sexual relations is procreation, as Plato, Aristotle, and other wise men had observed, and not aimless pleasure, as women, in their innocence, might imagine.[20]

In the concupiscence of the lady, however burdensome it might prove to her husband, the lover, on the other hand, found all his joy. The literature of the subject makes it amply clear that the medieval lady was thought to have resources to which her husband was forever a stranger. The lady usually appears in the troubadour *chansons* as a remote and unattainable vision of loveliness, but we are everywhere led to believe that once she was committed to love she was capable of giving such joy as would compensate the lover for all his patience:

> And this, Scripture shows us:
> When good fortune comes,
> A single day is worth a hundred.[21]

Indeed, when the lady of the song emerges in the round, she seems far from cold and far from shy; she foretells in no way Dante's Beatrice or Petrarch's Laura. In the *chansons* written by or attributed to women-poets, the poetess is never characterized in the role of the unattainable charmer. The ladies who speak in these songs do not admonish their knights to patience or urge them on to deeds of glory as we might expect. They do not even, like Sidney's Stella, cry, "No, no, no, no, no, no, my dear, let be." They are, on the contrary, depicted in their love-making exactly as if they were men, except that they are more passionate and more impulsive. Sometimes they are desperate with longing for their cold or faithless lovers; sometimes they sound a note of menace:

> I am forced to sing of something of which I have no desire to sing, so heavy is my complaint against him whose friend I am; for I love him more than anything else in the world, but neither courtesy nor mercy avail me with him, nor my beauty, nor my station, nor my wisdom: I am deceived, and betrayed just as if I were not desirable . . .
>
> I should be able to count on my prestige and my birth and my beauty, and above all on my true heart, and that is why I send this song yonder where you dwell, to be my messenger; and I desire to know, my fine handsome friend, why you show yourself so fierce and savage toward me. Is it pride or enmity? I do not know . . .
>
> And furthermore I wish you tell him, messenger, that in overmuch pride, many people find great trouble.[22]

It would appear then that the lady who sings in the courtly *chanson* represents a different stereotype from the lady who is sung to. The amorous lady closely resembles the amorous knight, but she is clearly not nearly as appealing a lover—she is more aggressive, more demanding; one is tempted to say, more masculine. From the dramatic viewpoint also, her role is altered. Noble and silent as a statue while she is the object of entreaty, the moment she finds a voice of her own she becomes unduly voluble. Evidently nobody troubled to devise a song for the unattainable lady: she had no need to sing. But once the proud beauty bestowed her love, her ideal character was lost. In the mind of the poet, she ceased to be a goddess; she became a woman, and took on the traditional infirmities of the sex. The roles were then reversed. It was she who pined and sighed for the knight, while he in his turn revealed himself as haughty and indifferent. The lovelorn lady entered, in short, the epic tradition, in which to love is to be at a disadvantage, helpless and vulnerable in a pitiless world.

To that tradition also belong the greater number of those early songs in French, the *chansons d'histoire* or *chansons de toile* which Bartsch grouped together under the heading of "romances."[23] All of these are songs of love or of complaint, objective in technique and dramatic in conception. The latest in point of time are those of Audefroi le Batard of Arras, which belong to the first half of the thirteenth century, but these are clearly the fruit of an attempt to revive a genre which belonged to an earlier day. Jeanroy considered that these are the only complete pieces we have which kept intact the conventions of the early lyric poetry in French which developed from the *chansons de geste*.[24] In fact, many exhibit traces of the influence of the courtly lyric of the Midi which made itself felt in the north after 1150, but it is obvious that these songs did not originate in that tradition.

In these songs the heroine is usually an unmarried girl of high parentage. She burns with love, and this passion she invariably expresses in the frank and straightforward manner that is characteristic of young girls in the French epic stories. The obstacles to this love are commonplace—the watchfulness of the parents, their opposition, the absence or the indifference of the gallant. The dramatic conception that binds together this body of verse is that of the languishing damsel and the self-sufficient male, the normal situation in all French poetry up to the middle of the twelfth century.

The knight in these songs is as shadowy as the lady in the troubadour *chanson*. It is invariably the girl who sings of love, and she is very expressive and vigorously characterized. These fair Yolandes and Aiglantines cannot attend to their affairs, so great is the weight of their longing. When they sew, they prick their fingers with the needle; when the man approaches they feel too faint to stand on their feet. The men, for their part, take the matter pretty much in their stride. Their attitude is magisterial, but receptive. Their feelings are delicate; they have to be apologized to with some frequency. It is obvious that these *personae* of the love-drama reflect the traditional relationship of knight and damsel in the *chansons de geste*, and these lyrics indicate, if anything, the popularity of the amatory situations depicted in those manly poems before the invasion of the southern love-poetry put a different face on the mode.[25]

The most interesting of the songs in Bartsch's collection is the group which Groeber, with singular acumen, called *sons d'amour*. He conjectured, on excellent evidence, that this genre had a full floriation in the last decades of the twelfth century. They are almost all *chansons de mal mariée*. This was hardly a diversified genre; with respect to their substance, the examples we possess differ very little the one from the other. The theme common to all is marriage, and this institution is handled in these songs with little respect and less than complete seriousness; in spite of their intensity these are on the whole comic songs.

The basis is a monologue spoken by the unhappy wife in dispraise of marriage and in praise of love. In the young wife's eyes marriage is a brutal captivity, endurable only because it is always possible to betray the jealous villain to whom ill-luck has bound her. The primitive form of the monologue is preserved only in a few examples; in *langue d'oc* there appear to be but two.[26] More usually the dramatic character of the song is emphasized in dialogue between the lady and her husband or the lady and her lover; sometimes the poet himself enters the action as witness or participant. These songs vary a good deal in quality, but the form was evidently very popular, for all of them are distinguished by a freshness of characterization which marks them off pleasantly from other contemporary forms. In general, the *mal mariée* has great verve, and she expresses herself with wit worthy of a better cause. Without exception the husband, "the Jealous One," is a sad and unsavory character who beats her, locks her up, threatens, and maltreats her—though naturally to no avail. Sometimes the husband is represented as physically repulsive, old and bald and thin and pale, and shaken by coughs. There are interesting caricatures:

Il est viels et rasotés
et glos come lous;
Si est magres et pelés
et si a le tous . . .[27]

It is only normal in such circumstances that the lady should make other arrangements. To distract her mind from the melancholy brute who afflicts her, she has a young and handsome lover to whom her heart is given:

j'ai bel amin
coente et joli,
a cui mes cuers s'otroie,

and she advises her husband to mind his own affairs if he knows what is good for him, for nothing can avert his doom:

ne soiés de moi jalous,
maix aleis votre voie,
car per Deu vos sereis cous
par riens ne me tenroie.[28]

The belle of these songs reveals, indeed, a sparkish humor which is in many ways reminiscent of her counterpart in English Restoration comedy. She is more than defiant. "Why," she asks in a gaily rhymed jingle, "why does he beat me and reproach me, my husband? Let him rage and bluster, the coward; all the more surely shall the beautiful, the blond, the jolly one have me. The jealous bore shall die of rage, and the sweet, savorous, amorous one shall have me:"

li jalous
enuious
de corrous
morra,
e li dous
savorous
amorous
m'avra.[29]

These songs, the fruit of a shockingly sophisticated conception of young womanhood, were surely not intended to be taken with solemnity. Their mood is gay, the rhythms are lilting, the spirit free. They are songs intended to excite laughter as well as a certain concupiscence. They constitute, of course, a wry comment on a plan of life which would make us shudder if we took a serious view of it. But these songs are far from didactic. In the gay outburst of the passionate young lady, there is no trace of the grave sententiousness with which the troubadour adorned his song. Decorum required here a different characterization. The mismarried lady did not argue. She asserted herself. But in her assertion, her predicament, her desire and her need—all too understandable—was implicit the whole system of *fin amor*. In these terms was most advantageously imagined the lady to whom the troubadour's song might be addressed—a lady neither distant nor haughty, but ripe, rebellious, ready, and eager—and above all, available. Such must have been the first step in the development of the character of the lady, if not in point of time, then in point of complexity. Psychologically, the lady who says yes comes first. All the other characterizations follow from this, from Guillaume IX's Dame Agnes to Dante's Lady Beatrice.

It is impossible to say with any certainty whether the *chanson de mal mariée* was in the relation of cause or consequence to the troubadour *chanson* of the Midi, and it is perhaps of no particular importance. The same set of conventions underly both genres, and the emotional patterns in which they are rooted are precisely the same. The difference is decisive in one point only—the one lady is easy, the other is difficult. It was the second lady who was destined to survive as a literary figure. It is upon her that the courtly poetry centers. Evidently the first had no great interest for those who wrote the knight's song: she was too willing. Nevertheless, in the drama of *fin amor* the *mal mariée* was indispensable. The loveless marriage is the very basis of the dramatic conception. It was not absolutely necessary to its plot that she should be charming; but unquestionably in her own *aria* the lady is charming. And it was in this genre particularly that the Jealous One got his comeuppance.

In the troubadour *chanson* the least obtrusive personage is that of the *gilos*, the jealous husband. Yet the character of True Love is necessarily influenced decisively by this menacing figure. Whether he is mentioned by the poet or not, the husband is always there, lurking in the shadows of the song. He is, of course, always ineffective; for, as we know, no man, however capable, is effective against Love. But he is always dangerous. In one of the earliest troubadour songs, in which we already find implicit the entire complex of the *mal mariée*, Guillaume IX gravely counsels the Jealous One regarding the hopelessness of his position:

> And I will tell you this, guardian, and give you this counsel, and it will surely be great folly not to believe me: It is hard to find a watchman who does not sometimes sleep.
>
> If you make it too costly for her to eat well, she will take whatever is at hand. If she cannot have a horse, she will get herself a palfrey.
>
> There is none among you who will dispute this with me: if by reason of an illness one were forbidden to drink strong wine, one would rather drink water than die of thirst.
>
> Anyone would rather drink water than die of thirst.[30]

This is about as much as the *gilos* ever gets from the *domneiador*, for, in general, communication between husbands and lovers is limited in this regard. But in the song of the mismarried lady, the poet let his fancy play freely over the domestic situation implicit in the *chanson d'amour*. That this situation had its comic aspects, we have seen, and the poet was well aware of their value as entertainment. In the celebrated May-song, *Kalenda Maya*, in the *Roman de Flamenca*, the dancers sing:

> Blessings on the lovely lady who does not make her lover languish; whom the fear of the jealous one and his punishments does not keep from going to her knight in the grove, the field or the orchard, and from taking him into her chamber, so that she may the better enjoy him, leaving the jealous one outside the gate. And if he speaks, may she reply: "Say

> no word, make yourself scarce, for I have my lover in my arms!" [31]

If this view of the matter seems lacking in verisimilitude, it may be supplemented from the many passages in the troubadour songs in which the lady is admonished by her lover to pay no attention to the beatings administered by her husband, since after all he can break only her bones, not her heart. So, in a famous song by Bernard de Ventadour, the lover exhorts his mistress:

> Lady, if my eyes do not see you, know that my heart does; do not afflict yourself any more than I do, for I know that you are watched on my account. But if the jealous one beats your body take care that he does not beat your heart. If he causes you pain, give him pain also; may he not have good from you in return for evil.[32]

But, of course, the *gilos* was not always depicted as a comic villain. He could be characterized also in tragedy, and in this aspect he quite captured the imagination. The horrible revenge of Raimon de Castel Rousillon who caused his wife to eat her lover's heart aroused, we are told, the rancor of all True Lovers, and they warred against the brutal *gilos* with blood and fire until he was destroyed.[33] It is only in the light of such horror-stories, the staple of the tragedy of jealousy, that we can appraise the magnitude of Shakespeare's genius in giving dignity and pathos to the role of the jealous husband. But Othello is an extraordinary characterization; in general, the role of the *gilos* lacked dignity. In his progress from the troubadour songs to the prose narratives of a later era, and ultimately to the stage, he preserved his canonical roles as clown and monster. It was to be many years before he would become an object of sympathetic interest.

Given these materials, it takes no great degree of imagination to bring the characters of the play of True Love into their proper dramatic relationship. The troubadour love-song involved, generally speaking, a single situation. The background was the loveless marriage. The *dramatis personae* consisted of the discontented wife, the jealous husband, the desirable lover—a trio with predictable interrelations. Since it was always the same, the underlying story did not have to be told; the various songs appropriate to it exhibited its several facets. The *chanson de mal mariée* was the song of the unhappy wife. The *chanson d'amour* was the song of the aspiring lover. The husband did not sing, and he had no song.

The little drama, invariable in concept and in structure, must be considered one of the prime literary creations of Western culture. It was endlessly reproduced and elaborated not only in the various forms of the love-lyric, but in every literary genre which came under the influence of the love-lyric. In the relations of these three characters, complicated by the intrigues of the *losengier*, the talebearer, there was apparently a plot of inexhaustible freshness which, after serving for centuries as a source of poetry, both lyric and narrative, furnished the novelist with stories and the dramatist with comedies, tragedies, and farces without number, and afterward with melodramas, problem plays, social comedies, and every other form which the stage supports. It is indeed remarkable that in this well-worn pattern writers should have found so constant a source of inspiration and audiences so unfailing a source of delight. But the reason is not obscure; the characters in this elementary drama are easily recognized. The situation is, from the genetic viewpoint, if not the first of the fantasies of childhood, at least the most readily available for literary purposes.

But whatever the source of the fantasy, its connections with adult reality can hardly be overlooked. Marriage in the upper classes, in medieval times, was not a particularly stable arrangement. Since a wife was acquired chiefly for her economic or political value, her desirability over a period of years was likely to fluctuate with some abruptness. At Roman law it had been a relatively simple matter to divorce a woman if such a course seemed desirable. As the Christian church gradually expanded its authority in domestic matters, divorce became progressively more difficult. Nevertheless the church was forced to take account of the practical requirements of an economy in which extensive real-estate operations were habitually conducted by means of the marriage contract.

In the eyes of the church, of course, a valid marriage was indefeasible. But a valid marriage was a rare thing. So various and so subtle were the impediments to wedlock that it was an extraordinary marriage in which a defeasance could not be discovered if it became desirable to find one.[34] In the Middle Ages, consequently, wives could be repudiated, exchanged, and put away with comparative ease and many a gallant lady found herself in the position of the ill-fated Eudoxia of Constantinople, who was repudiated by Guillaume VIII of Montpellier after twelve years of marriage, and had to end her life miserably in the convent into which her husband thrust her.

In such circumstances a woman might be excused for feeling that love afforded her a certain insurance against the uncertainties of marriage. Love was sanctified by an inner prompting and based upon a sincere choice. However illicit it might be from the point of view of religion and of society, it had the sanction of nature; as matters stood it was grounded upon firmer stuff than the marriage bond. The security, spiritual and economic, which the husband did not offer, the wife might well look for in the lover; at least, so the matter was rationalized.[35] Adultery was, of course, a grievous sin, but not beyond expiation. In any event, the church taught that even marriage provided no safeguard against this sin—it was adulterous to love one's husband out of measure.[36]

It is understandable, therefore, that a woman might regard the arrangements of the world of love as somewhat more reasonable than those of the world of marriage. The world of love had its god, its laws, its prophets, and its judges. In this world, it is true, the civil magistrate's writ did not run and one had to do without the blessing of the church, but strong social sanctions existed which might ensure a measure of stability. It was thus not altogether fantastic to conclude that the sacred link between man and woman was not the contract of marriage but the bond of love.

The literature of True Love is rich in expressions which profess to lift this relationship far above the sphere of sensual pleasure or social utility. Sincerity and constancy were of the essence of True Love. From its world the gay deceiver, the sensualist, and the vulgar pleasure-seeker were rigorously excluded. It was such people, the troubadours protested, who brought True Love into disrepute. Those base souls, *trichaires* and *enganadors*, who procured for themselves an ephemeral satisfaction by pretending a sincerity that they did not feel, belonged to the same class as the other *lauzenjadors* who infested the world of love, for of all the wrongs that could be committed in that world, the worst was to seek pleasure without love. This above all brought degradation to the knight and dishonor to the lady.[37]

The True Lover bound himself in the strongest language to eternal service and undying devotion, and was presumably "retained" only on these conditions. The consequence was the interesting rearrangement of the relations of wife, husband, and lover which lends a strange dignity to the literature of True Love. In the world of love, it was the lover who was the legitimate spouse. The husband was no more than a vulgar intruder. In the nature of things he had to be tolerated, but he had no portion in the realm of love. Love was eternal. But death loosed the bonds of marriage. Petrarch rejoiced in the thought that when he died, Laura would be waiting for him in heaven. As for her husband, whoever he might be, we hear nothing of him at all. Presumably he would not be in heaven; he was certainly not expected to play out his miserable role eternally among the angels.

In the creation of this wonderworld of lovers, the troubadours took a step toward what Burckhardt was to consider an essential aspect of the Renaissance, the transformation of life into a work of art. Doubtless the importance of this step can be exaggerated, yet we cannot doubt that certain social improvements resulted. In recreating their world in terms of the desire for beauty, the Provençal poets brought into being a system of morality and a concept of nobility which in many ways had more validity for their culture than the system it was intended to supplement or supplant. If we can believe those who wrote its history, the world from which this new system arose was utilitarian, materialistic, and corrupt, though it preserved the fable of knighthood and defended the blurred outlines of the feudal patriarchy. The troubadour's fantasy transformed this world into something that was idealistic, altruistic, and sincere. But the structure which they gave to this new culture which they imagined closely resembled matriarchy.

The system they professed naturally aroused the deepest opposition, especially in clerical quarters, and the ways of True Lovers were much condemned. Had the consequences of the courtly poetry been, however, that moral degradation of which the clerical writers complained, the threat to the existing order would in fact have been negligible, for the guilt-feelings of a class can always be aroused in terms of the moral standards by which it truly lives. The church in the thirteenth century moved with the utmost efficiency to mobilize such feelings among the Provenceaux, and in the atmosphere of the Inquisition there were the usual retractions and repentances. Although there is no evidence that the Inquisition really prosecuted troubadours as such, these poets ceased to ply their profession in the Midi soon after its establishment. But the cult of True Love was not destroyed. On the contrary, it had a new flowering in Italy and important literary consequences in the north of France. The troubadours, indeed, had developed no new licentious principle, but an ideal morality of their own. The love upon which this new morality was based was not, of course, such that it could possibly gain religious sanction, and it had as yet little basis in philosophy. But it was securely based in psychology, and the results were therefore far-reaching.

It is hardly possible to estimate at so far a remove of time the effect upon the idea of patriarchal authority of a widespread literature of erotic character which regularly depicted the lord as contemptible and hateful, and which conferred adoration and authority upon the lady. But it is inconceivable that it would have no effect. With the brutal *gilos* whose destiny it was to be forever outwitted, every husband was in some sense identified. In the domain of troubadour song, to be a husband was to be in a class with the odious King Mark, who was imprisoned by his own knights for his offenses against the gallant hero who openly cuckolded him, in a class with the repulsive cripple Gianciotto, whose handsome brother Paolo was the beloved of Francesca; to be a husband was to be the villain of a hundred tales and the hero of none. In this cabal of lovers, all, seemingly, were arrayed against the husband—the bachelors, the wives, the poets, the public, and even the husbands—it was as if each husband were the object of a general conspiracy to undo him. And not only was the falseness of his position as the owner of a wife repeatedly demonstrated to him in song and story, but in marshaling public opinion against him as they did for centuries, the poets found effective means of intimidating him in the event that it entered his head to make a public assertion of a husband's prerogatives. Nothing was more ridiculous than to be cuckolded and nothing more inevitable, as Panurge in his day was amply to discover. The only thing a husband could do in the face of such an array of forces was to join them. Five hundred years after the time of the first troubadours, Montaigne wrote, with admirable resignation:

> Chacun de vous a faict quelqu'un coqu: or nature est toute en pareilles, en compensation et vicissitude. La frequence de cet accident en doibt meshuy avoir moderé l'aigreur: le voylà tantost passé en coustume.[38]

Courtly literature in the Middle Ages thus mirrored a society in which, it would appear, cuckoldry was a universal pursuit and a universal complaint. Naturally there would be those who would wish to escape the penalty while they enjoyed the advantages of this system. Such practices the troubadours considered discourteous. Uc de Mataplana addressed a *sirventés* of admonition to his colleague Raimon de Miraval in which he took him severely to task for quarreling with his wife on account of her lover. It would be difficult, he was informed, to clear him of the charge of baseness, for, Mataplana justly observed, a husband who likes to enjoy himself at the expense of others must permit others to have the same privilege:

> Car maritz a cui platz jovens
> deu sofrir per so c'atressi
> sofran lui siei autre vezi.[39]

In the play of True Love, of course, jealousy at all times played a prominent part. But curious distinctions were made between various types of jealousy. The jealousy of the lover was praiseworthy; indeed, indispensable—it was the spring of self-perfection. But a husband's jealousy was tainted with aggression. It was the source of evil. "Love cannot exist without jealousy," explains the ingenious hidalgo of the seventh dialogue of *De amore:*

> Jealousy between lovers is commended by every man who is experienced in love, while between husband and wife, it is condemned throughout the world; the reason for this will be perfectly clear from a description of jealousy . . . there are three aspects of jealousy. A truly jealous man is always afraid that his services may not be sufficient to retain the love of the woman he loves, and he is afraid that she may not love him as he loves her, and he is so tormented with anxiety that he wonders whether she does not have another lover, although he believes that this cannot possibly be. But that this last aspect of jealousy is not proper for a married man is clearly apparent, for a husband cannot suspect his wife without the thought that such conduct on her part is shameful. Pure jealousy, in the case of the husband, takes a stain from the defect of its subject, and ceases to be what it was.[40]

It is for this very reason, according to Andreas, that love between husband and wife is impossible. Since the lady owes her lover nothing, he must continually strive to deserve the favors she bestows upon him. If he loses them, the fault is his. That uncertainty, however, which is a spur to the lover is intolerable to the husband. The constant doubt which makes the lover's special paradise makes marriage a hell.

The villain of the play of love was therefore not the husband as husband, but only the husband as *gilos.* It was in manifesting jealousy that the husband exhibited his impossible position. For in spite of the opprobrium he was certain to incur in asserting his conjugal rights, it was shameful for the husband to endure his wife's infidelity once he was made aware of its existence. Once he knew of his dishonor, he was expected to take remedial action, and the biographies of the troubadours are full of anecdotes which attest the ever present danger of the angry husband.

From the dramatic viewpoint, of course, this danger was essential to the design. Conflict was an integral part of the dream of love. For the purposes of the fantasy, the lover existed only on condition that the husband was there, and presumably the image of the *gilos* took form in the lover's mind at the very instant that the lady's image took possession of his heart. It was a situation which was charged from the start with the tensions suitable to tragedy. For this reason, doubtless, wisdom, discretion, and measure were the qualities with which the lover invariably recommended his passion, and it was generally conceded that in matters of love a man of wisdom and experience was much to be preferred to a young and dashing suitor.[41]

Here again the medieval poets demonstrated the practical turn which characterized their thinking, so far removed from the romanticism of a later age. The lovers who inhabit the troubadour literature do not give at all the impression of seeking a thrilling experience for which it is worth incurring a terrible penalty. What they profess to seek is a long and happy association; a design for living, not a beautiful death. That fever of delight, nourished by constant hope and heightened by constant frustration, which the troubadours called *joi,* was not supposed to end suddenly in an act of external violence. When Petrarch wrote wistfully of the beautiful death which only lovers know,

Che bel fin fa chi ben amando more,

he was thinking of dying, not at the hands of the jealous husband, but, like Rudel, in the arms of the beautiful wife.

Fin amor, as we can see from the more obviously dramatic genres, the *alba* especially, was conceived of as a graceful sport which involved a decided element of risk. It was, from one point of view, a warlike game; it might be called husband-baiting—how else is one to interpret an avocation which involved, at least in theory, the courtship of a married woman under the very nose of the dangerous husband? The conclusion is inescapable that the love-song, with all its stately elegance, derived its power and significance ultimately from the proximity of the avenging horn.

Consequently the capacity to take the necessary risk was as

important to the lover as the wisdom and skill upon which he staked his chance of success. The lover did not consciously seek danger—on the contrary, for the lady's sake it was his duty to avoid it; but danger was of the essence of *fin amor*. The extent of the risk was also in a sense the measure of the lover's worth. It conferred martial dignity on what might otherwise be considered an unmanly pursuit,[42] and the higher the lady was placed, the greater the risk. The play of True Love was knightly. It tested the skill and bravery of the lover; it measured the gallantry and wisdom of the lady; finally, it gauged the temper of the husband. Love was, in short, a test of courage and character. Like battle, it was the proof of the knight; and the qualities of the warrior might well be deduced from the behavior of the lover.

In sum, without the dark background of ever present danger, love would have appreciably less sparkle for the lovers.[43] But the jealous husband did more than give zest to this relationship; to him, paradoxically enough, it owed also its purity and its exalted quality. The peculiar joy of True Love depended upon the fact that the husband was in the unhappy position of attracting to himself the sum of aggression normally present in a libidinous relationship. Instead of venting their less amiable impulses upon each other, therefore, the lovers had a natural object of hostility. This arrangement, from a practical standpoint, left little to be desired. The lover and his lady shared the joy of love. The husband was the recipient of its fury. Evidently, if the jealous husband did not exist in this situation, he would have to be invented, and, of course, for the purposes of this fantasy, he always is.

But while the design of True Love was really ingenious from the standpoint of the lovers, it involved a certain menace for the social system in which it was rooted. It was, in fact, not a copy but a caricature of the feudal pattern. It aped it point for point, and, in fantasy, demolished it in detail. Whereas in the material world a vassal paid homage to his lord—the source, presumably, of all his good—in the world of love his homage was paid to his lady, the source of all his joy. All the service, loyalty, and constancy which in theory he owed to the lord he transferred to the lady, and the reward he hoped to gain for this treason was the opportunity ultimately to be guilty of another and even greater treason. This burning desire to commit the ultimate disloyalty, the knightly lover took pains to broadcast joyously to the world, so that in a little while the chorus of extra-marital love resounded from all the courts of civilized Europe. It is hardly possible to conceive of a more completely insolent repudiation of everything that patriarchal feudalism stood for, and the fact that this doctrine found encouragement among the very classes whose basis it attacked suggests to what an extent those classes must have been psychically oriented toward their own undoing.

The literature of *fin amor* may thus be properly considered a phenomenon of the decline of feudalism, a system in which the new chivalric class had actually no great stake. In the twelfth century we are already aware of the progressive encroachment upon the upper classes of the urban and money economy which the bourgeois were developing. While there was no abrupt dislocation of power in any of the countries in which the literary cult of woman was being propagated—northward in France, eastward in Germany, southward and westward in Italy, Spain, and Portugal —in all these regions the feudal authority was being progressively dissipated. During this period, nearly everywhere in Europe, vassals and communes were turning to the kings for protection against their immediate suzerains. This process was rebellious in its first intention, but in these circumstances rebellion was possible only in terms of another and more complete submission. The ultimate result, almost everywhere in Europe, was a strengthening and centralization of the temporal power. The outcome was monarchy.

In France, the Capetians, from Louis VI to St. Louis, took advantage of the internal stresses within the feudal structure to consolidate the civil power in the crown. In Provence no such centralization of power took place. The feudal authority in the Midi was in fact weakened to the point where the land could no longer be defended against invasion, and the royal and ecclesiastical authority was thereupon imposed from without. The royal *baillis* who assumed jurisdiction after the Albigensian crusade did not encourage the individualistic tendencies which the troubadours had expressed in song. The character of the southern courts was changed, and the poetry of *fin amor* in this region was extinguished.

Indeed, the tide of European culture was rising toward a paternalism stronger than anything feudalism could encompass. In medieval Europe everything was working toward the progressive unification of power in church and state, the ultimate unity, often projected, never realized, of "one empire, one monarch, and one sword." The end of the lyricism of Provence was marked by a great, but singularly unsuitable, monument, the *Comedy* of Dante, the supreme fantasy of a completely integrated universe presided over by the omnipotent Father, whose handmaid and angel was the lady of the song. But by the time this resplendent and serviceable angel had taken form, the last of the troubadours of Provence had vanished.

THE TROUBADOURS

The earliest examples of lyric poetry in a modern tongue are the work of Guillaume IX, Count of Poitiers and Duke of Aquitaine. Since Guillaume died in 1127 at the age of fifty-six, it is likely that the peak of his poetic activity had been reached some time before the turn of the century. The eleven songs by which he is known to us are written, like all the later troubadour poetry, in a language which, in accordance with a venerable tradition, is commonly called Provençal.

The existence of this language at so early a date points the first of the mysteries which surround the origins of the vernacular lyric. Literary Provençal was neither the dialect of Limousin nor that of the adjoining province of Poitou, still less the dialect spoken in Provence proper. It was a learned and courtly "grammar," native to no special area of the Midi but common to all. In this language, which Dante assigned to the region of southwest Europe and strangely enough called Spanish,[1] all the troubadours wrote, regardless of their native speech or the country in which they practiced their profession. It was thus not as a regional dialect that this Provençal developed, but as the language appropriate to a special type of poetry, a professional tongue which was itself a poetic creation.[2]

Although Guillaume IX is the first troubadour whose work is known to us, there is no reason to suppose that he invented the literary forms which he practiced. Nothing about the man or his work in the least suggests the primitive, nor does any contemporary speak of him as an innovator. As for himself, in the handful of songs he has left us in various styles and stanzas, he boasts manfully of all sorts of things, but never of being the first to celebrate in song the joy of love. On the contrary, in speaking of his verses he recommends his workmanship and invites comparison with others; like the later troubadours, he seems very conscious of his critics and his competitors, and clearly implies the existence of both at a time when we have little reason to be aware of either.[3]

> I should much like the world to know whether or not this verse is of a good color which I have brought out of my workshop, for in this mastery I bear off the flower, and that is the truth, and I shall bring the verse itself to witness when I have laced it up.[4]

Provençal poetry thus appears in literary history from the first as a *fait accompli*, a relatively learned and courtly form in an advanced stage of its development. There is no vestige of a preparatory period, nothing to indicate a slow evolution from popular or archaic forms. No lyrical fragment has come down to us which can justly be called quaint or primitive. What is preserved of this poetry from the earliest times is correct, sophisticated, adult, at home in its language, self-conscious in its expression, the fruit of a developed fantasy and a polished wit. It is therefore logical to suppose that in the closing decades of the eleventh century there was in existence in the Midi of France a vein of lyric poetry which had already been extensively worked. This poetry bears no sign of an exotic origin. It is quite possible that it was not, in the first place, indigenous. But however it came there, it was in the soil of France that it found its chief strength and in the culture of the Midi that it manifested its enduring character.

The interesting obscurity that veils the early history of the Provençal lyric extends also to those who wrote it. The Provençal poets were by no means anonymous. We have the names of upwards of four hundred poets of whose work some example remains.[5] Yet aside from their names, we have very little knowledge of them. In this respect, earlier students of the subject were more fortunate than we. They had the advantage of the extraordinarily informative work which Jehan de Nostredame published in 1575, *Les Vies des plus célèbres et anciens poètes provenceaux.* This lively work served as a veritable mine of information until Karl Bartsch, Paul

Meyer, and finally Charles Chabaneau demonstrated its fictional character. The demolition of Nostredame's *Lives*, unhappily, leaves us nothing to go on with respect to the troubadours save the manuscript biographies, and these are of such nature that no contemporary scholar can feel nearly as secure in his knowledge as were Raynouard in 1820 or Fauriel in 1832.

The early history of the vernacular lyric presents an instructive analogy to that of medieval art. It did not originate with the learned classes; obviously it could have owed nothing to the monasteries and little to the secular clergy. It was developed by a class of gifted artisans who were largely dependent for their livelihood upon the patronage of their betters.

Without the "lords" who paid for the building of churches and castles, Gothic art would never have had its extraordinary floriation. Similarly it was the enthusiasm of the wealthy nobility which chiefly stimulated the development of chivalric poetry. The nobles not only kept the poets alive by employing them to write their songs, they also manifested their delight in the poetic art by dabbling in it themselves. The songwriter's craft therefore had, like the craft of the mason, a double root. It was nourished by the artisan, but it owed a great deal also to the experienced taste and knowledge of the patron. To the church, although the church had nothing to do with it, it very likely owed the progressive idealization of the poetic concept which formed its basis. This process was perhaps involuntary, the result of pressure. Nevertheless it took place.

The poetry of the troubadours is known to us mainly through a number of manuscript anthologies compiled toward the end of the troubadour period. These songbooks evidently had a good vogue outside France. The manuscripts are by no means rare; some threescore are extant and more than half of them are of Italian origin. After the beginning of the fourteenth century the vogue of Provençal song was pretty well over in France, but in Italy the taste for troubadour music did not slacken, and the study of Dante and Petrarch increasingly directed attention to the Provençal poets whom the Italian masters had considered their teachers.

In size and format the troubadour songbooks vary a great deal.

Some are impressively elaborate tomes, others less ambitious and less expensive productions. In addition to the words, and sometimes the music, the best of the manuscripts contain biographical notes, *vidas,* set down either at the head of the section devoted to the author in question, or as a separate appendix to the whole. About a hundred poets are documented in this manner.

These "lives" are by no means uniform in length. A *vida* may consist of a few lines only—a terse statement regarding the birthplace and social position of the poet, a word or two concerning his life and loves, a brief estimate of his worth as an artist. Often enough the biographer took no trouble to conceal from the reader that he knew little about his author and cared less.

> Peire Bremon le Tort was a poor knight of Vienne. And he was a good poet and honored by all good men.
>
> Guillem de Montanhagol was a knight of Provence, and he was a good poet and a great lover, and he set his heart on Lady Jauseranda of the castle of Lunel and made for her many fine songs.
>
> Peire de Valeira was of Gascony of the land of Arnaut Guillem de Marsan. He was a jongleur of the time and age of Marcabru, and he made verses of the sort they made then, of little value, about leaves and flowers and songs and birds. His songs were worth little and he no more.[6]

Occasionally, however, the *vida* is an extensive composition in which the poet's best-known songs are "explained" in swift-moving anecdotes enlivened with dialogue, very suitable for recitation. But while these accounts are sometimes fascinating examples of medieval prose, the conclusion is unfortunately inescapable that the more interesting the biography, the less credible it is likely to be. As Gaston Paris long ago pointed out, in many cases the "explanations" are obvious embroideries upon the very material they purport to explain. Such is doubtless the case with the celebrated story of Jaufre Rudel and the lady of Tripoli, a little gem of medieval narrative which, it has been amply demonstrated, can owe nothing to history.

> Jaufre Rudel de Blaye was a man of very noble race, prince of Blaye, and he fell in love with the countess of Tripoli without ever having seen her, on account of the great good which he heard pilgrims speak of her who came from Antioch, and he made many songs about her with good music and poor words. And out of the desire to see her, he took the cross and put out to sea; and in the ship he fell ill, and was taken in Tripoli to an inn like a dead man. And this became known to the countess, and she came to his bedside and took him in her arms. And he knew it was the countess and recovered his sight and his hearing and his sense of smell, and he praised God who had prolonged his life until he might have sight of her. And thus he died in her arms, and she had his body buried in the house of the Templars with great honor. And that very day she became a nun on account of the sorrow she felt at his death.[7]

In addition to these *vidas*, certain manuscripts, chiefly of the fourteenth century, include prose commentaries called *razos*, Latin *rationem*, which introduce the text of the songs, identify the characters, and elucidate the circumstances of composition. These commentaries, like the *vidas*, very likely represent the end-product of oral traditions which, after having been elaborated successively by generations of jongleurs, eventually were set down by the troubadours who compiled the songbooks.[8]

The *razos*, as might be expected, show considerable variation in style and quality. Some are perfunctory introductions which lead by the shortest path to the formula "and he made the song which now you shall hear." Others are little works of art which run, as in the case of the *razo* of the song *Li doutz consire* of Guillem de Cabestaing, to some hundreds of lines, and represent a fairly advanced stage in the development of the *novella*. These anecdotes have in common a vital and rhythmic style and were obviously composed with care. Certain rhetorical formulas recur in them; occasionally there are passages of rhymed prose.[9] It seems entirely likely that the jongleurs interspersed their musical numbers with prose recitations of this sort in such a way as to provide an integrated program of entertainment.[10]

The troubadours who compiled the *chansonniers* were evidently quite aware of the advantages of a realistic technique. In the *vidas* and *razos,* they insist on the factual bases of their anecdotes, no matter how incredible they may seem. Some of these stories, no doubt, are pointless enough to be true. We are told, for instance, that Peirol was a poor knight who wooed the sister of his lord the Dauphin, until the Dauphin became jealous and sent him away, whereupon he found he could not earn his living as a knight and became a jongleur.[11] The more vivid stories give the impression of having been invented to serve as interesting background for the songs to which they relate, but the troubadours who set them down occasionally venture a solemn assurance that they themselves were present at the time of the occurrence, and therefore are in a position to report it *per auzir e per vezer.*[12] Thus Uc de Saint Circ sets our minds at rest with regard to the unlikely tale of Savari de Mauleon by attesting personally to the facts set forth in the *razo:*

> And know in truth that I, Uc de Saint Circ, who wrote these *razos,* was myself the messenger who went there and who bore the messages and the letters.[13]

In the absence of anything to contradict them, anecdotes so reassuringly set forth were certain to slip smoothly into the history of literature, and even such careful scholars as Diez and Chabaneau were willing to concede to these tales at least a general authenticity as realistic glimpses of life in the Middle Ages. Unhappily, further study has made it necessary to qualify as fiction almost everything in these stories save the names and provenience of the characters. Of the few troubadours who have left an independent trace in history—Guillaume IX, Rudel, Bertran de Born, Folquet de Marseille—the biographers tell us nothing that is at all consistent with the recorded facts. As it turns out, the troubadours were at such pains to embellish the tradition they were creating that now they barely emerge from their legends. With rare exceptions they are, and are likely to remain forever, artistic creations, the product of the same poetic imagination which was the source of their songs.[14]

But while we have only the vaguest notion of the lives of the troubadours as individuals, it has been possible to piece together a fairly adequate picture of the profession as a whole. Apparently there was at first no sharp distinction between the terms "troubadour" and "jongleur." In the biographies the terms are used interchangeably and sometimes applied indifferently to the same person. It was not until the last period of their activity that the troubadours manifested any marked sensitivity with regard to the epithet "jongleur." By that time, evidently, the social gap between performer and composer had widened so significantly that it had become insulting to call a troubadour a jongleur.

Jongleur—in Provençal *joglar,* from the Latin *jocare, joculare*—was the term regularly applied to the class of professional entertainers who performed feats of strength or skill in public. The word is not earlier than the eighth century, though the profession dates to the remotest antiquity. Greek vase-paintings depict comic figures which seem to correspond quite closely with what we know of the Roman *joculatores,* and it is likely that the nature of the wandering player changed little through the centuries from the time of that Thespis who, we are told, first trouped a show about the countryside on a cart.[15]

These vagabonds traveled in groups or singly, ragged, hungry, half-mad, and full of mischief. Very likely they differed little from the miserable creatures one still sees occasionally leading a mangy bear over the mountain passes between France and Italy, or the bands of wretched *baroni* depicted in the engravings of Callot. When, in the fullness of time, the poet and composer became differentiated from the ordinary mountebank, it became conventional to ascribe his pariah-like existence to the ravages of love, and this traditional idea of the troubadour was perpetuated even when the man himself had attained, as it sometimes happened, a settled position and superior social rank. It was, presumably, this madness—out of which he gained his livelihood—that drove him from the company of respectable men and condemned him to a life of solitude and restlessness. Love which consumed him also sustained him. It was love which transformed his inner torment into poetry and taught him how to sing for the delight of mankind. The troubadour was, in short, one possessed—such, at least, was the convention—a slave of a superior power, irresponsible like other madmen, yet somehow awesome and therefore to be listened to with the reverence due to those who are in touch with extraordinary forces. The line that divides the mountebank from the prophet has always been thin.

We are afforded occasional glimpses of these musical vagabonds trudging the roads of the Middle Ages, their stomachs and purses empty, their hearts full of pride. The description which comes soonest to mind is to be found in a sonnet of Petrarch's, one of the most famous, usually taken to be a self-portrait. Self-portrait it may be, but obviously not a portrait of the well-patronized poet; at the most it reflects his mental image of himself in the role of the idealized troubadour, very much as they portrayed themselves:

> Gloomy and thoughtful, I make my way alone with slow and dragging steps through the most empty places, with my eyes alert to flee the least sign of a human presence.
>
> No other screen can I find to shield me from the prying eyes of men for in my outward semblance devoid of joy can be read with ease how fiercely I burn inwardly.
>
> So that I believe, in truth, that only the mountains and the plains, the rivers and woods can know of what sort is this my life which is concealed from all others.
>
> Yet I cannot find a path so rough and wild but love comes always conversing with me, and I with him.[16]

The jongleur's lot has never been an enviable one. In Rome, from the earliest times, the entire acting profession labored under the stigma of civil disability. But the early empire was tolerant of actors, and it was not uncommon for exceptionally popular entertainers to achieve wealth and prestige. A great deal of amateur acting went on under the emperors, even in the best society, and knights and senators displayed their talents freely on the stage. In the sixth century, the celebrated mime Theodora became Justinian's empress and secured legislation which lightened the actor's lot very considerably. Nevertheless, at all times, the Roman moralists disapproved strongly of the scandalous practices of the profession, and the Christian church almost from the first anathematized all its branches as immoral and pagan.[17] By the fourth century, not only were the *scenici* excluded from the sacraments, but the clergy was absolutely prohibited from setting foot in the theaters.

It is, however, largely through the fulminations of the clergy that one is enabled to keep track of the movements of the players throughout the Dark Ages. Reviled and scolded wherever they went, the jongleurs established themselves as best they could in the French cities, or trudged the roads from festival to festival and from fair to fair, offering their services wherever they might be welcome. We hear of *mimes* and *histriones* at the court of Theodoric II at Toulouse; there is news of them at Soissons and at Paris in the fifth century. By the ninth century, judging by the rising chorus of clerical invective, their activity seems to have been widespread throughout the Midi of France. At the court of Charlemagne, Alcuin was untiring in his denunciation of the actors and dancers who daily brought the devil into the houses of their patrons.

It was generally agreed in clerical circles that the jongleurs were ministers of Satan, and the bishops made serious efforts to suppress "the songs of poets and the sentences and verses of comedians, which render the mind effeminate." [18] It was only when they began to sing the *chansons de geste* that the jongleurs were tolerated. Such songs celebrated Christian heroes, and while the knights might seem a little savage or a trifle lewd, their hearts at least were in the right place. Thus a distinction began to be made between jugglers, mountebanks, and singers of immoral songs and those who sang the lives of saints, *chansons de geste* and other edifying matter.[19]

There is, however, nothing to show that within the ranks of the jongleurs any sharp distinction was made between those who tumbled, juggled, or exhibited animals and those who sang, told stories and employed their talents, in the words of Guiraut Riquier, "to divert and to honor the nobility by the playing of instruments." The troubadour Guiraut de Calanson, writing about the year 1230, enumerated for the benefit of the jongleur Fadet an impressive list of the accomplishments necessary for the craft without making any mention at all of singing or recitation. Guiraut de Cabrera, on the other hand, drew up a stupendous list of poems which his jongleur Cabra should know by heart, and he said nothing about the skills of the juggler and tightrope walker.

It seems reasonable to suppose that different jongleurs had different specialties; the men who exhibited dancing bears did not, in all probability, develop the skills requisite to the troubadour. There were those who found it agreeable to specialize in music; such entertainers would be likely to add to their repertory of songs a collection of stories in prose and verse, and they would study to speak well, to sing pleasantly, to propose *jeux-partis* and other courtly games of wit. In order to function acceptably in court circles such entertainers would have to acquire courtly manners—as we are told, for example, of Peire Guillem of Toulouse that he was "ben avinenz d'estar entre las bonas genz." [20] This ability to behave properly in polite circles would presuppose a certain breeding, or at least the affectation of breeding. The troubadour, moreover, would try to look the part of the courtly gallant, at least when he could afford it, and having some share of learning, he might well aspire to the consideration due to a scholar.

Such, at least, would be a permissible inference from the "declaration" which the wise king Alfonso of Castille granted to the troubadour Guiraut Riquier in 1275. In this curious document the king recommends that to avoid confusion the Provenceaux would do well to imitate the Spanish in distinguishing among the four classes of jongleurs. In the first class should be placed the *bufos* who exhibit performing animals and who play instruments in the market place. After them should come the *joglars* who through their good manners are acceptable at court and who recite stories or sing songs composed by others. Above these should be ranked the *trobadors* who know how to fashion, according to the rules of art, *coblas, baladas,* and things of that sort. Those, however, who write *cansos* and *vers d'auctoritat,* who know how to instruct others in matters spiritual and temporal, who can explain the darker portions of their work and attain to the highest poetry, the *sobiran trobar,* those should be dignified with the title "doctor of poetry."

The absurd nature of Riquier's pretensions—for, as it has been remarked, there is every reason to believe that he himself drew up the *declaracio* attributed to the king as well as the *supplicacio* which requested it—must not blind us to the fact that by the end of the thirteenth century the art of vernacular poetry had developed to the point where it was possible to imagine such distinctions. When the perpetually needy Riquier, one of the last of the troubadours, assures the king that he would rather give up his calling than tolerate the epithet of jongleur, one hears the mountebank speaking; all the same, in the golden age of the troubadours, they did not take their profession quite so seriously. Many good reasons have been advanced to account for the decline of the troubadours in the course of the thirteenth century—the crusade, the Inquisition, the decline of the courts of the Midi, the exhaustion of the poetic vein—it is, in addition, possible that the profession fell of its own weight. In the fourteenth century, as the profusion of *chansonniers* suggests, the taste for troubadour love-poetry was perhaps still sufficient to support the unpretentious jongleur, but not the doctor of poetry. As a matter of fact, the doctor of poetry has seldom found adequate support in any age.[21]

Like the modern entertainer, the jongleur, in general, was not a creative artist. His talents were interpretive. Behind him stood the troubadour, the poet and composer who provided the material upon which the performer drew.[22] The type of talent required to compose a song is, of course, very far removed from the ability to deliver it effectively, but the two arts are not mutually exclusive and were certainly not considered so. We hear of some thirty jongleurs who learned the art of "finding" and who thus elevated themselves to the rank of troubadours.

It was evidently common practice for a troubadour to employ jongleurs to sing his verses. Guiraut de Bornelh, we are told, spent his winters in school, teaching, or studying, Latin. In the summer he went on tour with two jongleurs who sang his songs. Arnaut de Marueill employed the jongleur Pistoleta, who later became a composer in his own right, and "made songs with fine melodies"; Bertran de Born employed a certain Papiol.[23] In some of the *envois*, or *tornadas*, directions are given to the jongleur as to where and how he is to sing the song confided to him. It must be admitted that these directions are not always entirely comprehensible, but the general drift is clear enough. Guillaume IX commands his friend Daurostre to sing his song "down yonder," without howling; Peire Raimon begs his dear friend, his Diamond, to deliver his song in Toulouse. Jaufre Rudel asks those who learn his song from him to be careful not to mutilate it when they sing it.[24]

But the troubadours were performers as well as composers. They sang the songs which they themselves composed and they accompanied themselves on an instrument like the jongleurs. Apparently they did not always perform very well. Of Ricaut de Barbezieux we are told that he suffered severely with stage fright:

> He was a good knight at arms and handsome of his person. . . . He was very fearful of singing before people, and the more good people he saw the more confused he became and the less he remembered, and he always needed another to lead him on. But he sang very well and composed verses and melodies charmingly.[25]

The difference between the troubadour as singer and the jongleur, however, seems very clear. The jongleur offered a professional repertory of songs by many hands, while the troubadour would be expected, like the modern song-writer, to sing chiefly his own compositions. In the celebrated *sirventés*, *Chanterai d'aquetz trobadors*, composed about 1150 by the troubadour Peire d'Auvergne, we find a series of priceless caricatures of the troubadours of the last half of the twelfth century:

> Guiraut de Bornelh, who resembles an otterskin dried in the sun, with his thin complaints, like those of an old woman coming from the well, if he saw himself in a mirror, he would not value himself at the price of a thorn. . . .
>
> Limozi de Brive is the most beggarly jongleur from here to Benevento, and he looks like a sick pilgrim when he sings, the

> scoundrel, so much so that I almost feel pity for him myself. . . .
>
> Messire Guilhem de Ribas who is bad inside and out and sings his verses in a hoarse voice, and his stutterings are worthless, a dog can do as well, and his eyes look like those of a silver statue. . . .

After running in this engaging fashion through a dozen of his colleagues, the author concludes without false modesty:

> Peire d'Auvergne is gifted with a voice such that he sings equally well both high and low, and his melodies are sweet and pleasant to the ear. For this reason he is the master of them all; if only he would make his meaning a little clearer, for hardly anyone can understand it.[26]

From very early times, apparently, the art of song-making attracted amateurs from the highest nobility, so that barons of great wealth and dignity vied with the professional jongleurs as composers and entertainers. There is, moreover, reason to believe that noble poets without outstanding musical ability occasionally employed professional troubadours to set their verses. Of the school attributed to Eble, Vicomte de Ventadour, we know nothing except that it existed; but we have it on the authority of William of Malmesbury that Guillaume IX was in the habit of amusing his companions with comic songs—"*audientium rictus cacchino distendens*"—and Ordericus Vitalis tells us that this same Guillaume sang of his sad adventures in the Holy Land before the nobility.[27] Raimbaut, Count of Orange, one of the most original of the troubadours, wrote that love had brought him so low that people called him jongleur. It is noteworthy that his exalted rank entitled him to no special consideration in the *sirventés* composed by his contemporary Peire d'Auvergne. He is the ninth of the troubadours described in that rogue's gallery, and his verses are thoroughly disapproved of—his poetry has neither warmth nor joy,

> And I value as highly the pipers
> Who walk about begging for alms.[28]

But while kings, princes, and prelates amused themselves, and presumably their friends, by writing love-songs during this period, most of the troubadour songs were written by professional song-writers. These were drawn from every stratum of society. The petty nobility and the bourgeois and artisan classes supplied the greater number, as one might expect. The lowest classes would not ordinarily have the opportunity of acquiring the necessary education. Nevertheless, in the biographies, a certain number of troubadours are said to be of base extraction, like Bernard de Ventadour, "the son of the servant who heated the ovens in which the bread was baked for the castle of Ventadour." [29] But their low extraction did not always prevent them from becoming, like Bernard, *cortes et enseignatz,* or of receiving knighthood and lands from some appreciative patron, and attending upon the highest society.

The great jongleur Marcabru, we are told, was a foundling brought up by a rich man. After a period of apprenticeship to the troubadour Cercamon, he changed his name and became a troubadour in his own right. He appears to have been a rough diamond; but this may have been a professional pose, for his manner is, to say the least, imperious. Arnaut de Marueill was a clerk of low birth who, "because he could not live by his letters, went wandering about the world." Giraut de Bornelh, the "master of the troubadours," was a "man of low condition, but learned in letters and of natural good sense." There is no evidence at all that the base-born were at a disadvantage in this profession. This medieval tin-pan alley presents indeed a kaleidoscopic variety. Albert de Sisteron was the son of a jongleur; Aimeric de Peguilhan was the son of a cloth merchant; Peire Vidal, the son of a furrier; Guillem Figueira was a tailor. Arnaut Daniel was a gentleman; Aimeric de Belenoi, a clerk; Ricaut de Barbezieux, a poor vavasour; Raimbaut de Vaqueiras, like so many of the troubadours, was the son of a poor knight.

On the whole, the profession was a cross-section of the life of its time. It was by no means a respectable calling, nor very well rewarded; ordinary men did not enter it, but it had glamour. By the year 1210, the great days of the troubadours were pretty well over, yet there must have been still many a stage-struck youth who, like

Uc de Saint Circ, the son of a poor vassal, with many elder brothers, was sent by his family to college to become a clerk:

> They sent him to the school at Montpellier and while they thought that he was studying letters, he was learning *chansons* and verses and *sirventés* and *coblas*, and the deeds of great men and women, and stories of his own and of former times, and with this learning he became a jongleur.[30]

It is safe to surmise, however, that most of these singers were driven into vagabondage by grim necessity, like Gaucelm Faidit, who became a jongleur because he ruined himself at dice. Poor knights, vagabonds, beggars, the troubadours were, on the whole, shameless in their relations with their patrons. They flattered them broadly in their songs, naming them in the *envoi* by name or by *senhal*, celebrating or calumniating with the cynicism which has always characterized the profession of the publicist. Since they depended for their livelihood upon the generosity of the barons, they wrote songs in which they begged for the things of which they stood in need—a purse, a gown, a horse—sometimes with much grace, but seldom with much delicacy:

> Signor Dragoman, if I had a good horse, my enemies would find themselves in a losing battle, for as soon as they hear my name mentioned they fear me more than the quail the hawk, and they value their lives not a penny, so proud they know me to be, and savage, and brave.[31]

Their grace, their folly, their capacity to charm, to stir, and to amuse—such was the principal stock in trade of these minstrels, doubtless, and last of all the poetic skill of which they so often boasted. Like Machaut and Froissart in their time; like Dante in his exile; like Chaucer, Marot, Boiardo, Ariosto, Tasso, many were courtiers first and poets second. Many were wanderers all their lives, but it was their common hope to fill in the course of time a secure place with a prosperous patron, to be retained in a noble house where they might find, in the words of Guiraut Riquier, *mantenh e secors*. In such a house, among appreciative people, might be found, with luck, a long employment as a minstrel, or, better still, a permanent post as secretary, bodyguard, valet, or courier—whatever might serve to ensure a steady revenue. Such, beyond question, was the goal of the troubadour. The competition within the ranks of these vagabonds, like their need, was keen. There was a constant elbowing for attention; hence, no doubt, their gibes at each other's expense, their contests and debates, and the ceremonial boasting and chest-pounding with which they entertained their audiences.

That in these circumstances there would be little piety among them, and little virtue, is understandable. "They give themselves day and night to the vanities of the time," wrote Matfré Ermengaud, "to every folly, to every sin. So long as they can gain gowns and money, they feed people with lies fit to deceive fools." [32] They were dicers, drunkards, wenchers, the pillars of the tavern and the brothel. A few succeeded in attaining positions of trust and influence—Sordello, for example, in Italy, Gui D'Ussel and Elias de Barjols in Provence. There were also the famous examples of Raimbaut de Vaqueiras, who rose greatly in honor under his patron, and of Folquet de Marseille, a merchant-poet who renounced his sinful hobby and eventually became a bishop. But in general the fate of the troubadours was not a happy one. After a lifetime of wandering, many of them, even the most famous, ended their lives in misery or retired to a monastery to die.

The astonishing thing about these men is not that they were vagabonds but that they were poets. They were not, like the bulk of our modern song-writers, illiterates catering to the taste of illiterates. The best of them were, of course, great artists; but even the worst were highly skilled craftsmen. We may deplore in the work of some a certain lack of originality or mediocrity of conception, but their professional standards were amazingly high. Theirs was a poetry of high finish and of intricate workmanship, directed to an exclusive and discriminating audience. They worked in words with the same meticulous attention to detail which we admire in those of their contemporaries who worked in stone, in metal, and in glass. It may be conceded that, in general, they do not seem to have been gifted with the highest type of poetic imagination; their inspiration was limited by relatively narrow conceptual norms. Yet these vagabonds set the modes of lyric poetry for Europe for many centuries, and in some degree for the present day.

The story of Raimbaut de Vaqueiras gives us some notion of the life of a successful troubadour, and it has the advantage of coming from a document of almost unimpeachable character, the poet's own work. Raimbaut was born near Orange in Provence. He began his career as a jongleur, and eventually entered the service of one of the greatest soldiers of his day, Bonifacio, Marquis of Montferrat, who became King of Salonika. As minstrel and squire, Raimbaut followed his marquis through the wars in Sicily, thence to Constantinople, and eventually he was rewarded with knighthood and lands and became a companion in arms of the marquis. Before attaining to this eminence, however, Raimbaut had evidently drunk his fill of misery. In a spirited *tenson* with Albert, Marquis of Malaspina, whom he taunts with having robbed travelers on the highway in his time, he is treated to some revealing pleasantries—"I have seen you a hundred times trudging the road in Lombardy like a filthy jongleur, poverty-stricken and unhappy in love, and I did you a favor when I gave you to eat. . . ." [33]

Once he had entered the service of his *marques*, Raimbaut no longer knew want; nevertheless the *epistolas* in which he celebrates his master's exploits—and his own—are obviously intended to elicit a gift. Couched as they are in frank and familiar terms, these epistles are quite as shameless in their flattery as the analogous *épîtres* which, several centuries later, Clément Marot addressed to Francis I. After comparing his patron, in the usual terms, to Alexander and to Roland for his prowess, and to Bérart de Mondesdier for his courtesy, Raimbaut proceeds to praise his court, an earthly paradise:

> In your court reigns all good cheer, liberality and courtesy, fine clothes and fine arms, trumpets and games and viols and song, and never did it please you at mealtimes to set a porter to watch the gate as do the miserly rich.

At such a court, Raimbaut declares, he knows how to behave as a courtier and a lover should: "And I, lord, can boast this much, that in your court I knew how to live like a gentleman, to serve ladies, and to be patient and secret. . . ." But in addition to being courteous, Raimbaut declares, he is a man of valor. None can say "that ever in battle I left your side, nor that the fear of death deterred me from increasing your honor." In conclusion he asserts his claim upon his master's generosity, since he renders him threefold service as publicist, knight, and minstrel:

Et es razos, qu'en mi podetz trobar
Testimoni, cavalier e jocglar,
Senher Marques.[34]

Between this sort of retainer, nobly born but not of independent means, who could serve with the sword or the pen according to the occasion, and the Renaissance courtier as Castiglione described him two and a half centuries later, the relation seems tolerably clear. Even clearer is the analogy to the wretched courtiers who infested the mangy courts of the Italian princelings of the fourteenth and fifteenth centuries, whose complaints have come down to us in many a bitter phrase. If the troubadour tradition passes on the one hand through the great line of Renaissance lyricists—the line of Dante, Petrarch, Tasso, Ronsard, Spenser, Shakespeare, and Donne—on the other hand it loses itself in a labyrinth of such courtly rhymers as that Antonio Beccari of Ferrara who worked the courts of north and central Italy in the mid-fourteenth century, dogged all his days by passion and hunger. It is a far cry from the lowly jongleur to the sovereign poets Dante and Petrarch, but the distance did not seem as great to these masters as it does to us. Their scope, of course, was incomparably greater, and they had such genius as was granted, perhaps, to none of the troubadours; but they did not belong to a different order from that of their predecessors in the poetic art. They too were wanderers the greater part of their lives, and they too rendered to their patrons the sort of service which might properly be expected of a troubadour. The difference was that they were able to realize, each in his way, the ideal to which Guiraut Riquier aspired. They really became *doctors de trobar*.[35]

The poor jongleur tramping the roads of Lombardy seems a long way socially from the proud marquis who from time to time resorted to a little highway robbery to maintain, as he says, his reputation for generosity. But there was a relation between the two which gives color to the time. Both were poets; however wide the gulf that separated them, it was not impassable. They understood each other very well, shared a special gentility, and could berate each other wholeheartedly and on equal terms in their *tensons*. The existence of gifted patrons whose way of thought was not too far removed from that of the artist was an indispensable condition of the development of the art of poetry. It was in the courts that this art developed; it emerged in all respects a courtly art, devised by courtiers for the entertainment of courtiers, and adjusted to suit their interests and their emotional and intellectual requirements. Its nature is chiefly understandable in terms of the society which it served and expressed.

As the troubadour poetry had a vogue which lasted some two centuries, the requirements of this society might well be expected to change. Indeed, though the *chanson* continued to be written throughout the entire period, there was a very perceptible evolution of form and substance. The period during which the troubadour lyric was developed extends to about the year 1300. It has been divided, since the time of Diez, into three periods. The first is sometimes called archaic, and begins with the earliest date at which Guillaume IX might have been writing, sometime about the year 1090. It ends just short of the time of Bernard de Ventadour, in 1140. It therefore includes, besides Guillaume IX, only Cercamon and his pupil Marcabru, and Jaufre Rudel, and cannot be said to be very well represented. The "classic" period, between 1140 and 1250, includes most of the best-known names of the troubadour canon, but its continuity is interrupted by the Albigensian crusade which ravaged the Midi between 1209 and 1218. The last period, necessarily called decadent, extends from 1250 to 1293, the year in which died Guiraut Riquier, who called himself the "last of the troubadours." Since it seems quite as unlikely that Riquier was the last as that Guillaume IX was the first, the terminal date would perhaps not be taken too seriously, were it not that after 1300 no important poetry was written in *langue d'oc*.

This threefold division is, however, not especially useful in helping us to understand the evolution of the lyric tradition. Bernard de Ventadour marked a turning point in the development of the *chanson;* but the poets of the first period, while they differ rather markedly from those of the second, differ even more from each other, and hardly convey the impression of being archaic—in fact, three are among the most interesting of all those who wrote the *chanson*. In the decadent period, which marks the rise of the satirical and political song-writers, we come upon some of the freshest and most original of the troubadours, and to this period belongs one of the truest geniuses among the Provenceaux, Peire Cardenal. In this period also, Sordello, Montanhagol, and Riquier mark the transition which culminated in the *dolce stil* of Dante, and which through Petrarch and Bembo influenced a great deal of the lyricism of the Renaissance. It seems therefore somewhat more rewarding to follow, from the point of view of form, the lines along which developed the various poetic styles—*trobar clus, trobar ric,* and *trobar clar*—which, indeed, have had important consequences for the history of Western poetry; and, from the viewpoint of substance, the gradual refinement of the concept of love until in the fourteenth century it became passionless and lost itself in the poetry of religion on the one hand, and in philosophy on the other.

The forms which developed during these periods were extraordinarily diversified, quite as much by their content as by their structure. Some, like the *planh*, the dirge, were necessarily occasional. Others were based on a conventional situation of dramatic character—the *alba* and *pastorela.* The *tenso* and *partimen* were poetic debates. There were all sorts of songs for dancing, and many kinds of poetic whimsies such as the *descort*, the *vanto*, the *escondich*, the *enueg*, the *plazer*, and the nonsense-poem, the *no-sai-que-s·es*. The bulk of the troubadour poetry falls, however, under two main heads, the *chanson* and the *sirventés*. These did not differ at all in form. The substance of the *sirventés* was moral, political, vituperative, or didactic; it was used for persuasion, personal attack and defense, for instruction and for satire. As the troubadours were employed more and more as the propagandists of princes, they developed the *sirventés* quite fully and it is the characteristic form of the second half of the troubadour period. But the *chanson* was held most in honor throughout the entire extent of troubadour activity, and it accounts for the larger part of all the poetry the troubadours produced. The song-form was, of course, employed for many purposes. There were songs of war, pious songs, and pedagogical songs; but the normal theme of the troubadour *chanson,* endlessly varied and elaborated, was love.

The form that this love might take was far more rigidly prescribed than the form of the *chanson* which expressed it. Far from being an irresponsible tooting of adolescent passion in the spring, the Provençal love-song was based on a system of precise concepts of almost ritualistic character. It was a work of art drawn from an experience which was itself a work of art.

THE SONG

With the exception of the little *Doctrina de compondre dictatz*, composed at the end of the thirteenth century, the first attempt to study the prosody of the *chanson* was Dante's analysis in the second book of *De vulgari eloquentia*, a work which the poet unhappily did not finish.[1] To this task, Dante brought not only a very adequate knowledge of Provençal poetry, but the profound understanding of the art of poetic composition which one would expect from the greatest of masters. What Dante says, therefore, of the Italian *canzone* is of the greatest possible value in the analysis of the Provençal *chanson*, upon which the *canzone* was patterned.

The *chanson* had always a fervently confessional character. Yet there is no reason to believe that in Dante's mind the subject matter of the love-song had any more relation to external reality than that of any other poetic fiction. For Dante, art would be a reworking of experience in terms of the ideal, and the poetry of love would properly assimilate all love-experience to the archetype of *fin amor*. The nucleus of the love-song, consequently, would be a poetic fact, not a historical fact. At the core of the love-song was a fable; its truth would be a general truth, not necessarily a particular truth. And whatever specific truth the love-song might involve would have to be transformed in terms of the universal pattern before it could become the subject of song. Poetry, Dante tells us, properly considered, "*nihil aliud est quam fictio rethorica musicaque posita*—" is none other than a rhetorical fiction set to music.[2] He thus reaffirms the Aristotelian proposition that the basis of poetry is invention: poetry is a fiction developed according to the rules of art. And Dante includes in his definition that identification of poet and musician which we find in the prologue to

Terence's *Phormio,* and which troubadour practice everywhere exemplified.

In the *Poetics,* Aristotle made a clear distinction between the historian and the poet: "It is not the business of the poet to tell what has happened, but what may happen or what is possible . . . hence poetry deals more with things in a universal way, but history with each thing in itself." [3] In Aristotle's view, moreover, the poet was primarily a maker of fables, not of meters. But Dante, under the spell of Horace's *Art of Poetry,* was interested primarily in a discussion of form, and he did not go any further into the troublesome matter of poetic truth. Of the various sorts of vernacular poetry, he tells us, the *chanson* is, for a variety of reasons, the supreme form, the noblest, the most rewarding and most highly honored, comprising within itself the whole art of poetry, which is seen only partially in forms of lesser estimation such as the *ballata* and the sonnet.

Dante was much impressed with the flexibility of the *chanson.* In fact, the troubadours permitted themselves the utmost freedom with regard to the length of the line, the shape and length of the stanza, and the arrangement of the rhymes, and it was in variations of this sort that they chiefly displayed their ingenuity. As for substance, whatever fluidity the *chanson* might have had during the first period of its development, by the middle of the twelfth century it had taken on such definite character as all but defied innovation. In forms less noble and less demanding than the love-song, it was appropriate to display originality, but the *chanson* was as rigidly determined by its genre as the cathedral.

The troubadours took pride not only in the correctness and beauty of their verse, of which they often remind us in their songs, but also in the orthodoxy of their doctrine and the sincerity of their passion. An authentic inspiration was considered indispensable to the poet—the greater the devotion of the lover, the greater, supposedly, his mastery of the poetic art. Bernard de Ventadour wrote:

> It is no wonder if I sing better than any other singer, for my heart carries me closer to love and I am more completely sub-

> ject to his command. Body and heart and mind and sense, strength and power, I have given them all; the rein draws me so strongly toward love that I have no will to go anywhere else.[4]

Of Daude de Pradas, on the other hand—who has nevertheless left as proof of his popularity some twenty songs in as many songbooks—the anonymous biographer notes that his inspiration was not genuine: "He made songs with the skill of the poet, but they did not proceed out of love, so that they did not delight people and were not sung." [5] Evidently, the thirteenth century critic was concerned with the question of poetic sincerity quite as much as we are.

In the thirteenth century the conventional assumption would be that all excellence in the art of poetry proceeded from the power of love. Without love, the poet would have no true motive for singing and no real lyric afflatus. Beauty of substance and perfection of form in the song were ultimately no more than a reflection of that beauty which inspired the poet's desire. The one beauty was transformed into the other. The lady's image was impressed upon the poet's soul, and it was in the unswerving contemplation of this image and under its constant influence that the song was fashioned.[6] In the "finding" of the song, the poet was, accordingly, in a sense a passive recipient of inspiration. Through love the song came to his mind; the closer he came to love, the better he heard love's dictation.

Such was the convention; but obviously we can draw no conclusion as to the reality in any particular case of the emotions these formulas express. They might be used to include any degree of truth. It would be naïve for us to believe that each love-song was the transcription of a true-life situation. All the evidence points away from such a conclusion. On the other hand, the troubadour love-songs do not ever make the impression of being commercial valentines manufactured by hacks.

The troubadours were, as we have seen, in the main professional composers. The presumption therefore is logical that their songs were largely fictional, their emotions, imaginary, and all of True

Love may be thought to be, as Edouard Wechssler argued, mere professional gallantry. By extolling the desirability, and bewailing the obduracy of a patron's wife, the troubadour would naturally compliment his patron as well as his patroness, and we may conclude from this that much, if not all, of the troubadour poetry was written, as we say, on speculation, if not on assignment.[7] But such a view, while it recommends itself through its realistic approach to a problem which is too often treated sentimentally, is open to grave objections, of which the weightiest is that it affords us only the most superficial insight into the mind of a poet.

Undoubtedly these songs had their commercial aspects. We learn from the texts themselves that troubadours were occasionally hired to celebrate the charms of particular ladies, just as they were hired to compose songs of war, and political verses. Then, as now, all types of publicity fell within the limits of the poet's trade. But we can no more account for the poetry of love in this manner than for the poetry of heroism. The truth of life and the truth of art may not be the same, but the one necessarily hangs upon the other. The knight who sang in the love-song may never have quite existed as an individual, but as a social being his existence was of great significance to his time. The love-song portrayed the behavior of an ideal character in a situation which evidently had the utmost reality for the society to which it was addressed. There is no other way to account for the proliferation of the genre.[8] The poet may not have been "sincere," but the knight of the song would have to be, and the worth of the song would depend a great deal on the degree of emotion which it conveyed.

The poetry of love is ritualistic; it has at all times been expressed in stereotypes, and there have not been many. The troubadours were entirely conscious of the limited nature of their subject matter, and occasionally it distressed them to have nothing new to say. Gui d'Ussel wrote at the beginning of the thirteenth century:

> I should make songs more frequently, but it bores me to say each day that I sorrow and die for love, for all know how to say as much. That is why I must find new words set to a pleasant melody; but I can find nothing that has not already

> been said and sung. How then shall I pray to you, my love? I shall say that same thing in another fashion, so that in this way I may make my songs seem new. . . .[9]

Guillem Montanhagol, a half-century later, complained in the same manner, and he too promised to sing in a new fashion. But none of the troubadours sang in a new fashion. In matters of substance, evidently, the need to conform was paramount.

The prevailing mood of troubadour song was melancholy. It was, in general, a song of longing and complaint; but this was not the only permissible mood. While the archetypal lover specialized in the anguish of love militant, he also from time to time sang jubilantly of love triumphant—the genre certainly existed. Arnaut Daniel wrote jauntily:

> Life is good when joy sustains it; let him complain for whom it goes not well. I know of no reason to quarrel with my destiny, for, by my faith, I have my share of the best.
>
> She has no base heart, she whose friend I am; and there is none lovelier from here to Savoy. She pleases me so that I have more joy of her than Paris had of Helen, she of Troy.[10]

This is something different from complaint. It inclines toward another genre, the boast, the *vanto*. But even those songs which anticipate a successful courtship, instead of boasting of one, often put the lover's hopes in terms of an erotic fantasy which seems unduly detailed for purposes of compliment, and suggests quite another end. Arnaut Daniel wrote, in another song:

> May God, the courteous one, by whom were absolved the sins of Longinus the Blind, grant, if he please, that my lady and I may come to lie together in the chamber to which a precious assignation will bring us, a rendezvous from which I expect this great joy, that kissing and smiling, I may uncover her lovely body and gaze at it by the light of the lamp.
>
> Mouth, what have you said? I think that you have lost me such rewards as would honor the emperor of the Greeks, or the lord of Rouen, or the king who holds both Tyre and Jerusalem.

> Truly I am mad to ask so much that in the end I repent of my daring! For Love has not the power to preserve me, nor is any man wise who drives away his own joy.[11]

Fiction this may be, but surely not the fiction of the public-relations man. It is, if anything, the fiction of the novelist. Whatever the degree of "sincerity" in these verses, they are pretty clearly the fruit of an authentic emotional experience, an experience no doubt contemplated in professional tranquillity, nevertheless authoritative, and its purpose would be, not to compliment a lady, but to arouse an erotic train of thought in an audience.

It is reasonable to expect that love-songs should be written by lovers. To a considerable extent the poetic illusion involves this assumption, and, in the eyes of many, subjective poetry has little value unless it can be certified as true confession. But, of course, love-songs can be written for lovers as well as by lovers, and it would be a wise critic indeed who could distinguish those songs which are the fruit of passion from those which are the fruit of industry. It is doubtless unjust to compare the song-writer of the twelfth century with his counterpart in our time, since he has no counterpart in our time, but we have no better analogy at our disposal. In our day the manufacture of love-songs for the trade constitutes an important industrial operation, the details of which involve the nicest calculation of popular taste from year to year. The purpose of the contemporary commercial lyricist is principally to stimulate the emotions of an audience of young people, since careful analysis has established that it is this audience which chiefly supports the popular lyricism of our day. He writes therefore with all the sincerity of which he is capable in the character of an adolescent, although he is not, in general, an adolescent.

The troubadour wrote for an audience of knights and ladies. He wrote, accordingly, in the character of a knight, though he might not be a knight, and he wrote as a knight in love, though he might not be in love. As his audience evidently took delight in the contemplation of a particular dramatic situation, the poet reconstructed chiefly that situation, and with relation to it he doubtless took care to express such thoughts as were most likely to elicit a favorable response. The troubadour *chanson* is the song of the suppliant knight, but the troubadour was not necessarily a suppliant knight; he was a song-writer in the guise of a suppliant knight. What the song expressed was therefore not the details of his private life, but his emotions projected through the medium of the archetypal lover, whom he conceived in accordance with the normal expectation of the audience for which he worked.[12]

The troubadour who peddled his songs from court to court was, of course, in a somewhat different position from the noble amateur who wrote love-poetry for his own pleasure. Such a poet might well be expected to write love-songs when he was in love. But the man whose vocation it was to write love-songs could hardly wait for an immediate inspiration. He made his rounds during the good season, professionally lovelorn, with the repertory of songs which constituted his literary capital. The lady who had supposedly inspired these songs remained, according to the rules of the art, mysterious, and there was no need to suppose that she was always the same lady. Troubadours were accustomed, moreover, to writing songs in the character of various personages, male and female, in various dramatic situations. The protagonist of an Italian song of the thirteenth century, written by the falconer of Frederick II, Rinaldo d'Aquino, is a stock character, the distressed lady whose lover is departing on the crusade. As Rinaldo conceived her, the lady is sorrowful to the point of incoherence, and after running tumultuously through her complaint, she asks the jongleur Dolcietto to make her a proper love-song which she can send to her lover in Syria.[13]

Occasionally we are permitted a clear glimpse of the publicity man behind the figure of the "lover." Raimbaut de Vaqueiras wrote of a lady with whom he obviously was not in love: "She desires me to praise her merit and her beauty in my songs." Similarly, Folquet de Marseille—a respectable Genoese businessman, married, and the father of children—sang in the character of a jongleur: "If she deigns to retain me, she shall have her reward, for I shall cause her rare merit to resound at many a gathering." Such statements may well be conventional. From the very beginning of the troubadour tradition, it was part of the poet's blandishment that he would spread the fame of his lady throughout the land; even Guillaume IX offered his services in this respect in exchange for the lady's favor.

It would be easy for formulas of this sort to find echoes in the *vidas* of the troubadours. So we are told of Jordana d'Ebreun that the troubadour Gaucelm Faidit "*si la servi e la honra mout e la lauset e la fez grasir entre las plus valens domnas*"; indeed, he praised her so thoroughly "that no valiant man of Vienne or of all Provence thought himself worth a straw unless he had seen her." [14] This seems comically extravagant, yet it is impossible to rule out the possibility that it represents some degree of truth. Without doubt, an outrageous amount of haggling went into the troubadour's courtship, whether real or imaginary. Nevertheless, in their best work these poets aimed chiefly to develop the character-type of a lover who sang out of a pure and disinterested passion, and it is this character whose destiny the Renaissance lyricists most particularly worked out.

It would seem that the troubadour's expressions of desire were sometimes taken seriously by those who, with more or less justification, confused the protagonist of the song with its author. So, at least, one would judge from the *vidas* and *razos*, which, however untrustworthy they may be as history, yet reflect the views of the time more accurately than anything else we have. Some of these accounts were obviously meant to be lurid. Others are comic. In the biography of Peire Vidal we are astonished to read that a knight of St. Giles had the poet's tongue cut out quite early in his career because "he gave people to understand that he was the lover of his wife." And once, the biographer adds, when this same poet tried to kiss his patroness Azalais, the wife of Barral des Baux, she made a terrible outcry and had him hunted out of court so fiercely that he took refuge overseas with King Richard. This has the ring of truth about it. The *vida* of Aimeric de Peguilhan includes a story of another sort:

> Aimeric de Peguilhan was of Toulouse, the son of a bourgeois who was a merchant and had cloth to sell. And he learned *chansons* and *sirventés,* but he sang very badly. And he fell

> in love with a bourgeoise, his neighbor, and this love taught him to write poetry. And he made of her many fine songs, but the husband meddled with him and did him a dishonor, and Aimeric avenged himself; he wounded him in the head with a sword, and so he decided to leave Toulouse and go into exile. . . .[15]

In stories of this kind we are likely to smile at the quaint assumption, the matrix of many a saga of the films, that it is love which makes the artist. But it is undeniable that unless he is able to tap within himself a source of authentic emotion, the poet, however skilled he may be as *artifex*, must lapse into the merest professionalism. Sincerity of emotion, to be sure, is not enough to mark off the artist from the hack; many a foolish jingle has been rooted in the deepest and purest feeling. But those who are capable of arousing deep feeling in others are seldom people who have never themselves had a poignant experience. It is invariably from the recollection of an emotion, as Wordsworth long ago observed, that poetry is made; but we hardly need to be reminded in this psychological age, that the dynamic experience of the poet is imbedded in the unconscious and constitutes his artistic predisposition. Poets are doubtless made, not born; but they are made early in life. The love which teaches the poet how to sing is very likely not the result of an adult experience; nevertheless it is indispensable to his calling.

Consequently, it is always out of a deep and sincere feeling that the poet sings, though he himself may not be aware of its nature or its proper object. In consciously directing his emotional potential toward a specific person, the poet may well be motivated by rational or even mercenary considerations, but this does not alter the authenticity of the emotion which is at his disposal. To the inner image, the poet is always faithful, though it be an image which may be flashed on many screens. Thus all questions of poetic sincerity are divisible from the genetic point of view. The fundamental question concerns the complex out of which poetry is made, without which all such activity is mere craftsmanship. In the thirteenth century this complex was called the gentle heart. Next after that comes the question of the particular cause through which the latent capacity emerges as a work of art, in accordance with the rules of art.

"No one can sing well unless the song comes from the heart," wrote Bernard de Ventadour, "and for the song to come from the heart it is necessary that the heart be full of true love. If my song is excellent it is because I direct wholly to the joy of love my mouth and my eyes and my heart and my brain." [16] But although love furnished the motive and the substance, the work itself was a considerable labor which required both skill and patience. No troubadour thought of a song as a spontaneous welling forth of the heart's emotion. To make a song, words were carefully interlaced, woven and twisted together like a fabric; or else the song was forged and filed like metal, or planed, joined, polished, and gilded, in the fashion of the woodworker. The material offered a certain resistance; it was hard and precious. Arnaut Daniel wrote:

> On this gay and graceful air, I fashion words, and I plane and smoothe them, and they will be true and sure when I have gone over them with the file; for Love at once polishes and gilds my song, which moves from her who maintains and governs worth.[17]

Another passage to the same effect illustrates its point with extraordinary concision:

> Obre e lim
> Motz de valor
> Ab art d'amor.[18]

Jaufre Rudel thought of a song as a delicate and fragile piece of mechanism:

> Good is this verse, for never did I fail; everything that is in it is in its place; may he who learns it from me be careful not to break it nor put it in pieces. So may it be received in Quercy by Lord Bertrand, the Count at Toulouse.[19]

The *chanson*, ostensibly an unrestrained outpouring of deepest feeling, was in fact as carefully and conventionally ordered as everything else in medieval art. Out of his song, carved in language as dense as stone, the knight gazes at us with the polite and inscrutable smile of the Gothic statue, at once intimate and impersonal. With disarming frankness, the troubadours divulge to the world the innermost secrets of the heart; but these secrets are always the same secret, the heart is the heart of nobody in particular. It is the heart of all the troubadours.

When we say, therefore, that the troubadour song is subjective in nature, we are really speaking of its ostensible and formal, not necessarily its true, quality. The *chanson* is a genre in which the poet speaks to us directly and confidentially about a secret love, the object of which he could not confide to his closest friend; such is the convention. In reality, the *chanson* is an *aria,* a stage monologue, the attitudes, moods, and emotions of which are derived from a dramatic fable of invariable design; and the poet, while seemingly he confronts us in every line, remains anonymous up to the point where he emerges in his own proper person at the end in the *envoi,* the *tornada.* The troubadour's song thus corresponds precisely to Dante's definition of poetry. It is a rhetorical fiction set to music, the lover's song in the drama of True Love. It would be vain to expect any substantial originality in a genre which was conceived in this manner, and in fact, as we have noted, it is exceptional to meet with any.

This is not to say that True Love had no existence outside literature. Doubtless the *chanson* was as faithful a reflection of the realities of its time as, let us say, an *aria* out of *La Traviata* or a song in a contemporary musical comedy. But it is important to remember that the troubadour, like the modern playwright, was the creator of the drama which he set forth, and not necessarily its protagonist. Whatever the immediate state of his emotions, the goal of his artistic endeavors would be a song, and not a lady.

It was not until the end of the twelfth century that the formal characteristics of the troubadour song were established with precision. Before that time, the term *chanson* had not come into general use; the early troubadours called their songs *vers.* According to the *vida* of Peire d'Auvergne, it was Giraut de Bornelh who first wrote *chansons*. Whatever this may mean, the fact is that until the middle of the thirteenth century the terms *vers* and *chanson* were used interchangeably. After that time a distinction appears to have been made on the basis of a fanciful etymology which derived *vers* from *verus*, true. The term *vers* was then considered applicable to those songs which contained matter of truth, that is, to songs of a moral, didactic, or satiric nature, formerly called *sirventés*, but not to songs which contained matter of love. These were regularly called *chansons*.[20]

By the end of the twelfth century, the term *chanson*, in Provençal *canso* or *chanso*, had come to mean a love-song of some half-dozen stanzas of identical structure, usually, but not always, set to a new melody, a melody especially composed for it. The *chanson*, like the liturgical hymn, was in general monostrophic—each strophe was meant to be sung to the same tune—and the stanzas were consequently matched with great exactness, line for line, syllable for syllable.[21] The musical thought of the *chanson* was thus completely contained within the single stanza, and each stanza was an independent unit of song. One supposes that the effect would be varied by the singer in accordance with the mood and sense of the verse, nevertheless the reiteration of a single melody would conduce to a certain insistence, and this is characteristic of troubadour music.[22]

When narrative matter was set to music in this way, as in the English ballad, the story itself gave a kind of movement to the composition. In the lyric, a new departure was ordinarily made with each stanza, the logical links between stanza and stanza were weak or lacking, and the effect is of a recurrence rather than of a progression. To the modern ear, conditioned to a musical development which proceeds more or less climactically to a resolution, the troubadour music is likely to convey the feeling of a pleasant excursion which gets nowhere, and this mood is by no means inconsistent with the general tenor of the verse.

Although, necessarily, we discuss the verse, the *dig*, apart from the melody, it is unlikely that the troubadours thought of their songs in this way. Usually the poet who arranged the words also composed the music; he must have thought therefore in terms not only of the line of verse but also of the musical phrase. Needless to say, the effect of these songs when they are sung is quite different from the impression they make upon us when we see them on the printed page. These songs were designed to strike the ear, not the eye. The artificiality of separating the words from the music becomes particularly apparent when we try to comprehend what Dante has to say with reference to the structure of the stanza, since his statement has to do primarily with the musical division and only secondarily with the composition of the poem.

In an oft-quoted passage in *De vulgari eloquentia,* Dante describes the arrangement of the stanza with relation to the melody to which it is set. Some stanzas, he writes, are set to a continuous melody which is neither divided nor repeated, and he gives as examples the type of *chanson* written by Arnaut Daniel, and also a *sestina* of his own, *Al poco giorno,*

> quia quaedam sunt sub una oda continua usque ad ultimum progressive, hoc est sine iteratione modulationis cuiusquam et sine diesi . . .

Other stanzas, however, are divisible, and the division—the turn or *diesis*—marks a change of melody. This change, so Dante tells us, always takes place in connection with a repetition of the original melody. When the repetition takes place before the *diesis,* the stanza is said to have feet, *pedes,* and usually it has two feet, though it may have more. The stanza then has the form AA B. If the repetition of the melody takes place after the *diesis,* the stanza is said to have verses: its form is then A BB. Where the melody is not repeated before the *diesis* (A BB), the stanza is said to have a front, *frons.* If there is no repetition after the *diesis* (AA B), it is said to have a tail, *cauda.* Thus a divisible stanza may have a front and verses (A BB), or feet and tail (AA B), or feet and verses (AA BB). Where there is repetition of the melody, of course, the feet must be exactly symmetrical, syllable for syllable, and so the verses.[23]

Dante does not use the term "tripartition." But it follows from his description that a stanza which has feet and tail, or front and verses, will be tripartite in structure, while a stanza which has feet and verses will be divisible in two or in four. Judging from the verse-forms alone, without reference to the music in the songbooks, it is observable that it was a common, though by no means a universal, practice for the troubadours to compose their stanzas on the scheme AA B, with feet, that is, and tail. In such stanzas the feet were often composed of elements rhymed *abab* or, inversely, *abba*, while the tail was of varying length, but seldom less than three lines long. This arrangement would result in a tripartite stanza of seven lines, a very common pattern up to the time of Bernard de Ventadour, who made frequent use of it, in the form, for example, *abab bcc*. As time went on, however, the tripartite structure was evidently felt to be banal, and the adepts of the *trobar ric* preferred other forms, particularly the through-composed stanza which Dante attributes to Arnaut Daniel.

When a tripartite stanza had feet, the form and length of the first sections of the stanza were necessarily fixed. Variety in stanzaic structure could then be achieved only by lengthening the tail. The classic stanza rarely exceeded eight or nine lines in length; the tail would then be only slightly longer than the feet. In later times, as the tail grew longer, there ceased to be much sense in the threefold division from the standpoint of either poetic or musical design. The tail, indeed, in some cases grew to unconscionable lengths. Giraut de Bornelh wrote stanzas twenty-four lines long. Aimeric de Peguilhan has a song with stanzas of forty-two lines, the longest in the troubadour canon.[24]

Aside from the melodic structure, rhyme was the essential element in the design of the stanza. In some of the songs, it is all too clear that the pattern of thought was chiefly dictated by the exigencies of the rhyme. But even where this was not the case, it was mainly through the rhyme-pattern that the poet gave form and movement to the stanza and unity to the composition. Where the poet's primary intention was to rhyme rare and difficult words in a spectacular way—*rimas caras*—the consequence was often a strange hodgepodge of ideas tumbled together heedlessly as the rhyme pulled the sense this way and that. In this style of poetry it is understandable that the words seem nebulous; the poem is, in fact, not much more than a tissue of sound intended for singing, and it is only through a miracle of craftsmanship that it makes any sense at all.

A consequence of the narrowness of the love-song from the point of view of substance was the extraordinary elaboration of its form. By the end of the twelfth century the troubadours had devised much of the artifice with which European lyricism was to be burdened for the next five centuries. Aside from the work of the great masters, it is unusual to find anything new or fresh in the way of an expression of feeling, but on all hands we encounter stupendous feats of versification.

To enlarge their rhetorical apparatus, the troubadours ransacked the bestiaries and lapidaries for similitudes and metaphors. Certain favorite figures were pressed repeatedly into service—the ship, the salamander, the elephant, the lovelorn Tristan, the phoenix, the lodestone, Narcissus. Apostrophes were regularly addressed to various personifications, to Love, to Mercy, to the poet's heart and his eyes. Such entities were made to enter into debates with each other and with the poet—they admonished, reproached, and instructed each other; they had quarrels. There was a vogue for dialogue-songs in which the lover was put through his paces by an imaginary interlocutor. Along with these devices came the systematic use of antithesis to mark the conflict in the soul of the lover, the use of enumeration, and of similitudes in series. But the true genius of the Provenceaux was expressed not so much in rhetoric as in the elaboration of the rhyme. The choice and disposition of the rhymes was considered of prime importance. Fearful ingenuity was expended in the use of internal rhymes, initial rhymes, equivocal rhymes, double rhymes, derivative rhymes, in such tricks of design as *coblas capfinidas* or *vers encadenat*, in which each strophe begins with the word which ends the preceding strophe, and such verbal marvels as the *canso redonda*, in which the same rhymes revolve through successive strophes in a predetermined, but constantly varied order.[25]

The earliest troubadours did not scruple to employ a new set of rhymes for each stanza of a song. About half the songs of

Guillaume IX are composed in this simple fashion. In the fourteenth century manual of prosody, the *Leys d'amors,* these are called *rims singulars.* The next step in complexity was to link up stanzas in pairs, so that the rhyme changed in every other stanza—*coblas doblas.* Formal perfection was achieved by the use of the same rhymes in the same order throughout all the stanzas of the song, *coblas unissonans.* The practice of writing unisonant songs was common from the earliest times; one of the most famous of the songs of Guillaume IX, *Mout jauzens me prenc en amar,* was composed in this manner, almost all the songs of Cercamon, about a quarter of those of Marcabru, and most of Jaufre Rudel's.

But before long, the troubadours became too sophisticated for this sort of perfection, and they broke the harmony of the uniformly recurrent rhyme by interpolating lines which had no echo in the stanza, but which rhymed with the corresponding line in the succeeding stanzas, *rimas dissolutas.* There might be any number of these odd lines within a stanza. When a stanza was composed exclusively of lines of this character, there was, of course, no effect of rhyme within the stanza at all, but the stanza, taken as a unit, rhymed line for line with all the succeeding stanzas of the song in the pattern *abcdefg . . . n.* Such a pattern, while it imposed a rigorous outline upon the stanza, virtually gave the effect of unrhymed verse, for it would take an acute ear to pair rhymes which answered each other at such remote distances, and in different units of the song. The end-product of the troubadour's elaboration of rhyme was, consequently, a virtuosity so great that it all but silenced the rhyme, thus combining the greatest difficulty with the least effect, the last word in subtlety of craftsmanship.

Through such devices poetry was rendered progressively exclusive until its beauties could be savored fully only by the connoisseur. The result was the rich style of which, in the classical period, Arnaut Daniel was the chief proponent, the *trobar ric.* What principally characterized this style was the elevation of difficulty to the rank of an aesthetic principle; indeed, with certain poets the beauty of difficulty took precedence over all other artistic considerations. At the other extreme from the facile rhymers of the light style, Daniel and his colleagues made a point of combining the rarest and most difficult sounds in rhythmical patterns of the greatest possible intricacy.[26]

At the core of the *trobar ric* there was, of course, a social motive, the sophisticate's horror of being caught in some banality of expression. But, as we have already noted, it occurred to nobody who practiced this style to avoid banality of idea. In a great deal of the troubadour poetry, as in most of the lyric poetry of the sixteenth century which was derived from it, the intellectual content of the poem—the substance—was really no more than the material vehicle in which the form of the poem was realized. It is therefore necessary to reverse the usual application of these terms in order to appreciate the poet's achievement in these genres. The matter was, or in the course of time became, conventional. It was the design, in sound, color, and poetic texture, that chiefly interested the poet. The design was the controlling idea, the germ of the poem. When Raimbaut d'Orange wrote

> Rare, dark and colored words I weave together,
> Sadly pensive . . .[27]

he described the process of composition quite clearly—the poet began with a mood, not an idea, and out of this mood, he made a pattern of light and sound. In the best examples of this poetry, the texture and color of the poem accord beautifully with the mood which they express. When the mood is smooth, the verse is smooth; grief, anger, despair are matched with corresponding sounds, rough, sharp, grave, dark, shrill. In the instrumentation of the mood, every sort of rhetorical device was pressed into service—internal rhymes, displaced rhymes, broken stanzas, puns and alliterative tricks, sound-effects of all sorts, sometimes amazing in their virtuosity, sometimes annoying, but seldom boring.

Arnaut Daniel's celebrated song *L'aura amara* is a good example of a piece written in the *trobar ric*. It consists of six stanzas and a *tornada*, with a few rhyming lines set among *rimas dissolutas* in a jagged pattern of undeniable richness. The song itself seems to shiver in the bitter wind which its sharp sounds evoke, and the sense stutters forth spasmodically, as if forced out between the chattering teeth of the poet. While the intention is completely representational, mimetic, the effect borders upon the abstract, and the modernists of the twentieth century were much indebted to it, without quite understanding what was involved:

> L'aura amara
> Fa·ls bruoills brancutz
> Clarzir
> Que·l doussa espeissa ab fuoills
> E·ls letz
> Becs
> Dels auzels ramencs
> Ten balps e muts
> Pars
> E non pars;
> Per qu'eu m'esfortz
> De far e dir
> Plazers
> A mains per liei
> Que m'a virat bas d'aut
> Don tem morir
> Si·ls afans no m'asoma.[28]

In a literal translation, the poverty of the conception becomes painfully evident. The cold wind prevents the birds from singing, therefore the poet will do their office in order to delight the beloved tyrant of his heart:

> The bitter wind
> Makes the branchy groves
> Clear
> Which the soft thickens with leaves
> And the joyous
> Beaks
> Of the boughy birds
> Are stuttering and mute,
> Pair
> And non-pair;
> For which reason I strive

To do and say
Pleasant things
For her
Who has cast me down from high
So that I fear to die
If she does not still my pain.

Written in a sort of poetic algebra, *L'aura amara* permits a certain glimmer of meaning to come through, but the interest of the poem is obviously not in the stereotypes which it reiterates. It is upon the intricacy and originality of the pattern that the poet has chiefly concentrated his effort. This sort of poetry, obviously, is not for the beginner; but it is difficult not because the poet has been at pains to conceal his thought, but because in striving for an unusual effect he has compressed and distorted the expression out of any resemblance to the norms of speech.

The *trobar clus* was a somewhat different style. Here the poet was concerned not with verbal marvels but with the effect of mystery, the pleasure of the enigmatic. Difficulty remained the writer's central preoccupation, but the burden was shifted. The poem was not difficult to write; it is difficult to read. The difficulty in this sort of poetry is not ordinarily a matter of syntax. It is only that the poet has erected an intellectual barrier between himself and his audience. Often enough, the words are clear. We simply cannot decide what they mean.

The best of the *trobar clus* is characterized by a parabolic quality, the result of a studied ambiguity which implies a reserve of meaning beyond the comprehension of the average intelligence. The poem communicates a feeling that more is meant than meets the eye, and what meets the eye is by no means certain. We are thus aware of penumbral significances which may or may not have been intended, as well as of a general exasperating breakdown of communication. Such poetry teases the mind into poetic activity on its own account. It elicits an athletic response which is in pleasant contrast with the more passive pleasure of easy poetry, and thus brings about an enhanced participation on the part of the listener or the reader, who has a feeling, if he succeeds in penetrating the poet's meaning, of greater intimacy than less exclusive types of poetry can afford. Of those who practiced the closed style among the troubadours, none was able to compose a masterpiece of the magnitude of Donne's "A Nocturnall Upon S. Lucie's Day," but the seventeenth century poet's relation to his predecessors in the closed style is unmistakable.

In one direction, inevitably, this sort of poetry bordered upon allegory. It was noted quite early in the development of the *chanson* that any sort of aspiration could be expressed "in semblance of love." The lady of the song could easily be taken, for example, to connote the Blessed Virgin; in time it became possible to address in "*sembianza d'amore*" whatever was conceived of as the object of desire—the Ideal, Wisdom, Justice, Beauty, Glory, or Salvation. Not many of the troubadours were in any sense scholars, but in the Middle Ages love and the symbolic method were equally inescapable. Between the allegorical methods of scriptural interpretation transmitted through Augustine and applied with the greatest freedom by the doctors of the church, and the methods for the interpretation of secular matter illustrated by Dante in the *Convivio,* and later by Ficino and Pico, the most obvious relation exists. The type of *sovrasenso* which Bruno extracted from the love-sonnets of *Gli eroici furori* was the natural outcome of this line of thought, and this extraordinary work is, of course, by no means an isolated example of the allegorical exegesis of love-poetry in the time of the Renaissance.[29]

Accordingly, the poems in which Rudel sings of his far-off love do not permit us to decide whether this *amor de lonh* is sacred or profane, concrete or abstract, a mood or an aspiration; whether the far-off lady is an ideal of unattainable happiness, or the Blessed Virgin, or simply a lady who lived on the other side of the mountains or the sea.[30] Without question, the play of imagination which this ambiguity sets up in the mind adds immeasurably to their interest. It is a similar technique which gives the *Vita Nuova* of Dante its strangely mysterious air, both in its poetry and in the prose which transforms this poetry into another poetry still. But this is not at all the sort of obscurity which characterizes the *trobar clus* of Marcabru. This strange minstrel, who is usually credited with the invention of the sibylline style, was a specialist in verbal complexities, double-entendres, obscure allusions, strange words, paradoxes. As he himself tells us, he is rich in ingenuity; he lights a fire with one hand and puts it out with the other. He confesses his obscurity with proud candor:

> I hold him wise without any doubt who can guess in my song what each word means, and how the theme unfolds, for I myself am subject to error when I interpret dark words . . .[31]

Good examples of the *trobar clus* in the style of Marcabru are therefore impossible to translate.

Although the reaction against the obscure style was severe and unremitting, this poetry influenced many of the troubadours, and poets continued to "skim" their verse and to "entangle" their words long after the vogue of this *trobar* had ostensibly passed. Judging by what the troubadours said of it, the motive for practicing this style of writing was twofold. It was at the same time defensive and esoteric. Peire d'Auvergne wrote: "I like to sing in words that are tight and closed, so that people will hesitate to mock at them."[32] On the other hand, there was an aggressive element in it; the closed style was militantly exclusive.

The famous *tenson* between Giraut de Bornelh and the troubadour "Linhaure," on the subject of the *trobar clus*, has been called the first literary debate in a modern tongue:

> I should like to know, Giraut de Bornelh, why and for what reason you keep blaming the closed poetry. Tell me, if you value so highly what is common to all, will not everyone be equal?

Giraut answers that in his view of the matter a song is loved and esteemed all the more when it is within reach of all. But Linhaure takes a different stand:

> Giraut, I do not wish my poetry to fall into such a muddle that people will prize equally the good and the bad, the little and the great. Never shall it be praised by fools, for they neither know nor care about what is finest and best.

> Giraut, so long as I put forth the best and express it swiftly and vividly, I care little how widely it is known, for great abundance was never dainty fare; that is why people prize gold more than salt, and it is the same with song.[33]

The upshot of the controversy is that Giraut permits himself to be completely convinced by his adversary and he gives up his half-hearted attempt to uphold the easy style. "Linhaure," he concludes, "a true lover is full of good counsel," and so, he says, even if this enigmatic style causes him difficulty, he intends in future to stand by it.

But interesting as the closed style was, and has always been, to the experienced reader, it necessarily had a limited appeal and it was hardly suited to serve the needs of those who had to live in the twelfth century by the popularity of their writings. Courtly taste in those times was tickled by some spice of the bizarre and difficult, but on the whole it inclined to easy poetry. Even the noble amateur Raimbaut d'Orange—"*bons trobaires, mas mout s'entendeit en far caras rimas e clusas*"—was forced to descend occasionally from his exalted perch. He wrote proudly: "Since easy poetry is so highly prized, I shall be sorry not to excel in that also." [34] Giraut de Bornelh who, as a professional, was much more at the mercy of his public, eventually capitulated also, though with a show of reluctance:

> There was a time when I pleased myself rather—for at that time it was permitted me—with these broken stanzas, these words folded back on themselves, subtly and tightly joined, which people nowadays hardly understand . . .[35]

But in other songs he again confirmed his faith in the difficult style:

> I shall be told that if I gave myself a little more trouble, I should sing more simply and that this would suit me better. Not at all: richness of meaning and rarity of form add to the value of a poem. My belief is that the best songs are never understood the first time.[36]

> As for me, to set my song better, I seek out and bring back as if by the bridle, beautiful words laden with strange and natural meaning, which not everyone can discover . . .[37]

Judging by the frequency with which Giraut de Bornelh returned to this theme, the controversy, toward the end of the twelfth century, as to whether poetry should be difficult or easy must have been of considerable interest to the courtly audience. Eventually, so Giraut tells us, he went over to the simple style and became its champion:

> I begin with difficulty a verse which I intend to make easy, for yesterday I resolved that I would write it so that all should understand, so that it should be easy to sing, and this for the greater pleasure of all.
>
> I could easily make it more difficult, but a song has not its full value unless it is within the reach of everyone. In spite of what people say, I take pleasure in hearing my songs sung everywhere, at will, in voices both clear and hoarse, and in seeing women take them to the well.
>
> When I wish to give myself to closed poetry, I do not think that I can find my equal, but I think as much skill is needed to observe reason as to entangle words.[38]

Unhappily, it was not in the nature of this poet to be simple, and although he began a song with the brave words, "I shall make a song such that even my grandson can understand it," his style from first to last seems thorny and full of snags, and though he is seldom profound, "the master of the troubadours" is never clear.

The vogue of the *trobar clus*, as such, did not outlast the twelfth century, but its influence in one form or another was felt for a very long time. As late as the middle of the thirteenth century, we find the Italian troubadour Lanfranc Cigala protesting vigorously against the excesses of those who practiced this style, and, not long after, the closed style became associated with Cavalcanti's celebrated *canzone Donna mi prega*, the precise meaning of which no one has ever quite succeeded in fathoming. Eventually the taste for this sort of poetry found its way through the Italian poets to France, and, toward the end of the sixteenth century, to England, where its influence is traceable in the work of Shakespeare and Donne.

The main current of Provençal lyricism, however, turned to a reasonably simple style which, though wonderfully concise, yet was easy to understand. This was the light style, *trobar leu*, or *trobar clar*, which had already been amply developed by Peire Roger and Bernard de Ventadour. With this change of emphasis, came a renewal of interest in the subject matter of the *chanson*. The love-song was now extended in the direction of wit, with Peire Vidal; of passion, with Raimon de Miraval; of philosophy, with Folquet de Marseille, Sordello, and Montanhagol; of religion, with Guiraut Riquier. In none of these directions, it must be admitted, was its development impressive; nevertheless, some strides were made.

The *trobar ric* and the *trobar clus* were important side roads in the evolution of troubadour love-poetry, but the main line of growth was marked by such poets as Peire Roger, Bernard de Ventadour and Arnaut de Marueill, all of whom practiced a clear and elegant style without eccentricity. In this line of development, which culminates in Petrarch, are found most of those who wrote the *chanson* during the twelfth and thirteenth centuries. If Bernard de Ventadour seems to our taste the greatest of these, it is not because he was markedly different from the others; it is only because he was a better poet. A lyric genius of the first rank, he was able to bring the love-song to the highest perfection of which the troubadour style was capable.

The *chanson* which this group of poets transmitted was subject to little formal variation after the great age of troubadour poetry, the period 1180–1210. What was evolved was a dignified and courtly song consisting of six to eight stanzas of medium length, of relatively complex structure, but with little concession to the cult of rare rhymes, newfangled words, or other stylistic wonders. From the earliest times it had been customary to begin the song with a short prelude which involved an allusion to the season of the year, usually, but not necessarily, spring. It was usual, also, to end the song with one or, more often, two *envois*, called in Provençal, *tornadas*.

Whatever the origin of the *départ printanier*, its function in the love-song was seldom other than conventional: it appears to have curiously survived its efficacy as a substantial part of the composition. It would be a mistake to conclude from this that the troubadours had no real interest in nature. If the nature prelude was often no more than a perfunctory gesture in the direction of the outer world, it was because the world of the love-song was the inner world, to which external nature served as a bridge. The temptation to linger a little on this bridge was evidently strong. The few lines which the poet normally consecrated to the birds, the hawthorn, and the budding boughs show keen observation and a genuine feeling for nature, and more often than not they give the *chanson* a delightful air of having been composed outdoors beside running streams amid green foliage in woods and orchards.

Of all the formulas of troubadour poetry, the nature-prelude seems by far the happiest, the most simple and unaffected. The identification of the longing of the lover with the universal longing of nature in the *renouveau* of spring, the deep feeling of correspondence between the world of nature and the world of man, give a shade of philosophical importance to what might otherwise be considered a trivial subject matter. It is impossible to say how new this formula was when Guillaume IX first used it, but it seems fresh:

> In the sweetness of the new time the woods put out their leaves, and the birds sing, each in his own tongue, the verses of the new song. It is well, then, that a man also should take his pleasure of that which men most desire.[39]

Marcabru, a few years later, struck a more usual note:

> Since the winter of this year has passed and the sweet time of flowers has returned, since I hear in the fields the songs of young birds, the green fields and the thick foliage have given me such joy that I have begun to sing.[40]

With Jaufre Rudel, the prelude took a more elaborate turn:

> When the brook once more runs clear from the spring, according to its custom, and the flower of the eglantine appears, and the little nightingale on the branch turns and modulates and draws out his sweet song, refining it, it is right that I also should sing of what is mine.[41]

It must be admitted, they are really enchanting, these glimpses of an April morning long ago. It is true they all make but a single picture; but the picture is unforgettable—the clear brook, the birds' song, the boughs vibrant with the new leaf; and the knight riding through the green forest, feeling in his heart the joy which thrills through the world, and in his soul the sadness of desire which is its human counterpart. How much of the beauty of the French countryside, the steep green valleys of the Dordogne, the skies of Poitou and of Provence, has been distilled into these stereotypes:

> I like it when the wind breathes upon me in April, before May comes in, and all through the calm night the nightingale sings and the jay, each bird in his tongue, in the freshness of the morning taking joy of love as each hovers close to its mate.[42]

Of course, it is all quite abstract, this description. It is no particular morning in no particular spring. It is the archetypal spring morning complete with leaves and birds, equally useful for the decoration of a song, a tapestry, a parchment or a chapel-window; it is an example of decorative art. But how fortunate that it is there!

By the time of Peire Roger, the nature-prelude had already bred its corollary. The spring morning was no longer necessary to the poet's joy. In the dead of winter, love made its own springtime:

> Neither rain nor wind prevents me from thinking of poetry; the cruel cold takes away neither my song nor my laughter, for love guides me and sustains my heart in the perfect joy of nature; it nourishes, leads and supports me; no other thing rejoices me; no other thing makes me live.[43]

Inevitably another stereotype took shape, the idea that the splendor of the lady was brighter than all other earthly splendor, and that she alone was the source of the poet's joy:

> When the fresh grass appears, and the leaf, and the blossoms open on the bough, and the nightingale lifts his voice high and clear in song, I have joy of the bird and joy of the flower and joy of myself, but of my lady greater joy; on all sides I am surrounded and girt with joy, but she is a joy that is beyond all other joys.[44]

For the *chanson Can vei la lauzeta mover,* Bernard de Ventadour composed what is doubtless the most beautiful, as it is certainly the most famous, of these preludes. In this case, it is neither from the season nor from the landscape that the song takes its leap, but from the joy of the skylark, in a superb figure:

> When I see the lark moving its wings in joy against the light until at last it forgets and lets itself fall by reason of the sweetness that fills its heart, oh, such envy comes to me of those whose happiness I see that I marvel that my heart does not melt away at once with desire! [45]

Beyond this point the nature-prelude did not evolve. It became progressively less frequent in the course of the twelfth century, and by the beginning of the thirteenth it was already old-fashioned as a lyric introduction. But by this time it had passed into the narrative genres, and many a romance began with the canonical figure of the new leaf, the April sun, and the little birds making melody each in his own tongue. It was in this fashion that the Sicilian Guido delle Colonne began his Latin *Historia trojana,* and Boccaccio his *Filocolo* and his *Ameto,* and in the prologue of *The Canterbury Tales* Chaucer made it imperishable in English.[46]

The *tornada* with which the love-song often ended was, unlike the *départ,* rather businesslike in character. This was a short stanza, more often two and sometimes three, an *envoi* which addressed or dedicated the song to a particular person or commended the poet to his patron, or gave instructions to the jongleur who was to sing it or the messenger who was to transmit it. Sometimes, by a pleasant fiction, this messenger was the song itself:

> Messenger, go and run
> And tell the gentlest one
> Of the pain and the grief
> That I feel, and the torment.[47]

In the early period, the *tornada* was sometimes no more than an emphatic repetition of the last lines of the song:

> At Narbonne, since I am not going there, may this my song be presented, and I desire that for this praise it be my warranty.
>
> To my Esteve, since I am not going there, may this my song be presented, and I desire that for this praise it be my warranty.[48]

Later practice did not favor this sort of repetition and the effect of summing up was then limited to the rhyme only, since the *tornada* regularly repeated the final rhymes of the concluding stanza. In a very common form of *tornada,* Giraut de Bornelh "turns" to his patron at the end of his song:

> To God I commend my Sobre-totz, the Joyous One, and it would please me much if I were with him.[49]

This formal parabasis in which the poet affirmed, by way of compliment, the bond which subsisted between him and his patron, frequently identified the patron only by a *senhal,* a pseudonym. In this case the *senhal* might be transparent, since there was no particular reason for secrecy with regard to one's patron. Thus Peire Vidal turns his song to Barral des Baux and his wife, using the *senhal* by which his patron was commonly known, Rainier:

> Dame Vierna, mercy of Montpellier, Lord Rainier, now you will love your knight. Since my joy has always increased through you, I praise God.[50]

When, however, the poet addressed the beloved lady in the *tornada,* the *senhal* by which she was designated was normally impenetrable. Indeed, the epithet or pseudonym chosen for the *senhal* was such that the lady herself would not be expected to recognize it, so great was the lover's discretion and so rigid the requirements of True Love. The poet, such was the convention, simply broadcast the song, hoping that it would find its secret mark, or directed that it be sung at a given court, but the *senhal* did not limit its application; the song might be sung by anyone to anyone, anywhere. Such *senhals* as Good Neighbor—*Bon Vezi*, Lovely Face—*Bel Vezer*, Superwoman—*Mielhs que Domna*, might or might not have been intended to attach in a given case to a particular person. It would, in any case, be all but impossible to discover who that person might be—that was the poet's secret.

Between the *départ* and the *tornada* the song was held together by the rhyme and the music, and generally by no more than that. The *chanson* had very little of that internal unity which we now consider essential to a work of art. The controlling principle was not one of logical progression. The song was a revery, a train of thought revolving about a central theme. This is quite apparent from almost any troubadour song, even the most carefully written; for example, Bernard de Ventadour's *Tant ai mo cor ple de joya*, a true masterpiece in this genre:

> So full of joy is my heart that it transfigures everything for me. To me, the ice is white flowers and red, and yellow, and my happiness increases with the wind and the rain, so that my power mounts and grows, and my song improves. So much love have I in my heart, so much joy and sweetness, that in my eyes the hail is blossoms and the snow, verdure.
>
> I may go about without clothes, naked in my shirt—true love protects me from the chill wind. The more fool he who loses his self-restraint and behaves improperly. But I have taken thought of myself, from the time when first I begged the most beautiful for her love, from which I expect so much good that in exchange for this riches I would not take all of Pisa.
>
> She withholds her love from me, but I have great faith, for at least I have achieved its semblance, and I have had so

much good from her that I can feel no sadness the day I see her. She has taken my heart with love so that the spirit runs to her where she is, but the heart remains here, apart, far from her dwelling in France.

I have good hope of it, but little it helps me, for she keeps me in the balance like a ship in the sea. From the sadness that torments me, I know not where to hide; all night long it twists and throws me about the bed; I feel a pang of love greater than ever did Tristan the Lover who suffered so much pain for Iseult la Blonde.

Ah God, if I were a swallow and could fly through the air, to come in the deep night to the place where she makes her dwelling! Noble lady, full of joy, your lover is dying! I fear that my heart will melt if this endures. Lady, for your love I join my hands and adore you! Lovely body, fresh of hue, you have made me bear great pain.

There is naught in the world which absorbs me so much that when I hear her name mentioned my heart does not turn to her, and my face lightens so that, no matter what you have heard me say about her, you will see at once that I wish to smile. So much I love her with true love that often I weep because sighs taste better after weeping.

Messenger, go run, tell the Loveliest One of the pain and the sorrow I endure for her sake, and the torment.[51]

Obviously, this composition has escaped the tyranny of logic. The poet is full of joy, then full of sadness; he has great hope, and he is in the depths of despair. All the things that troubadours say are in this poem. As a description of the precarious state of the lover, it is complete. Nevertheless, the song conveys a living impression of the joy of love and its sadness, perhaps a stronger impression than a closely integrated statement could transmit. There is something poetically convincing, undeniably, about the seeming inconsequentiality of this succession of ideas. The development of the mood from joy to grief and from grief to joy, undisciplined as it seems, has the vascular quality of a living experience.

This disjunctive movement of the troubadour love-song is certainly not the result of an absence of art. The pattern of thought exemplifies a morphological principle somewhat different from the classic, but it is more than adequate to convey mood and meaning. The poem has no logical sequence; the filaments which bind together thought to thought are of the slenderest; but the song has a psychological integrity which is quite as defensible as a principle of art as the rationalistic principle which we inherit.

This technique becomes clearer when we compare what is perhaps the most widely admired example of troubadour song, the *chanson Can vei la lauzeta mover*, the prelude of which has already been quoted:

When I see the lark moving its wings in joy against the light until at last it forgets and lets itself fall by reason of the sweetness that fills its heart, oh, such envy comes to me of those whose happiness I see that I marvel that my heart does not melt away at once with desire!

Alas, how much I thought I knew of love, and how little I know! For I cannot keep from loving her from whom I shall never have any good. She has all my heart, and all of me, and herself and all the world besides, and when she withdraws herself from me, she leaves me nothing but my desire and my longing heart.

Never more did I have power over myself nor belong to myself from that hour when first she let me look into her eyes, a mirror that pleased me much. Mirror, since first I saw myself in you, my deep sighs have killed me; thus I lost myself, as the handsome Narcissus lost himself in the spring.

I despair of women. Never more will I trust them, and as much as I have been accustomed to defend them, now I shall speak against them. Since I see that not one of them comes to aid me against her who kills and confounds me, now I doubt and mistrust them all, for well I see that they are all alike.

In this she shows herself very much a woman, my lady, for which I reproach her, for she wants nothing that others wish, and what is forbidden, that she does. I have fallen into an evil case, like the madman on the bridge, and I know not why this happened to me, save that I pushed too hard against the mountain.

Mercy is lost, indeed, and I never knew it till now, for she who should feel it most of all has none; where then shall I find it? Ah, how little one would think, to see her, that she would permit a lovelorn wretch to die, who without her cannot recover, without giving him aid.

Since neither prayer avails with my lady nor pity, nor the rights which I have; since it pleases her not that I love her, never more will I speak of it to her. Now I part from her and I renounce her. Since she has given me death, with death I reply, and I go, since she does not retain me, wretched, into exile, I know not where.

Tristan, you shall have no more from me, for I go, wretched, I know not where. I have finished with song. I renounce it, and I hide from joy and from love.[52]

In this song the mood is more evenly sustained than in the previous example. One would say the poet intended here a closer integration of the thought; nevertheless his ideas do not flow one into the other; the stanzas are not composed in a necessary sequence. Each stanza is an independent element. The whole makes a design; but the stanzas might conceivably be rearranged without any essential alteration of the total effect. Only the first and last stanzas and the *tornada* have a necessary position.

In the development of *Can vei la lauzeta mover*, the mind is made to turn in an orbit about the thematic core passing in turn from thought to thought, from mood to mood; from melancholy to hopelessness, to resentment, to reproach, to despair. In the seventh stanza, the poem comes to a true culmination. It is in this respect somewhat unusual, and probably for this reason more satisfactory to the modern taste than the first example, which is left unresolved. But this conclusion, while it is perfectly consistent with the rest of the song, does not follow inevitably from what precedes it. The song might have ended equally well on another note.

In general, the Provençal love-song has not, in the Aristotelian sense of the term, an end nor, strictly speaking, a beginning. This is not terminology appropriate to its structure any more than it would be suitable to the analysis of a stained-glass window. The song has a point of inception, and necessarily a termination, but not necessarily a conclusion. The strophes are conceived of as autonomous and collateral units; they do not develop syllogistically. What the *chanson* illustrates is a method of composition, essentially Gothic, which involves the juxtaposition, not the subordination of units. It is this principle, almost universal in medieval art, which gives to the *chanson* its characteristic quality.[53]

It would be useless to apply to this poetic the principle with which, in a later age, Tasso resolved the long debate regarding the unity of the epic—the principle that the unity of a poem should be such that nothing can be added or taken away without impairing the whole. Only the most general ideas determined the length of the *chanson* or the range of its content. If one had to revise or emend such a song, it would be difficult to find a principle of excision or of addition. There was ordinarily no reason why a song should have seven stanzas instead of six or eight or nine. The length of the song was a matter of taste with the troubadour and of memory with the jongleur. The manuscripts, accordingly, show a great deal of variation in the texts, not only in the number, but in the order of the strophes, and an editor cannot always establish a text with conviction.

Nothing is more unlikely, however, than the idea that the characteristically disjunctive quality of the *chanson* was due to some constitutional inability of the troubadours to integrate a logical sequence or to fit it into a rhyme-pattern. The troubadours were virtuosi. No poets in the history of Western literature have demonstrated a surer mastery of their medium. They were certainly capable—as we can see from poetic forms other than the love-song

—of achieving when they wished a completely unified and consequential expression. The *chanson* was conceived in a different spirit. Like the moods which it expressed, it rejected the dictation of logic in favor of a stream of association, and the *tornada* ended the song only by interrupting it.

What seems true of the verse seems equally true of the music. For their melodies, the troubadours made use of the various modes of the ecclesiastical system, and occasionally also of the major, which the Gregorian generally avoided, since this mode was considered exciting and lascivious. To the modern ear, in any case, these melodies do not seem unduly stimulating. Beautiful as they often are, they have, if anything, a plaintive quality that is eventually hypnotic.

The tendency toward tripartition was, as we have seen, by no means universal; but, on the whole, this body of song represents an important advance in the direction of symmetry and balance in musical expression. On the other hand, the lack of a terminal principle distinguishes troubadour practice rather clearly from the melodic habit of later times. Except for those melodies which employ the major, the end of a troubadour song is likely to make upon an ear conditioned by nineteenth century influences the effect of an indefinite suspension in space rather than of a firm descent to the ground. The troubadours did not, as a rule, seek the sort of musical finality to which we are accustomed in our time. Their melodies have little propulsive force. The dynamism which began to characterize Western melody in the fifteenth century with Josquin, which was developed more fully in the seventeenth with Lassus and Monteverdi, and which in Bach and Handel, and finally in Beethoven, became despotic in its urgency, was not in the least characteristic of troubadour song. In his music, as in his poetry, the troubadour was greatly interested in the arrangement and pattern of his phrases, but he obviously did not feel the need to build to a climax, and his melodies make the effect of a pleasant and seemingly endless recurrence. They tease the mind through a pattern of departure and return, but they do not submit to the authority of the leading tone.

To the modern ear, the troubadour songs therefore seem to

go pleasantly round and round. Their pace is grave, their movement majestic. They have little excitement, but they have persistence. Like the love which they express and celebrate, they look for fulfillment, but only at infinity.

TRUE LOVE

The basis of the troubadour love-song, and of all the lyric and narrative forms which in time came under its influence, was the concept of *fin amor*. The adjective *fin, fis,* from Latin *fides,* had the sense of faithful, honest, sincere, true. The expression *fin amor,* frequently rendered as honest love, pure love, perfect love, or, after Gaston Paris, courtly love, is very well translated as true love, a phrase which has much the necessary connotation in English.

In Renaissance England both the term and the concept were still widely current, and the cult of true love had more than literary significance throughout Europe in the seventeenth century. By that time, of course, the idea had suffered some dilution. In Sir Thomas Elyot's *The Defence of Good Women* (1545), for example, Candidus speaks of true lovers in terms which make us think of nothing more fervent than the polite intercourse of the salon:

> Nay truly; true lovers, of which company I confess myself to be one, are in no part of their conditions. For only delighting in the honest behavior, wisdom and gentleness of ladies or other matrons, we therefore desire to be in their companies, and by mutual devising, to use honest solace.

What true love meant to the troubadours is another question. All the troubadours were concerned in celebrating the joy of love; all professed themselves true lovers. But it would be a mistake to think of *fin amor* as an ironclad system. The concept perhaps had a certain rigidity; the troubadours had not.

It is clearly quite as important to take account of the diversity of the troubadour poetry as to arrive at a formulation of its essential character. It is also more difficult. When we speak of the troubadours, we may have in mind Bernard de Ventadour or Arnaut Daniel, but we are in fact speaking of a body of upward of four hundred poets of every sort and condition—the King of Aragon, the jongleur Pistoleta, the Count of Poitou and the tailor Guillem Figueira. It is astonishing that the theory of love which these poets developed should be as consistent as it is, the more so since it was only in the period of decadence that the troubadours acquired the habit of setting down theoretical matter in didactic form. But it would be a mistake to believe that we can reduce the mass of amatory verse that the troubadours have left us to a definite and consistent system of rules. At the most what we have is a spectrum of attitudes. Much depends therefore upon our point of departure. When we look for consistency in the troubadour poetry, we are surprised to find it all so much alike; but when we look for variety we find astonishing discrepancies.

Quite early in the history of the courtly poetry, genres were developed which treated love from very different viewpoints, from the most coarse and sensual to the most refined and idealistic. What is commonly described as the official love-theory of the troubadours represents in the main the poetic substance of the *canso maestrada*, the full-dress love-song—a form which was subject to more rigorous scrutiny than the forms which grew up around it—supplemented by the doctrine set forth in some of the didactic pieces. Thus with the aid of certain impressive specimens indispensable to the anthologist, we are able to chart a fairly smooth course through the tangle of courtly poetry, but we must remember that these are convenient landmarks, and that landmarks are convenient precisely because they are somewhat set apart from the surrounding country.

The troubadour love-song reproduced little of the turbulent gaiety which we associate with the rich courts of the Midi. Sensual these songs are, without doubt, but theirs is a sensuality thrice abstracted. In general, true love makes the impression of an erotic cult so highly disciplined that it savors of the monastic. It is a poetic mood well suited to the grim romantic castle imagined by Vernon Lee as the cradle of *fin amor,* a castle filled with lonely men under the spell of a single lovely lady. It seems less appropriate to the château of the noble song-writer Eble II de Ventadour—"*valde gratiosus in cantinelis usque ad senectam alacritatis carmina dilexit,*" so Jaufre de Vigeois describes him—who could serve an unexpected visitor from Poitiers with his hundred knights a sumptuous banquet without appearing to disturb his steward or his butler. The poets who sang of true love in the courts of the Midi were, indeed, capable of many moods. They could be brutally or comically misogynistic, cynical, ironic, obscene, suggestive. But the central fantasy which determined all these variants was the song of the suppliant knight, and this had always an idealistic character.

The love which the suppliant offered his lady was in general illicit and as a rule adulterous. The knightly lover of the troubadour song did not usually address his suit to a girl he hoped to marry.[1] As a matter of fact, songs of courtship in which the lover's intentions are, as we say, honorable appear to be in the minority in Western literature, though as time goes on they become more frequent. What is chiefly characteristic of European lyricism, especially during the Middle Ages and the Renaissance, is the love of the moth for the star, a passion at all times carefully distinguished from the analogous desire of the moth for the flame:

Ab bel semblan que fals' Amors adutz
S'atrai vas lieis fols amans e s'atura
Col parpaillos qu'a tant folla natura
Queis fer al foc per la clardat que lutz.[2]

The art of courtship was called *domnei*—from Provençal *dompna,* lady; the practice of courting ladies was *domneiar;* the practitioner of the art, a *domneiaire* or *entendedor.* By *domnei* and *drudaria*—from *drutz,* a lover—were meant the practice of true love. Those who practiced love falsely were deceivers, *trichaires,* and the troubadour songs do not advance the aspirations of such people. True love was not usually successful, we are told, but that was not the lover's fault:

> De domnas m'es veyaire
> Que gran falhimen fan
> Per so car no son gaire
> Amat li fin aman. . . .[3]

The posture of the true lover is so familiar that we have come to accept it as the hallmark of medieval culture. A seal attributed to the noble *trouvère* Conon de Bethune (1150–*c*.1220), for example, represents it perfectly. This depicts, in an oval cartouche, an armed knight on his knees before a lady. His body is shrouded in a mail hauberk. His head is completely concealed in his helmet. He wears spurs but no sword. The lady stands at arm's length, chastely robed, her regular nondescript features framed in long braids, presumably blonde, and between her outstretched palms the knight's hands are placed in the formal gesture of homage. Within the cartouche, in the space above the helmet of the kneeling knight is inscribed the single word: *Merci.*[4]

The entire concept of *fin amor* is implicit in this image. The relation of the knight and the lady is obvious. As for the motto, if we could digest the entire corpus of courtly love-poetry into a single word, the word would be *merci.* The *trouvère* Thibaut de Champagne described the situation precisely in a French *chanson* of the early thirteenth century which might serve as a caption to this ideograph:

> Dame, en la vostre baillie
> Ai mis cuer et cors et vie.
> Por Dieu, ne m'oubliez mie.
> La ou fins cuers s'umelie,
> Doit on trouver
> Merci, aie,
> Por conforter.[5]

Chiefly significant is the knight's attitude. He has chosen to have himself depicted before all the world in perpetual submission to a woman. He is her man, her vassal, and to her, in some sense, all his deeds revert. But the situation is static. In return for his service, the knight hopes one day to receive "mercy," a boon which the lady cannot fully grant him without immediately destroying the relationship depicted in the seal. Knight and lady are thus frozen in these attitudes for eternity, the knight forever suppliant, the lady forever holding and withholding. In this manner the eternal feminine leads him on, within the frame of a concept as fixed and changeless as the seal itself. Without doubt, there is in this idea some element of the tragic, and this element, however attenuated, is traceable also in the songs in which the knight exhibits his love. As the logic of the situation admits of no alteration of the design, these songs necessarily resemble each other. Each constitutes, one might say, another impression of the seal.

The *impresa* of Gérard de Saint-Amand, of approximately the same date as that of the Flemish poet Conon, adds an important character to the drama of true love—not the lady's husband, of course, for in general the *gilos* is kept outside the cartouche—but the knight's horse, which in this instance stands impatiently behind his master, ready to bear him off the moment he rises from his knees. Within the cartouche the knight kneels, constant, fixed and motionless forever, but the artist evidently desires us to understand that this passive pose is the posture of his soul, not his body. The knight's heart is fixed and submissive, his body is free; the active life thrusts its horse's head boldly into the circle of true lovers. The motto reads: *Secretum meum mihi*, a phrase which had a profoundly religious connotation, and is surmounted by a cross, indicating that Saint-Amand combined the service of his lady with the service of his Lord. The sense of the motto is not mysterious—in the perfection of true love, the identity of the beloved lady would be an enigma never to be revealed, not even to the lady herself who served, unwittingly, as the guiding star of the knight.[6]

The image of true love was thus based upon a metaphor which equated love with feudal service, and this conceit was the shaping principle of the whole design. The knight was the lady's vassal; she was his lord, his leader, and his guide. "To her who is the guide of honor," wrote the troubadour Miraval, in a typical passage, "I have sworn myself as liegeman, with joined hands, on my knees." To be received in this manner by the lady was, of course, a considerable privilege, for the feudal relation involved reciprocal obligations—the vassal's obligation to serve and to defend was predicated upon the suzerain's duty to maintain and to support. The height of the troubadour's ambition was in many cases simply to be accepted, to be "retained." "I remained before her," wrote Gaucelm Faidit, "hands joined, on my knees, weeping, until she took me into her service. And at first she was astonished at my boldness, but when she saw my humility, she received my homage, for she understood that I was sincere. I am her liegeman and her servant." [7]

So convincing are such humble protestations of the lover's desire to be retained that one might be tempted to wonder if the poor troubadour were doing any more than applying for a position. But the lover's humble posture had no connection with the relative rank or wealth of the lady; it was merely an elaboration of the conceit. If Bernard de Ventadour, the son of a *sirven,* addressed his lady, presumably the Duchess Eleanor of Aquitaine, in terms of abject humility: "I am at her mercy; she may give me away or sell me, as she pleases," it was in precisely similar terms that the Duke of Aquitaine addressed his lady also:

> For so completely do I give and deliver myself to her that she may inscribe my name in her charter. And deem me not mad if thus I love my fine lady, for without her I cannot live, so great need have I of her love.[8]

What the true lover offered, therefore, regardless of his social position, was a complete reversal of the normal relation of man and woman. As Ronsard was to write in his day,

> C'est devenir valet au lieu de maistre,
> C'est mille fois le jour mourir et naistre.[9]

The consequence of being retained was, naturally, by no means definite. The situation might be imagined as forever static, in which case the lover would have every reason for multiplying his complaints. The lyric seldom went much further than this.

But the situation was well suited to narrative development; and the wonderfully powerful plot of *The Changeling*, for instance, shows how these materials would in time be adapted for the stage. The first step in love's progress was necessarily an offer of service. In this the lover did not ordinarily haggle. Bernard de Ventadour wrote at the end of a deeply passionate song:

> Noble lady, I ask nothing of you save that you should accept me as your servant. I will serve you as a good lord should be served, whatever the reward may be. Here I am, then, at your orders, sincere and humble, gay and courteous. You are not, after all, a bear or a lion, and you will not kill me, surely, if I put myself between your hands.[10]

It is almost in these words that De Flores recommends himself to the beautiful Beatrice-Joanna in Middleton and Rowley's play.

Doubtless when these poetic fancies were translated into everyday realities of behavior, situations would develop of which we gain some inkling from the imaginary conversations in the treatise of Andreas Capellanus. We may be sure that the conventional protestations of the love-song were bandied about freely in conversation, and that they were received and parried with such feminine grace as the recipient could command. In *The Book of the Courtier*, Castiglione makes it apparent that the gallant conversations of the time of Andreas were equally suitable to the sixteenth century salon, and that expertness in love-discourse was a necessary accomplishment of the Renaissance court-lady, who could hardly avoid the *ragionamenti d'amore* which

> every gentleman uses as a means to acquire favor with the ladies . . . not only when impelled by passion, but often to do honor to the lady to whom he speaks, since he believes that the pretense of loving her is a testimony of her worthiness to be loved.[11]

The submissive posture assumed by the lover during his courtship of the lady was not a temporary phase of their relationship, as it is in the form of courtship which leads to marriage. His submission was, in theory, perpetual. Presumably, in the course of time, this relationship might lead to difficulties. In a *tenson* between Marie de Ventadour and Gui d'Ussel, written some time before 1222, Gui advances a somewhat radical view of the relation which should subsist between lovers. A lady, he says, once she has resolved to give herself to love, should do as much for her lover as he for her, without any regard for rank, since between friends there should be no superior. To this opinion, the Vicomtesse Marie is indignantly opposed:

> Gui, whatever he desires the lover must implore as a mercy, but the lady may command him, although sometimes she should request him; and the lover must fulfill her requests and her commands as proceeding from her who is at once his beloved and his sovereign; but the lady must honor him as her friend, not as her lord and master.
>
> Gui d'Ussel, this is not at all the way lovers speak in the beginning. On the contrary, when they have a mind to someone, kneeling, with their hands clasped, they say, "Lady, permit me to serve you humbly, as your liegeman," and it is in this way that she accepts him. I therefore judge him, in all justice, a traitor if, having given himself as a servant, he tries to become an equal.[12]

One would judge, however, that Gui was not altogether committed to the side he chose in this debate, for in a *tenson* with his cousin Elias, already quoted in another connection, he takes the more usual position that as a lover cannot, in all decency, maintain a submissive attitude in a conjugal relation, love and marriage are never compatible. Thus, he argues, as the young Ibsen was to argue seven centuries later, the only way to preserve one's love is not to marry its object:

> Elias, if I refuse to take my lady to wife, I do her no dishonor, and if I leave her it is only out of fear and out of the great honor in which I hold her; for if I marry her and afterwards court her, I cannot commit any greater fault, and if I treat her rudely and brutally, I am guilty of a wrong toward love, and my courtship is destroyed.[13]

As Elias is cast in this *tenson* in the role of realist, he answers his cousin's arguments with exceptional good sense:

> Cousin, you might take me for a villain if, were I in a position to have her whom most I love to myself, without guardian, co-tenant or lord, I should ask for anything better. A husband has his joy without torment, but a lover has it mixed with pain. And so I prefer, whatever people may say, to be a joyful husband rather than a tortured lover.[14]

From this sort of debate, it may be gathered that the idea that conjugal love was possible and even preferable to true love was by no means unheard of in chivalric literature. Nor was it unheard of to proffer true love to a maid.[15] But it was to be some time before these ideas received a full development.

Since love brought about a drastic change in the normal relations of man and woman, the enamorment was an event of great importance. As Andreas Capellanus described it, love was the result of a prolonged meditation upon the lady's charms, after desire was aroused by the sight of them. But many of the troubadours thought of the enamorment as a sudden event, unexpected and immediately conclusive. The lady's bright glance was an arrow, a dart which penetrated the lover's eye and lodged in his heart. The conceit was already traditional in the twelfth century:

> Never was archer able to draw more straight than she who shot into my heart the sweet death of which I wish to die, unless she restore my joy with a glance of love.[16]

Once he was attacked in this manner, the poor man had no recourse but to beg for quarter:

> A thousand times a day I wish to die, so much the dart pains me with which Love has wounded my heart . . .[17]

> I have yielded myself to your mercy, lady, for life or for death, and if it should please you to kill me, may God never save me if I should wish to recover.[18]

The conceit of the arrow of love was, of course, by no means original with the troubadours. It was of classical origin, and they doubtless borrowed it more or less directly from Ovid. They did not use it with any precision. It was never quite clear, for example, where these darts came from—whether it was the lady who loosed them, or whether the god of love shot them through the embrasures of her eyes, or from some other point of vantage. Occasionally the poet's language bordered upon the scientific, but to no great purpose. Uc Brunec, for example, used the jargon of the schools in explaining the phenomenon of enamorment:

> Love is a courteous spirit who lets himself be seen only in his semblance, for he shoots his sweet arrows from the eyes to the eyes, and passes from the eyes to the heart and from the heart to the thoughts.[19]

One is hardly prepared for the vast consequences of this conceit in the literature of the following centuries. But the troubadours did not exploit the metaphor much beyond this point. It remained for Guido Cavalcanti to borrow from the schoolmen the terminology which would transform the art of love into a science.

Nevertheless, the troubadours were agreed that love was in the first place a lesion of the eye. It was born of light, of an image which, after penetrating the eye, descended to the heart and lodged there, kindling desire. It was thus in the heart's heat that love was nourished. Peire Vidal wrote:

> The flame, the fire and the blaze of love is born in the heart; there desire nourishes it and it engenders that meditation which masters the heart a hundredfold.[20]

In time the thermal aspects of this process became impressive. Three hundred years after the time of Peire Vidal, we find, in the sonnets of Antonio Tebaldeo, that the fire in the poet's heart burns so brightly that it threatens to scorch his limbs and his garments, and the heat is so intense that it causes the snows of winter to melt at his approach.[21]

None of the troubadours showed any such interest in the

psychology or physiology of love as the Italian lyric writers of the following ages; nevertheless, the spiritual aspects of the matter were often the subject of troubadour song. Particularly the troubadours discussed the inner conflict of the lover in terms of the organs responsible for his plight. "Three enemies I have," wrote Uc de Saint Circ, "and two evil lords who plot night and day to destroy me. The enemies are my eyes and my heart who make me desire her who is not for me." [22] But of all those who discussed the question of the eyes and the heart, only Aimeric de Peguilhan appears to have had an interesting thought, the idea that beauty is a preconceived ideal:

> True Love, I assure you, has not, and cannot have of himself, force or power, or any authority either small or great, unless the eyes and the heart give it to him. . . . For the eyes are the dragoman of the heart, and the eyes seek out what it pleases the heart to retain; and when they are well accorded all three, and firmly of one mind, then True Love is born from that which the eyes make pleasing to the heart. . . . And so, let all true lovers know that Love is a true affection which is born of the heart and of the eyes, without doubt, that the eyes make it flower and the heart causes it to bear fruit—Love, the fruit of the true seed.[23]

Troubadour love was typically at first sight, but the idea that a man might fall passionately in love with a lady he had never seen, either because destiny had implanted her image in his heart at birth, or through having his imagination inflamed by reports of her beauty, as in the case of Jaufre Rudel or of Raimbaut d'Orange, seems to have fascinated the medieval audience. It was also very acceptable to fall in love with a face seen in a picture, a mirror or a vision. There were many ways in which a beautiful image might enter the soul. But, normally, sight was the spark that set off the train of love. Andreas Capellanus considered that the blind were incapable of love because "a blind man cannot see anything upon which his mind can reflect immoderately, and so love cannot arise in him." [24] The dart of love, as we can see from the detailed description in Cligès,[25] was the image of the lady herself, her face and figure. It was this which entered the heart and perturbed the spirit; upon this the fancy, in the words of Andreas, immoderately dwelt until at last the man "proceeded to action."

These commonplaces were given the widest currency in the course of the thirteenth century. When the Sicilian Giacomo da Lentino undertook to explain the nature of love in a sonnet, one of the first ever written, it was in complete accordance with the troubadour theory:

> Love is a desire that comes from the heart through the abundance of great delight; and the eyes first of all engender Love, and the heart gives it its nourishment.[26]

A generation later, in the time of Guido Guinizelli, the thunderbolt and the darts of love must have been so common in Italian poetry as to make people yawn at the very thought, but Guido dutifully developed the conceit:

> There appeared a flash of splendor which, passing through my eyes, came to strike my heart; it is this which put me in such a state. It was the beautiful eyes full of love which struck desire into my heart as a bird is struck by an arrow.[27]

The military aspect of the situation appealed more strongly to the other Guido. It was Guido Cavalcanti who principally transmitted the idea of the sweet and ruthless enemy against whom it is useless to struggle, and whose glance brings death:

> It was through the eyes that the battle came at first and all my strength was at once broken, and with the blow my mind was destroyed . . .[28]

Few of the troubadours wrote in this vein; obviously, this lacked measure. But the Italian poets developed it further and further in the direction of absurdity. No conceit, perhaps, in all the history of literature has been labored so assiduously as this, yet apparently, the more it was used, the more useful it became. Through Petrarch and the Petrarchists, it became an almost indispensable element in Renaissance love-poetry. Thus when Portia's invisible musicians sang the question, "Tell me where is fancy bred?" for the perplexed Bassanio, very likely there was nobody in Shakespeare's audience who had not at his fingers' tips the answer to this august mystery.

The dart of love was not ordinarily fatal, but it appears to have resulted in considerable discomfort to the lover. The symptoms of love-sickness were traditional. For the Greeks in classic times, love was normally a female ailment, the sort of thing a Phaedra might experience; it was not a disease appropriate to men. The Romans were less immune. The troubadours came to know the symptomatology of love through Ovid, if not through personal experience, and love-sickness soon became widespread in Western literature.

Love was the occupational disease of the leisure class. It was also a special hazard of the poet's trade, for it was chiefly out of the pain of love that poetry was made. The symptoms of love-illness, *hereos*, Chaucer called it, were often described; from the *Viaticum* of Constantinus Africanus in the eleventh century to Burton's *Anatomy* in the seventeenth, the love-syndrome varied little. In the initial stages the symptoms were not unbecoming—sleeplessness, loss of appetite, loss of flesh, and the characteristic pallor of the lover, together with love of solitude and a tendency to weep, particularly when music was played. But, we are told, unless the disease was cured, it became dangerous—the lover might pass into a melancholy, waste away, and die. So Hamlet, as Polonius diagnosed his illness,

> Fell into a sadness, then into a fast,
> Thence to a watch, thence into a weakness,
> Thence to a lightness, and by this declension
> Into the madness wherein now he raves . . .[29]

The physiology of love-sickness was simple. Joy was "a medicine to the body." It expanded the heart, which thereupon sent the vital spirits coursing through the arteries. Hence the joyful lover, as Bernard de Ventadour wrote, felt warm in deepest winter, and the joy that emanated from Guillaume IX's lady renewed and refreshed the body of the lover. But grief caused the heart to contract, and the blood and the melancholy humor to descend and to "muster" round the heart from the periphery of the body. Thus oppressed, the heart labored and languished. The cold humor quenched the animal heat, the radical moisture was dried up, and as the spirits were progressively extinguished, the man grew feeble, and at last he died.[30]

Such an outcome, of course, would be considered both tragic and deplorable, and Alain Chartier was much criticized for his anti-feminism in causing the hero to die in *La belle dame sans mercy*. Such inflexible virtue as would cause a man's death was not encouraged in women, the less so as it was considered shameful in the suzerain to let a vassal die for lack of succor.[31] But it was not considered inappropriate for the lady to cause the lover to suffer on her account such torments as only martyrs can endure. On the contrary, the mercy which the lover sought was properly won only through the greatest labor and pain. The lover sighed incessantly. Since each sigh came from the heart and cost it a drop of blood, his face grew pale, betraying his anemia. For lack of spirit, his bodily members failed. He froze and burned with love's fever, trembling constantly, consumed inwardly with excessive heat, outwardly chilled. In addition he suffered psychic tortures beyond description—jealousy, doubt, and fear, and incessant inner debate. He cut indeed a pitiable figure in the eyes of the world:

> When I see her, it is at once evident in my eyes, in my face and in my color, for I shake with fear like a leaf in the wind. I have not enough sense left for a child, so greatly am I taken with love; and of a man so completely vanquished, a woman should have great pity.[32]

Love was a madness. A lover's mind could not function properly because the inner image of the beloved absorbed his attention to the exclusion of everything else. Therefore lovers could not be expected to act quite rationally. They might lapse suddenly into a kind of coma, totally abstracted from the world. "Many times," wrote Folquet de Marseille, "people speak to me and I don't know what they say; they greet me and I hear nothing." [33] In the same way, Lancelot in the *Roman de la charrete* "totally forgets himself and he knows not whether he is alive or dead, forgetting even his own name." Apparently after a time there was nothing to do in this predicament but to take to one's bed:

> I keep sighing in my feeble heart, for I see that I deceive myself, I see myself get thinner every day, my body and my spirits fail as if the life were going to leave me. My sighs fill me with anguish; soon they will be exhaled even to the last.[34]

Even successful love was a painful experience. The true lover had not an easy moment—jealousy and fear were essential elements of his mental state. "Indeed," wrote Andreas Capellanus, "he fears so many things that it would be difficult to tell them all." [35] Fear, indeed, was that spice which gave true love its special savor. Chrétien de Troyes remarked in *Cligès:*

> Amors sanz crieme et sans peor
> Est feus sanz flame et sanz chalor,
> Jorz sanz soleil, bresche sanz miel,
> Estez sanz flor, iverz sanz giel.

> Love without fear and without apprehension is fire without flame and without warmth, day without sun, hive without honey, summer without flower, winter without frost.[36]

It was natural that love so highly spiced with pain should evoke a reaction. In a *chanson* which celebrated deliverance from passion, Peire Cardenal summed up comprehensively the conventional torments of the lover, and he sang the joy of not loving:

> Now in truth I have every reason to praise Love: he takes away neither my appetite nor my sleep, nor does he make me feel cold nor heat; I neither yawn nor sigh on his account; I do not wander about at night from place to place; I am neither vanquished nor tortured, nor sad nor complaining; I need not pay a messenger; I neither betray nor am I betrayed, and I leave the game with the dice.[37]

But in the conventional troubadour song, the pain of love was indistinguishable from joy. The very song in which Bernard de Ventadour draws his most pitiful picture of the lover's plight is at the same time an affirmation of his happiness:

> He is dead who feels not in his heart something of the sweet savor of love. And of what use is it to live without merit, a source of mischief to others! May the Lord God never hate me so much as to let me live a month or a day when I become a mischief-maker and have no desire for love.[38]

Most of the troubadour songs are sad, not with the sadness of regret or of reminiscence, but the sadness of unfulfillment. The knight of the song accepted this sadness as part of his lot in life, and assimilated it to pleasure. It became part of the joy of love to be sad:

> But the sorrow is for me pleasure, laughter and joy, for in thinking of her, I am a lecher and a glutton: ah, God! if I could ever possess her otherwise! [39]

Yet this sadness was not considered to be a permanent state in the lover. It was a complex emotion, but essentially love was gay:

> I am sad, I am happy; often I sing, often I sorrow, now I grow thin and now put on flesh, for love has divided himself in my heart into joy and sadness; in laughing and in weeping, in dreaming and in playing, Love shows me his qualities in the midst of laughter and tears.[40]

In love, joy was everywhere. It underlay all of love's torments. The pain of love arose only from the denial or the deferment of joy. The lover's submission, his servitude, the long torment patiently endured, the glorious and dangerous quests valiantly sought out and achieved, all these were undertaken in joy and in the hope of greater joy to come. The art of love was, after all, a *gai saber*, and if so much of the *gai saber* seems sad, it is because sadness too has its joys.

It is in the poetry of Guillaume IX that we first come upon the joy of love, in a charming song through which the word *joi* is made to echo and re-echo like a hunting call. Guillaume does not tell us what this joy is. All we can gather is that joy of love is a spiritual exaltation which gives poetic quality to the sexual relationship and transforms it into something rare and beautiful, of great therapeutic power.

> Never has man been able to understand what it is, in wish or in desire, in thought or in imagination; such joy cannot find its equal, and whoever would praise it properly would not be able to accomplish this task, not if he tried for a year.
>
> Through her joy she can heal the sick, and through her anger she can kill the healthy, and of the wise man make a fool, and cause the handsome one to lose his beauty, and brutalize the most courteous and give courtesy to every brute.[41]

Evidently the joy of love was such as might properly inspire reverence. But the noble poet seems to have been as uncertain of its nature as people have been ever since, and what was already vague he did his best to confuse even further by using the term *joi* in several ways all at once. Love's ecstasy is *joi*. But the lady herself is a joy, and joy is an effluence which emanates from her, and joy is what they experience who are admitted to her presence. Moreover the word *joia* was rich in its associations; it could signify "jewel" as well as "delight." These joys, clearly, all had their basis in sexual intimacy, but in a relation which was blessed and—at least in fantasy—guiltless; a delight which was also a benediction. The consequence of this joy was an enhancement of the physical and spiritual vigor of the lover. It made him strong and brave and magnanimous beyond his normal capacity. Guillaume IX said that it refreshed the heart and renewed the flesh so that it never grew old.[42] We find much the same idea in a *tenson* between Marcabru and Uc Catola:

> Marcabru, when I am tired and ill, and my sweet lady welcomes me with a kiss when I undress, I rise again whole and healthy and cured.[43]

The joy of love was the joy of life, a genial and enthusiastic surge of vitality which could be felt throughout the whole of creation. In man it was felt most potently in the joy of courtship, the affirmation of man's youth and virility. It might be felt in every season, but in spring most potently, and it was in his desire to share in this universal joy that the lover turned to the loveliest of creatures. Because the joy of love was wholly within the lady's power to give or to withhold, the knight knelt at her feet, for this joy must be given freely, and received with humility; like mercy, it could not be constrained.

Out of joy came virtue. "It is joy which nourished my childhood and my youth," wrote Peire Rogier in a song not quite Wordsworthian, "and without it I should be nothing. And I see that all actions of men debase, degrade, and disgrace them except love and joy." [44] Raimbaut d'Orange set great store by gaiety:

> I have the right to laugh and I often laugh; I laugh even in my sleep. My lady laughs so sweetly that it seems to me the laughter of God, and this laughter causes me more joy than the laughter of four hundred angels charged to assure my gaiety.[45]

Because joy was good and predisposed men to good, while melancholy was evil and predisposed men to ill, Sordello wrote that it is a man's duty to be gay: "A man lives only when he lives in joy. Whoever lives in affliction cannot sincerely perform deeds that are fine and pleasing." [46]

Unhappily, the joy of love was difficult to sustain. In developing the fantasy of an amorous relationship without guilt, the troubadours attached themselves psychologically to a tradition more ancient than Zeus, which had nothing to do with husbands and fathers. In this situation, both historically and genetically, joy, power and authority were vested in the wise and beautiful mother, and it was in this delightful image that the troubadour created the beloved lady of the song. But it was one thing to dream up such a fantasy, another to liberate it sufficiently from the fears and anxieties habitual to the human condition, so that the dream could be exhibited even in poetry without the usual compensatory devices. The ghostly figures excluded from the paradise of true lovers returned at once to haunt it in another guise, and even in fancy a thousand obstacles obtruded themselves between the lover and the lady. Invisible eyes observed their every movement, malevolent tongues whispered everywhere. There were constant misunderstandings. There was great need of patience and self-restraint, many tears. The joy of love surpassed all understanding, but this joy had to be won, like all forbidden things, with infinite pain and at greatest cost, and it was not a thing that could be long retained.

So few of the troubadour songs celebrate a successful courtship that one is tempted to conclude that the concept of true love was not framed to include success. The true lover did not set his mind upon an easy conquest; he made it as hard for himself as he could. The lady of his "intention" was not only of exalted station, she was of the most exalted station, quite simply the most beautiful, the noblest, wisest, and most desirable of earthly creatures, a being so perfect that one trembled at the very thought of proposing an intimacy.

The precise nature of the *guerredon*, the reward, which might properly be expected from the service of so exalted a creature was rarely made explicit. Unquestionably it was in all cases some form of physical intimacy. At the least it would be a token—a smile, a ribbon, a glove, a ring, a kiss. This was received as a pledge of more to come, the *plus* or *sobreplus*. But the *sobreplus* was not always forthcoming. In *The Art of Honest Love* of Andreas Capellanus, the clerical gentleman of the eighth dialogue explains to the lady of the higher nobility whom he is courting:

> I want to explain to you something . . . which I know many keep hidden in their hearts . . . and that is, that one kind of love is pure and one is called mixed. It is the pure love that binds together the hearts of two lovers with every feeling of delight. This kind consists in the contemplation of the mind and the affection of the heart; it goes as far as the kiss and

> the embrace and the modest contact with the nude lover, omitting the final solace, for that is not permitted to those who love purely.

The pure love he speaks of is undoubtedly what the later troubadours regarded as the perfection of *fin amor*—

> This love is distinguished by being of such virtue that from it arises all excellence of character, and no injury comes of it, and God sees very little offense in it. No maiden can ever be corrupted by such love, nor can a widow or a wife receive any harm or suffer any injury to her reputation. This is the love I cherish, this I follow and ever adore, and never cease urgently to demand of you. But that is called mixed love which gains its effect from every delight of the flesh and culminates in the final act of Venus. . . . This kind quickly fails, and it lasts but a short time, and one often regrets having practiced it; one's neighbor is injured and the Heavenly King is offended by it, and from it come very grave dangers. . . . But mixed love too is real love, and it is praiseworthy, and we say that it is the source of all good things, although from it grave dangers threaten also.[47]

It is unfortunate that the learned lover is not more explicit in this passage, for we have no other precise statement on this point. Yet there is enough here to furnish a clue to much that is puzzling in the poetry of true love. It seems tolerably clear that the terms "honest love," "chaste love," and "perfect love" were in general meant to be synonymous with the pure love of Andreas. Therefore true love ideally would involve a courtship of limited objective, resulting in a not quite adulterous relationship. Such love would not be, strictly speaking, sinful, illicit, or illegal. It pushed its frontiers to the very borders of adultery, but its merit was that it did not transgress them. The true lover had, accordingly, a positive and definite way of differentiating himself from the false lover, the traitor, the hypocrite, and the *losengier*. There was no question of degree. The moment the line which divided intimacy from adultery was crossed, the nature of love was altered, the lady was compromised and endangered, and the joy of love changed its quality.

The danger of transgression in a situation of such singular delicacy would be, of course, enormous, and it was precisely on this point that the true lover was expected to warrant his reliability. But, human nature being what it is, even with the best intentions, *amor purus* was likely to change without notice into *amor mixtus*, and the learned clerk of *De amore* could evidently not go so far as to exclude *amor mixtus*, in this strictly secular discussion, from the category of true love.

Although the concept of love refined almost to the point of the ideal is to be found in the earliest troubadour songs, in general, troubadour love was frankly sensual. Guillaume IX expressed himself with forthright virility, even in his "idealistic" songs:

> I remember still a morning when we made an end of war, and she gave me so great a gift, her love and her ring. May God let me live long enough to have my hands once again under her mantle.[48]

Other troubadours sang with equal or greater freedom of getting —or desiring—kisses and embraces, of looking forward to the hour when they might lie beside the lovely lady, or contemplate her charms, or clasp her body, white, plump, and smooth, or possess her completely. It is obvious that many of these songs were meant to inflame the imagination:

> She will be merciful if henceforth she puts an end to the long struggles through which she leads me; if she will give me first a kiss, and afterwards more, according to my deserts; and then we shall take a little journey together along a short and frequently travelled road which her lovely body full of delight has shown me.[49]

Most of the *chansons*, however, breathe a highly refined sensuality. The troubadours developed the poetry of obscenity in appropriate poetic forms, ribald, coarse, Rabelaisian. In the *chanson* their expression was restrained by that *mesure* which was considered essential to true love, and the erotic images they evoked were few, relatively innocent, and curiously stereotyped.

The fact is there was a good deal of smoke, but not much fire in the *fin aman;* he burned, but with a flame so cool that, as he constantly assured his lady, it was a hazard only to himself. The ideal lover was neither impulsive in his actions nor aggressive in his manner. On the contrary, in matters of love he was fearful and timid as a girl, and his contact with the beloved lady was principally musical. "I die of love for you, and I do not dare pray to you save in my songs," wrote Arnaut de Marueill.[50] This was a typical formula. Arnaut Daniel complained: "I dare not say who it is that inflames me." [51] Peire Rogier gives us a very precise idea of the nature of this secret love:

> Neither I nor anyone has told her, nor does she know of my desire; but I love her in secret as much as if she had made me her lover . . .
>
> I am the truest of lovers; I ask nothing of my lady, neither little favors nor a smiling countenance; wherever she may be, I am her lover and I court her, hidden, dissimulated, and concealed. She does not know the good she does me, nor that through her I have joy and merit . . .[52]

Secretum meum mihi: to some extent all the troubadours, even the most outspoken, participated in this attitude of diffidence and reserve, for timidity in matters of love became the knight quite as much as aggressiveness in matters of war. Ideally it was enough that the lady's image was enshrined in his heart, the object of his continual contemplation. It was not necessary that anyone should know; and from the self-restraint with which he sealed off this inner life from the world the knightly lover derived his characteristic tension and his power. Love was, in the first place, an inner dedication. Not everyone could keep it within bounds, but the merit of doing so was very great. To be as stout as Launcelot in battle and as meek as Launcelot in love implied the possession of an exceptionally flexible personality, capable of assigning all the savagery of its aggressiveness to one sphere of activity, and all the charm of its passivity to another. It was a triumph of chivalric culture.

Such an ideal would result, naturally, in interesting complexities of character. We find it difficult to reconcile the "sure master" of the bragging songs of Guillaume IX with the timid lover of his *vers d'amour;* in fact, they are not reconcilable, though they exist side by side. They are different facets of a personality; they give rise to different poetic genres and have different consequences in literary history. The epic knight of the *chanson de geste* was caricatured as a mighty swashbuckler, a Herculean character who did not mince words as to his capacities:

> I am called the sure master; never will my love have me one night without wishing to have me again the next. I am, I dare boast, so well taught in this mastery that I can earn my bread with it in every market.[53]

This is a vaunt, a *vanto,* a comic genre; after Ariosto it would be called a *rodomontade.* Peire Vidal, toward the end of the century, treated it with the gusto of a court jester:

> When I have put on my strong double hauberk, and girded about me the brand which once was given me by Don Gui, the earth quakes where I set down my foot, and I have no enemy so proud that he does not promptly open a path and a way for my advance, so greatly do they fear me when they hear my step.
>
> In boldness I exceed Roland and Oliver, and in courtship Berard de Montdidier; for my prowess is such, and my repute so great, that messengers come to me constantly with a golden ring, with a ribbon white and black, with such salutations as fill my heart with joy.
>
> In all things I show myself a good knight; and so I am, and I know all the mastery of love and all that belongs to courtship, for never did you see anyone so pleasing in a chamber nor, when armed, so terrible and powerful; and therefore I

> am loved and feared by those who neither see me nor hear me.[54]

It is a self-confident character of this type who is pictured by Guillaume IX in the celebrated affair of Dame Agnes and Dame Ermessen and their cat.[55] The knight of the love-song was at the other pole from this. Guillaume IX described him:

> I do not dare send word to her by another, so much I fear that it may make her angry, nor do I myself dare to make a strong show of my love before her, so much do I fear to transgress; therefore she herself must find my remedy, since she knows that it is through her alone that I may recover.[56]

The most interesting of the "self-portraits" of the timid lover is to be found in a *chanson* by a little-known troubadour of the thirteenth century, Arnaut de Tintignac:

> In anxiety and in sorrow and in great perplexity am I and in great desire, partly out of folly and partly out of good sense, for I dare not reveal my heart to her whom most I desire, nor can I feel any other love.
>
> Love troubles me greatly; because of love I am often sad, for she has not taken me into her service, this Love whom I desire and long for, who makes me sigh and languish, for above all things that I see and can choose, I desire her.
>
> *Mesure* has encumbered me much and taught me an excess of politeness, so that I restrain myself from provoking her displeasure or incurring her anger, although she does not now deign to welcome me. I am so fearful of being rebuffed that I dare not reveal my good thoughts to her.
>
> I have such a light and noble heart, and I go to her full of daring, and the words are true and complete which I have ready to address to her before the noble court, but when I see her I can say nothing, and it seems to me that it is better to suffer in silence than to hear a cruel word that may cast me into despair.[57]

Such characterizations resulted not in broad comedy as in the case of the braggart soldier, but in a more subtly comic figure which was destined in time to see long service on the stage as well as in the lyric and narrative genres. The timid lover was a stereotype toward which the character of the true lover naturally inclined, even without the conventions involved in the feudal conceit. The reason seems clear. To make poetry is, after all, not quite the same thing as to make love. The real lover tends to make children, not songs; and his love, in spite of all measure, is likely to be sadly mixed. In the case of the poet, the psychic tension is discharged in the poem. The poem itself is an act of creation, an act of love, beyond which the lover, as poet, has neither any great desire nor any need to go.

For the poet, then, the ultimate object of love is not so much the lady as the fantasy of the lady—and this fantasy the song sufficiently embodies. It was, accordingly, chiefly as a suppliant that the troubadour portrayed himself, and while the nature of the ultimate longed-for reward was never in doubt, the knight was usually content with something on account, and the *sobreplus* was postponed as long as possible, perhaps forever. Aimeric de Peguilhan put it in commercial terms:

> At least if she does not pay me the whole of the account, I have gained so much honor from her that I have well recovered my investment.[58]

True love was, ideally, a perpetual courtship, an end in itself, a work of art which owed little to the work of Venus. It was quite unnecessary for the lover to declare this love. His secret was best kept to himself.

Thus the situation out of which Shaw made *Candida* was one of the oldest dramatic situations in the history of modern literature. It was necessary to alter the traditional relations of the poet, the husband, and the lady very little in order to make a contemporary comedy of them; and there is in fact no better example of *fin amor* in the theater of our time than the affair Candida-Marchbanks. Exactly as in the case of Shaw's poet-lover, the goal to which the *fin aman* aspired was an intermediate position which assured him of progress without unduly involving him in the dangers of success.

As the true lover's desire was not so much to possess as to be possessed, any mark of acceptance was enough to give him joy. Physical union would be, in itself, no more than the ultimate symbol of this acceptance, and while this, or something near it, was doubtless at the end of the lover's thoughts, other tokens would do as well and perhaps even better. The act of physical union was in any case not particularly appropriate to the situation of true lovers, since it necessitated a drastic reorganization of their psychic relationship. Besides, the husband commanded such union at his pleasure, and presumably gained no joy by it. The true lover did not desire a fleeting satisfaction of this sort. What he sought was permission to enjoy a state of perpetual desire. For this a sign was required from the lady.

The first reward of love-service was recognition. By acknowledging that she was aware of his existence, the lady established the indispensable basis for further communication. The lady's salutation was therefore considered in itself a mark of distinction, a guerdon. "When you deign merely to salute me," wrote Bernard de Ventadour, "it is high recompense that you give me." In a song by Miraval, the lover manifests even greater modesty: all his desire is limited, he says, to the lady's greeting and salutation. In time, since it gave joy, the salutation took on mystical significance, to which the double meaning of *salut*, both greeting and salvation, contributed. Aimeric de Peguilhan, for example, saw special virtue in his lady's greeting: "By reason of your salutation, without more, every man thought himself ennobled and cured of ill." [59] It was on such groundwork that Dante elaborated the famous passage in *Vita Nuova* XI on the extraordinary effect of Beatrice's salutation.

The entire corpus of troubadour literature separates the robust vitality of Guillaume IX from the mysterious doctrine of Dante, but the timid lover, as Guillaume characterized him in the beginning, is still recognizable in the later poet; the tradition was not broken. The system of love-service which defined the writings of the poets of the *dolce stil* differed not at all from that which was already developed when the first of the troubadours was writing.

Si·m vol mi dons s'amor donar
Pres suy del penr'e del grazir,
E del celar e del blandir
E de sos plazers dir e far
E de sos pretz tener en car
E de son laus enavantir.

> If my lord is willing to give me her love, I am ready to receive it and to be grateful for it, and to be secret and to court her, and to do and say what pleases her, and to be careful of her honor, and to spread her praises everywhere.[60]

In these verses, which Guillaume IX must have written at the very end of the eleventh century, we come for the first time upon an offer of true love. It seems clear from the tone of the song that the terms which Guillaume engaged himself to accept already constituted an established form of servitude. Where it came from is an enigma, but there was to be no deviation from this pattern as long as troubadour poetry endured.

The Count of Poitou illustrates from the very beginning the curious custom of addressing the lady as "my lord," *midons*, instead of "my lady," *ma dompna*. This peculiarity of troubadour song has been identified with an analogous custom in Arabic poetry, the rationale of which is said to be that since it was considered indecent to address verses of love to a woman, the convention became established of using the masculine pronoun. In Provençal love-poetry, however, the feminine pronoun was used freely, and it was not considered indecent to write verses to women. It seems reasonable, therefore, to suppose that the use of *midons* in addressing a lady was simply a consequence of the feudal conceit upon which the idea of true love was based. Since homage was due normally to the lord, the lady to whom love-service was proffered might properly be considered as belonging to the order of human beings in whom lordship resided. She was therefore in Dante's words "not woman merely," but a superior being; no mistress, but a master.

The true lover offered himself to the lady in a fourfold capacity —as her lover, her vassal, her champion, and her poet. As vassal, he was the agent of her will; as champion, the custodian of her reputation and the herald of her fame. Armed with her token, he represented the warlike aspect of her beauty, and he was expected to maintain her pre-eminence convincingly by force of arms. Finally, as poet, he was expected to exhibit his lady's valor in song by force of rhetoric. It was the beauty of the lady which made the beauty of the song, and the cruelty of which the lover incessantly complained was also the measure of her worth and her power.

These ideas, which characterize not only the lyric of love but also the romance, were taken quite as seriously in the sixteenth century as in the twelfth. In the *Courtier*, the lady Emilia instructs the poet Unico Aretino in terms which might have been taken verbatim from any troubadour:

> He who sets his mind to love ought also to set his mind to please his beloved and to accommodate himself wholly to her wishes, and according to these to govern his own, and make his own desires her slaves, and his very soul an obedient handmaid which should never think of anything but to be transformed, if it is possible, into that of his beloved, and to account this his highest felicity, for thus they do who love truly.[61]

Aside from his service as knight and poet, the true lover assumed also the obligations of courtship and of secrecy, *blandir e celar*. The expanded formula thus became *servir, onrar, celar, sofrir*. Of these, the most important duty, the *conditio sine qua non* of true love was *celar*, to conceal.

True love could thrive only in secrecy. It was an order to which it was honorable for a woman to belong only on condition that nothing could be proved against her. Therefore all suppliants absolutely guaranteed their discretion. In Andreas' treatise, the clerical suitor especially recommends the amatory qualities of the clergy because of the discretion and measure traditionally cultivated by that profession:

> We find that a clerk is in every respect more cautious and prudent than a layman and conducts himself in his affairs with greater restraint, and is accustomed to keeping everything within proper bounds; that is because a clerk, as Scripture tells us, has an experienced knowledge of all things. Therefore in love he is to be preferred to a layman . . .[62]

These are almost exactly the terms in which Tartuffe recommends himself to Elmire in Molière's play:

> Mais les gens comme nous brûlent d'un feu discret,
> Avec qui pour toujours on est seur du secret.
> Le soin que nous prenons de vostre renommée
> Répond de toute chose à la personne aimée
> Et c'est en nous qu'on trouve, acceptant nostre cœur,
> De l'amour sans scandale et du plaisir sans peur.[63]

The reasons for the mystery in which true love was enveloped seem to go far beyond any practical considerations. Danger was, as we have noted, the traditional climate of chivalric love, and the ever-present menace of the irate husband is attested in many a blood-curdling tale. But there is a ritualistic similarity about these stories which suggests that they belong to the mythology rather than to the history of love. The story, for example, of the lover's heart, served up at dinner by the jealous husband, was reproduced in so many forms and places—*Cabestanh*, The *Lai Guiron*, *Ignaurès*, *Le Chatelain de Couci*, *Reinmann von Brennenberg*—that the suspicion is inescapable that we are dealing here with a widespread Thyestean fantasy.[64] The *chansons* of true love, like the romances, doubtless reflected in some way the realities of their time but, as we have noted, there is little reason to believe that they were other than fictions. The troubadour promised secrecy and *mesure* in his song because secrecy and *mesure* would normally be essential to a love affair. The lover's song necessarily reproduced the conditions of love. These gave it verisimilitude, not truth.

The drama of love, as the songs developed it, had always the vividness of reality. The lady remained ritualistically vague, but she was never treated as an abstraction or a symbol. Wonderful and beautiful as she was, she was constantly subject to the tattlings of the talebearer. It was the lover's duty to see that no breath of scandal should touch his lady, no matter how careless she herself might become. In a *tenson* between the Comtesse de Die and a lover whom the biographer obligingly identifies as Raimbaut d'Orange, the passionate lady reproaches the knight for his excess of precaution, while he excuses himself firmly—and doubtless hypocritically—on the ground that his first thought must be for her reputation:

> Lady, I fear the scandalmongers, they are resolved on your ruin; let us leave off. It is not that my heart has changed since I have been away from you, but their tattlings have set up fatal ambushes for you and we shall never more be able to enjoy a day of happiness.
>
> Friend, that is no excuse. May the evil that may come to me never prevent you from coming to see me when I ask you; and if you become more anxious than I about my honor, I shall consider you unfaithful. . . .[65]

In addition to looking after the lady's honor, the lover had to be continually on his guard lest he himself be defamed in her eyes by a false accusation. The lady was, *ex hypothesi,* the wisest and noblest of living creatures, but she was at the same time passionate, irresponsible, impulsive and open to flattery, gullible and easy to deceive. Cast paradoxically in two molds, at once the matriarch and the child, the lady could not be depended on for a moment. In the poet's fantasy, the flatterers and scandalmongers who at all times surrounded her took every opportunity to cast aspersions on her true lover's behavior. Therefore a significant part of courtship was devoted to the denial of calumny.

The losengers, as Chaucer calls them, were the villains of the piece. It was out of fear of these talebearers that the lady responded coldly, or not at all, to the lover's advances; the *losen-*

giers' sharp eyes kept the lovers from meeting; it was their evil tongues which sooner or later turned the lady from her faithful servant. The *losengiers* insinuated themselves falsely into the lady's graces by pretending to be true lovers when in fact they were self-seekers, deceivers, and hypocrites. Their flatteries were intended to advance their own selfish interests; they strove to promote their ignoble affairs by defaming others better than themselves. Rarely defined, without any precision of outline, they were felt to be everywhere, shapeless and mysterious figures who lurked in the shadows of the song, always guessed at, never seen.

Of all the *dramatis personae* of true love, the *losengier* seems the least fictive. We have little precise information about the courts of the twelfth century, but the very full body of literature in dispraise of court life in the following centuries affords us clear glimpses of the self-seekers who elbowed each other in every court. Three centuries after the death of the "last troubadour," Spenser still considered the *losengier* the chief enemy of the courtier. In the *Amoretti,* it is a *losengier* who at last causes the lovers to part. The Blatant Beast who is somewhat absent-mindedly chased by the Knight of Courtesy through the cantos of the sixth book of *The Faerie Queene* is obviously none other than the enemy of true lovers in allegorical shape.[66]

The *losengier* was never individualized. He represented in the most general way the undifferentiated mass of inimical forces which the lover felt to be arrayed against him. Ultimately, of course, the *losengier* was no more than the imaginary *voyeur* implied in all fantasy, the all-seeing eye which springs into being the moment something is concealed.[67] This force was a shaping principle of the lover's song: because of it the whole had to be suffused with mystery. For fear of the *losengier* the lady had to be not only anonymous but featureless, and the poet was sadly hampered in his efforts to spread abroad her praise. "I should be very happy if I dared to praise her," wrote Giraut de Bornelh, "but I fear to be heard by the false, perfidious, felonious, and unrestrained *losengiers.*" [68]

The ladies of the song therefore all look very much alike. They have no individual traits. Their charms are every bit as stereotyped as the landscape they inhabit. They are, each of them, simply unique, the noblest and best of living creatures. The lady's image in the poet's heart, the constant object of his contemplation, was completely assimilated to the universal mold of beauty, the ideal. The process was entirely conformable with the theory of art which in the sixteenth century Michelangelo developed in his sonnets to Vittoria Colonna. The result was a curiously impersonal art-form. Guillaume IX compared his lady's color to that of ivory—he went no further in describing the object of his passion; no more did Dante. But it was hardly necessary to describe her. Her face and figure were to be seen everywhere in the Middle Ages, pictured in miniatures and tapestries, sculptured on the porches of cathedrals, described over and over in the same terms precisely in the songs and romances of chivalry. She was the medieval glamour-girl, blonde and slender, round-armed, straight-nosed, grey-eyed, white-skinned, with her small red smiling mouth, her sparkling teeth, her small firm breasts and slim waist:

Huelhs clars ab boca rizen,
Dens plus blancas que cristals,
Neus blanca non es aitals
Cum sos belhs cors de joven;
Fresca, vermelha, ses menda
Es la cara sotz la benda:
Tot y es, quant y cove . . .[69]

This lady lived well on into the Renaissance. Botticelli painted her. Poliziano described her, in his *Giostra,* in the very terms which Arnaut de Marueill had found appropriate to his own time:

> Your graceful body, your beautiful blonde hair, and your forehead that is whiter than the lily; your beautiful, clear, laughing eyes, your straight and well-formed nose, the fresh colors of your face, white and more rosy than a flower . . .[70]

A century after the time of Arnaut de Marueill, Boccaccio envisaged his Fiammetta in about the same way:

> Fiammetta, whose hair was curly, long and golden, and falling over her white and delicate shoulders, and her round face with a coloring blended of white lilies and red roses, all splendid, with two eyes which seemed like those of a peregrine falcon, and a little mouth whose lips seemed like two rubies.[71]

It is almost exactly the face which looks out at us from Eustache Deschamps' charming *virelai:*

> J'ay vers yeulx, petis sourcis,
> Le chief blont, le nez traitis,
> Ront menton, blanche gorgete.
> Sui-je, sui-je, sui-je belle?

Behind the mask of the ideal, the lady of the song preserved, at least in theory, complete anonymity, for the knight of the *chanson* was a deeply suspicious person, mistrustful even of his closest friends. "There is no man so loyal that I do not consider him a felon if he inquires into my love," wrote the troubadour Cadenet; and Bernard de Ventadour, Giraut de Bornelh, and many others wrote to the same effect.[72] The result of these pressures was to impart to the dance of love its characteristic rigidity and restraint. Under the watchful eyes of the *losengiers,* the true lover had to preserve his countenance, his distance, and his decorum. The lady must appear immensely remote. The song itself had to keep within bounds. In this dance, so we are given to understand, it was the *losengier* who called the tune; therefore the measure was slow and grave, solemn and courtly, a very different matter from the impetuous surge of passion which we associate with the loves of such tragic butterflies as Romeo and Juliet. Love was a madness; on this point all the troubadours were agreed. But in true love, at least, there was method. Patience was the basis of true love, the lover's fundamental aptitude, and the spring of all love's benefits:

> He knows little of love who does not await mercy, for love desires us to suffer and to wait; then in a little time love repairs and amends all the pain he has made us endure so long, and that is why I prefer to die having known true love

> than to live with a high heart empty of love, for so love fated me from the beginning.[73]

It was through the delays and sufferings of constantly frustrated longing that the commonplace relationship of a man and a woman was transformed into a rich and complex experience. The troubadour Perdigon wrote:

> Blessed be the pains, the sorrows and the cares which I have long suffered because of love. Because of them I taste a thousand times more intensely the good which love now makes me feel. So much do the ills of the past cause me to enjoy my present happiness that it seems to me that if there were no evil one would hardly be able to savor the good. Thus evil enhances good, and therefore every evil should be welcomed when it comes.[74]

The lady's obduracy had also a more practical purpose. As Arnaut Daniel put it:

> Not because of the torment I endure do I turn from loving well, though this keeps me in solitude, for thus I make the words rhyme on this theme.[75]

Out of the richness of his experience, prolonged and intensified by the lady's obduracy, the knight made poetry. The song was born in pain and sung in joy; and since she reflected the pain as well as the joy of love, the lady of the song took on a curiously dual character. She was cruel and merciless, a she-wolf; she was also wise, kindly, and noble, an angel. It was in her angelic role that Montanhagol, for example, depicted her:

> For she who receives my songs and my praise bears off the flower of earthly beauty. But I tell you, in truth, that we should rather think that her beauty comes from the highest heaven; so much does it resemble the work of paradise that hardly does her beauty seem to be of this world.[76]

Thus while the pitiless lady might be reviled and reproached, it was customary at the same time, particularly among the later poets, to express gratitude for her obduracy, since this obduracy was the fruit of her superior virtue and wisdom, and the source of all the lover's good:

> I owe to her all the glory that my beautiful verses and my fine actions have brought me, for it is from her that I hold the talent and the learning; it is she who made me gay and who made me a poet; all that I do well comes to me from her.[77]

> I rejoice in the long and sweet desire, for often it has made me dream and achieve songs of mastery . . .[78]

The true lover had also his special virtue, the quality called *mezura*, measure, that inner restraint which governs the appetites and keeps them subject to the intellect. This was both an aesthetic and an ethical concept, and obviously it had some relation to Greek *sophrosyne*. In the twelfth century it was closely identified with courtesy. "He may boast of courtesy," wrote Marcabru, "who knows well how to keep measure." [79] For Daude de Pradas, it was the fourth of the virtues, the equilibrating principle of the soul.[80] Valor and measure were considered equally important knightly attributes. Without measure, the knight's valor was profitless. Bertran de Born wrote in a *sirventés*: "Without measure, nothing succeeds; he who acts without restraint gets nowhere." [81] Two generations later, the more scholarly Montanhagol summed up the matter in a *sirventés* which assimilated *mezura* to the Aristotelean concept of the golden mean:

> Nothing in the world is more highly prized than measure. And measure is simply that which amends the defect in what is too much and too little. Reason forms it midway between these two, and makes a virtue out of the two vices by taking from each what it contains of evil.[82]

Montanhagol was by no means unique among the troubadours in advancing these more or less scholarly ideas. His Venetian contemporary Bartolome Zorzi echoed substantially the same doctrine; so too did Guiraut d'Olivier.[83] Thus, in the thirteenth century, the *mezura* of the early Provenceaux took on classical coloring. In this new form it established itself as a principle of gentlemanly behavior, and eventually this concept merged in the philosophical tradition which in the sixteenth century furnished Castiglione, Guazzi, and Spenser with the basis of their ethical system.

As a semi-classical virtue, the fruit of the intellectual faculty, *mezura* was primarily a male attribute. In consequence, the love-theorists found themselves once more in a paradoxical position with respect to the lady. She was on the one hand the source and teacher of measure; on the other hand, she was reputedly quite lacking in that quality herself. No attempt was made to reconcile these attitudes. In the songs addressed to them, the ladies have so much measure that they are constantly reproached with their coldness and cruelty; but when ladies sing of love in their own person, it is usual for them to show no measure at all. On the contrary, it is they who accuse their knights of an unseemly lack of enthusiasm. The songs of the troubadour and the *troubairitz* were thus exactly similar, save that the women's songs exhibited—as in the case of the Comtesse de Die—less measure than those of the men.[84] It is not very easy to understand in what way women were made to acquiesce in this tradition, but unquestionably they did. Long after the time of the mysterious Comtesse de Die, we find gallant ladies such as Gaspara Stampa in Venice and Louise Labé in Lyon addressing sonnets of passionate reproach to cold and haughty gentlemen in very much the style of the female troubadours.

The standard of love was, however, not the degree of its heat, but the degree of its refinement. Through the slow and mysterious operation of the flame of love, whatever was base and gross in the lover's nature was supposedly consumed and dissipated until at last only the pure and noble spirit remained. There was no way of attaining to the highest human distinction save through love's alchemy. For this reason true love was an end in itself. "Love is the key to merit," wrote Arnaut Daniel.[85] Aimeric de Belenoi developed the idea further:

> If one wishes to know if a lover loves well, let him consider his spirit and his valor and how he bears himself. If he is

> really in love, his actions, his words and his qualities will be finer than what is needful . . . we owe all fine actions to true love.[86]

Self-restraint, self-control, self-mastery—these were the qualities comprised in *mezura.* They were qualities which could be developed, but not acquired. Measure was an essential quality of the gentle heart. Through love's discipline, the gentle spirit was schooled and perfected, and the effect was visible in all the facets of the personality. Thus the true reward of love was perfection, although the ostensible goal was something else, and the lady, even unwittingly, led the true lover through desire step by step toward ideal manhood.

These ideas, commonplace by the beginning of the thirteenth century, were already current in the first troubadour period. Marcabru had written:

> Never will I believe, no matter who swears it, that the wine comes not from the grape, and that the man taken by love does not become better because of it, for never have we learned that a single one became worse; and I myself have attained the greatest worth thanks to the best of women—nevertheless I am uncertain, for I dare not boast for fear of her who is the object of my hope.[87]

Thereafter it became very usual to sing of love as the source of all virtue and all goodness. "True lovers know," wrote N'At de Mons in a typical passage, "that through love the haughty become humble and the base are ennobled, and the lazy become skilled, and the simple, wise." [88] The similitude of the refining flame was also taken up widely. Peirol used it: "The flame of love consumes me day and night, and thus I am refined like gold in the fire." Peire Cardenal made the figure even more explicit: "Just as silver is refined in the burning flame, so the poor, good patient one is softened and refined in his burning pain." It was generally agreed that only by becoming virtuous, brave, wise, and gentle could a lover hope to deserve the love of the lady who was herself all these things. The knight was thus led into virtue and nobility by the most carnal of his appetites, but this appetite, progressively refined, was the most effective civilizing force at the disposal of humanity.[89]

By the end of the thirteenth century the doctrine of the ennobling power of love was so thoroughly established in romantic literature that nothing henceforth would serve to dislodge it. In courtly circles it was considered that no force had greater efficacy in the education of a gentleman than the desire inspired by the beauty of a lady. This idea was destined to have the fullest possible development. By the time Boccaccio reproduced it in his story of Cimone and Iphigenia it had already taken on a more special coloring, but the troubadour source is unmistakable:

> Love's arrow having, then, through Iphigenia's beauty penetrated into Cimone's heart, where no teaching had ever availed to win an entrance, in a very short time, proceeding from one idea to another, he . . . not only learned letters, but became very eminent among the students of philosophy and—the love which he bore Iphigenia being the cause of all this—he not only reduced his rude and rustic speech to seemliness and civility, but he became a master of song and music, and very expert and brave in riding and in martial exercises both by land and by sea. In short, . . . the fourth year was not ended from the day of his first falling in love before he had become the brightest and most accomplished gentleman of all the young men of Cyprus . . .
>
> What then, charming ladies, shall we say of Cimone? Truly nothing other than that the lofty virtues implanted by heaven in his generous soul had been bound with very strong bonds by jealous fortune and shut in some narrow corner of his heart until Love, mightier than fortune, broke and burst these bonds asunder, and as the awakener and quickener of drowsy and sluggish wits, urged forth these virtues into the daylight, which till then had been darkened by a barbarous obscurity, thus showing clearly from what depths it can uplift those

> souls that are subject to it, and to what heights it can conduct them with its rays.[90]

In much the same way, Petrarch informs St. Augustine in the third dialogue of his *Secretum* that it is to Laura that he owes all his fame and his glory:

> —to her I owe whatever I am, and I should never have attained such little renown and glory as I have unless she by the power of this love had quickened into life the feeble germ of virtue that nature had sown in my heart. It was she who turned my youthful soul away from all that was base . . . and forced me to look upward.[91]

By the sixteenth century this idea had become one of the most familiar stereotypes of amatory poetry. In the meantime, as the ennobling influence of love was emphasized more and more by the later troubadours, the ideal of true love was refined to the point where the sensual component all but vanished. That excess of sensuality which Marcabru had inveighed against in his time as "against reason," Francesco da Barberino a century later condemned in the most unequivocal terms: "Illicit love cannot properly be called by the name of love at all, but by the consent of all honest people it is called madness." [92]

The intervening century had seen the rise and decline of the taste for the troubadour love-song, the invasion of the Midi of France by Simon de Montfort, and the extension of the power of Rome over the conquered regions. It is thus quite likely that the vogue of pure love gained ground as a concession to the growing pressures of the church. But the concept of a love so pure that it was virtually unobjectionable can be seen at work in those who lived in the gay time long before the Dominicans were influential in the Midi. The idealistic strain which is perceptible in the songs of Marcabru and Cercamon, and afterward in the work of Alegret and Bernard Marti, became dominant in the time of the *stilnovisti* and found its perfection in Dante, but there was no period in which it had not its exponents. In the golden age of troubadour activity, we find the amiable Monk of Montaudon stoutly insisting on the purity of his intentions:

> I am the guardian of her honor, and if human fragility causes an unruly desire to be born in me, I shall triumph over it by the strength of my love.

A generation later, in the time of the crusade, such sentiments were echoed on every hand.

The Italian troubadour Sordello, by no means blameless in his own personal life, associated himself wholeheartedly with this doctrine, so much so that he was thought by some of his contemporaries to have originated it. In a *chanson* which became famous, he turned the tables on the lady by asking her not to give him what he ought not to have, even if he begged for it. As the lady now became the guardian of the knight's virtue, the frustrated lover was able, by an ingenious twist of thought, to derive profit from his very lack of success:

> Lady, the greater grows the desire in which I languish, since you do not return my love, the greater grows my desire to praise your merit; for, my beloved, there cannot come to me complete joy from you if your merit must suffer by it. Your honor is as dear to me as your beautiful body.
>
> To you, whose worth is without equal, I have given myself loyally and sincerely, and I would rather die of grief than receive from you a joy which would result in an injury to your honor; and if ever I should come to desire you otherwise, may you have neither pity nor regard for me.
>
> No knight can love his lady truly if he does not love her honor as much as her self. That is why I beg you, beautiful and charming person, never to do what I ask you if it is contrary to your honor . . .[93]

This doctrine, so reassuring for the lady, evidently caused surprise in certain quarters, though it was by no means new. In a *tenson* with Sordello, Peire Guillem of Toulouse took a traditionalistic position:

> Messire Sordel, no lover was ever seen of such color as you, for other lovers desire kisses and embraces, but you say you do not prize what other lovers desire . . .[94]

The troubadour Granet wrote somewhat more skeptically of "the usage of Don Sordel," while Bertran d'Alamanon expressed some mild regret that his colleague had taken leave of his senses.[95] But of course this was not the only strain that Sordello could pipe. In a *vanto, No·m meravilh,* he characterized an altogether different type of lover:

> I do not wonder that husbands are jealous of me, so well do I understand the science of love. There is no lady in the world so virtuous that she can defend herself against the charm and sweetness of my prayers, therefore those who complain of me should not be blamed, for all husbands suffer whose wives receive me; but provided that their ladies disrobe in my company, I care little for their suffering and their clamor. May no husband complain of my happiness, for it is my destiny that whatever I want of love I shall have, and therefore neither protests nor clamor will prevent me from being a lady-killer.[96]

In giving prominence to the song of the pure lover, Sordello attracted attention, doubtless, because he was a step ahead of the mode. But in a little while the chaste lover was to become a very familiar literary figure.

Guillem Montanhagol of Toulouse appears to have felt the sobering effects of the Albigensian crusade more keenly than most. He took a strongly partisan stand against the excesses of the clergy, and, sometime between 1233 and 1237, addressed to his patron Raimon VII, Count of Toulouse, a *sirventés* in which he reminded him in no uncertain terms of the iniquities of the invading horde of clerks. It is possible that, as his position with regard to the Inquisition was not strong, he wished to defend himself and his profession from the reproach of promoting immorality. At any rate, he took up the cudgels in behalf of true love in a manner which argues a new interest in the subject:

> Truly, lovers must serve love with all their hearts, for love is not sin but a virtue which makes the wicked good and the good better, and puts a man in the way of doing good every day; and out of love comes chastity, for whoever truly gives his mind to love cannot thereafter do evil.[97]

Like Marcabru and the Monk of Montaudon, Montanhagol drew a sharp distinction between true love and false:

> I cannot call that man a lover who uses deceit in love. . . . He who asks his lady to commit a fault neither loves nor deserves to be loved; for a lover should on no account desire anything of his lady that might tend to her dishonor. The object of love is to elevate that which is truly loved. He who asks anything else of his beloved betrays the name of lover.
>
> Passion has never dominated me to the point of making me desire anything wrong of her to whom I have given myself, nor would I take pleasure in anything which might bring her shame. A true lover should value the honor of his lady a hundred times more than his own satisfaction.[98]

This pure love was, in Montanhagol's view, entirely acceptable to God:

> False lovers deserve false love, but to him who follows the right, God grants every good sooner or later, and in any case after death . . .[99]

The whole idea of the consummation of true love in the afterlife was inherent in these lines, but Montanhagol did not develop it. It remained for Dante and for Petrarch to carry this idea, each in his way, to a conclusion. But if Montanhagol was not quite capable of ushering in the new style, at least it was he who announced it. Unlike Gui d'Ussel, he did not feel that everything worth saying on the subject of love had already been said. On the contrary, he felt that he had hit on something new and important, though he does not seem to have understood just where its importance lay. What was involved, in fact, was the reconciliation of the love of woman with the love of God, but the idea did not become explicit until after the time of Guido Guinizelli, a generation later. When it did, it gave rise to a whole new poetry of love, quite as Montanhagol had foretold:

> The old troubadours did not sing so much on the subject of love, in their time when all was gay, that it is no longer possible for us to make good songs, new, pleasing and sincere. We can, indeed, sing what has not been sung before; for no poet is fine and good until he makes songs that are new, graceful and well set, with new words put together with new skill . . .[100]

The doctrine of pure love which he was advocating in his *sirventés*, Montanhagol naturally referred to the golden age of chivalry when morals were pure and love was true:

> The noble knights of old sought nothing in love save honor, and those in whom beauty dwelt did nothing which they should not have done . . . Nowadays honor is held in scorn; lovers have other ideas, which bring shame and damage to many. I shall very likely be attacked by all false lovers on account of this song, and by those women in whose heart falseness dwells. But whoever tolerates evil takes part in it. The good man hates all evil, and the duty of the wise is to protect fools against their errors.[101]

This is very much the same language as that used by Sir Thomas Malory in the next century to contrast the fickle lovers of his day with the more robust lovers of the golden age of chivalry, as he imagined it to have been:

> But nowadays men can not love seven night but they must have all their desires: that love may not endure by reason; for where they be soon accorded and hasty heat, soon it cooleth. Right so fareth love nowadays, soon hot soon cold: this is no stability. But the old love was not so; men and women could love together seven years, and no licours lusts were between them, and then was love, in truth and faithfulness: and lo, in like wise was used love in King Arthur's days.[102]

The paradox with regard to love and chastity had been enunciated long before by Andreas Capellanus:

> Oh, what a wonderful thing is love, which makes a man shine with so many virtues and which teaches everyone, no matter who he is, so many good traits of character! There is another thing about love which we should not praise in a few words: it adorns a man, so to speak, with the virtue of chastity, because he who shines with the light of one love can hardly think of embracing another woman, even a beautiful one. For when he thinks deeply of his beloved, the sight of any other woman seems to him rude and rough.[103]

That chastity which Montanhagol had in mind when he wrote "*d'amor mou castitatz*" would therefore have been in the first place no more than the constancy on which the true lover prided himself, that voluntary morality which was traditionally associated with *fin amor*. But the requirements of *mesure* and the lover's obligation to guard his lady's reputation gave it a deeper significance than simply an aversion to promiscuous relations. No troubadour appears to have developed the ideal of a purely intellectual bond such as that which linked, in their age, the saintly Vittoria and the aged Michelangelo. The distinction which seemed important to the troubadours was that between pure love and the mixed love which, we are told in the eighth dialogue of *De amore*, "injures one's neighbor and offends the Heavenly King." It was from this mixed love, real and praiseworthy but, in the clerk's opinion, sinful and dangerous, that Sordello and Montanhagol turned in virtuous abnegation. From pure love, of course, "chastity" proceeded, provided the lovers were capable of the necessary self-restraint. Thus in his *Secretum*, Petrarch tells St. Augustine, who in his time had also struggled for chastity, of his youthful struggle with Laura in the way of *fin amor:*

> —but unmoved by my entreaties, unyielding to my caress, she safeguarded her woman's honour, and in spite of her youth and mine, in spite of a thousand circumstances that could have bent a heart of adamant, she stood her ground,

> resolute and unsubdued. Yes, this womanly soul taught me what should be the honour and duty of a man, and to preserve her chastity she did, as Seneca expresses it
>
> "What was to me at once an example and a reproach"
>
> And at last, when she saw the reins of my chariot were broken, and that I was rushing to the abyss, she chose rather to part from me than to follow where I went.
>
> —Now I know what I wish and what I desire and I have at last made firm my staggering soul. She for her part has ever been firm in her mind and always the same. The more I understand this woman's constancy, the more I admire it; and if sometimes I regretted her resolution, now I rejoice in it and I give thanks.[104]

The bourgeois lover in the first dialogue of Andreas' treatise is instructive on this head:

> From ancient times, four distinct stages have been established in love; the first consists in the giving of hope, the second in the granting of the kiss, the third in the enjoyment of an embrace, and the fourth culminates in the yielding of the whole person.[105]

It was in the fourth stage only, in the judgment of the troubadours, that true love came in conflict with the laws of marriage and thus incurred the sanctions of society. Upon the step which divided the third stage of love from the fourth, therefore, was concentrated much, if not all, of the age-long discussion of false love and true, and good love and bad.

Obviously, smiles, kisses, and an occasional embrace would not in themselves result in any considerable social or economic disorder; they might, with discretion, be indulged in without much fear of the consequence. But the social and psychic taboos applicable to the fourth stage of love were enormous. Hence, as time went on more and more weight appears to have been placed on the capacity of the *fin aman* to content himself with the joys of a love that stopped short of fulfillment. The ideally poetic relationship was an eternal courtship. The moment this courtship was brought to its ultimate conclusion, true love was transformed into another, and perhaps more honest relationship, but one that was no longer blessed. "Time makes it so that the greatest gift of love, men would rather hope for than attain. . . . When love has no further to go, in a moment, it turns into not-caring," thus wrote Uc Brunec. "It changes heart and turns into despair, and the lover blames what once he loved." [106]

The treacherous lovers of whom we hear so much in the troubadour poetry were doubtless those who, having promised pure love, took advantage of their situation to overpass the bounds of honesty, and thus brought dishonor and damage to the lady. It became, consequently, very usual for the knight of the song to disclaim any *folle pensée*. Unfortunately, pure love went so far in its permissible stages that the degree of measure required of the lover to abstain from the fourth and fatal stage could not be considered within the reach of all. In a *tenson* with Aimeric de Peguilhan, Elias d'Ussel indicates with gentle cynicism the forseeable consequences of this sort of lovemaking:

> Don Elias, I ask your counsel regarding her whom I love more than myself or anyone else, for she tells me that she will lie with me for a night, on condition that I swear that I will not force her beyond her wish, but will content myself with embracing her and kissing her. Tell me now how it seems to you —is it better for me to suffer and endure this condition, or to go beyond her wish and perjure myself?
>
> Don Aimeric, my advice to you is if she will lie with you, do it joyfully, for he who holds his lady in his arms is mad if he goes looking for her elsewhere . . .
>
> . . . For if I were lying by her whom I love more than myself, I would not ask her for any more, but laughing and playing gently, I should gain my desire . . . then I should go on a pilgrimage as far as Syria to beg God's forgiveness for my perjury.[107]

The power of measure to bring about such miracles of self-control as the successful practice of pure love required was an evident proof of the nobility of the passion. Strange as it seems to us, this sort of asceticism evidently recommended itself to the Renaissance mind as an example of virtue not far removed from sainthood. In the third book of *The Courtier*, Cesare Gonzaga invites the company to marvel at what must be considered a remarkable instance:

> What will you say of another lady who, for the space of six months, lay almost every night with a very dear lover, and nevertheless in this garden rich with the sweetest fruits, urged on by the utmost ardor of her own desire, and by the prayers and tears of one who was dearer to her than her own life, abstained from tasting them, and although she was imprisoned and bound naked in the strong chains of those beloved arms, she never gave herself up as conquered, but conserved immaculate the flower of her purity.[108]

It would be too much to expect, however, that these refinements would recommend themselves to everyone. The *gilos* would find the ways of true love little to his taste. Othello, for one, is shocked at the idea of pure love, as Iago suggests it to him:

> IAGO: Or to be naked with her friend in bed
> An hour, or more, not meaning any harm?
> OTHELLO: Naked in bed, Iago, and not mean harm?
> It is hypocrisy against the devil.
> They that mean virtuously, and yet do so
> The devil their virtue tempts, and they
> tempt heaven.[109]

But then, true love was never really at home in England.

If the school of "idealistic" poetry which Sordello and Montanhagol represented did not at once flower into something new and wonderful, the reasons are not far to seek. The idea of a purely spiritual love was simply no part of the troubadour way of thought; it was as yet a strictly clerical concept. Refined as it might become, true love was seldom an abstraction. Although it denied itself the ultimate satisfaction in the interest of that spiritual joy which was its constant object, it was firmly based upon the carnal appetite. Therefore Montanhagol, having announced his intention to write of love as nobody had written of it before, went on to write of it as everyone had written of it before. He dreamt of a *noel dig*, a new poetry, but the desires which he felt as he contemplated the beautiful image of the lady were the normal desires of the troubadour. These the lady might properly satisfy without "committing a fault," and it was the constant burden of his song that women take too long to grant their lovers the joy which they deserve:

> Women commit a great folly in making so many difficulties before they permit themselves to be loved. For a lady who realizes that her lover is true commits a fault if she makes him wait. We live, indeed, shorter lives than our ancestors. I should wish therefore that this annoying custom of long delays should cease, for, in my opinion, people would live longer if they knew the joys of love.[110]

Upon the recalcitrance of women, indeed, he blamed the decline of virtue in his day:

> Ladies are much to blame if joy is lost and honor has left us. For if they consented to love, the world would be as gay as once it was, and the knights would hold themselves high, and each would seek virtue for himself, but now everything turns to treachery.[111]

The type of abstract love which moves our wonder in the three songs which Jaufre Rudel wrote, long before, concerning the far-off lady, is almost unique in troubadour poetry. None of the troubadour songs goes to such lengths as this in attempting to portray the remoteness of the lady, though the lady is distant in all of them. Rudel makes the feeling of distance explicit, not only in the conception but in the design of a song in which the word *lonh* is made to echo and re-echo in each stanza. But the idea of a love without a definite object, an unlocalized longing, touching as it is, has also its comedic aspects, and Rudel did not scruple to ridicule the mood he had invented:

> Let no one be surprised at me if I love that which will never see me, for my heart has joy of no love save that which I have never seen; no other joy gives it such delight, and I know not what good can come of it, ah, ah.
>
> Well I know I have never had joy of her, that she will never have joy of me, nor have me for her friend, nor ever promise herself to me; never has she told me the truth and never has she lied to me, and whether she will or no, I know not, ah, ah.[112]

Rudel's songs touch the imagination in an altogether extraordinary way, but they had not much to do with the doctrine of true love. So little, indeed, was Rudel's mood in these songs comprehensible to his audience that his commentators invented the story of the lady of Tripoli to bring his songs within the conventional frame of troubadour love-making.

It was Guiraut Riquier who marked the final phase in the development of true love. In his hands, the line projected by Montanhagol and Sordello was carried to the point where the lover rejoices that he has received, and required, nothing whatever of his lady. Many troubadours had protested, like Peire Rogier, that they required nothing by way of guerdon but the privilege of secret adoration. Riquier took a more extreme position. He celebrated a relationship in which his lady, *Belh Deport*, increased her prestige and his own worth by paying no attention to his love, thus keeping their relationship on the purest possible plane:

> I hold myself well rewarded by my talent which came to me through having well loved my lady without being loved in return, for my name is known, and I have the sympathy of the great. And as my lady of the lovely body which I honor, adorned with all the graces, was never reproached nor blamed, not even for an evil thought, I love her the more perfectly and with greater fear; for it seems to me that had she granted me the least favor contrary to duty, both she and I would have been degraded by it. For I would not have been called a man of learning nor a man of taste had I achieved my desire, but

> because this joy was denied me I have grown in wisdom to the point where vile hopes no longer please me.[113]

He was a sad poet, very conscious of the evils of the time, conscious too that he was bringing a period to a close, that he had come into the world, as he says, too late.[114] The great period of Provençal lyricism was definitely over. In the last quarter of the thirteenth century, very likely it was necessary for a troubadour to come to terms with the church if he was to survive at all. In the end, Riquier brought himself, like so many others, to recant the central doctrine of his profession. In his various works, he had depicted the lover in almost every character of the repertory from the braggart to the devotee of the Blessed Virgin. Now, in a *chanson*, the practical purpose of which seems painfully evident, he renounced that love which, in his words, "makes one do all proper things and gives one the qualities which accompany honor." After a quarter-century devoted to the celebration of the joy of love, he conceded at last that love was nothing but "foolish desire," and he turned from it to that higher love which guarantees eternal bliss.[115]

In itself, of course, this recantation is hardly impressive. In the thirteenth century, recantations were the rule. Many troubadours had turned their song in the end to the adoration of the Blessed Virgin, and nothing is more common in the *vidas* than the final statement that the minstrel, after a more or less exciting life, retired to a monastery to die. But Riquier presents himself to us in the character of the last troubadour, and there is undeniably something interesting in this repudiation of true love by the "last" of true lovers.[116]

Toward the end of the century, Riquier had found refuge in one of the last centers of troubadour activity, the court of Henry II Comte de Rodez. There, in the year 1285, he was assigned the task of writing a poetic commentary on the *canso Celeis cui am*, a work of the early thirteenth century, very likely based on a passage in the treatise of Andreas Capellanus. In this song, a work of no great obscurity, the troubadour Guiraut de Calanson had described in allegorical language the architecture of the palace of love. The power which dwelt and reigned in this palace, Calanson called "the inferior third" of love, since the whole of love, as he explained, included two other thirds—a superior love to which belongs "sincerity" and "mercy," and that sovereign love which is celestial. From the palace of this inferior love to which all the great ones of the earth were subject, the vulgar, the ill-bred, and the faithless were excluded, leaving more than half the world to lodge outside the barriers. Those who gained admittance mounted to the palace by four steps, and there were five doors to open. Calanson had written:

> In his palace, where he goes to take his pleasure, are five portals, and whoever can open the two can, with difficulty, pass the three, but it is not easy to depart; and in joy he dwells who can remain there.[117]

In his "exposition" of Calanson's poem, Riquier sadly reaffirmed the ephemeral nature of carnal love. There were, he agreed, three sorts of love—celestial love, natural love, which was the mutual love of parents and children, and carnal love. This last, the inferior third, was not rational; it listened only to the will, and while its beginnings were agreeable, it ended in "torments, cares, and sorrows." The four steps were *onrar, celar, servir, sufrir.* Of the five gates by which one entered the palace, Riquier identified the fourth with the kiss, and, he wrote, "if one went no further, love would never end and never die." But the fifth and fatal gate was "the deed which kills love in the heart of him who has passed it." For this reason, in Riquier's judgment, all were transients who entered there. It was not easy to depart, as Calanson wrote, but whoever passed all five gates had nothing to do but to go his way, for "once desire is satisfied there is nothing left." Those, however, Calanson had observed, who were capable of remaining dwelt forever there in joy. "But," Riquier remarked, "nobody has the power to remain there once he has had his desire." [118] It was the "deed" therefore which put an end to true love, that deed from which, unhappily, the lovers of his time had not the moral strength to abstain. The case was far otherwise, of course, with celestial love, and therefore the poet prayed God to grant him one day a sight of that other high palace in which there is "peace without end, love without limit, perfect good without evil, pleasure without sadness and joy without desire." [119]

Thus Riquier, without absolutely abandoning earthly love, turned his song to the love of higher things. He lost nothing by it professionally. He was no stranger to religious poetry. About one-fourth of his songs are pious in character. In entering the service of the Blessed Virgin, whose true lover he declared himself to be, about the year 1288, he found it unnecessary to change his customary *senhal.* In a song dated 1288, the Blessed Virgin became Belh Deport. Indeed, so nearly similar was the tone of his pious *chansons* after this date to that of his secular songs that, were it not for a few allegorical phrases, it would hardly be possible to say whether in the former he was addressing an earthly beauty or the Queen of Heaven:

> I often thought in the past to sing of love, but I knew it not, for I called my folly love; now Love makes me love a lady such that I can neither honor nor fear her sufficiently, nor love her as she deserves . . .
>
> Through her love, I hope to grow in merit, in honor, in riches and great joy; it is to her alone that my thoughts and my desires should turn; since through her I can obtain all the good which I desire, for I am loved by her, provided I conduct myself toward her according to the code of the true lover . . .
>
> She has so great a beauty that nothing can diminish it; nothing is lacking there, she shines day and night . . . My lady I can name, rightly, Belh Deport . . .[120]

Other troubadours of the last period do not leave us in much doubt as to the object of their adoration. After 1250 the song of love in profane form directed to the Virgin became increasingly common.[121] The Confrérie du Rosaire had been established in Provence at the same time as the Inquisition, and under its auspices the cult of the Blessed Mother little by little absorbed most of the worship and all of the rhetoric which had formerly been bestowed upon the ladies of the Midi.

Thus, at last, the cult of true love found its proper object within the new social frame, and the adoration of woman was sanctified to a pious purpose. But in directing their longing toward an ideal of sacred character, the troubadours cut the living vein which nourished their art. The sensual component was absolutely essential to their tradition, and if this was to develop further, a link would have to be forged between earthly and heavenly love, and between sensual and spiritual beauty. The troubadours had assembled all the materials necessary for this nexus, but none of them had managed to bring it about. It was in Italy that the next advance took place.

THE SICILIANS

The first of the jongleurs whose arrival in Italy can be dated with any precision was Raimbaut de Vaqueiras, who found himself a place at the court of Bonifacio de Montferrat about 1180. Some decades later, Peire Vidal was working the road from Pisa to Milan, apparently with great success, for he professed himself enchanted with his reception in Lombardy. Before the end of the twelfth century, Aimeric de Peguilhan also had found employment in Italy, at the courts of the Estensi and the Malaspina.

In the first decades of the thirteenth century, the troubadours began to swarm in earnest over the Italian countryside, and before long they were to be met with everywhere in Tuscany and Lombardy. In 1225 we hear of troubadours brawling in a tavern in Florence. By 1288 French jongleurs had become so much of a nuisance in Bologna that the authorities found it necessary to curtail their activities.[1]

The Italians did more than extend a welcome to the jongleurs from France. With typical enthusiasm, they seized upon the literary baggage of these visitors, and made it their own. In an incredibly short time the paladins of Charlemagne were naturalized in Italy, and their doings, endlessly supplemented and embroidered, remained a matter of concern to the Italians long after the taste for these stories had spent itself in France. The Provençal love-poetry, similarly, took root firmly in the Italian cities, and, shedding its original language little by little, it became Italian.

In the sixteenth century, after passing through the hands of the Italian masters, the lyrical tradition of Provence was transmitted once again to the northern countries. By that time it had become

Platonized, refined and exalted, and though fundamentally it was unaltered, its Italianization was complete. The Provençal poetry, however, did not die. Bembo was able to say at the beginning of the sixteenth century that more than a hundred Provençal poets were still read in Italy; but it is true that he represented special tastes, recondite and antiquarian. The poetic vocabulary upon which the French formed their own lyric patterns in the time of the Renaissance was imported from Italy; the models were Italian models—in the sixteenth century it was the turn of France to borrow back what in the first place she had lent. From Italy the new poetry passed also to Portugal and Spain, which had felt the Provençal influence some centuries before, and to England, which had also felt these influences, if less powerfully. Thus the troubadour tradition circulated in the course of four centuries among the countries of Europe, taking on in each language and country a characteristic color and idiom, yet itself essentially unchanged.

In Italy the vogue of the Provençal poetry continued unabated throughout the fourteenth century, and in consequence a good deal of the Provençal material which has come down to us is Italianate. In describing the form and metric of the *canzone* in *De vulgari eloquentia*, Dante made no distinction between the practice of the Italians and that of the Provenceaux. It is clear that he thought of vernacular poetry as an international tradition developing concurrently in several dialects.

From the end of the twelfth century, the Italian troubadours—the Genoese Folquet de Marseille, Lanfranc Cigala, the Dorias and Bonifacio Calvo; the Venetian Bartolomeo Zorzi; the Torinese Nicoletto; the Mantuan Sordello—had written exclusively in Provençal, competing with the troubadours of the Midi in Italy, in Spain, and in Provence. When courtly poetry began to be written in Italian, the Italian poets simply adapted their practice to the troubadour forms. There was no transition, merely a translation. The same poetic forms were practiced in the two languages, the one elegant, self-conscious, sophisticated, the other stuttering still in its efforts to accommodate an insufficient vocabulary to the requirements of a complex subject-matter and a highly developed formal mold.

The earliest school of courtly poetry in Italian took shape in the third decade of the thirteenth century. Since it was associated with the imperial court at Palermo, it was called Sicilian, though its members were by no means all insular Sicilians.[2] Frederick encouraged his courtiers to write in Italian in imitation of the Provenceaux, but the new poetry did not supplant the Provençal for some time. The Siculo-Tuscan school lasted until the fourteenth century. The troubadour Sordello was alive in 1266, and the master of the Sicilian school, the notary Giacomo da Lentino was his contemporary. The troubadour Lanfranc Cigala lived until 1300 and was a younger contemporary of Cino da Pistoia and of Dante. There was obviously nothing antique about the Provençal poetry in the eyes of the poets of the *trecento.* It was still a living stream, from which they derived ample nourishment.

Although the Emperor Frederick himself, as well as his son Enzo and his minister Pier della Vigna, set the example of rhyming in Italian, the first fruits of this attempt to establish a national literary tradition were not spectacular. The Sicilians brought nothing to the poetry of true love save their language, which was not yet ready, and their ardor, which seems moderate. Of the dozen poets who made up this group, none, with the exception of the imperial Notary, had talent.

The Notary, however, was a poet. He had nothing new to say, it is true. Nevertheless, his poetic achievement is impressive. His editor, Langley, attributes to him thirty-eight pieces of undisputed authorship, besides an equal number of poems of more or less doubtful authenticity. It is to Giacomo that the honor belongs of rooting the poetry of true love in Italian soil. But he seems to stand at the end, not the beginning, of a tradition. Of the dozen *canzoni* which are said to be his, the greater number exhibit all the formal extravagances of the more ornate troubadours, while in substance they exemplify only the most familiar molds. The Notary's innovation in naturalizing the Provençal matter was, doubtless, great enough; he seems to have had no idea of going beyond his models.

The pitiless lady, more cruel than a viper, whose beauty no

similitude can suggest, seems no different in Italian than in Provençal. She is, in fact, the same lady, and the timid lover who fears to arouse her anger by declaring his love very properly paraphrases in Italian all the clichés of Provençal rhetoric. It has been customary since the time of Lorenzo de' Medici [3] to speak disparagingly of the Notary, but it was no mean goal he set himself, and no small achievement to transplant the entire apparatus of *fin amor* in a language which had, in some sense, to be created for it. As Giacomo did not hesitate to borrow a *canzone* (*Troppo son dimorato*) [4] more or less intact from the troubadour Perdigon (*Trop ai estat*), it is possible to follow his method of translation with some insight into the nature of his problem. It is clear that he had not the mastery of form of the Provenceaux, nor the concision which characterizes their style; nevertheless he was able to achieve a poetic level which is seldom very far below that of the poets he imitated.

The immediate difficulty in adapting the Provençal matter to Italian was the lack of technical vocabulary. The Sicilians solved this difficulty in the simplest possible manner by using the Italian cognate whenever it was convenient, regardless of the difference in meaning. In this way, a number of Italian words took on special connotations in the poetry of love—*virtù, valore, pietà, mercede, gentilezza, superbia.* Other words changed meaning in conformity with the Provençal: Italian *umile* came to mean simple, kind or modest; *error* meant love's torment; *canoscenza* became wisdom; *voluntate* and *talento,* desire; *cattivo,* unhappy; *invidia,* longing, as well as envy; *noia,* dislike, hatred or fear; *fino,* true or pure; *sofferenza,* patience; *caro,* rare; *orgoglio,* arrogance as well as pride; *ira,* grief as well as wrath. By means of this new vocabulary, it became possible to deal adequately in Italian with the various situations peculiar to the literature of *fin amor.* At the same time, these borrowings served to limit the poet to the time-honored patterns which the Provençal terminology represented.

Though in substance the Italians at first added nothing to the troubadour poetry, the sonnet form was new. We have no sonnets prior to those of the Notary. Of the thirty-five Sicilian sonnets which have been preserved, he wrote at least a score, and it is altogether possible that he devised the form. The brevity of the sonnet encouraged the poet to unify and point his thought in a way that was foreign to the Provençal mode. The sonnet had both fluidity and a strong terminal principle. Though it had little amplitude, its form was well suited to melodic setting. Like the *chanson* stanza, from which it was perhaps adapted, it might be arranged in tripartite fashion. Its very limitations gave it a sort of austerity, and it presented none of the artistic intricacy of the *chanson.*

The form came full-fledged into the history of literature. All of the Sicilian sonnets are written in fourteen hendecasyllabic lines, divided into octave and sestet. The octave is invariably composed of two quatrains in alternate rhyme, *abab, abab,* and it always ends in a full stop. The sestet is usually distinguished logically from the octave; the musical *volta* was evidently accompanied by a turn of thought. The subdivision of the sestet into tercets is common in Giacomo's sonnets, but he experimented also with the sequence of couplets *cd cd cd.* The result is a relatively simple and flexible song form, learned and courtly in its association, but, unlike the majestic *canzone,* very suitable for casual rhyming.[5]

The gap that divided the Sicilians from the school that sprang up in Tuscany was little more than geographic. By the middle of the thirteenth century, the Notary was in all likelihood dead; the master of the Tuscan school, Guittone d'Arezzo, was a young man of twenty-five, actively involved in the turbulent political situation, and prolific in the production of sonnets and *canzoni* of love. Like Giacomo, Guittone did not innovate. But he developed the Italian style to the point where it can really be said to exist, and his two dozen disciples, in Bologna, Lucca, Pistoia, Siena, Pisa and Florence, carried on his method with deference.

In the course of a full life, Guittone covered the subject of love very thoroughly and from all sides. The poems he wrote in praise of love and his songs of courtship seem entirely orthodox, and altogether pedantic. In one *canzone* he appoints himself the champion of women and undertakes their defense before all the world. Women are more loyal in love than men, he declares; they are more noble and dearer to God, because they were made of nobler stuff than men—God made man of earth, but woman was made of man. Men have perhaps more wisdom and strength than women, but it is the hope of woman's love that gives man his prowess—without that hope, man would know how to do almost nothing but eat and sleep.[6]

His *trattato d'amore,* consisting of twenty-three sonnets in the style of a troubadour's *ensenhamen,* developed with some acumen the subject of how to win success in love. In one of these poems, a distant ancestor of Shakespeare's 130th sonnet, he takes issue with those who praise women by means of comparisons which cannot do justice to their subject,

> For when he wishes to praise his lady he says she is as beautiful as a flower and that she seems like a jewel and that her face is colored in grain . . .

This, says Guittone, is no way to praise a creature whom nature has made superior to all others, with the possible exception of man. The rest of his love-songs offer no great novelty, though they show clearly the drift toward a pedantic display of learning which characterizes the last stages of troubadour poetry. It is evident that, even before he became an ascetic, Guittone thought of himself as a teacher and a moralist.

The moral songs which Fra Guittone wrote after his conversion represent a complete recantation with respect to love and the adoration of women, and he furnishes us with an interesting example of that turn from profane to sacred poetry which astonishes us in the work of so many poets of the Renaissance. All the pedantic subtlety which had gone into his love-lyrics, he turned now to the service of God and the Blessed Virgin, and the ardor which formerly he spent in praising love he now employed to decry it. In an introductory *canzone,* he denies categorically that love is the poet's inspiration. Nothing so mad as love can possibly produce wisdom, he declares, and he issues a formal defiance:

> Now it will be seen whether I shall know how to sing and whether I shall be worth as much as before, since I flee from love and disclaim it entirely, and since it displeases me more

> than anything else. I hear it said that a man not pierced by love cannot write poetry and is not worth a jot. But this is far from true. . . .[7]

In another song he regrets his youth, misspent in the service of his vices, though luckily—like Dante and Donne—he was saved "*a mezza etate.*" The rest of his moral verses very properly celebrate that "*vero amore*" which is the love of God.[8]

Although Guittone does not greatly impress us with the force of his genius, he did more than anyone to develop the courtly lyric in Italy, and in his day he had the fame of a *chef d'école.* Guido Guinizelli, whom Dante hailed as "father of me and of those of my betters who ever used sweet and graceful rhymes of love," had in his day called Guittone father,[9] and Guittone was the literary ancestor also of Chiaro Davanzati, one of the chief links between the troubadours and the Italian school. After Guittone, true love traveled with an Italian passport. But almost at once, a break was perceptible in the lyric tradition, and before long there developed, between the disciples of Guittone and the Florentine school which formed about Cavalcanti and Dante, a polemic of some importance.[10]

The school of Guittone looked chiefly to the past for its models and its inspiration. In the period between Guillaume IX and Guiraut Riquier, still alive and active in the Midi when Guittone was an old man, the troubadour tradition had hardly varied in any essential aspect. But times were changing fast, and the history of the new poetry illustrates clearly the accommodation of this tradition to the tastes of a changing world.

The thirteenth century aspired greatly to knowledge. Two generations of extraordinary scholars had already organized the scattered Biblical and Patristic texts in such a way as to form a consistent body of learning. Now, under Aristotelian influence, these materials were assimilated to the vast orderly conspectus of the ancient cosmos. Suddenly, for once in the history of mankind, everything became comprehensible. Through revelation, with the aid of logic, all the mysteries of the cosmic order were at last unraveled for the benefit of rational man, the masterpiece of nature, the peer and even, it seemed, the superior of the angels. After the long darkness of ignorance, the flood of light shed by the theologians must have been dazzling. The eye of man searched every corner of the universe. It probed the atom; it looked into the mind of God, weighed His purposes, defined His structure, inquired curiously and with extraordinary confidence into the relations and limitations of the angelic substances; it searched the human soul and explored its possibilities. Never had there been such certainty, such majesty, such faith in the power and reach of human thought.[11]

It was a period of exceptional enthusiasms, a time when everything seemed possible and the stars of heaven swam almost within arm's reach. Joachim of Flora looked to the proximate coming of the Third Kingdom, the reign of the Holy Spirit, somewhere about the year 1260. Suitable preparations were made in various quarters to receive it. Meanwhile new universities sprang up everywhere. Bologna, Reggio, and Modena were already centers of learning. The first half of the century saw the establishment in Italy of nine important schools—Vicenza, Arezzo, Padua, Vercelli, Naples, Piacenza, Pavia, Siena, Rome.

The heavens themselves resounded with the effort of human aspiration. The great monastic effort at church building had spent itself; now came the turn of the bishops. Between 1150 and 1300, the mounting wave of Gothic art swept over Europe, and on its crest rode the cathedrals, thrusting their sculptured prows into the sky. In central Italy mysterious spiritual forces arose like winds, sweeping irresistibly north and south, fanning into flame every sort of religious frenzy. The burning desire of the Dominicans to search out God through logic, the flaming ardor of the Franciscans to come to Him through love, were translated on lower levels of aspiration into the aimless wanderings of armies of hysterical children, and the grim parades of masochistic fanatics in search of they knew not what. It was, in short, a marvelous and a terrible time in which might be found everything save that *mezura* and *retenemen* on which the chivalric poets had based an ideal of human behavior.

In this fervent climate, in the latter and more turbulent half of the thirteenth century, the Florentine school of the *dolce stil novo* took form. "School" is perhaps too precise a term for what was possibly not even a literary *cénacle*. The seven young men, mostly Florentines, who have traditionally been called *stilnovisti* were certainly related by a common style and an affinity of conception, but they differed widely in character and poetic temper. For a time these poets made a common cause in literature. They exploited with almost monotonous insistence a common stock of ideas, praised one another's efforts, and exchanged verses of correspondence. They also attacked, reproached, and insulted each other, and wrangled poetically quite in the manner of competing troubadours. All of them seem to have felt the influence of Guittone; but they appear to have come early under the influence of Guittone's divergent pupil, Guido Guinizelli. Thence they passed into the sphere of Guido Cavalcanti, the most considerable of the Italian poets before Dante. It was very likely Cavalcanti, more than anyone else, who gave coherence to the group which owes its name and its place in history to Dante, his "first friend."

The *dolce stil novo* was a new departure in the poetry of true love. Its influence was widespread, and in some measure inescapable in this period, but the new style did not by any means absorb all the poetic energies of Italy at the end of the thirteenth century. In the *Rime* of Dante, even, we find a good proportion of songs and sonnets which are relatively free of stilnovist influence. The concept of intellectual love, which the sweet new style initiated, was too difficult and too narrow to engage the main current of the lyric tradition. That stream was chiefly transmitted through the school of Guittone, through Chiaro Davanzati and his followers, and Petrarch passed it on to the Western world after infusing it with his own genius. Nevertheless, it is exceptional to find any idealistic love-poetry after Dante which is completely free from the influence of the *stilnovisti*.

With the parallel course of the "realistic" poetry which the troubadours bequeathed in generous measure to their Italian descendants, we need not here greatly concern ourselves. To this genre, earthy, libertine, masculine, misogynistic, even the stilnovist poets occasionally contributed, although it was never their specialty. Along with the cult of the ideal there developed a cult of frank sensuality. As a pendant to the taste for beauty there was elaborated a sophisticated taste for ugliness, and in its service the ugliest sounds were pressed into service and the ugliest sights were scrupulously depicted.[12] Those who practiced the poetry of love experimented also with the poetry of hate and the poetry of evil. The gentle Cino, Dante's friend, who specialized as a timid and susceptible lover, wrote the savage *enueg Tutto ch'altrui aggrada me disgrada;* Cecco Angiolieri, professionally misanthropic, vented his spleen in furious and violent visions of death and destruction.[13]

Thus, concurrently with the poetry of the gentle heart, and in reaction to it, there was cultivated the poetry of lust, hatred, and carnality. It was perceived that sin, ugliness, and vice had a certain human splendor which, however shocking, was transmissible in art. The screams which echoed from hell were a source of pleasure, as St. Bernardino of Siena had noted, to the ears of the blessed in heaven. Besides, beauty, like paradise, had more than one avenue of access. The period which chiefly developed the idealism of love was correspondingly fertile in the antithetical genre, the poetry of the aggressive impulse, hedonistic, comical, skeptical, grotesque, and brutal. There was nothing new in this; the tradition could be traced back as far as Guillaume IX. It would culminate in the magnificent cacophony of Rabelais.

The *stilnovisti,* however, had something new by way of a poetic idea. It was, indeed, the first new idea that had come to enrich the patterns of *fin amor* in many years, and their enthusiasm is understandable. Like the French Pléiade in later times, the *stilnovisti* announced themselves with impressive fanfare. After two centuries of bowing and scraping, the poet of love was about to enter the sacred portals of philosophy. It was the advent of important poetry. The moment was solemn.

THE NEW STYLE

The poets of "the sweet new style" were not courtiers and did not write for a courtly audience. Their literary and political activity centered upon Florence. But in this bourgeois setting, they were not bourgeois. They represented tastes which were, if anything, more exclusive and more aristocratic than those of that chivalry whose nobility the troubadours had labored to define, and in the very bosom of the middle class they sought manfully to defend an inaccessible ideal. Love, as always, pointed the way, but the way was long and difficult, and the goal incomprehensible to the greater part of mankind. "Oh, blessed are those few who sit at that table where the bread of the angels is eaten," wrote Dante, "and wretched are those who share the fodder of the sheep!" [1]

Of the half-dozen poets who from time to time munched the bread of the angels, none appears to have been of low condition. All were either nobles or men of law, save perhaps that Gianni Alfani of whom we know only that he was a friend of Cavalcanti and that he went into exile for political reasons. Guido Cavalcanti belonged to the great feudal family of the Uberti; Cino da Pistoia and Dino Frescobaldi both came of important families; Dante traced his ancestry proudly back to the knight Cacciaguida; Lapo Gianni was an imperial notary. The temper of the *stilnovisti* was predominantly upper-class, haughty, and in the main Ghibelline, but they based their nobility upon a more exclusive concept than birth or wealth. They developed to the full the central tenet of troubadour theory, and claimed the highest nobility possible to man on the basis of the gentle heart and the intellect developed through the love of beauty.

As they were neither jongleurs nor professional poets dependent on the favor of patrons, but a group of more or less noble amateurs, the *stilnovisti* could afford to indulge fully that scorn of the vulgar profane which had characterized the practitioners of the more recondite *trobars*. The *stilnovisti* wrote difficult poetry and they affected in literary matters a refined snobbery. In time this became a principle of art and served to widen even further the gap between poetry and life. They regularly warned their songs in the *envoi* to stay away from those who had not noble natures and a refined understanding. They scorned to explain themselves. "I have adorned you sufficiently," Cavalcanti wrote to his *canzone, Donna mi prega,* "so that you will be praised by people of understanding. You have no wish to visit with others." [2]

Since the sort of beauty they worshiped had aspects beyond the physical, the *stilnovisti* considered that their perceptions and intuitions were beyond the grasp of ordinary people. Cavalcanti wrote of his lady: "Her beauty is not known to the base, for its quality requires too lofty an intellect to comprehend it." [3] No troubadour wrote in this vein; the beauty of the lady of their songs was manifest to all; no special aptitude was necessary to see it. But the beauty which moved the interest of the *stilnovisti* was not primarily sensual in its character. It required an effort of the intellect to perceive its nature. For these poets love was an intellectual longing, a desire which had almost nothing in common with the yearnings of the unlettered for sensual gratification.

Often enough, it is true, the mysteries of this intellectual love were no more than mystifications. In commenting, for example, on his paradoxical language in *Vita Nuova* XIV, Dante disdains to clarify his explanation for the benefit of the puzzled reader:

> True it is that among the words in which the cause of this sonnet is made manifest dubious words are written, as when I say that love kills all my spirits, but the visual spirits remain alive but outside their proper instruments. And this enigma is impossible to solve for anyone who is not an adept of love [*fedele d'amore*] in a similar degree; and to those who are, what would solve the doubtful words is clear; and yet it

> is not proper for me to explain this riddle, since my explanation would be either vain or superfluous.

When we consider what is involved in the sonnet in question, all this must seem mere youthful pompousness; nevertheless, these puerile mysteries undoubtedly contribute something valuable to the atmosphere which distinguishes this extraordinary work. Besides, a modicum of learning was really necessary to the proper understanding of these obscurities, and this learning was apparently a source of considerable satisfaction to those who possessed it. Guido Guinizelli pointed out loftily to a detractor:

> God has established degrees in nature and in the world; he has created minds and intellects of unequal power; for this reason it is better not to say whatever pops into one's head.[4]

It is unnecessary to take expressions of this sort with complete solemnity; doubtless they were not written without some spark of humor, but they indicate the nature of that humility upon which the *stilnovisti* prided themselves. If they abased themselves before the lady's beauty, they displayed the greatest arrogance with regard to the rest of the world. Naturally, the timid lover of the song had to be characterized very differently from the proud poet involved in literary controversy. We rarely miss in the controversial rhymes of the *stilnovisti* the professional asperity of the jongleur; but there is something more, something new. The new poets affected the lofty disdain not of the troubadour absorbed in love, but of the philosopher absorbed in learning. Superficial or profound, the new poetry reeked of the schools.

The *stilnovisti* were in fact involved in a special sort of scholarship. They speculated deeply on the nature and the mechanism of love, its causes, formal and final; its consequences, proximate and ultimate. The troubadours had sometimes touched upon such questions. But the *stilnovisti* undertook the inquiry armed with such science as the troubadours never aspired to; they had something to go on besides common sense, and they took these matters seriously. It fascinated them that love should be invisible and intangible and yet powerfully efficient. They wondered whether it was substance or accident, a thing or a quality. The mechanism of enamorment attracted them especially. It seemed extraordinary to them that the sight of the lady's face even at a distance should have so electrifying an effect on the lover's heart, and they explored the physiology of these affections with the greatest interest. The lover bore the lady's image within himself wherever he was—he had only to close his eyes in order to see her—how was it to be explained that a person who was not present was nevertheless constantly before one's eyes? Such questions, obviously, were of a different order from the practical and moral problems which had engaged the interest of the chivalric audience. But the *stilnovisti* found subjects of this sort very suitable for rhyming.

The *stilnovisti* were scientifically minded, but they were not scientists. They were poets. In an age that was much given to metaphysical speculation, they desired to adapt their subject matter to the intellectual temper of the time. They desired not only to sing of love, but to rationalize their subject matter according to the best authorities. Their poetry exhibits therefore a peculiar blend of attributes. It is elaborately ornamented, rich and musical, but too often it seems precise, dry, and technical in its content. It combines strangely the passionate and the rationalistic.

This mood was in fact transitional between troubadour gallantry and Renaissance intellectualism; it marks a most important stage of literary development. The complex was, naturally, not stable. With the *stilnovisti* love went to school, but it could not stay there indefinitely. The scientific marvels which in their youth these poets found enthralling seemed less interesting to the poets of a later age. In the mature Dante the scientific postures of youth became a truly philosophic attitude; the conceits of the *dolce stil* became metaphysical concepts. Petrarch, for his part, rejected the scientific approach in favor of a deeper subjectivity and a more conventional style. Very likely the intellectual problems of the *dolce stil* seemed old-fashioned in the later fourteenth century to those who were already looking to newer sources of learning and a more authentic humanism. At any rate, the vogue for scientific poetry passed quickly. Petrarch's obscurities derived quite simply from his interest in the methods of the *trobar ric* and the *trobar clus,* not from any attempt to interpret physiologically or metaphysically the lover's state of mind or the movements of his soul. It was to be some time before, under Platonic influence, the stilnovist attitudes were revived.

The poets of the *dolce stil* were, in any case, far from systematic. They employed a learned jargon, but their subject matter was often trivial, their science in general no more than a manner. It was, of course, a manner which sought to bridge the gulf between *domnei* and the high realm of theology, but the bridge itself, to begin with, amounted only to a metaphor. In time, the meaning of intellectual love became more or less clear, but it is safe to say that not everyone who wrote of it really understood what he was writing. It is probably vain to look for logical consistency in the mass of contradictions in which this poetry is entangled.

Of all the poets of this school only Dante left a consistent system, and Dante arrived at this only by constantly overhauling his work, reinterpreting his early poems in the *Vita Nuova,* allegorizing his *canzoni* in the *Convivio,* integrating the whole, ultimately, in the grand synthesis of the *Commedia.* It is to a very considerable extent in the light of Dante that we are able to understand the work of his colleagues; it is therefore possible that in some cases we are tempted to give greater significance to their poetic achievement than it deserves. No one can doubt the intellectual pre-eminence of Cavalcanti; for the rest, their contribution was striking, but modest. Even if we include with the *stilnovisti* the handful of Florentines who carried this style into the next age—Ventura Monachi, Franceschini degli Albizzi, Sennuccio del Bene, and Cino Rinuccini—the whole of this poetry may be contained within the covers of a small book. The influence of the *dolce stil* was extremely pervasive, and in consequence this poetry has been very carefully studied, but its bulk is by no means great, and its doctrine is by no means clear.

Primarily this poetry makes the impression of existing in a world of its own devising, a twilight city in which marvelous ladies appear and vanish like figures in a dream. These ladies are infinitely more mysterious than the ladies who inhabit the troubadour songs. We have no idea of where they come from or where they go; their very nature is in doubt, whether human or divine. We have no precise idea of how they seemed, tall or short, blonde or dark, nor what it was, precisely, that the poet wanted of them. The troubadour lady has a certain solidity which supports the given characterization. She is remote, but she is existent. The stilnovist lady exists chiefly in the lover's heart. It is there that she is contemplated, not in the world of light and shade; therefore she takes on her various semblances with the fluidity of thought. She is now an angel with laughing eyes, now a wolf, ravenous and fierce. It is obvious that the poet is concerned chiefly with states of mind, his own mind, not with objective things. The beauty of the lady is a reflection of the poet's desire; her cruelty is a projection of his aggression. The poet describes himself first and always. Ultimately, this poetry has little to do with women.

Troubadour poetry, however conventionally conceived, has often an outdoor feeling, a healthy freshness of meadow and wood. The stilnovist poetry has no landscape—it takes place in the depths of the poet's soul. When, as in Cavalcanti's *Fresca rosa novella,* the outer world frames the fantasy, the effect is charming, but the poem does not really belong to the *dolce stil.* The love which is the basis of the stilnovist poetry does not quite skirt the areas of physical desire, but it becomes a fever of the intellect, and in the resulting confusion the outer world is all but lost.

The school of poetry of which Dante was master had its origin, by his own attribution, in the verses of the Bolognese lawyer Guido Guinizelli. In the *Comedy,* Dante places Guinizelli in purgatory among the adulterers, for this Guido had not, in Dante's opinion, broken with the carnality of true love; nevertheless he hails him reverently as his ancestor in the poetic art. When Dante was writing the *Purgatorio,* Guinizelli had been dead nearly a half-century; very likely, he was no longer alive in 1276, when Dante was a boy of eleven. Almost nothing is known of Guinizelli, but there is no doubt that he was considered an innovator in his day, for the Luccan poet Bonagiunta Orbicciani took the trouble to attack him in a satirical sonnet on the obscurity of his style and his recondite matter:

> Now that you have changed the manner of the
> pleasant songs of love, their form and essence,
> so as to overgo all other poets,
> You have become as a torch which shines in the
> darkness but which pales wherever the sun sheds
> its light, which far exceeds your own.
> Indeed, you surpass all the world in subtlety, and
> there is no one who can interpret your language
> properly, so dark it is!
> But it is considered a strange business—although
> learning comes to us from Bologna—to make
> love-songs out of science.[5]

For his elegance of expression, Bonagiunta was compared in his day—perhaps ironically—to Folquet de Marseille and Peire Vidal, but a certain Maestro Francesco da Firenze, reproaching him for plagiarizing the Notary, reminded him forcefully of the fate of the crow with the borrowed feathers.[6] It was, indeed, only through the *Comedy* of Dante that Bonagiunta achieved any sort of immortality.

In the *Comedy*, Dante describes himself as coming upon Bonagiunta, sadly emaciated, in that part of purgatory reserved for repentant gluttons. After some obscure mutterings, the Luccan poet inquires, marveling, if this living being who stands before him is really "he who invented the new rhymes beginning *Donne ch'avete intelletto d'amore*." Dante does not favor him with a direct answer. He answers obliquely, with becoming modesty, "I am one who takes note when Love inspires me, and what he dictates to me inwardly, that I set forth." This is all Bonagiunta needs to hear; comprehension comes upon him like a flash of lightning:

> Oh, brother, he said, now I see the knot which
> kept the Notary and Guittone and me short
> of the sweet new style which I hear.

> Truly, I see how closely your pens follow after
> him who dictates, which certainly was not the
> case with us.
> And he who sets himself to search further has
> lost all sense of difference between the one
> style and the other . . .[7]

It was from this passage that the sweet new style took its name. But while comprehension came quickly to Bonagiunta in purgatory, the same cannot be said for those who, in this world, have often turned Dante's words over in an attempt to discover in them some principle by which to understand the *dolce stil novo* which Bonagiunta recognized so easily. Whatever interpretation one may prefer of this passage, and there are many, it is clear that Dante had no idea of citing himself as the sole innovator in the *uso moderno*. In *De vulgari eloquentia* he constantly associates himself and his style with his friend Cino da Pistoia. In the *Vita Nuova* he acknowledges his dependence upon Cavalcanti; in the *Comedy*, his debt to Guinizelli and the troubadours. Even if there were no apparent similarities in the work of these poets, we should have to look, following Dante's directions, for the links that bound them together.

Evidently, Dante had his reasons for marshaling among the repentant sensualists on the purgatorial terraces those of his literary forebears whom he considered to have had a hand in the development of the new poetry. Nevertheless, in the *Purgatorio* he not only refrains from defining the new style which Bonagiunta recognizes in the single tercet which Dante bestows upon him, but he also discourages any inquiry into its nature beyond the fact that its practitioners follow closely the dictates of love. Bonagiunta, in his weakened condition, gladly concurs, and we should be happy to follow his example, save that the critical principle enunciated by Dante sheds no light whatever on the issue which Dante apparently had it in mind to resolve in this passage.

The question of what the novelty of the new style might consist in has been debated with unusual fervor. It has been argued with great cogency on the one hand that it was by reason of its substance that the new poetry was new; on the other hand, excellent arguments have been adduced to show that its novelty was entirely a matter of the form.[8] Few scholars have taken literally Dante's dictum in *Purgatorio* XXIV, 52, that the chief difference between his style and that of the older poets was that Dante wrote simply and sincerely what he felt in his heart, while they did not. Such declarations of sincerity were a commonplace of troubadour literature; but they had as little relation to the poetic practice of the troubadours as to that of Dante. For the troubadours, as for Dante, poetry would be a transmutation of inner experience according to the rules of art. In the thirteenth century no poet sang simply from the heart. This was reserved for birds. The poet might follow closely the inner dictates of love, as Dante said he did, but love was not a voice. It was a system.

Dante was a master of poetic artifice. Bonagiunta and his colleagues were its servants. The difference between his work and theirs leaps to the eye. But it would require a critical spirit of supernatural keenness to determine where in the scale of poetic artifice the old style left off and the new began. From the time of the Notary to the time of Dante, vernacular poetry in Italian had improved by leaps and bounds. In the hands of the *stilnovisti*, Italian poetry became for the first time capable of the utmost sonority and the most varied music. Such progress in the art of poetry hardly came about through the inspiration of love alone. It reflected, progressively, an exquisitely sharpened awareness of the musical possibilities of the language, and this awareness was doubtless shared by many. There is every reason to suppose that in the discussion of sound and rhyme in *De vulgari eloquentia*, Dante represented not only his own practice but the conscious practice of all those poets of his acquaintance whose work he cites in illustration of his doctrine.[9]

The Toulousan Guilhem Molinier saw no inconvenience in giving to his manual of Provençal prosody the title *Laws of Love*. For Molinier, as for Dante, the laws of love and the laws of poetry would be the same. Passion was all sorts of things, but love was poetry. Therefore the dictates of love came out of the rhetoric book to an extent which is all but incomprehensible in an age which has been conditioned by the romantic attitudes of the nineteenth century. For the Middle Ages, love was no untutored longing. It was a work of art, and involved a thorough grasp of the necessary masteries. Accordingly, when in the *Convivio*, Dante assigned to the seven arts their appropriate places in heaven, it was in the Third Heaven, the heaven of Venus, that he placed Rhetoric, "sweetest of the sciences." [10]

It seems likely that there was some difference of opinion among the disciples of Guittone as to the type of rhetorical figure appropriate to the love-song. Guittone's sonnet on the ineffectiveness of similitudes to describe the lady's beauty may, of course, have been intended as mere gallantry, but the tone of the verse indicates that he meant to express his disapproval of hyperbolic comparisons. Bonagiunta took Guinizelli to task particularly for his use of learned conceits in a song of courtship. In fact, Guinizelli was the first of the learned poets to write in Italian, and the intellectual cast which he gave to his *canzone Al cor gentil* was a totally new departure in the poetry of love.

Many troubadours had written of serious matters in the form of a *chanson*, but none had combined the scientific and the gallant in so daring a manner. In *Al cor gentil* Guinizelli merged *vers* and *canso;* while explaining the nature and quality of love, he made love—the lecture was part of the courtship. Moreover, while the troubadours had explored many areas as a source for poetic figures, none had thus far embarked upon a conceit which fitted human love so brilliantly into the cosmic scheme. Guinizelli's innovation represented an important step in the enlargement of the poetic horizon. With the *canzone Al cor gentil*, Guinizelli initiated the vogue of metaphysical poetry.

The *dolce stil*, insofar as it derived from Guinizelli, was a style, not a philosophy; but it was a style which made use of certain conceits which implied clearly the outlines of an underlying philosophical scheme. It remained for others to make this scheme explicit, yet in the main the metaphysical basis of the *dolce stil* may be traced to Guinizelli without difficulty. As Guinizelli had something in mind, unlike most of his contemporaries, it was necessary for him to find a more allusive form of expression than the school of Guittone commonly used. His *canzone* therefore bristles with comparisons, and it is quite possible that it was this characteristic which drew Guittone's criticism with regard to the ineptness of similitudes. As a matter of fact, the clarity of Guinizelli's expression was not enhanced by the demands of his over-elaborate rhyme scheme, and he was certainly inclined, like all the metaphysical poets, toward the obscure style. He had not, to be sure, the elegance of Cavalcanti nor the smoothness of Cino. But he had something interesting to say, and this is perhaps one of the fundamental requisites of a sweet style.

It is not at all difficult to understand why Dante declined in the *Purgatorio* to discuss the character of the new poetry with the second-rate Luccan poet whom he selected to represent the older school. Nothing is more difficult to define than style. Yet Dante's answer seems insultingly evasive. Presumably, all those who wrote songs "in the semblance of love" wrote under love's dictation; from the time of Bernard de Ventadour no formula was more commonly expressed than this. Peirol had written: "Well must I sing since it is love who teaches me and gives me the talent to make fine songs; without that I should not have been a poet"; Arnaut Daniel: "Love inspires me and sets my words to music"; Montanhagol, that it was love that gave him his learning.[11] Even the mystic Richard of St. Victor, whose twelfth century treatise on the degrees of love was certainly known to Dante, repeated this commonplace: "He alone speaks of that subject worthily who composes his words according to the dictates of his heart." [12]

In the *Purgatorio*, nevertheless, Bonagiunta concedes readily that, not having listened closely enough to love's dictation, he had not been able to attain in his lifetime that poetic felicity which his interlocutor was demonstrating at that very moment. The sweet style in question, Dante tells us, he himself derived from Guido Guinizelli, and Guido, hearing these words, at once points to Arnaut Daniel, his neighbor in the refining flame, as a better master in the vernacular art.[13]

In making Guinizelli acknowledge the link that bound him to the troubadours, Dante very properly demonstrated his sense of tradition, but he did not hail Daniel as his own literary progenitor.

The troubadour, in Dante's opinion, was the greatest of the vernacular stylists, yet he had not pointed the way to a new subject matter. Guinizelli had. Through him, love had vastly broadened its scope. Without quite relinquishing its foothold on earth, it now reached far into the skies, and the poet of love was able to employ his intellect, his learning, and his imagination for the first time to some purpose.

What Bonagiunta was made to realize in the course of his brief literary discussion in purgatory was the value of the metaphysical style which Guinizelli had inaugurated and which Dante was even then exhibiting in its high perfection. The *canzone Donne ch'avete* which Dante had selected for Bonagiunta to admire was the first *canzone* of the *Vita Nuova,* an excellent example of the philosophical love-song in the manner of Guinizelli. But the latest and surest evidence of the value of the sweet new style was, of course, not the youthful *Vita Nuova* but the *Comedy.* It was this divine poem two-thirds complete which Dante now exhibited in fancy to the imaginary Bonagiunta, as he himself climbed the steps toward paradise, attended at no great distance by pagan Virgil and Christian Statius. With the new style, so Bonagiunta was given to understand, vernacular rhyme had at last reached its majority. It could now be called poetry, and it took its place among the great literatures of the world.[14]

Thus, in Dante's view, the "knot" which had hampered Bonagiunta and his colleagues was not simply their sensuality. Dante had often accused himself of that, and he had the father of the *stilnovisti* even then expiating his sensuality in the flames of the upper cornice. It was the limitation of love-poetry to the things of this earth which had kept Bonagiunta and the Notary from advancing in the poetic art; and Guittone, because he had not understood how far love could reach, had betrayed its inspiration. It was in freeing, not the lover, but the poetry of love from the knot of the flesh that Dante, following Guinizelli and Cavalcanti, had found a new style in which to write the love-song. Thus Bonagiunta, hearing Dante speak in the very poem which was the triumphant vindication of the metaphysical style, at last understood what he had not understood when he reproved Guinizelli for making love-songs out of science; namely, that it is Love himself who dictates the philosophical system which is based upon love, and that therefore the path of true love leads inevitably to theology, which is the highest poetry.[15]

Dante, of course, represents the new style in its perfection. But the poets of the Florentine *cénacle* had much in common with the early Dante; they shared among them the whole formulary of the *dolce stil.* All of them sought an expression that was "sweet, graceful, and subtle," and this *dolcezza,* this *leggiadria* and *sottilezza* were essential elements also in the characterization which lovers assumed in the new poetry. More than any other single element, the use of this character-type bound together the poets of the *dolce stil.*

The stilnovist poet did not sing in the character of a knight. By this time Italian poetry had shed the chivalric trappings of troubadour poetry, and we are no longer able to place the singer in a feudal context. The lover of the stilnovist song is somewhat vaguely situated in a world in which he has no certain place. He depicts himself as pitifully timid and shy; his manner is humble and self-conscious, punctilious, courteous, gentle. His mood is somewhat less stable even than that of his counterpart in the Provençal songs. The lady inspires him with such terror that he dares not look at her, lest the sight prove fatal to him, but he is compulsively fixed upon her, and he vacillates constantly between exaltation and despair.

A certain sweetness exudes from this poetry; it is not altogether healthy; it smells of death. Its source is a tender piety, an air of resignation which is occasionally enlivened with imprecations and laments. We are invited to picture the poet not as a cavalier trotting his horse down a leafy path, but as a pale youth walking slowly along a narrow street, or sitting pensive in a city square, tense with repressed passion. This lover speaks much of dying. Introspective to an unusual degree, he accentuates the normal subjectivity of the troubadour into a kind of hypochondria, a neurotic interest in the troubled workings of his own psyche.

How far this character-type diverges from the nature of the

turbulent spirits who created it—revolutionists like Dante, firebrands like Cavalcanti, politicians like Cino—a glance at their biographies will show. This poetry obviously has little to do with the sort of reality out of which biography is made. The stilnovist lover has no external life. Once his eyes have betrayed him by admitting into his heart the image of the fatal lady, he has no further business in the material world. Henceforth his eyes look inward, and his life is passed, presumably, in a rapture of self-contemplation.

For the *fin aman*, a practical lover with a definite goal in mind, an art of love sufficed. But the stilnovist was interested less in the conduct of love than in its phenomenology; he developed a science of love. For this purpose Cavalcanti borrowed what was necessary from the best and newest sources—the Averroistic writings then in vogue as well as the various treatises of Albertus Magnus and the *Summae* of Thomas Aquinas.[16] Under such influences, the *batalha d'amor* of the troubadours took an unexpected turn. It ceased to be a conflict of man and woman, and became a psychic conflict within the individual, involving the mutual relations of the eyes, the mind, the soul, the heart, and the spiritual mechanism which bound these faculties together.

The poetry which resulted from these procedures was by no means to the taste of everyone. The poet Onesto da Bologna, for example, attacked Cino in a pungent sonnet, the sentiments of which many a modern student has doubtless fervently echoed:

> *Mind* and *humble* and more than a thousand basketfuls of spirits and your air of walking in your sleep make me think that there is no way to make sense of you in your rhyming mood. I know not what makes you do it, whether love or death, but with your philosophic airs you have wearied even the strongest of those who hear your beautiful, conceited song. Moreover we all find very burdensome your colloquies of three with another person, and your four-voiced discussions with yourself. Truly, all human burdens seem sweet in comparison with what you cause a man to endure who reads you.[17]

While the troubadours had occasionally ventured into philosophical matters, none of them had seriously pretended to any unusual degree of learning. But the *stilnovisti* wished to be thought of as teachers and doctors, and they attempted to elevate the poet's vocation as far as possible. Dante spoke of Guinizelli as "the sage"; Juvenal and Virgil also were sages; [18] and Dante's immediate predecessors in the poetic art were dignified as doctors of poetry in a passage of *De vulgari eloquentia* which makes the literary pretensions of Guiraut Riquier seem less absurd.[19] The love-theory appropriate to such scholarly poets was naturally much more abstruse than anything that would have recommended itself to the poets of Provence. It involved a thoroughgoing excursion into the physiology of the subject.

The physiological doctrine upon which Cavalcanti founded his theory of love was a well-integrated system of classical origin which, having answered its purpose for a great many years, still held the field in the sixteenth century. It was an entirely sensible system based largely on the writings of Aristotle, Praxagoras, Hippocrates, and Galen, and its shortcomings were not evident at a time when it had not yet been observed that the lungs are the organs of respiration and that the blood circulates in its vessels. In the Galenic system it was the function of the heart to pump air into the arteries through its systolic and diastolic movements, while the lungs acted as a bellows to cool the heart and keep the radical heat from burning the humors, which it distilled. The blood ebbed and flowed from the heart; otherwise it lay inert in its vessels, while through it the spirits flowed in accordance with the movements of the soul. The heart was the center of the complex cuisine by means of which the soul utilized and renewed the material body. It was also the seat of the passions or emotions, the motive powers of the sensitive soul.[20]

The troubadours had resolved the problem of enamorment by assuming, partly on Ovidian authority, that love was in the first place brought about by an amorous glance. This glance, shot out like an arrow, carried through the lover's eyes into his heart. Then, as Andreas explained, an intellectual process was initiated, and out of excessive meditation upon the lady's image now lodged in the heart there developed that desire which eventually caused the lover to pass from potency to action, from *passio* to *virtus*. Upon this theoretical groundwork, Guinizelli and Cavalcanti elaborated with the enthusiasm of pioneers. The result was the development of a type of poetry which amply demonstrated the inconvenience of making "love-songs out of science."

The fundamental tenet of the scientific system at their disposal was the Aristotelian division of the human soul into three elements, vegetative, sensitive, and rational.[21] To explain the connection of the immaterial soul with the material body, the Greek physiologists had assumed the existence of an intermediary substance which partook of the nature of each and could therefore act upon the one by virtue of the other. This substance was the spirit, a hot vapor of great subtlety extracted in the liver, refined by coction in the heart and further refined in the brain. By means of the spirit, resident in the arterial system and constantly renewed, the soul could transmit its impulses to the bodily members and maintain its communications with the organs of sense and cerebration as well as with the outer world.[22]

The workings of this microcosm corresponded precisely to the workings of the cosmic organism. As we learn in the treatise *De anima*, attributed to Hugh of St. Victor, the soul is completely present at the same time in all parts of the body, just as God is completely present everywhere in the universe which His spirits operate in accordance with His will. Since the human soul, like its Creator, is at the same time triple and one, it has three spirits corresponding to its three faculties. To the natural faculty corresponds the natural spirit, resident in the liver. The vital spirit resides in the heart. The animal spirits reside in the brain.[23]

In the Galenic theory, the liver—the function of which it is to supply nourishment to the body—is the center and origin of the venous system. The product of digestion, the chyle, is sent from the stomach to the liver. There, by a second digestion, the blood and the other primary humors are produced, as well as the more highly refined natural spirit from which all other spirits are made. The natural spirit ascends along the veins to the left ventricle of the heart, and there it is refined by the heart's action into the more subtle *spiritus vitalis,* which is then incorporated in the arterial system. Moving through the blood along the pulsatile veins, the vital spirit brings heat to the bodily members, and eventually it moves into the ventricle of the brain. In that place, further heated and refined, it is converted into the animal spirits, which, sent along the nerves to the sense-organs, furnish communication to the perceptive faculty of the soul. Some of these spirits remain in the ventricle to serve the general sensitivity, or common sense, and the imagination; some pass to the middle cell of the brain to serve the rational faculty; some pass into the posterior cell of the brain, where they serve the memory. The rest flow into the motor nerves in the spinal marrow.[24]

The mechanism of enamorment thus became explicable in terms of a movement of spirits from the soul of one person to that of another. Light was the intermediary. The bright glance which issued from the laughing eyes of the lady consisted of a fiery beam of spirits which pierced the eye of the beholder, and made its way to his heart. These visual spirits were of great potency. In the case of the basilisk, Albertus Magnus informs us, the *spiritus visivus* can kill.[25] In the case of the lady, the result might be almost as dangerous, for once lodged in the heart, the invading spirits were capable of disordering the entire vital mechanism. The *stilnovisti* evidently found this process enchanting. They did not weary of describing it:

> From her eyes, wherever she turns them, come burning spirits of love which strike the eyes of those who look at her and, passing through these, each of them pushes as far as the heart.[26]

No one who undertook to describe the nature of love felt it possible, apparently, to avoid a more or less detailed allusion to the way in which the sight of beauty aroused desire. Castiglione, writing in the first years of the sixteenth century, transmitted this concept pretty much as it was formulated in the *trecento:*

> Those living spirits that issue from the eyes, being generated near the heart, and entering now by the eyes at which they

> are aimed like an arrow at the mark, naturally penetrate the heart as if it were their own place, and there they mingle with the other spirits and, with that most subtle quality of blood which they have in them, they infect the blood in the neighborhood of the heart to which they have come, and heat it and make it like themselves, apt to receive the impression of that image which they bear with them. And little by little these messengers, going back and forth along the way from the eyes to the heart, and bringing back with them the tinder and steel of beauty and grace, fan with the breath of desire that flame which burns so ardently and never consumes itself because they are always bringing it matter of hope to feed on.[27]

The first consequence of this invasion of visual spirits was the awakening of desire, a movement of the sensitive soul. But presently the image, now resident in the imagination, was perceived by the intellectual faculties. These apprehended it, abstractly, as idea. Then, in those beings who were capable of it, love proceeded on a higher plane. The desire of the sensitive soul was motivated solely by the beautiful object. For the rational soul, the object of desire was the beauty of the idea. This was, of course, not a sensual but an intellectual longing, the desire of the soul to unite with the beauty of another soul and thus to participate more fully in the beauty of the absolute.[28]

The love of the rational soul supplemented, but did not necessarily supplant, the desire of the sensitive faculty. It was of a nobler and more permanent order, the specific attribute of humanity, as distinguished from animal desire. The desire which centers upon the sensual object, we are often told, comes and goes and varies in accordance with the sensual image, but

> Love is not love
> Which alters when it alteration finds
> Or bends with the remover to remove. . . .

The love which is fixed upon the ideal, the ever-fixed mark in the intellect, does not vary once it is awakened. The lady ages and dies; but the idea of her beauty is not subject to modification. The love of the idea is unchanging. It was this love, primarily, though by no means exclusively, that the *stilnovisti* sang.

This refinement of *fin amor* was the chief contribution of the school of the *dolce stil.* As their doctrine had little to do with tangible realities, the new poets completed the retreat from the sensible and practical which the later troubadours had initiated, and with them poetry became truly exclusive. Theirs was an abstruse concept, difficult to express, difficult to control, and easily misunderstood. Nevertheless, much of the idealistic poetry of the Renaissance stems from this root. Ficino's interpretation of the *Symposium* owed almost as much to the *stilnovisti* as to Plato, and in time stilnovism merged with the Platonism of the new age so thoroughly that the two became hardly distinguishable.

The *stilnovisti* based their love-theory in the first place on the most familiar of philosophic commonplaces, the dualism of form and matter. Since matter was Protean and could have no beauty save that which form imparted, the true object of love must ultimately be form, and form was apprehensible to the intellect only as idea. To the sensitive soul, however, form was manifest only in its material representation, the physical being. This ephemeral shape was, of course, not a rational object of desire; therefore sensual love was a confusing and frustrating experience. The consequence was the lover's torment—the never-ending strife between the soul and the tyrannical image which struggled with it for the mastery. But when, by the operation of the intellect, the will was motivated toward the true object of desire, love could be directed rationally toward beauty itself rather than toward the material object. In this direction, ultimately, lay the lover's happiness.

In developing these concepts the *stilnovisti* made use of a theory of knowledge which owed as much to the commentaries of Averroës as to Aristotle. It was generally considered that the faculty concerned with knowing must consist of two agencies, one passive, one active. The passive, or possible intellect was in the first place a *tabula rasa* capable of receiving and storing impressions, but it could receive these only as ideas. The intellect therefore could have no direct knowledge of particular things. These were perceived by the sensitive soul as images—*phantasmata*—exactly as animals perceived them, classified by the common sense and stored in the imagination. They were so far unintelligible, for the rational soul had no contact with the images of the outer world save through the imagination, the "mind's eye." Now through the working of the active intellect, the images apprehended by the sensitive soul were stripped of their modes and contingencies and reduced to absolute form. The moment an image was thus reduced to its essence, there took form in the possible intellect a corresponding likeness which represented the image intelligibly as idea. When the rational soul had thus received the idea of the external object perceived by the senses, it referred this to the phantasm stored in the imagination. Thus, by a kind of reflex, the rational soul was able to know what the sensitive soul perceived.[29]

From this standpoint it became comprehensible that the soul's desire might proceed independently along several levels. The sensitive soul moved toward the satisfaction of wants which were other than those of the rational soul. Flesh desired to unite with flesh, animal with animal, but intellect with intelligence—the intellect desired to possess beauty in the only way in which, ultimately, beauty can be possessed, through knowledge. The senses moved blindly toward their goal, which was ultimately not different from that of the intellect; but the ardor of the intellect was enlightened, it knew what it wanted. For the rational faculty, love was not an inexplicable urge, nor an instinctual drive to carry out nature's ends in reproduction; it was a desire to attain perfection, to unite with higher forms, to unite, finally, with the absolute, with God. In this manner, the rational soul transcended the blind urge to couple with whatever beautiful object might come its way, in an intelligent awareness of the nature, the process and the purpose of love.

Since the intellectual faculty was considered to be the distinguishing characteristic of the human being, to love humanly was to love intellectually. The highest quality of the beautiful woman would thus be her transparency, the quality which permitted the lover to glimpse the soul, the ideal, through the fleshly envelope;

and the function of the beauty of woman would be to set man on the upward path, making manifest to him in the first place through his senses that beauty which his intellect could afterward follow upward to its source in the absolute.

By the middle of the thirteenth century, the philosophic basis of the *dolce stil* was already commonplace among the learned. The works of Albertus Magnus and Thomas Aquinas gave these ideas the widest currency, and there is evidence that by this time also a good deal of interest had been generated in the Italian universities, particularly at Padua, in the epistemological superstructure which Averroës had erected upon the Aristotelian foundation. The consequence was the integration of the system of true love in the theological synthesis which the learned doctors of the thirteenth century had so brilliantly brought about.

In the *Summa theologica* (I–II, Qu. 26) St. Thomas had assembled and coordinated all the available philosophic material relevant to love and its operation in the Christian cosmos. For St. Thomas love has a twofold aspect. From the viewpoint of the attracting object it is passion; from the viewpoint of the striving subject, it is force. Love is in every case the origin of motion, and its object is always the good.

All manifestations of the spirit, in this view, are experienced as drives or urges. To the three parts of the human soul there correspond the three drives, *motus naturalis, motus appetitus, motus rationalis.* Since the soul is the principle, but not the subject, of the corporeal organism, the vegetative and sensitive activities are bound to the body, but the intellectual faculties have no such corporeal bond and are therefore available to the soul after death. The highest love therefore transcends time and mortality, and its object is the eternal.

Love belongs to the appetitive powers, and there is a grade of love corresponding to each of these powers. The natural appetite follows nature's purpose. The sensitive appetite also is governed by external necessity—in animals, always; in man it is free insofar as it obeys reason. But the rational appetite obeys reason only and is always free.

The appetitive drive, St. Thomas apprises us, is a circular motion. It proceeds out of the desired object, affects the soul and moves the appetite, which then strives to reach the object and to unite with it. When it has done so, the circle completed, it comes to rest. All motions in the universe are, in this way, the consequence of love in some grade. The force of gravity is *amor naturalis;* hunger is *amor sensitivus;* but man rises to God through *amor rationalis.*

The nature of love makes it clear in what direction human love should direct itself. It is natural to love what is like ourselves; at the same time it is normal to desire only what we lack. Accordingly, it is rational to love ourselves, our equals, and our inferiors in the scale of creation with benevolent love, but without longing. For what is above us in the cosmic scheme, the higher beings, it is reasonable to feel longing; but when we desire in this manner what is below us in the scale of creation we strive not for absolute but for relative good, *bonum secundum quid,* and this is irrational. Thus sensual pleasure is a good only for the senses, except insofar as it furthers reproduction, and it has no part in that *virtus concupiscentiae boni* which directs the soul upward.[30]

Since in the chain of creation woman is a lower being than man, or at best of equal rank with him, man may love woman reasonably with friendship or benevolence, but not with desire. Such was the outcome of the scholastic doctrine available to the poets of the *dolce stil.* As for the literary tradition which they inherited from the Provenceaux, it involved, we have seen, a fundamental ambiguity with regard to the status of woman. The troubadours did not, in general, consider that women were superior to men,[31] but they celebrated the beloved woman in each case as nature's masterpiece, a being above all other living creatures. It was therefore theoretically possible for the *stilnovisti* to square the love-theory of the Provenceaux with orthodox theological doctrine on condition that the beloved lady were qualitatively distinguishable from the rest of womankind, if such a thing were conceivable. This was, in fact, the solution which the *stilnovisti* adopted.[32]

By assimilating the desire for the beauty of woman to the longing of the soul for the absolute, the *stilnovisti* put the entire relation of true love on a new footing. The lady became an ideal. Unhappily, once the beauty of the lady was abstracted to the archetypal form, the lady as an individual lost her significance for the lover; she merely symbolized on the material plane the ideal beauty which was the true object of his desire. To preserve the individuality of the lady and yet make her defensible as the object of a rational love, it was necessary to exalt her to the status of a higher being, an intelligence or angel. In either case love, whether of the ideal or the angel, had to be completely sublimated, that is to say, desexualized, before it could be considered a rational desire. In exalting the beloved lady to the point where she might be loved with intellectual love, it was necessary to divest her of her womanhood. The poet's love now acquired the necessary nobility; but the lady vanished.

The transformation lady-into-angel necessarily involved some confusion on the lover's part. The beautiful creature presented herself in the first place to the sensual eye, and the process of detaching the rational from the sensual desire which she inspired was accompanied, if we may believe Dante, by considerable inner stress. Much of the poetry of the *dolce stil* centered upon this process. Often initiated, seldom resolved, the lover's conflict became a prime subject for poetry. The conflict between the two loves, and its consequences, furnished Petrarch with the central theme around which he arranged his *Rime* and also a good part of his *Secretum*. After Petrarch this subject matter became the basis of much, if not most, of the serious love-poetry of the Renaissance.

These complexities were naturally not altogether comprehensible to the uninitiated. Traditionally a song of love was a song of courtship, and it was not very clear to those of the old school what it was that the new poets wanted of women. Cavalcanti wrote in a "sonnet" addressed to Guido Orlandi, his friend:

> . . . You may know how to wind a crossbow and hit the beam of a roof squarely, and you may have read Ovid a little, and shot some arrows, and made bad rhymes, but that does not mean that your mind can reach the place where Love

> teaches, softly and subtly, how to sing of his ways and of his state. That is not a thing, believe me, that one carries about in the hand; such as you are, He is of another sort; by the speech alone one can tell who has been there. And it is no wonder that my former sonnet did not touch you: Love himself wrought the object which I file.[33]

If the celebrated *canzone Donna mi prega* was intended to enlighten the world regarding the intricacies of love conceived in this fashion, it must be confessed that Cavalcanti succeeded only in obscuring still further what was never altogether clear. The poem, as he tells us, was written for the benefit of an inquiring lady. The identity of this lady is not mysterious. She was none other than the same Guido Orlandi who had proposed in a sonnet addressed to Cavalcanti a series of questions concerning the nature of love.[34]

These questions Cavalcanti answered *seriatim* in his *canzone,* a *trattato d'amore* of scholastic cut, with a decidedly Averroistic coloring. Love, Cavalcanti explains, in terms which Dante echoed in the prose of the *Vita Nuova,* is not a substance but an accident. It resides in the region of the memory, and is the result of a shadow cast by Mars. It proceeds from a visible shape which, once it is made intelligible, passes into the possible intellect. Love never exerts its power in that quarter because there the form has its universal character only, and therefore shines perpetually on itself, affording not pleasure but meditation. Love, however, is not a rational urge. It is sensual, and therefore disturbs the rational judgment, and since it substitutes intention for reason, in a vicious nature it would be a bad guide. Love is a rare thing, most often seen in noble natures. It is indivisible, beyond color and outside being. Sealed in darkness, it radiates light, and he who is worthy of faith says that only from love is born mercy.[35]

The dark words of *Donna mi prega,* couched in the style of the *trobar clus* and further obfuscated by the rigors of a complex rhyme-pattern and a technical terminology, seem to have had the greatest influence upon Cavalcanti's contemporaries. Dante referred to it twice in *De vulgari eloquentia,* once in the *Convivio.*

Dino del Garbo published a lengthy commentary. Frequently glossed and commented on, it was one of the prime vehicles of scholastic love-theory and, though it cannot be said to have clarified its subject in any substantial way, it formed the nucleus of a considerable literature.[36]

In *Donna mi prega*, Cavalcanti was concerned with sensual love exclusively. His *canzone* treats with the necessary reverence a dangerous and irrational urge which it is impossible for certain natures to resist. Intellectual love is, of course, of another order, but it is related in its origin to that longing which does not lead to heaven. In his *ballata Veggio negli occhi*, Cavalcanti described the relation in terms of a striking conceit:

> In my lady's eyes I see a light full of spirits of love which brings wonderful delight into my heart, so that it is filled with joyous life;
>
> Such a thing befalls me when I am in her presence that I cannot describe it to the intellect: It seems to me that as I gaze at her there issues from her semblance a lady of such beauty that the mind cannot grasp it, and from this at once another is born of wondrous beauty out of which it seems that there issues a star which says: "Behold, your blessedness is before you."
>
> When this beautiful lady appears, a voice goes forth before her which celebrates her meekness so sweetly that if I try to repeat it, I feel that her greatness is such that it makes me tremble, and in my soul stir sighs which say: "Lo, if you gaze at this one you will see her virtue ascended into heaven."[37]

What Cavalcanti's lady would gather from this, if she could fathom the meaning, was that her image, when the poet saw her, made a joyous tumult in his heart, but in his mind it aroused another sort of experience, neither joyous nor sad, but wonderful. There the image of the lady was rendered intelligible as an essence of wondrous beauty and, glowing in the intellect as a celestial intelligence, a star, it foretold the salvation of the poet if he could but follow this beauty to its source in heaven. Of all the *stilnovisti,* only Dante attempted such an excursion, and that effort led into another kind of poetry, in which the beauty of the lady became a progressive revelation until at last it was quenched in a greater beauty still, the ineffable beauty of God. For Cavalcanti, however, as for Dante in the *Vita Nuova,* the intuition sufficed, at least for the time. It gave a supernatural radiance to the beauty of the lady, but it did not calm the fever of the flesh.

In the light of these imaginings, the ladies who appeared to these young men in Florence were invested with such glamour as no women had ever had before. "Who is this who comes?" the poet asks in wonder. "All men gaze at her; she causes the very air to tremble with her brightness, and brings Love with her so that no man can utter a word, but each one sighs aloud." [38] Their splendor was dazzling:

> One cannot speak of this lady; she came adorned with such beauty that the human mind could not bear it long enough for the intellect to apprehend her . . .[39]

And even when the mind was able to grasp this beauty, the shock was so great that the poet cried out in pain:

> Have pity, great Lord, you who clasp the high heavens . . . have pity on the tumult of my soul where you depict that image which my intellect contemplates . . .[40]

All the *stilnovisti* took pleasure in describing in detail the devastation caused by the lady's beauty: it was their specialty. The troubadour love-song, we have seen, was essentially dramatic in character, a lyric which could be fitted into an imaginary plot of conventional character. The *stilnovisti* perpetuated the dramatic character of the lover's song, but the stage was no longer set in objective reality. The play of love now became an inward thing; the poet set his stage in the depths of the lover's soul. It became difficult to imagine the scene. These scenes were lit only by an internal radiance, but these radiances were felt to be of vast trajectory; they were shafts which opened into paradise. The conventional *dramatis personae*, the lover, the lady, the jealous one, and the *losengier*, became peripheral characters. The poet now depicted the mutual relations of his heart and his senses, his soul and his intellect. In this new drama, a sort of morality play in embryo, the personified heart became the protagonist; the antagonist was the lady's image, or Love itself enthroned in the bosom, and the interior castle became peopled with troubled spirits which sped on mysterious errands, confused by the disputes of the faculties which commanded them.[41]

In this system the lady hardly existed. She was the occasion of all the turmoil, but her appearance was momentary. After the first encounter the lover seldom saw her and could hardly abide her presence when he did, so powerful was her influence. When Beatrice's eyes knew that they were victorious over his reason, Dante tells us, they departed, "taking with them the standards of love," and he never more saw them in their conquering aspect; but, the poet continues, "the image of this lady resides still on the summit of my soul, where Love placed her, who was her guide."[42] This image of the lady was infinitely more cruel than the lady. As personified by the lover, it mocked him brutally for the sufferings it occasioned his soul, whose power it usurped. A lady, conceivably, may feel pity, but an image can feel no pity:

> More beautiful now than ever and more joyful, it seems that she smiles and raises her murderous eyes and cries out against the weeping soul which laments its exile: "Wretch, depart! Out! Away!" So too cries the voice of desire which, as always, makes war against me; but I suffer less from that because my sensuality is much less alive and much closer to the term of its suffering.[43]

Under the influence of the tyrannical image in his heart, the normal functioning of the lover's soul was completely disrupted. The vital spirits no longer attended to their affairs, the soul was driven from its proper seat, all was confusion. The sensitive appetite, no longer obedient to reason, was no longer free.[44] All this took place in a twinkling. Lapo Gianni described the first onslaught of love with a sure eye for the dramatic possibilities of the conceit:

> Within your heart there arose a little spirit which issued from your eyes and came to wound me as I gazed at your lovely face, and it pushed its way through my eyes so rapidly and so savagely that it made my heart and my soul run away—the one had been asleep and the other was terrified—and when they felt it coming so proudly and the blow so strong they feared that death in that moment would exercise its power. But when the soul was reassured, it called to the heart, "Are you dead then, that I don't feel you any longer in your place?" The heart, which had little life left in it, wandering alone and comfortless, almost speechless for trembling, answered: "Oh, soul, help me up and lead me again to the castle of life." And thus together they went to the place whence he had been driven.[45]

It is apparent from descriptions of this sort that the gentle heart was endowed with enormous recuperative powers. It died constantly, yet lived to die another day, passing from *more* to *amore* with the regularity of clockwork. This was theoretically defensible. When the vital spirit, *anima,* was driven from the heart by the fiery spirits which composed the lady's image, the heart was bereft of life, and it died. Such was the normal consequence of the separation of body and spirit. But the interruption was momentary. The lover felt faint, his heart missed a beat, then the spirits surged back and resumed their functions more or less as usual.[46] But since the lady's spirits were now firmly ensconced in the lover's heart, this organ might properly be said to belong henceforth to her. It was in this manner that the poet "lost" his heart.

In the elaboration of these conceits, it must be admitted, the *stilnovisti* used their terms with very little precision. The terms *cor, anima,* and *mente*—heart, soul, and mind—were used with the most varied application. But when we consider that the very considerable perturbations of these faculties described by Lapo Gianni in *Angelica figura* is only an interesting way of saying that the sight of the beautiful lady caused the poet to gasp with admiration, we hardly feel the necessity for a more exact terminology. The important thing was to convey a sense of internal dissension, the disruption of the interior economy which love brought about, and this the incessant bickering of *cor, anima,* and *mente* amply illustrated, whether the terms were used precisely or not.

The case with the spirits is not less confusing to the modern reader, since spirit meant impulse or tendency as well as mind or soul, and the term was also frequently used in its technical sense of inter-substance between soul and body. From the point of view of function, the bodily spirits corresponded to the spirits which moved the cosmic organism, the angelic substances in the sky which visibly radiated light and heat, and which, sending their rays into the souls of men, penetrated them also and moved them. Properly considered, the virtue of the lady in Cavalcanti's *ballata Veggio negli occhi* ascended to the heavens because in the first place it had descended from the heavens. The lady's visible radiance, her beauty, which astonished everyone, was in fact an angelic power. This fact was, of course, not perceptible to the sensitive faculty, which was capable of knowing only appearances, but the rational faculty perceived the truth. It saw the lady as she was, a celestial intelligence sojourning for a time on this sphere. Thus it was that with the sensitive soul the poet loved the lady, but with the rational soul he loved the celestial spirit which reflects and distributes the light of God.[47]

Accordingly, when the poet spoke of his lady as a radiant star —*lucente stella*—he paid her a double compliment. This radiant spirit shone in the corporeal world in the appearance of a woman, sending out of the windows of her soul rays of high potency with which to move the hearts of men. This was a conceit. It meant that the lady was so lovely that all men came under her influence who beheld her. On the higher plane, however, it was manifest that the lady was of the species of the heavenly spirits, moving men's souls upward through beauty. She was a link with heaven, and her influence was of cosmic significance. This was not intended as a conceit. It was advanced as fact. The beauty of the lady whose image perturbed the heart of the poet was literally compounded of celestial light, for the light which glowed in her eyes—her *luci* and *lumi*—was akin to the light which radiated from the star of the third heaven. It was the light of Venus. "Angelic shape newly come from heaven to spread your blessings among men," so begins Lapo Gianni's *canzone*, "the high god of love has placed in you all his powers . . ." [48]

It was small wonder that ladies of such potency should have unusual effect upon the susceptible male. They were, of course, not for everyone. Just as it was necessary to have eyes to perceive their beauty, it was necessary also to possess the requisite psychic endowment to apprehend the quality and meaning of this beauty. Beauty summoned all men; but only to some was given the capacity to heed the summons; and these elect were thereafter undone for the things of this world. They were raised to the skies; but the price was a kind of death. Beauty, the image that glowed in the imagination, might set any brute afire with longing. But the beauty that flamed in the intellect was of another sort, it revealed its provenience; and therefore the susceptible one was struck dumb with terror; he trembled and fainted and hid his head, for he knew that this beauty was a superhuman power, and even as he surrendered, he feared to be overwhelmed by its terrible strength. Such was the destiny of those to whom nature accorded the gentle heart.

It is perhaps for this reason that the stilnovist lover seems infected with a strange hysteria. The troubadour lover was normally timid, and sometimes the lady terrified him, but with the *stilnovisti* all reactions were heightened beyond reason. Cavalcanti wrote:

> She is so noble that I cannot imagine that any man in this world can dare to look at her without first trembling; and I myself would die if I should look at her! [49]

The nature of the phenomenon which the poet described, in fact, made any but a hyperbolic style unsuitable, for the love of a man for a celestial being can hardly be described in normal language. We look in vain in this psychic environment for that *mezura* upon which the troubadour founded his system. The poetry of the *stilnovisti* was not public poetry like that of the troubadours; it was infinitely more exclusive, and it was unnecessary in poetry of so private a nature to promote a purely social ideal. For the chivalric poets, measure was of the essence of love. It was a practical concept, the lover's warranty. For the *stilnovisti,* ostensibly completely self-absorbed, love's pressures were extreme and uncontrollable. Against love, Cavalcanti wrote, neither force nor measure was of avail:

Amor mi sforza,
Contra cui no val forza—ni mesura.[50]

Measure, indeed, had never protected the lover. Even in troubadour theory, it was a protection only for the lady. The consequence of the invasion of the intellect by love was that now not even intellectual love could be said to be under the control of the intellect. To the fever of the flesh succeeded the fever of the mind. The desire for knowledge became a furor attended with all the inconveniences of high-pulsed passion, of which the best and latest example may be found in *Gli eroici furori* of Giordano Bruno. It was perhaps inevitable that the stilnovist poets in their attempt to treat their subject matter with the calm rationality of the philosopher should fall at once into the sphere of the mystic.

In the Franciscan view of the matter, man's highest good was the ecstatic union with God, and love alone was the key to this beatitude. Love was the highest power in the universe. Studies could do no more than to confuse the soul in its longing to unite with the absolute. Even according to the treatise of the neoplatonic Dionysius, a work of compelling influence for the time, it was only in surrendering all knowledge that one arrived at the transcendental ray of divine darkness. The seeds of anti-rationalism were inherent in any philosophic system which emphasized the role of love. The consequence was clearly discernible in the writings of Joachim of Flora, on the one hand, of St. Bonaventure on the other. In his day, Iacopone openly scorned philosophy as a needless confusion, and in his poetry he drew further and further from the restraints of lyrical form until at last—at the other extreme from the precisely ordered art of the troubadours—he gave expression to his passion in incoherent cries.

The *stilnovisti* did not trouble to reconcile the Franciscan and Dominican positions with regard to the primacy of love or knowledge as the way to God. It was no part of their business as poets. Only Dante went so far into theology as to attempt such a synthesis. In the stilnovist lyrics the love of love and the love of knowledge coexisted peacefully. At no time was this poetry free from sensuality. Centuries later, when Michelangelo wrote, "The life of my love is not my heart," he had gone a good distance further along the road to Platonism than any of the *stilnovisti* ever ventured or desired to go.[51] For them the fountain of love was always the heart, its immediate object always a woman.

But the fervor of the intellect was essential to their poetry. In the poetry of the *dolce stil* all things were suffused with *amor*, yet every step in love's progress awakened a flash of intellectual insight, a perception of correspondence. For these poets, the Creator spoke to the intellect in sensual terms only; therefore they understood and communicated largely in terms of analogy and metaphor. Their intuitions were expressed as conceits. They could persuade the mind, but not convince it. In these circumstances a certain display of force was indispensable—the result was the hyperbolic style which is characteristic of their work.

For this style the *stilnovisti* were, of course, indebted to the troubadours, but they found it necessary to go much beyond them. In the poetry of the *dolce stil*, everything is vast in scale and of extraordinary intensity. Cino's lady outshines the sun. Cavalcanti's lady leaves the beholder gasping. Beatrice is a miracle. Crowds gather on the street to gaze upon her when she passes. Her powers are superhuman. Her presence confers goodness. Her greeting is a benediction—the analogy with Christ has been often remarked. At the thought of Beatrice, the poet bathes the earth in tears. When she appears before his eyes his tremors are so great that the very stones of the street invite him to die. Even in heaven the beauty of Beatrice astonishes the angels; it surprises the Lord Himself.[52]

Therefore when one of these ladies dies the event must be

considered a supreme disaster. The troubadours had not scrupled in their dirges to invite whole provinces to mourn. Lanfranc Cigala, for instance, had written of his dead lady:

> Everything that was lovely in the world is dead; what made the heroes valiant, and the poets sing, and all true lovers worthy; the reason why merit was esteemed and why it was worth while striving to become better. Therefore let all men weep, for a thousand years have passed since death committed so great a crime. . . . And now, why does not the whole province die in which once she lived? [53]

This was a relatively restrained expression of grief, a style in which the poet was followed by Marot in his dirge for Louise de Savoie, and by Spenser in his lament for Dido in *The Shepherd's Calendar*. Pons de Capdueil however announced in a *planh* that by "this death the whole world was annihilated." This was the proper style for the stilnovist song of mourning. But while the troubadours' hyperbole might be thought of as mere professional exaggeration, or the result of an excess of grief, the *stilnovisti* had some basis for rationalization. Since, in their view, the radiant lady who sojourned on earth for a time was an organizing principle sent by God Himself, her displacement was certain to bring about important cosmic repercussions. These phenomena might be expected to match the portents that accompanied the deaths of heroes and Caesars, and in some degree they were reminiscent of the upheavals which attended the departure of Christ from this world, more particularly as St. Bernard had depicted them. If the lady was identified with the soul of the world, her passing involved the death of the world, and it took no great stretch of the imagination to go a step further, as Donne was to do in his day, and anatomize the carcase.[54]

The *stilnovisti* felt that they, of all men, were privileged to experience the highest ecstasies and deepest torments of humanity. Words could hardly reach so far as to convey the intensity of their experience. Therefore the sweet style was a tense style; it strained to express the inexpressible. Love, constantly disappointed, constantly weeps in these verses. The lovers seldom smile;

their view of life is tragic. Dante's eyes "desire to die"; Cavalcanti calls himself *l'angoscioso*, the sorrowful one; Cino feels that he looks grim: "I am the visible image of death; my shadow must frighten men." [55]

All the *stilnovisti* pity themselves deeply. Betrayed by the lady's eyes, Dante says, "So greatly do I pity myself that this pity gives me as much pain as my martyrdom." [56] And all arouse pity by their sad aspect, in everyone, that is, but the lady. These lovers sigh constantly, and their sighs dispirit them, for the sigh is an exhalation of the breath of life, it comes from the heart. For this reason, sighs may be wet with tears, since the soul weeps internally, exuding radical moisture. Cavalcanti wrote:

> My sorrowful and fearful soul goes weeping among the sighs which it finds in the heart so that they issue forth bathed in tears.[57]

Moreover, since the sigh is spirit, it can gather and convey intelligence to the heart. In the last sonnet of the *Vita Nuova*, Dante describes the flight of the spirit soaring to seek the heart's desire. The conceit is one of the most beautiful examples of the *dolce stil*; indeed, the poem is one of the supreme examples of poetic imagination, to which translation, even the most artless, can render no service:

> Beyond the sphere which turns most distant, passes the sigh which issues from my heart. A strange intelligence, which Love, weeping, gives it, draws it ever upward. When it has come where it desires to be, it sees there a lady who receives such honor and such light that by her own splendor this pilgrim spirit sees her. It sees her such that when it returns to tell me of her, I do not comprehend, so subtly does it speak to the sorrowing heart which questions it. All I know is that it speaks of that gentle one, because I hear it mention Beatrice often, and that I understand quite well, dear ladies.[58]

In adapting the patterns of troubadour love-poetry to the metaphysics of the schoolmen the *stilnovisti* made a magnificent contribution to Western poetry. But it was a strange world of fantasy that resulted. Apprehended in this way, the world of streets and houses took on the transparency of a dream. Matter was reduced to potency, an unimaginable sea in which forms took shape and vanished in ever-changing flux. In this spirit world the lady of the song all but lost her being; she became an image in the lover's soul, a phantasm more real than its objective counterpart.

The concept of material beauty also suffered a certain change. The lady was beautiful because her soul was beautiful. Her face and its expressions but mirrored the movements of the invisible spirit. Muffled in its noncommittal veil of flesh, the soul was manifested mysteriously as water reveals the passage of the invisible wave. Each movement of the body, a blush, a smile, a glance, represented the action of a special spirit, a *spiritello*,[59] in the service of a greater spirit still, and the sum of all these spirits was the personality, a luminous point in the continuum which connected the meanest entity with the splendor of highest heaven. In love all was spirit:

> A subtle spirit wounds through the eyes which causes a spirit to arise in the soul from which is born a spirit of love such that all other spirits are made gentle through it.
>
> No vile spirit can feel it, such is the power of this spirit! This is the spirit that makes one tremble and the spirit which gives sweetness to the lady.
>
> And afterward from this spirit proceeds another sweet and gentle spirit which is followed by a spirit of mercy, so that from this first spirit spirits rain, and of all the spirits it has the key by virtue of the spirit which sees.[60]

Between the world of partly spiritualized matter and the world of pure spirit, the link was the beauty of woman. The lady's influence, thus conceived, was very great. In the lady's presence all evil thoughts vanished, all offenses were pardoned. She radiated charity and put one in the way of salvation. Through her the action of the play of love was seen to proceed simultaneously on every level from the inmost heart of the lover to the cosmic stage on which was played the universal drama of good and evil. Through her the desire of the lover merged in the longing of the universe for its creator.

The lady of the troubadour song was perfect; and her beauty was such that the true lover strove for self-perfection in order to become worthy of her. But she was entirely of this world. Therefore, for the true lover love was a career, but not a religion. The old genre did not die when the new came in. Cino repeated the true lover's creed exactly as a troubadour would have sung it:

> If I can boast of having become something out of nothing, I thank love for it who, thanks to his mercy and out of his courtesy, so honors me that in my heart he resides and dwells; and if a true boast is no disgrace, I say that of his grace he grants me that I should bring out of my heart the songs I sing, for which reason I am ready to die for his faith. And yet love has given me an even richer gift, for he has given me into the power of such a lady that the sun when she appears is conquered by her radiance, wherefore, since in every land is heard the rumor of her worth, I shall never cease to sing of her.[61]

The transformation of the lady into an angel took place by a natural transition. As early as the time of Guillaume IX, we have seen, the lady of the song was said to have extraordinary powers—she could heal the sick with the joy that emanated from her and this joy kept her lover from growing old. These were perhaps not superhuman traits—it may be that any really desirable girl can do as much—but undeniably they had something about them of the occult. The next step was implied in the lady's traditional perfection. After earthly perfection had reached its highest superlative, the troubadours looked to heaven for suitable comparisons.[62] The lady's exaltation to the heavenly sphere followed as a matter of course.

Long before the *stilnovisti* pre-empted the field, the Notary had made a more or less pious gesture in the necessary direction. Taking his departure from the troubadour stereotype that the true lover would refuse to go to paradise unless his lady were there,

Giacomo indulged a more orthodox wish in a sonnet which really has a charming quality:

> I have set my heart on serving God so that I may go to paradise, to the holy place where I have heard there is every pleasure, sport, and laughter.
>
> Without my lady I should not wish to go there, she of the blonde head and shining face, for without her I should not enjoy myself, being separated from my lady.
>
> But I say this not in the sense that I should wish to commit a sin in that place; all I desire is to look at her fine figure and her lovely face and languorous eyes, for it would give me great delight to contemplate my lady in her glory.[63]

From the wish to contemplate the lady's charms in paradise to the idea that the lady was sent from paradise to delight mortal eyes with the beauty of the other world was no great step. Montanhagol had already taken it. The Sicilian poet Inghilfredi took it in his stride:

> Her wisdom and her sweet language, her beauty and her amorous aspect cause me great torment when I think of them. It is Jesus Christ who conceived her in Paradise; then he made her by clothing an angel with flesh.[64]

The idea that the lady resembled an angel was certainly far from new in the time of Guido Guinizelli. Guittone d'Arezzo himself had anticipated his disciple in this respect in a prose epistle in which was set forth almost everything that the next generation of poets was to say regarding the angelic lady:

> My noble lady, almighty God has put in you such marvelous perfection that in your acts, your words, and all your aspect you seem rather an angel than an earthly creature; so that those who understand best find everything wonderful that they see in you. We were not worthy to find so marvelous and so admirable a creature living among the human generation of this mortal sphere—but, as I think, it pleased God to put you among us to make us marvel, so that we might have a

> mirror in which every worthy lady and every brave man might arrange himself so as to avoid vice and follow virtue.[65]

It was, however, Guinizelli who gave the angelic lady her status in Italian poetry. His *canzone Al cor gentil* was compendious. It organized for the first time in Italian what was essential to the doctrine of true love, brought the whole system up to date, and added the crowning compliment to the lady in an unforgettable figure, vivid and witty. It had important consequences, without doubt, but it cannot be taken seriously as philosophical poetry. It is, after all, an exercise in similitudes which ends in a metaphysical conceit. Yet it was studied, quoted, paraphrased, and commented on as if it were philosophy. For Dante it was the cornerstone of the new style.

Guinizelli's *canzone* begins incisively with the idea that love and the gentle heart are in the relation of act and potency; the one was created for the other:

> Love comes always to the gentle heart
> As a bird seeks the green of the grove;
> Nor did nature make love before the gentle heart,
> Nor the gentle heart before love . . .[66]

To illustrate the working of love upon its proper object, Guinizelli drew upon a familiar fact in the lapidary lore of the time. Certain stones, after being refined alchemically by the rays of the sun, derived their special virtue from being exposed to the radiation of the appropriate star:

> . . . after the sun has drawn out through his strength what is vile in it, the star gives it worth and power. Thus to the heart which is made by nature candid, pure, and gentle, woman like a star brings love.

The similitude is perhaps not entirely successful, but it conveys the idea. The radiant woman ignites that love which is latent in the heart refined by nature. Moreover, this process takes place only in noble natures,

> A depraved nature, with love, acts as water with fire: the cold draws out the heat . . .

This nobility has, of course, nothing to do with birth. It is nature's gift:

> The sun shines full upon the mud all day,
> Mud it remains, nor the sun less splendid.
> The haughty man says: I am gentle by birth;
> He is as mud. The sun is inner worth;
> Regard not whence a man may be descended,
> Nor think that one may gentle be
> According to his ancestry.
> But him whose heart is made, in virtue, tender,
> Nature alone can gentle render:
> Though the ray of the star may not kindle the sea,
> The star loses none of its splendor.

From this consideration of the relation of love and the noble nature of man, Guinizelli passes by a sudden transition to a higher plane. The leap seems brilliant. But it is quite natural, from the viewpoint of the theory of correspondences, to pass from microcosm to macrocosm. The one exactly reflects the other; here the similitude is perfect:

> Upon the Intelligence of the heavens shines God the Creator, brighter than the sun in our eyes, and she who understands the will that commands her from beyond the heavens moves to obey him, turning the sky, and at once achieves the blessed fulfillment of the just God. Thus the lovely lady should make manifest the reality of the gentle desire which shines in her eyes to him who never swerves from obeying her.[67]

Guinizelli did not, like Cavalcanti, reduce the world to a play of spirits moving in a sea of matter. But he was among the first to appreciate the poetic force of the scholastic world-view, and certainly the first to apply it to the troubadour doctrine. God moved the world through love by means of intermediate substances created for the purpose, and these intelligences worked simply by knowing the Creator's will. Gazing upon the light of God, they transmitted it in action, themselves radiant with the light they received. In the same way, the spirits of the human organism moved the flesh in accordance with the soul's desire. When this soul in its turn contemplated a higher spirit, and, through love, obeyed it, it reflected the working of the cosmic mechanism all along the chain of being. The lady who thus dominated the lover's soul might properly be compared with an angelic intelligence. St. Thomas was informative on this point:

> All material bodies are governed by the angels. And this concept is sustained not only by all the doctors of the church, but also by all the philosophers who have admitted the existence of spiritual beings . . . Aristotle supposed that the stars are moved by spiritual substances, but he does not admit that they exercise an immediate influence on inferior bodies . . . but we are forced to recognize that the angels have an immediate power not only over the stars but also over inferior bodies . . . St. Augustine says that every being in this world has an angel who governs him . . .[68]

In his commentary on the *canzone Voi che 'ntendendo,* Dante explained further:

> These movers move by their understanding alone those bodies which are committed to each of them. The most noble celestial sphere, the principle of which is passive, turns because it is touched by the moving force of the angel's thought, and I say touched, not corporeally, but by the contact of a power which is directed upon it.[69]

In this manner, by the influence of her beauty, the radiant lady moved the souls which entered her orbit. She touched them only with her spirit, but it was enough; they were moved. Then, ablaze with desire, pleading for pity, sighing and weeping, and full of the joy of love, they revolved about the angelic figure which controlled them. The lover might believe, of course, as had the troubadours, that this figure was the end of his desire. In his ignorance he might confuse the fleshly envelope with the abiding soul. But the sage lady would be sure to set him right until he came to understand his position clearly. He revolved about her, but she revolved about God, and he had no alternative to following her trajectory.[70]

As the mercy of the lady was of a higher order than the guerdon that he craved, the lover's lot was not a happy one. The angelic lady could be depended on to see that he got nothing save what was good for him. What was good for him was in the moral order, virtue, and in the intellectual order, wisdom. It was not easy to acquire these—nor was it entirely pleasant; the gentle heart had much to endure. To be rescued from the carnality of this world, it was perhaps necessary to go through hell, like Dante, or through the lifelong terrestrial torment of Petrarch; but the sage lady could bring it about if the lover were constant. Then, after instruction and purgation, he might at last perceive the true nature of that light which in the lady's eyes first kindles love:

> We are inflamed by thy gift and are carried upward, we wax hot within and we go on; we ascend the paths that are in our heart and we sing a song of degrees . . .[71]

> Look that you spare not your eyes, they said. We have placed you before the emeralds whence Love once shot his shafts at you. A thousand desires hotter than flame held my eyes bound to the shining eyes which remained forever fixed upon the griffin. As the sun in a mirror, exactly, the twofold beast was blazing within them, now with the attributes of one, now of the other nature.[72]

It is quite probable that Guinizelli did not have in mind so exalted an outcome when he wrote *Al cor gentil,* and that the desire aroused by the lady's splendor bore still a considerable resemblance to troubadour sensuality. The *stilnovisti* never escaped wholly from the flesh. Beatrice reproaches Dante for something of this sort, certainly, in the famous passage in *Purgatorio,* XXXI, 34–63 in which she takes him to task for his inconstancy. At any rate, Guinizelli, in his *canzone,* developed the conceit of the angelic lady only to retract it immediately, reproved for even thinking of such a comparison:

> Lady, God will say to me one day when my soul is before him, "How dared you? You traversed the heavens and came as far as me in order to find in me a similitude of vain love? Truly, to me alone is worship due and to the Queen of this high realm in which no lies are uttered!" I might answer Him then: "She resembled an angel who might be of your kingdom. It was no sin in me to place my love in her." [73]

In this manner Guinizelli turned his philosophic *canzone* into harmless gallantry. It is difficult to believe that there is any question here of a serious retraction or of an earnest reconciliation of earthly and heavenly love. The song is built upon a series of similitudes: love is like a bird, like light, like fire, like a magnet, like the sun. The last figure compares the light in the lady's eyes with the light of God. It is too much; and the poet apologizes gracefully for his daring. *Al cor gentil* goes no further than this.

It would be, of course, a considerable extravagance to affirm seriously that the young married women who aroused the interest of the poets of central Italy were in fact angels, and Guinizelli never went so far. But he trifled with the idea. In the sonnet *I' vo del ver,* he ventured to tinge with religious color the wonderful qualities of the troubadour lady. In another sonnet, *Vedut' ho la lucente stella diana,* he developed the conceit of the angelic lady somewhat further:

> I have seen the bright star of the morning take on a human semblance and give off radiance, as it seems to me, beyond all other beings . . .

This was still the language of compliment. It had so far occurred to no one to take the conceit of the starry lady with any more seriousness than any other figure, and Guittone d'Arezzo lumped the star together with the gem, the flower, and the pomegranate in his list of inept comparisons.[74] The transition from a poetic conceit to a philosophic theory was of course largely a question of emphasis. It is impossible to say how seriously any of the *stilnovisti* intended the angelic lady to be taken, but her poetic utility was immense, and there was a considerable body of dogma to substantiate the conceit once it was seriously advanced. It remained for Cavalcanti to advance it seriously.

Guinizelli had used the idea of the angelic lady as a similitude: the lady resembled an angel. Cavalcanti proposed it as an authentic intuition: the lady whose radiance made one think of a star was in fact a star. As the stars were radiant spirits flaming in the sky, so the angelic spirits embodied on earth could be recognized through the splendor which attended them, and chiefly through the miraculous light that shone in their eyes, the windows of the spirit. In *Veggio negli occhi*, Cavalcanti represents the lady revealed to the intellect in her true light. She is an angel. And if she is an angel, then it becomes possible for her lover to follow her to the very steps of the throne of God.[75]

The effrontery of this proposal is really impressive. Nothing could be further from orthodox ecclesiastical doctrine than the idea that a woman, the traditional source of all temptation, should be an angel of God. It is true that in mystical quarters it was commonly considered necessary to initiate the progress of the soul from the love of the sensual object. "It is by the exterior beauty," Albertus Magnus had written, "that the spirit is led to understand the interior beauty," and St. Bernard had enlarged generally upon this topic. But none of the doctors of the church had any idea of involving the female form in the ladder which led to heaven. It was perhaps necessary for man in the confused state of his soul to take the first steps upward from the carnal level, but it was not reasonable to go down in order to ascend.[76]

The line which divided love, even the truest, from charity had aways been jealously guarded, and the singular asperity with which Matfré Ermengaud and Andreas Capellanus anathematized the subject of their treatises indicates how completely unacceptable the doctrines of true love were from the standpoint of religion. But there was a loophole in the wall which divided the one love from the other. As St. Augustine had indicated, love and charity had a common basis. Charity was inescapable in the universe, and the difference between the one and the other love was simply a question of the ultimate object of desire. If woman was loved for her own sake, this passion was reprehensible; but if she were loved for the sake of God, this love was charity.[77]

In Augustine's view it was not irrational to use the things of this world so that "through what is material and temporal we may seize what is spiritual and eternal." But it was not practical to rest in and enjoy these things lest we "stop by the way and place our hope of beatitude in man rather than in the angel." [78] Thus the clerical objection to true love was put on practical grounds —this love stopped short of its proper object. However valuable ethically the lady might appear as a guide to virtue, she remained an obstacle to salvation.

In transforming the object of true love from a lady into an angel, the *stilnovisti* took the shortest way from love to charity, but the issue became confused. There was no precedent, even among the mystical writers, for singing songs of true love to angels. Latin love-songs of some fervency had been written, it was true, by the clerks of the school of Angers—Marbodius, Hildebert, Baudry de Bourgeuil—in the time of Guillaume IX, to the great ladies of Normandy.[79] But these songs had enjoyed little currency, and in any case they were addressed to ladies whose power was strictly of this world. The stilnovist poets were not clerks. They were not mystics, and they do not appear to have been people of more than ordinary piety. Cavalcanti was reputed an atheist. There was not the slightest reason to suppose that the conceit of the angelic lady could possibly recommend itself in clerical quarters.

Nevertheless the idea that supernatural beings of great beauty lived and moved upon the earth could not be summarily dismissed. The fact that on at least one occasion the angels of God had been amorously involved with the human race was handed down on the highest authority.[80] Augustine had not doubted that the angels who appeared to Abraham were of solid construction,[81] and St. Thomas took the view that angels who visit the earth take on human bodies. The influence of angels on the affairs of this world was also not in doubt. In the opinion of St. Thomas the angels enlightened men not only as to what they should believe, but also as to what they should do.[82]

The idea that the beautiful lady to whom the poet directed his worship was a messenger from heaven thus derived a certain cogency, but the lady became more enigmatic than ever. It is, of course, frivolous to question whether or not these young men thought they were really in love with angels. The world of stilnovist song was even more of a dream world than the world created by the troubadours. For literary purposes it was quite enough that the lover in the song should think he was in love with an angel. It is not astonishing that the new poetry aroused ridicule on the part of those who continued to practice the older style. The character-type had changed too radically to pass unchallenged. The protagonist of the troubadour song was a knight in love with a lady. The protagonist of the stilnovist song was a young scholar in love with a star.

For a personage thus conceived, love was, as always, a process of education; but the course of study was advanced: the lover began to understand the reasons for love's torment. Cino da Pistoia wrote in one of the *cor-anima-mente* sonnets:

> The intellect of love which alone I possess has so accurately depicted this gentle lady to my mind that I can see her, though she is far away, and yet take comfort;
>
> So that for a space my dead heart rests from weeping, while my sorrowful soul sees her, inwardly, so beautiful that it confesses that what from the viewpoint of pity is wrong may perhaps be right after all.
>
> Thus I am made to change opinion and I am often turned from my first belief by this gentle and high intelligence in which shines the divinity of love, shed upon me through the supreme beauty of this lady of so great worth.[83]

In the phrase, intellect of love—Dante's phrase is intelligence of love—was suggested that essential relation between the heart and the mind, the unity of the sensitive and rational souls, which made it possible for the desire of the senses to be elevated into an intellectual aspiration. Sensual love was a property of the sensitive soul. It could never be entirely eradicated while life endured. But in those who had "intelligence of love," it could be understood and in some degree controlled. In those of the gentle heart, love was an intuition of the good. It was through the desire of what was beautiful that one arrived at what was good: at the summit of the intellectual scale the *summum pulchrum* and the *summum bonum* were seen to be the same. But the lover received the ray of the third heaven through the eyes of the beloved lady first of all in his heart—it was there that he was chiefly susceptible. It was only secondarily that the influence of the lady was exerted in his mind. So long as the angelic lady remained in the flesh, therefore, the quality of the desire she evoked remained complex and equivocal, for these earthbound stars had bodies which, unlike the heavenly bodies, aroused concupiscence. It was only when the angel was distant or, better still, dead, that stilnovist love could be purified of its carnal component. And even then it was possible, as Petrarch was to demonstrate at length, to love the spirit carnally.

It was at this point, midway between earth and heaven, that stilnovist love was fixed, precisely reflecting the human condition. Between the love of the flesh and the love of the spirit the gentle heart ceaselessly vibrated, and this vibration was the motor of the poetry of the gentle heart. Whatever else it might be, the stilnovist poetry was the record of an authentic psychic conflict; for this reason, doubtless, it remains to this day viable, modern, and essentially comprehensible. No considerable body of poetry has so intensely concentrated the torment of the human spirit.

For, remarkably introverted and self-centered as they were, these poets were yet profoundly conscious of the beauty of the outer world. Dante constantly astonishes the reader with the sharpness of his observation. Cavalcanti, in one of the finest sonnets of the period, compares the beauty of the world with that of the lady in a series of comparisons which shows how well he loved that world which had to be renounced for love:

Beauty of woman of noble heart, and armed knights of gentle breeding, birds singing, and talk of love, brave ships running swiftly on the sea,

Soft breezes at the break of dawn, and white snow falling in the still air, green river banks, and fields of flowers, jewels of gold and silver, and azure ornaments,

These the beauty and the nobility of my lady and her gentle heart so far surpass that they seem base to the beholder,

So far she exceeds all other beauty as the heavens exceed the earth; good comes soon to one of such nature.[84]

For these young men, deeply involved in the political storms which rocked central Italy in their day, the beauty of woman was doubtless a refuge. It was also a prison. The yoke of love, as they imagined it, was calculated to weigh much more heavily upon them than that assumed by the troubadours. In the chivalric tradition the lover preserved at least some part of his manhood, but the stilnovist lover condemned himself to complete passivity with regard to the angelic lady, and he resented his position even more than the troubadour, since he had no objective guerdon for which to hope. The tension between the external world and the narrow world of fantasy to which the lover retreated may be sensed in all the poetry of this school. Almost all the stilnovist songs include a protest, and in many ways we are made aware of a mood that is not quite idealistic. Cino, for example, wrote in a *canzone:*

As I certainly believe, God selected you from among the most beautiful of his angels and, in order to create a marvelous thing, He caused you to assume the human condition: so sovereign and noble a creature you are that the world owes its joyous state only to the presence among us of your lovely face.

Lady, by God, consider: if He made you so marvelous and so wonderfully pleasing it was so that in seeing you men

> should praise Him; it was for this that He gave you beauty, that you should make manifest His supreme power.
>
> Therefore, let it not displease you if I gaze fixedly at your wonderful face which has wounded my heart but which lightens all my heavy pain; certainly God did not make you in order that your beauty might be the death of anyone.[85]

This is, perhaps, pious language, but the manner is certainly reminiscent of Andreas' manual of seduction. The lover in Cino's *canzone* is not only impudent, he is gallant. He brings to the conquest of heavenly beauty, somewhat to our astonishment, the bantering tone of the man about town; he seems experienced. But it was precisely of the essence of stilnovist love that it was dual in its mode and its tendency.

In the *dolce stil*, the lover is always conscious of the duality of his nature. He is on intimate terms with his inner mechanisms and follows their workings with interest. He knows that the levels of the soul are absolutely distinguishable, but that the soul is one. It has a faculty that is involved with the flesh, and another that is not, but the two are inextricable; so long as we live there is no way of quite detaching the one from the other.

Consequently, the debate of the heart and the mind was inescapable, so too was the lover's anguish. Love was the heart's poor intellect by which it strove, confusedly and blindly, to reach its good. The heart was aroused by the beauty of the flesh just as the intellect was aroused by the beauty of the immaterial form, the idea. The external world was in the same relation to both faculties—the image which set the heart racing with desire set the mind ablaze with wonder. On all levels love groped in darkness toward the star whose splendor it apprehended as it could.

Torn in this manner, the lover was seldom well; no earthly guerdon could appease his torment. But his illness was the promise of his salvation, and the nobility of the gentle heart was revealed precisely in this spiritual malaise which set off love's elect from the rest of mankind. The lover was always pale and always melancholy. Typically, he was depicted in mid-career along the scale of love, loath to relinquish the attraction of the flesh, yet striving mightily toward the things of the spirit. The stilnovist songs, and after them many of the Petrarchan sonnet-sequences, were the record of the joy and the agony of this effort, but more of its agony than of its joy.

This record was too often set forth in terms of the ponderous rhetorical apparatus inherited from the troubadours, the accumulation of centuries, for the stilnovist insisted on carrying all his baggage up the ladder with him. Among the *stilnovisti*, aside from Dante and Cavalcanti, only Dino Frescobaldi showed originality in the choice of figures, and his are the most strained and hyperbolic of all. In him the conflict—*questa spietata guerra e faticosa* —seems sharpest, the tyranny of love most cruel:

> A high star, of such extraordinary beauty that its light takes away the shadow cast by the sun, shines in the heaven of love with such power that it enraptures me with its brilliance.
>
> And now it becomes so fierce, as it sees how its rays pierce my heart, that it takes with those rays which it induces from above, the highest place in the firmament,
>
> And, in the guise of a woman, this wonderful star makes it appear that it displeases her that I should live, and in her disdain she too has arisen to the zenith.
>
> Love, which speaks to me in my mind, makes arrows out of her brilliance and a target of the little life that is left me.[86]

In Frescobaldi's conceit, out of the image of the lady is born the she-wolf of desire. The lady, of course, is blameless. It is our unfortunate nature which makes love so cruel a tyrant. The fierceness of desire, constantly augmented by the spirits that emanate from the angelic creature, results in a new creature of the spirit, a monster which ravages the lover's heart:

> Lady, from your eyes, it seems, there moves a ray which enters into my soul, and when it is there, it seems that often it passes into the desire which it finds there.

> From this union there appears in my soul a wondrous figure which becomes a she-wolf and finds itself powerful and rules so cruelly that it seems that every torment comes from it to my heart.[87]

But Frescobaldi could depict also a softer and gentler figure of the order of Dante's Pargoletta, neither the devouring beast of the heart nor the angel which glimmers in the mind, but a figure with the innocence of a beautiful child:

> . . . a lady of joyous youth who gives forth the light of her beauty softly as the morning star or the pearl. With her hands this one places in my heart a little, gentle soft spirit which there assumes the sovereignty of love.[88]

On this level, a measure of sanity could be found. It was not necessary, after all, for the star to devastate the lover with its ray. The light from the third heaven could guide one gently and sweetly and, in Frescobaldi's opinion, this was the true way of love:

> This highest star which is seen in its splendor nevermore abandons me: He gave her to me who from his heaven grants me every grace that my intellect requires. And the wondrous dart which he bears in his hand gives sweetness to her who is concerned with me. Love knows that in no other way was man subjected in the past, or now, or ever.[89]

The *stilnovisti* carried the conceit of the angelic lady no further than this. The next step was in the direction of allegory. In the *Convivio,* Dante set forth the method whereby a love-lyric could be given through symbolism a succession of meanings. In time the allegorical method of the *Convivio* would result in a flood of *trattati d'amore* of the order of Lorenzo de' Medici's *Commento* and *Gli eroici furori* of Giordano Bruno, but as yet the new style had nothing to do with the symbolic method. It merely provided the material from which a *sovrasenso* could be extracted.

The next step, obviously, would involve a heavy investment in scholastic learning. Cavalcanti died young; neither he nor any of his fellows developed the ideas of the new poetry into a system. It remained for Dante to devise a compliment to a woman's eyes in which was involved all the history of the world and the hope of mankind. The prelude to this crowning achievement in the *Commedia* was the *Vita Nuova.*

NEW LIFE

The action of the *Vita Nuova* developed as naturally out of the songs of the *dolce stil* as the drama of true love out of the troubadour *chansons.* We have no difficulty in identifying the plot of Dante's early masterpiece. It is the old story, adapted conformably with the new setting and the new age in which it was rooted.

The *Vita Nuova* reflects in detail the changes which had come over the chivalric tradition in its process of naturalization in the Italian cities. It is urban in its environment and bourgeois in its tone. In its breadth of action it is narrow, but far deeper and higher in its spiritual scope than its Provençal counterpart, and infinitely more imaginative, occult, and mysterious. As narrative, unquestionably, the prose is somewhat static and uncertain; the work belongs principally to the lyric genre. Its affinities are with the introspective novel or the bourgeois tragedy, certainly not with chivalric romance. If we think of the narrative possibilities of the troubadour fantasy of true love—the story of Cabestanh, for example, or the story of Bertran de Born—the story of Beatrice seems almost too simple to be useful. Yet in its basic outline the story is the same as that of all other stories of true love, and the characters are the same. Somewhere in Dante's story the *gilos* exists, although he plays no part in the action and is never mentioned, and because of him and the ever-present *losengiers—maldicenti,* Cino calls them—the action proceeds in mystery, insofar as it may be said to proceed at all.

The figures which so strangely people the *Vita Nuova* doubtless inhabited all the poetry of the *dolce stil,* but it is rarely that we are made aware of any outward reality in these songs, and we do not observe them. It is in the *razos*—the *ragioni*—of Dante's book that the material action takes place. The songs around which the narrative is arranged have no action; they differ in no way—save perhaps in quality—from the *sonetti, ballate,* and *canzoni* of the other writers of this school. Even in Dante's *ragioni,* the realistic touches are few. The story which binds the songs together gives rather the illusion than the reality of a true and intense experience.

Out of the songs of the *Vita Nuova* Dante developed a psychic drama which appears, indeed, to have consequences on every plane save that of material reality. From the microcosmic standpoint the love which is the subject of the work is treated as a perturbation of the soul which ends in spiritual illumination. As we have seen, this was essential in the new style. In its macrocosmic aspect, this love is an aspiration of universal magnitude which involves in the *amours* of a Florentine young man, God Himself, the angelic host, the saints, the calendar, and the entire cosmic mechanism. Played on this scale, the plot of love's drama no longer has to do with the more or less comprehensible efforts of a young lover to engage the interest of a haughty lady in despite of her husband and the surrounding busybodies. It becomes a play of dreams and spirits, of fleeting contacts of unutterable significance, visions and premonitions of disaster, symbols and portents of occult character—a mystical experience of great depth and moment. The relation of the *Vita Nuova* to the rest of the literature of the new style seems unequivocal. It made explicit, rationalized, and interpreted, insofar as it was possible, in a more or less orderly narrative sequence what was already intrinsic and implicit in the stilnovist poetry up to the period of its composition. It is a synthesis and an epitome, not an innovation.

As a record of the ascent of the spirit through love, it is true, the *Vita Nuova* went no further than the initial stages. It is in the *Convivio* that Dante recorded the necessary preparations, and in the *Comedy,* the actual adventure of the soul. *The Vita Nuova,* however, laid the substantial groundwork for the *Comedy.* It preceded it as Lady Vanna precedes Lady Beatrice, and perhaps at no greater distance, for Dante was certainly of mature years when he put this work together, and the final prose indicates that he was already thinking of the greater work.

But while it seems quite clear that the one work grew out of the other, Dante's two masterpieces belong to entirely different levels of poetic development, just as the love which each work celebrates is in a different stage of evolution. Love appears in the *Vita Nuova* simultaneously with the first appearance of "the glorious lady of my mind who was called Beatrice by many who knew not how she was called," and then and there takes up its residence in the poet's soul.[1] The final wish of the poet is addressed to Love, "the Lord of Courtesy," that it may please him to let his soul see the glory of his lady who now gazes gloriously into the face of God.[2] Between these two stages is unfolded the story of the carnal love of Beatrice.

The *Vita Nuova* records the adventure of the heart. The *Comedy* records the voyage of the soul. Heart and soul are, indeed, present in both ventures, but in different emphasis. In the *Vita Nuova* the willing spirit goes as far as the heart can send it. The sigh with which the heart explores the reaches of heaven in search of its beloved proceeds from the heart and returns to the heart, a spirit bearing incomprehensible tidings. But the *Comedy* is the adventure of the highest soul, the intellect, and, led by beauty, it reaches beyond the stars, in knowledge more and more precise, as far as thought can reach.

The *Vita Nuova* describes the first movements of that love which seeks the stars. It was normal that this love should see heaven first of all in the sparkle of a woman's eyes. Only when this light had failed did Love cause the gaze of the poet to turn upward where the true stars have their being. Before the death of Beatrice there had been some premonitions, but it was only when she was dead that the intellect came truly into play in the desperate effort to comprehend, and now there began for the lover another story and another life. The *Vita Nuova* has really only two phases. They are both governed by the same love—the love of the living woman and the love of the dead, the love of the spirit in the body and the love of the bodiless spirit. The intellect is deeply concerned in this love, which possesses all of the soul; but, even in its second phase, it is still, in St. Bernard's words, the love of the spirit according to the flesh. It is only in the *Paradiso,* in the last cantos, that the poet achieves the love of the spirit according to the spirit.

The term *Vita Nuova* was left ambiguous, like so many other things in this cryptic work. Very likely the poet himself was unwilling to be limited with regard to its meaning, and no one has since succeeded in defining what Dante left indefinite. The poet informs us in the opening lines that there is a chapter-heading in the book of his memory—if indeed *mente* in this place means memory and not mind or soul—a Latin rubric which reads *Incipit vita nova.* When Dante wrote these lines, he had, conceivably, other chapters in mind also; at any rate, in his later works, he referred to this as his *Vita Nuova,*[3] and the work took on an independence which perhaps it was not at first intended to have.

At this time *nuovo* in Italian meant young, strange, wonderful, early, beautiful, rare and nine, as well as new, and the *stilnovisti* used it in all of these senses. The possibilities for rhetorical equivocation were therefore endless. *Vita Nuova* as a title really tickled the mind; it had precisely the kind of ambiguity which suited the closed style in which much of this work is couched. The work dealt with the poet's early life, his youth, an extraordinary youth ruled by an extraordinary love; a period spent in the contemplation of a miracle of feminine beauty the earthly manifestations of which occurred in a periodicity of nine, the number of perfection, yet not so perfect a number as the divine number, the decad. The title, however, lent itself to a more deeply pious connotation since, after the time of Augustine, new life was often used to signify the life of the spirit regenerated in Christ, and Dante himself made an analogy between Beatrice and Christ in the *Vita Nuova.*[4]

To the love-theory of the *dolce stil,* the *Vita Nuova* added only one idea that was new—the love of the disembodied spirit. This idea was largely developed in the prose. The poetry summed up the *dolce stil* authoritatively both in substance and in form. The songs and sonnets which Dante arranged for this work represented pretty well the entire range of the new poetry, from the merest gallantry to the ultimate intuition of divine love. As they are evidently pieces written at various times over a considerable period, they have no intrinsic principle of sequence, and fall chiefly into two categories, songs written to a living lady, and songs which lament her death. It is by no means certain that any of these songs was written especially for the *Vita Nuova*, though it seems quite probable that a few were written to round out the poetic frame of the work. It is the prose which gives narrative sequence to these songs, marshals them in a meaningful pattern, and in a sense re-writes them in the service of a unified concept.

The more closely we read the songs of the stilnovist canon, the more obvious it becomes that there is nothing absolutely new in the *Vita Nuova* except the scheme itself. All the poetic materials can be identified without difficulty in the work of Dante's contemporaries or predecessors. The lady is a miracle, an angel from heaven who is awaited in heaven; her beauty dazzles the world; her salutation is a benediction; her death a public calamity and the occasion of universal mourning—by this time these were all well-established elements of amatory poetry. In the same way the poet's timidity, his inner torment, his relations with the god of love, his visions, his intuitions, his sorrow and his joys are familiar themes; their novelty lies only in the skill with which they are developed poetically. The verse exemplifies most of the poetic modes that were current at the time in Dante's circle—the song of praise, the complaint, the plea for pity, the reproach, the excuse, the vision, the *planh*, together with some didactic forms which do not have to do directly with courtship.

The prose narrative is a work of art of the highest poetic value. In themselves, the songs are tolerably simple and clear, but the narrative develops to the full the visionary quality which distinguishes the *dolce stil*. By means of the prose the songs are set in a strange world in which personages, symbols, and events occur and recur as in a dream. The difference between this prose and the *razos* of the troubadours is very marked. The troubadours employed an objective technique in the narratives with which they "explained" the songs in their anthologies; it is chiefly in the songs themselves that we find the subjective element. Since Dante was explaining his own songs, his *ragioni* have an intimate and personal character which is foreign to the troubadour songbooks, and the result is an integrated work of "autobiographical" character, quite unlike anything which had been written in the lyric tradition up to that time.

Central in the plan of the *Vita Nuova* is the conception of the principal character, the lover. He is nameless, of course, and unlocalized, but the year of his birth is established with precision.[5] He speaks in verse in the first person, as all lovers do in the forms related to the *canso*, but he speaks in the first person in prose as well, so that the temptation is irresistible to identify the character and the author, and to assume that the extraordinary spiritual happenings which the *Vita Nuova* relates really took place more or less as they were set forth. It would be impertinent at this stage of the discussion to suggest that the *Vita Nuova* is obviously a work of the imagination, a sort of novel like *Fiammetta,* were it not that ever since Boccaccio wrote his life of Dante, in 1364, it has been traditional to ascribe a certain historicity to these events and to assume that the daughter of that Folco Portinari who died on 31 December, 1289, the Bice Portinari who married Simone de' Bardi, was in fact identical with the Bice of the sonnet *I mi sentii svegliar* and the Beatrice of the *Vita Nuova.* Perhaps she was. But the fact is that the tradition which connects the glorious Beatrice, the "blessing of Florence," with the wife of a Florentine merchant is based chiefly on the testimony of a "trustworthy person" almost three-quarters of a century after the event; and, from a scholarly point of view, this is disturbing. From every other standpoint, the tradition is as strong as steel. Whatever validity it may have as fact, its validity as legend is beyond discussion.

But whatever the relation may have been between Dante and the daughter of Folco Portinari, it is clear that the Beatrice of the *Vita Nuova* is not a woman but a poetic concept, marking a stage of that spiritual evolution which the *stilnovisti* so often and so carefully described. With this idealized Beatrice, the daughter of Folco would have had in any case only the remotest connection. In the same way the gentle and timid youth, of whose exterior semblance we catch an occasional glimpse as he pauses in the street to speak respectfully to a group of ladies or sits bemused drawing pictures of angels, can hardly be confused with the stern figure which Boccaccio drew. Whatever his connection with Dante, the lover of the *Vita Nuova* is a poetic construction of more or less conventional cut, exactly as is Beatrice. Both are personages designed to play a certain action in a drama conceived according to the patterns of the stilnovist lyric, and this is their principal reality. Much the same may be said of Petrarch's Laura, and, in general, of all the ladies who in the following years became the subject of the Renaissance lyric sequences of love.

In the *Vita Nuova* the lover has, naturally, more solidity as a character than the lady. Like almost all the troubadour ladies, Beatrice is depicted in terms of the ideal. She has little to distinguish her as an individual; we know only that she was of the color of pearl, perfect and pitiless. The lover, as always, is much more interested in himself than in the lady. He describes his comings and goings with some realism, and his inner life in great detail. Nevertheless this personage, while individualized in some degree, is at bottom an archetype like the other; both may be found in almost any song of the *dolce stil* pretty much as Dante portrays them, the lady remote and coolly radiant, the lover troubled and feverish. They are reciprocally conceived counterparts in the relation of form and potency: the one is made for the other as love for the gentle heart.

As these characters rarely meet, only that action which takes place within the lover's soul may be called truly dramatic. The thread of the narrative, as Dante devised it, involves mainly three stages, all of them traditionally the subject of poetry—the enamorment and courtship; the death of the lady; and its sequel—the lover's temporary infidelity and his return to the true way of love. These phases of the story are developed largely in the prose. It seems obvious that a good many of the poems would be equally appropriate to one or another section of the narrative.

The numerological system by which Dante governed the arrangement of the songs among the prose *ragioni* is chiefly interesting because of the manner in which it points the stages of the narrative. The system is not immediately apparent to the reader, and the numerological schemes of such later sequences as Scève's *Delie* would seem to derive rather from the more obvious number symbolism of the *Comedy* than from the *Vita Nuova.* The sections of the *Vita Nuova* were, indeed, not numbered by the author but by his editors, and it was not until the time of Norton that the numerology of the *Vita Nuova* became the subject of close study.

By the time of Dante, numerology had long aroused interest in scholastic circles. In the wake of the Pythagorean traditions which identified form with number, Augustine had written, "Divine wisdom is seen in the numbers impressed on all things,"[6] and after him various patristic writers had written on the properties and virtues of certain numbers; but the church had no abiding interest in this type of symbolism, and the subject never acquired any degree of precision. Nevertheless, the Creator was believed to have apportioned the rhythms and quantities of the universe according to the virtues of numbers, and Dante also proportioned his work in accordance with a hidden numerological principle. This principle, symbolically meaningful, served also an artistic purpose. It was a principle of design and imposed upon the units of the work an extrinsic order which added yet another dimension of significance.

For the formal principle of the *Vita Nuova,* Dante chose the number nine. As he tells us in *Vita Nuova* XXIX, this number was closely associated with Beatrice because the nine spheres of heaven were perfectly related at the moment of her generation, and for this and other reasons she was herself a nine, a miracle, *cosa nova.* All manifestations of Beatrice in the *New Life* of Dante are conformable, or are made conformable, with the number nine. Presumably the perfect life of Beatrice was completely expressed in harmonies of nine, but all we know of it is her comings and goings in the life of Dante, both in the flesh and in the three visions which center upon her, so that the *Vita Nuova* is in reality Dante's life of nine, his life, so to speak, of Beatrice.

The consequence of this numerological conception is to give a cosmic dimension to the entire Dante-Beatrice relationship, every event of which is precisely timed in accordance with a supernatural schedule in which the stars themselves are concerned. Thus the life of Dante-and-Beatrice is conceived of as having design, rhythm, and purpose, like a poem, and the *Vita Nuova* is the poet's transcription of a love-poem composed by no less a poet than God Himself.[7]

Dante's transcription, however, comes somewhat short of perfection. The numerical basis of the *Comedy* is three, and it is all marvelously built of threes. But the *Vita Nuova* was a compilation. It naturally offered a certain resistance to the superposed design, and the result is a little uncertain. For the poetry, apparently, ten and not nine is the principle of arrangement. There are three decads of poems and a final sonnet: three and one, a trinity. Of Beatrice's number nine, we are constantly reminded in the prose, and this number vibrates curiously with the poetic arrangement in tens. The poems themselves have still another principle of order. They are founded in the main on the fourteen-line stanza, all the sonnets and the three *canzoni.*

The distribution of the poems among the prose *ragioni* is carefully ordered so as to point the three stages of the love-story, of which the first has to do with earthly love, the second with death, and the third with the love of the spirit. The adult Beatrice first appears and speaks in *Vita Nuova* III. The consequence is the first vision of Love, and this event is at once announced in a sonnet addressed to the *fedeli d'amore,* the brotherhood of the gentle heart. In the tenth section the *gentilissima* expresses her dislike for the ways of *fin amor* by withholding her salutation. This motivates a *ballata* of apology, an apology which is also a declaration of love. In the fourteenth section, the lover is reduced to tears by Beatrice's mockery, her *gabbo,* and some sections later he resolves henceforth to write only in praise of Beatrice, and no longer about himself. He thus enters upon a "new and more noble matter." The first example of his new matter is the *canzone* *Donne ch'avete,* in which the death of Beatrice is foreshadowed, and this song initiates the second decad of poems.

Donne ch'avete, to which Dante gave the honor of representing the sweet new style in *Purgatorio* XXVI, is in fact a compendium of all that is most characteristic of the stilnovist manner. The lady of the song is not said to be an angel, it is true. But her soul shines on earth so brightly that it is visible in heaven, which would be perfect if she were there; her power is such that any woman appears noble who accompanies her; in her presence Love chills all evil thoughts; whoever can bear to look at her face becomes at once noble or else dies; whoever receives her greeting is filled with peace and forgets all wrongs; and God has granted that whoever speaks with her cannot come to a bad end. This lady is of the color of the pearl, a masterpiece of nature; it is by her pattern that beauty is measured, and from her eyes move flaming spirits of love which reach the hearts of all who gaze upon her. Nothing more appropriate could have been selected to exemplify the new style, and if this is what Dante set down at Love's dictation, we can only marvel at Love's thoroughness. He covered the ground.

Nevertheless there is in *Donne ch'avete* an unmistakable feeling of grandeur, and if we look closely it becomes evident that it centers upon the second strophe. Here we feel the pure strong thrust of the imagination, and the song gains suddenly a higher level:

> An angel cries out in the divine Intelligence and says: "Lord, in the world is seen a marvel in the act which proceeds from a soul which gleams as far as here." Heaven, which has no defect save the lack of her, asks her of its Lord, and all the saints implore this favor. Only Pity takes our part, for God says, and it is of my lady that he means to speak: "My beloved ones, now suffer in peace that the lady of your hope may dwell for as long as it may please me down yonder where there is one who expects to lose her, and who will say in hell: "O ye ill-fated! I have seen the hope of the blessed in heaven."

In these lines one may see, as one chooses, a prophecy of the *Comedy*,[8] or simply a compliment of more than ordinary magnificence. In either case this remarkable conceit, which ranges over the entire universe, taking hell, earth, heaven, and God

Himself to witness the wonder of the lady, is of the very essence of the new style. Its pedantry makes us smile—the angel speaks to the Almighty as if He were in a classroom. Yet the audacity of the conception makes us marvel. This, too, is characteristic of the new style. It has scale.

Ten sections later, in the twenty-eighth chapter of the *Vita Nuova,* occurs the death of the most gentle lady, and the *canzone Li occhi dolenti* (Section XXXI) initiates the third decad of poems. It is in the thirty-fifth section that the other gentle lady distracts the poet from his devotion to the ideal Beatrice; but in the thirty-ninth section, the vision of the beatified Beatrice dressed in her first colors rescues him from his dilemma, and he determines henceforth to be faithful to this love alone. He is then rewarded with the final and indescribable vision which ends the last decad.

From every point of view, artistic, conceptual, and numerical, the entire design is composed around the *canzone Donna pietosa,* in which for the second time the death of Beatrice is foreshadowed. This song, by any reckoning, occupies the precise center of the composition. It is the fifth poem of the second decad, and it occupies a central position between the other two *canzoni* of the *Vita Nuova,* the first of which looks forward to the death of Beatrice and the second of which, *Li occhi dolenti,* looks back upon it. *Donna pietosa* has eighty-four lines. Its exact midpoint is the line in which the death of Dante himself is foreseen:

> Visi di donne m'apparve crucciati
> Che mi dicean pur: Morra' ti, morra' ti.[9]

The *New Life* therefore centers upon death.

The true beginning of the new life is death, to which love is the prelude—this is the "meaning" of the *Vita Nuova.* It is the sight of Beatrice as an infant angel which first arouses love in the poet, and the vision of this resplendent child clothed in crimson, the color of charity, recalls him in the end to that love which is the earnest of his beatitude. Between the two visions is comprehended the brief life of Beatrice on earth, the prelude to the eternity of Beatrice in heaven. It is love which puts Dante in the way of salvation. It is death which rescues him from the folly of sensual desire. Death shows him the way that leads from the vanity of *fin amor* to that intellectual love of beauty, the ultimate object of which is God. In the *Vita Nuova* this process is not completed. It is begun. And therefore the rubric with which the book begins very properly reads: *Incipit vita nova.*

Thus the "vain imagining" of Dante in the *canzone Donna pietosa*, when, after many signs and portents, he sees his lady's soul borne aloft by angels singing Hosanna, does not depress him. The dream of death, on the contrary, brings him joy and peace. It is in this mood that he sees his lady, still alive and healthy, pass by in the street, preceded by her friend Vanna, Cavalcanti's lady, and it occurs to him that Vanna in more than one sense is the precursor of Beatrice.[10]

There is not much difference in the first part of the *Vita Nuova* between Beatrice and the lady Vanna whom Cavalcanti had created in his love-songs. It is only after the vision of death in *Donna pietosa* that the character of love is changed for Dante. His conversion is accomplished through the simplest and most traditional means; it is classic. During a period of illness, he experiences the sudden realization that Beatrice is mortal and will die, and with that it comes to him that he too will die one day. With this vivid realization of death comes a crucial change in his attitude toward Beatrice. From this point on, Beatrice begins to teach him the lesson which is summed up for him ultimately at the gates of paradise:

> Never did nature and art present to you any pleasure so great as the fair members in which I was enclosed and which are now scattered in dust,
>
> And if the highest pleasure thus failed you by my death, what mortal thing ought then to have drawn you to desire it?
>
> Truly, at the first arrow of deceitful things, you should have risen up after me who was such no longer.[11]

In Cavalcanti's conception, love was never free of the sensual appetite. Therefore in *Donna mi prega* love is said to be kindled by a dark ray from Mars, for love of this sort overshadows the intellect and arouses the endless conflict of mind and heart. This conflict Dante resolved in the death of the earthly Beatrice. In dying, Beatrice kindled a beacon in the sky toward which a more rational desire than sensual love could rise, and thus she initiated that movement of the soul which was to end, for Dante, only in the presence of the Heavenly Father. The lover of Vanna was earthbound, sad and restless. But the beauty of Beatrice led her lover first to the summit of human goodness, thence through knowledge to that place where the soul at last comes to rest.

The idea that man could ascend to God in this manner through the pure love of a woman had occurred in turn to Guinizelli and to Cavalcanti, but neither had devised the means—probably because, bound as they were to the troubadour tradition, they were unwilling to relinquish the lover's guerdon. For Dante the guerdon was not essential; at the end of the first decad of poems in the *Vita Nuova,* he put it from his mind.[12] His guerdon was in any case no more than Beatrice's salutation. This was, he tells us, his only happiness; and in giving it up he found another happiness within himself, the joy of devoting himself to her praise. Many troubadours, as we have seen, had gone over this ground in the past; what was new was that for Dante not only the guerdon but the lady herself was expendable. *Donne ch'avete* therefore involves a declaration of independence from the tyranny of sensual love, even the purest. The lady shone in this world with celestial light; she was irresistible, it was true, but only for a time. It was logical therefore to worship the source rather than the mirror of this splendor. This would perhaps not be possible without aid from above, but this aid was immediately forthcoming. Indeed, it was Beatrice herself who, by denying Amor, indicated the way of charity.[13]

We are thus able to understand why, immediately after the vision of death in the *Vita Nuova,* Dante interpolated the episode of Vanna and Beatrice and the sonnet *I mi sentii svegliar* together with the digression explaining why Vanna was called Primavera.[14] It is because at this point in the narrative it becomes evident that Cavalcanti's lady was in fact the historical precursor of the lady of Dante's devising. The one concept, indeed, follows the other both logically and chronologically, and in this passage Dante serves notice that with respect to the angelic lady he has overgone his "first friend" and made something new and wonderful. The somewhat astonishing analogy of Beatrice and Christ, which is further developed in *Purgatorio* XXXI, now becomes comprehensible also. After the living Beatrice, who did not differ essentially from Cavalcanti's lady Vanna, there comes the ideal Beatrice, glorified and blessed, the savior of man through the New Life of love.

In this progression, the final step led inevitably to another and more exalted poetry. The *Comedy* of Dante Alighieri is obviously rooted in the lyric tradition. Without the lady of the troubadour song, without *Bon Vezi*, without Vanna, there could have been no Beatrice. Step by step in the course of two centuries Beatrice took form, and now through the perfection of Beatrice the well-schooled lover was able to intuit the perfection toward which the cosmos strives. Through the love of her beauty, he was able to achieve the supreme vision of the world which follows in all its various aspects from the comprehension of the universal Beatrice. This revelation was the guerdon which the lady bestowed upon her lover in the fullness of time. So love "restored in one day all the wrongs he had done elsewhere"—

> q'Amors
> Restaura tot en un dia
> Qant qe a mesfait alhors . . .

and here, at last, Love and the lady transcended the third heaven.

In this manner, the successive transformations of the lady of the song reached their apogee and came to an end. There was to be no more. The Renaissance added some Platonic touches, but in the main these patterns controlled the progress of the idealistic lyric until the middle of the seventeenth century, certainly, and perhaps much longer. The most gentle lady had, in all conscience, gone as far as she could. Since the troubadours themselves had begun at the top of the scale of perfection, the succeeding degrees could be but few. But these steps were the most difficult and, to encompass them, the art of pleasing ladies had to be transformed into a branch of theology. Out of the perfect lady of the troubadours was born the angelic lady, Cavalcanti's star, an angel in the flesh. Of this sort were Vanna, Cino's Selvaggia, Dante's Pargoletta, Sennuccio's Lisetta, and the countless others who were to appear in the course of the next centuries. Beatrice, however, held greater promise. In the *Vita Nuova,* Dante's lady shed her fleshly aspect and became pure spirit. It was then no longer possible to love the beauty of Beatrice in the flesh; it had to be loved in its spiritual aspect exclusively, the beauty of a blessed soul in heaven, a pure ideal. The ultimate step in the idealization of the lady of the song was, accordingly, her effacement from the earth.

The love of the earthly Beatrice led Dante, as he tells us, to a life of virtue, humility, and charity, and this simply in anticipation of his guerdon, the salutation in which was all his beatitude.[15] Love had done as much, or almost as much, for the troubadour lover. But the love of the heavenly Beatrice, the true Beatrice, led Dante to God. The process which begins with the premonition of the death of Beatrice in the *Vita Nuova* ends only when in Paradise Beatrice steps aside, and the lover whom she has led to the Empyrean sees standing in her place the glorious elder who points the way to the seat of the All-Highest. From this moment on, Beatrice recedes further and further still from her lover's eyes until she takes her appointed place in the heavenly rose of which she forms a part; and her splendor, hitherto dazzling, is seen to be but a ray of the supreme and eternal light.[16]

True love, which in the beginning had expressed the knight's revolt against the patriarchy which encompassed and limited him, thus returned by a most circuitous route to its point of departure. In true love, everything had conspired to deny the father and his authority as lord and master. But these aggressions, though inexhaustible at root, had spent themselves for the time, together with the system out of which they grew. In time *fin amor* became attenuated to the point where it could scarcely be considered reprehensible. With the poetry of the *dolce stil,* the wheel came full circle.

If in the ideal love of another man's wife there still lingered some trace of troubadour sensuality, certainly it was blameless to love the beauty of a disembodied spirit. Death terminated the marriage contract. Love was eternal. From the poet's point of view the idea was stupendous. It can occasion no surprise therefore that, after Dante, the rate of mortality among angelic ladies should rise abruptly and alarmingly. In terms of the stilnovist conceit, obviously, the best thing a lady could do for her lover was to die. It became familiar practice to write love-songs to the lady *in morte* after having courted her, more or less unsuccessfully, *in vita.*

But if Beatrice furnished the pattern, she did not long remain the model for those who wrote of ideal love. For the fourteenth century, the *Comedy* of Dante was a *summa* and the author a theologian. His worth as a poet was savored chiefly by a few connoisseurs like Pucci and Villani and a few poets like Boccaccio, and it is questionable whether even Boccaccio understood quite what the *Comedy* was about. It was Petrarch who set the fashion of ideal love for the Renaissance.

Petrarch's lady resembled Vanna and Selvaggia much more nearly than the radiant lady of Dante's devising, but in her poetic function she followed the Beatrice of the *Vita Nuova.* Petrarch's *Rime* were arranged as a poetic record of the uneasy ascent of the spirit through love. The influence of the *stilnovisti* upon Petrarch was profound, no doubt, but far from exclusive. Much of his verse echoed the troubadour styles directly or indirectly. Nevertheless he developed to the full the spiritual conflict which lay at the core of the new poetry, and he transmitted what was essential in terms which were generally understandable. Most of the song and sonnet sequences of the Renaissance followed the pattern of Petrarch's *Rime.* It is safe to consider the greater portion of sixteenth century love-poetry in Italy as an exercise in poetic virtuosity; it exhibits no important departure from the theme of *fin amor* as Petrarch understood it. In France the Délies, Olives, Cassandres, Idées, Pasithées, Maries, Cléonices, Hélènes; in England, the Stellas, Ideas, Coelias, Diellas, Dianas, Phillises, Delias of the later age, together with their numberless counterparts in the other countries of Europe, owed much, if not all, to Petrarch's Laura. It is rarely that one catches more than a glimpse of Beatrice in any of these angels.

The she-wolf had another history, long and interesting, if not glorious. Petrarch had made her into a raging lion; for Ronsard she became a tigress; Jodelle planned a vast series of vituperative sonnets, of which a few survive.[17] For Wyatt she was, among other things, a tiger; a Medusa for Stirling; a poisonous toad for Gabriel Harvey; an evil spirit for Shakespeare. But in Renaissance poetry, on the whole, the lady's nature was angelic, her heart was generous, her role ministerial. It was her high task to assume the place of mediatrix between the life of the senses and the life of the spirit: she was the principal nexus between heaven and earth for those of noble nature who felt the power of love. The role was appropriate to the time, and it became classic. No longer an independent entity, but the handmaid of a higher power, the lovely lady radiated splendor in accordance with the divine will and, kindling love in the gentle heart, insensibly and irresistibly she drew her lover to the feet of his Lord.

"All'alta fantasia qui mancò possa."

A SELECTIVE BIBLIOGRAPHY

Albertus Magnus, *Opera omnia, cura Augusti Borgnet*. Parisiis, 1890–1899.

Andraud, P., *La Vie et l'œuvre du troubadour Raimon de Miraval.* Paris, 1902.

Andreae Capellani regii Francorum De amore libri tres, ed. E. Trojel. Havniae, 1892.

———, *The Art of Courtly Love* by Andreas Capellanus, translated by J. J. Parry. New York, 1941.

Anglade, J., *Anthologie des troubadours.* Paris, 1927.

———, *Histoire sommaire de la littérature méridionale.* Paris, 1921.

———, *Les Troubadours, leurs vies, leurs œuvres, leur influence.* Paris, 1919.

———, *Le Troubadour Guiraut Riquier.* Paris, 1905.

Appel, C., *Bernart von Ventadorn, seine Lieder.* Halle, 1915.

———, *Die Lieder Bertrans von Born.* Halle, 1932.

———, *Die Singweisen Bernarts von Ventadorn.* Halle, 1934.

———, "L'Enseignement de Garin le Brun" in *Révue des langues romans,* XXXIII (1889), pp. 404–432.

———, "Petrarka und Arnaut Daniel" in *Archiv für das Studium der neueren Sprachen und Literaturen,* CXLVII (1924), pp. 212–235.

———, *Provenzalische Chrestomathie.* 5th edition, Leipzig, 1920.

———, "Zu Marcabru" in *Zeitschrift für romanische Philologie,* XLIII (1923), pp. 403–469.

Aubry, P., *Trouvères et troubadours.* Paris, 1909.

Audiau, J., et R. Lavaud, *Nouvelle anthologie des troubadours.* Paris, 1928.

Axhausen, K., *Die Theorien über den Ursprung der provenzalischen Lyrik.* Marburg, 1937.

Azzolina, L., "Dante e i 'fedeli d'amore' " in *Convivium,* II (1930), pp. 801 ff.

———, *Il dolce stil nuovo.* Palermo, 1903.

Babb, L., *The Elizabethan Malady*. East Lansing (Michigan State College Press), 1951.

Bartoli, A., *I primi due secoli della letteratura italiana*. Milano, 1880.

Bartsch, K., *Altfranzösische Romanzen und Pastourellen*. Leipzig, 1870.

———, *Chrestomathie de l'ancien français*. 12th edition, Leipzig, 1927.

———, *Chrestomathie provençale*. 6th edition, ed. E. Koschwitz, Marburg, 1904.

———, *Grundriss zur Geschichte der provenzalischen Literatur*. Elberfeld, 1872.

Beauchet, L., *Histoire du droit privé de la république athénienne*. Paris, 1897.

Beck, F., *Dantes Vita Nova*. München, 1896.

Beck, J., *La Musique des troubadours*. Paris, n.d.

———, *Les Chansonniers des troubadours et des trouvères publiés en fac-simile et transcrits en notation moderne*. Paris and Philadelphia, 1927.

Beck, J. and L., *Les Chansonniers des troubadours et des trouvères*. 2 vols. Philadelphia, 1938.

Belperron, P., *La Joie d'amour*. Paris, 1948.

Bergert, F., *Die von den Trobadors genannten oder gefeierten Damen*. Halle, 1913.

Berry, A., *Florilège des troubadours*. Paris, 1930.

Bertacchi, G., *Poesie predantesche*. Milano, n.d.

Bertoni, G., *Il canzoniere provenzale di Bernart Amoros*. Fribourg (Suisse), 1911.

———, *Il duecento* (*Storia letteraria d'Italia*). Milano, 1930.

———, *I trovatori d'Italia*. Modena, 1915.

Bezzola, R., *Les Origines et la formation de la littérature courtoise en occident*. Paris, 1944.

Bird, O., "The *Canzone d'Amore* of Cavalcanti according to the commentary of Dino del Garbo" in *Medieval Studies*, II (1940); III (1942), pp. 117 ff.

Bloch, M., *La Société féodale*. 2 vols. Paris, 1940.

Bonfante, G., "Lucevan gli occhi suoi più che la stella" in *Italica*, XXI (1944), pp. 116 ff.

Bonifacio, G., *Giullari e uomini di corte nel 200*. Napoli, 1907.

Boutière, J. et A.-H. Schutz, *Biographies des troubadours*. Toulouse-Paris, 1950.

Briffault, R., *Les Troubadours et le sentiment romanesque*. Paris, 1945.

———, *The Mothers*. 3 vols. New York, 1927.

Brinkmann, H., *Entstehungsgeschichte des Minnesangs*. Halle, 1926.

———, *Geschichte der lateinischen Liebesdichtung im Mittelalter*. Halle, 1925.

Brunner, H., *Deutsche Rechtsgeschichte*. 2 vols. Leipzig, 1887–1892. 2nd ed., Leipzig, 1906, 1928.

Bundy, M. W., *The Theory of Imagination in Classical and Medieval Thought*. Urbana, 1927.

Burdach, K., "Ueber den Ursprung des mittelalterlichen Minnesangs . . . " in *Vorspiel, Gesammelte Schriften zur Geschichte des deutschen Geistes*, Vol. I, pp. 253 ff. Halle, 1925.

Butler, A. J., *The Forerunners of Dante*. Oxford, 1910.

Canello, U. A., *La vita e le opere del trovatore Arnaldo Daniello*. Halle, 1883.

Capefigue, J. B. H. R. de, *Histoire de Philippe-Auguste*. Paris, 1829.

Casini, T., *Le rime dei poeti bolognesi del secolo XIII*. Bologna, 1881.

Cavalcanti, Guido, *Rime, con introduzione e appendice bibliografica di E. Cecchi*. Lanciano, 1913.

Cesareo, G. A., "Amor mi spira" in *Miscellanea di studi critici in onore di Arturo Graf*. Bergamo, 1903.

———, *La poesia siciliana sotto gli Svevi*. Catania, 1894.

Chabaneau, C., *Les Biographies des troubadours*. Toulouse, 1885.

Chaytor, H. J., *The Troubadours*. Cambridge, 1912.

———, *The Troubadours and England*. Cambridge, 1923.

Chrétien de Troyes, *Cligès*, ed. W. Foerster. *Romanische Bibliothek*, Vol. I. Halle a/S., 1889.

———, *Erec et Enide*, ed. W. Foerster. Halle, 1896.

———, *Perceval le Gallois, publié par C. Potvin*. Mons, 1866–1871.

———, et Godefroy de Laigny, *Le Roman du chevalier de la charette*, ed. P. Tarbé. Reims, 1860.

Christ, W. von, "Geschichte der griechischen Literatur" in I. von Müller, *Handbuch der Altertums Wissenschaft*. 6th edition, München, 1912–1924.

Cian, V., *I contatti letterari italo-provenzali*. Messina, 1900.

Cino da Pistoia, *Rime, con prefazione di D. Fiodo*. Lanciano, 1915.

Cochin, H., *Vita Nova*. Paris, 1914.

Coulet, J., *Le Troubadour Guilhem Montanhagol*. Toulouse, 1898.

Crescini, V., *Manuale per l'avviamento agli studi provenzali.* 3rd edition, Milano, 1926.

———, *Nuove postille al trattato amoroso d'Andrea Capellano.* Venezia, 1909–1910.

Cross, T. P. and Nitze, W. A., *Lancelot and Guenevere, a Study on the Origins of Courtly Love.* Chicago, 1930.

D'Ancona, A. and Comparetti, D., *Le antiche rime volgare secondo la lezione del Codice Vaticano 3793.* 5 vols. Bologna, 1875–1888.

Dante, *Le opere, testo critico della Società Dantesca Italiana.* Firenze, 1921.

De Bartholomaeis, V., *Poesie provenzali storiche relative all'Italia.* 2 vols. Roma, 1931.

———, *Rime giullaresche e popolari d'Italia.* Bologna, n.d. (1926).

Dejeanne, J. M. L., *Poésies complètes du troubadour Marcabru.* Toulouse, 1909.

Del Monte, A., "Dolce stil novo" in *Filologia romanza,* III, pp. 254–264.

De Lollis, C., "Dolce stil novo e 'noel dig di nova maestria' " in *Studi medievali,* I, pp. 5 ff. Torino, 1904.

———, "La fede di Dante nell'arte" in *Nuova antologia,* August 1, 1921.

———, *Vita e poesie di Sordello di Goito.* Halle, 1896.

Denomy, A. J., "Courtly Love and Courtliness" in *Speculum,* XXVIII (1953), pp. 44–63.

———, "Fin'amors, The Pure Love of the Troubadours," in *Medieval Studies,* VII (1945), pp. 139–207.

———, *The Heresy of Courtly Love.* New York, 1947.

Di Benedetto, L., *Rimatori del dolce stil novo.* Bari, 1939.

Diez, F., *Die Poesie der Troubadours.* 2nd edition, Leipzig, 1883.

———, *Leben und Werke der Troubadours.* 2nd edition, Leipzig, 1882.

Doctrina de compondre dictatz, ed. P. Meyer, in *Romania,* VII, pp. 355 ff.

D'Ovidio, F., *Studii sulla Divina Commedia.* Milano-Palermo, 1901.

Du Bus, Gervais, *Le Roman de Fauvel,* ed. Långfors. Paris, 1914–1919.

Dumitrescu, M., *Les Poésies du troubadour Aimeric de Belenoi.* Paris, 1935.

Ercole, P., *Guido Cavalcanti e le sue rime.* Livorno, 1885.

Ermengaud, Matfré, *Le Breviari d'Amor*, ed. G. Azaïs. Beziers, Paris, 1862–1881.

Faral, E., *Les Jongleurs en France au moyen âge*. Paris, 1910.
Fassbinder, K., *Der Trobador Raimbaut de Vaqueiras, Leben und Dichtung*. Halle, 1929.
Fauriel, C., *Histoire de la poésie provençale*. Paris, 1846.
Feuerlicht, I., "Vom Ursprung der Minne" in *Archivum romanicum*, XXIII (1939), pp. 36 ff.
Figurelli, F., *Il dolce stil novo*. Napoli, 1933.
Fletcher, J. B., *The Religion of Beauty in Woman*. New York, 1911.
Frank, G., "The Distant Love of Jaufré Rudel" in *Modern Language Notes*, LVII (1942), pp. 528 ff.
Frank, I., *Répertoire métrique de la poésie des troubadours*. Paris, 1953.
———, *Trouvères et Minnesänger, Recueil de textes*. Saarbrücken, 1952.
Frey, D., *Gotik und Renaissance als Grundlagen der modernen Weltanschauung*. Augsburg, 1939.
Friedlander, L., *Darstellungen aus der Sittengeschichte Roms*. 10th *edition* (Wissowa), Leipzig, 1920–1922.
Friedmann, W., *Arnaut de Marueill*. Halle a/S., 1910.

Galen, Claudius, *De humoribus liber* in *Claudii Galena opera omnia*, ed. Kühn. 20 vols. Vol. XIX. Leipzig, 1821–1833.
Gaselee, S., *The Transition from the Late Latin Lyric to the Medieval Love Poem*. Cambridge, 1931.
Gautier, L., *La Chevalerie*. 3rd ed. Paris, n.d.
———, *Les Épopées françaises*. Paris, 1865–1869.
Gennrich, F., *Altfranzösische Lieder: I Teil*. Halle, 1953.
———, *Grundriss einer Formenlehre des mittelalterlichen Liedes . . .* Halle, 1932.
———, *Zur Ursprungsfrage des Minnesangs*. Halle, 1929.
Gerold, T., *La Musique au moyen âge*. Paris, 1932.
Gide, P., *Étude sur la condition privée de la femme*. Paris, 1867.
Gilson, E., *La Théologie mystique de S. Bernard*. Paris, 1934.
Gist, M. A., *Love and War in the Middle English Romances*. Philadelphia, 1947.
Grillo, E., *Early Italian Literature. Vol. I, Pre-Dante Poetical Schools*. London, 1920.

Guittone d'Arezzo, *Rime, a cura di Francesco Egidi* (*Scrittori d'Italia*). Bari, 1940.

Gunn, A. M. F., *The Mirror of Love*. Lubbock, Texas, 1952.

Guthrie, R., *Marcabrun*. New York, 1926.

Hartmann, M., *Das arabische Strophengedicht. Teil I: Das Muwassah*. Weimar, 1897.

Hauser, A., *The Social History of Art*. 2 vols. New York, 1952.

Hauvette, H., *Dante, introduction à l'étude de la Divine Comédie*. Paris, 1911.

Hill, R. T., and T. G. Bergin, *Anthology of the Provençal Troubadours*. New Haven, 1941.

Histoire littéraire de la France. 37 vols. Paris, 1733–1938.

Hoepffner, E., *Aux origines de la nouvelle française*. Oxford, 1939.

———, "Deux notes sur le troubadour Guiraut de Borneil" in *Romania*, LXIII (1937), pp. 204 ff.

Jeanroy, A., *Histoire sommaire de la poésie occitane*. Toulouse, Paris, 1945.

———, *La Poésie lyrique des troubadours*. Toulouse, Paris, 1934.

———, *Les Chansons de Guillaume IX*. Paris, 1927.

———, "Les Femmes poètes dans la littérature provençale au XIIIe siècle." In *Mélanges Salverda de Grave*. Groningen, 1933.

———, *Les Poésies de Jaufré Rudel*. Paris, 1914.

———, *Origines de la poésie lyrique en France*. 2nd edition, Paris, 1904.

———, et J.-J. Salverda de Grave, *Uc de Saint-Circ*. Toulouse, 1913.

Johnson, R. C., *Arnaut de Marueill*. Paris, 1935.

Jolowicz, H. T., *Historical Introduction to the Study of Roman Law*. Cambridge, 1952.

Jones, W. P., *The Pastourelle, A Study of a Lyric Type*. Cambridge, Massachusetts, 1931.

Kastner, L. E., "Marcabru and Cercamon" in *Modern Language Notes*, XXVI (1931), pp. 91 ff.

Kirby, T. A., *Chaucer's Troilus, A Study in Courtly Love*. Baton Rouge, Louisiana, 1940.

Klein, O., *Die Dichtungen des Mönchs von Montaudon*. Marburg, 1885.

Kolsen, A., *Dichtungen der Trobadors*. Halle, 1916–1919.

———, *Sämtliche Lieder der Trobadors, Guiraut de Bornelh.* 2 vols. Halle, 1910–1935.

Krabbes, T., *Die Frau in altfranzösischen Karls-Epos.* Marburg, 1884.

Kussler-Ratyé, G., "Les Chansons de la Comtesse Beatrice de Dia" in *Archivum romanicum,* I (1917), pp. 161 ff.

Labusquette, R. de, *Les Béatrices.* Paris, n.d.

Lamma, E., *Lapo Gianni e Gianni Alfani, Rime.* Lanciano, 1912.

Långfors, A., *Les Chansons de Guillem de Cabestanh.* Paris, 1914.

Langley, E. F., *The Poetry of Giacomo da Lentino.* Cambridge, Massachusetts, 1915.

Lapa, M. Rodrigues, *Das origens da poesia lírica en Portugal na idade-média.* Lisboa, 1929.

Latini, Brunetto, *Li Livres dou tresor,* critical edition by F. J. Carmody. Berkeley, 1948.

Lavaud, R., *Les Poésies d'Arnaut Daniel.* Toulouse, 1910.

Lea, H. C., *A History of the Inquisition of the Middle Ages.* 3 vols. New York, 1922.

Lévy, E., *Provenzalisches Wörterbuch.* 8 vols. 1894–1924.

Lewent, K., "An Old Provençal *Chanson de Mal Mariée*" in *Romanic Review,* XXXVII (1946), pp. 3–19.

———, "Das altprovenzalische Kreuzlied" in *Romanische Forschungen,* XXI (1908), pp. 321–448.

———, "Les Chansons du troubadour Aimeric de Belenoi" in *Annales du Midi,* LII (1946), pp. 22–49.

———, "The Troubadours and the Romance of Jaufre" in *Modern Philology,* XLIII (1945–1946), pp. 143–169.

Lewis, C. S., *The Allegory of Love.* Oxford, 1951.

Lipari, A., *The Dolce Stil Novo according to Lorenzo de' Medici.* New Haven, 1936.

Lommatzsch, E., *Provenzalisches Liederbuch.* Berlin, 1917.

Lorris, Guillaume de et Jean de Meun, *Le Roman de la rose,* ed. E. Langlois. Paris, 1914–1924.

Lot-Borodine, M., *La Femme et l'amour au XIIe siècle d'après les poèmes de Chrétien de Troyes.* Paris, 1909.

———, *Le Roman idyllique au moyen âge.* Paris, 1913.

———, "Sur les origines et les fins du service d'amour" in *Mélanges Alfred Jeanroy,* pp. 223–242. Paris, 1928.

Lote, G., *Histoire du vers français. Tome III, 1ère partie: Le Moyen âge.* Paris, 1955.

Lowes, J. L., "The Loveres Maladye of Hereos" in *Modern Philology,* XI (1914), pp. 491–546.

Lowinsky, V., *Zum Geistlichen Kunstlied.* Berlin, 1898 (extract from *Zeitschrift für französische Sprache und Literatur,* XX [1898], pp. 163 ff.).

Luchaire, A., *La Société française au temps de Philippe-Auguste.* Paris, 1909.

Mahn, C. A. F., *Gedichte der Troubadours in provenzalischer Sprache.* 4 vols. Berlin, 1856–1873.

———, *Die Werke der Troubadours in provenzalischer Sprache.* 4 vols. Berlin, 1846–1853.

Marie de France, *Die Lais de Marie de France, hrsg. von K. Warnke.* Halle, 1885.

———, *Poésies,* ed. B. Roquefort. Paris, 1820.

Marti, M., *Cultura e stile nei poeti giocosi del tempo di Dante.* Pisa, 1953.

Massèra, A. F., *Sonetti burleschi e realistici dei primi due secoli.* Bari, 1940.

Maus, F. W., *Peire Cardenals Strophenbau in seinem Verhältniss zu dem anderer Trobadors.* Marburg, 1882.

Melanchthon, *Liber de anima. Philippi Melanchthonis opera quae supersunt omnia,* Vol. XIII, ed. C. G. Bretschneider. Halle, 1834–1860.

Menéndez Pidal, R., *Poesia juglaresca y juglares.* Madrid, 1924.

Meyer, P., "Des Rapports de la poésie des trouvères avec celle des troubadours" in *Romania,* XIX (1890), pp. 1–62.

———, *Le Roman de Flamenca.* 2nd edition, Paris, 1901.

Migne, J. P., *Patrologiae cursus completus. Series Latina* (*PL*). Parisiis, 1845–1855. *Series Graeca* (*PG*). Parisiis, 1856–1866.

Milá y Fontanals, M., *Los trovadores en España.* Barcelona, 1889.

Molinier, Guilhem, *Las leys d'amor,* ed. J. Anglade. 4 vols. Toulouse, Paris, 1919–1920.

Monaci, E., *Crestomazia italiana dei primi secoli.* Citta di Castello, 1912.

Montaigne, Michel de, *Essais,* ed. A. Thibaudet. (La Pléiade). Paris, 1950.

Moore, E., "Beatrice" in *Studies in Dante, 2nd series.* Oxford, 1899.

Moore, O. H., "Jaufré Rudel and the Lady of Dreams" in *Publica-*

tions of the Modern Language Association (PMLA), XXIX (1914), pp. 517–536.

Nardi, B., "L'averroismo del 'primo amico' di Dante" in *Dante e la cultura medievale.* 2nd edition, Bari, 1949.

———, "La filosofia dell'amore" in the same.

Nicholson, R. A., *A Literary History of the Arabs.* Cambridge, 1930.

Nostredame, Jehan de, *Les Vies des plus célèbres et anciens poètes provençaux, nouvelle édition, préparée par C. Chabaneau et publiée par J. Anglade.* Paris, 1913.

Novati, F. and A. Monteverdi, *Le origini.* (*Storia letteraria d'Italia*). Milano, 1920.

Nykl, A. R., *A Book containing the Risala known as The Dove's Neck-Ring about Love and Lovers composed by Abu Muhammad' Ali ibn Hazm al-Andalusi.* Paris, 1931.

———, *El cancionero de Aben Guzmán.* Madrid, 1933.

———, *Hispano-Arabic Poetry and Its Relations with the Old Provençal Troubadours.* Baltimore, 1946.

Nyrop, K., *Storia dell'epopea francese nel medio evo,* translated by E. Gorra. Torino, 1886.

Ordericus Vitalis, *Historiae ecclesiasticae libri tredecim,* ed. A. le Prévost. 5 vols. Parisiis, 1838–1855.

Paetzold, A., *Die individuellen Eigentümlichkeiten einiger hervorragenden Trobadors.* Marburg, 1897.

Paris, G., *La Littérature française au moyen âge.* 4th edition, Paris, 1913.

———, "Les Origines de la poésie lyrique en France au moyen âge" in *Journal des Savants,* 1892.

Pattison, W. T., "The Background of Peire d'Alvernhe's *Chantarai d'aquest trobadors*" in *Modern Philology,* XXXI (1933), pp. 19–34.

———, *The Life and Works of the Troubadour Raimbaut d'Orange.* Minneapolis, 1952.

Pérès, H., *La Poésie andalouse en arabe classique au XI*[e] *siècle.* Paris, 1953.

Pertz, G. H., *Monumenta historica Germaniae, epistolae Karolini aevi.* Berolini, 1895.

Petrarch, *De contemptu mundi* in *Opera omnia*. Basel, 1581.

Piccolomini, Aeneas Sylvius, *Opera omnia*. Basel, 1551.

Pillet, A. and H. Carstens, *Bibliographie der Troubadours*. Halle, 1933.

———, "Zur Ursprungsfrage der altprovenzalischen Lyrik" in *Schriften der Koenigsberger gelehrten Gesellschaft*, 1928, Geisteswiss. Hefte No. 4, pp. 359 ff.

Pound, E., *The Spirit of Romance*. Norfolk, Connecticut, 1952. (London and New York, 1910).

Rajna, P., "Guglielmo Conte de Poitiers, trovatore bifronte" in *Mélanges Alfred Jeanroy*. Paris, 1928.

———, *Le origini dell'epopea francese*. Firenze, 1884.

———, "Tra le penombre e le nebbie della Gaia Scienza" in *Miscellanea* V. *Crescini*. Cividale, 1927.

Rauhut, F., "Selbstdarstellung bei den ältesten Trobador" in *Formen der Selbstdarstellung, Festgabe für Fritz Neubert*, ed. G. Reichenkron and E. Haase. Berlin, 1956.

Raynouard, F. J. M., *Choix des poésies originales des troubadours*. 6 vols. Paris, 1816–1861.

———, *Lexique roman*. 6 vols. Paris, 1838–1844.

Reese, G., *Music in the Middle Ages*. New York, 1940.

Reich, H., *Der Mimus*. 2 vols. Berlin, 1903.

Remy, P., *La Littérature provençale au moyen âge*. Brussels, 1944.

Renan, E., *Averroès et l'averroisme*. Paris, 1861.

Rho, E., *Il dolce stil nuovo e G. Cavalcanti*. Arezzo, 1922.

Riquer, Martín de, *La lírica de los trovadores. Tomo I, Poetas del siglo XII*. Barcelona, 1948.

Rivalta, A., *Le rime di Guido Cavalcanti*. Bologna, 1902.

Robin, P. A., *The Old Physiology in English Literature*. London, 1911.

Rohde, E., *Der griechische Roman und seine Vorlaüfer*. 2nd edition, Leipzig, 1900.

Rossi, V., "Il 'dolce stil nuovo' " in *Le opere minori di Dante Alighieri*. Firenze, 1906. Also in *Scritti di critica italiana*, Vol. I. Firenze, 1930.

Salvadori, G., *La poesia giovanile e la canzone d'amore di Guido Cavalcanti*. Roma, 1895.

———, *Liriche e saggi*. Vols. II and III. Milano, 1933.

Salverda de Grave, J.-J., "Giraut de Borneil et la poésie obscure" in *Mélanges J. van Ginneken*. Paris, 1937.

Sapegno, N., *Il trecento* (*Storia letteraria d'Italia*). 3rd edition, Milano, 1948.

Savj-Lopez, P., "Jaufre Rudel, questioni vecchie e nuove" in *Rendiconti della Reale Accademia dei Lincei*, XI (1902), pp. 212–225.

Scarano, N., *Beatrice*. Siena, 1902.

———, "Fonti provenzali della lirica petrarchesca" in *Studi di filologia romanza*, Vol. II. Roma, 1886.

Scheludko, D., "Beiträge zur Entstehungsgeschichte der altprovenzalischen Lyrik: I. Klassisch-lateinische Theorie," in *Archivum romanicum*, XI (1927), pp. 273 ff. "II. Die arabische Theorie," *ibid.*, XII (1928), pp. 30 ff.

Schultz, O., *Die provenzalischen Dichterinnen*. Leipzig, 1888.

Schultz-Gora, O., *Altprovenzalisches Elementarbuch*. 3rd edition, Heidelberg, 1915.

———, *Die Briefe des Trobadors Raimbaut de Vaqueiras an Bonifaz I, Markgrafen von Montferrat*. Halle, 1893.

———, *Provenzalische Studien. I.* Strasburg, 1917. *II.* Berlin-Leipzig, 1921.

Schutz, A. H., *Daude de Pradas*. Toulouse, Paris, 1933.

———, "Were the *Vidas* and *Razos* recited?" in *Studies in Philology*, XXXVI (1939), pp. 565–570.

Shaw, J. E., "Dante and Bonagiunta" in *Annual Reports of the Dante Society*. Cambridge, Massachusetts, 1936.

———, *Guido Cavalcanti's Theory of Love: The Canzone d'Amore and other Related Problems*. Toronto, 1949.

Shephard, W. P. and F. M. Chambers, *Aimeric de Peguilhan*. Evanston, 1950.

Singleton, C. S., *An Essay on the Vita Nuova*. Cambridge, Massachusetts, 1949.

Sordello, *Le Poesie*, ed. M. Boni. Bologna, 1954.

Spenser, Edmund, *The Faerie Queene* in *The Works of Edmund Spenser, A Variorum Edition*. 8 vols. Baltimore, 1932–1938.

Spiers, A. G. H., "*Dolce Stil Nuovo*, The Case of the Opposition" in *PMLA* (ns), XVIII (1910), pp. 657–675.

Spitzer, L., "Bemerkungen zu Dantes Vita Nuova" in *Publications de la Faculté des Lettres de L'Université d'Istanbul*, II (1937), pp. 162–208.

———, *L'Amour lointain de Jaufré Rudel et le sens de la poésie des troubadours*. Chapel Hill, 1944.

Stronski, S., *La Légende amoureuse de Bertran de Born*. Paris, 1914.

———, *La Poésie et la réalité aux temps des troubadours*. Oxford, 1943.

———, *Le Troubadour Folquet de Marseille*. Cracovie, 1910.

Summa Theologica (*S.Th.*) in *Sancti Thomae Aquinatis doctoris angelici opera omnia iussu impensaque Leonis XIII P.M. edita*. Vols. 4–12. Romae, 1882–1948.

Tallgren, O. J., *Rinaldo d'Aquino*. Helsingfors, 1917.

Taylor, H. O., *The Medieval Mind*. 4th edition, 2 vols., New York, 1925.

Thomas, A., *Francesco da Barberino et la littérature provençale en Italie au moyen âge*. Paris, 1883.

———, *Poésies complètes de Bertran de Born*. Toulouse, 1888.

Topsfield, L. T., "Raimon de Miraval and the Art of Courtly Love" in *Modern Language Review*, LI (1956), pp. 33–41.

Torraca, F., "Federico secondo e la poesia provenzale" in *Studj su la lirica italiana del Duecento*, pp. 235–341. Bologna, 1902.

Utley, F. L., *The Crooked Rib*. Columbus, 1944.

Vallone, A., *La cortesia dai provenzali a Dante*. Palermo, 1950.

———, *Cortesia e nobiltà nel Rinascimento*. Asti, 1955.

Vic, C. de and J. Vaissette, *Histoire générale du Languedoc*. 2nd edition, Toulouse, 1872–1904.

Vossler, K., *Der Troubadour Marcabru und die Anfänge des gekünstelten Stiles*. München, 1913.

———, *Die philosophischen Grundlagen zum "süssen neuen Stil."* Heidelberg, 1904.

Waddell, H., *The Wandering Scholars*. 5th edition, London, 1930.

Wallensköld, A., *Les Chansons de Conon de Bethune*. 3 vols. Paris, 1921.

———, *Thibaut de Champagne, roi de Navarre, Chansons*. Paris, 1925.

Wechssler, E., "Frauendienst und Vassalität" in *Zeitschrift für französische Sprache und Literatur*, XXIV (1902), pp. 159 ff.

———, *Das Kulturproblem des Minnesangs, I: Minnesang und Christentum*. Halle, 1909.

Weigand, H. J., *Three Chapters on Courtly Love in Arthurian France and Germany*. Chapel Hill, 1956.

Weinhold, K., *Die deutschen Frauen in dem Mittelalter*. Wien, 1882.

Westermarck, E. A., *The History of Human Marriage*. 3 vols. 5th edition, New York, 1922.

Wettstein, J., *Mezura, l'idéal des troubadours, son essence et ses aspects*. Zurich, 1945.

Wilamowitz-Moellendorff, U. von, *Hellenistische Dichtung in der Zeit des Kallimachos*. Berlin, 1924.

———, and B. Niese, *Staat und Gesellschaft der Griechen und Römer*. Berlin and Leipzig, 1910.

Zenker, R., *Die Lieder Peires von Auvergne*. Erlangen, 1900.

NOTES

LOVE AND THE POETRY OF LOVE

1. C. S. Lewis, *The Allegory of Love* (Oxford, 1936; 5th ed., 1951), p. 4.
2. C. S. Lewis, *loc. cit.*
3. Thomas Aquinas, *Summa theologica,* I, 92, art. 1; I, 99, art. 2. Aristotle, *De generatione animalium,* II, 3 (737a 27).
4. André Tiraqueau, *De legibus connubialibus, Œuvres* (Paris, 1574), I, 1.
5. *Epist. sen.,* XIV, 3. Cf. the discussion in *De contemptu mundi,* in *Opera omnia* (Basel, 1581), I, 355.
6. Aeneas Sylvius Piccolomini, *Opera omnia* (Basel, 1551), 609.
7. L. B. Alberti, *Opere volgare,* I, 43: "*Tutte sono pazze e piene di pulci, le femmine.*" For Alberti's ideas on the subject, see his essay "Amator" in *Opera inedita* (Florence, 1890), 1–18.
8. Plato, *Laws,* VI, 773 ff.
9. *Hippolytus,* 616 ff., trans. Hadas and McLean, *The Plays of Euripides* (New York, 1936), p. 125.
10. *Medea,* 629 ff., trans. Hadas and McLean, *op. cit.,* p. 78. Cf. *Antigone,* 781 ff.
11. Cf. R. Briffault, *The Mothers* (New York, 1927), I, 523 ff.
12. E. A. Westermarck, *The History of Human Marriage* (1922), II, 334; Briffault, *op. cit.,* I, 521.
13. Pindar, *Pythian* IX, 67 f.
14. Cf. Erwin Rohde, *Der griechische Roman* (2nd ed., 1900), pp. 68 ff.
15. Xenophon, *Oeconomicus,* IX, trans. E. C. Marchant.
16. Ps. Dem. 59, 122. On the status of Greek woman in marriage, see Wilamowitz-Moellendorff and Niese, *Staat und Gesellschaft der Griechen und Römer,* pp. 35 ff.
17. Thucydides, 2, 45.
18. *Eumenides,* 365, trans. E. D. A. Morshead.
19. *Eumenides,* 658 ff., trans. A. W. Smyth (Loeb).
20. Aristophanes, *Ecclesiazusae,* 224.
21. L. R. Farnell, *The Cults of the Greek States* (London, 1896–1909), III, 83, 89, 100; J. E. Harrison, *Themis* (Cambridge, 1912), pp. 36 ff., 386 ff. Plutarch, himself a priest, tells us that Dionysos is the generative principle which gives life to all. (*De Iside et Osiride,* xxxiv; cf. *idem, Quaesti de arate signis,* vii.)
22. The classical work on the subject, often disputed, is J. J. Bachofen, *Das Mutterrecht* (Stuttgart, 1861).
23. *Hippolytus,* 406. The literature on the psychoanalytic question is ex-

ceptionally rich and varied. For what is especially relevant to the present subject I shall cite only Edmund Bergler, *The Basic Neurosis* . . . (New York, 1949), pp. 14 ff., 46 ff., 137 ff., a somewhat unorthodox but most instructive approach to the problem.

24. See Lewis, *Allegory of Love*, p. 3.

25. *Ion*, 886 ff., trans. Hadas and McLean.

26. "Toward the maid I went, to hear what she was saying. I saw her white and comely and of simple countenance: she did not disdain my words. Now without delay, I asked for her love." *Pastourelle: Quant voi la flor nouvele*, in Bartsch, *Romanzen und Pastourellen* (Leipzig, 1870), p. 192.

27. "Before my eyes I see my heart and my aching wounded soul, dying of a blow which love dealt it in that very moment when I saw my lady." Guido Cavalcanti, *I prego voi*, in *I rimatori del dolce stil novo*, ed. G. R. Ceriello (Milan, 1950), p. 64. The text is Di Benedetto's.

28. *Hippolytus*, 616 ff.

29. G. Salmon, "Saturninus," in Smith and Wace, *Dictionary of Christian Biography*, IV, 587. Athanasius, *In passionem et crucem Domini*, XXX, in Migne, *PG* 28, 236; *idem*, *De virginitate*, *PG* 28, 279. Tertullian, *De monogamia*, III, in *PL* 2, 932. Justin, *Apologia I pro christianos*, XXIX, in *PG* 6, 373. Ambrose, *Exhortatio virginitatis*, in *PL* 16, 343. Jerome, *Epistola* XXII, 2, in *PL* 22, 395.

30. St. Augustine, *De civitate Dei*, XIV, 23 ff., in Migne, *PL* 41, 430 ff.

31. Thomas Aquinas, *S. Th.*, I, 98, art. 1–2; I–II, 77, art. 1.

32. Clement of Alexandria, *Paedagogus*, II, 2, in Migne *PG* 8, 429; *Stromata*, VII, 12, *PG* 9, 497.

33. *S. Th.*, II–II, 152, art. 3. Tridentine Council, 24th session, 10th canon, in *Canones et decreta SS. oecumenici Concillii Tredentini* (Romae, 1845).

34. Thomas Aquinas, *S. Th.*, I, 37, art. 1; I–II, 26, art. 2, art. 3. Augustine, *De civ. Dei*, XIV, 7; *Confessions*, XIII, 9; *De Trinitate*, XV, 19.

35. *Paradiso*, XXVII, 109. The text I translate is the *Testo critico della Società dantesca italiana* (Firenze, Bemporad, 1921).

36. *Paradiso*, I, 74; *Convivio*, II, 4.

37. *Paradiso*, XXIV, 150. Cf. Thomas Aquinas, *S. Th.*, I, 60, art. 1; I–II, 26, art. 1; Augustine, *Conf.*, XIII, 9.

38. *Psalms* 63, 1. *Psalms* 84, 2.

39. Albertus Magnus, *De laudibus virginis Mariae*, VI, *Opera omnia*, ed. Borgnet, XXXVI, 337.

40. *De Isaac et anima*, I, 4–6, in Migne, *PL* 14, 533 f.

41. *Sermones de diversis*, VIII, 9, in Migne, *PL* 183, 565. Cf. Richard of St. Victor, *Tractatus de quatuor gradibus violentiae charitatis*, *PL* 196, 1220; St. Bonaventura, *Itinerarium mentis in Deum*, *Opera omnia*, ed. Quaracchi (1891), V, 295.

42. St. Thomas, *S. Th.*, I–II, 26, art. 3. Cf. St. Augustine, *De civ. Dei*, XIV, 7.

43. St. Augustine, *De doctrina christiana*, III, 10, in Migne, *PL* 34, 72.

44. St. Bonaventura I *Sententiarum*, 3, 1, 2, *Opera omnia*, ed. Quaracchi I, 72.

45. St. Augustine, *De doctrina christiana*, I, 4, in *PL* 34, 20.

46. Petrarch, *Secretum*, dialogue 3.

47. Tertullian, *Liber de exhortatione castitatis*, IX, in Migne, *PL* 2, 924. For a discussion of this point, see Briffault, *The Mothers*, III, 249.
48. Peter of Blois, *Sermon* XII, in Migne, *PL* 207, 597.
49. It is, of course, possible to exaggerate the abruptness of this change. Michelet wrote: "In the thirteenth century, God changed his sex." He has often been taken to task. See, e.g., L. Gautier in Petit de Julleville, *Histoire de la littérature française* (Paris, 1896), I, 144.
50. Cf. Thomas Aquinas, *S. Th.*, I–II, 77 art. 4: "Concupiscence, whereby a man desires good for himself, is reduced to self-love as to its cause. . . ." Cf. Aristophanes' speech in the *Symposium* of Plato.
51. Trojel's ed. (Copenhagen, 1892), II, 8th dialogue, p. 182; Parry's translation (New York, 1941), p. 122.
52. *Symposium*, 189 ff., Jowett's translation.
53. J. M. L. Dejeanne, *Poésies complètes du troubadour Marcabru* (Toulouse, 1909), XXXI, 73 ff.
54. J. M. L. Dejeanne, *op. cit.*, p. 179. Jeanroy believes that by pure love Marcabru means love of God (*Poésie lyrique des troubadours* [1934], II, 17).
55. Marie de France, *Poésies*, ed. Roquêfort (Paris, 1820), I, 84.
56. Rufinus, *Greek Anthology* (Loeb), V, 70.
57. Rufinus, *op. cit.*, V, 66. Cf. Alfred Koerte, *Die hellenistische Dichtung* (1925), pp. 166 f.
58. Sappho, *Lyra Graeca*, I.
59. Catullus, *Ille mi par esse deo videtur.*
60. Ovid, *Ars amatoria*, II, 288 ff.
61. Giraut de Bornelh, *Ailas, com mor*, Mahn, *Werke*, II, 51.
62. *Argonautica*, III, 947 ff.
63. *Phaedrus*, 246 ff., trans. Jowett.
64. D. Scheludko, "Beiträge zur Entstehungsgeschichte der altprovenzalischen Lyrik," *Archivum romanicum*, XI (1927), pp. 273 ff., pp. 305 ff.
65. *Greek Anthology* (Loeb), V, 144.
66. *Ibid.*, V, 292.
67. *Ibid.*
68. *Ibid.*, V, 242 (Eratosthenes); V, 269 (Agathias).
69. For the various theories in the field, see: D. Scheludko, "Beiträge zur Entstehungsgeschichte der altprovenzalischen Lyrik," *Archivum romanicum*, XI (1927), pp. 309 ff.; Henning Brinkmann, *Entstehungsgeschichte des Minnesangs* (1926), pp. 17 ff.; Étienne Gilson, *La Théologie mystique de Saint Bernard* (1934), pp. 215 ff.; Gaston Paris, "Les Origines de la poésie lyrique en France au moyen âge," *Journal des Savants*, 1892, pp. 424 ff.; Konrad Burdach, *Über den Ursprung des mittelalterlichen Minnesangs* (1918); A. R. Nykl, *The Dove's Neck-Ring* (Paris, 1931), pp. lxxviii ff. The best general discussion of the question is still to be found in A. Jeanroy, *La Poésie lyrique des troubadours* (Paris-Toulouse, 1934), I, 61–80, but the weight of authority has shifted very significantly in the last two decades toward the theory of Arabic origins. See further, in the Bibliography, the relevant works of Axhausen, Bezzola, Briffault, Feuerlicht, Gennrich, Hartmann, Lapa, Nicholson, Nykl, Pérès, and Pillet.

THE KNIGHTS

1. Léon Gautier, *La Chevalerie*, pp. 246–247 and 270 ff.; Marc Bloch, *La Société féodale* (1940), II, 49 ff.

2. Pio Rajna, *Le origini dell'epopea francese* (Firenze, 1884), p. 389; Gautier, *La Chevalerie*, pp. 256 ff.; J. B. de Capefigue, *Histoire du temps de Philippe Auguste* (Paris, 1829), I, 28; H. O. Taylor, *The Medieval Mind*, (2nd ed., 1914), I, 543 ff.; M. Bloch, *La Société féodale*, I, 224 ff.

3. Westermarck has collected some interesting citations to bear on this point. *The History of Human Marriage*, II, 341 ff.

4. Cf. H. Brunner, *Deutsche Rechtsgeschichte* (Leipzig, 1887–1892), II, 202 ff., 243–302.

5. So in a charter of the Abbey of St. Victor cited by J. B. H. R. de Capefigue, *Histoire du temps de Philippe Auguste* (Paris, 1829), I, 35.

6. Hans Naumann, *Deutsche Kultur im Zeitalter des Rittertums* (1938), p. 4; Louis Reynaud, *Les Origines de l'influence française en Allemagne* (1913), p. 167; Marc Bloch, "La Ministerialité en France et en Allemagne," *Revue historique de droit français et étranger* (1928), p. 80; Paul Kluckhohn, "Ministerialität und Ritterdichtung," *Zeit. für Deutsches Altertum*, vol. 52 (1910), p. 137. Cf. Taylor, *The Medieval Mind*, I, 545 ff. and 574 ff.

7. The relation of the two strata of nobility is carefully defined for the sixteenth century in *The Courtier*, particularly in Books I and IV which treat of the mutual obligations of the courtier and his prince.

8. Boethius, *Consolatio*, III, pr. 6 and m. 6.

9. *Benefits*, III, 28. The passage is cited in Andreas, *De amore*, I, VI.

10. Arnaut de Marueill, *Razos e mezura*, Raynouard, *Choix*, IV, 410.

11. *Partimen: Perdigos, ses vassalage*, in C. Appel, *Provenzalisches Chrestomathie* (Leipzig, 1895), no. 95.

12. "Encore lor fes une demande:
En issirent il a cheval?"

Gervais du Bus, *Le Roman de Fauvel*, ed. Långfors (Paris, 1914–1919), ll. 1089 ff.

13. *Li livres dou tresor*, livre II, part. II, chap. L, ed. P. Chabaille (Paris, 1863), p. 343. Cf. *Il Tesoretto*, ed. Wiese, Cap. XVI, ll. 1695 ff. (Strasbourg, 1907), p. 64.

14. *Convivio*, IV, 24.

15. *Le dolce rime d'amor*, ll. 101 f., in *Convivio*, IV.

16. *Monarchia*, II, 3, ll. 10 ff.

17. Egidio Romano, *De regimine principum*, I, 4, 5.

18. Sordello, *Aissi co·l tesaurs es perdutz*, ll. 613–622 and 635–640, in *Sordello, le poesie*, ed. Marco Boni (Bologna, 1954), p. 216.

19. *Romance of the Rose*, ll. 18595 ff., ed. Ernest Langlois (Paris, 1922), IV. The anonymous author of *De eruditione principum* (lib. I, cap. 4), ascribed to the school of Aquinas, says much the same thing in scholastic terms. Cf. Boethius, *Consolatio*, III, pr. 4.

20. Guinizelli, *Al cor gentil*, in *I rimatori del dolce stil novo*, ed. G. R. Ceriello (Milano, 1950), p. 20.

21. See, for example, Chaucer, *Gentilesse* and also *The Wife of Bath's Tale*, ll. 1109–1169. J. L. Lowes, *MP*, XIII, pp. 19 ff.

22. So, in *Morte d'Arthur*, in the case of Arthur, Kay, Beaumains, Galahad; so too with Tor, son of Aries the cowherd, whose mother on the way to the milking managed a brief, but sufficient, encounter with the stern knight King Pellinore (Malory, *Morte d'Arthur*, III, 4.) Behind this sort of story is, of course, the plot of the traditional *pastourelle*. Cf. the story of Griflet, *fise de Dieu* (*ibid.*, I, 22). Cf. E. K. Chambers in *English Association Tract* no. 51 (1892).

23. Gaetano Salvemini, *La dignità cavalleresca nel commune di Firenze* (Firenze, 1896).

24. Perdigon, *Ben aio·l mal e·l afan e·l cossir*, stanza 4, Raynouard, *Choix*, III, 345. H. J. Chaytor, *Les Chansons de Perdigon* (Paris, 1926), p. 6.

25. See, for example, Malory, *Morte d'Arthur*, X, 74, X, 80.

26. C. Nyrop, *Storia dell'epopea francese*, pp. 323 ff.; Gautier, *La Chevalerie*, p. 75.

27. *Gesta Regis Ricardi* in *Chronicles and Memorials of Great Britain and Ireland during the Middle Ages*, Rolls Series (London, 1858), vol. 38, no. 1803, p. 143.

28. See P. Meyer and A. Longnon, *Raoul de Cambrai* (Paris, 1882), pp. xvi ff.

29. Pier-Candido Decembrio, *Vita* in Muratori, *Rerum italicarum scriptores* (Bologna, 1925–1940), XX, 985.

30. Aeneas Sylvius, *Commentarii*, p. 92; *Opera inedita* (Cugnoni), p. 509.

31. In the *Morte d'Arthur*, the coming of Galahad is set 454 years after the passion of Our Lord, i.e., in the fifth century (Bk. XIII, ch. 2).

32. "The order of chivalry . . . is the art of indulging in every excess and of leading a life of folly. Our knights . . . despoil and ransom the subjects of the church; they crush down the poor . . . they seek in the sufferings of others the satisfaction of their illicit lusts and boundless licence. Our knights of the present day . . . vie with one another in debauchery and drunkenness." *Petri Blesensis epistolae*, XCIV, in Migne, *PL* 207, 293. For a collection of citations to illustrate this point, see R. Briffault, *The Mothers* (New York, 1927), III, 382 ff.

33. See J. Bédier, *Les Légendes épiques* IV (1921), 432.

34. L. Gautier, *La Chevalerie*, pp. 290 ff.; M. Bloch, *La Société féodale*, II, 51 ff.; M. Andrieu, *Les Ordines romani du haut moyen-âge I. Les Manuscrits* (Louvain, 1931), pp. 112 ff., p. 445.

35. *Raoul de Cambrai*, ed. Meyer et Longnon, p. 195. Cf. *Aiol*, ed. Normand et Raynaud, ll. 2172 ff. On ladies' forwardness, A. Luchaire, *La Société française au temps de Philippe Auguste* (Paris, 1909), p. 376; T. Krabbes, *Die Frau in altfranzösischen Karls-Epos* (Marburg, 1884), p. 20. On the hero's attitude toward women, see Nyrop, *op. cit.*, pp. 348 ff.

36. E.g. in *Enfances Vivien*, ed. Wahlund und v. Failitzen, p. 265; cf. P. Meyer, "Mélanges de poésie Anglo-Normande," in *Romania*, IV, 394.

37. *Ider*, in *Histoire littéraire de la France*, XXX, 208. *Le Chevalier du perroquet*, *ibid.*, p. 107. *Morte d'Arthur*, X, 38. Cf. C. Nyrop, *Storia dell'epopea francese nel medio evo* (Torino, 1886), pp. 351 ff.

38. *Le Roman de Tristan par Thomas*, ed. J. Bédier (Paris, 1902–1905), I, 133.

39. C. Nyrop, *Storia dell'epopea francese*, p. 351; L. Gautier, *La Chevalerie*, p. 343.

40. *Perceval le Gallois*, ed. C. Potvin, V, 57.

41. *Lai de Graelent, Poésies de Marie de France*, I, 506.

42. Chrétien de Troyes et Godefroy de Laigny, *Le Chevalier de la charette*, ed. P. Tarbé (Reims, 1849), 1302 ff.

THE LADIES

1. Aristotle, *Politics*, I. Beauchet, *Histoire du droit privée de la république athénienne* (Paris, 1897), II, 327; U. v. Wilamowitz-Moellendorff and Niese, *Staat und Gesellschaft der Griechen und Römer*, pp. 35 ff.

2. Theodor Mommsen, *History of Rome*, I, 74.

3. H. T. Jolowicz, *Historical Introduction to the study of Roman Law* (Cambridge, 1952), pp. 112, 243. Paul Gide, *Étude sur la condition privée de la femme* (Paris, 1867), p. 129. L. Friedlander, *Darstellungen aus der Sittengeschichte Roms*, 10th ed., Wissowa (Leipsic, 1920–1922), I, chap. 5.

4. Gaius, *Institutes*, ed. E. Poste, I, 145–194; III, 44. *Digesta* XXIII, 2.21; *Codex Justinianus*, V, 4.14; O. Karlowa, *Römische Rechtsgeschichte* (Leipzig, 1885–1901), II, 174.

5. *Edictus Rothari*, 205.

6. Karl Weinhold, *Die deutschen Frauen in dem Mittelalter* (Wien, 1882), I, 303; H. Brunner, *Deutsche Rechtsgeschichte* (Leipzig, 1887–1892), I, 76.

7. "*E·l coms Anfos de Proensa . . . det lor moillers a Barjols e terra,*" in Boutière et Schutz, *Biographies des troubadours*, p. 92. See P. Gide, *op. cit.*, pp. 396 ff.

8. Philippe de Beaumanoir, *Coutumes de Beauvaisis*, ed. Salmon (Paris, 1900), XLIII, 27.

9. St. Paul, 1 Cor. 11. Cf. 1 Cor. 14; 1 Tim. 2, 12. Chiaro Davanzati, *E si mi piacie vedere Pulzella*, l. 12: "*E cio c'ama il marito degi amare,*" in A. D'Ancona, *Le antiche rime volgari* (Bologna, 1875–1888), IV, 279. For citations on the necessity for castigating women, see Gide, *op. cit.*, p. 413. See also Karl Bücher, *Die Frauenfrage im Mittelalter* (Tübingen, 1910).

10. "Husband and wife may be joined together by every sort of affection, but this feeling cannot take the place of love." Andreas, *De amore*, I, VI, 7. Cf. Briffault, *The Mothers*, I, 221; I, 523; II, 1; Westermarck, *The History of Human Marriage*, II, 339 ff.; H. O. Taylor, *The Medieval Mind*, I, 586. See also E. Langlois, *La Société française au XII*[e] *siècle d'après dix romans d'aventure* (2nd ed., Paris, 1904).

11. Gui d'Ussel, *Gui d'Ussel, be·m pesa de vos*. ll. 23–24, Audiau et Lavaud, *Nouvelle anthologie des troubadours*, p. 200.

12. For examples, see Briffault, *The Mothers* I, 531 ff. Cf. Westermarck, *The History of Human Marriage*, II, 339 ff.

13. Two of the romances of Chrétien de Troyes, *Erec and Enid* and *Cligès*, explore the possibility. In the Renaissance, Pontano and Rota wrote love-songs to their wives. Jacques d'Ostun sings of his wife (P. Meyer, *Recueil*, no. 351).

But these must be considered curiosities of literature, so uncommon is the genre.

14. Cf. The Monk of Montaudon, *Fort m'enoia,* ll. 12 f., in Hill and Bergin, *Anthology of the Provençal Troubadours* (New Haven, 1941), p. 109.

15. *Ara·m digatz,* stanza 3, Audiau, *Les Poésies des quatre troubadours d'Ussel,* p. 69.

16. Montaigne, *Essais,* III, 5, *On some verses of Virgil,* ed. Thibaudet, La Pléiade (1950), pp. 952, 955. Cf. *Essais,* I, 30; *op. cit.,* p. 235.

17. *L'Imposteur,* II, 2.

18. Andreas Capellanus, *De amore,* ed. Trojel, p. 353; translated as *The Art of Courtly Love,* by J. J. Parry (New York, 1941), p. 208. Cf. Thomas Aquinas, *S. Th.,* II–II, 149, 4.

19. Matfré Ermengaud, *Le Breviari d'Amor,* ed. G. Azais (Beziers-Paris, 1862–1881), ll. 18740 ff. Cf. *ibid.,* ll. 18504 ff.

20. E.g., Francisco Barbaro, *De re uxoria* (Amsterdam, 1639), Lib. II, cap. iv, pp. 128 f.; Poggio Bracciolini, *An seni sit uxor ducenda,* ed. Wm. Shepherd (Liverpool, 1807), p. 27; Leonardo Bruni, *Oeconomicorum Aristotelis* (1508), p. 9.

21. Bernard de Ventadour, *Lo tems vai e ven e vire,* stanza 6, Audiau et Lavaud, *Anthologie,* p. 28. This is a commonplace of troubadour poetry. To the same effect, Aimeric de Peguilhan, *Chantar vuilh,* ll. 36 ff., ed. Shepherd and Chambers, p. 35.

22. Comtesse de Die, *A chantar m'er,* stanzas 1, 5, 6, Audiau et Lavaud, *Anthologie,* p. 51, Raynouard, *Choix,* III, 22.

23. The terms were used in the Middle Ages: story-songs or cloth-songs, so called because presumably women sang them while sewing. P. Paris first called them romances in 1833, because he thought they resembled the Spanish romances. They were first published by Karl Bartsch under the title *Romanzen und Pastourellen* (Leipzig, 1870).

24. Alfred Jeanroy, *Les Origines de la poésie lyrique en France,* 2nd ed. (Paris, 1904), pp. 226 ff.

25. See K. Bartsch, *Romanzen,* nos. IV, VI, IX; VIII, XIV, XVII. See also G. Groeber, *Die altfranzösischen Romanzen und Pastourellen* (Zurich, 1872), pp. 10 ff.

26. Bartsch and Koschwitz, *Provenzalische Chrestomathie,* 6th ed. (Marburg, 1904), p. 245.

27. *Un petit devant le jor,* stanza 5, Bartsch, *Romanzen,* I, 38.

28. Bartsch, *op. cit.,* I, 351.

29. *Ibid.,* I, 51.

30. Guillaume IX, *Compaigno non puosc mudar,* ed. Jeanroy (Paris, 1927), no. II, p. 3. Cf. Juvenal, VI, 247: "Have her locked up. Who will watch your watchman? Your wife knows her way about. She will begin with them."

31. P. Meyer, *Le Roman de Flamenca* (Paris, 1901), ll. 3244 ff.

32. *Quan par la flors,* ll. 41 ff., in C. Appel, *Bernart von Ventadorn,* p. 232.

33. *Vida* of Guillem de Cabestaing, in J. Boutière et A.-H. Schutz, *Biographies des troubadours* (Paris, 1950), pp. 158 ff.

34. Not only was any degree of consanguinity a bar to a valid marriage, whether the relationship was legitimate or not, but a spiritual affinity, such as a relationship through god-parents, was sufficient to preclude proper wedlock.

The arguments advanced for the nullification of the marriage of Henry VIII of England and Catherine of Aragon, for example, were mere legal commonplaces which, in other circumstances, would have been deemed amply sufficient. See F. Pollock and F. W. Maitland, *A History of English Law before the time of Edward I*, vol. II, pp. 369 ff.

35. See, for instance, the story of Raimon de Miraval, *Razo* of Pillet, 406.12, in Boutière et Schutz, *Biographies des troubadours*, p. 289.

36. Alanus de Insulis, *Epitome of the Art of Preaching*, ch. XLV; Jerome, *Against Jovinian*, I, 49; Peter Lombard, *Sentences*, IV, 31; Clement of Alexandria, *Paedagogus*, II, 10; Andreas, *De amore*, I, VI, 7.

37. Marcabru, *Al son desviat*, ed. Dejeanne, p. 19; Arnaut Daniel, *Lancan son passat*, stanzas 2 and 3, ed. Canello, p. 98, ed. Lavaud, p. 37.

38. *Essais*, ed. A. Thibaudet, III, 5, p. 973.

39. *D'un sirventes m'es pres talens*, P. Andraud, *Raimon de Miraval*, p. 138. Cf. the *Razos* in Boutière et Schutz, pp. 289, 300.

40. *De amore*, I, VI, dial. 7; Parry's translation, p. 102.

41. *De amore*, I, VI, dial. 8; Parry, p. 125. Cf. Boccaccio, *Filocolo*, Bk. IV, Question 3.

42. Cf. the situation in *Erec and Enid*, in which the knight, having married the lady, is considered shamefully lacking in manliness when he devotes himself to love-making.

43. *De amore*, I, VI, dial. 7; Parry, p. 100: "What is love but an inordinate desire to receive passionately a furtive and hidden embrace?"

THE TROUBADOURS

1. *De vulgari eloquentia*, I, 8.

2. Since the term "Provençal" was never properly applicable to the language of the troubadours, other terms have from time to time been employed to designate it. The most widely used have been "romance" and "romanic," which became rare locutions after the twelfth century in this connection, and "occitan" and "occitanic," derived from *langue d'oc*, the term which Dante used in his classification of the vulgar dialects in *De vulgari eloquentia* I, 8. The term "Provençal" goes back to the historians of the first crusade, who distinguished the northern French, whom they called *Franci* or *Francigenae*, from the French of the Midi, whom they called *Provinciales*. Very likely it was the influence of Jehan de Nostredame's famous work, *Les Vies des plus célèbres et anciens poètes provenceaux* (1575), which established the term so firmly in literary history that all efforts to supersede it have failed. See C. Chabaneau, "Sur la langue romane du Midi de la France," in *Histoire de Languedoc*, ed. Privat, X, 68 ff.; P. Meyer, "La langue romane du Midi de la France et ses differents noms," *Annales du Midi*, I (1889), pp. 1 ff.; A. Jeanroy, *La Poésie lyrique des troubadours*, I, 45 ff.

3. Cf. F. Diez, *Leben und Werke der Troubadours* (1829), Leipzig, 1883, pp. 3 ff.; E. Wechssler, "Frauendienst und Vassalität," *Zeitschrift für franz. Sprache*, XXIV, 159; Jeanroy, *Chansons de Guillaume IX*, 2nd ed. (Paris, 1927), p. xviii. Cf. R. Bezzola, "Guillaume IX et les origines de l'amour courtois," *Romania*, LXVI (1940), 145 ff.

4. *Ben vuelh que sapchon li pluzor*, Jeanroy, *Guillaume IX*, p. 13.

5. Jeanroy, *Poésie lyrique*, I, 326 ff.: *liste bio-bibliographique des troubadours des origines au milieu du XIVe siècle*. See also Alfred Pillet and Henry Carstens, *Bibliographie der Troubadours* (Halle, 1933).

6. Boutière et Schutz, *Biographies*, pp. 223, 175, 234.

7. Boutière et Schutz, *Biographies*, p. 202. See G. Paris, "Jaufre Rudel" in *Revue Historique*, LIII (1893), pp. 225 ff.; *idem*, *Mélanges de littérature française du moyen-âge*, pp. 498 ff. Cf. J. Anglade, *Les Troubadours*, p. 34; Jeanroy, *Poésie lyrique*, I, 106 ff.

8. Of these compilers only two have identified themselves, Uc de Saint Circ and Miguel de la Tor.

9. See *Razo* of Pillet, 242.55, in Boutière et Schutz, p. 199.

10. See A.-H. Schutz, *Studies in Philology*, XXXVI (1939), p. 565 ff.

11. Boutière et Schutz, *Biographies*, p. 251.

12. E.g., *Vida* of Cadenet, Boutière et Schutz, p. 78.

13. Boutière et Schutz, p. 319.

14. See S. Stronski, *La Légende amoureuse de Bertran de Born* (Paris, 1916); *idem*, *Poésies de Folquet de Marseille* (Cracow, 1919), Introduction; N. de Wailly, *Récits d'un ménéstrel de Reims* (Société de l'histoire de France, Paris, 1877).

15. Suidas, s.v. Thespis.

16. Petrarch, *Solo e pensoso i più deserti campi*, sonnet 28, *Rime* no. 35.

17. See, for example, Tertullian, *De spectaculis*, in Migne, *PL* 1, 703 ff., 722 f., 730 ff.

18. Leidrad, *Epistolae*, in G. H. Pertz, *Monumenta Historica Germaniae, epistolae Karolini aevi* (Berolini, 1895), II, 541.

19. E. Faral, *Les Jongleurs en France au moyen-âge* (Paris, 1910), pp. 24, 67, and Appendix III, nos. 1–13. See also L. Gautier, *Les Épopées françaises*, II, 11; C. Nyrop, *L'epopea francese* (Torino, 1888), p. 279; W. Hertz, *Spielmans-Buch*, p. 317; F. Guessard et C. Grandmaison, *Huon de Bordeaux* (Paris, 1860), pp. vi ff.

20. Boutière et Schutz, p. 227.

21. Text of Riquier's *declaracio* in Mahn, *Werke*, IV, 163. See J. Anglade, *Le Troubadour Guiraut Riquier*, ch. VI; R. Menéndez Pidal, *Poesia juglaresca y juglares*, pp. 14 ff.; A. Jeanroy, *Poésie lyrique*, I, 146.

22. The word "troubadour," Provençal *trobador*, is derived from *trobar*, to find, or invent, a melody or poem. The French form was *trouvère*.

23. "Vida de G. de Bornelh," in Boutière et Schutz, p. 191. "Vida de A. de Marueill," *ibid*., p. 256. "Vida de B. de Born," *ibid*., p. 35.

24. Guillaume IX, *Farai chansoneta nueva*, ll. 28 f. Peire Raimon, *Ar ai ben d'amor apres* in Audiau et Lavaud, *Anthologie*, p. 97. Jaufre Rudel, *No sap chantar*, ll. 34 f., Hill and Bergin, *Anthology*, p. 29.

25. Boutière et Schutz, p. 309.

26. Hill and Bergin, *Anthology*, pp. 71 ff.; also in Audiau et Lavaud, *Anthologie*, p. 131. Cf. the famous *sirventés* of the Monk of Montaudon, *Pos Peire*, R. Lavaud, *Les Troubadours cantaliens*, II, 244.

27. C. Chabaneau, *Les Biographies des troubadours* (Toulouse, 1885), p. 6.

28. "Per so pretz aitan los pipautz/ Que van las almornas queren," *Chanterai d'aquetz trobadors,* ll. 59 f., Hill and Bergin, p. 73.

29. *Vida* in Boutière et Schutz, p. 23.

30. *Vida,* Boutière et Schutz, p. 331; *Uc de Saint Circ,* ed. Jeanroy et Salverda de Grave, pp. xxxvi ff.

31. Peire Vidal, *Dragoman senher,* Mahn, *Werke,* I, 229; Hill and Bergin, *Anthology,* p. 96.

32. Matfré Ermengaud, *Breviari d'Amor,* 18421 ff.

33. *Aram digatz, Rambaut,* ll. 23 ff. in Hill and Bergin, *Anthology of the Provençal Troubadours* (1941), p. 119.

34. Raynouard, *Choix,* II, 260. See further, Klara Fassbinder, *Der Trobador Raimbaut de Vaqueiras, Leben und Dichtung* (Halle, 1929).

35. Dante did not hesitate to use this term in connection with the Provenceaux: "Et hoc omnes doctores perpendisse videntur, cantiones illustres principiantes ab illo. . . ." *De vulgari eloquentia,* II, 5.

THE SONG

1. This was certainly composed before 1305. The evidence is summarized in N. Zingarelli, *Vita di Dante,* I, 566. It therefore antedates G. Molinier's *Leys d'amors* by some fifty years.

2. *De vulgari eloquentia,* II, 3.

3. *Poetics,* 51 a 36; 51 b 19.

4. *Non es meravelha,* stanza 1, C. Appel, *Bernart von Ventadorn* (Halle, 1915), p. 186; Hill and Bergin, *Anthology,* p. 39.

5. *Vida,* in Boutière et Schutz, *Biographies,* p. 91.

6. Cf. Chrétien de Troyes, *Roman de la charette* (Reims, 1860), ll. 1–30; Arnaut Daniel, *En cest sonet,* ll. 5–7, in Canello, *Arnaldo Daniello,* p. 128.

7. E. Wechssler, "Frauendienst und Vassalität," in *Zeitschrift für franz. Sprache und Litteratur,* XXIV (1902), pp. 159 ff. *Idem, Das Kulturproblem des Minnesangs, I: Minnesang und Christentum* (Halle, 1909). Reviewed by E. Faral in *Annales du Midi,* XXIII (1911), 218.

8. Cf. I. Feuerlicht, "Vom Ursprung der Minne," in *Archivum romanicum* XXIII (1939), p. 36.

9. *Ben feira chanzos,* ed. Audiau, *Poésies des quatre troubadours d'Ussel,* p. 27.

10. *Can chai la fueilla,* stanzas 3 and 6, in U. A. Canello, *Arnaldo Daniello* (Halle, 1883), p. 97.

11. *Doutz brais e critz,* stanzas 5 and 6, in Canello, *op. cit.,* p. 111.

12. The question of the poet's "sincerity" has been discussed often and well. Most serious students of the subject have been inclined to agree with Diez that the troubadour's love is generally fictional in character. F. Diez, *Die Poesie der Troubadours,* p. 122; C. Appel, *Bernart von Ventadorn,* pp. xxiv ff.; N. Zingarelli, "Su Bernart di Ventador," *Studi Medievali,* I, 392; Anglade, *Guiraut Riquier,* p. 241; E. Wechssler, *Das Kulturproblem des Minnesangs,* p. 214. S. Stronski, *Folquet de Marseille,* p. 68; *idem, La Poésie et la réalité aux temps des troubadours* (Oxford, 1943).

13. *Giammai non mi conforto,* in O. J. Tallgren, *Rinaldo D'Aquino* (Helsingfors, 1917), p. 107.

14. Boutière et Schutz, *Biographies,* p. 122.

15. Boutière et Schutz, *Biographies,* p. 3; cf. *vida* of Guirardo lo Ros: "*e l'amors qu'el ac en leis l'enseignet a trobar,*" *ibid.,* p. 188. A very common formula.

16. Bernard de Ventadour, *Chantars no pot gaire valer,* stanza 1, Bergin and Hill, *Anthology,* p. 36.

17. *En cest sonet coind'e leri,* stanza 1, ed. U. A. Canello, *Arnaldo Daniello,* p. 128. Same text in R. Lavaud, "Les Poésies d'Arnaut Daniel," *Annales du Midi,* XXII (1910), p. 300.

18. "I forge and file words of value according to the art of love," *idem, Chanson do·ill mot,* ll. 12–14, in Canello, p. 95; Lavaud, p. 26.

19. Jaufre Rudel, *No sap chantar,* stanza 6, in A. Jeanroy, *Jaufré Rudel* (Paris, 1924), p. 16.

20. In the *Doctrina de compondre dictatz* (c. 1275) we read: "If you wish to make a *vers* you must treat of truths, examples, proverbs, or praises, but not in the semblance of love on a new melody; and the difference between the *chanson* and the *vers* is that the subject is not the same." (Ed. by P. Meyer, *Romania,* VII, 355.)

21. Not all chansons were set to a new melody. Marcabru, for example, writes: "singing on a borrowed air, I shall see if I can make a *vers* on false love." (*Al son desviat,* stanza 1, in Dejeanne, *Marcabru,* p. 19.) And not all chansons were monostrophic. Guiraut Riquier has a song, for instance, in which the first, third, and fifth stanzas, we are told in the MS., are meant to be sung on one melody and the second and fourth on another. (*Res no·m val mos trobars,* in Mahn, *Werke,* IV, p. 69.)

22. It is usually considered that the troubadours derived the *chanson* from the hymn. The *lai,* which is polystrophic, was doubtless derived from the sequence. See G. Reese, *Music in the Middle Ages* (New York, 1940), p. 219; J. Beck, *La Musique des troubadours* (Paris, n.d.), p. 86; P. Aubry, *Trouvères et troubadours* (Paris, 1910), p. 191.

23. *De vulgari eloquentia,* II, 10. Cf. Jeanroy, *Poésie lyrique,* II, 70. Strangely enough, Jeanroy calls the feet in the arrangement AAB, *frons.*

24. In Diez, *Poesie,* 2nd edition (Leipzig, 1883), p. 308.

25. For a collection of examples, see Jeanroy, *Poésie lyrique,* II, 80 ff.

26. See, for example, Arnaut Daniel, *Doutz brais e critz,* in Canello, p. 111. Cf. Raimbaut d'Orange, *Cars, douz e fenhz,* and *En aital rimeta prima,* in Pattison, *Raimbaut d'Orange,* pp. 65 ff. and 72 ff.

27. "Cars bruns et teintz motz entrebesc/ Pensius pensanz . . ." (*Cars, douz e fenhz,* in Appel, *Raimbaut d'Orange,* p. 86, ll. 19 f.; W. T. Pattison, *Raimbaut d'Orange* (University of Minnesota Press, 1952), p. 65.

28. Arnaut Daniel, *L'aura amara,* stanza 1, in Canello, p. 105; Hill and Bergin, *Anthology,* p. 75.

29. See, for example, Angelo Lipari, *The Dolce Stil Novo according to Lorenzo de'Medici* (Yale University Press, 1936), pp. 100 ff.

30. Cf. C. Appel, "Wiederum zu Jaufre Rudel," in *Archiv für das Studium der neueren Sprache,* CVII (1902), p. 338; A. Stimming, *Der Trobador Jaufre*

Rudel (Kiel, 1873); Olin Moore, "Jaufre Rudel and the Lady of Dreams," *PMLA*, XXIX (1914), p. 517; A. Jeanroy, *Les Chansons de Jaufré Rudel* (Paris, 1924), p. iv; G. Frank, "The Distant Love of Jaufre Rudel" in *Modern Language Notes* LVII (1942), pp. 528 ff.; L. Spitzer, *L'Amour lointain de Jaufré Rudel et le sens de la poésie des troubadours* (Chapel Hill, 1944).

31. Marcabru, *Per savi·l tenc ses doptanssa*, stanza 1, ed. Dejeanne, XXXVII; cf. *ibid.*, XIV, ll. 49–54. See K. Vossler, *Der Troubadour Marcabru*, pp. 61 ff. On *trobar clus* see also *Peire d'Auvergne*, ed. Zenker, p. 65; J. Coulet, *Mélanges Chabaneau*, p. 786; Jeanroy, *Poésie lyrique*, II, 32; Pattison, *Raimbaut d'Orange*, p. 52.

32. *Peire d'Auvergne*, ed. R. Zenker (Erlangen, 1900), XIV, 1. 5.

33. *Era·m platz, Giraut de Bornelh*, in Appel, *Chrestomathie*, 5th ed., p. 126; Hill and Bergin, *Anthology*, p. 62.

34. Raimbaut d'Orange, *Pos trobars plans*, in *Revue de littérature romaine*, XL, 414; Pattison, *Raimbaut d'Orange*, p. 118; *Vida* in Boutière et Schutz, *Biographies*, p. 264.

35. *Si·l car no·m ministr' a drech*, ll. 7 ff., in *Giraut de Bornelh, Saemtliche Lieder*, ed. A. Kolsen (Halle, 1910), I, 78.

36. *La flors del verjan*, ll. 18 ff., Kolsen, I, 140.

37. *Si·m sentis fizels amics*, ll. 50 ff., *ibid.*, I, 152.

38. *A penas sai comensar*, stanzas 1–3, ed. Kolsen, I, 15.

39. Guillaume IX, *Ab la dolchor del tems novel*, stanza 1, ed. Jeanroy (Paris, 1927), X, p. 24.

40. Marcabru, *Pois l'iverns d'ogan*, ed. Dejeanne, XXXIX, p. 191.

41. Rudel, *Quan lo rius de la fontana*, ed. Jeanroy (Paris, 1924), II, p. 3; Hill and Bergin, *Anthology*, p. 24.

42. Arnaut de Marueill, *Bel m'es*, Raynouard, *Choix*, III, 208; Hill and Bergin, *Anthology*, p. 55.

43. Peire Roger, *Tan no plou ni venta*, Mahn, *Werke*, I, 120.

44. Bernard de Ventadour, *Can l'erba fresch'e·lh folha par*, in Appel, *Bernart von Ventadorn*, XXXIX, stanza 1; Hill and Bergin, *Anthology*, p. 43.

45. *Can vei la lauzeta mover*, Appel, *op. cit.*, XLIII, stanza 1; Hill and Bergin, *Anthology*, p. 45.

46. For the relation to Chaucer, see A. S. Cook, *Transactions of the Connecticut Academy of Arts and Sciences*, XXIII, 1 ff.

47. Bernard de Ventadour, *Tant ai mo cor*, Hill and Bergin, *Anthology*, p. 46.

48. Guillaume IX, *Pus vezem de novelh florir*, stanzas 8 and 9, ed. Jeanroy, VII, p. 19.

49. Giraut de Bornelh, *Jois e chans*, stanzas 8 and 9, ed. Kolsen, I, 298.

50. *Dragoman senher*, Hill and Bergin, *Anthology*, p. 97. On the *tornada* see also Jeanroy, *Poésie lyrique*, II, 93, note 2. Cf. Dante, *Convivio*, II, 11.

51. Bernard de Ventadour, *Tant ai mo cor*, in Appel, *Bernart von Ventadorn*, p. 257; Hill and Bergin, *Anthology*, p. 46.

52. Bernard de Ventadour, *Can vei la lauzeta mover*, in Appel, *Bernart von Ventadorn*, XLIII; Hill and Bergin, *Anthology*, p. 45.

53. Cf. Dagobert Frey, *Gotik und Renaissance als Grundlagen der modernen Weltanschauung* (Augsburg, 1929), pp. 38, 194.

TRUE LOVE

1. Jeanroy writes that in the poetry of the French *trouvères* also there are no examples of a written song that has to do with other than illicit love. A. Jeanroy in Petit de Julleville, *Histoire de la littérature française* (Paris, 1896), I, 372.

2. "By the fine-seeming which false love puts on, it attracts to itself mad lovers, just as the butterfly has so mad a nature that it is driven into the fire by the splendor with which it burns." Folquet de Marseille, *Sitot me soi*, stanza 2, in S. Stronski, *Le Troubadour Folquet de Marseille* (Cracow, 1910), I.

3. "Truly it seems to me that ladies in this err greatly, that true lovers are never loved." The stanza continues: "It is not for me to reproach them for what they may desire, but it saddens me that a false deceiver is able through his cunning to get as much as a true lover gets of love, or even more." Bernard de Ventadour, *Can la frej aura venta*, stanza 3, Appel, p. 212; Hill and Bergin, *Anthology*, p. 41.

4. Credited to the *Archives nationales de France*, in P. Lacroix, *Vie militaire et réligieuse du moyen-âge* (Paris, 1877), p. 8. Bloch reproduces a similar seal in *La Société féodale*, I, plate IV.

5. "Lady, in your power I have placed my heart, my body and my life. For the love of God, do not forget me. Where the true heart humbles itself, there one should find mercy, ay, to comfort it."

6. Saint-Amand's seal is reproduced in Lacroix, *op. cit.*, p. 7. The motto was referrable to *Isaiah* 26:16–17, in which the church fathers saw a clear reference to the Blessed Virgin. The words *Secretum meum mihi* are used in this connection by Albertus Magnus, *De laudibus mariae, Prologos primus*, in *Opera*, ed. Borgnet, vol. 36, p. 1.

7. Gaucelm Faidit, *Sitot ai tarzat*, Raynouard, *Choix*, III, 290.

8. Guillaume IX, *Farai chansoneta nueva*, stanza 2; ed. Jeanroy, p. 20.

9. *Œuvres*, ed. Blanchemain, I, 216.

10. *Non es meravilha s'ieu chan*, stanza 7, in Hill and Bergin, *Anthology*, p. 39.

11. Castiglione, *Il libro del cortigiano*, III, 53, ed. M. Scherillo (Milan, 1928), p. 324.

12. *Gui d'Ussel, be·m pesa de vos*, stanzas 3 and 5, Audiau et Lavaud, *Anthologie*, p. 199.

13. *Aram digatz*, Audiau, *Les Quatre troubadours d'Ussel*, p. 69. Cf. Henrik Ibsen, *Love's Comedy*, 1862; G. B. Shaw, *Man and Superman*, Act IV (New York, Brentano's, 1905), p. 159.

14. The last couplet involves a pleasant pun, or paronomasia:

Per q'ieu am mais, cals qu'en sia lo critz,
Esser maritz gauzens que drutz marritz.

15. Cf. the discussion in Boccaccio's *Filocolo*, Bk. IV, Question 9.

16. Rigaut de Barbezieux, *Be volria saber d'Amor*, stanza 5, in Chabaneau et Anglade, *Rigaut de Barbezieux* (Montpellier, 1919), p. 22.

17. Sordello, *Aitant ses plus*, ll. 29 f., in M. Boni, *Sordello* (Bologna, 1954), p. 10.

18. Sordello, *Dompna, meillz q'om pot pensar,* ll. 51 ff., in Boni, p. 25.

19. Uc Brunec, *Cortezamen mou en mon cor,* in Raynouard, *Choix,* III, 315.

20. *Lai on cobra,* Raynouard, *Lexique roman,* I, 415; Anglade, *Peire Vidal,* XXXV, 25 ff.; cf. *Romance of the Rose,* ll. 4613 ff.; Andreas, *De amore,* I, 1.

21. *Antonio Tebaldeo Ferrarese, l'opere d'amore* (Venezia, 1534), sonnets 37 and 59. Cf. Serafino, sonnet 101, in *Serafino dall' Aquila, le rime* (Bologna, 1894).

22. Uc de Saint Circ, *Tres enemics,* stanza 1, in Bartsch, *Chrestomathie provençale* (4th edition, Elberfeld, 1880), p. 158. Cf. the debate of the eyes and the heart in Chrétien de Troyes, *Cligès,* ll. 441 ff.

23. Aimeric de Peguilhan, *Anc mais de ioy ni de chan,* stanzas 3–4, in Mahn, *Gedichte,* III, no. 737, p. 40; Shepard and Chambers, *Aimeric de Peguilhan,* p. 74.

24. *De amore,* I, 5; Parry, p. 33.

25. *Cligès,* ll. 600 ff.

26. *Amor e un disio,* in Langley, *Giacomo da Lentino,* p. 61. This sonnet was surely written before 1250.

27. *Dolente lasso,* in G. R. Ceriello, *I Rimatori del dolce stil novo* (Milano, Rizzoli, 1950), p. 33. This is an edition of Di Benedetto's anthology of 1944, of the same title.

28. *L'anima mia vilment'è sbigottita,* in Ceriello, *Rimatori,* p. 56.

29. *Hamlet,* II, 2, 141 ff. Cf. Chaucer, *Knight's Tale,* ll. 1372 ff.; J. L. Lowes, "The Loveres Maladye of Hereos," *Modern Philology,* XI (1914), 491. See also Lawrence Babb, *The Elizabethan Malady* (Michigan State College Press, 1951), pp. 128 ff.

30. Pierre de la Primaudaye, *The French Academie,* trans. T. B. C. (London, 1618), p. 455.

31. See A. Piaget, "La belle dame sans merci," in *Romania,* XXI, XXIII, XXX, XXXIV (1901–1905).

32. Bernard de Ventadour, *Non es meravilha,* stanza 6, Hill and Bergin, *Anthology,* p. 40.

33. Folquet de Marseille, *En chantan m'aven,* Raynouard, *Choix,* III, 160.

34. Peire Raimon, in *Breviari d'Amor,* l. 28976.

35. *De amore,* I, 1; cf. I, VI, dialogue 6, Parry, p. 102.

36. *Cligès,* ed. W. Foerster, ll. 3893 ff.

37. Peire Cardenal, *Ar mi puesc be lauzar d'amor,* in Bartsch, *Provenzalische Chrestomathie,* 174.

38. Bernard de Ventadour, *Non es meravilha,* Hill and Bergin, *Anthology,* p. 40.

39. Arnaut Daniel, *Sols sui qui sai,* ll. 33–35, in Canello, p. 115.

40. Rigaut de Barbezieux, *Atressi com lo leos,* stanza 4, in Chabaneau et Anglade, *Rigaut de Barbezieux,* p. 59.

41. Guillaume IX, *Mout jauzens me prenc en amar,* stanzas 4, 6; Hill and Bergin, *Anthology,* p. 8.

42. In *Mout jauzens me prenc en amar,* ll. 35 f.

43. *Amics Marchabrun,* ll. 49 ff., Hill and Bergin, *Anthology,* p. 21.

44. Peire Rogier, *Tant ai mon cor,* Raynouard, *Choix,* II, 34.

45. Raimbaut d'Orange, *Ab nou cor*, Raynouard, *Choix*, III, 16; Pattison, *Raimbaut d'Orange*, p. 185.

46. Sordello, *Aitant ses plus*, stanza 1, Boni, *Sordello*, p. 8.

47. Andreas, *De amore*, I, VI, dialogue 7; trans. Parry, p. 122.

48. Guillaume, IX, *Ab la dolchor del temps novel*, stanza 4, ed. Jeanroy, p. 25.

49. Arnaut de Marueill, *Bel m'es*, stanza 4, in Audiau et Lavaud, *Anthology*, p. 62; Hill and Bergin, p. 55.

50. In *Breviari d'Amor*, l. 30860.

51. Arnaut Daniel, *Anc ieu non l'aic*, l. 27, in Canello, p. 125.

52. Peire Rogier, *Per far esbaudir*, stanzas 3 and 4, Raynouard, *Choix*, III, 32.

53. Guillaume IX, *Ben vuelh*, ed. Jeanroy, p. 15.

54. Peire Vidal, *Dragoman senher*, stanzas 2, 3, 4, in J. Anglade, *Peire Vidal* (2nd edition, Paris, 1923), p. 40; Hill and Bergin, *Anthology*, p. 96. Cf. *Baros de mon dan* and *Neus ni gels*, in Anglade's edition, for other examples of this genre by the same author.

55. Guillaume IX, *Farai un vers, pos mi sonelh*, Hill and Bergin, *Anthology*, p. 4.

56. Guillaume IX, *Mout jauzens*, stanza 8, ed. Jeanroy, p. 24; Hill and Bergin, p. 7.

57. *En esmai et en consirer*, stanzas 1–4, in Audiau et Lavaud, *Anthologie*, p. 103.

58. Aimeric de Peguilhan, *Totz hom qui so blasma*, ll. 47–48, in W. P. Shepard and F. Chambers, *Aimeric de Peguilhan* (Northwestern University Press, 1950), p. 241.

59. Aimeric de Peguilhan, *De tot en tot*, ll. 35–6, Shepard and Chambers, *op. cit.*, p. 129.

60. *Mout jauzens*, stanza 7, ed. Jeanroy, p. 23; Hill and Bergin, *Anthology*, p. 8.

61. Castiglione, *Il Cortigiano*, III, 63; ed. Scherillo (Milano, 1928), p. 335.

62. Andreas, *De amore*, I, VI, 6; Parry's translation, p. 125.

63. Molière, *L'Imposteur*, III, 3.

64. Gaston Paris, *Romania*, XI (1883), p. 359.

65. Comtesse de Die, *Amicx, ab gran cossirier*, in Raynouard, *Choix*, II, 188.

66. Cf. the Beast Galtissant whom it was the task of Sir Palomides to pursue—"in his body there was such a noise as it had been the noise of thirty couple of hounds questing." *Morte d'Arthur*, IX, 12.

67. Jeanroy thought the *losengiers* were simply rival poets. *Poésie lyrique*, II, 113.

68. *Er ai gran joi*, stanza 3, Kolsen, *Giraut de Bornelh*, I, p. 4.

69. Uc de Saint Circ, *Servit aurai franchamen*, stanza 5, Raynouard, *Choix*, III, 333.

70. Arnaut de Marueill, *Dona genser qu'ieu non sai dir*, stanza 1, Raynouard, *Choix*, III, 199.

71. *Decameron* 4, 10.

72. *Breviari d'Amor*, ll. 31829, 33506. Giraut de Bornelh, *Er ai gran joi*, stanza 4, Hill and Bergin, *Anthology*, p. 56; Kolsen, *op. cit.*, I, p. 4.

73. Rigaut de Barbezieux, *Pauc sap d'amor,* stanza 1, in Chabaneau et Anglade, *Rigaut de Barbezieux,* p. 76.

74. Perdigon, *Ben aio·l mal,* stanza 1, Raynouard, *Choix,* III, 344; Chaytor, *Les Chansons de Perdigon,* p. 4.

75. Arnaut Daniel, *En cest sonet coind'e leri,* stanza 6, in Canello, p. 128.

76. Montanhagol, *Non an tan dig,* ll. 20 ff., in J. Coulet, *Guilhem Montanhagol* (Toulouse, 1898), p. 111.

77. Peire Vidal, Mahn, *Werke,* I, 224.

78. Guiraut Riquier, *De midons e d'amor,* ll. 37 ff., Mahn, *Werke,* IV, 29. Cf. Cino da Pistoia, *S'io mi riputo,* in *Rimatori del dolce stil novo,* p. 149. And cf. Spenser, *Faerie Queene,* Bk. IV, introd., stanza 2.

79. Marcabru, *Cortesamen vuoill comenssar,* stanza 4, ed. Dejeanne, XV, p. 61.

80. Cited in Anglade, *Guiraut Riquier,* p. 292.

81. Bertran de Born, *Volontiers feira sirventes,* stanza 2, in Hill and Bergin, *Anthology,* p. 86.

82. Guillem Montanhagol, *Qui vol esser agradans,* ed. Coulet, XIII, ll. 18 ff., p. 162. On the general question, see A. Jeanroy, *De nostratibus medii aevi poetis, etc.,* pp. 51 f.

83. For citations on this point see Anglade, *Guiraut Riquier,* pp. 272 ff.

84. See, for example, Comtesse de Die, *A chantar m'er de so,* in Audiau et Lavaud, *Anthologie,* p. 51.

85. Arnaut Daniel, *En breu brisara,* l. 9, Canello, p. 129.

86. Aimeric de Belenoi, *Pos lo gai tems,* Mahn, *Gedichte,* III, 904, p. 140.

87. Marcabru, *Bel m'es quan son li fruich madur,* stanza 4, Dejeanne, XIII, p. 53.

88. N'At de Mons in Mahn, *Gedichte,* I, 182.

89. Peirol, *Quoras que·m,* in Raynouard, *Choix,* III, 276; Peire Cardenal, *Pus ma boca,* in Raynouard, *Choix,* IV, 354. And see the discussion in F. Diez, *Die Poesie der Troubadours,* 2nd ed. (Leipzig, 1882), pp. 123 ff.

90. *Decameron* 5, 1.

91. Petrarch, *De contemptu mundi,* dialogue 3, *Opera omnia* (Basel, 1581), I, 355. Draper's translation. *Petrarch's Secret, translated by W. H. Draper* (London, 1921), p. 121.

92. A. Thomas, *Francesco da Barberino* (Paris, 1883), p. 56.

93. *Quan plus creis, dompna,* stanzas 1–3, in M. Boni, *Sordello* (Bologna, 1954). Cf. *Dompna mieils qu'om,* in Boni, p. 26.

94. *En Sordel, que vos es semblan,* stanza 3, in Boni, *Sordello,* p. 79.

95. Granet, *Pos al comte es vengut en corage,* in Mahn, *Gedichte,* III, no. 1017, p. 203. *Bertran d'Alamanon,* ed. Salverda de Grave, p. 95.

96. Sordello, *No·m meravilh,* in Boni, *op. cit.,* p. 195.

97. *Ar ab lo coinde pascor,* ed. J. Coulet, *Le Troubadour Guilhem Montanhagol,* II, ll. 11 ff. Cf. the *sirventés, Del tot vey remaner valor,* in Coulet, p. 87; Audiau et Lavaud, p. 167.

98. Montanhagol, *Nulhs om no val,* in Coulet, X, ll. 10 ff., p. 108.

99. *Ibid.,* ll. 33 ff.

100. Montanhagol, *Non an tan dig,* Coulet, VII, ll. 1–8, p. 111.

101. Montanhagol, *Nulhs om no val,* stanzas 5 and 6, Coulet, p. 141.

102. *Le Morte Darthur,* XVIII, 25; ed. A. W. Pollard (London, 1908), II, 404.

103. *De amore,* I, IV, trans. Parry, p. 31.

104. Petrarch, *De contemptu mundi,* dialogue 3. Draper's translation, *Petrarch's Secret,* pp. 130, 131.

105. *De amore,* I, VI, 1. Parry, p. 42.

106. Uc Brunec, *Pus lo dous tems,* stanzas 5, 6, in Raynouard, *Choix,* IV, 430.

107. *N'Elias, conseill vos deman,* in Raynouard, *Choix,* IV, 22. The point was often the subject of debate. Cf. *Rofin digatz,* Raynouard, V, 437, and Thibaut de Champagne, in *Histoire littéraire,* XXIII, 797.

108. Castiglione, *Il cortegiano,* III, 43, ed. M. Scherillo (Milano, 1928), p. 307.

109. *Othello,* V, 1.

110. Montanhagol, *Non an tan dig,* ed. Coulet, VII, stanza 4, p. 111.

111. *Leu chansoneta m'er a far,* ed. Coulet, VI, stanza 3. On the question of Montanhagol's contribution see Coulet's introduction to his edition (Toulouse, 1898), and the studies of C. de Lollis, *Studi di filol. rom.,* Vol. VIII (1899), pp. 163 ff.; *idem,* in *Sordello* (1896), pp. 79, 280; *idem:* "Dolce stil novo e 'Noel dig di nova maestria' " in *Studi medievali* (Torino, 1904), I, 5–23.

112. *No sap chantar,* stanzas 2, 5, ed. Jeanroy, VI, p. 16. Cf. Guillaume IX, *Farai un vers de dreyt nien,* and Raimbaut d'Orange, *Escotatz, mas no sai que·s es.* The reference in Rudel's song is clearly to the *amor de lonh* which forms the subject of songs II and V in Jeanroy's edition.

113. Guiraut Riquier, *Mout me tenc per ben pagatz,* stanzas 1–3, ed. Pfaff, Mahn, *Werke,* IV, p. 30. See the discussion in J. Anglade, *Le Troubadour Guiraut Riquier* (Bordeaux-Paris, 1905), p. 249.

114. Guiraut Riquier, *Be·m degra de chantar tener,* l. 16, in Mahn, *Werke,* IV, 79.

115. Guiraut Riquier, *Ieu cuiava soven d'amor chantar,* Mahn, *Werke,* IV, p. 75. See also: *Humils, forfaitz, repres e penedens,* Mahn, *Werke,* IV, p. 31.

116. On the question of the monastic terminus of a troubadour's life see the excellent discussion in V. Lowinsky, *Zum geistlichen Kunstlied* (Berlin, 1898).

117. Guiraut de Calanson, *Celeis cui am,* stanza 4, in Hill and Bergin, p. 160. Cf. *De amore,* I, VI, 5; Parry, p. 71.

118. *Als subtilz aprimatz,* ll. 489–567, in Mahn, *Werke,* IV, pp. 210 ff.

119. *Ibid.,* ll. 885 ff. For a full discussion of this poem see Anglade, *Guiraut Riquier,* pp. 254 ff.

120. *Ieu cuiava soven d'amor chantar,* stanzas 1, 2, 6 in Mahn, *Werke,* IV, p. 75. See the discussion in Anglade, *Guiraut Riquier,* pp. 285 and 296.

121. See Anglade, *op. cit.,* pp. 301 ff.; V. Lowinsky, *Zum geistlichen Kunstlied* (Berlin, 1898), pp. 30 ff.

THE SICILIANS

1. See G. Bertoni, *I trovatori d'Italia* (Modena, 1915), pp. 3–25.

2. Dante, *De vulgari eloquentia,* I, 12.

3. "Epistola a Federigo d'Aragona," in D'Ancona e Bacci, *Manuale della letteratura italiana* (Firenze, 1921), II, 84.

4. In E. F. Langley, *The Poetry of Giacomo da Lentino* (Harvard University Press, Cambridge, 1915), p. 24.

5. See Langley, *Giacomo da Lentino*, pp. xxv f.; *idem*, "The Extant Repertory of the Early Sicilian Poets," in *PMLA*, XXVIII (1913), pp. 454 ff.

6. Guittone d'Arezzo, *Ahi lasso*, in Francesco Egidi, *Le Rime di Guittone d'Arezzo* (Bari, 1940), *Canzone* XX, p. 44.

7. *Ora parrà s'eo saverò cantare*, in Egidi, *Guittone d'Arezzo*, *Canzone* XXV, p. 61.

8. *Ibid.*, XXVI, XXVII, for example, in Egidi's edition, pp. 61, 65.

9. Dante, *Purg.* XXVI, 97; Guido Guinizelli, *O caro padre meo*, in G. R. Ceriello, *I Rimatori del dolce stil novo* (Milano, 1950), p. 37.

10. See Cavalcanti, *Da più a uno face un sillogismo*, *Rimatori*, p. 84.

11. *S. Th.*, I, 20, art. 4; I, 108, art. 8; cf. *Convivio*, III, 7.

12. See, for example, Cavalcanti's sonnet *Guata, Manetto*, in *I rimatori del dolce stil novo*, p. 68.

13. Cino da Pistoia, *Tutto ch'altrui*, in *Rimatori*, p. 209. Cecco Angiolieri, *Tre cose solamente*, in F. Monaci, *Crestomazia italiana dei primi secoli* (1955), p. 567; *idem*, *S'i fosse foco*, in A. F. Massèra, *Sonetti burleschi e realistici dei primi due secoli* (2nd ed., 1940), p. 112.

THE NEW STYLE

1. *Convivio*, I, 1. Cf. *De vulgari eloquentia*, II, 4 ff.

2. *Donna mi prega*, stanza 6, in *Rimatori*, p. 42.

3. Cavalcanti, *Posso de gli occhi*, *Rimatori*, p. 62.

4. *Omo ch'è saggio non corre leggiero*, in *Rimatori*, p. 38.

5. Bonagiunta, *Poi ch'avete mutata*, in Monaci, *Crestomazia* (1955), p. 350. See also D. Pierantazzi, "Bonagiunta Orbicciani, campione del 'trobar leu,' " in *Convivium* (1948), pp. 873 ff.

6. See the anonymous sonnet *Poi di tutta bontà* in Monaci, *Crestomazia* (1955), p. 355, and Maestro Francesco da Firenze, *Di penne di paone*, *ibid.*, p. 356.

7. *Purgatorio* XXIV, 52 ff.

8. G. A. Cesareo, "Amor mi spira," in *Miscellanea di studi critici in onore di Arturo Graf* (Bergamo, 1903), pp. 515 ff. L. Azzolina, *Il "dolce stil nuovo"* (Palermo, 1903); K. Vossler, *Die philosophischen Grundlagen zum "süssen neuen Stil"* (Heidelberg, 1914); V. Rossi, "Il 'dolce stil nuovo' " in *Scritti di critica letteraria* (Firenze, 1930), I, 19 ff.; P. Savij-Lopez, "Il dolce stil nuovo" in *Trovatori e poeti* (Palermo, 1906). Cf. also Zingarelli, *La Vita, i tempi e le opere di Dante*, I, 585; II, 1120 ff., and the excellent discussion in N. Sapegno, *Il Trecento* (Milano, 1948), pp. 11 ff. and pp. 60 ff.

9. *De vulgari eloquentia*, II, 7; II, 13. Cf. *Convivio*, IV, 25.

10. *Convivio*, II, 13. Cf. the sonnet *Da quella luce*, if it is his. All the same, Dante made a careful distinction between the goodness and the beauty of a poetic statement: its goodness lay in the meaning (*sentenza*), while its beauty was in the ornament of the language. *Convivio*, II, 11; *De vulgari eloquentia*, II, 1.

11. See Bernard de Ventadour, *supra*, p. 116; Peirol, *Ben dei chantar*,

stanza 1, in Raynouard, *Choix*, III, 273; Arnaut Daniel, *Autet e bas entre·ls prims fuelhs*, in Raynouard, *Choix*, V, 38; Montanhagol, *Non an tan dig*, in Coulet, no. VII, ll. 15–16, p. 110. The *stilnovisti* generally echoed this sentiment: see Cavalcanti, *De vil matera*, in *Rimatori*, p. 82; Lapo Gianni, *Ballata, poi che ti compuose amore, ibid.*, p. 95; Cino, *Qua' son le cose, ibid.*, p. 255.

12. ". . . *Solus proinde de ea digne loquitur qui secundum quod cor dictat verba componit*," Hugh of St. Victor, *Tractatus de gradibus charitatis* in Migne, *PL* 196, 1195. See also Mario Casella in *Studi danteschi*, XVIII (1934), 108.

13. *Purgatorio* XXVI, 97.

14. Cf. *De vulgari eloquentia*, II, 4; II, 5.

15. Cf. Boccaccio, *De genealogia deorum*, XIV.

16. See on this point Bruno Nardi, *Saggi di filosofia dantesca* (Milano, 1930), pp. 1–39.

17. Onesto da Bologna, *Mente e umile*, in T. Casini, *Le rime dei poeti bolognesi del secolo XIII* (Bologna, 1881), no. XLVI, p. 93.

18. *Vita Nuova*, XX; *Convivio*, IV, 13; *Inferno*, VII, 3.

19. *De vulgari eloquentia*, I, 10; I, 12.

20. *Claudii Galeni Opera Omnia*, ed. Kuhn (Leipzig, 1821–1833), XIX, 490 ff.

21. *De Anima*, 413ª–414ª; *Nic. Ethics*, 1102ª–1103ª.

22. Cf. Philip Melanchthon, *Liber De anima* (1540), *Opera*, ed. C.B. Bretschneider (Halle, 1834–1860), XIII, 88.

23. Hugh of St. Victor, *De anima*, II, 13, in Migne, *PL* 40, 788. Cf. Albertus Magnus, *De somno et vigilia*, I, 7, *Opera omnia*, ed. Auguste Borgnet (Paris, 1890), IX, 121; *idem*, *De spiritu et respiratione*, I, 2, 13, Borgnet, IX, 213; *idem*, *De anima*, I, 2, 13, Borgnet, V, 176.

24. With the passages cited in Albertus Magnus, cf. Bartholomaeus Anglicus, *Liber de proprietatibus rerum* (Strassburg, Husner, 1491), III, 22. Cf. *Batman upon Bartholome* (London, 1582), fols. 12–17; Melanchthon, *Opera*, XIII, 88.

25. Albertus Magnus, *De animalibus*, 25, in *Opera omnia*, ed. Borgnet, XII, 549.

26. Dante, *Donne ch'avete*, ll. 51 ff., in *Vita Nuova*, XIX; *Amor e'l cor gentil*, ll. 9 ff., in *Vita Nuova*, XX; *Voi che 'ntendendo*, ll. 10 ff., in *Convivio*, II. Cf. *Convivio*, II, 6, et seq., in which the ray is attributed to the star in the heaven of Venus.

27. Castiglione, *Il libro del cortegiano*, III, 66, ed. M. Scherillo (Milano, 1928), p. 337.

28. Cf. Thomas Aquinas, *S. Th.*, I–II, 23, 4.

29. Thomas Aquinas, *S. Th.*, I, 14; I, 15; I, 26, 2; I, 57, 2; I, 74; I, 79; I, 86. B. Nardi, "L'averroismo del 'primo amico' di Dante," in *Studi danteschi*, XXV (1940), reprinted in *Dante e la cultura medievale* (2nd ed., Bari, 1949); for a further discussion of Cavalcanti's Averroism, see G. Salvadori, *La poesia giovanile e la canzone d'amore di Guido Cavalcanti* (Roma, 1895), pp. 41 ff.; K. Vossler, *op. cit.*, pp. 74 ff. On the question of medieval psychology, see M. W. Bundy, *The Theory of Imagination in Classical and Medieval Thought* (Urbana, 1927), chap. IX.

30. *S. Th.*, I–II, 26, 4.

31. A. Thomas, *Francesco da Barberino et la littérature provençale,* p. 174 f., cites the Comtesse de Die, Arnaut Catalan, and Peire Vidal to the effect that women are higher beings than men. Guittone d'Arezzo says something of the sort also in *Ahi, lasso, che li boni,* F. Egidi, *Guittone d'Arezzo* (Bari, 1940), p. 44. Most of the defenders of women in the course of the *querelle des femmes* follow a line similar to Guittone's. It is rarely made convincing.

32. On this point, which seems obvious to me, most scholars appear to be agreed. See K. Vossler, *op. cit.*, "Die Liebesfrage," and his most ardent critic, V. Rossi, in the essay "Dolce stil novo" in the miscellany, *Le opere minori di Dante Alighieri* (Firenze, 1906), p. 41. But see C. S. Singleton, *An Essay on the* Vita Nuova (Harvard University Press, 1949), p. 69 and note, for a contrary view; namely, that this solution was reached only by Dante in the *Vita Nuova.*

33. Cavalcanti, *De vil matera,* ll. 5–16, in Ceriello, *Rimatori,* p. 82.

34. Guido Orlandi, *Onde si move e donde nasce amore?* in E. Cecchi, *Rime di Guido Cavalcanti* (Lanciano, 1910), p. 42.

35. Mario Casella has published a critical edition of this *canzone* in *Studi di filologia italiana,* VII (1944), 97, with a full interpretation.

36. *Donna mi prega* in *Rimatori,* p. 42; *De vulgari eloquentia,* II, 13; *Convivio,* IV, 20.

37. Cavalcanti, *Veggio negli occhi,* in *Rimatori,* p. 63.

38. Cavalcanti, *Chi è questa che ven,* in *Rimatori,* p. 47.

39. Cavalcanti, *Io non pensava,* in *Rimatori,* p. 50.

40. Cino da Pistoia, *Quando potrò io dir,* in *Rimatori,* p. 223.

41. Cf. Spenser, *The Faerie Queene,* II, 9, 33 ff., in which are described in allegorical terms the heart, the soul, and the attendant spirits.

42. Dante, *E m'incresce,* ll. 43 ff., *Opere di Dante* (Società dantesca, Firenze, 1921), p. 79.

43. *Ibid.*, ll. 47 ff. Cf. *Convivio,* II, VI, 8, in which *anima* and *spirito* are equated with the lady's image and the lover's ego, *Opere,* p. 183.

44. "Another is the appetite which does follow the apprehension of its subject, but out of necessity and not out of free choice. And such is the sensual appetite of the brute, which however in the human being participates to some extent in liberty insofar as it obeys reason." *S. Th.*, I–II, 26, 1.

45. Lapo Gianni, *Angelica figura,* ll. 5 ff., in *Rimatori,* p. 94.

46. See *Convivio,* II, 10.

47. Cf. Dante, *E m'incresce,* ll. 14–32. Cf. *S. Th.*, I–II, 60.

48. *Angelica figura,* ll. 1–4, in *Rimatori,* p. 94. Cf. *Convivio,* II, 6.

49. *Li occhi di quella,* stanza 3, in *Rimatori,* p. 65.

50. *Fresca rosa novella,* ll. 43 f., in *Rimatori,* p. 48.

51. *Paradiso,* XI–XIII. Michelangelo, *La vita del mie amor non è 'l cor mio* in *Le rime di Michelangelo Buonarroti,* ed. Cesare Guasti (Firenze, 1863), p. 186.

52. Cino da Pistoia, *S'io mi reputo,* in *Rimatori,* p. 149; Cavalcanti, *Chi è questa che ven, Rimatori,* p. 47; Dante, *Vita Nuova,* XII, XV, XXVI; *idem, Li occhi dolenti, Vita Nuova,* XXXI. Cf. A. Marigo, *Mistica e scienza nella Vita Nuova* (Padova, 1914), pp. 45 f.

53. Lanfranc Cigala, *Eu non chant ges per talan de chantar,* stanzas 3–4, in G. Bertoni, *I trovatori d'Italia* (Modena, 1915), p. 347.

54. Pons de Capdueil, *De tots chaitius,* in M. v. Napolski, *Ponz de Capduoill* (Halle, 1879), XXIV, p. 85, an interesting example of the troubadour manner in the dirge. Cf. Bonifacio Calvo, *S'ieu ai perdut, no s'en podon jauzir,* in M. Pelaez, "Bonifacio Calvo," *Giornale storico della letterature italiana* (Torino, 1897), XXIX, 336. Clément Marot, *Complainte de Madame Loyse,* in *Œuvres complètes* (Paris, 1894). Spenser, *The Shepheardes Calender,* "November," in *The Minor Poems,* vol. I (Johns Hopkins Press, 1943), p. 104. John Donne, *An Anatomie of the World,* in *Complete Poetry and Selected Prose* (London and New York, 1932), pp. 195 ff.

55. Dante, *Ciò che m'incontra, Vita Nuova,* XV; Cavalcanti, *Li occhi di quella gentil foresetta,* in *Rimatori,* p. 65; Cino, *Come in quelli occhi,* in *Rimatori,* p. 230.

56. *E m'increscе,* ll. 1–3, in *Opere* (Società dantesca), p. 79; cf. Cavalcanti, *A me stesso di me,* in *Rimatori,* p. 61.

57. Cavalcanti, *S'io prego questa donna,* ll. 9–11, in *Rimatori,* p. 57.

58. *Oltre la spera, Vita Nuova,* XLI, in *Opere* (Società dantesca), p. 53.

59. See *Convivio,* III, 8, the commentary on *Amor che nella mente.*

60. Cavalcanti, *Per gli occhi,* in *Rimatori,* p. 61.

61. Cino, *S'io mi reputo,* in *Rimatori,* p. 149.

62. E.g., Montanhagol, in Coulet, VII, ll. 20 ff., p. 111.

63. Giacomo da Lentino, *Io m'agio posto in core,* Langley, p. 73.

64. Inghilfredi, *Audite forte cosa,* in G. Bertacchi, *Poesie pre-dantesche,* p. 59.

65. Guittone d'Arezzo, *Epist.* V, in E. Monaci, *Crestomazia italiana dei primi secoli* (1955), p. 207.

66. *Al cor gentil ripara sempre amore,* in *Rimatori,* p. 20; cf. Dante, *Amor e'l cor gentil,* and the *ragioni* in *Vita Nuova,* XX; See also *Purgatorio,* XVIII, 19.

67. Stanza 7. For this difficult passage I translate the text established by L. Di Benedetto, reprinted in *Rimatori,* p. 22.

68. Thomas Aquinas, *S. Th.,* I, 110, art. 1.

69. *Convivio,* II, 5.

70. Dante, *Amor che ne la mente, Convivio,* III, ll. 19 ff.; cf. *Convivio,* III, 7.

71. St. Augustine, *Confessions,* XIII, 9.

72. *Purgatorio,* XXXI.

73. *Al cor gentil,* Stanza 6.

74. Guinizelli, *I' vo del ver,* in *Rimatori,* p. 32; *Vedut' ho la lucente stella diana,* in *Rimatori,* p. 31; Guittone d'Arezzo, *S'eo tale fosse,* ed. Egidi, p. 194.

75. Cavalcanti, *Veggio negli occhi,* in *Rimatori,* p. 63. Cf. Lapo Gianni, *Dolc' è il pensier,* in *Rimatori,* p. 77; *Angelica figura, ibid.,* p. 94; Dante, *Io mi son pargoletta,* in *Opere* (Società dantesca, 1921), p. 93.

76. St. Bernard, *De diligendo Dei,* ed. Williams and Mills (1926), XII, pp. 60 ff.

77. "Charity I call that movement of the soul which aims at the enjoyment of God for himself alone, and of oneself and one's neighbors for His sake;

cupidity, however, is the movement of the soul to enjoy oneself and one's neighbors and other corporeal things not for the sake of God." *De doctrina christiana,* III, 10 in *PL* 34, 72.

78. *De doctrina christiana,* I, 33; cf. St. Bonaventure, I *Sententiarum* 3, 1, ed. Quaracchi, I, 72.

79. See H. Brinkmann, *Geschichte der lateinischen Liebesdichtung im Mittelalter* (Halle, 1925).

80. Genesis 6.

81. St. Augustine, *De civitate Dei,* XVI, 29.

82. St. Thomas, *S. Th.,* I, 51, 2; I, 111, 1.

83. *Lo intelletto d'amore ch'io solo porto,* in *Rimatori,* p. 176.

84. *Beltà di donne,* in *Rimatori,* p. 47.

85. *Sì mi stringe l'Amore,* stanzas 3–4, in *Rimatori,* p. 182.

86. *Un' alta stella,* in *Rimatori,* p. 122.

87. Dino Frescobaldi, *Donna, da gli occhi tuoi,* in *Rimatori,* p. 124.

88. Dino Frescobaldi, *Poscia ch'io veggio,* ll. 6 ff., in *Rimatori,* p. 126.

89. *Quest' altissima stella,* in *Rimatori,* p. 126.

NEW LIFE

1. *Vita Nuova,* II; cf. *E m'incresce,* ll. 57 ff., in *Opere,* p. 79.

2. *Vita Nuova,* XLII.

3. E.g., in *Convivio,* II, 12, 4, in *Opere,* p. 192.

4. *Vita Nuova,* XXIV; cf. *Purgatorio,* XXX: "This man was such in his new life potentially—"; cf. 2 Cor. 4, 16; 5, 14.

5. *Vita Nuova,* II and XXIX. Beatrice names him in the *Commedia.*

6. St. Augustine, *De libero arbitrio,* II, 16; cf. Isidore Hispalensis, *Liber numerorum,* in Migne, *PL* 83, 190. See, too, E. Mâle, *L'Art réligieux au XIIIe siècle,* p. 25.

7. Cf. C. S. Singleton's brilliantly poetic interpretation in the first section of his *Essay on the* Vita Nuova (Harvard University Press, 1949).

8. So Henry Cochin, *Vita Nova* (Paris, 1914), pp. 211 ff.

9. *Donna pietosa,* ll. 41–42, *Vita Nuova,* XXIII.

10. *Vita Nuova,* XXIV.

11. *Purgatorio,* XXXI, 49 ff.

12. *Vita Nuova,* XVIII.

13. Cf. St. Augustine, *De doctrina christiana,* III, 10, *PL* 34, 72, a passage I have already quoted.

14. *Vita Nuova,* XXIV; cf. *Purgatorio,* XI.

15. *Vita Nuova,* XI, 1 ff.

16. *Paradiso,* XXXI, 64; *Paradiso,* XXXIII, 67 ff.

17. Étienne Jodelle, *Contr'Amours,* in *Les Amours et autres poésies,* ed. van Bever (1907).

INDEX

The Discovery of Talent

The Walter Van Dyke Bingham Lectures on the Development of Exceptional Abilities and Capacities

The Discovery of Talent

Edited by
Dael Wolfle

The Walter Van Dyke Bingham Lectures on the Development of Exceptional Abilities and Capacities

Harvard University Press
Cambridge, Massachusetts
1969

Distributed in Great Britain by Oxford University Press, London

Library of Congress Catalog Card Number: 69–18046

Printed in the United States of America

Introduction

"Finding the talented, encouraging their advancement, making known their potentialities" serves two purposes: individuals are helped to fulfill their promise, and society is enriched. To aid individuals or to enrich society—the emphasis has sometimes been on one and sometimes on the other of these complementary goals—man has long engaged in a talent search. Many cultures, in many ages, in many parts of the world have nurtured their talented youth. Ancient China sought young scholars who could excel in the rigorous civil service examinations that selected servants of the state. The medieval Catholic Church reared many of its cardinals and at least half of its popes from among the humbly born. Indian tribes of British Columbia prepared the most skillful young hunters and fishermen for roles of leadership. These societies and others have shared the common purpose of identifying and encouraging the kinds of talent each prized most highly.

Western Europe and the United States have not only shared this common purpose but in the present century, more deliberately than men have ever done before, have also sought to understand the nature of human talent.

The eleven lectures in this volume describe both aims: to try to understand what talent is, and to try to understand how talent may be recognized and developed. The lectures do not, however, provide a fully rounded treatment of all facets of these two aims. The lecturers were not selected for that purpose, but rather to give recognition to individuals who had in some significant fashion contributed to the better identification of the talented. Each wrote of his own work or of the area in which his interest had centered. Consequently, some matters which other speakers would have chosen to emphasize are not included here, or treated only lightly. For example, it would be of interest to include a history of the means various societies have used to identify the kinds of talent each wanted to cultivate, but no one chose this topic.

Nevertheless, with different degrees of comprehensiveness and detail, the central issues were considered by one or more of the eleven lecturers. The themes they developed could be analyzed in a variety of ways. I choose to take them up under three headings:

1. The nature of human ability and the reasons for its variability.
2. The structure of human ability.
3. The methods of measuring, predicting, and fostering the development of human ability.

The Nature of Human Ability and the Reasons for its Variability

Philosophers, psychologists, and educators have wrestled with the problem of defining *intelligence* or *aptitude* or *ability* or whatever other term one attaches to those qualities that permit some persons to perform socially valued tasks more accurately, more rapidly, or with greater power than do others. Some scholars have assumed the existence of an underlying aptitude which is given to a child by his genes and which exists whether or not it becomes manifest in the particular environment in which he is reared. There is justification for this position, but it often hides the importance of other variables that contribute to human accomplishment. Stalnaker was criticizing such one-sidedness when he said that "the IQ is overrated. Unfortunately, parents and even many teachers regard the IQ as an infallible and crucially significant index. As a result, they ignore the importance of the many other characteristics which contribute to attainment. In the final analysis it is not how bright one is, but what one has accomplished that counts."

Many characteristics of the life history of two men help explain why one accomplishes more than the other. Heredity, education, health, physical energy and work habits, motivation (and all that word encompasses), parental advantage, the often irrelevant aspects of physical appearance or manner of speech, and the quite unpredictable accidents that put one person in the right place at the right time—all such matters may help to explain A's success and B's failure.

Intelligence is a useful concept, but none of the lecturers attribute all of the differences in achievement to differences in intelligence. Eight of the eleven—Terman, Burt, Strong, Wolfle, Stalnaker, MacKinnon, Ghiselli, and Mackworth—explicitly point out that other factors are involved, and several of them devote most of their lectures to these other factors. Terman discusses personality traits that make for success, and Strong describes the efforts he and others have made to measure vocational interests. Burt considers the inheritance of emotional and temperamental qualities that affect the way one works and the amount one achieves. MacKinnon, Ghiselli, and Mackworth concentrate on important kinds of ability that are not well measured by any of the available tests of "intelligence."

Intelligence is not the only variable, but in a society that puts much emphasis on formal education, on the ability to deal with symbols and abstractions, and on the ability to use language effectively, it has rightly been one of the most thoroughly studied. Much of this study has centered on the long-continuing debate over the relative contributions of heredity and environment in creating differences in human achievement. Heredity and environment have each been given credit as the major contributor, and each has its supporter in these pages.

Burt is more assured than any of his colleagues on the heredity-environment problem; for him, hereditary differences far outweigh environmental differences. His analysis of the intelligence-test scores of schoolchildren leads him to conclude that "nearly 23% of the total variance appears due to nongenetic influences, i.e., to environment or to unreliability, and about 77% to genetic factors." When he makes adjustments to allow for what appear to be erroneous scores, he finds that "only about 12% (or slightly more) is apparently due to nongenetic influences and 88% to genetic factors."

Others disagree. Terman, without being statistical or quantitative about the matter, emphasizes the importance of the zeitgeist in determining the abilities that will be fostered, rewarded, developed, and hence varied. Vernon emphasizes environmental determinants, and most of the other lecturers give them substantially greater weight than does Burt.

Had other lecturers been chosen for the series, it is probable that other answers to the heredity-environment question would have been given. I recall an international conference of a dozen years ago in which a distinguished British geneticist announced that 50 percent of the variance in human ability was due to differences in heredity and 50 percent to differences in environment. I asked whether this precise balancing of importance resulted from experimental evidence or represented his best guess about a situation which admitted of no final answer. I was assured that the evidence supported the 50–50 division.

The gentleman gave the wrong answer. He was wrong for two very significant reasons, although it seems to have taken an unduly long time for us to come to understand their significance. One reason is that the relative importance of heredity or environment differs in different populations. All of the difference between two identical twins is attributable to nongenetic factors. Much of the difference between a normal child and a congenital idiot is genetically determined. The relative importance of environment increases with age. In short, the relative contributions of heredity and environment depend upon the population in which they are studied.

Most scholars would recognize this point, as does Burt, and would probably reply that they agree but that in attempting to assess the relative contributions of the two factors, they were dealing with a "normal" population, usually a population of "normal" schoolchildren. Even so, the argument has probably helped draw attention away from the wide variety of environmental variables that affect intellectual growth. In the final address of the series, Vernon offers much the most sophisticated treatment of the problem. In addition to genetic factors, he lists nine environmental determinants of children's performance on standardized tests. Expressed in terms of handicaps, they are: malnutrition and disease, perceptual deprivation in the preschool years and conceptual deprivation during school years, repression of independence and constructive play, family insecurity and lack of planfulness, female dominance, defective education, linguistic handicaps, the conceptual and grammatical structure of the child's native language, and the unattractiveness of adult roles that are visible and the resultant lowering of adolescent aspirations.

Vernon's list of environmental variables provides a good introduction to the second reason why the British geneticist was wrong in saying that exactly 50 percent of the variance could be attributed to inherited and 50 percent to environmental differences. That statement overlooked what the statisticians call interaction. The effects of heredity plus the effects of environment, each acting independently, do not account for 100 percent of the variance; the interaction between heredity and environment must also be included in the equation. As Vernon points out, it is necessary "to get away from the notion of intelligence as a definite entity, an autonomous mental faculty, which simply matures as children grow up. Rather we have to think of it in terms of a cumulative formation of more and more complex and flexible [ways of dealing with situations] which develop through interaction between the growing organism and its environment." The genetically superior infant and his less well endowed brother react differently to the sights and sounds and other stimuli that affect them both. Reacting differently, the superior infant develops a different method of responding to other environmental variables and of dealing with the information he receives. And these differential methods of reacting provide different kinds and amounts of practice in developing inherited traits or tendencies. Thus the interaction builds up. Hereditary differences influence the ways in which the child responds to the environment. Differential responses to the environment influence the manner and speed of development of inherited potentialities. By the time the child is old enough to become a subject for the psychologist's or the geneticist's investigation, a large part of what he does is no longer attributable to either variable acting alone, but must be explained in terms of their interaction.

This view of the matter—sensible and obvious as it seems now—was a long time in developing. It would not be right to say that the earlier scholars who argued as if two definite and immutable figures which add up to 100 could be found were wasting their time. But it is correct to say that the percentages are not immutable, that the problem is now formulated in a more insightful fashion, and that attention can now be turned to problems which stand a greater chance of leading to socially useful ideas for improving child development.

The Structure of Human Ability

So far we have been discussing differences in human ability as if they could all be scaled along a single continuum, as if human ability were a unitary trait. That this is a gross oversimplification of the true situation has been evident for far longer than there have been systematic studies of the nature of ability. It must have been evident for millennia that the person who excelled in one kind of activity did not necessarily reach an equal standard of excellence in other kinds of activities. At least for centuries, some persons have been known as musical geniuses, others as mathematical geniuses, and still others as particularly competent in other areas. There has also been interest in those peculiar individuals who are generally considered stupid but who can remember long strings of numbers heard only once, or who perform surprisingly well in some other fashion.

Statisticians and psychologists have studied, analyzed, and interpreted these differences in an extensive literature on mental factors. Broadly speaking, there have been three schools of thought concerning the underlying structure of human ability.

One is the idea that there is a large and pervasive factor of general intelligence and a relatively restricted number of special factors. Charles Spearman did more than anyone else to establish this view.

The second theory holds that there are a number of relatively independent and more or less co-equal factors which combine in different patterns to account for the differences in performance on different kinds of tasks and tests. Among contributors to this theory, the leader was L. L. Thurstone, who was chosen to give the second lecture in the series. Unfortunately, his lecture was never delivered. Ill health forced a postponement, and Dr. Thurstone's death a few months later terminated a career of brilliant contributions to the study of human ability.

Adherents of the third position hold that intelligence consists of a large number of rather narrow or specific kinds of abilities. The name of Godfrey Thompson is most closely associated with this position.

None of the lecturers are avowed supporters of Godfrey

Thompson's theory of many highly specific factors, but both Spearman's theory of a general factor (usually symbolized by the letter *g*) and Thurstone's theory of group factors claim supporters among the eleven lecturers. Sometimes support is based on theoretical grounds, sometimes on pragmatic grounds.

Terman and Ghiselli brush the factor problem aside by saying or implying that whatever the underlying structure may be in theory, they consider the matter pragmatically and therefore treat intelligence in an unanalyzed fashion. Terman is the more specific: "Both the evidence on early mental development of historical geniuses and that obtained by follow-up of gifted subjects selected in childhood by mental tests point to the conclusion that capacity to achieve far beyond the average can be detected early in life by a well-constructed ability test that is heavily weighted with the *g* factor." Vernon, for both theoretical and practical reasons, also follows Spearman in emphasizing the *g* factor.

Among the lecturers who devote considerable attention to the underlying structure of ability, Guilford is the most positive and enthusiastic. He follows Thurstone more avidly than Thurstone ever followed his own pioneering ideas.

Guilford defines the object of his search in these words: "Each intellectual component or factor is a unique ability that is needed to do well in a certain class of tasks or tests." He identifies some 50 separate factors, which he arranges in a three-dimensional model called "the structure of intellect." On one dimension are arrayed four classes of intellectual content with which one may work: figural, symbolic, semantic, and behavioral or social. The second dimension is defined by five kinds of operation performed: evaluation, convergent thinking, divergent thinking, memorization, and cognition. "When a certain operation is applied to a certain kind of content, as many as six general kinds of products may be involved." These six products constitute the third dimension: units, classes, relations, systems, transformations, and implications. This model, with the three axes divided, respectively, into four, five, and six segments, includes 120 spaces or cells.

According to Guilford, there should be a factor for each cell. Not all have been found, but he has identified about 50. To complicate the matter, however, some of the 120 cells contain more than one factor, and so, he concludes, "we may end up with more than 120 abilities," each of which would be "a unique ability."

Vernon, whose position as the final lecturer in the series gave him an opportunity to get in the last word on several controversial points, rejected Guilford's model. He points out that the intercorrelations among tests—the prime data which the factor analysts analyze—are determined not only by the test content and whatever underlying abilities may be involved, but also "by the form or technique of the tests, its speededness, level of difficulty of the items, whether multiple-choice or creative response, whether analogies, series or classifications, and so forth," and summarizes his position by quoting Quinn McNemar's characterization of "fragmentation of ability into more and more factors of less and less importance."

There is a middle ground in this argument. It goes something like this. Factor analysis is useful in studying the interrelations among a variety of tasks or performances. The number and nature of the factors one finds depend, however, upon the nature, number, and variety of tasks or tests included in the original battery from which the intercorrelations are derived and upon the method used to factor analyze these intercorrelations. There is no unique set of factors that describes once and for all the varieties of intellectual performance. On the practical side, factor analysis helps to give an understanding of the interrelations among different kinds of performance or different tasks. But for personnel selection, or for educational or vocational guidance, little is added by going much beyond the general factor (if one believes in g) or a small number of group factors (if one prefers the multiple-factor approach).

In a general and qualitative fashion, one can relate this conclusion to the earlier discussion of the nature of human ability and the reasons for its variability. The determiners of human ability are multiple and the relations among them complex. They have acted in different combinations, with different effects, at different times, on different individuals. There is wide variety in the kinds of material (verbal, pictorial, arithmetical, symbolic, and so forth) that can be dealt with by human beings, and there is also wide variety in the kinds of tasks that involve these varied materials. One must therefore expect to find varying patterns of correlations when different sets of tasks, involving different types of materials, are presented to different groups of subjects. That there is no unique set of underlying factors that can "explain" all the varieties and differences in human ability is the only reasonable conclusion.

Nevertheless, there are consistencies in human performance. There are major trends or themes in human development and in education. Factor analysis provides a sometimes useful means of identifying and of coming closer to understanding these consistencies.

Measuring, Predicting, and Fostering the Development of Human Ability

When Terman was young, the slogan "early ripe, early rot" was widely accepted. Egalitarianism leads to such beliefs. The precocious child is expected to burn out. The backward one is expected to be a late bloomer. The person who excels in one field is deficient in another. And of course there is some truth in these generalizations. Some bright children do not reach the levels expected of them. Others accomplish more than early indications would lead one to predict. People do have their strengths and their weaknesses.

But there is also consistency in human performance. No one has done more than Terman to demonstrate that intellectual superiority in childhood is generally followed by intellectual superiority as an adult. Who better than Terman could have started off this series of addresses with solid, empirical evidence that talented youngsters become talented adults, that the stories about the backward boyhoods of the great men of history lack foundation, that the slogan "early ripe, early rot" is in fact rot?

Terman's evidence (and, of course, the evidence from other sources) that bright children become able, productive adults, the evidence that there is consistency in human performance both over time and over a range of related tasks, makes possible not only research on the structure of ability but also makes possible, and socially useful, a variety of practical efforts to identify and cultivate talents. Several of the lecturers deal with such efforts.

Stalnaker describes "how the problem of discovering and encouraging talent on an extensive scale has actually been handled" by the National Merit Scholarship Program. Starting with about 600,000 high school juniors who took the Merit Program preliminary selection test in 1960, a succession of hurdles reduced the group a year later to about 5,000 who received college scholarships and another 30,000 who received honors or commendations. Accompanying the scholarship program is a continuing series of research studies on methods of selection and on the subsequent performance of the very superior high school students who go through the selection process. Stalnaker's data agree with Terman's in showing that the very bright tend to be superior in other respects and that their high performance continues in later years.

MacKinnon and Mackworth discuss creativity or originality. MacKinnon studied mature, professional men judged by their colleagues to be high in creativity. Architecture was the field he used to illustrate his work. In such groups, all of whose members are at least moderately intelligent, he found the relationship between intelligence, as usually measured, and rated creativity to be essentially zero. The creative architect is not necessarily more "intelligent" than the uncreative one, but somehow he uses his abilities differently. His childhood experiences and early family environment and treatment also differed typically from those of the less creative architects, as did a number of the personality traits MacKinnon investigated. But what kinds of training or experiences are effective in producing high creativity is still a puzzle. As a student, the truly creative individual may be rebellious, sometimes uncertain and in some turmoil, and thus hard for the teacher to accept. The warning to teachers is not to quell creativity by insisting on docility.

Mackworth's analysis of scientific originality differentiates between scientists who are able to solve problems and the more imaginative and seminal ones who advance scientific thought by formulating new problems. Because the latter are fewer and more precious, he goes on to discuss the arrangements, methods of support, and working relationships that might favor research productivity.

Strong and Ghiselli also depart from the general emphasis on intelligence to discuss other elements involved in career choice and performance. Strong raises questions about the role of interests, attitudes, goals, and satisfactions in determining vocational choice and in contributing to vocational success. Despite general agreement on the importance of these elements of the human makeup, Strong's lecture is evidence of how little we know about them.

Ghiselli's examinations of managerial talent show that intelligence is only one of the elements required for success, and that at the very highest levels intellectual ability may even be a detriment: "It is possible that these individuals at the very extreme high levels of capacity to deal with abstract ideas and concepts do not find in managerial activities the intellectual challenge they need." In agreement with Strong, Ghiselli also finds interests, attitudes, and personality variables significant determiners of managerial competence.

Paterson deals primarily with problems of vocational guidance and vocational training and considers both effective and successful people and some who are not. He considers the ill effects of discrimination in preventing the normal development of talent and regrets the talent that is lost to society because we fail to develop it adequately.

The urgent social problem of preventing potential talent from being killed or stunted has been coming into increasingly sharp focus in recent years. It has taken time to realize the importance of this problem; it was so easily passed over by those with strong beliefs in heredity. Burt quotes Karl Pearson's explanation: "It is not so much that the slums create the dullards, but rather that the duller stocks gravitate automatically to the slums." Growing knowledge of the lifelong effects of early childhood experience and more sophisticated notions of genetic heterogeneity now give the slums more credit for creating dullards than Pearson was willing to concede.

Vernon considers the importance, and the current ignorance, of the specific effects of child-rearing customs and methods. The opportunity and motivation for intellectual development in a child born into a home marked by ambition, school orientation, cultural and intellectual interests, and eagerness to help the child explore ideas and sensory experiences or try out and improve his skills, differ so tremendously from the opportunity and motivation of a child born into a home in which these positive factors are all lacking that the two youngsters start off on completely different roads toward maturity.

We know too little about the specific effects of different child-rearing customs, as Vernon points out, and as Wolfle emphasizes in describing Strodtbeck's comparison of equally bright boys in Jewish and Italian families in the United States. As we acquire more knowledge concerning the specific effects of early childhood differences, we can expect to learn how to develop more high talent, how to develop more talent of moderate levels, and also how to avoid some of the talent loss we now suffer.

The strategy of talent development is Wolfle's theme. Agreeing with Stalnaker, Ghiselli, MacKinnon, and others that the selection of students for promotion to higher levels should take into consideration variables other than the easily and customarily measured ones—school grades and intelligence-test scores—and agreeing with Paterson and Vernon on the need to study the social and cultural factors that stimulate or retard intellectual development, he emphasizes the importance of intellectual diversity and tries to outline a socially useful strategy for talent development. That such a strategy can be presented only in bare and tentative outline reflects the fact stressed by a number of the lecturers that there are large gaps in our knowledge. Much has been learned about the nature of human ability and about how it develops. But there is much that is still unknown.

Retrospect

Walter Van Dyke Bingham, pioneer American applied psychologist, who gave none of these lectures, was responsible for all of them. In his autobiography, Bingham describes one of his major interests as "finding the talented, encouraging their advancement, making known their potentialities."[1] He worked at this self-assigned task consciously, deliberately, and effectively. As he anticipated the end of his own life, this dominant purpose, sup-

1. Walter Van Dyke Bingham, *A History of Psychology in Autobiography*, Vol. IV, pp. 1–26, Clark University Press, Worcester, Mass., 1952.

ported by "a fondness for looking ahead, planning, and *initiating a cooperative enterprise,*" [2] led him to propose the "Discovery of the Talented" project. With his will, he left a memorandum expressing the wish that an annual series of lectures might be established to "rivet attention . . . on the great value of accurate identification of exceptionally promising young people" and also to honor those persons who had made significant contributions to the improvement of methods for the discovery and development of talent. The generosity of his wife, Millicent Todd Bingham, and the cooperation of the American Psychological Association made it possible to carry out that wish. Through 12 lectures, including the one Thurstone was unable to deliver, the "Discovery of the Talented" project continued, each year with a different lecturer, and each year at a different university, a university selected because it had been the site of notable work on talent identification or development. This first phase of the carrying out of Bingham's wish is now ended. Mrs. Bingham has provided for its continuation, however. From now on, the lectures, under the new name of the Walter Van Dyke Bingham Lectures, will be sponsored by and presented at Carnegie-Mellon University—the new name of the Carnegie Institute of Technology, where Dr. Bingham founded the first American department of applied psychology and where his papers and memorabilia are preserved.

Now, more than fifteen years after Dr. Bingham's death, how does the idea seem? The answer was given in part by one of the critics who read the lectures when Harvard University Press was considering bringing them together in book form. He wrote:

> The lectures represent a wide-ranging presentation of a number of current ideas concerning talent by persons who have been closely concerned with research on that topic.

Ibid.

> These papers are written in a way which should make the content accessible to a broad audience of interested persons extending well beyond the category of professional psychologists . . . for example, to persons concerned with all aspects of education, with business, with government, and with the arts.

In a larger sense the lectures have been part of a great national and international effort to develop more fully the potentialities of able young people. Private foundations, industry, state governments, and particularly the Federal Government provide vast sums to improve education and to assist students. Special efforts are being made to discover young people whose high potential would otherwise remain hidden. Studies of creativity and other types of accomplishment are vigorously pursued. John Gardner's phrase "the pursuit of excellence" has been so widely used that it has become a cliché. It is neither possible nor worthwhile to determine how much the Discovery of the Talented project contributed to this upsurge of interest in the identification and education of talented young persons. The significant fact is the upsurge itself.

At the same time, there has come to be widespread recognition of the huge social loss we suffer in all ranges of the ability distribution. Far too many children are born into homes that give them little intellectual stimulation, in which their potentialities cannot mature, in which attitudes and customs are so rigid that originality and creativeness cannot flourish, in which the traits and abilities required for effective participation in a complex technological society have little chance to develop. The stultifying effect of these early handicaps on the whole course of life are being realized as never before, and so is their social cost in poverty, apathy, delinquency, crime, inability to compete for jobs in a technological society, and the probability that the unsuccessful will pass on to their children their own frustration, alienation, and what the anthropologist Oscar Lewis has called the "culture of poverty."

Compassion for the individuals who are so trapped, and concern for the health of the society of which they are a part, have now led to the beginnings of massive efforts to remedy the handicaps of a deficient home environment, to overcome the cancer of poverty, and to raise the deprived closer to the level of the average in education, marketable abilities, and self-esteem. These efforts are mandatory, for to the extent that they succeed, they will raise the whole tone and level of accomplishment of society as well as the level of satisfaction and well-being of its members.

But by themselves, these efforts are not enough. Herbert J. Muller, philosophizing on what makes a civilization succeed or fail, concluded that the most reasonable ideal is a democratic society in which there is "culture and education for all, within their capacity." But he went on to remind us that achievement of this ideal requires special attention to those who can contribute most.

> The creative achievements of civilization to date have been primarily the work of an elite, and the greatest achievements will always be due immediately to the gifted few. Ideally, democracy would mean not merely a general rise in the culture of the masses but an elite that is freely recruited, that may be enlarged and constantly invigorated by special talent from the ranks. . . .
>
> For us, the last word is a challenge to the educated, privileged classes. The problem today is not merely a matter of improving the minds and tastes of common men. It is also a question of whether the elite can provide better political, intellectual, and spiritual leadership than it has in all previous societies. For if the creative achievements of civiliza-

> tion have been due primarily to the elite, so too have the failures of civilization.[3]

"Finding the talented, encouraging their advancement, making known their potentialities" will continue to serve two high purposes: gifted individuals will be helped to fulfill their promise and civilization will be enriched.

Washington, D.C., October 21, 1968 Dael Wolfle

3. Herbert J. Muller, *The Uses of the Past,* Oxford University Press, Oxford, 1952, and New American Library, New York, 1954.

Contents

The Discovery of Talent

The Walter Van Dyke Bingham Lectures on the Development of Exceptional Abilities and Capacities

Lewis M. Terman

The Discovery and Encouragement of Exceptional Talent[1]

I am deeply sensible of the honor of being invited by the American Psychological Association, through its special committee, to give the initial lecture in the Walter V. Bingham Lectureship series.

I am especially happy that Chancellor Kerr and the psychology department of the University of California graciously acceded to my request that the address be given here, where I have many friends and where so much notable research has been done on the mental, physical, and personality development of children; where such famous experiments have been made on the purposive behavior of rats, both gifted and dull; where authoritarian minds have been so exhaustively probed; and where the recently established Institute of Personality Assessment is engaged in such promising investigations.

Before beginning my lecture I should like to pay tribute to the life work of the late Walter Van Dyke Bingham, at whose request

1. This paper is based on the first Walter Van Dyke Bingham Lecture, given at the University of California at Berkeley, March 25, 1954. It was first published in the *American Psychologist,* 1954, vol. 9, no. 6 (June), pp. 221–230.

this lectureship was established by Mrs. Bingham. Born in Iowa in 1880, young Walter early demonstrated his exceptional gifts by skipping both the third and fourth grades and by graduating from high school at the age of 16. As a freshman in college he was the youngest in his class and the only one to make a straight A record. After graduating from Beloit College he taught in high schools for four years, then entered the graduate school of the University of Chicago and in 1908 won his doctorate in psychology with honors. From 1908 to 1910 he was instructor at Teachers College and assistant to Edward L. Thorndike. In 1910 he was appointed assistant professor at Dartmouth to teach all their classes in psychology, but when he left there five years later the staff included an instructor and two full professors, all selected by Dr. Bingham. His rare ability to recognize exceptional talent is indicated by the fact that both of these professors became college presidents.

From 1915 to 1924 Dr. Bingham was professor of psychology and head of the division of applied psychology at the Carnegie Institute of Technology, and it was here that he found the opportunity he had long wanted to promote large-scale investigations in applied psychology. The faculty he assembled for that purpose was one of the most distinguished ever brought together anywhere in this country. Among them were J. B. Miner, L. L. Thurstone, Walter Dill Scott, Kate Gordon, and E. K. Strong. Three others appointed as consultants were F. L. Wells, G. M. Whipple, and Raymond Dodge. It was this faculty that, under the wise leadership of Dr. Bingham, laid the solid foundation for vocational and industrial psychology in America.

When our country entered the war in 1917, nearly all of the Carnegie group were soon engaged in psychological work either for the Surgeon General or for the War Department or for both. Dr. Bingham was a member of Yerkes' committee of seven that devised the army mental tests, in 1917–18 was a member of the Committee on Classification of Personnel (the committee charged with devising and administering vocational tests in all the army camps), and in 1918–19 was Lt. Colonel in the Personnel Branch of the Army General Staff.

During World War II even greater service was rendered by Dr. Bingham as chief psychologist for the Office of Adjutant General from 1940 to 1946. In this capacity he and his committee were responsible not only for the Army General Classification Test that was administered to the many millions of inductees, but also for advising on the entire program of psychological services in the armed forces. In this capacity too he was in position to influence the selection of men best qualified to head the various branches of military psychology. I have no doubt that the extraordinary success of the work accomplished by psychologists during the war was largely due to his leadership and to his judgment of men.

If time permitted, I should like to tell you about his more than 200 publications, about the great variety of problems they dealt with, and the contributions they made in several fields of psychology, but I am sure that if Dr. Bingham were here he would want me to get on with our scheduled program.

I have often been asked how I happened to become interested in mental tests and gifted children. My first introduction to the scientific problems posed by intellectual differences occurred well over a half-century ago when I was a senior in psychology at Indiana University and was asked to prepare two reports for a seminar, one on mental deficiency and one on genius. Up to that time, despite the fact that I had graduated from a normal college as a Bachelor of Pedagogy and had taught school for five years, I had never so much as heard of a mental test. The reading for those two reports opened up a new world to me, the world of Galton, Binet, and their contemporaries. The following year my MA thesis on leadership among children (Terman, 1904) was based in part on tests used by Binet in his studies of suggestibility.

Then I entered Clark University, where I spent considerable time during the first year in reading on mental tests and precocious children. Child prodigies, I soon learned, were at that time in bad repute because of the prevailing belief that they were usually psychotic or otherwise abnormal and almost sure to burn themselves out quickly or to develop postadolescent stupidity. "Early ripe, early rot" was a slogan frequently encountered. By the time I reached my last graduate year, I decided to find out for myself how precocious children differ from the mentally backward, and accordingly chose as my doctoral dissertation an experimental study of the intellectual processes of fourteen boys, seven of them picked as the brightest and seven as the dullest in a large city school (Terman, 1906). These subjects I put through a great variety of intelligence tests, some of them borrowed from Binet and others, many of them new. The tests were given individually and required a total of 40 or 50 hours for each subject. The experiment contributed little or nothing to science, but it contributed a lot to my future thinking. Besides "selling" me completely on the value of mental tests as a research method, it offered an ideal escape from the kinds of laboratory work which I disliked and in which I was more than ordinarily inept. (Edward Thorndike confessed to me once that *his* lack of mechanical skill was partly responsible for turning *him* to mental tests and to the kinds of experiments on learning that required no apparatus.)

However, it was not until I got to Stanford in 1910 that I was able to pick up with mental tests where I had left off at Clark University. By that time Binet's 1905 and 1908 scales had been published, and the first thing I undertook at Stanford was a tentative revision of his 1908 scale. This, after further revisions, was published in 1916. The standardization of the scale was based on tests of a thousand children whose IQ's ranged from 60 to 145. The contrast in intellectual performance between the dullest and the brightest of a given age so intensified my earlier interest in the gifted that I decided to launch an ambitious study of such children at the earliest opportunity.

My dream was realized in the spring of 1921 when I obtained a generous grant from the Commonwealth Fund of New York City for the purpose of locating a thousand subjects of IQ 140 or higher. More than that number were selected by Stanford-Binet tests from the kindergarten through the eighth grade, and a group mental test given in 95 high schools provided nearly 400 additional subjects. The latter, plus those I had located before 1921, brought the number close to 1,500. The average IQ was approximately 150, and 80 were 170 or higher (Terman, 1925).

The twofold purpose of the project was, first of all, to find what traits characterize children of high IQ, and secondly, to follow them for as many years as possible to see what kind of adults they might become. This meant that it was necessary to select a group representative of high-testing children in general. With the help of four field assistants, we canvassed a school population of nearly a quarter million in the urban and semiurban areas of California. Two careful checks on the methods used showed that not more than 10 or 12 percent of the children who could have qualified for the group in the schools canvassed were missed. A sample of close to 90 percent insured that whatever traits were typical of these children would be typical of high-testing children in any comparable school population.

Time does not permit me to describe the physical measurements, medical examinations, achievement tests, character and interest tests, or the trait ratings and other supplementary information obtained from parents and teachers. Nor can I here describe the comparative data we obtained for control groups of unselected children. The more important results, however, can be stated briefly: children of IQ 140 or higher are, in general, appreciably superior to unselected children in physique, health, and social adjustment; markedly superior in moral attitudes as measured either by character tests or by trait ratings; and vastly superior in their mastery of school subjects as shown by a three-hour battery of achievement tests. In fact, the typical child of the group had mastered the school subjects to a point about two grades beyond the one in which he was enrolled, some of them three or four grades beyond. Moreover, his ability as evidenced by achievement in the different school subjects is so general as to refute completely the traditional belief that gifted children are usually one-sided. I take some pride in the fact that not one of the major conclusions we drew in the early 1920's regarding the traits that are typical of gifted children has been overthrown in the three decades since then.

Results of thirty years' follow-up of these subjects by field studies in 1927–28, 1939–40, and 1951–52, and by mail follow-up at other dates, show that the incidence of mortality, ill health, insanity, and alcoholism is in each case below that for the generality of corresponding age, that the great majority are still well adjusted socially, and that the delinquency rate is but a fraction of what it is in the general population. Two forms of our difficult Concept Mastery Test, devised especially to reach into the stratosphere of adult intelligence, have been administered to all members of the group who could be visited by the field assistants, including some 950 tested in 1939–40 and more than 1,000 in 1951–52. On both tests they scored on the average about as far above the generality of adults as they had scored above the generality of children when we selected them. Moreover, as Dr. Bayley and Mrs. Oden have shown, in the twelve-year interval between the two tests, 90 percent increased their intellectual stature as measured by this test. "Early ripe, early rot" simply does not hold for these subjects. So far, no one has developed postadolescent stupidity!

As for schooling, close to 90 percent entered college and 70 percent graduated. Of those graduating, 30 percent were awarded honors and about two-thirds remained for graduate work. The educational record would have been still better but for the fact that a majority reached college age during the great depression. In their undergraduate years 40 percent of the men and 20 percent of the women earned half or more of their college expenses, and the total of undergraduate and graduate expenses earned amounted to $670,000, not counting stipends from scholarships and fellowships, which amounted to $350,000.

The cooperation of the subjects is indicated by the fact that we have been able to keep track of more than 98 percent of the original group, thanks to the rapport fostered by the incomparable field and office assistants I have had from the beginning of the study to the present. I dislike to think how differently things could have gone with helpers even a little less competent.

The achievement of the group to midlife is best illustrated by the case histories of the 800 men, since only a minority of the women have gone out for professional careers (Terman, 1954). By 1950, when the men had an average age of 40 years, they had published 67 books (including 46 in the fields of science, arts, and the humanities, and 21 books of fiction). They had published more than 1,400 scientific, technical, and professional articles; over 200 short stories, novelettes, and plays; and 236 miscellaneous articles on a great variety of subjects. They had also authored more than 150 patents. The figures on publications do not include the hundreds of publications by journalists that classify as news stories; editorials, or newspaper columns; nor do they include the hundreds if not thousands of radio and TV scripts.

The 800 men include 78 who have taken a PhD degree or its equivalent, 48 with a medical degree, 85 with a law degree, 74 who are teaching or have taught in a four-year college or university, 51 who have done basic research in the physical sciences or engineering, and 104 who are engineers but have done only applied research or none. Of the scientists, 47 are listed in the

1949 edition of *American Men of Science.* Nearly all of these numbers are from 10 to 20 or 30 times as large as would be found for 800 men of corresponding age picked at random in the general population, and are sufficient answer to those who belittle the significance of IQ differences.

The follow-up of these gifted subjects has proved beyond question that tests of "general intelligence," given as early as six, eight, or ten years, tell a great deal about the ability to achieve either presently or 30 years hence. Such tests do not, however, enable us to predict what direction the achievement will take, and least of all do they tell us what personality factors or what accidents of fortune will affect the fruition of exceptional ability. Granting that both interest patterns and special aptitudes play important roles in the making of a gifted scientist, mathematician, mechanic, artist, poet, or musical composer, I am convinced that to achieve greatly in almost any field, the special talents have to be backed up by a lot of Spearman's *g*, by which is meant the kind of general intelligence that requires ability to form many sharply defined concepts, to manipuate them, and to perceive subtle relationships between them; in other words, the ability to engage in abstract thinking.

The study by Catharine Cox of the childhood traits of historical geniuses gives additional evidence regarding the role of general intelligence in exceptional achievement. That study was part of our original plan to investigate superior ability by two methods of approach: (*a*) by identifying and following living gifted subjects from childhood onward; and (*b*) by proceeding in the opposite direction and tracing the mature genius back to his childhood promise. With a second grant from the Commonwealth Fund, the latter approach got under way only a year later than the former and resulted in the magnum opus by Cox entitled *The Early Mental Traits of Three Hundred Geniuses* (1926). Her subjects represented an unbiased selection from the top 510 in Cattell's objectively compiled list of the 1,000 most eminent men of history. Cox and two able assistants then scanned some 3,000 biographies in search of information that would throw light on the early mental development of these subjects. The information thus obtained filled more than 6,000 typed pages. Next, three psychologists familiar with mental age norms read the documentary evidence on all the subjects and estimated for each the IQ that presumably would be necessary to account for the intellectual behavior recorded for given chronological ages. Average of the three IQ estimates was used as the index of intelligence. In fact two IQ's were estimated for each subject, one based on the evidence to age 17, and the other on evidence to the mid-twenties. The recorded evidence on development to age 17 varied from very little to an amount that yielded about as valid an IQ as a good intelligence test would give. Examples of the latter are Goethe, John Stuart Mill, and Francis Galton. It was the documentary information on Galton, which I summarized and published in 1917 (Terman, 1917), that decided me to prepare plans for the kind of study that was carried out by Cox. The average of estimated IQ's for her 300 geniuses was 155, with many going as high as 175 and several as high as 200. Estimates below 120 occurred only when there was little biographical evidence about the early years.

It is easy to scoff at these post-mortem IQ's, but as one of the three psychologists who examined the evidence and made the IQ ratings, I think the author's main conclusion is fully warranted; namely, that "the genius who achieves highest eminence is one whom intelligence tests would have identified as gifted in childhood."

Special attention was given the geniuses who had sometime or other been labeled as backward in childhood, and in every one of these cases the facts clearly contradicted the legend. One of them was Oliver Goldsmith, of whom his childhood teacher is said to have said "Never was so dull a boy." The fact is that little Oliver was writing clever verse at 7 years and at 8 was reading Ovid and Horace. Another was Sir Walter Scott, who at 7 not only read widely in poetry but was using correctly in his written prose such words as "melancholy" and "exotic." Other alleged childhood dullards included a number who disliked the usual diet of Latin and Greek but had a natural talent for science. Among these were the celebrated German chemist Justus von Liebig, the great English anatomist John Hunter, and the naturalist Alexander von Humboldt, whose name is scattered so widely over the maps of the world.

In the cases just cited one notes a tendency for the direction of later achievement to be foreshadowed by the interests and preoccupations of childhood. I have tried to determine how frequently this was true of the 100 subjects in Cox's group whose childhood was best documented. Very marked foreshadowing was noted in the case of more than half of the group, none at all in less than a fourth. Macaulay, for example, began his career as historian at the age of 6 with what he called a "Compendium of Universal History," filling a quire of paper before he lost interest in the project. Ben Franklin before the age of 17 had displayed nearly all the traits that characterized him in middle life: scientific curiosity, religious heterodoxy, wit and buffoonery, political and business shrewdness, and ability to write. At 11 Pascal was so interested in mathematics that his father thought it best to deprive him of books on this subject until he had first mastered Latin and Greek. Pascal secretly proceeded to construct a geometry of his own and covered the ground as far as the 32nd proposition of Euclid. His father then relented. At 14 Leibnitz was writing on logic and philosophy and composing what he called "An Alphabet of Human Thought." He relates that at this age he took a walk one afternoon to consider whether he should accept the "doctrine of substantial forms."

Similar foreshadowing is disclosed by the case histories of my gifted subjects. A recent study of the scientists and nonscientists among our 800 gifted men (Terman and Oden, 1947) showed many highly significant differences between the early interests and social attitudes of those who became physical scientists and those who majored in the social sciences, law, or the humanities. Those in medical or biological sciences usually rated on such variables somewhere between the physical scientists and the nonscientists.

What I especially want to emphasize, however, is that both the evidence on early mental development of historical geniuses and that obtained by follow-up of gifted subjects selected in childhood by mental tests point to the conclusion that capacity to achieve far beyond the average can be detected early in life by a well-constructed ability test that is heavily weighted with the *g* factor. It remains to be seen how much the prediction of future achievement can be made more specific as to field by getting, in addition, measures of ability factors that are largely independent of *g*. It would seem that a 20-year follow-up of the thousands of school children who have been given Thurstone's test of seven "primary mental abilities" would help to provide the answer. At present the factor analysts don't agree on how many "primary" mental abilities there are, nor exactly on what they are. The experts in this field are divided into two schools. The British school, represented by Thomson, Vernon, and Burt, usually stop with the identification of at most three or four group factors in addition to *g*, while some representing the American school feed the scores of 40 or 50 kinds of tests into a hopper and manage to extract from them what they believe to be a dozen or fifteen separate factors. Members of the British school are as a rule very skeptical about the realities underlying the minor group factors. There are also American psychologists, highly skilled in psychometrics, who share this skepticism. It is to be hoped that further research will give us more information than we now have about the predictive value of the group factors. Until such information is available, the scores on group factors can contribute little to vocational guidance beyond what a good test of general intelligence will provide.

I have always stressed the importance of *early* discovery of exceptional abilities. Its importance is now highlighted by the facts Harvey Lehman has disclosed in his monumental studies of the relation between age and creative achievement (Lehman, 1953). The striking thing about his age curves is how early in life the period of maximum creativity is reached. In nearly all fields of science, the best work is done between ages 25 and 35, and rarely later than 40. The peak productivity for works of lesser merit is usually reached 5 to 10 years later; this is true in some twenty fields of science, in philosophy, in most kinds of musical composition, in art, and in literature of many varieties. The lesson for us from Lehman's statistics is that the youth of high achievement potential should be well trained for his life work before too many of his most creative years have been passed.

This raises the issue of educational acceleration for the gifted. It seems that the schools are more opposed to acceleration now than they were thirty years ago. The lockstep seems to have become more and more the fashion, notwithstanding the fact that practically everyone who has investigated the subject is against it. Of my gifted group, 29 percent managed to graduate from high school before the age of 16½ years (62 of these before 15½), but I doubt if so many would be allowed to do so now. The other 71 percent graduated between 16½ and 18½. We have compared the accelerated with the nonaccelerated on numerous case-history variables. The two groups differed very little in childhood IQ, their health records are equally good, and as adults they are equally well adjusted socially. More of the accelerates graduated from college, and on the average nearly a year and a half earlier than the nonaccelerates; they averaged higher in college grades and more often remained for graduate work. Moreover, the accelerates on the average married .7 of a year earlier, have a trifle lower divorce rate, and score just a little higher on a test of marital happiness (Terman and Oden, 1947). So far as college records of accelerates and nonaccelerates are concerned, our data closely parallel those obtained by the late Noel Keys (1938) at the University of California and those by Pressey (Pressey, 1949) and his associates at Ohio State University.

The Ford Fund for the Advancement of Education has awarded annually since 1951 some 400 college scholarships to gifted students who are not over 16½ years old, are a year or even two years short of high school graduation, but show good evidence of ability to do college work. Three quarters of them are between 15½ and 16½ at the time of college entrance. A dozen colleges and universities accept these students and are keeping close track of their success. A summary of their records for the first year shows that they not only get higher grades than their classmates, who average about two years older, but that they are also equally well adjusted socially and participate in as many extracurricular activities (1953). The main problem the boys have is in finding girls to date who are not too old for them! Some of them have started a campaign to remedy the situation by urging that more of these scholarships be awarded to girls.

The facts I have given do not mean that all gifted children should be rushed through school just as rapidly as possible. If that were done, a majority with IQ of 140 could graduate from high school before the age of 15. I do believe, however, that such children should be promoted rapidly enough to permit college entrance by the age of 17 at latest, and that a majority would be better off to enter at 16. The exceptionally bright student who is kept with his age group finds little to challenge his intelligence and all too often develops habits of laziness that later wreck his college career. I could give you some choice examples of this in my gifted group. In the case of a college student who is preparing for a profession in science, medicine, law, or any field of advanced scholarship, graduation at 20 instead of the usual 22 means two years added to his professional career; or the two years saved could be used for additional training beyond the doctorate, if that were deemed preferable.

Learned and Wood (1938) have shown by objective achievement tests in some 40 Pennsylvania colleges how little correlation there is between the student's knowledge and the number of months or years of his college attendance. They found some beginning sophomores who had acquired more knowledge than some seniors near their graduation. They found similarly low correlations between the number of course units a student had in a given field and the amount he knew in that field. Some with only one year of Latin had learned more than others with three years. And, believe it or not, they even found boys just graduating from high school who had more knowledge of science than some college seniors who had majored in science and were about to begin teaching science in high schools! The sensible thing to do, it seems, would be to quit crediting the individual high school or the individual college and begin crediting the individual student. That, essentially, is what the Ford Fund scholarships are intended to encourage.

Instruments that permit the identification of gifted subjects are available in great variety and at nearly all levels from the primary grades to the graduate schools in universities. My rough guess is that at the present time tests of achievement in the school subjects are being given in this country to children below high school at a rate of perhaps ten or twelve million a year, and to high school students another million or two. In addition, perhaps two million tests of intelligence are given annually in the elementary and high schools. The testing of college students began in a small way only 30 years ago; now almost every college in the country requires applicants for admission to take some kind of aptitude test. This is usually a test of general aptitude, but subject-matter tests and tests of special aptitudes are sometimes given to supplement the tests of general aptitude.

The testing movement has also spread rapidly in other countries, especially in Britain and the Commonwealth countries. Godfrey Thomson devised what is now called the Moray House test of intelligence in 1921 to aid in selecting the more gifted 11-year-olds in the primary schools for the privilege of free secondary education. This test has been revised and is given annually to about a half million scholarship candidates. The Moray House tests now include tests of English, arithmetic, and history. In 1932 the Scottish Council for Research in Education (1933) arranged to give the Moray House test of intelligence (a group test) to all the 90,000 children in Scotland who were born in 1921, and actually tested some 87,000 of them. The Stanford-Binet tests have been translated and adapted for use in nearly all the countries of Europe and in several countries of Asia and Latin America. Behind the Iron Curtain, however, mental tests are now banned.

I have discussed only tests of intelligence and of school achievement. There is time to mention only a few of the many kinds of personality tests that have been developed during the last thirty-five years: personality inventories, projective techniques by the dozen, attitude scales by the hundred, interest tests, tests of psychotic and predelinquent tendencies, tests of leadership, marital aptitude, masculinity-femininity, et cetera. The current output of research on personality tests probably equals or exceeds that on intelligence and achievement tests, and is even more exciting.

Along with the increasing use of tests, and perhaps largely as a result of it, there is a growing interest, both here and abroad, in improving educational methods for the gifted. Acceleration of a year or two or three, however desirable, is but a fraction of what is needed to keep the gifted child or youth working at his intellectual best. The method most often advocated is curriculum enrichment for the gifted without segregating them from the ordinary class. Under ideal conditions enrichment can accomplish much, but in these days of crowded schools, when so many teachers are overworked, underpaid, and inadequately trained, curriculum enrichment for a few gifted in a large mixed class cannot begin to solve the problem. The best survey of thought and action in this field of education is the book entitled *The Gifted Child,* written by many authors and published in 1951 (Witty, 1951). In planning for and sponsoring this book, The American Association for Gifted Children has rendered a great service to education.

But however efficient our tests may be in discovering exceptional talents, and whatever the schools may do to foster those discovered, it is the prevailing *Zeitgeist* that will decide, by the rewards it gives or withholds, what talents will come to flower. In Western Europe of the Middle Ages, the favored talents were those that served the Church by providing its priests, the architects of its cathedrals, and the painters of religious themes. A few centuries later the same countries had a renaissance that included science and literature as well as the arts. Although presumably there are as many potential composers of great music as there ever were, and as many potentially great artists as in the days of Leonardo da Vinci and Michelangelo, I am reliably informed that in this country today it is almost impossible for a composer of *serious* music to earn his living except by teaching, and that the situation is much the same, though somewhat less critical, with respect to artists.

The talents most favored by the current *Zeitgeist* are those that can contribute to science and technology. If intelligence and achievement tests don't discover the potential scientist, there is a good chance that the annual Science Talent Search will, though not until the high school years. Since Westinghouse inaugurated in 1942 this annual search for the high school seniors most likely to become creative scientists, nearly 4,000 boys and girls have been picked for honors by Science Service out of the many thousands who have competed. As a result, "Science Clubs of America" now number 15,000 with a third of a million members —a twenty fold increase in a dozen years (Davis, 1953). As our need for more and better scientists is real and urgent, one can rejoice at what the talent search and the science clubs are accomplishing. One may regret, however, that the spirit of the times is not equally favorable to the discovery and encouragement of potential poets, prose writers, artists, statesmen, and social leaders.

But in addition to the over-all climates that reflect the *Zeitgeist,* there are localized climates that favor or hinder the encouragement of given talents in particular colleges and universities. I have in mind especially two recent investigations of the differences among colleges in the later achievement of their graduates. One by Knapp and Goodrich (1952) dealt with the undergraduate origin of 18,000 scientists who got the bachelor's degree between 1924 and 1934 and were listed in the 1944 edition of *American Men of Science.* The list of 18,000 was composed chiefly of men who had taken a PhD degree, but included a few without a PhD who were starred scientists. The IBM cards for these men were then sorted according to the college from which they obtained the bachelor's degree, and an index of productivity was computed for each college in terms of the proportion of its male graduates who were in the list of 18,000. Some of the results were surprising, not to say sensational. The institutions that were most productive of future scientists between 1924 and 1934 were not the great universities, but the small liberal arts colleges. Reed College topped the list with an index of 132 per thousand male graduates. The California Institute of Technology was second with an index of 70. Kalamazoo College was third with 66, Earlham fourth with 57, and Oberlin fifth with 56. Only a half-dozen of the great universities were in the top fifty with a productivity index of 25 or more.

The second study referred to was by Knapp and Greenbaum (1953), who rated educational institutions according to the proportion of their graduates who received certain awards at the graduate level in the six-year period from 1946 to 1951. Three kinds of awards were considered: a PhD degree, a graduate scholarship or fellowship paying at least $400 a year, or a prize at the graduate level won in open competition. The roster of awardees they compiled included 7,000 students who had graduated from 377 colleges and universities. This study differs from the former in three respects: (*a*) it deals with recent graduates, who had not had time to become distinguished but who could be regarded as good bets for the future; (*b*) these good bets were classified according to whether the major field was science, social science, or the humanities; and (*c*) data were obtained for both sexes, though what I shall report here relates only to men. In this study the great universities make a better showing than in the other, but still only a dozen of them are in the top fifty institutions in the production of men who are good bets. In the top ten, the University of Chicago is third, Princeton is eighth, and Harvard is tenth; the other seven in order of rank are Swarthmore 1, Reed 2, Oberlin 4, Haverford 5, California Institute of Technology 6, Carleton 7, and Antioch 9. When the schools were listed separately for production of men who were good bets in science, social science, and the humanities, there were eight that rated in the top twenty on all three lists. These were Swarthmore, Reed, Chicago, Harvard, Oberlin, Antioch, Carleton, and Princeton.

The causes of these differences are not entirely clear. Scores on aptitude tests show that the intelligence of students in a given institution is by no means the sole factor, though it is an important one. Other important factors are the quality of the school's intellectual climate, the proportion of able and inspiring teachers on its faculty, and the amount of conscious effort that is made not only to discover but also to motivate the most highly gifted. The influence of motivation can hardly be exaggerated.

In this address I have twice alluded to the fact that achievement in school is influenced by many things other than the sum total of intellectual abilities. The same is true of success in life. In closing I will tell you briefly about an attempt we made a dozen years ago to identify some of the nonintellectual factors that have influenced life success among the men in my gifted group. Three judges, working independently, examined the records (to 1940) of the 730 men who were then 25 years old or older, and rated each on life success. The criterion of "success" was the extent to which a subject had made use of his superior intellectual ability, little weight being given to earned income. The 150 men rated highest for success and the 150 rated lowest were then compared on some 200 items of information obtained from childhood onward (Terman and Oden, 1947). How did the two groups differ?

During the elementary school years, the A's and C's (as we call them) were almost equally successful. The average grades were about the same, and average scores on achievement tests were only a trifle higher for the A's. Early in high school the groups began to draw apart in scholarship, and by the end of high school the slump of the C's was quite marked. The slump could not be blamed on extracurricular activities, for these were almost twice as common among the A's. Nor was much of it due to difference in intelligence. Although the A's tested on the average a little higher than the C's both in 1922 and 1940, the average score made by the C's in 1940 was high enough to permit brilliant college work, in fact was equaled by only 15 percent of our highly selected Stanford students. Of the A's, 97 percent entered college and 90 percent graduated; of the C's, 68 percent entered but only 37 percent graduated. Of those who graduated, 52 percent of the A's but only 14 percent of the C's graduated with honors. The A's were also more accelerated in school; on the average they were six months younger on completing the eighth grade, 10 months younger at high school graduation, and 15 months younger at graduation from college.

The differences between the educational histories of the A's and C's reflect to some degree the differences in their family backgrounds. Half of the A fathers but only 15 percent of the C fathers were college graduates, and twice as many of A siblings as of C siblings graduated. The estimated number of books in the A homes was nearly 50 percent greater than in the C homes. As of 1928, when the average age of the subjects was about 16 years, more than twice as many of the C parents as of A parents had been divorced.

Interesting differences between the groups were found in the childhood data on emotional stability, social adjustments, and various traits of personality. Of the 25 traits on which each child was rated by parent and teacher in 1922 (18 years before the A and C groups were made up), the only trait on which the C's averaged as high as the A's was general health. The superiority of the A's was especially marked in four volitional traits: prudence, self-confidence, perseverance, and desire to excel. The A's also rated significantly higher in 1922 on leadership, popularity, and sensitiveness to approval or disapproval. By 1940 the difference betwen the groups in social adjustment and all-round mental stability had greatly increased and showed itself in many ways. By that time four-fifths of the A's had married, but only two-thirds of the C's, and the divorce rate for those who had married was twice as high for the C's as for the A's. Moreover, the A's made better marriages; their wives on the average came from better homes, were better educated, and scored higher on intelligence tests.

But the most spectacular differences between the two groups came from three sets of ratings, made in 1940, on a dozen personality traits. Each man rated himself on all the traits, was rated on them by his wife if he had a wife, and by a parent if a parent was still living. Although the three sets of ratings were made independently, they agreed unanimously on the four traits in which the A and C groups differed most widely. These were "persistence in the accomplishment of ends," "integration toward goals, as contrasted with drifting," "self-confidence," and "freedom from inferiority feelings." For each trait three critical ratios were computed showing, respectively, the reliability of the A–C differences in average of self-ratings, ratings by wives, and ratings by parents. The average of the three critical ratios was 5.5 for perseverance, 5.6 for integration toward goals, 3.7 for self-confidence, and 3.1 for freedom from inferiority feelings. These closely parallel the traits that Cox found to be especially characteristic of the 100 leading geniuses in her group whom she rated on many aspects of personality; their three outstanding traits she defined as "persistence of motive and effort," "confidence in their abilities," and "strength or force of character."

There was one trait on which only the parents of our A and C men were asked to rate them; that trait was designated "common sense." As judged by parents, the A's are again reliably superior, the A–C difference in average rating having a critical ratio of 3.9. We are still wondering what self-ratings by the subjects and ratings of them by their wives on common sense would have shown if we had been impudent enough to ask for them!

Everything considered, there is nothing in which our A and C groups present a greater contrast than in drive to achieve and in all-round mental and social adjustment. Our data do not support the theory of Lange-Eichbaum (1932) that great achievement usually stems from emotional tensions that border on the abnormal. In our gifted group, success is associated with stability rather than instability, with absence rather than with presence of disturbing conflicts—in short with well-balanced temperament and with freedom from excessive frustrations. The Lange-Eichbaum theory may explain a Hitler, but hardly a Churchill; the junior senator from Wisconsin, possibly, but not a Jefferson or a Washington.

At any rate, we have seen that intellect and achievement are far from perfectly correlated. To identify the internal and external factors that help or hinder the fruition of exceptional talent, and to measure the extent of their influences, are surely among the major problems of our time. These problems are not new: their existence has been recognized by countless men from Plato to Francis Galton. What is new is the general awareness of them caused by the manpower shortage of scientists, engineers, moral leaders, statesmen, scholars, and teachers that the country must have if it is to survive in a threatened world. These problems are now being investigated on a scale never before approached, and by a new generation of workers in several related fields. Within a couple of decades vastly more should be known than we know today about our resources of potential genius, the environmental circumstances that favor its expression, the emotional compulsions that give it dynamic quality, and the personality distortions that can make it dangerous.

References

Cox, Catharine C. *The early mental traits of three hundred geniuses.* Vol. II of *Genetic studies of genius,* Terman, L. M. (ed.). Stanford: Stanford Univer. Press, 1926.

Davis, W. Communicating science. *J. atomic Scientists,* 1953, 337–340.

Keys, N. The underage student in high school and college. *Univer. Calif. Publ. Educ.,* 1938, 7, 145–272.

Knapp, R. H., & Goodrich, H. B. *Origins of American scientists.* Chicago: Univer. of Chicago Press, 1952.

Knapp, R. H., & Greenbaum, J. J. *The younger American scholar: his collegiate origins.* Chicago: Univer. of Chicago Press, 1953.

Lange-Eichbaum, W. *The problem of genius.* New York: Macmillan, 1932.

Learned, W. S., & Wood, B. D. The student and his knowledge. *Carnegie Found. Adv. Teaching Bull.,* 1938, No. 29.

Lehman, H. C. *Age and achievement.* Princeton: Princeton Univer. Press, 1953.

Pressey, S. L. *Educational acceleration: appraisals and basic problems.* Columbus: Ohio State Univer. Press, 1949.

Terman, L. M. A preliminary study in the psychology and pedagogy of leadership. *Pedag. Sem.,* 1904, *11,* 413–451.

Terman, L. M. Genius and stupidity: a study of some of the intellectual processes of seven "bright" and seven "dull" boys. *Pedag. Sem.,* 1906, *13,* 307–373.

Terman, L. M. The intelligence quotient of Francis Galton in childhood. *Amer. J. Psychol.,* 1917, *28,* 209–215.

Terman, L. M. (ed.), *et al. Mental and physical traits of a thousand gifted children.* Vol. I of *Genetic studies of genius,* Terman, L. M. (ed.). Stanford: Stanford Univer. Press, 1925.

Terman, L. M., & Oden, M. H. *The gifted child grows up.* Vol. IV of *Genetic studies of genius,* Terman, L. M. (ed.). Stanford: Stanford Univer. Press, 1947.

Terman, L. M. Scientists and nonscientists in a group of 800 gifted men. *Psychol. Monogr.,* 1954, Vol. *68,* no. 7, 1–43.

Witty, P. (ed.). *The gifted child.* Boston: Heath, 1951.

Bridging the gap between school and college. New York: The Fund for the Advancement of Education, 1953.

The intelligence of Scottish children. Scottish Council for Research in Education. London: Univer. of London Press, 1933.

Donald G. Paterson

The Conservation of Human Talent[1]

When I began thinking about the subject matter of tonight's lecture, I planned to discuss the interrelation of ability, achievement, vocational interests, and job satisfaction and, especially, the perplexing lack of relationship between measured vocational interests on the one hand and achievement and job satisfaction on the other. Later on, when I decided to discuss the conservation of human talent, I found myself concerned not so much with the technicalities primarily of interest to the vocational and personnel psychologist but rather with an attempt to portray the role of vocational and personnel psychology in a free America. Thus, my intent is to appeal to a wider audience in the hope that, perhaps, my remarks may help to secure a better public understanding of what my professional colleagues are attempting to do. It is my conviction that Walter Bingham would want this type of emphasis just as much as he would approve a talk emphasizing the more technical aspects of our work.

The subtitle of my topic is "The Role of Vocational Psychology

1. This paper is based on the Walter Van Dyke Bingham Lecture given at the Ohio State University, April 17, 1956. It was first published in the *American Psychologist,* 1957, vol. 12, no. 3 (March), pp. 134–144.

in Manpower Management." Perhaps it would be well, at the outset, to provide a few definitions.

We define vocational psychology as the study of the relationship of personality to vocational and occupational adjustment. The term "personality" is used in a broad sense to include abilities, aptitudes, interests, attitudes, and all other personal characteristics. The term "occupational adjustment" refers to the extent to which a person's unique characteristics are in harmony with the short-run and the long-run demands of the vocation or occupation in which he finds himself.

By manpower management we mean the conservation and optimal utilization of our human resources in our total economy. In addition, we emphasize that the idea of manpower management should be broadened to include the idea of manpower self-management. In a free, democratic society, we cannot achieve an optimal utilization of our human resources without recognizing the importance and dignity of the individual and his right to choose freely the occupation for which he feels he is fitted. It is this emphasis that differentiates our task in America from what goes on in a totalitarian state. Here, we assume that the state exists to serve the individual, whereas totalitarianism assumes that the individual exists to serve the state.

My own interest in this topic goes back to my graduate student days here at Ohio State University before World War I. My major advisor—the late Dr. Rudolf Pintner—was busy helping to create a psychology of individual differences by quantitative studies of a wide variety of groups of children and adults. And he had the knack of enlisting the energies of his students in this exciting quest. He and his students studied the feebleminded, the delinquent, the deaf, the blind, the unemployed. In these studies we used available mental test methods, improved existing tests, and devised new tests. The immediate aim was to get a better understanding of the educational, occupational, and social adjustment problems of children and adults. The ultimate aim, however, was to aid the individual to make better educational, occupational, and social adjustments.

This experience was followed by the great adventure of World War I when we were given the opportunity to apply psychological methods to the solution of military manpower problems. In this work, we learned to work with the medical profession, with the psychiatrists, with personnel managers from business and industry, and with line and staff officers at all levels of authority and responsibility. Here again, we adapted available psychological tests and rating scales, improved existing methods, and devised new methods. The aim, of course, was to aid our armed forces to utilize the talents of our civilian-soldiers with a minimum of waste in time and in manpower. The slogan behind all of this effort became "the right man in the right place."

Following World War I, great efforts were made to apply this experience to business and industry and to education. We witnessed the slow growth of vocational psychology and personnel administration during the 1920's. Then came the depression of the 1930's. With it came an accelerated attack on problems of employment, unemployment, and relief. I refer to the work of the Minnesota Employment Stabilization Research Institute in the early 1930's followed by the Adjustment Service in New York City which put on a one-year demonstration of the values of the vocational and avocational counseling of some 12,000 unemployed persons. Then came the Occupational Research Program of the United States Employment Service most ably directed by Drs. W. H. Stead, M. R. Trabue, and C. L. Shartle. This enterprise resulted in an improved public employment service with testing and counseling services available in the principal cities of the United States. Improved programs for the vocational counseling of the physically handicapped in various states of the union as well as intensive vocational counseling services for our veterans have been introduced on an unprecedented scale. In addition, our more progressive business and industrial organizations have organized more effective employment and personnel departments to improve the selection and placement of men and women in jobs for which they are best fitted.

During the 1930's a similar attack on manpower problems was being made in education. I refer to the work of the American Council on Education and its committees on student personnel work and its work in developing the cooperative testing program now taken over by the Educational Testing Service of Princeton, New Jersey. This has led to state-wide testing programs at the secondary school level, the introduction of student counseling programs in colleges and in high schools, and the attempt of secondary schools and colleges to adjust their curricular offerings to the wide range of individual differences in aptitudes, abilities, and interests found in any representative group of youngsters and adults. In short, all possible efforts are now being made to individualize mass education at every level of education.

I must add that World War II and events since World War II have greatly expanded our efforts in all these directions. And this has been accompanied by increased recognition of the need for improved professional competence of all those who are responsible for aiding each individual to make an optimal educational and occupational adjustment in our increasingly complex world of work. If this objective could be fully attained, the proportion of our population which is properly labeled "occupationally maladjusted" would be held to a minimum.

Time precludes discussion of the multiplicity of causes of occupational maladjustment. I would, however, like to mention widespread discrimination in education and in employment of members of minority groups, of younger workers lacking job experience, of older workers, of women, and of the physically handicapped. In addition, there is, in our culture, the white collar complex, the "hitching your wagon to a star" idea, and the "log cabin to the White House" tradition which leads youth and adults alike to strive for the highest occupational levels regardless of whether or not they possess the necessary aptitudes, abilities, and interests needed for even minimum success at these levels. William Proctor and Helen Ward (1923) of California, in the early 1920's, showed that high school youngsters with IQs below 100 overwhelmingly chose the top occupational levels, whereas a follow-up four years later showed most of them to be in the unskilled and semiskilled levels of work. Details are shown in Table 1. There is no reason to believe that youngsters today are much more realistic or rational in their vocational aspirations. It appears that four-fifths of our youth aspire to high level jobs in which only one-fifth of our labor force is employed. Furthermore, this same type of wishful thinking characterizes adult workers as well.

To a considerable degree, this phenomenon appears to be due to false job values permeating our society. I refer to the prestige hierarchy of occupations which was first established by Counts in 1925. In 1945, in discussing this problem before a group of high

Table 1. Occupational choices of low IQ (80–99) high school pupils.

Occupational Level	Occupational Choice	Occupation Engaged in Four Years Later
I Professional	30%	0%
II Business, Clerical	26%	5%
III Skilled Trades	44%	32%
IV Semiskilled	0%	35%
V Unskilled	0%	28%

school counselors, I presented the data by Counts and was immediately assailed because they were certain that these prestige values had been destroyed by the depression of the 1930's, by experiences during World War II, by the growth of courses in occupational information, and by the introduction of educational and vocational counseling services in the high schools. This led us (Deeg and Paterson, 1947) to duplicate the 1925 study in 1946, with the results shown in Table 2. Surprisingly enough, the results remained substantially the same as shown by a correlation of + .97 between the 1925 rank order and the 1946 rank order. If we really believed in the essential dignity of labor, no matter how menial, and that the welfare of our society is really dependent upon the contributions of workers in every

Table 2. Social status ranks of twenty-five occupations obtained in 1925 and in 1946.

Occupations	Rank Order 1925	Rank Order 1946	Occupations	Rank Order 1925	Rank Order 1946
Banker	1	2.5	Electrician	13	11
Physician	2	1	Insurance Salesman	14	10
Lawyer	3	2.5	Mail Carrier	15	14
Supt. of Schools	4	4	Carpenter	16	15
Civil Engineer	5	5	Soldier	17	19
Army Captain	6	6	Plumber	18	17
Foreign Missionary	7	7	Motorman	19	18
Elem. School Teacher	8	8	Barber	20	20
Farmer	9	12	Truck Driver	21	21.5
Machinist	10	9	Coal Miner	22	21.5
Traveling Salesman	11	16	Janitor	23	23
Grocer	12	13	Hod Carrier	24	24
			Ditch Digger	25	25

occupational group, the prestige hierarchy of occupations would disappear and each occupation would be ranked as equal to every other occupation. Since this is not so, the vocational counselor is confronted by tremendous resistance to wise occupational choices by innumerable youngsters and adults who seek jobs with high prestige rather than jobs for which they are best fitted.

Another type of evidence pointing to widespread occupational dissatisfaction is provided by surveys which asked the adult worker this question: "If you could go back to the age of eighteen and start life over again, would you choose a different career or occupation?" Roper (1938) made this nationwide survey with the following results: (*a*) 41 percent of the total sample answered "Yes," they would change; (*b*) a slightly larger proportion of men than of women would change; (*c*) a slightly larger proportion of older workers than of younger workers would change; and (*d*) a *much* larger proportion of factory workers than of professional workers would change. This last fact points to an occupational hierarchy of job satisfaction in which so-called higher level jobs have the largest proportion of satisfied workers with a constant increase in the proportion of dissatisfied workers as we descend to the semiskilled and unskilled levels of work.

In 1940, our Research Staff at Minnesota working on problems of employment, unemployment, and relief made an opinion survey of selected occupational groups in St. Paul and, among others, used this same question. The results (Paterson and Stone, 1942) were quite similar, as shown in Table 3. Those who answered "Yes" were then asked: "What occupation or career would you choose?" The results, as shown in Table 4, for the three occupational groups having the largest proportion of "Yes" answers indicated a striking tendency to choose the higher level prestige occupations. This suggests that the same tendency to choose high level occupations as was revealed by Proctor and

Ward for high school youngsters in the early 1920's is manifested by adult workers in the early 1940's. There is no reason to believe that the facts would be much different at the present time.

Table 3. Dissatisfaction with life work.[a]

Occupational Group	Percent Desiring Change
Streetcar Operators	80
City Firemen	63
Unemployed	61
Relief Clients	60
Clerical Workers	46
Social Workers	26
Employers	19
All Groups	52

[a] Selected Occupational Groups, St. Paul, Minnesota, 1941. $N = 1{,}405$.

Table 4. Type of work preferred by those desiring change of life work.

Type of Work Preferred	Percentage Choosing Type of Work		
	Streetcar Operators	City Firemen	Clerical Workers
	$N = 162$	$N = 126$	$N = 102$
Professional & Executive	34	47	82
Clerical & Sales	5	5	5
Skilled Trades	22	15	0
Semiskilled	0	1	0
Unskilled	0	0	0
Service	4	8	1
Farm Work	9	2	1
Don't Know	26	22	11
Total	100	100	100

Another important cause of occupational maladjustment is the failure of our educational system to prepare youngsters adequately and, many times, even minimally, for occupational competition upon entering the labor force. All too frequently youngsters are kept in school until age 16, 17, or 18, or even longer, without being given appropriate vocational training needed for economic competition. This results in a sort of wholesale negative vocational guidance program whereby youngsters drop out of school as failures in our characteristically academic types of education. Many are then forced into the labor market with few positive assets that can be used to classify them properly for available jobs. At this point, business and industry frequently make a fatal mistake in classifying such youngsters as fitted for only the unskilled, semiskilled, or other types of work that require little prejob or on-the-job training. If this be in error, the youngster gets trapped in a vicious employment circle. He acquires job experience and as he moves from employer to employer he is tagged by job labels that merely perpetuate his occupational misclassification. This is because of the widespread practice of classifying applicants for employment primarily on the basis of their work histories.

Clear-cut evidence on this point was obtained by our St. Paul study in 1940–41 of a 10 percent sample of applicants for employment in the local Public Employment Office (Yoder *et al.*, 1948). The busy employment interviewers, at that time, were forced to classify applicants primarily on the basis of work histories and a brief interview. Our research staff, on the contrary, classified these same applicants on the basis of complete case histories that included extensive interviewing covering the entire life history of the individual with especial emphasis on home background, education and training, detailed work histories, claimed interests, attitudes, and motivations, plus the administration of general and special aptitude tests, trade tests, achievement tests, interest tests, personality tests, and, finally, clearance reports from previous schools attended, from previous employers, and from social service agencies. Our research staff classifications were aimed at occupational fields that the applicants could enter immediately or that the applicants could probably succeed in if they secured appropriate pre-employment or on-the-job training. The results, as shown in Table 5, reflect a disturbing lack of agreement between the two sets of primary job classifications (ibid., p. 140). There is perfect agreement for only 100 of the 233 male applicants. Thus, there was agreement in only 43 percent of the cases. What is even more disturbing is the extent of the disagreements among the other 57 percent of the applicants.

One of the outstanding findings is the amount of misclassification that appears in the case of those men who were tagged by the Public Employment Service as "semiskilled" or "unskilled." A total of 122 were so classified. There was agreement between the Employment Service Classification and the Research Staff Classification in only 35, or 29 percent, of these applicants. And, what is more important, a considerable number of these so-called semiskilled and unskilled applicants could function in the labor market as skilled workers, in sales work, in clerical types of work, and, in four instances, the appropriate classification would have placed these individuals at the professional, semiprofessional, or managerial levels of work.

If we assume, for the moment, that the Research Staff classifications are correct and that the Employment Service classifications where there is disagreement are incorrect, it is obvious that here is evidence of a tremendous waste of our manpower resources. In other words, our traditional methods fail to classify men properly for work opportunities, and thus there is a violation of the concept of conservation of talent in our society.

The skeptic, however, may believe that the Research Staff

Table 5. Employment Service primary job classifications of 233 male unemployed registrants compared with Research Institute primary job classifications of the same individuals (1940–41).

Employment Service Classifications	Research Institute Classifications								
	Professional, Semiprofessional, and Managerial	Clerical	Sales	Service	Farm	Skilled	Semi-skilled	Unskilled	Total
Professional, Semiprofessional, and Managerial	8	4	2	–	–	–	1	1	16
Clerical	1	17	5	1	–	2	2	2	30
Sales	1	5	4	–	–	1	–	–	11
Service	–	1	–	7	3	–	1	–	12
Farm	–	–	–	–	–	–	–	–	–
Skilled	–	1	–	1	–	29	7	4	42
Semiskilled	2	4	3	2	7	11	27	6	62
Unskilled	2	7	4	7	10	7	15	8	60
Total	14	39	18	18	20	50	53	21	233

classifications are as likely to be in error as the Employment Service classifications. For evidence on this point, we can point to the accuracy of our Research Staff classifications made on a similar basis in 1932 as revealed by a follow-up study of the occupation engaged in ten years later (ibid., p. 147). The results are presented in Table 6. These 144 adults were tested, classified, and counseled in 1932, and predictions were later made as to the probable type and level of occupational competition to be expected in 1942. There was perfect agreement in 77 percent of the cases, underprediction in 13 percent and overprediction in 10 percent. Analysis of the case records in the 23 percent of disagreements indicates a variety of factors at work, the most important of which seemed to be unusually good or poor motivation or personality and temperamental difficulties.

To go back to the misclassification of "unskilled" workers shown in Table 5, perhaps a case history of one such individual will best dramatize what is involved.

> *Family Background.* Mr. Harolds was one of nine children whose father was a skilled worker in the building trades. The family lived in several small towns. Mr. Harolds graduated from high school in the mid-thirties at age 19.
>
> *Physical Handicap.* Mr. Harolds was unable to enter the labor market for three years after high school graduation because of a bone condition that developed following surgery.
>
> *Rehabilitation Service Experience.* When sufficiently recovered, Mr. Harolds was put in touch with the State Vocational Rehabilitation Service. Because he was a high school graduate, this Service sent him to a business college to take a ten-month secretarial course. But Mr. Harolds could not become interested in this type of course and withdrew after six months.

Table 6. Relation between future occupational group as predicted in 1932 and actual occupational group in 1942.[a]

Occupational Group as Predicted in 1932	Actual Occupational Group in 1942										
	Professional, Scientific	Professional, Verbal	Professional, Managerial	Clerical, Skilled	Clerical, Routine	Sales, Personal	Sales, Routine	Mechanical, Skilled	Mechanical, Unskilled Semiskilled	Casual	Total
Professional, scientific	2	–	–	–	–	–	–	1	–	–	3
Professional, verbal	–	3	1	–	–	–	–	–	–	–	4
Professional, managerial	–	1	2	–	–	–	–	–	–	–	3
Clerical, skilled	–	–	2	9	–	–	1	–	–	–	12
Clerical, routine	–	–	1	–	15	–	–	1	1	2	20
Sales, personal	–	1	–	–	–	2	–	–	–	1	4
Sales, routine	–	–	–	–	–	–	1	–	–	–	1
Mechanical, skilled	–	–	–	1	–	–	–	25	1	–	27
Mechanical, unskilled, semiskilled	–	–	2	–	2	1	–	1	34	6	46
Casual	–	–	1	–	1	–	1	–	3	18	24
Total	2	5	9	10	18	3	3	28	39	27	144

[a] From Farabaugh, Mary. A longitudinal study of vocational adjustment during the depression years. Unpublished doctor's dissertation, University of Minnesota, 1946.

Work Experience, 1938–1942. Mr. Harolds entered the labor market in 1938 and held a number of seasonal jobs. These included working as a house painter, farm laborer, surveyor's helper, stock boy and sales worker in a general store, and window washer. He was not interested in any of these jobs, and employer reports reflected this lack of interest. When he applied for work in the St. Paul Public Employment Office in 1942, he was classified as "Unskilled." He happened to turn up in our Employment Research Institute 10 percent sample of applicants.

Research Staff Classification. He was classified as fitted for potential "professional levels of work." This classification was based chiefly on the test scores obtained at the time and also on his earlier test and scholastic record at time of high school graduation.

Test Data. 1. General Ability. Mr. Harolds made a high score on the Pressey Classification Test—96th percentile on adult norms. His College Ability Test percentile rank at time of high school graduation was 92 and his High School Scholarship Rank was at the 93rd percentile in a graduating class of over 100.

2. Clerical Ability. His clerical ability was poor. He was at the 10th and 15th percentiles on the two parts of the Minnesota Clerical Test and in the lowest third on the USES Worker Analysis Section Test of Clerical Ability. Had the Rehabilitation Service tested this man seven years earlier, they probably would not have assigned him to a business college secretarial course.

3. Dexterities and Mechanical Ability. No outstanding scores were made on these tests.

4. Personality Tests. Scores on the Bell Adjustment Inventory revealed him to be "Very retiring" in the social area and to be somewhat disturbed in the emotional area. He reported to the vocational counselor that he was discouraged, that he felt he was quite a disappointment to his parents and to himself because he had been out of high school so long without making any real progress. The counselor wrote: "I feel that *if* he can make a satisfactory job adjustment, his personality difficulties will clear up."

5. *Interests.* There were no crystallized vocational interest patterns on Strong's Vocational Interest Blank except for two B+'s in the verbal-linguistic occupations (Lawyer and Author-Journalist).

Counselor's Judgment. In view of all ascertained facts concerning Mr. Harolds' family background, failure in clerical training, and poor work history, but with his superior high school record, and superior college ability test scores, the counselor urged him to enter college and attempt to prepare himself for a professional career. The problem was primarily one of motivating him to attempt college work even though he would have to be entirely self-supporting. After many counseling sessions, Mr. Harolds decided to carry out this plan.

Subsequent Thirteen-Year History. Mr. Harolds entered the University of Minnesota in September, 1942, and graduated in June, 1946, receiving the BA degree magna cum laude, together with membership in Phi Beta Kappa. He majored in one of the social sciences. He then earned his MA in 1948 and his PhD in 1950 in the same social science. Since then he has made steady progress in the academic world beginning as an Assistant Professor in a midwestern state university.

Our latest report, in December, 1955, indicates continued success and satisfaction with his professional attainments.

Implications. Time does not permit adequate discussion of

the implications of the case of Mr. Harolds. The following, however, appear to be worthy of emphasis.

1. In the mid-thirties, there was no adequate program of educational and vocational counseling in the high school attended by Mr. Harolds. No one apparently recognized the high potential of this youngster, at least to the extent of counseling him to prepare for a professional type of work by going to college.

2. In the mid-thirties, rehabilitation work for the physically handicapped was prescientific in the sense that Mr. Harolds was forced into a ten-month secretarial training program without its being realized that he lacked clerical aptitude and measured clerical interests. This action was taken in spite of his own expressed distaste for clerical work. The decision seemed to have been based primarily on the fact that this person was a high school graduate and could be prepared for job competition in a relatively inexpensive ten-month secretarial training program which would also be compatible with his physical handicap. This action proved to be wasteful of taxpayers' funds and only served to embark Mr. Harolds on a program of job failure. This is a case of "penny-wise and pound-foolish."

3. The Public Employment Service in 1942 misclassified Mr. Harolds as an "unskilled laborer" primarily on the basis of his "job-hopping" work history for a period of some four years.

4. The Employment Research Staff, because of its comprehensive testing and interviewing program plus its consulting of school records and of all previous employers, was able to recognize this man's potential assets and to take the necessary steps to translate a record of job marginality and job failure into a record of outstanding achievement at the PhD level of professional training. Here is a concrete example of the kind of vocational counseling needed to conserve human talent in our society.

I would now like to present another case history because it dramatizes and points up earlier failures of our society in a number of important respects. This is the story of Mr. Edwards, who was born before 1890.

Family Background. His mother died when he was an infant. His father died when he was nine years old. He then lived with relatives in New York City until age thirteen when he left home.

Schooling. He left school at age 12 with a fourth grade education and went to work. This was at the turn of the century when compulsory schooling laws were not rigidly enforced and when child labor legislation was almost unheard of.

Work Experience, 1900–1913. (1) Unskilled worker in wallpaper factory, four months; (2) Steam fitter's helper, plumber's helper, printer's helper, about one year; (3) Operator of drill press and punch press (learned work), about eight months in shop work; (4) Handbill distributor, house-to-house, four months; (5) Janitor in an institution, six months; (6) Tinsmith's helper, four months; (7) Itinerant worker in hotels around the country, bellhop, houseman, porter, six years; (8) Farm laborer in different parts of country, three years; and (9) Railroad car repairman's helper and bridge repairman's helper, six months.

Accident in 1913. While riding the rods on a freight train in 1913, he fell under the wheels, and both legs were amputated just below the knees. He was fitted with artificial limbs but never learned to use them. Upon recovery from amputation he was advised by the physician-in-charge to go into the field of selling on street corners. This vocational advice reflects 1913 attitudes toward crippled persons. The view was that industry could not use such people and that they could "earn a living" only by publicly displaying their handicap.

Work Experience, 1913–1943. Sold newspapers, miniature

Bibles, shoelaces, and lead pencils on street corners and was on and off of private relief and of public relief for a period of thirty years.

Vocational Guidance Service. Mr. Edwards came to the vocational guidance service of a city department of public relief in 1943 at the age of 55. The counselor's judgment was that this man had never made a satisfactory vocational adjustment from 1900 to 1913 nor from 1913 to 1943. The chief causes seemed to be: broken home, poor family background, limited schooling, inadequate training for the labor market, and entering labor market in the days when child labor was tolerated. Following his accident and the amputations, there were no adequate physical or vocational rehabilitation services available, and social services were also inadequate. This picture began to change, however, toward the end of the depression years. Thus, from 1941 to 1943, this man, who had married shortly after his accident and was blessed with two children, was aided by the "Lone Craftsman" organization to learn to mix paints and to paint plates at home, where it was necessary for him to stay most of the time because his wife had become bedridden with a chronic affliction. He kept house and took care of his wife, getting around with or without crutches.

Vocational Counselor's Judgment at First Interview. Mr. Edwards claimed he was in good physical condition with no complaints. He was quite a reader of newspapers and magazines and had followed the events of World War II with keen interest. The counselor reported that Mr. Edwards was clean of person, pleasant, cooperative, and extremely interested in the possibilities of work or of placement training. He claimed to have interests in art work, believed he could learn lettering and become a sign painter, or that he could learn machine-shop work, or that he would like to prepare for personnel work. The man appeared to have the following vocational liabilities: advanced age, crippled condition, limited schooling, poor work history, long record of dependency, and a difficult home situation. There appeared to be few, if any, vocational assets except his eagerness to become self-supporting.

Test Results.

1. Mr. Edwards made surprisingly high "general intelligence" test scores. In spite of the fact that his formal schooling was limited to the fourth grade which he completed at age twelve, his intelligence test scores were equal to those of the top quarter of Minnesota adults. This would be equivalent to three or four years of high school work.

2. High scores on the four Minnesota Spatial Relations Form Boards and the Minnesota Paper Form Board suggested mechanical aptitude of a high order. He ranked at the 83rd percentile and 85th percentile points of Minnesota adults on these two tests.

3. Surprisingly good scores were made on the Bell Adjustment Inventory. These probably reflect an eagerness to put his best foot forward in order to facilitate his job-planing and job-getting ambitions.

4. On the Kuder Preference Record his peak scores were 70th percentile in Mechanical, 90th percentile in Artistic, 70th percentile in Social Service, and 64th percentile in Clerical. He was, however, at the 12th percentile in Persuasive which corresponds with his "*Retiring*" score on the Bell. Both of these low scores are incompatible with the sales work he had attempted from 1913 to 1943.

Vocational Plans. He was enthusiastic about entering a defense plant machine-shop on-the-job training program where he would be required to work ten hours a day. He was placed in such a plant in June, 1943. The employer had already learned that physically handicapped persons with better than average mechanical ability could quickly learn to become good production workers.

Follow-up. Two weeks after placement, he reported he was having difficulty reading micrometers because his glasses were so scratched and in such poor repair. An eye examination and new glasses removed this difficulty.

Two months later, he reported he was working 60 hours a week and enjoying the work. His employer also reported that he was making an excellent job adjustment.

In November, he reported he was still working 60 hours a week, was well satisfied with his job but that he became exhausted before the end of the shift. He was fearful that he would not be able to keep up to the quality-of-work standards. He believed a reduction in hours per day would be helpful and was advised to consult his employer.

In the middle of December, he discussed his home situation and what could be done medically for his wife. Social Services aided at this point.

In 1946, three years after reporting to the Vocational Guidance Service, he came in voluntarily to report on his war and postwar work experiences. The record is as follows: (1) He spent one year in the defense plant which then laid off most of the workers because of defense cutbacks; (2) he then spent four months at another company but was laid off because of reduction in force; (3) he spent one year in another company but was laid off because of shortage of materials; (4) he next spent four months at another company but was laid off because of shortage of materials; and, finally, (5) he was rehired for the same job by the same company but was laid off after one month because of shortage of materials.

At this time, follow-up reports from his several employers

indicated that he had established a good work history and a good reputation as a competent worker on each job he held from 1943 through March, 1946. Furthermore, he had become a self-respecting, tax-paying citizen and at no time was in need of private or public relief. But disaster struck when he lost all of his possessions in a fire and, with unemployment compensation benefits terminated, it was necessary for Mr. Edwards to go on relief again. He is now receiving his old age pension and social security benefits and has remained out of the job market since March, 1946.

Implications. The case of Mr. Edwards illustrates a general failure of our society, in the past, to recognize and to utilize "better than average scholastic and mechanical aptitude" from the time he left school at the turn of the century to the time of a national emergency. It also illustrates that an occupationally maladjusted person, even though handicapped educationally, physically, occupationally, and by age for job competition, can, through appropriate vocational testing and vocational counseling, become a productive and self-respecting worker. Had adequate educational, guidance, and social service facilities been available when this man was a youngster it is probable that he might have made a far greater contribution to society throughout his life. Here, again, is a concrete example of what we mean when we stress the importance of the conservation and optimum utilization of our human resources. Manpower shortages are centering attention on this problem area with the result that we are making real headway in utilizing hitherto neglected sources of manpower.[2]

2. An excellent survey of the current situation has been reported by Dael Wolfle in *America's Resources of Specialized Talent*, Harper and Brothers, 1954.

At the present time there is widespread concern that a considerable proportion of our abler high school graduates do not go on to college. The provision of vastly increased funds for scholarships will help, but the problem is not due solely to lack of finances. There is a serious motivation problem, too, that needs attention. Early identification of the gifted and intensification of our educational and counseling efforts with such youngsters, together with the extension of our counseling programs to include the parents of the gifted, will be needed to cope with this problem of under-utilization.

The current shortage of engineers and scientists is receiving nationwide attention at the present time. Positive programs to interest more youngsters in these fields by improving instruction in mathematics and science in our high schools and by investing vast sums of money in museums of science and industry in our larger centers of population are needed and will undoubtedly be effective. But those responsible for these programs must not impose them upon youngsters who are lacking in mathematical aptitude or who have no genuine interests in science or engineering. It might also be well to point out that engineering colleges and industry must accept the challenge of optimally utilizing the scientists and engineers who are now in and will continue to enter the labor market. Perhaps we need to develop educational programs that will train increased numbers of draftsmen and scientific aids who can release many engineers and scientists from wasting their talents on routine tasks. It is with a view to facilitating this kind of attack that the University of Minnesota Industrial Relations Center has undertaken to develop specialized functional engineering vocational interest scales for Strong's Vocational Interest Blank. Dr. Wilbur Layton of our Student Counseling Bureau has constructed an effective aptitude test for freshman engineers. In addition, Dr. Marvin Dunnette has developed the Minnesota Enginering Analogies Test (1955) to aid in the selection and differential placement of engineering graduates. In brief, we would emphasize the importance of providing for and improving the vocational counseling of prospective engineers and scientists in high schools, colleges, engineering schools, graduate schools, and in industry. If these provisions are not made all along the line, it is likely that frantic efforts being made to remedy current shortages will involve a tragic maladjustment of many individuals who should have been oriented toward other occupational goals and objectives.

Other neglected sources of manpower have already been touched upon, such as those who are occupationally misclassified in the labor market. Hope for prevention of such occupational misclassification lies in the direction of improved counseling services in the schools, gearing the vocational portions of our educational programs to the real needs of business and industry, expanding the testing and counseling work in the local offices of our public employment service, and the adoption of a differential placement point of view in personnel departments in business and industry. I would like to emphasize this last point. The widespread practice of having separate employment departments in a given company for the hiring of factory workers, of clerical workers, and of salesmen is based on the false assumption that applicants for work can and do correctly classify themselves. Many applicants, however, are unaware of their own potentialities and accept whatever occupational classification may have been imposed upon them by their work histories and their prior experiences in the labor market. This merely perpetuates whatever occupational misclassifications have occurred. To overcome these serious errors, the personnel department of each company should supervise the hiring for all segments of the business and should assume responsibility for properly classifying all applicants for employment with that company. This vocational guidance point of view has only recently been hinted at in Tiffin's *Industrial Psychology* (1942) and in Robert Thorndike's book on *Personnel Selection* (1949). And, now, what I call "the Minnesota point of view" toward personnel work in business and industry is set forth in elaborate detail in the recent book by Drs. C. Harold Stone and William Kendall entitled *Effective Personnel Selection Procedures* (1956).

Another neglected source of manpower has already been hinted at earlier. I refer to the under-utilization of the physically handicapped. Systematic efforts to aid in the rehabilitation of the physically handicapped veteran and nonveteran go back to the early 1920's. The aim was worthy, but the means available were inadequate. It is a fact that rehabilitation workers, then, were almost wholly untrained. The procedure consisted primarily of asking the physically handicapped person what training he desired and then promptly providing it. If and when failure to profit from training ensued, the physically handicapped person was transferred to some other training course or school without inquiry as to whether or not it, too, was inappropriate. This process continued during the 1920's and 1930's with an appalling waste of time and money, and was accompanied by frustrated ambitions on the part of the handicapped persons and the rehabilitation workers as well. During the mid-thirties a radical shift was made in Minnesota when vocational psychologist Donald Dabelstein was put in charge of the state program. At about the same time, a demonstration of vocational counseling procedures was introduced into the Minneapolis VA Hospital. This was followed by the development of VA Guidance Centers during World War II and the development of Vocational Counseling Services in VA hospitals. But this tremendous expansion of vocational counseling services fell far short of the type and quality of services needed because of the lack of properly trained and qualified vocational counseling psychologists. This lack is now being remedied by the PhD vocational counselor training program inaugurated by the VA in 1952 and by the Federal sponsorship of a similar MA training program for vocational counselors of the physically handicapped at the state level which was begun in 1955. The net results of these two training programs will be to increase rapidly the numbers of well-trained vocational counselors of the physically handicapped. And I am proud to announce that another Minnesota trained PhD who has specialized in this area of work is author of a soon-to-be-published textbook on this subject. The author is Lloyd H. Lofquist, and the title of his book is *Vocational Counseling with the Physically Handicapped,* published in the Century Psychology Series.

May I add just a word of warning about the responsibilities of those who benefit from these improved training programs in our graduate schools? It would be a calamity if these newly trained vocational counselors should become so engrossed in theories about personality development and the counseling process itself that they failed to aid the counselee in formulating practical plans that really led to jobs and good job adjustments.

In the meantime, education of employers and of their personnel directors has been intensified to the point where resistance to the hiring of properly qualified, physically handicapped persons has been steadily reduced. There is every reason for optimism today over the prospects for a vast improvement in our utilization of the physically handicapped. Here, again, is an area in which the idea of maximum conservation of human talent is on the threshold of realization.

Another neglected source of manpower lies in our failure to utilize the ever increasing number and proportion of older persons in our society. Private pension plans force compulsory retirement of thousands who are able and willing to continue at productive work. These same plans, plus unfavorable attitudes toward the productivity of older persons, tend to set arbitrary hiring-age limits at about 40 or 45. Thanks to Dr. Lillien J. Martin, Dr. Walter R. Miles, Dr. Sidney L. Pressey, Dr. Irving Lorge, and others, the facts are now rapidly accumulating to show that age alone is a poor index of competence. Our own Industrial Relations Center has also conducted research on this problem and, more recently, has cooperated with the Public Employment Service in attempting, through research, to measure the magnitude of the problem and to study ways and means of coping with it. It is our hope that adequate age norms can be set up for the better aptitude tests now available. We also urgently need to conduct controlled experiments on the efficacy of the vocational counseling and differential placement of older persons in business and industry. Here is a major challenge that must be attacked and solved if we are to maximize the conservation of human talent among our senior citizens.

One final neglected source of manpower comprises minority groups. Because of widespread discrimination in employment, many members of many minority groups are never permitted to realize their full employment potential. Since vocational psychology must adhere to the principle of employment on the basis of merit, the vocational counselor is necessarily thrust into the midst of controversy. He will, therefore, welcome FEPC laws on the national, state, and local level. At the present writing such laws seem to be spreading at the state and local level. In Minnesota, our first FEPC law came in Minneapolis on January 1, 1947, and finally after five biennial sessions of the legislature it became state law in 1955. And other cities in our state have also adopted local ordinances setting up Fair Employment Practices Commissions. At the present time, state FEPC laws have been adopted in thirteen states, and local FEPC ordinances have been adopted in eleven communities. In addition, an increasing number of state and local Councils on Human Rights and Councils on Human Relations are paving the way for more FEPC legislation to come.

The breaking down of discrimination barriers not only serves to open up employment opportunities to qualified applicants regardless of race or creed, but it also tends to force employers to adopt more objective and scientific employment procedures. Employers must do so in order to protect themselves against unfounded charges of discrimination. This fact has accelerated the demand by employers for professionally trained personnel workers and personnel psychologists to install objective methods of hiring qualified applicants regardless of creed or color.

FEPC laws, however, are not self-enforcing. Their effectiveness, obviously, depends upon public opinion. For this reason, the vocational psychologist must aid citizens and citizen groups who are engaged in the struggle to open up and to maintain nondiscriminatory employment opportunities for everyone in our democratic society. Of course, this also means that our educational and training opportunities must likewise be provided on a nondiscriminatory basis in order that the potential abilities of every person may be identified and developed to the highest possible degree. Until this total program is fully realized in the East, the West, the North, and the South, we shall perpetuate the present inexcusable waste of precious human resources.

I have attempted to present some of the challenging problems involved in the conservation of human talent. In doing so, I have stressed the importance of vocational psychology with emphasis on the role of educational and vocational counseling in reducing and preventing occupational maladjustment in our society. Although we have made substantial progress in this regard, we are now only on the threshold of achieving some of the goals set forth so ably by the pioneers in this field. I refer, of course, to the work of Muensterberg, Thorndike, Yerkes, Terman, Scott, Hollingworth, Poffenberger, Bingham, Strong, Thurstone, Viteles,

Burt, and Toops. Fortunately, a growing number of our younger psychologists have seen the same vision and will carry on with even greater vigor and competence.

References

Counts, G. S. The social status of occupations: a problem in vocational guidance. *Sch. Rev.*, 1925, *33*, 16–27.

Deeg, Maethel E., & Paterson, D. G. Changes in social status of occupations. *Occupations*, 1947, *25*, 205–208.

Dunnette, M. *Manual for the Minnesota Engineering Analogies Test.* New York: The Psychological Corporation, 1955.

Paterson, D. G., & Stone, C. H. Dissatisfaction with life work among adult workers. *Occupations*, 1942, *21*, 219–221.

Proctor, W. M., & Ward, Helen. Relation of general intelligence to the persistence of educational and vocational plans of high school pupils. *J. educ. Res.*, 1923, *7*, 277–288.

Roper, E. The fortune quarterly survey: XI, Part 5. *Fortune*, 1938, *17*, 86–88.

Thorndike, R. *Personnel selection.* New York: John Wiley & Sons, Inc., 1949.

Tiffin, J. *Industrial psychology.* New York: Prentice-Hall, Inc., 1942.

Stone, C. H., & Kendall, W. *Effective personnel selection procedures.* New York: Prentice-Hall, Inc., 1956.

Yoder, D., Paterson, D. G., *et al. Local labor market research.* Minneapolis: University of Minnesota Press, 1948.

Cyril Burt

The Inheritance of Mental Ability[1]

The Problem of Individual Differences

In Britain as in America, the earliest applications of the new techniques of mental testing were concerned chiefly with the lower end of the intellectual scale. They were readily accepted as practical aids to the doctor in diagnosing the mentally deficient, and to the teacher in discriminating the temporarily retarded from the irremediably dull. It was Bingham's firm belief that: "in the long run it would be even more profitable to discover and aid the bright and the supernormal than to ascertain and provide for the dull and defective."

In this country the traditional method of dealing with the problem was by means of what was popularly known as "the scholarship system." British teachers and parents were apt in those days to think of scholarships rather as a means for rewarding hard work than as a device for detecting and assisting im-

1. This paper is based on the Walter Van Dyke Bingham Memorial Lecture given at University College, London, May 21, 1957. It was first published in the *American Psychologist,* 1958, vol. 13, no.1 (January), pp. 1–15.

pecunious talent. But considerable misgiving was felt over the erratic local distribution not only of scholarship winners but also of defectives. It was indeed widely affirmed that these variations in the numbers were "largely the result of the injustice of the ordinary methods of examination." Accordingly, in 1913 the London County Council took the unprecedented step of appointing an official psychologist. His chief duties were to act as referee for what were sometimes known as "problem children"—particularly in disputed cases of feeblemindedness and of scholarship ability.

In the surveys that I carried out in this capacity I found that, in the poorer districts of the East End, there were three times as many certified defectives, eight times as many backward pupils, but only one-tenth the number of scholarship winners as were reported in the well-to-do areas of London. Who or what was to blame: the teachers, the homes, the traditional examination in arithmetic and English? Or the fact that the varying modicum of ability bestowed on each child was irretrievably fixed at birth? Environment or heredity, those seemed to be the alternative explanations; and each had its own enthusiastic advocates. As a rule the social reformers gave one answer and the psychologists the opposite.

During the nineteenth century the main champions of social reform were the philosophical radicals: Bentham, James and John Mill, and their various followers. Their motto was the maxim of Helvétius: *l'éducation peut tout;* or, as James Mill put it, "if education cannot do everything, there is hardly anything it cannot do." In psychology, their one basic law was the law of association; and the wide differences between one individual and another they attributed solely to the cumulative effects of association, through the operation of "habit, custom, training, and environmental opportunity or deprivation."

By the beginning of the twentieth century, however, most

British psychologists had abandoned this simple creed. Impressed by the novel doctrines of the evolutionary school, they began to follow Darwin, Spencer, Huxley, and Galton in holding that the laws of heredity and individual variation applied to men as well as to animals, to mind as well as to body. "It is not so much," said Karl Pearson, "that the slums create the dullards, but rather that the duller stocks gravitate automatically to the slums." It followed that the only cure would be to start breeding citizens as we bred race horses, prize rabbits, or pedigree pups. Huxley's celebrated essay on the "Natural Inequality of Man" won over the few who still wavered. Most teachers were already converted by firsthand experience under the new scheme of universal education.

However, during the last few decades psychologists have been gradually discovering that the problem is far more complicated than either side had originally assumed. And, largely as a result, there has been yet another swing of the polemical pendulum. In part this is due to a reluctance to support what G. K. Chesterton once described as "the modernized dogma of predestination—a dogma calculated to paralyse all progress towards a welfare state"; in part it has been due to a fuller appreciation of the possibilities of experience and learning, which in turn has involved a reversion to something like a rejuvenated belief in the fundamental law of association.

To the British psychologist the experimental work on "conditioning" seemed to offer a more precise interpretation, on a more adequate basis, of the traditional doctrine of association as preached by Hartley and Mill; and the behaviourist school was widely welcomed as substituting a more profitable line of practical research for inconclusive speculations about heredity and innate endowment. As a result, we find contemporary educationists reminding each other of Bagley's well known dictum that, "except for a few cases of pathological deficiency, the factor of heredity plays a very small part in human life, as compared with the factor of environment" (1912); while several of their psychological colleagues quote with approval the pronouncements of Watson: "there are inheritable differences in structure, but we no longer believe in inherited capacities." "Give me," he adds, "a dozen healthy infants, and my own world to bring them up in, and I'll guarantee to train any one of them to become any type of specialist I might select—doctor, lawyer, artist, merchant-chief, and even beggar-man or thief" (1931, p. 104).

A glance through the current literature will show that, for the most part, the hypotheses which our younger psychologists desire to challenge are the two propositions which, at the beginning of the century, were accepted almost without question as justifying the organization of our system of education: first, the hypothesis of general ability, i.e., the view that "up to adolescence the chief differences distinguishing individual pupils are differences in 'general intelligence' "—a view which led the Chief Inspector of Schools to declare that, "with a few exceptions, each pupil may be taught in the same class for every subject, or, if mentally defective, sent to a special school on the ground that he is defective all round"; secondly, the hypothesis of mental inheritance, i.e., the view that the wide differences in the degree of general ability exhibited by various pupils were due mainly to genetic endowment.

The Hypothesis of General Ability

Of these two hypotheses the first was firmly rejected by the report of the "Norwood Committee"—a report which strongly influenced the reorganization of our national education as envisaged in the Education Act of 1944. The committee maintained that children differed far more in quality of ability than in amount; and recommended a tripartite classification of "secondary" schools, based on the doctrine that pupils fall into three main types: a literary or abstract type, to be educated at "grammar schools"; a mechanical or technical type, to be educated at "technical schools"; and a concrete or practical type to be educated at "modern schools." This conception was supported by several leading psychologists who argued that "the statistical analyses of Thurstone disclose no evidence for Spearman's factor of general ability, but only a number of 'primary abilities,' each more or less specialized" (Burt, 1943b).

The scheme has not worked out in actual practice so successfully as was hoped; and the proposal itself at once stimulated a large number of new inquiries. Those who still defend the tripartite theory seem to overlook the vast and varied character of the evidence that has since become available on the issue thus raised. As a rule they content themselves with citing one particular line of reasoning—usually the statistical. If, however, we take a wider view, we shall find that there are three or four independent chains of converging arguments, none perhaps irrefragable by itself, but all of them tending to rehabilitate the older view. The evidence on which these inferences rest is drawn from many different fields: introspection, observation, biology and neurology, as well as statistical research.

In point of fact, the distinction between "general ability" and "special abilities" was due, not (as is so widely supposed) to Spearman but rather to Francis Galton, from whom Spearman, as he expressly states in his earlier papers, originally borrowed it. Spearman, however, went on to deny the existence of "special abilities" which Galton had supported, on the ground that they were "just relics or revivals of the obsolete theory of faculties" (1927). It is this aspect of the Spearman doctrine that the modern educationist repudiates, and with it he is a little too ready to discard "general intelligence" as well.

However, even Galton had been partly anticipated by previous writers who, in a vague and inchoate fashion, had inculcated a somewhat similar doctrine on the basis of speculative arguments, partly introspective, partly biological. Introspection, so the faculty school had claimed, revealed a sharp distinction between intellectual or cognitive qualities on the one hand and emotional or orectic qualities on the other. Spencer and his followers accepted this distinction, and supplemented it with biological arguments, which in those days were almost equally conjectural. During the evolution of the animal kingdom, and again during the development of each individual, the fundamental capacity which Spencer termed intelligence

> . . . becomes [so he tells us] progressively differentiated into a hierarchy of more specialized cognitive capacities—sensory, perceptual, associative, and ratiocinative, much as the trunk of a growing tree ramifies into boughs and twigs (1870, Part iv).

Later writers were not so sure that the term cognition really furnished the best differentia: for them the real distinction was between directive or adaptive processes on the one hand and valuative or dynamic processes on the other; "intelligence," said Sully, "steers like a rudder; emotion and interest supply the steam." A similar reinterpretation has more recently been proposed by Piaget in his book on *The Psychology of Intelligence* (1950, pp. 4ff.).

Far more convincing to my mind is the neurological evidence. The alternative doctrine of distinct and independent abilities drew much of its support from early experiments on cerebral localization. These, it was claimed,

> . . . appear to indicate that distinct functions—motor, sensory, perceptual, associative, linguistic, and the like—can be assigned to distinct and definite centres or areas within the brain.

And this conclusion was apparently corroborated by the maps of cell structure subsequently produced by histologists like Campbell, Brodmann, and von Economo. Their inferences, however, have been severely criticized by more recent workers, like Bok, Lorente de Nò, and, at University College, by D. A. Sholl (1956). Few of the older map makers (he says) realized "the enormous amount of variability that exists between individual human brains." In their studies of comparable cortical areas from different specimens of *Ateles* Lashley and Clark have shown that the differences between different individuals are at least as large as the differences upon which the distinction of "architectonic areas" was based (1946). Hence it now seems clear that the charts that used to figure in popular textbooks "greatly exaggerated the amount and the definiteness of the alleged localization, both as regards structure and as regards function."

After all, as Sherrington so frequently pointed out, in any one individual each anatomical tissue—skin, bone, hair, or muscle—tends to be of the same general character all over the body: minor local variations are often discernible; but in the same individual the variations are much slighter than those between one individual and another; and we should naturally expect the same to hold good of nerve tissue. Bolton's studies of the cerebral cortex, both in normal and defective persons, suggest that the quality of the nervous tissue in any given individual tends to be predominantly the same throughout: in low-grade defectives, for example, the nerve cells tend to be "visibly deficient in number, in branching, and in regularity of arrangement in every part of the cortex." The clinical work of Hughlings Jackson, the experimental researches of Sherrington, and the microscopical studies of the infant brain carried out more recently by Conel and de Crinis, seem in many ways to provide increasing confirmation for Spencer's theory of a "hierarchy of neural functions," developing stage by stage out of a simpler basic activity into higher and more specialized forms. Even if we cannot wholly accept Lashley's doctrine of the "mass action" of the brain, nevertheless the actual facts that he has reported are far more in keeping with a theory of general ability (and minor special abilities) than with a theory of major "special abilities" and no general factor. And Sholl himself concludes that "intelligence," like retentivity, is a "general attribute of all cortical tissue" (1956, p. 111).

Each of the foregoing arguments—from introspection, from biology, and from neurology—is admittedly inconclusive. The most we could so far claim is that, when taken in combination, the evidence from each of these separate fields sets up a fairly strong a priori probability in favour of Galton's twofold theory of general abilities plus special. It is at this point, therefore, that the psychologist is tempted to invoke the aid of statistical analysis. In my view, the function of statistics, at any rate in psychological research, is simply to provide a more rigorous method of testing alternative hypotheses. How then do the various hypotheses that confront us stand up to this ordeal?

Each of the three main suggestions leads to distinctive corollaries which are open to statistical verification. First of all, if, as Thorndike held, there was no such thing as a general factor, but only a set of independent abilities, then the cross-correlation between the tests or assessments for those abilities should be zero, or at least nonsignificant. They are not: they are always both significant and positive. Secondly, if, as Spearman maintained, there were no such thing as special abilities but only a single general factor, the intercorrelations for every test should diminish proportionately in the same descending order (except, of course, for nonsignificant deviations due to sampling and the like): in technical language, the table of intercorrelations should constitute a matrix of rank one. It does not.

The third hypothesis assumes the presence of both general and special abilities. In the early article (1909) to which I have already referred,[2] I endeavoured to apply to the correlations between mental tests the procedure which Karl Pearson had already elaborated for use with measurements of bodily characteristics. In this way I sought to compare each of my various tables of observed coefficients with the best fitting set of theoretical values deduced from the hypothesis of a single "general ability" only; this hypothetical ability was redefined as the "highest common factor" entering into all the processes measured in any given table.[3] The fit was moderately good, but by no means perfect. The differences between the observed and the theoretical values were accordingly tested for statistical significance; and the result was to disclose small but significant clusters of residual correlations, common to certain limited groups of tests

2. Those to whom this earlier (1909) paper is inaccessible will find the essential figures from one of the tables reproduced in books by Freeman (1926) and Thorndike (1914); Garnett (1921) reprints not only the observed values, but, beneath them, the theoretical values, the discrepancies, and the probable errors, as I myself had done. It should be noted that the procedure subsequently developed by Spearman (1927) was rather different. He preferred to secure independent assessments for intelligence, based on teachers' ratings, examination results, or, in later inquiries, the results of one or two accredited tests, and use them as "reference values." In other words, he used an *external* criterion; whereas I have used an *internal* criterion or "factor" derived from the intercorrelations themselves. My reasons were that both examination results and teachers' assessments were commonly influenced by the child's capacity to learn, i.e., by his memory, rather than by his sheer intelligence, and thus often reflected what the child had actually acquired rather than his innate capacity.

3. The simplified formula used for this purpose in most of these earlier researches (1917, p. 53) was the same as that subsequently adopted by Thurstone under the name of the centroid formula (1935, p. 94, Equation 13). When in addition "special abilities" were studied as well as "general ability," they were regarded as "group factors" obtainable by an arithmetical rotation of the "bipolar" factor matrix. I may add that we encountered a certain amount of evidence indicating that several of these special abilities were also largely dependent on heredity, but space does not permit me to deal with them here.

only, thus plainly indicating the presence of certain supplementary abilities. This seemed definitely to clinch the double hypothesis put forward by Galton. Precisely the same conclusion was reached in many later analyses carried out both by myself and by other workers with larger numbers of pupils and a greater variety of tests (Burt, 1914–1931, 1917).

The factorization of correlations between persons and between successive occasions (with the same persons and tests) revealed, or at least very plainly confirmed, the constant presence of a random factor, which appeared to be due, not merely to sampling as ordinarily understood, but to something essentially characteristic of the working of the mind or brain. A somewhat similar conclusion has been independently reached by neurologists like Beurle, Cragg and Temperley, and Uttley and Sholl. Thus the type of "neuronal connectivity" suggested by the histological study of dendritic fibres strongly suggests "the semi-random arrangement of a machine working largely in accordance with the principles of probability" (Sholl, 1956).[4] This partly

4. This is not the same as the "sampling theory" of Thomson, which maintains that the apparent emergence of "factors" is "a result of the laws of chance and not of any psychological laws": like all simplified theories, it seems to amplify just one aspect of mental process, at the expense of denying all the rest. What is needed is a model which will combine the "integrative action" of the nervous system with its "stochastic action." As I have suggested elsewhere (*Psychometrika,* 3, p. 160), the mathematical model which most effectively does this is a classificatory model derived from Pearson's method of principal axes. The mechanical model would resemble, not the homeostat of Ashby or the mechanical tortoise of Grey Walter, but rather a classification machine like that proposed by Uttley and Sholl. Similarly a stochastical induction machine would seem to reproduce the results of human learning far better than the model adopted by Hull and his followers. It is therefore tempting to suggest that what has been called the A/S ratio—i.e., the proportionate amount of "association cortex" with which either a species or an organism is endowed at birth—would form an index primarily of the amount of its intelligence and only incidentally of its capacity to learn.

agrees with, though it is by no means identical with, the doctrine of "equipotentiality" put forward by Lashley; and thus further supports the value of factorial procedures as a means of investigating variations in mental ability.

However, what is far more important from the practical standpoint of educational guidance is this: in nearly every factorial study of cognitive ability, the general factor commonly accounts for quite 50% of the variance (rather more in the case of the young child, rather less with older age groups) while each of the minor factors accounts for only 10% or less. With increasing age, the "group factors," which represent special abilities, contribute increasing amounts to the total variance; and this fact lends further support to the view that, as a result of maturation, cognitive ability progressively differentiates and tends to become more and more specialized (Burt, 1954).

Be that as it may, whatever be our views on the various biological or neurological issues, we may, I think, safely say this: for purposes of prediction—forecasting what this or that individual child is likely to do in school or in after-life—the general factor is by far the most important, though admittedly not our only, guide. For all practical purposes, almost every psychologist—even former opponents of the concept of general intelligence, like Thorndike, Brown, Thomson, and Thurstone—seems in the end to have come round to much the same conclusion, even though, for theoretical purposes, each tends to reword it in a modified terminology of his own. And thus today, save for one or two occasional attacks, current psychological criticism is not so much concerned with the problem of "general intelligence," but is directed rather against the second of our two initial propositions: the assumption, namely, that individual differences in intelligence are hereditary or innate.

The Genetic Component

Here three distinct questions seem to be involved: (*a*) what evidence is there for the *fact* of inheritance, (*b*) what precisely is the *mode* in which intelligence is inherited, and (*c*) what is the *relative importance* of the genetic factor as compared with the environmental?

The Fact. In controversies about the facts of mental heredity most critics have tended to assume that the two causal agencies commonly discussed—heredity and environment—are not merely antithetical but mutually exclusive. The environmentalists apparently suppose that, once they have shown that intelligence tests are affected by environment, it follows that all differences in intelligence are due to nothing but environment. Similarly the thoroughgoing hereditarian is apt to talk as though he believed that differences in intelligence were due to nothing but genetic constitution. This is the old familiar fallacy which I am tempted to label "nothing-buttery." In point of fact, with a few rare exceptions, like eye colour or serological differences in the blood, every observable characteristic that geneticists have studied has proved to be the product of the joint action of both heredity and environment. There are, in short, no such things as hereditary characters: there are only hereditary tendencies.

Now, where two contributory factors, such as heredity and environment, are likely to be involved, the obvious procedure will be to keep first one and then the other as constant as possible, and observe the results in either case.

1. *Uniform environment.* As psychological consultant to the London County Council, I had free access to orphanages and other residential institutions, and to the private files of case records giving the history of the various inmates. My co-workers and I were thus able to study large numbers of children who had been transferred thither during the earliest weeks of infancy, and

had been brought up in an environment that was much the same for all. To our surprise we found that individual differences in intelligence, so far from being diminished, varied over an unusually wide range. In the majority of cases, they appeared to be correlated with differences in the intelligence of one or both of the parents. Some of the most striking instances were those of illegitimate children of high ability: often the father (so the case records showed) had been a casual acquaintance, of a social and intellectual status well above that of the mother, and had taken no further interest in the child. In such cases it is out of the question to attribute the high intelligence of the child to the special cultural opportunities furnished by the home environment, since his only home has been the institution.[5]

2. *Uniform heredity.* To secure cases in which the children's genetic endowment is the same, we may turn to assessments obtained from monozygotic or "identical" twins. The mother is not infrequently unable or unwilling to bring up two children at the same time, and one twin is consequently sent to a relative or to a foster home. Owing to the strong popular prejudice against separating twins, she not unnaturally tries, as a rule, to keep these arrangements secret. But patient and tactful inquiries show that cases of twins brought up in different environments almost from birth are in fact much commoner than is usually believed. We have now collected over 30 such cases (1943c, 1955). I re-

5. Details are given in the various *Annual Reports of the Psychologist to the London County Council* (Burt, 1914–1931) and are summarized in Burt, 1943c. In the recent symposium on *Quantitative Inheritance* (1952), Woolf, quoting a later paper of mine, regrets that I have "based such far reaching conclusions on the study by Barbara Burks . . . covering only 214 foster children" (1928). But the principal basis for my own conclusion was a series of investigations in residential schools under the LCC covering in the course of years over 600 cases. I cited Burks' inquiry merely to show how an independent investigator in a different country had arrived at much the same figures as my own.

produce the more important correlations for the twins in Table 1 and have added for comparison corresponding coefficients obtained from other pairs, both related and unrelated. As regards intelligence the outstanding feature is the high correlation between the final assessments for the monozygotic twins, even when reared apart: it is almost as high as the correlation between two successive testings for the same individuals. On the other hand, with school attainments the correlations are much lower for twins reared separately than for twins reared together in the same home.

Several of our critics—Heim and Maddox, for example—have cited the account of analogous cases (described by Newman and others) as proving that intelligence is dependent on environment. Thus, to take an oft-quoted pair, "Helen," who had been trained as a teacher, scored with the Stanford-Binet tests an IQ of 116; whereas her twin sister, "Gladys," brought up for much of her childhood in an isolated district of the Canadian Rockies, scored only 92. But, says Newman, her score

> . . . was higher than we might expect considering her scant education; and . . . it seems certain that the great deficiency in education had inhibited the development of the rather high grade of mental ability with which she was *endowed by heredity* (1942, pp. 136–144).

Thus Newman's interpretation in no way conflicts with ours.

It is sometimes alleged (Maddox, 1957) that, since twins are born at the same time, the intrauterine environment must have been the same for both before birth, even if later on their environments differ widely, and that quite conceivably it is the former that is crucial. As it happens, however, this rather gratuitous assumption reverses the actual facts. Embryological and obstetric records show that, particularly with twins developed from split ova, the position of each in the uterus, and the subse-

Table 1. Correlations between mental and scholastic assessments.

	Identical twins reared together	Identical twins reared apart	Nonidentical twins reared together	Siblings reared together	Siblings reared apart	Unrelated children reared together
Mental						
"Intelligence"						
Group Test	.944	.771	.542	.515	.441	.281
Individual Test	.921	.843	.526	.491	.463	.252
Final Assessment	.925	.876	.551	.538	.517	.269
Scholastic						
General Attainments	.898	.681	.831	.814	.526	.535
Reading and Spelling	.944	.647	.915	.853	.490	.548
Arithmetic	.862	.723	.748	.769	.563	.476

quent development, is liable to differ widely (Burt and Howard, 1956, pp. 123ff. and refs.).

I think, therefore, that it may be safely said that, apart from the influence of some preconceived theory, few psychologists nowadays would be inclined to contest the mere fact of mental inheritance: the most that can be plausibly alleged is that its influence is comparatively slight and distinctly elusive.

The Mode of Inheritance. The majority of those who still question the importance of mental inheritance, and many of those who support it, seem by preference to adopt entirely antiquated notions of the way in which inheritable characteristics are transmitted. If, as I have maintained, mental capacities are dependent on the physical characteristics of the brain (or, to speak a little more precisely, on the structural and biochemical qualities of the nervous system), then we should expect those capacities to be inherited in accordance with the same principles that govern the inheritance of physical characteristics; and these principles (except for obscure and apparently exceptional instances of extranuclear heredity) are essentially those commonly associated with the name of Mendel. Many British psychologists, however, feel a strong and not unreasonable prejudice against applying "atomistic theories like Mendel's" to explain the facts of mental life, and consequently, so far as they admit the possibility of mental inheritance at all, still cling to the old Darwinian principle of blended inheritance. On this view heredity means "the tendency of like to beget like" (the definition quoted by one of them from the *Oxford English Dictionary*). As a result, they commonly assume that the arguments for inheritance must consist in demonstrating resemblances between the parent and his children by means of correlations. When the two parents differ, then the child is still expected to consist in an intermediate blend of both.

The approach of the modern geneticist is the reverse of all

this. As he views it, the real problem is rather to explain why in so many instances "like begets unlike." Both for the environmentalist and for the believer in blended inheritance, one of the most puzzling phenomena is the appearance, not merely of extremely dull children in the families of the well-to-do professional classes, but also of extremely bright children in families where both the cultural and the economic conditions of the parents would, one might imagine, condemn every child to hopeless failure. With the Mendelian hypothesis these anomalies are just what we should anticipate. However, the few critics who are familiar with the Mendelian explanation appear, as a rule, to suppose that it can apply only to discontinuous variations; and point out that intelligence, like stature, exhibits not discontinuous but continuous or graded variation. Hence, so they contend (sometimes citing the experiments of De Vries on "pure lines"), the apparent differences in intelligence between one individual and another must be due almost entirely to differences in environmental conditions.

Mendel himself was the first to indicate how his theory could be extended to account for this particular difficulty. When supplementing his experiments on the hybridization of peas by hybridizing beans, and (as before) crossing white flowered plants with purple, he found, that, whereas with peas the two types always sorted out with no hint of any intermediate color, with beans the offspring displayed "a whole range of hues from white to deep purple." This, he suggested, might be explained by postulating that with beans the color was determined, not by a single pair of alternative factors, but by a *number* of such pairs, each positive factor, when present, contributing a small additional amount of color. And if, as before, the recombinations are the effects of chance unions, then the resulting frequencies would obviously approximate to those of the normal curve.

However, in our early surveys of London children (1914–1931, 1917), we found that, when complete age groups were tested, the distribution of intelligence departed significantly from that of a perfect normal curve: there was a swollen tail at the lower end, due to an excess of mental defectives, and a smaller enlargement at the upper end. This and other considerations led me to put forward the tentative hypothesis that innate variations in intelligence are due partly to unifactor and partly to multifactor inheritance: i.e., they result from Mendelian factors of two main kinds (no doubt overlapping), viz., (*a*) major genes responsible for comparatively *large* deviations, usually of an abnormal type, and (*b*) multiple genes whose effects are *small, similar,* and *cumulative.*

Karl Pearson (1904) endeavoured to test the Mendelian theory in its multifactorial form by comparing its implications with actual figures obtained for height, arm length, and similar physical measurements, collected by himself and Alice Lee, from over 2,000 students and their relatives. The expected correlations which he deduced for various degrees of kinship were in every case far smaller than the observed coefficients. He therefore emphatically rejected the hypothesis of Mendelian inheritance, and fell back on the older theory of blending. However, in deriving his formulae and his expected values, Pearson relied on an oversimplified model. Contrary to what we now know to be the case, he assumed that the effect of assortative mating—the tendency of like to marry like—could be ignored as negligible, and that dominance would in every case be perfect. Ronald Fisher has since undertaken the rather formidable task of deducing more appropriate formulae, which allow for these and other complicating factors (1918). And with these refinements the calculated correlations fit Pearson's own figures as well as could be wished.

My colleagues and I have applied Fisher's methods (suitably modified) to assessments for intelligence (Burt and Howard, 1956). The data were secured in the course of surveys of the entire school population in a representative London borough, and covered nearly 1,000 pairs of siblings, together with ratings for parents, and (so far as they were accessible) grandparents, uncles and aunts, and first cousins. The final assessments for the children were obtained by submitting the marks from the group tests to the judgment of the teachers who knew the children best: where the teacher disagreed with the verdict of the marks, the child was interviewed personally, and subjected to further tests, often on several successive occasions. The assessments for the adult members of the family were naturally far less accurate. Nevertheless, in almost every case the correlations computed from the actual data agreed with the theoretical values deduced from the multifactorial hypothesis far better than with the values deduced from any other hypothesis hitherto put forward. The only appreciable discrepancy occurred in the case of first cousins. Here, as for stature, the observed correlation for intelligence is larger than the theoretical; but the difference is not statistically significant, and could readily be explained if (as has been suggested above) variations in intelligence are affected by a few major genes as well as by numerous minor genes. I may add that on sorting out figures for cousins of maternal, paternal, and mixed kinship there is also some slight evidence suggestive of sex linkage.

The Relative Influence of Heredity and Environment. In practical work, however, the question most frequently raised is, not whether differences in intelligence are inherited, nor even how they are inherited, but rather what is the relative influence of heredity as compared with environment. To an omnibus inquiry like this there can be no single answer. We can only try to determine, for this or that type of environment, for this or that population, and for this or that type of assessment, how far the observable results appear to be influenced by each of the two main groups of factors.

As Fisher's analysis has shown, formulae analogous to those used to deduce the expected correlations from the theoretical variances can also be devised for deducing the amount of the constituent variances from the observed correlations. I have ventured to amplify Fisher's methods (mainly on the lines of later work by Mather and Sewall Wright) so as to allow for unreliability and for the systematic effects of environment, i.e., of environmental influences which are correlated with those of heredity, as well as for random effects. The genetic contribution may be regarded as comprising two distinguishable portions: that due to the "fixable" component (or, as Fisher expresses it, to the "essential genotypes") and that due to the "nonfixable" (i.e., deviations due to dominance and similar influences). The data analysed consist of (*a*) the marks obtained from intelligence tests of the ordinary type taken just as they stand and (*b*) adjusted assessments obtained by the supplementary methods already described (Burt and Howard, 1956).

From Table 2 it will be seen that, with the crude test results, taken just as they stand, nearly 23% of the total variance appears due to nongenetic influences, i.e., to environment or to unreliability, and about 77% to genetic factors; with the adjusted assessments only about 12% (or slightly more) is apparently due to nongenetic influences and 88% to genetic factors. This of course means that the common practice of relying on tests alone—usually a group test applied once only—is by no means a satisfactory method of assessing a child's innate ability. Better assessments are obtained by submitting the test scores to the teachers for criticism or correction, and where necessary adjust-

Table 2. Analysis of variance for assessments of intelligence.

Source	Unadjusted test scores	Adjusted assessments
Genetic component:		
fixable	40.51	47.92
nonfixable	16.65	21.73
Assortative mating	19.90	17.91
Environment:		
systematic	10.60	1.43
random	5.91	5.77
Unreliability	6.43	5.24
Total	100.00	100.00

ing them by the methods described above. But such intensive inquiries would be too costly for routine use except in borderline cases.

Environment appears to influence the test results chiefly in three ways: (*a*) the cultural amenities of the home and the educational opportunities provided by the school can undoubtedly affect a child's performance in intelligence tests of the ordinary type, since so often they demand an acquired facility with abstract and verbal modes of expression; (*b*) quite apart from what the child may learn, the constant presence of an intellectual background may stimulate (or seem to stimulate) his latent powers by inculcating a keener motivation, a stronger interest in intellectual things, and a habit of accurate, speedy, and diligent work; (*c*) in a few rare cases illness or malnutrition during the prenatal or early postnatal stages may, almost from the very start, permanently impair the development of the child's central nervous system. The adjusted assessments may do much towards eliminating the irrelevant effects of the first two conditions; but it is doubtful whether they can adequately allow for the last.

Limitations Involved in These Conclusions

As in almost all scientific investigations, the hypothetical model which has formed the basis of our inquiry involves of necessity certain minor simplifications. In particular we have assumed, for purposes of calculation, a sharp distinction between the "major genes" of unifactor inheritance and the "polygenes" of multifactor inheritance, and have treated the latter as contributing equal and additive doses to the sum total of each child's innate intelligence. We have then supposed that the effects of the former would on the whole be excluded if the few obviously pathological cases (mostly found in special schools or institutions) were omitted from our final calculations. However, these assumptions have led several critics to accuse us of

> . . . disrupting the individual personality into atomic bits and discrete pieces which have subsequently to be joined together like a mosaic. . . . Personality [it is argued] is not a mosaic but a seamless whole, and hence the entire Mendelian hypothesis with its particulate genes, each producing a unit-character or adding another unit to the same character, is quite inapplicable to the facts of conscious behavior, and therefore to the study of mental capacity.

Objections of this kind could of course be used just as well to prove that a neuronic theory of the central nervous system is incompatible with the facts of conscious behaviour or of individual variations in ability, since nerve cells or "neural bonds" are equally "particulate." Nevertheless, even those neurologists who prefer to start from a "field theory" do not wholly reject the neuronic hypothesis (cf. Sholl, 1956). In both cases the difficulties raised owe their force chiefly to the fact that there is a vast series of elusive processes intervening between theory and observable results which the critic is exceedingly apt to forget.

Moreover, criticisms like those just cited plainly rest on an obsolete version of the Mendelian doctrine. No geneticist today, I imagine, accepts the hypothesis of the autonomous corpuscular gene; and the genotypic endowment of the individual can only affect the phenotypic resultant through the mediation of innumerable obscure biochemical steps.

In our original papers Howard and I tried carefully to guard against recurrent objections of this type. As we pointed out, the phrase "multiple factors" may be used to cover either (*a*) relatively numerous loci each with only two allelomorphs or (*b*) a single locus (or relatively few loci) each with numerous allelomorphs, or possibly (*c*) some combination of the two. Hypothesis *b* by itself would hardly seem to fit the facts. We are inclined to think that factors of all the various types may be operative in varying degrees, and that the attempt to classify factors or genes should not be too severely pressed.

We further assumed that in all probability the influence of such factors on the individual's observable intelligence was mainly the indirect result of their influence on the development of his central nervous system, and was presumably effected by modifying growth rates. And we expressly stated that the ultimate influence of any one "gene" upon intelligence might be but one of its multifarious consequences, and possibly a comparatively remote consequence at that. Some genes may have a larger share in the final result; others a smaller; and the rough classification of genes into "major" genes and "minor" was adopted primarily with a view to simplifying our general discussion.[6] We

6. If Mather's view that "the major genes occur only in euchromatin, while heterochromatin contains only polygenes" (Darlington and Mather, 1949, p. 151) is eventually confirmed there would be more adequate grounds for retaining a sharp distinction between the two modes of inheritance. However, this view is not universally accepted. For an alternative interpretation of the experimental results on which Mather largely relies, see the papers by Reeve and Robertson quoted in our article (Burt

ourselves find the "theory of chromosomal hierarchy," advanced by Goldschmidt (1955), especially attractive as a basis for the ultimate hierarchical differentiation of mental ability.

However, this is not the place to enlarge on these speculative interpretations. We fully admit that the simplifications involved in our hypothetical model mean that the figures finally deduced can be no more than approximations. But we maintain that the error of approximation, however large, will nevertheless be smaller than the amount of "unreliability" inevitably involved in all such measurements.

In any case we must repeat that the conclusions reached are at best only valid in reference to the particular conditions under which they were obtained. They would not necessarily hold good (*a*) of other mental traits, (*b*) of different methods of assessment, (*c*) of a population of a different genetic composition, or (*d*) of a population at a different cultural level: much less would they hold good if there were any subsequent change (*e*) in the present distribution of environmental and genetic characteristics, or (*f*) in the influences affecting their mutual interaction.[7]

The Inheritance of Other Mental Qualities

The mental trait in which we have been chiefly interested is the general factor of "intelligence." This, we readily concede, is but one psychological ingredient in ordinary everyday behaviour. Our critics are accustomed to reproach us for apparently ignoring the rest. There are several obvious reasons why we have dealt

---

and Howard, 1956, p. 116). These writers incline more to what in the text I have called hypothesis *b*. But, as Howard and I contended, their alternative interpretation would affect only the method, not the results, of our statistical deductions.

7. A more detailed reply to the criticisms urged by Woolf, Heim, and Maddox appears in the issue of the *Brit. J. statist. Psychol.*, 1954, Part i.

less fully with other determinants. The first and the most conclusive is that comparatively little evidence is as yet available in regard to the genetic composition of other mental factors. We have, however, in the course of our surveys, met with an appreciable number of cases which strongly suggest the inheritability of certain specific abilities and disabilities, or rather of certain ill-defined tendencies that presumably underlie such disabilities —particularly in our studies of memory, of visual, auditory, and kinaesthetic imagery, and of verbal, numerical, artistic, and musical aptitudes (Burt, 1914–1931). We have encountered other cases which suggest the inheritability of general emotional instability, of temperamental qualities like introversion and extraversion, and of certain quasi-instinctive tendencies like sex and bad temper (or "pugnacity," as McDougall would have termed it). But emotional tendencies are always much more liable to be influenced and altered by postnatal experiences, and in any case undergo considerable changes during the developmental stages, so that all attempts at assessment are apt to be precarious. The most convincing evidence is afforded by the family histories of children brought up in orphanages or residential institutions (Burt, 1941, especially p. 14). In all these instances the evidence, such as it is, appears to indicate that each of the characteristics mentioned, cognitive and temperamental alike, is influenced both by unifactor and by multifactor modes of inheritance—the latter tending on the whole to predominate, but in varying degrees. This after all is what is commonly found in investigations on physical characteristics. Characteristics depending mainly (though not entirely) on the development of the long bones—such as arm length, leg length, stature, and perhaps the longer dimensions of the face and head—yield correlations of much the same magnitude as those obtained for general intelligence. Others, like cephalic index, breadth at hips, and particularly facial characteristics, seem to be rather more subject to the influence of single (or relatively few) genes, which often appear to exhibit almost perfect dominance. Variations in the cartilaginous features, and particularly those depending on flesh and fat, are far more readily affected by environmental influences (for data, see Tanner, 1953).

But secondly there is a practical reason for concentrating attention first of all, and chiefly, on the inheritability of general intelligence. General intelligence, as we have seen, accounts for four times as much of the variance as any other identifiable factor. Galton's pronouncement is thus fully borne out by our own results:

> . . . general ability appears far more important than special gifts; and, where the allowance granted by nature is inadequate, the keenest will and the stoutest industry must strive in vain.

Moreover, the child's innate endowment of intelligence sets an upper limit to the best he can possibly attain. No one would expect a Mongolian imbecile, with the most skilful coaching in the world, to achieve the scholastic knowledge of an average child. In the same way, no should expect a child who is innately dull to gain a scholarship to a grammar school, or one whose inborn ability is merely average to win first class honors at Oxford or Cambridge. No doubt, in any individual case the ascertainment of this upper limit can never be a matter of absolute certainty: an IQ derived from tests alone falls far short of a trustworthy indication. Hence education authorities, like life insurance companies, have to follow Butler's maxim, and take probability for their guide. They cannot, however, afford to risk a lavish expenditure on cases where there are fairly heavy odds against success.

Nevertheless, it must be owned that, in Britain at any rate, the existing administrative machinery is far less efficient than it might be. In an inquiry made just before the introduction of the Education Act of 1944 we found that "approximately 40 percent of those whose innate abilities are of university standard are failing to reach the university" (Burt, 1943c). The new arrangements proposed by the act, and the postwar changes in the economic circumstances of the various social classes, have appreciably altered the entries to "grammar schools"; but it is too early to say how far they have affected the composition of the universities. For grammar schools the entries vary considerably from one area to another and even from year to year. The general aim is apparently to provide a grammar school education for the brightest 20% of each age group; this corresponds to a border line of about 113 IQ. On this basis the round figures in Table 3 represent estimates deduced from the information so far available.

A more intensive survey of two contrasted areas ("industrial" and "prosperous") has just been published by J. E. Floud and her colleagues. Briefly their conclusion is that, in both areas, gross material handicaps have been greatly lessened, though not entirely eliminated. Nevertheless, in their view, the "problem of social wastage" is by no means overcome. The fact that, even today, a large proportion of the children from the working classes fail to reach the higher levels of scholastic instruction Floud her-

Table 3. Estimates for grammar school entries.

	General population[a]	Proportions over +0.85 SD	Expected entries	Actual entries
Middle Class	20%	.40	.08 (40%)	55%
Manual Class	80%	.15	.12 (60%)	45%
Total	100%		.20 (100%)	100%

[a] The *Census of Great Britain* (1951) gives an estimate of 81.7 for males over 15, occupied or retired, falling into the classes of "Skilled," "Mixed," and "Unskilled" workers: these I have pooled in a single broad group.

self attributes to the way in which the "educational ladder" is still widely regarded as a "middle class prerogative," to be anxiously watched and jealously preserved (1956).

I myself should be inclined to look rather to a difference in the aims and aspirations which are traditional in the different classes. The consequences seemed clearly revealed by the differences in the after-careers of LCC scholarship winners from the lower and the middle classes respectively whom my colleagues and I have been able to follow up (cf. 1914–1931, Burt and Howard, 1956).[8] The figures show that the abler children from the working classes, even when they have obtained free places or scholarships at secondary schools of the "grammar" type, frequently fail to stay the course: by the time they are sixteen the attractions of high wages and of cheap entertainment during leisure hours prove stronger than their desire for further knowledge and skill, and easily overcome their original resolve to face a long prospect of hard sedentary work *in statu pupillari.* As a headmaster of a secondary school which receives both types of boy has put it:

8. Additional evidence is furnished by the report of the Central Advisory Council for Education (England) on *Early Leaving.* In 1953, at the age of entry to the grammar school (11 plus), 66% of the top intelligence group were the children of manual workers; at the end of the grammar school period the proportion had fallen to 47%. Of those who drop out, some are "premature leavers," i.e., they leave voluntarily, as soon as they are legally able to do so; others fail to reach the top form and so leave at 16: of these many even fail to secure a school leaving certificate. In such cases, the award of a special place in the grammar school would seem itself to have been a wasted effort. Nevertheless, in the long run there may be certain compensating advantages to the community as a whole: even the early leavers may have gained something from the higher education to which they have been for a while subjected, and it would surely be a misfortune were all the brightest youngsters to forsake the social class into which they were born. Their continued presence there must help, not only to elevate its tone, but also (a point too often overlooked) to prevent its genetic constitution from being wholly depleted of its better elements.

> The working class parent wants his boy to be "selected" chiefly to prove that "his child is a good as anybody else's"; having done so, he will withdraw him at the earliest possible opportunity: I do not press them, for the presence of those whose chief interest in life is television, Hollywood films, football pools, "the dogs," and "the girls" has not improved the tone of my school. And too often these "ignobler attitudes and crude ambitions" are shared by, and encouraged by, both parents and friends.

On the other hand, if I may quote the report of an experienced university teacher:

> That section of the middle class which seeks, by paying fees that it can ill afford, to assist its children to climb, *via* a "public school" or an independent "grammar school," to a University education and a good honours degree in the humaner subjects, is animated by a traditional morale which is comparatively rare in children and parents from the other classes: those who nowadays come here on grants, at no cost to themselves or their parents, are, on the whole, most irregular attendants, and the least satisfactory students.

Or, to quote a still more recent pronouncement of the High Master of St. Paul's:[9]

> The parents are themselves imbued with four traditional ideals which they hand on to their posterity: self-discipline, a community spirit, the Christian religion, and a readiness to accept social responsibility even at the sacrifice of material enjoyments—a genuine *noblesse oblige.*

Underlying all these differences in outlook I myself am tempted to suspect an innate and transmissible difference in

9. A. N. Gilkes, *Independence in Education,* 1957.

temperamental stability and in character, or in the neurophysiological basis on which such temperamental and moral differences tend to be built up. Tradition may explain much: it can hardly account for all. However, it would be idle to pursue such speculations here in the absence of more adequate data.[10]

Need For Further Research

To my mind the most pressing need at the moment is for more extensive research. Hitherto the most active investigators have been research-students, with little or no experience of the ways of children or the conditions of the classroom. For the requisite

10. Since my lecture was written and delivered, some further information has become available in the data published by the Association of Universities of the British Commonwealth (*Report of an Inquiry into Applications for Admissions to Universities,* 1957). It appears that at Oxford and Cambridge only 12% of the men and 7% of the women had fathers in manual occupations; at other universities the proportions were somewhat higher, namely, 31% and 19%, respectively. Among the general population 72% of the population would fall into the manual category. The report points out that to a large extent the decline must occur during the school period, and the real reason, it is suggested, is more often lack of zeal than lack of the requisite ability. "Differing environmental influences and aspirations seem mainly responsible for the fall from 66% at the point of entry to the non-fee-paying grammar school and 36% at the point of university entry. . . . Discrimination against those of humble social origin can be virtually ruled out."

Most education authorities nowadays tend to use what are misleadingly termed "intelligence tests" as tests of suitability for a grammar school. (Such tests, as I have argued elsewhere, should rather be termed "tests of scholastic aptitude.") The original intention was that the "intelligence test" should, so far as possible, assess innate ability. Bright children with special verbal or literary abilities and interests were then to be allocated to grammar schools; and those with practical or mechanical abilities or interests, to technical schools. But for the majority the age of 11 plus is too early to make a satisfactory distinction. Hence the brightest still seem likely to be sent to secondary schools of the grammar type rather than to a technical school, even if more suited to the latter.

facilities, and for any supplementary information they may want, they have to rely on the goodwill of the busy teacher. And one important factor is still more often overlooked: the motivation of the children themselves. This takes two obvious forms. There is first what may be called direct or short distance motivation. As actual trial has repeatedly shown, neither pupils nor students are likely to exert their full powers in a test conducted merely in the interests of someone else's research; but when the examinees' entrance to a grammar school or university depends on their performances, the average score may rise 5 to 10 IQ points higher. Secondly, there are the effects of indirect or long distance motivation: the influence of parental attitudes, of teachers' exhortations, and (most of all perhaps with British lads) of the social pressure that arises from the opinions and the comments of their school fellows, and from the tone and atmosphere of the school or class to which the pupil belongs. It is therefore hardly surprising if the results obtained in mere academic researches are at times disappointing, and evince a comparatively low reliability.

I myself had the good fortune to be appointed a member of the school inspectorate, and so not only acquired a firsthand knowledge of the schools, teachers, and pupils, but enjoyed full authority to interrupt the timetable, examine private records, and requisition whatever information might be wanted. Here therefore I must again record my indebtedness both to the London County Council for facilitating these inquiries and financing their publication, and to the teachers, social workers, and school medical officers, who rendered such wholehearted cooperation in all our investigations. It is to be hoped that other education authorities will in the near future perceive the practical value of systematically organized inquiries of this kind, conducted on an official basis by those who know the schools from inside.

The basic researches must be carried out on children rather than on students or adults. With adults, it is much harder to achieve accurate assessments; innate tendencies are already obscured and overlaid; and detailed family histories difficult to obtain. In allocating adults to appropriate occupations, whether in civil life or in the fighting services, innate capacities are of little consequence, and accordingly tend to be ignored. As a result the severest critics of researches on heredity are generally those whose experience of mental testing has been gained in the adult field. This was manifest during the symposium recently arranged by the Psychological Section of the British Association. Several contributors, for instance, echoed remarks like those of H. E. Jones that "potential investigators should now be advised that the nature-nurture controversy has been shown to be an unproductive field of research" (Carmichael, 1946); and similar conclusions have more recently been voiced by writers like Maddox (1957), Renshaw (1957), and others, who deplore what they call "the resurrection of the nature-nurture controversy" as "wholly anachronistic."

But whether or not this is now the prevailing view among psychologists, it is not the opinion of leading geneticists. Goldschmidt, Snyder, Calvin Hall, and Calvin Stone all deplore the neglect of genetic inquiries by psychologists of the present day. Goldschmidt in particular has criticized "the extreme belief of contemporary psychologists in the power of environment"—a belief which he ascribes to the "doctrine of universal conditioning, which has, until lately, dominated the behaviourist school" (Dunn, 1921). In this country eminent authorities like R. A. Fisher (1919, 1950) and Fraser Roberts (1957) have not only urged the importance of genetic studies for psychology, but have made noteworthy contributions of their own.

Mere statistical inquiries, however, can never suffice. In this country one of the most obvious needs is a series of intensive studies of able boys and girls similar to those already carried out on the backward, the defective, the neurotic, and the delinquent.

The brilliant investigation of 1,000 gifted children, started by Terman and his colleagues over 30 years ago, and so assiduously followed up, furnishes an admirable model (1925, 1954). But nothing like conclusive answers can be given to the questions here raised until far more extensive research has been undertaken on the fundamental problems of psychogenetics. An adequate understanding of the basic processes can be secured only if we start with carefully planned experiments on lowlier creatures, where pure strains can be obtained, breeding controlled, and successive generations more speedily raised. When we know more about the genetics of intelligence in animals, we may be able to construct with greater confidence a more exact hypothesis regarding the transmission of intelligence in man.

Social Implications

After all, the practical importance of the issues involved is so profound and so far-reaching that it would be fatal to dismiss the problem as "unproductive" or "anachronistic" without attempting to settle it one way or the other. No democratic state can afford to pass it by. If in the end the views of the early pioneers should turn out to have been approximately correct—if "innate intelligence varies between limits at least as wide as IQ's of 50 and 150," and if too "the average intelligence of the general population at maturity is little if at all above that of an average child of thirteen or thirteen-and-a-half"—then the bearing of genetic variation on the national and social questions of the present day would be all too obvious.

In our laudable eagerness to improve the lot of our own generation, we have been tempted to close our eyes to the effects of present policy on the generations to come. The over-all efficiency of the citizens who make up a nation or a state must in the last resort depend on what has been called its "chromosomal pool."

Improved environmental amenities can of themselves ensure no lasting results; but the changes in a nation's genetic constitution are likely to prove irreversible. Throughout almost the entire Western world, and to a less extent in other areas as well, the last half-century or so has witnessed radical modifications in the conditions that previously governed marriage and fertility. Increased mobility, enhanced freedom, new means of production, new methods of government, the progressive reduction of the traditional barriers separating different peoples and different social groups, and, in our own country, the recent extensions of the educational ladder, all these transformations are visibly disturbing the stability alike of classes and of races. Almost inevitably they must alter the genetic constitution of what have hitherto been the dominant nations and the dominant stocks within those nations.

From history and from past experience we know full well how changes in the balance between inbreeding and outbreeding[11] can affect the later destinies of populations, remoulding them sometimes for good, sometimes for ill. Geneticists have repeatedly drawn attention to the processes at work, and indicated the need for studying the possible effects of contemporary trends (cf., e.g., Darlington and Mather, 1950, pp. 49ff. and Fisher, 1950, pp. 170ff.). Yet current sociological textbooks seem almost wholly

11. British readers will find it instructive to compare current copies of such works as *Who's Who* with those of (say) 60 years ago, and note the changes in the pedigrees of the British clergy (who in the nineteenth century were probably the most inbred profession in the country) and in the ancestry of members of the British cabinet and Civil Service during that period. The recent work of Ginsberg, Glass, and Moss has shown very plainly how the extension of the educational ladder is altering the composition of the different social groups, though none of the writers has considered the possible genetic consequences. The most illuminating discussion is still that contained in the concluding chapters of Fisher's book on *The Genetical Theory of Natural Selection* (1930), especially Chap. X, "Reproduction in Relation to Social Class."

to ignore them. Surely it is high time that the social psychologist should now take up the question and plan a systematic series of investigations on the intricate but highly important issues involved. May I therefore conclude by endorsing, in the strongest possible terms, the verdict of Stone (Dunn, 1921), quoted by Bingham in the last letter he wrote to me:

> It is a matter of shame and regret that only an amateurish beginning has been made by psychologists in applying modern genetic methods to fundamental study in the nature-nurture area.

And may we hope that in the near future Bingham's "deepest wish" may be fulfilled, and that "a small band of enthusiasts will come forward to explore afresh this urgent and many-sided field of research."

References

Bagley, W. C. *The educational process.* New York: Macmillan, 1912.

Burks, Barbara. *27th Yearbook National Society for the Study of Education,* 1928, *1,* 219.

Burt, C. Experimental tests of general intelligence. *Brit. J. Psychol.,* 1909, *3,* 94–177.

Burt, C. The inheritance of mental characteristics. *Eugen. Rev.,* 1912, *4,* 168–200.

Burt, C. *Annual reports of the psychologist to the London County Council.* London: London County Council, 1914–1931.

Burt, C. *The distribution and relations of educational abilities.* London: P. S. King & Son, 1917.

Burt, C. Is the doctrine of instincts dead? *Brit. J. educ. Psychol.,* 1941, *11,* 155–172; 1943, *13,* 1–16a.

Burt, C. The education of the adolescent: the psychological implications of the Norwood Report. *Brit. J. educ. Psychol.,* 1943, *13,* 126–140b.

Burt, C. Ability and income. *Brit. J. educ. Psychol.*, 1943, *13*, 83–98c.

Burt, C. The differentiation of intellectual ability. *Brit. J. educ. Psychol.*, 1954, *24*, 76–90.

Burt, C. The evidence for the concept of intelligence. *Brit. J. educ. Psychol.*, 1955, *25*, 158–177.

Burt, C., & Howard, M. The multifactorial theory of inheritance and its application to intelligence. *Brit. J. statist. Psychol.*, 1956, *9*, 95–131.

Campbell, F. *Eleven plus and all that.* London: Watts, 1956.

Carmichael, L. (ed.). *Manual of child psychology.* New York: Wiley, 1946.

Darlington, C. D., & Mather, K. *The elements of genetics.* London: Allen & Unwin, 1949.

Darlington, C. D., & Mather, K. *Genes, plants, and people.* London: Allen & Unwin, 1950.

Dunn, L. C. (ed.). *Eugenics in the twentieth century.* New York: Macmillan, 1921.

Fisher, R. A. Correlation between relatives on the supposition of Mendelian inheritance. *Trans. roy. Soc., Edin.*, 1918, *52*, 399–433.

Fisher, R. A. The causes of human variability. *Eugen. Rev.*, 1919, *11*, 213–220.

Fisher, R. A. *The genetical theory of natural selection.* Oxford: Clarendon Press, 1950.

Floud, J. E., Halsey, A. H., & Martin, F. M. *Social class and educational opportunity.* London: Heinemann, 1956.

Freeman, F. N. *Mental tests.* New York: Houghton Mifflin, 1926.

Galton, F. *Hereditary Genius.* London: Macmillan, 1869.

Garnett, M. *Education and world citizenship.* Cambridge: Cambridge Univer. Press, 1921.

Goldschmidt, R. B. *Theoretical genetics.* Berkeley: Univer. California Press, 1955.

Lashley, K. S., & Clark, G. The cytoarchitecture of the cerebral cortex of *Ateles:* a critical examination of architectonic studies. *J. comp. Neurol.*, 1946, *85*, 223–305.

Maddox, H. Nature-nurture balance sheets. *Brit. J. educ. Psychol.*, 1957, *27*, 166–175.

Newman, H. H. *Twins and super-twins.* London: Hutchinson, 1942.

Pearson, K. On a generalized theory of alternative inheritance with special reference to Mendel's laws. *Phil. Trans.*, 1904, *203*, 53–87.

Piaget, J. *The psychology of intelligence.* London: Kegan Paul, 1950.

Reeve, F. C. R., & Waddington, C. H. (eds.). *Quantitative inheritance.* London: H. M. Stationery Office, 1952.

Renshaw, T. Burt's concept of intelligence. *Brit. Psychol. Soc. Bull.,* 1957.

Roberts, J. A. F. *An introduction to medical genetics.* Oxford: Oxford Univer. Press, 1940.

Sholl, D. A. *The organization of the cerebral cortex.* London: Methuen, 1956.

Spearman, C. *Abilities of man.* London: Macmillan, 1927.

Spencer, H. *Principles of psychology.* London: Williams & Norgate, 1870.

Stone, C. P. Methodological resources for the experimental study of innate behaviour as related to environmental factors. *Psychol. Rev.,* 1947, *54,* 342–347.

Tanner, J. M. The inheritance of morphological and physiological traits. In A. Sorsby, *Clinical genetics.* London: Butterworth, 1953.

Terman, L. M. (ed.). *Genetic studies of genius.* Stanford: Stanford Univer. Press, 1925, 1947.

Terman, L. M. The discovery and encouragement of exceptional talent. *Amer. Psychologist,* 1954, *9,* 221–230.

Thorndike, E. L. *Educational psychology.* New York: Teachers College, Columbia University, 1914.

Thurstone, L. L. *The vectors of mind.* Chicago: Univer. Chicago Press, 1935.

Watson, J. B. *Behaviourism.* London: Paul, Trench Trubner, 1931.

Edward K. Strong, Jr.

Satisfactions and Interests[1]

The topic is "Satisfactions and Interests." During the last 37 years I have learned some things about interests, but I confess I have taken satisfaction for granted—which I think is pretty much what most psychologists have done. The term is employed in everyday language and defined in the dictionary. It plays an important role in all theories of motivation. For over three decades surveys of job satisfaction of employees have been conducted costing thousands of dollars. Nevertheless I am very doubtful if any ten experts would agree on a specific definition of the term.

Years ago I contended that there was "no better criterion of a vocational interest test than that of satisfaction enduring over a period of years" (Strong, 1943, p. 385). I have actually never used satisfaction as a criterion on the ground that there seemed to be no good way to measure it. Such correlations as have been reported between interest scores and satisfaction have been for the most part too low to be of practical significance.

1. This paper is based on the Walter Van Dyke Bingham Memorial Lecture given at the University of Minnesota, April 10, 1958. It was first published in the *American Psychologist,* 1958, vol. 13, no. 8 (August), pp. 449–456.

Job Satisfaction and Job Success

Most people have assumed that job satisfaction or morale contributes to production. It came as a shock to me, as it must have done to many others, to read Brayfield and Crockett's (1955) review of the literature and to learn that there is little or no evidence to support the assumption. In a still more recent review, Herzberg, Mausner, Peterson, and Capwell (1957) report some relationship between morale and production, but in most of the investigations where there were positive relations they were low correlations. Reading these two reviews and that of Viteles (1953) and many of the articles on which these reviews are based leaves one bewildered. Definitions of the key terms are conspicuous by their absence and must differ greatly, judging by the context. Many statements by one writer are contradicted by another.

What is satisfaction? Some say it is a kind of feeling as simple as pleasantness; others contend it is a complex of feeling, emotion, and sensation. If the latter, do the proportions of these three ingredients vary each time? Contrast the satisfaction of eating dinner and resting afterwards with a full stomach with the satisfaction of finding a house to rent after hunting many weary days. The mother tells her daughter as she leaves the home to have a good time and asks when the girl returns: "Did you have a good time?" Is having a good time what is meant by satisfaction?

Employee surveys are called attitude or job satisfaction or morale surveys. The terms are sometimes used synonymously and sometimes not. In the absence of generally accepted definitions it is suggested that job satisfaction be employed when the worker is thought of as an individual and that morale be used when the worker is thought of as a member of a group. Perry defines morale as "a state of mind which characterizes groups of men when they are engaged in some action . . . The essence of it is that the group holds together and holds to its objective, despite events that are calculated to divide and dishearten" (1942). An employee is an individual and a member of one or more groups. It is appropriate to consider both his job satisfaction and his morale. But seemingly there should be some difference in the inventories designed to measure these two attitudes towards one's job. Inventories regarding morale should contain items relative to the man's involvement with his company, his union, and the members of his department. Are the low correlations between production and job satisfaction caused in part at least by inadequate measurement of job satisfaction? Consider briefly how job satisfaction has been measured.

Employee surveys since the pioneer days of Houser have typically consisted of two parts: the first part asking a few questions as to the man's overall satisfaction with his job; the second asking whether he liked or was satisfied with all manner of factors, such as income, supervision, cafeteria, pension system, and so on. A summary of the responses in the first part was supposed to measure the employee's overall satisfaction. Responses to the items in the second part that pertained to each job factor were summarized in order to show how satisfied or dissatisfied employees were regarding the various factors. The purpose of such surveys has been to aid management to improve production by determining the causes of dissatisfaction and by identifying the departments with low morale. Much of the literature is devoted to the causes or job factors presumably associated with dissatisfaction, their relative importance, and what can be done to improve conditions. Surveys have been worthwhile to the extent that management has made intelligent use of the results—which has not always been done.

One reason why job satisfaction inventories do not correlate with production is that the items do not furnish good measures of the specific job factors. In one investigation, for example, four questions were used to measure each of four factors; the intercorrelations among the four items ranged from .39 to .52. A summary of the responses of four such questions can only roughly approximate what they purport to measure.

Even if we had good measures of job factors, which we do not have, some of the factors would not correlate particularly with production. Seemingly, health should be directly related to production. But some employees who suffer from poor health plug along regardless, and other employees absent themselves whenever they have the sniffles. Consider one very simple example of physical condition, that of toothache. If we rate production on a scale of −3 to +3 (where −3 represents absence from work and zero production, and +3 represents maximum production) and similarly rate satisfaction-dissatisfaction from toothache (where −3 represents such severe pain the man is absent at his dentist, the rating of −2 represents a decrease of 2 from normal rating in production, and the rating of −1 represents a decrease of 1 from normal production), then we will have a correlation of .42 when 35% of employees have ratings of −3, −2, and −1 in dissatisfaction from toothache. If the percentage of employees so affected drops to 15%, the correlation is .26; if the percentage is further decreased to 10%, the correlation is .20. It is unlikely that the percentage of employees seriously affected by toothache is ever as high as 10%, so that the correlation would be appreciably below .20 although the data were arranged so that there was high correlation between suffering from toothache and decrease in production.

In order to obtain a significant correlation between satisfaction-dissatisfaction and production, we must have a situation where dissatisfaction produces decrease, and satisfaction produces increase, in production; and, furthermore, where a fair percentage of employees rate the factor high or low. It is doubtful if most job factors are so related to production.

Consider a second condition, that of being in love. Here we might obtain very high or very low overall satisfaction-dissatisfaction responses depending upon the current behavior of the loved one. It seems probable that those suffering from this malady, whether satisfied or not, would exhibit decrease in production since the employee's attention would be distracted by daydreaming about last night and what will happen on the next date.

The factor of age has a curvilinear relationship with production. The youngest and oldest employees are more satisfied than those about 30 years of age. The factor of age will reduce the correlation when it is mixed in with other factors.

Those of you who are interested should consider how satisfaction-dissatisfaction relative to each aspect of a job could be related to success on the job and also estimate what percentage of employees would be particularly satisfied or dissatisfied on any one day.

A still more serious difficulty arises when responses to all the items on an inventory are summarized on the assumption that, if job satisfaction is to be measured, all aspects of the job should be taken into account. Here, inadequate measures of each factor are combined without much consideration as to the relationships between the factors—a procedure which makes our statisticians fairly froth at the mouth. A way must be found to consider only those who are really satisfied or dissatisfied with each job factor and to disregard those who don't really care about the factor. In the case of toothache there may be perfect correlation with production among the very few suffering with toothache and zero correlation among the great majority. Data based on all of them will not correlate as high as .10. How can you expect to learn how production is related to satisfaction with the job and with expectation of advancement when people with such attitudes are combined with girls who expect to marry and quit work? We need to develop adequate measures of each factor and determine the relationship to an adequate criterion before attempting a summary of all factors.

One way to discover what a test should measure is to note the nature of its items. Four types of questions are found in survey questionnaires: questions asking for facts, opinions, likings, and satisfactions. The proportions of these types vary greatly among survey inventories.

The evidence is clear that facts and opinions about working conditions are colored by feeling—as is every aspect of behavior. It is therefore appropriate to use fact and opinion questions to indicate feeling. Responses should, however, differ according as one is asked: Does your supervisor treat all alike? Do you like your supervisor? Are you satisfied to work under your supervisor? Most inventories ask many interest questions: "Do you like or dislike this and that?" Considering that the inventory is to measure job satisfaction or morale, it is surprising that there are not more items which ask: "Are you satisfied or not with this and that?" Relatively few items inquire as to the man's involvement with his fellows and the company.

The correlations between job satisfaction and production are low not only because measures of job satisfaction are inadequate but because measures of success on the job are also inadequate. It is well recognized that production is not a complete measure of success on the job. There is possibly no more difficult problem in industrial psychology than the determination of adequate criteria of success. Furthermore, in a surprisingly high proportion of jobs there is no way to measure amount of production, and in many cases where it can be measured, as on an assembly line, the measure is far more a measure of flow of work, determined by management, than it is a reflection of the man's ability and willingness to do the work. It is not surprising that psychologists resort so often to ratings of supervisors as their criterion of success. Psychologists have so far contributed relatively little to this task. I have great faith in the ability of psychologists to develop an adequate test of any specifically defined activity; but, if the activity is not definitely defined, the first step should be to define the activity, not to attempt to devise tests that correlate .20, maybe .30, with something that it is hoped represents the activity. It would seem at the present time that both psychologists and management should concentrate on what is meant by success on a given job. When that is accomplished, management ought to be able to measure success on the job, and psychologists should aid in the analyses and devise tests which will predict in advance who will be successful and, I hope, also who will be interested and reasonably satisfied.

What shall be done with job surveys? Three alternatives are evident. First, continue the surveys for their practical value to business management but discontinue trying to prove that morale increases production appreciably. Second, accept the necessity of morale for its own sake. Modern personnel practice stresses that men must be selected so as to be both useful and happy. Maybe we should assume that good morale means general contentment, happiness, satisfaction on the part of all, top management as well as employees. No instructor, supervisor, or army officer wants the people under him to be complaining and criticizing everything that has to be done. Third, develop adequate measures of morale and success on the job. If there were adequate measures, might there not be much higher correlations between them?

Unquestionably much has been learned from job satisfaction surveys of practical use to business and of theoretical value to psychology. It is doubtful, however, if additional surveys will add much more of theoretical value. It now seems highly desirable to isolate and define the basic components and find some way to measure each of them. These are problems for psychologists to tackle. They are not easy or we would know more about them than we do today.

Opinion, Attitude, Interest, and Satisfaction

Consider now four basic concepts: opinion, attitude, interest, and satisfaction. First, what is *opinion,* often referred to as attitude? An opinion is a mental reaction to the relationship between this and that. Many items in an employee survey are opinion items, such as: "Do you work better on a clear or rainy day?" Responses to the questions are either "Yes" or "No" based on facts, more or less, but primarily indicating belief or disbelief. Belief is a feeling comparable to pleasantness, liking, and satisfaction. Opinions concerning religion and membership in the Republican or Democratic party are about as stable as anything we have in life. But many judgments are based on conversation, hearsay, no personal experience, and change about as readily as styles. The hullabaloo following the appearance of Sputnik is a striking example of a whole country losing faith in what they had previously believed. Because opinion items are not as stable as interest items, it is doubtful that they can be as useful as interest items in predicting future behavior. Research is needed to answer this and many other related problems well set forth by Sherif and Cantril (1945) and by McNemar (1946).

A second term is *attitude.* This term has a great vogue today. But what does it signify? Nelson (1939) lists 23 rather distinct characterizations of the term. Sherif and Cantril tell us the term is in a very confused state, and McNemar reminds us that "no one has ever seen an attitude." Seemingly its best usefulness is its ambiguity. When a psychologist does not want to disclose his real purpose, as is typically the case with employee surveys, he may call his inventory a job attitude survey.

Several have given definitions of attitude. Peak's definition of attitude is useful here. She defines attitude (1955) as "a hypothetical construct which involves organization around a conceptual or perceptual nucleus *and* which has affective properties." Concepts and percepts are acquired reactions to a combination of sensations. They are mental activities, and most of them initiate overt activities. It is not merely that sensations are organized into a concept so that no two persons have exactly the same concept but that such concepts are *used* in some manner that is important. What happens when I say the word "baseball"? Do you see the word, or think of keeping score, as you used to do in high school, or do you think of watching a game, or of playing the game, of playing short stop, or knocking out a home run? If the concept is emphasized, then according to Peak we have an attitude; if the activity is emphasized, we have a habit, a skill, or an interest. Psychologists are prone to call activities by many names depending upon the aspect that is emphasized. Thus the activity of skating is called a habit or a skill when its motor coordination acquired by repetition is emphasized; it is called an interest when its feeling quality is emphasized.

Five characteristics of *interests* may be mentioned. First, they are acquired in the sense that feeling becomes associated with the activity. We are not referring to the learning of an activity itself, such as writing one's name, which usually requires many repetitions. We are referring to the associating of feeling with an activity. Such association results from one or only a few experiences—once stung by a bee, one dislikes bees the rest of his life. About all that can be said about the associating process is that, when an activity is useful, aids in reaching some goal, pleasant feeling is attached to it; when the activity is not useful, brings some disagreeable consequence, unpleasant feeling is attached.

Second, interests are persistent. Sometimes disliking is replaced by liking and vice versa; many start out disliking olives and acquire a taste, a pleasant feeling, for them. But, all in all, interests are surprisingly permanent.

A third characteristic of interests is intensity. One can not only immediately indicate whether he likes or dislikes an activity, but one can also immediately indicate his relative preferences for different activities.

The fourth and fifth characteristics are acceptance-rejection and readiness to act. For example, the waitress says: "Will you have some garlic bread?" My wife's response is, "Yes, please"; my own response is, "No, thanks." She likes garlic and goes toward it, I dislike garlic and reject it. Such acceptance-rejection implies action, direction, choice. Such preferences typify readiness to act in the sense that a habit or memory is a readiness to act. The query of the waitress is a stimulus, and the already acquired interest, habit, memory, whatever one wants to call it, functions. The associated value, or feeling quality, determines whether the activity will be accepted or rejected, whether the organism will go toward or away from it, whether it will continue the status quo or discontinue it. It must also be noted that many activities develop in time so as to bring sufficient pleasure to be employed for their own sake. So we smoke, chew gum, play bridge, or golf for the fun of it.

It is not surprising that interest tests predict the direction in which a person will go, for each item is indicative of preference, choice, direction to go. Interest tests are diagnostic because no two persons have acquired the same list of activities nor are the activities classified in the same manner as liked or disliked. Moreover, people engaged in an occupation have to a marked degree similar interests, and so people in one occupation can be differentiated from the members of other occupations.

How shall *satisfaction* be defined? Here again there are many definitions of satisfaction, but most of them emphasize three aspects: first, arrival at a goal, Webster says "fulfillment of a need or desire"; second, pleasant feeling or contentment; and third, a relatively quiescent condition. A sleepy cat purring on a rug, or contented cows, come to mind. But satisfaction occurs not merely when the goal is reached but also long before. These two satisfactions may be referred to as actual and anticipated satisfaction. Anticipation of one's date next Friday night is often much more exciting than the actuality.

Dissatisfaction is the opposite of satisfaction as far as feeling goes, but the overt activities accompanying satisfaction and dissatisfaction are quite different. In the case of actual satisfaction, the series of activities has been completed or nearly so, tension is released, and quiescence follows. In the case of anticipated satisfaction, activities may continue for years, as in the case of the boy planning to be a physician. Here is long range planning, continuing effort. Dissatisfaction arises because the individual is prevented from reaching his goal. He must find some way to circumvent the obstacle, or he must forego his desire. Any interference with one's purpose is frustrating with release of energy and anger. Such explosive behavior is very different from the quiescence of reaching a goal or the long term planning associated with anticipated satisfaction. Expressed in another way, anticipated satisfaction accompanies progress toward a goal, while dissatisfaction arises when progress is prevented.

I have had a lot of fun asking my colleagues what is the difference between interests and satisfactions. They start out quite sure they know and often end up quite confused. One distinction is that interests are associated with activities, and satisfactions are not. It is true that there are certain activities regularly employed to satisfy bodily needs, but the striking characteristic in securing satisfaction is that one uses whatever activities are available and may use a different combination of activities each time a goal is sought. Aside from the final, consummatory activity, satisfaction cannot be identified in terms of activities, as can interests.

Can interests and satisfactions be differentiated in terms of feeling? Interests are liked or disliked; there seems to be no qualitative difference in the liking of different activities. Satisfactions of bodily needs differ in quality. But possibly this is so because of the presence of different sensations. If the sensations were eliminated, would the remaining satisfactions be similar in such cases? What about goals other than bodily needs? Are there qualitative differences in the satisfactions of earning an *A* grade, in winning the high jump, in finding a house to rent, and so on? On the negative side, disliked activities tend to be ignored. But if one is forced to employ a disliked activity, as fixing a flat tire, the reaction is more typically dissatisfaction than disliking; then one grumbles, complains, swears, and even exhibits all the symptoms of anger.

Finally how can satisfaction-dissatisfaction be measured? We have already mentioned how job satisfaction is measured and that improvements are greatly needed before adequate measurements can be obtained as to how much satisfaction-dissatisfaction is associated with each job factor. Before considering a different procedure, let us eliminate measurement of satisfaction-dissatisfaction of past events on the grounds that they cannot be measured with any accuracy; and even if they could, they would be of little value.

A man who liked to fish and to golf but no longer does so because of old age continues to say he likes such activities. It is possible that, if he were asked to arrange a long list of activities in order of preference, he would not rank fishing and golf as high as he would have done 20 years earlier. Nevertheless he still likes them. The question is: Can one feel satisfaction for past events in similar fashion? I once hiked through heavy brush in hot weather for over 24 hours without food or water. It must have been very rugged, but I cannot now conjure up the thirst and fatigue I must have experienced. I can only recall the incident and enjoy talking about it as I am doing now. My old friend Hollingworth would have exclaimed: "That exemplifies the oblivescence of the disagreeable." My present feeling of pleasure at having done it is very different from how I must have felt at the time. Consider another incident. A violent argument arises in the machine shop as to how a job is to be done. The man who wins feels satisfied, the other dissatisfied. Now, if as so often happens the incident is forgotten the next day and there is no bad feeling on either side, then there is no existing satisfaction or dissatisfaction. And if so, is there any value today in trying to measure the feelings of yesterday? But if the loser in the argument continues to be sore, then such existing dissatisfaction may have a bearing on his overall satisfaction-dissatisfaction.

What about satisfaction-dissatisfaction concerning a goal not yet attained? Here three components are evident: the goal, the dissatisfaction of today, and the anticipated satisfaction of tomorrow. The difference between the last two is, however, more significant than either, or both, considered separately.

In attempting to explain persistence of motivation Peak suggests that it is the "discrepancy rather than the affect which is the important source of continuing action." It is the difference between "Harry's feeling about his present job . . . and his feeling for the ideal job that he imagines" that is the source of persistent efforts to achieve the ideal. This agrees with what I have long taught: that motivation, or "intensifying the want of a prospect in selling, involves, first, making him realize how unpleasant his present situation is, and second, making him anticipate as much as possible the enjoyment he will have when he reaches his desired goal" (1938). Morse (1953) has this same conception in mind when she says that "satisfaction depends basically upon what an individual wants from the world and what he gets." We would suggest substituting what "he expects to get" for "what he gets."

Measurement of Motivation

What we are proposing is the measurement of motivation rather than satisfaction of a given moment. Motivation is a more dynamic aspect of behavior than satisfaction and should prove more useful in predicting future behavior. It is worthwhile to know how an employee feels towards this or that right now, today. But it is more important to know whether he is going to continue in his present type of work, to continue with the company, or to do something else. Job surveys have asked: "How satisfied are you with this and that?" In contrast we ask: "What do you want?" "What do you expect to get?" and "What do you think are the chances you will get what you want?" The difference between aspiration and expectation affords a basis of estimating degree of dissatisfaction; but likelihood that the expectation will be achieved must also be taken into account. The greater the expectation, the greater is the anticipated satisfaction.

It should be noted in passing that measurement of motivation is similar to measurement of interests in that neither predicts how far or how fast one will go, for success is primarily a matter of ability, but both indicate direction, which of many activities will be engaged in.

Specific goals must be considered as well as present dissatisfaction and anticipated satisfaction. It is futile to compare the feelings of a girl who is working hard to make good and become office manager with those of a girl who is planning to quit work, marry, and have a home of her own, even though at the moment they are both dissatisfied with their progress toward their different goals.

Goals are phantasies, wishes, daydreams, aspirations, plans.

Goals are often called needs. Some of them are needs but most have evolved as the result of social pressures, often expressed as "Keeping up with the Joneses." Many of these seem imperative, but does one have to keep up with the Joneses in every respect?

Have we any idea how many different goals the men and women in this country possess, if all were expressed in standard terminology? Does a given man possess during his lifetime all possible goals or only a few? If the latter, why has he these particular goals? Again, how many goals does a man have at a given time? It is also important to know whether each goal is accompanied by its own satisfaction-dissatisfaction quality or do all these qualities more or less fuse together? In other words, does unhappiness because of one's wife affect one's attitude toward one's job, and vice versa? Does the dissatisfaction at being fired from one's job and the satisfaction from one's girl's promise to marry him alternate so that he fluctuates from dissatisfaction to satisfaction; or do the two fuse, and if so is the fusion a mere average or a weighted average in terms of their relative significance?

Goals differ also in complexity. There are simple goals as getting to class on time and complex goals such as planning to graduate from college while still in high school. Such long distant goals necessitate careful planning in terms of many subgoals, as selecting the courses necessary to enter college, getting good enough grades, selection of a college, etc.

It is necessary to determine not only a man's goals but the chance, the likelihood, of his attaining his goal. Likelihood is dependent here not upon the actual facts but upon the man's opinion or belief. A former student resigned because he saw no future in being moved from one job to another, not knowing that he was being groomed for an important position. The greater the chance, the greater is the anticipating satisfaction; the less the chance, the greater is the dissatisfaction. When there is no chance, the man may quit (a friend of mine committed suicide), or nurse a grudge, or abandon his goal (often not easy to do), or find a substitute goal. Likelihood may be expressed in terms of money as in buying an auto or home; or it may be expressed in terms of effort, that is, practice or study; or in terms of willingness to forego other goals, often called pleasures.

With many goals there is a cycle from dissatisfaction to satisfaction, repeated over and over. A simple example is eating. Three times a day we want to eat, are satisfied, and quit thinking about eating for a short while. Another example pertains to salary. Start with dissatisfaction, then anticipated satisfaction when the grapevine reports there will be raises, then satisfaction when the increase is received, then little thought of the subject gradually changing to dissatisfaction. Answers to the static question, "Are you satisfied with your salary?" depends upon where the man is in such a cycle. The more dynamic questions of: "What salary do you want a year hence, five years hence?" and "What do you think the chances are of obtaining such salaries?" should provide a more forward-looking picture of the man's reaction to his salary. Whether men can look five years ahead or not is something to be determined. A few years ago I tried out such questions with college seniors; the great majority could not or would not give anything like definite answers.

Satisfaction in the long run necessitates improvement, progress. A golfer who had never had a better score than 85 would be elated with 84. But if he had 84 every time for several weeks, he would become steadily more dissatisfied; only an 83 or better would give him satisfaction. Many investigators have pointed out that men about 30 years old are more dissatisfied than younger and older men. Is this not due to the fact that such 30-year-old men have come to realize that future progress is limited, that they are not going to realize their aspirations? Some remain disgruntled, but many seek satisfaction in other activities.

The term "level of aspiration" has considerable vogue today. Presumably it represents fairly well formulated to clear-cut formulation of one's goals. Why does one young man aspire to be a lawyer and his brother follow in the footsteps of his father, a coal miner? We always come back to the old, old problem: did the two go in different directions because of environmental educational pressures or because their genes were different? I have a hunch that many adult goals have evolved out of phantasies and daydreams. A 10-year-old girl dreamed of accompanying Allan Quartermain on wild adventures in Africa; later on she has always said "Yes" to her husband's harum-scarum expeditions. Is there any connection? Why did she indulge in exploration and physical danger instead of being a movie actress, a princess, or a Cinderella? How can one ascertain what daydreams a person has, considering that daydreams are usually viewed as too personal, too self-revealing, to be divulged to anyone? No psychologist will achieve fame by predicting future behavior on the basis of well-formulated plans; the really tough task is to predict behavior in terms of the antecedents of such plans.

I hope it has occurred to you that there are two great problems: What can this person do, what are his abilities, what can he accomplish if his abilities are properly trained; and, second, what does he want to do, which way does he want to go in life? His satisfaction, happiness, contentment is dependent upon the direction he is permitted to go. Happiness and success are interrelated, but all counseling services both educational and industrial must seek reasonable success for their counselees and also happiness now and in the future. Such counseling is dependent upon a determination of capacities on the one hand and goals on the other hand. We have made far more progress in measuring capacities than in ascertaining men's goals.

I have asked many questions for which I don't know the answers. There are hundreds of difficulties in all this—I am tempted to say a million difficulties. A good research man ought not to be dismayed; rather he should glory in the complexities—a tough job is far more fun than an easy one.

References

Brayfield, A. H., & Crockett, W. H. Employee attitudes and employee performance. *Psychol. Bull.*, 1955, *52*, 396–424.

Herzberg, F., Mausner, B., Peterson, R. O., & Capwell, D. F. *Job attitudes: review of research and opinion.* Pittsburgh: Psychological Services of Pittsburgh, 1957.

McNemar, Q. Opinion-attitude methodology. *Psychol. Bull.*, 1946, *43*, 289–374.

Morse, N. C. *Satisfaction in the white-collar jobs.* Ann Arbor: Institute for Social Research, 1953.

Nelson, E. Attitudes: I. Their nature and development. *J. gen. Psychol.*, 1939, *21*, 367–399.

Peak, H. Attitude and motivation. In *Nebraska symposium on motivation*, 1955.

Perry, R. B. National morale. *Educ. Rec.*, 1942, *23*, Suppl. No. 15.

Sherif, M., & Cantril, H. The psychology of attitudes. Part I. *Psychol. Rev.*, 1945, *52*, 295–319.

Strong, E. K., Jr. *Psychological aspects of business.* New York: McGraw-Hill, 1938.

Strong, E. K., Jr. *Vocational interests of men and women.* Stanford: Stanford Univer. Press, 1943.

Viteles, M. S. *Motivation and morale in industry.* New York: Norton, 1953.

J. P. Guilford — *Three Faces of Intellect*[1]

My subject is in the area of human intelligence, in connection with which the names of Terman and Stanford have become known the world over. The Stanford Revision of the Binet intelligence scale has been the standard against which all other instruments for the measurement of intelligence have been compared. The term IQ or intelligence quotient has become a household word in this country. This is illustrated by two brief stories.

> A few years ago, one of my neighbors came home from a PTA meeting, remarking: "That Mrs. So-And-So, thinks she knows so much. She kept talking about the 'intelligence *quota*' of the children; 'intelligence *quota*'; imagine. Why, everybody knows that IQ stands for 'intelligence *quiz*.'"
>
> The other story comes from a little comic strip in a Los Angeles morning newspaper, called "Junior Grade." In the first picture a little boy meets a little girl, both apparently about the first-grade level. The little girl remarks, "I have

1. This paper is based on the Walter Van Dyke Bingham Memorial Lecture given at Stanford University, April 13, 1959. It was first published in the *American Psychologist*, 1959, vol. 14, no. 8 (August), pp. 469–479.

> a high IQ." The little boy, puzzled, said, "You have a what?" The little girl repeated, "I have a high IQ," then went on her way. The little boy, looking thoughtful, said, "And she looks like such a nice little girl, too."

It is my purpose to speak about the analysis of this thing called human intelligence into its components. I do not believe that either Binet or Terman, if they were still with us, would object to the idea of a searching and detailed study of intelligence, aimed toward a better understanding of its nature. Preceding the development of his intelligence scale, Binet had done much research on different kinds of thinking activities and apparently recognized that intelligence has a number of aspects. It is to the lasting credit of both Binet and Terman that they introduced such a great variety of tasks into their intelligence scales.

Two related events of very recent history make it imperative that we learn all we can regarding the nature of intelligence. I am referring to the advent of the artificial satellites and planets and to the crisis in education that has arisen in part as a consequence. The preservation of our way of life and our future security depend upon our most important national resources: our intellectual abilities and, more particularly, our creative abilities. It is time, then, that we learn all we can about those resources.

Our knowledge of the components of human intelligence has come about mostly within the last 25 years. The major sources of this information in this country have been L. L. Thurstone and his associates, the wartime research of psychologists in the United States Air Force, and more recently the Aptitudes Project[2] at the University of Southern California, now in its tenth year of research on cognitive and thinking abilities. The results from the Aptitudes Project that have gained perhaps the most atten-

2. Under Contract N6onr-23810 with the Office of Naval Research (Personnel and Training Branch).

tion have pertained to creative-thinking abilities. These are mostly novel findings. But to me, the most significant outcome has been the development of a unified theory of human intellect, which organizes the known, unique or primary intellectual abilities into a single system called the "structure of intellect." It is to this system that I shall devote the major part of my remarks, with very brief mentions of some of the implications for the psychology of thinking and problem solving, for vocational testing, and for education.

The discovery of the components of intelligence has been by means of the experimental application of the method of factor analysis. It is not necessary for you to know anything about the theory or method of factor analysis in order to follow the discussion of the components. I should like to say, however, that factor analysis has no connection with or resemblance to psychoanalysis. A positive statement would be more helpful, so I will say that each intellectual component or factor is a unique ability that is needed to do well in a certain class of tasks or tests. As a general principle we find that certain individuals do well in the tests of a certain class, but they may do poorly in the tests of another class. We conclude that a factor has certain properties from the features that the tests of a class have in common. I shall give you very soon a number of examples of tests, each representing a factor.

The Structure of Intellect

Although each factor is sufficiently distinct to be detected by factor analysis, in very recent years it has become apparent that the factors themselves can be classified because they resemble one another in certain ways. One basis of classification is according to the basic kind of process or operation performed. This kind of classification gives us five major groups of intellectual abilities: factors of cognition, memory, convergent thinking, divergent thinking, and evaluation.

Cognition means discovery or rediscovery or recognition. Memory means retention of what is cognized. Two kinds of productive-thinking operations generate new information from known information and remembered information. In divergent-thinking operations we think in different directions, sometimes searching, sometimes seeking variety. In convergent thinking the information leads to one right answer or to a recognized best or conventional answer. In evaluation we reach decisions as to goodness, correctness, suitability, or adequacy of what we know, what we remember, and what we produce in productive thinking.

A second way of classifying the intellectual factors is according to the kind of material or content involved. The factors known thus far involve three kinds of material or content: the content may be figural, symbolic, or semantic. Figural content is concrete material such as is perceived through the senses. It does not represent anything except itself. Visual material has properties such as size, form, color, location, or texture. Things we hear or feel provide other examples of figural material. Symbolic content is composed of letters, digits, and other conventional signs, usually organized in general systems, such as the alphabet or the number sytem. Semantic content is in the form of verbal meanings or ideas, for which no examples are necessary.

When a certain operation is applied to a certain kind of content, as many as six general kinds of products may be involved. There is enough evidence available to suggest that, regardless of the combinations of operations and content, the same six kinds of products may be found associated. The six kinds of products are: units, classes, relations, systems, transformations, and implications. So far as we have determined from factor analysis, these are the only fundamental kinds of products that we can know. As such, they may serve as basic classes into which one might fit all kinds of information psychologically.

The three kinds of classifications of the factors of intellect can be represented by means of a single solid model, shown in Figure 1. In this model, which we call the "structure of intellect," each dimension represents one of the modes of variation of the

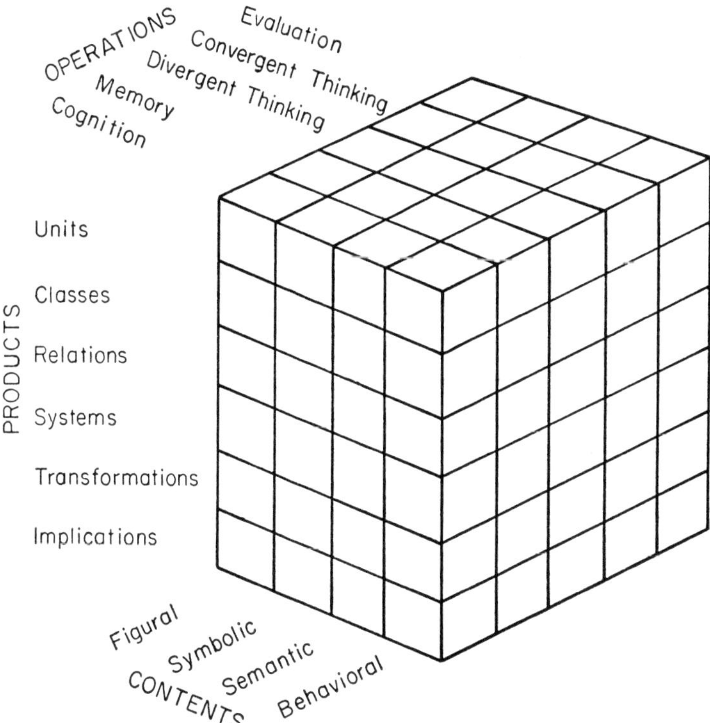

Fig. 1. A cubical model representing the structure of intellect.

factors.[3] Along one dimension are found the various kinds of operations, along a second one are the various kinds of products, and along the third are various kinds of content. Along the dimension of content a fourth category has been added, its kind of content being designated as "behavioral." This category has been added on a purely theoretical basis to represent the general area sometimes called "social intelligence." More will be said about this section of the model later.

In order to provide a better basis for understanding the model and a better basis for accepting it as a picture of human intellect, I shall do some exploring of it with you systematically, giving some examples of tests. Each cell in the model calls for a certain kind of ability that can be described in terms of operation, content, and product, for each cell is at the intersection of a unique combination of kinds of operation, content, and product. A test for that ability would have the same three properties. In our exploration of the model, we shall take one vertical layer at a time, beginning with the front face. The first layer provides us with a matrix of 18 cells (if we ignore the behavioral column for which there are as yet no known factors) each of which should contain a cognitive ability.

The Cognitive Abilities

We know at present the unique abilities that fit logically into 15 of the 18 cells for cognitive abilities. Each row presents a triad of similar abilities, having a single kind of product in common. The factors of the first row are concerned with the knowing of units. A good test of the ability to cognize figural units is the Street Gestalt Completion Test. In this test, the recognition of familiar pictured objects in silhouette form is made difficult for

3. For an earlier presentation of the concept, see Guilford (1956).

testing purposes by blocking out parts of those objects. There is another factor that is known to involve the perception of auditory figures—in the form of melodies, rhythms, and speech sounds—and still another factor involving kinesthetic forms. The presence of three factors in one cell (they are conceivably distinct abilities, although this has not been tested) suggests that more generally, in the figural column, at least, we should expect to find more than one ability. A fourth dimension pertaining to variations in sense modality may thus apply in connection with figural content. The model could be extended in this manner if the facts call for such an extension.

The ability to cognize symbolic units is measured by tests like the following:

Put vowels in the following blanks to make real words:

P__W__R
M__RV__L
C__RT__N

Rearrange the letters to make real words:

R A C I H
T V O E S
K L C C O

The first of these two tests is called Disemvoweled Words, and the second Scrambled Words.

The ability to cognize semantic units is the well-known factor of verbal comprehension, which is best measured by means of a vocabulary test, with items such as:

GRAVITY means ________
CIRCUS means ________
VIRTUE means ________

From the comparison of these two factors it is obvious that recognizing familiar words as letter structures and knowing what words mean depend upon quite different abilities.

For testing the abilities to know classes of units, we may present the following kinds of items, one with symbolic content and one with semantic content:

Which letter group does not belong?
XECM PVAA QXIN VTRO

Which object does not belong?
clam tree oven rose

A figural test is constructed in a completely parallel form, presenting in cach item four figures, three of which have a property in common and the fourth lacking that property.

The three abilities to see relationships are also readily measured by a common kind of test, differing only in terms of content. The well-known analogies test is applicable, two items in symbolic and semantic form being:

JIRE : KIRE : : FORA : KORE KORA LIRE GORA GIRE
poetry : prose : : dance : music walk sing talk jump

Such tests usually involve more than the ability to cognize relations, but we are not concerned with this problem at this point.

The three factors for cognizing systems do not at present appear in tests so closely resembling one another as in the case of the examples just given. There is nevertheless an underlying common core of logical similarity. Ordinary space tests, such as Thurstone's Flags, Figures, and Cards or Part V (Spatial Orientation) of the Guilford-Zimmerman Aptitude Survey (GZAS), serve in the figural column. The system involved is an order or arrangement of objects in space. A system that uses symbolic elements is illustrated by the Letter Triangle Test, a sample item of which is:

—
d —
b e —
a c f ?

What letter belongs at the place of the question mark?

The ability to understand a semantic system has been known for some time as the factor called general reasoning. One of its most faithful indicators is a test composed of arithmetic-reasoning items. That the phase of understanding only is important for measuring this ability is shown by the fact that such a test works even if the examinee is not asked to give a complete solution; he need only show that he structures the problem properly. For example, an item from the test Necessary Arithmetical Operations simply asks what operations are needed to solve the problem:

A city lot 48 feet wide and 149 feet deep costs $79,432. What is the cost per square foot?

A. add and multiply
B. multiply and divide
C. subtract and divide
D. add and subtract
E. divide and add

Placing the factor of general reasoning in this cell of the structure of intellect gives us some new conceptions of its nature. It should be a broad ability to grasp all kinds of systems that are conceived in terms of verbal concepts, not restricted to the understanding of problems of an arithmetical type.

Transformations are changes of various kinds, including modifications in arrangement, organization, or meaning. In the figural column for the transformations row, we find the factor known as visualization. Common measuring instruments for this factor are the surface-development tests, and an example of a different kind is Part VI (Spatial Visualization) of the GZAS. A test of the ability to make transformations of meaning, for the factor in the semantic column, is called Similarities. The examinee is asked to state several ways in which two objects, such as an apple and an orange, are alike. Only by shifting the meanings of both is the examinee able to give many responses to such an item.

In the set of abilities having to do with the cognition of implications, we find that the individual goes beyond the information given, but not to the extent of what might be called drawing conclusions. We may say that he extrapolates. From the given information he expects or foresees certain consequences, for example. The two factors found in this row of the cognition matrix were first called "foresight" factors. Foresight in connection with figural material can be tested by means of paper-and-pencil mazes. Foresight in connection with ideas, those pertaining to events, for example, is indicated by a test such as Pertinent Questions:

> In planning to open a new hamburger stand in a certain community, what four questions should be considered in deciding upon its location?

The more questions the examinee asks in response to a list of such problems, the more he evidently foresees contingencies.

The Memory Abilities

The area of memory abilities has been explored less than some of the other areas of operation, and only seven of the potential cells of the memory matrix have known factors in them. These cells are restricted to three rows: for units, relations, and systems. The first cell in the memory matrix is now occupied by two factors, parallel to two in the corresponding cognition matrix: visual memory and auditory memory. Memory for series of letters or numbers, as in memory span tests, conforms to the conception of memory for symbolic units. Memory for the ideas in a paragraph conforms to the conception of memory for semantic units.

The formation of associations between units, such as visual forms, syllables, and meaningful words, as in the method of paired associates, would seem to represent three abilities to remember relationships involving three kinds of content. We know of two such abilities, for the symbolic and semantic columns. The memory for known systems is represented by two abilities very recently discovered (Christal, 1958). Remembering the arrangement of objects in space is the nature of an ability in the figural column, and remembering a sequence of events is the nature of a corresponding ability in the semantic column. The differentiation between these two abilities implies that a person may be able to say where he saw an object on a page, but he might not be able to say on which of several pages he saw it after leafing through several pages that included the right one. Considering the blank rows in the memory matrix, we should expect to find abilities also to remember classes, transformations, and implications, as well as units, relations, and systems.

The Divergent-Thinking Abilities

The unique feature of divergent production is that a *variety* of responses is produced. The product is not completely determined by the given information. This is not to say that divergent thinking does not come into play in the total process of reaching a unique conclusion, for it comes into play wherever there is trial-and-error thinking.

The well-known ability of word fluency is tested by asking the examinee to list words satisfying a specified letter requirement, such as words beginning with the letter "s" or words ending in "-tion." This ability is now regarded as a facility in divergent production of symbolic units. The parallel semantic ability has been known as ideational fluency. A typical test item calls for listing objects that are round and edible. Winston Churchill must have possessed this ability to a high degree. Clement Attlee is reported to have said about him recently that, no matter what problem came up, Churchill always seemed to have about ten ideas. The trouble was, Attlee continued, he did not know which was the good one. The last comment implies some weakness in one or more of the evaluative abilities.

The divergent production of class ideas is believed to be the unique feature of a factor called "spontaneous flexibility." A typical test instructs the examinee to list all the uses he can think of for a common brick, and he is given eight minutes. If his responses are: build a house, build a barn, build a garage, build a school, build a church, build a chimney, build a walk, and build a barbecue, he would earn a fairly high score for ideational fluency but a very low score for spontaneous flexibility, because all these uses fall into the same class. If another person said: make a door stop, make a paper weight, throw it at a dog, make a bookcase, drown a cat, drive a nail, make a red powder, and use for baseball bases, he would also receive a high score for flexibility. He has gone frequently from one class to another.

A current study of unknown but predicted divergent-production abilities includes testing whether there are also figural and symbolic abilities to produce multiple classes. An experimental figural test presents a number of figures that can be classified in groups of three in various ways, each figure being usable in more than one class. An experimental symbolic test presents a few numbers that are also to be classified in multiple ways.

A unique ability involving relations is called "associational fluency." It calls for the production of a variety of things related in a specified way to a given thing. For example, the examinee is asked to list words meaning about the same as "good" or to list words meaning about the opposite of "hard." In these instances the response produced is to complete a relationship, and semantic content is involved. Some of our present experimental tests call for the production of varieties of relations, as such, and involve figural and symbolic content also. For example, given four small digits, in how many ways can they be related in order to produce a sum of eight?

One factor pertaining to the production of systems is known as expressional fluency. The rapid formation of phrases or sentences is the essence of certain tests of this factor. For example, given the initial letters:

with different sentences to be produced, the examinee might write "We can eat nuts" or "Whence came Eve Newton?" In interpreting the factor, we regard the sentence as a symbolic system. By analogy, a figural system would be some kind of organization of lines and other elements, and a semantic system would be in the form of a verbally stated problem or perhaps something as complex as a theory.

In the row of the divergent-production matrix devoted to transformations, we find some very interesting factors. The one called "adaptive flexibility" is now recognized as belonging in the figural column. A faithful test of it has been Match Problems. This is based upon the common game that uses squares, the sides of which are formed by match sticks. The examinee is told to take away a given number of matches to leave a stated number of squares with nothing left over. Nothing is said about the sizes of the squares to be left. If the examinee imposes upon himself the restriction that the squares that he leaves must be of the same size, he will fail in his attempts to do items like that in Figure 2. Other odd kinds of solutions are introduced in other items, such as overlapping squares and squares within squares, and so on. In another variation of Match Problems the examinee is told to produce two or more solutions for each problem.

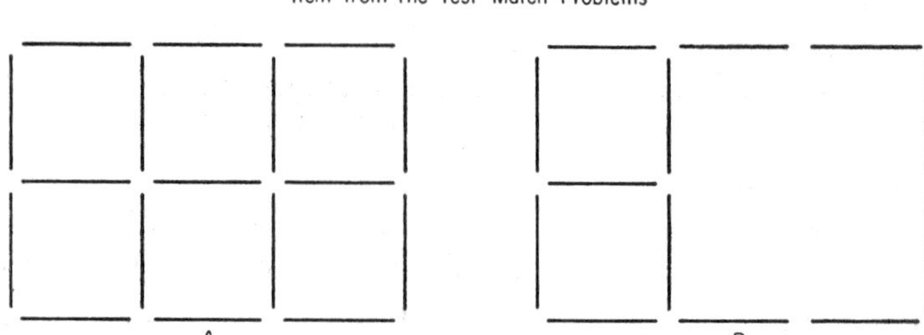
Item from the test Match Problems
A
B
Take away four matches in A, leaving three squares and nothing more.
Answer: B

Fig. 2. A sample item from the test Match Problems. The problem in this item is to take away four matches and leave three squares. The solution is given.

A factor that has been called "originality" is now recognized as adaptive flexibility with semantic material, where there must be a shifting of meanings. The examinee must produce the shifts or changes in meaning and so come up with novel, unusual, clever, or farfetched ideas. The Plot Titles Test presents a short story, the examinee being told to list as many appropriate titles as he can to head the story. One story is about a missionary who has been captured by cannibals in Africa. He is in the pot and about to be boiled when a princess of the tribe obtains a promise for his release if he will become her mate. He refuses and is boiled to death.

In scoring the test, we separate the responses into two categories, clever and nonclever. Examples of nonclever responses are: African Death, Defeat of a Princess, Eaten by Savages, The Princess, The African Missionary, In Darkest Africa, and Boiled by Savages. These titles are appropriate but commonplace. The number of such responses serves as a score for ideational fluency. Examples of clever responses are: Pot's Plot, Potluck Dinner, Stewed Parson, Goil or Boil, A Mate Worse Than Death, He Left a Dish for a Pot, Chaste in Haste, and A Hot Price for Freedom. The number of clever responses given by an examinee is his score for originality, or the divergent production of semantic transformations.

Another test of originality presents a very novel task so that any acceptable response is unusual for the individual. In the Symbol Production Test the examinee is to produce a simple symbol to stand for a noun or a verb in each short sentence, in other words to invent something like pictographic symbols. Still another test of originality asks for writing the "punch lines" for cartoons, a task that almost automatically challenges the examinee to be clever. Thus, quite a variety of tests offer approaches to the measurement of originality, including one or two others that I have not mentioned.

Abilities to produce a variety of implications are assessed by tests calling for elaboration of given information. A figural test of this type provides the examinee with a line or two, to which he is to add other lines to produce an object. The more lines he adds, the greater his score. A semantic test gives the examinee the outlines of a plan to which he is to respond by stating all the details he can think of to make the plan work. A new test we are trying out in the symbolic area presents two simple equations such as $B - C = D$ and $z = A + D$. The examinee is to make as many other equations as he can from this information.

The Convergent-Production Abilities

Of the 18 convergent-production abilities expected in the three content columns, 12 are now recognized. In the first row, pertaining to units, we have an ability to name figural properties (forms or colors) and an ability to name abstractions (classes, relations, and so on). It may be that the ability in common to the speed of naming forms and the speed of naming colors is not appropriately placed in the convergent-thinking matrix. One might expect that the thing to be produced in a test of the convergent production of figural units would be in the form of figures rather than words. A better test of such an ability might somehow specify the need for one particular object, the examinee to furnish the object.

A test for the convergent production of classes (Word Grouping) presents a list of 12 words that are to be classified in four, and only four, meaningful groups, no word to appear in more than one group. A parallel test (Figure Concepts Test) presents 20 pictured real objects that are to be grouped in meaningful classes of two or more each.

Convergent production having to do with relationships is represented by three known factors, all involving the "education of correlates," as Spearman called it. The given information includes one unit and a stated relation, the examinee to supply the other unit. Analogies tests that call for completion rather than a choice between alternative answers emphasize this kind of ability. With symbolic content such an item might read:

pots stop   bard drab   rats ?

A semantic item that measures eduction of correlates is:

The absence of sound is ______.

Incidentally, the latter item is from a vocabulary-completion test, and its relation to the factor of ability to produce correlates indicates how, by change of form, a vocabulary test may indicate an ability other than that for which vocabulary tests are usually intended, namely, the factor of verbal comprehension.

Only one factor for convergent production of systems is known, and it is in the semantic column. It is measured by a class of tests that may be called ordering tests. The examinee may be presented with a number of events that ordinarily have a best or most logical order, the events being presented in scrambled order. The presentation may be pictorial, as in the Picture Arrangement Test, or verbal. The pictures may be taken from a cartoon strip. The verbally presented events may be in the form of the various steps needed to plant a new lawn. There are undoubtedly other kinds of systems than temporal order that could be utilized for testing abilities in this row of the convergent-production matrix.

In the way of producing transformations of a unique variety, we have three recognized factors, known as redefinition abilities. In each case, redefinition involves the changing of functions or uses of parts of one unit and giving them new functions or uses in some new unit. For testing the ability of figural redefinition, a task based upon the Gottschaldt figures is suitable. Figure 3 shows the kind of item for such a test. In recognizing the simpler figure within the structure of a more complex figure, certain lines must take on new roles.

In terms of symbolic material, the following sample items will illustrate how groups of letters in given words must be readapted

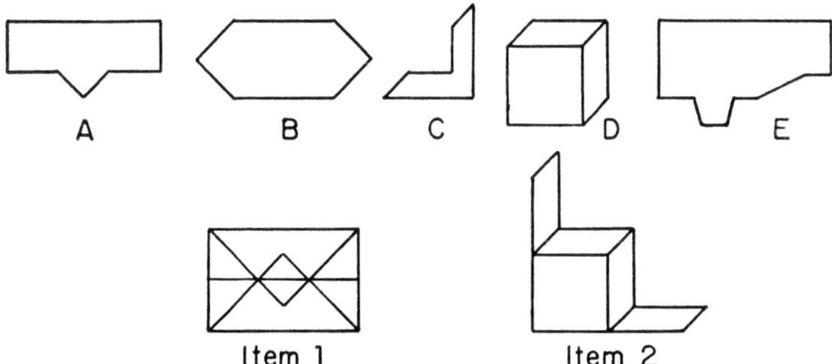

Fig. 3. Sample items from a test Hidden Figures, based upon the Gottschaldt figures. Which of the simpler figures is concealed within each of the two more complex figures?

to use in other words. In the test Camouflaged Words, each sentence contains the name of a sport or game:

> I did not know that he was ailing.
> To beat the Hun, tin goes a long way.

For the factor of semantic redefinition, the Gestalt Transformation Test may be used. A sample item reads:

> From which object could you most likely make a needle?
>
> A. a cabbage
> B. a splice
> C. a steak
> D. a paper box
> E. a fish

The convergent production of implications means the drawing of fully determined conclusions from given information. The well-known factor of numerical facility belongs in the symbolic column. For the parallel ability in the figural column, we have a test known as Form Reasoning, in which rigorously defined operations with figures are used. For the parallel ability in the semantic column, the factor sometimes called "deduction" probably qualifies. Items of the following type are sometimes used.

> Charles is younger than Robert
> Charles is older than Frank
> Who is older: Robert or Frank?

Evaluative Abilities

The evaluative area has had the least investigation of all the operational categories. In fact, only one systematic analytical study has been devoted to this area. Only eight evaluative abilities are recognized as fitting into the evaluation matrix. But at least five rows have one or more factors each, and also three of the usual columns or content categories. In each case, evaluation involves reaching decisions as to the accuracy, goodness, suitability, or workability of information. In each row, for the particular kind of product of that row, some kind of criterion or standard of judgment is involved.

In the first row, for the evaluation of units, the important decision to be made pertains to the identity of a unit. Is this unit identical with that one? In the figural column we find the factor long known as "perceptual speed." Tests of this factor invariably call for decisions of identity, for example, Part IV (Perceptual Speed) of the GZAS or Thurstone's Identical Forms. I think it has been generally wrongly thought that the ability involved is that of cognition of visual forms. But we have seen that another factor is a more suitable candidate for this definition and for being in the very first cell of the cognitive matrix. It is parallel to this evaluative ability but does not require the judgment of identity as one of its properties.

In the symbolic column is an ability to judge identity of symbolic units, in the form of series of letters or numbers or of names of individuals.

Are members of the following pairs identical or not?

825170493_____825176493
dkeltvmpa_____dkeltvmpa
C. S. Meyerson_____C. E. Meyerson

Such items are common in tests of clerical aptitude.

There should be a parallel ability to decide whether two ideas are identical or different. Is the idea expressed in this sentence the same as the idea expressed in that one? Do these two proverbs express essentially the same idea? Such tests exist and will be used to test the hypothesis that such an ability can be demonstrated.

No evaluative abilities pertaining to classes have as yet been recognized. The abilities having to do with evaluation where relations are concerned must meet the criterion of logical consistency. Syllogistic-type tests involving letter symbols indicate a different ability than the same type of test involving verbal statements. In the figural column we might expect that tests incorporating geometric reasoning or proof would indicate a parallel ability to sense the soundness of conclusions regarding figural relationships.

The evaluation of systems seems to be concerned with the internal consistency of those systems, so far as we can tell from the knowledge of one such factor. The factor has been called "experiential evaluation," and its representative test presents items like that in Figure 4 asking "What is wrong with this picture?" The things wrong are often internal inconsistencies.

A semantic ability for evaluating transformations is thought to be that known for some time as "judgment." In typical judgment tests, the examinee is asked to tell which of five solutions to a practical problem is most adequate or wise. The solutions frequently involve improvisations, in other words, adaptations of

Fig. 4. A sample item from the test Unusual Details. What two things are wrong with this picture?

familiar objects to unusual uses. In this way the items present redefinitions to be evaluated.

A factor known first as "sensitivity to problems" has become recognized as an evaluative ability having to do with implications. One test of the factor, the Apparatus Test, asks for two needed improvements with respect to each of several common devices, such as the telephone or the toaster. The Social Institutions Test, a measure of the same factor, asks what things are wrong with each of several institutions, such as tipping or national elections. We may say that defects or deficiencies are implications of an evaluative kind. Another interpretation would be that seeing defects and deficiencies are evaluations of implications to the effect that the various aspects of something are all right.[4]

Some Implications of the Structure of Intellect

For Psychological Theory

Although factor analysis as generally employed is best designed to investigate ways in which individuals differ from one another, in other words, to discover traits, the results also tell us much about how individuals are alike. Consequently, information regarding the factors and their interrelationships gives us understanding of functioning individuals. The five kinds of intellectual abilities in terms of operations may be said to represent five ways of functioning. The kinds of intellectual abilities distinguished according to varieties of test content and the kinds of abilities distinguished according to varieties of products suggest a classification of basic forms of information or knowledge. The kind of organism suggested by this way of looking at intellect is

4. For further details concerning the intellectual factors, illustrative tests, and the place of the factors in the structure of intellect, see Guilford (1959).

that of an agency for dealing with information of various kinds in various ways. The concepts provided by the distinctions among the intellectual abilities and by their classifications may be very useful in our future investigations of learning, memory, problem solving, invention, and decision making, by whatever method we choose to approach those problems.

For Vocational Testing

With about 50 intellectual factors already known, we may say that there are at least 50 ways of being intelligent. It has been facetiously suggested that there seem to be a great many more ways of being stupid, unfortunately. The structure of intellect is a theoretical model that predicts as many as 120 distinct abilities, if every cell of the model contains a factor. Already we know that two cells contain two or more factors each, and there probably are actually other cells of this type. Since the model was first conceived, 12 factors predicted by it have found places in it. There is consequently hope of filling many of the other vacancies, and we may eventually end up with more than 120 abilities.

The major implication for the assessment of intelligence is that to know an individual's intellectual resources thoroughly we shall need a surprisingly large number of scores. It is expected that many of the factors are intercorrelated, so there is some possibility that by appropriate sampling we shall be able to cover the important abilities with a more limited number of tests. At any rate, a multiple-score approach to the assessment of intelligence is definitely indicated in connection with future vocational operations.

Considering the kinds of abilities classified as to content, we may speak roughly of four kinds of intelligence. The abilities involving the use of figural information may be regarded as "concrete" intelligence. The people who depend most upon these abilities deal with concrete things and their properties. Among these people are mechanics, operators of machines, engineers (in some aspects of their work), artists, and musicians.

In the abilities pertaining to symbolic and semantic content, we have two kinds of "abstract" intelligence. Symbolic abilities should be important in learning to recognize words, to spell, and to operate with numbers. Language and mathematics should depend very much upon them, except that in mathematics some aspects, such as geometry, have strong figural involvement. Semantic intelligence is important for understanding things in terms of verbal concepts and hence is important in all courses where the learning of facts and ideas is essential.

In the hypothesized behavioral column of the structure of intellect, which may be roughly described as "social" intelligence, we have some of the most interesting possibilities. Understanding the behavior of others and of ourselves is largely nonverbal in character. The theory suggests as many as 30 abilities in this area, some having to do with understanding, some with productive thinking about behavior, and some with the evaluation of behavior. The theory also suggests that information regarding behavior is also in the form of the six kinds of products that apply elsewhere in the structure of intellect, including units, relations, systems, and so on. The abilities in the area of social intelligence, whatever they prove to be, will possess considerable importance in connection with all those individuals who deal most with other people: teachers, law officials, social workers, therapists, politicians, statesmen, and leaders of other kinds.

For Education

The implications for education are numerous, and I have time just to mention a very few. The most fundamental implication is that we might well undergo transformations with respect to our conception of the learner and of the process of learning. Under the prevailing conception, the learner is a kind of stimulus-response device, much on the order of a vending machine. You put in a coin, and something comes out. The machine learns what reaction to put out when a certain coin is put in. If, instead, we think of the learner as an agent for dealing with information, where information is defined very broadly, we have something more analogous to an electronic computer. We feed a computer information; it stores that information; it uses that information for generating new information, either by way of divergent or convergent thinking; and it evaluates its own results. Advantages that a human learner has over a computer include the step of seeking and discovering new information from sources outside itself and the step of programing itself. Perhaps even these steps will be added to computers, if this has not already been done in some cases.

At any rate, this conception of the learner leads us to the idea that learning is discovery of information, not merely the formation of associations, particularly associations in the form of stimulus-response connections. I am aware of the fact that my proposal is rank heresy. But if we are to make significant progress in our understanding of human learning and particularly our understanding of the so-called higher mental processes of thinking, problem solving, and creative thinking, some drastic modifications are due in our theory.

The idea that education is a matter of training the mind or of training the intellect has been rather unpopular, wherever the prevailing psychological doctrines have been followed. In theory, at least, the emphasis has been upon the learning of rather specific habits or skills. If we take our cue from factor theory, however, we recognize that most learning probably has both specific and general aspects or components. The general aspects may be along the lines of the factors of intellect. This is not to say that the individual's status in each factor is entirely determined by learning. We do not know to what extent each factor is determined by heredity and to what extent by learning. The best position for educators to take is that possibly every intellectual factor can be developed in individuals at least to some extent by learning.

If education has the general objective of developing the intellects of students, it can be suggested that each intellectual factor provides a particular goal at which to aim. Defined by a certain combination of content, operation, and product, each goal ability then calls for certain kinds of practice in order to achieve improvement in it. This implies choice of curriculum and the choice or invention of teaching methods that will most likely accomplish the desired results.

Considering the very great variety of abilities revealed by the factorial exploration of intellect, we are in a better position to ask whether any general intellectual skills are now being neglected in education and whether appropriate balances are being observed. It is often observed these days that we have fallen down in the way of producing resourceful, creative graduates. How true this is, in comparison with other times, I do not know. Perhaps the deficit is noticed because the demands for inventiveness are so much greater at this time. At any rate, realizing that the more conspicuously creative abilities appear to be concentrated in the divergent-thinking category, and also to some extent in the transformation category, we now ask whether we have been giving these skills appropriate exercise. It is probable that we need a better balance of training in the divergent-thinking area as compared with training in convergent thinking and in critical thinking or evaluation.

The structure of intellect as I have presented it to you may or may not stand the test of time. Even if the general form persists, there are likely to be some modifications. Possibly some different kind of model will be invented. Be that as it may, the fact of a multiplicity of intellectual abilities seems well established.

There are many individuals who long for the good old days of simplicity, when we got along with one unanalyzed intelligence. Simplicity certainly has its appeal. But human nature is exceedingly complex, and we may as well face that fact. The rapidly moving events of the world in which we live have forced upon us the need for knowing human intelligence thoroughly. Humanity's peaceful pursuit of happiness depends upon our control of nature and of our own behavior; and this, in turn, depends upon understanding ourselves, including our intellectual resources.

References

Christal, R. E. Factor analytic study of visual memory. *Psychol. Monogr.*, 1958, *72*, No. 13 (Whole No. 466).

Guilford, J. P. The structure of intellect. *Psychol. Bull.*, 1956, *53*, 267–293.

Guilford, J. P. *Personality.* New York: McGraw-Hill, 1959.

Dael Wolfle

Diversity of Talent[1]

A problem of continuing concern is the extent to which we are properly developing and utilizing the nation's intellectual resources. For both realistic and practical reasons it is desirable that we make better provisions than we have in the past for the full development of human talent. The more fundamental reason is that one of the basic ideals of a free society is the provision of opportunity for each person to develop to his full capacity. This ideal has been expressed in many ways, yet from time to time we need to remind ourselves that it lies at the very cornerstone of our form of society. *The Pursuit of Excellence,* the Rockefeller report on education, of which John Gardner (1958) was the principal author, phrased it this way:

> The greatness of a nation may be manifested in many ways —in its purposes, its courage, its moral responsibility, its cultural and scientific eminence, the tenor of its daily life.

1. This paper is based on the Walter Van Dyke Bingham Memorial Lecture given at Columbia University, May 10, 1960. It was first published in the *American Psychologist,* 1960, vol. 15, no. 8 (August), pp. 535–545.

> But ultimately the source of its greatness is in the individuals who constitute the living substance of the nation.
>
> . . . .
>
> Our devotion to a free society can only be understood in terms of these values. It is the only form of society that puts at the very top of its agenda the opportunity of the individual to develop his potentialities. It is the declared enemy of every condition that stunts the intellectual, moral, and spiritual growth of the individual. No society has ever fully succeeded in living up to the stern ideals that a free people set themselves. But only a free society can even address itself to that demanding task.[2]

The idealistic reason for fostering the full development of talent is expressed in the quotation just read. There is also an urgent practical reason: the nation has an increasing need for many kinds of highly developed talent. Earlier in our history, the most critical need was for land for an expanding agriculture and then later for financial capital for an expanding industry. But now the critical need is for men and women with ideas and highly developed talents, men and women who can teach, who can roll back the boundaries of ignorance, who can manage complex organizations, who can perform the diverse and demanding tasks upon which the further development of a free, industrial society depends.

World War II marks the time at which there began to be clear recognition that the need for resources of land and capital had been surpassed by the need for resources of human talent. Prior to World War II we lived through the worst depression in our history. It was not people that we needed, but rather work for

2. From *The Pursuit of Excellence: Education and the Future of America.* Copyright © 1958 by Rockefeller Brothers Fund, Inc. Reprinted by permission of Doubleday & Company, Inc.

the people we had. In the years before the depression, most of the labor force was engaged in farming and in those trades and vocations that make relatively little demand upon man's higher intellectual capacities. It was in World War II that we were pinched for men and brains. It was then that we also began to recognize that invention could be deliberately planned. The scientific and engineering achievements of the war period provided dramatic evidence that some major problems could be solved and some major new inventions produced when imaginative and talented men set their minds to the task. With this wartime demonstration as a model, it seemed likely that organized research could be fruitfully applied on a large scale to industrial problems. There followed a great growth in industrial research, in industrial production, and in interest in the nation's supply of intellectual resources.

My personal involvement in the study of the nation's intellectual resources began in 1950 when I became Director of the Commission on Human Resources and Advanced Training. This commission was established by the American Council of Learned Societies, the American Council on Education, the National Academy of Sciences, and the Social Science Research Council. When the commission's report was published (Wolfle, 1954), it brought together a considerable range of information concerning the supply of talented persons in the United States, the demand for their talents, and the potential supply from which we might draw in the future. Since 1954, public interest in the problem of making fuller use of our intellectual resources has been increased by other studies, by the technological achievements of the USSR, and by a growing recognition of our obligation to help less fortunate nations climb to a higher level of industrial, educational, and personal well-being.

One of the studies of the Commission on Human Resources and Advanced Training dealt with the extent to which the United

States succeeds in educating those young persons who have the intellectual capacity for higher education. Our statistics on this point have been widely used. But the figures we published in 1954 are now out of date and should be replaced. I am glad, therefore, to have the permission of Donald S. Bridgman to quote more recent figures which he has compiled and which will soon be published by the National Science Foundation.

Bridgman was one of my colleagues on the Commission on Human Resources and Advanced Training. He has continued to be interested in how many bright students we are getting, or failing to get, into college. He has considered—as have others—that students in the top 30% of the ability distribution are qualified for college work. Of young men in this ability range, Bridgman's figures show that approximately 45% now graduate from college. Of the 55% who do not, approximately one-fifth fail to finish high school, two-fifths finish high school but do not enter college, and two-fifths enter college but do not finish. Thus we are getting into college about two-thirds of the upper 30% of boys, and about two-thirds of those who enter stay to graduate.

The figures for girls show fewer completing college and more dropping out at earlier stages. Of 100 girls in the top 30% in ability, approximately 30 graduate from college. Of the 70 who do not, about 10 fail to finish high school, 40 finish high school but do not enter college, and 20 enter college but do not graduate.

Of the top 30% in general intellectual ability, for the two sexes combined, nearly 60% enter college, and close to 40% earn bachelor's or higher degrees. If we examine a smaller and more highly selected group, say the top 10% or the top 5% on the intelligence distribution, the retention rates are appreciably higher.

How should we judge these figures? If we compare them with figures from other countries, we have a right to be proud of our record. If we compare them with our own performance in earlier years, we can take pride in the improvement. But if we examine them in terms of our growing need for persons with high ability and advanced education, the current figures give us reason for concern. We should seek to increase the percentage of able young men and women who receive a higher education, but even as we seek that increase we can already foresee the limits on future improvement under our present methods of selection and education. As we look to the future, we must consider how to make better use of our resources of talent.

The Encouragement of Talent

The obvious first response to this problem is that we should be more active in the encouragement of talented young persons. Thus Charles H. Brower (1960), President of the advertising firm Batten, Barton, Durstine, and Osborne, said recently to the Advertising Federation of America:

> I ask only that we look for talent and excellence as avidly as we look for . . . many of our less valuable natural resources.
>
> . . . .
>
> Our educators, our ministers, our editors, our businessmen, our unions, and our organizations . . . should join in a mammoth talent hunt to uncover [the] treasure of brains which . . . is hiding in unlikely places all over America.

In actuality, a talent hunt has long characterized both the American culture and a number of other cultures. Part of this hunt has been systematically organized; much of it has been informal, unorganized, and on an individual basis.

Walter Bingham once told me that he approached the end of high school with no thought of entering college. One day one of his teachers took him aside and planted the idea that led him to enroll at Kansas University the following fall. I wonder how often a similar scene has occurred in the early lives of men and women who later entered the professional or learned fields. George Beadle, who was awarded the 1958 Nobel Prize in Physiology and Medicine, tells an almost identical story: a Nebraska farm boyhood, a father uninterested in higher education, and an inspiring teacher who urged the future Nobel laureate to enter the University of Nebraska. There must be many other eminent men and women who could tell similar stories: bright, industrious students with potentialities far exceeding the range of vision acquired from home and community, whose sights were lifted by a teacher or an older friend who took the trouble to encourage talent. I am glad that Bingham told me how he was encouraged to go to college, for perhaps that experience helps to explain his abiding interest in the identification and encouragement of talented youngsters.

The incident also illustrates the principle to which I wish to give first attention. The principle is this: talent requires encouragement. Certainly there are exceptions, or at least apparent exceptions: each of us could name greatly gifted men who rose from poor surroundings, overcoming great obstacles, seemingly driven by a force that no hardships and no obstacles could impede. There may be exceptions, but it is neither safe nor realistic to assume that high ability is always accompanied by high motivation, that human talent will override obstacles to find its own way to fruition. Nor is it safe to assume that the necessary inspiration or encouragement will always be provided by the family.

In an illuminating study of the role of personal encouragement in the lives of bright students, Swanson (1955) interviewed men who, some twenty years earlier, had been superior high school seniors. Some of these men had gone to college; others had quit at the end of high school. Swanson tried to find out what influences had determined which of these men had gone to college and which had not. One of the clearest differences was the simple fact that someone—a teacher, a minister, a relative, or a friend—had encouraged some of the men to go to college, while others could not recall that anyone had ever suggested that they should continue formal education beyond high school. Certainly other factors than this one were involved; much besides a few conversations on the topic determines how long a student stays in school. But it is significant that the men who went to college were usually actively encouraged to do so, sometimes encouraged by several people, while those who did not enter college could not recall this kind of personal encouragement.

Walter Bingham might or might not have attended college had his teacher not encouraged him. I think perhaps he might, for another story of his youth shows a character already marked by determination and self-confidence. He made straight A's his first year in college, a good record for a 16-year-old boy who was the youngest student on the campus. But he established no firm friendships and did not want to return to Kansas University. Where should he go? He applied to two colleges, he told me. One promptly accepted him; the other did not reply. When summer came to an end and it was again time to go off to college, in which direction should he head: to the college that had accepted him or to the one that had ignored him? The safe and cautious solution would have been to go to the college that had accepted him, but young Walter was more venturesome. He concluded that the college that was eager to have him must not have many good students and that the college that did not seem to care whether he came or not must therefore be the better institution. So, off he went to Beloit, the college that had not acknowledged his application, but that did accept him on arrival and that turned his interest toward psychology. I suspect that a 17-year-old boy who possessed the self-assurance evident in this decision might well have gone to college anyway, whether or not a particular teacher had urged him. But we cannot be sure. Perhaps we are able to honor Bingham because we are in reality also honoring the high school teacher who recognized his talent and encouraged him to develop it.

Anecdotes are useful if they illustrate a significant principle, but it is time to return to the principle: talent requires encouragement if it is to reach its full development. The encouragement may come from parents or other interested individuals, or encouragement may be built into the customs and traditions that characterize a particular social group. Scotland has produced an unusually large number of notable men. This high intellectual productivity has been explained as resulting from widespread interest among the Scots in seeking out and encouraging talent. Whether this explanation would withstand critical analysis, I do not know, but that there are major differences in intellectual productivity among different social and ethnic groups is completely clear.

Social Factors in Talent Development

About ten years ago the Social Science Research Council's Committee on the Identification of Talent began an investigation of some of these differences. The committee received a substantial grant from the John and Mary R. Markle Foundation and decided that this grant should not be used in attempts to improve aptitude tests or other existing methods of identifying talent, but should rather be used to investigate some of the social conditions that help to determine how talent manifests itself and how it is stunted or made to blossom. One of the studies that we supported was by Fred Strodtbeck (1958). Strodtbeck started by selecting a number of bright, teen-age boys. Half were Jewish, half Italian. He then set out to analyze the Italian-Jewish cultural differences and to determine how these differences influence the aspirations and education of growing boys. This he did by studying the values that characterized the thinking of the families of each of his subjects, and the patterns of social interaction among the father, the mother, and the bright son. He found that in a number of quite detailed respects Jews have values more likely to promote high achievement than do Italians and that there is greater agreement among Jewish family members on these values.

I do not want to go into detail concerning Strodtbeck's study, but I cite it as an example of the possibility of investigating the social factors that influence the extent to which potentially high ability will actually be developed. I might have cited other studies, such as the Quincy (Illinois) Youth Development Project of Robert F. De Haan and Robert J. Havighurst, or the different approach of Anne Roe, or the still different works of Samuel Stouffer. Instead of extending this list, let me merely call attention to the importance of learning more than we now know about the social conditions that influence the development and utilization of talent. We need better information concerning the family as a social system, the school as a social system, and the ways in which these social systems encourage talent or hinder its development.

Policy for Talent Development

The encouragement of talent is clearly desirable, and so is the better understanding of the social conditions that aid or hinder its development, both because the individual with talent is thus more likely to reach closer to his full potential and because the nation is more likely to gain the advantage of his high ability. But it is not sufficient simply to say that we should encourage talent wherever we find it. There is an additional, and psychologically more interesting, question to take up.

This psychologically more interesting question has to do with the development of an underlying policy or strategy of talent development. If one of us were suddenly assigned responsibility for developing a national policy of talent development, I wonder what he would do. No single one of us is likely to be given this responsibility, but collectively it is shared by many persons, whether they realize it or not. Every person who constructs or interprets a test or other measure for the selection of scholarship or fellowship winners, every college admissions officer, every guidance counselor, every educational philosopher or administrator, and every teacher daily makes decisions that in fact do help to determine how the nation's intellectual resources are developed and utilized. Their actions constitute our unanalyzed, but nonetheless determining, present policy.

We have, in the past, concerned ourselves chiefly with the techniques of identifying talented persons and furthering their education. So long as our work is controlled primarily by techniques, the major directions will be determined by the techniques themselves, the criteria that we find most reliable, and relevant statistical and experimental considerations. These factors should continue to concern us. But by themselves they are not enough. It is time to give consideration to questions of social value, purpose, or ultimate objective. I suggest that it is time for those of us who are professionally most concerned to consider the policy issues and to try to develop a strategy that will maximize the achievement and social value of the persons whose talents we seek to identify and develop.

Two aspects of such a policy are obvious. First is the desirability of encouraging the full development of all forms of socially useful talent. Of this point I have already spoken. Second is the need for a better understanding of the social and cultural factors that stimulate or retard the development of talent. Of the need for research I have also spoken.

After these two points, what comes next? In addition to identifying talented youngsters and helping them to secure an education commensurate with their abilities, in addition to conducting research, we must also consider how the talent we are developing can be so distributed as to result in the greatest accomplishment. The recommendation that I will make on this point is likely to be controversial. In order to point up the issue clearly, I will start with what may seem to be an extreme point of view.

The Value of Diversity

In the selection and education of persons of ability, it is advantageous to a society to seek the greatest achievable diversity of talent: diversity within an individual, among the members of an occupational group, and among the individuals who constitute a society.

In speaking of diversity among individuals, I am using words in their ordinary meaning; but when I speak of diversity within an individual, the expression sounds strange. There is no customary term for the idea I am trying to express, for the adjectives with good connotations mean the opposite of what I am trying to say. I am not talking about the well-rounded individual, or the broad scholar, or the man of many talents. These are qualities we ordinarily respect; but I wish to make a case for the opposite, for the man who has developed some of his talents so highly that he cannot be well-rounded, for the one who may be called uneven or one-sided but in whom at least one side has been developed to the level of real superiority. For the sake of symmetry with the concept of diversity among individuals, I have called this kind of development diversity within an individual. If the expression still seems strange, its meaning will become clearer as we go along.

One further explanation is essential. I do not wish to maximize variance or diversity by having some persons very bright and others very dull. Obviously we want each person to reach the highest level of which he is capable. But even if we were doing as well as we know how to do in the identification and education of talented persons, the problem of optimal deployment of their various talents would still be a question of undiminished psychological and social interest. Even under these circumstances, a strong case can be made for the proposition that the value of a nation's intellectual resources—or the total achievement—would be maximized by maximizing the variety of abilities within and among individuals. This is not a new idea; but the point needs repetition and also needs analysis, for even though we agree upon the value of diversity, strong forces are constantly at work in the opposite direction. These forces tend to make us more, rather than less, alike and tend to prevent the uneven development of a talented individual.

Many of the methods that have been developed for dealing with people in groups have the effect of reducing the variability among the group members. Examples are the use of uniform lesson assignments and the use of general aptitude measures and the average grade or the rank in class as devices for selecting students for the next higher educational level. Advertising procedures, trade union policies, wage scales, and a variety of other forces also work in the direction of uniformity rather than diversity. These tendencies are supported by popular attitudes that place a premium on uniformity and conformity rather than upon diversity and individuality. Lyle Spencer quotes the mother of three bright children as saying: "I'm not interested in geniuses, all I want to do is to raise my kids to be normal, well-adjusted adults." Many parents would agree; they want their children to be like other children, and not to be different. Teachers, too, sometimes express this attitude. De Haan and Havighurst (1957) quote a teacher as saying: "When I am finished with my class in June, the slow children are a little faster, and the fast have slowed down a bit."

Years ago, Truman Kelley protested this attitude and leveled his guns against school teachers and officials who exhibit it. He called them pedagogical plainsmen and accused them of preferring intellectual plains to intellectual hills and valleys. They were, he wrote, so obsessed with averages and norms that they devoted themselves to "the weary process of shovelling to fill valleys and steady erosion to remove mountains of human capacity."

Had Harold Benjamin not already pre-empted the title, I might have called this address "The Cultivation of Idiosyncrasy," for the major point of my argument is that the cultivation of diversity is desirable both for the individual young persons whose futures lie in our hands and for the society in which they will live and work. I cannot use Benjamin's title, but I can quote a few of his paragraphs (1955). The wit and humor with which he approached serious problems has illuminated many an educational discussion, and the fable he used in opening the Inglis lecture at Harvard in 1949 illustrates the point I want to make. The fable is the story of the school in the woods.

> All the animals had to take all the subjects. Swimming, running, jumping, climbing, and flying made up the required curriculum.
>
> . . . .
>
> Some animals, of course, were better students than others. The squirrel, for example, got straight A's from the first in running, jumping, and climbing. He got a good passing grade, moreover, in swimming. It looked as though he would make Phi Beta Kappa in his junior year, but he had trouble with flying. Not that he was unable to fly. He could fly. He

> climbed to the top of tree after tree and sailed through the air to neighboring trees with ease. As he modestly observed, he was a flying squirrel by race. The teacher of flying pointed out, however, that the squirrel was always losing altitude in his gliding and insisted that he should take off in the approved fashion from the ground. Indeed, the teacher decided that the taking-off-from-the-ground unit had to be mastered first, as was logical, and so he drilled the squirrel day after day on the take-off.
>
> ....
>
> The squirrel tried hard. He tried so hard he got severe Charley horses in both hind legs, and thus crippled he became incapable even of running, jumping, or climbing. He left school a failure, and died soon thereafter of starvation, being unable to gather and store nuts.

Benjamin continued the fable to relate the difficulties of the snake, the eagle, and the gopher. I shall quote only the story of the eagle.

> The eagle was a truly brilliant student. His flying was superb, his running and jumping were of the best, and he even passed the swimming test, although the teacher tried to keep him from using his wings too much. By employing his talons and beak, moreover, he could climb after a fashion and no doubt he would have been able to pass that course, too, except that he always flew to the top of the problem tree or cliff when the teacher's back was turned and sat there lazily in the sun, preening his feathers and staring arrogantly down at his fellow students climbing up the hard way. The teachers reasoned with him to no avail. He would not study climbing seriously. At first he turned aside the faculty's importunities with relatively mild wisecracks and innuendoes, but as the teachers put more pressure upon him he reacted

> with more and more feeling . . . [and finally quit school altogether].

I wonder how many human students have been similarly frustrated and had their talents stunted by being required to climb slowly step by step, instead of being encouraged to soar rapidly to the heights of which they were capable.

I have said that it is socially valuable to maximize diversity. Now let me try to prove the point. I should like to be able to give a rigorous proof; for, if the assertion is correct, there flow from it a number of implications for the professional work of psychologists, guidance counselors, teachers, and all who deal professionally with the identification, education, and utilization of talented persons. The proof cannot be rigorous, for we do not have adequate measures of amount of talent, of achievement, or of the social value of achievement. But it is possible to analyze these variables and to examine their interrelationships. The exercise leads convincingly to the conclusion that maximum diversity results in maximum social value.

Let us start the analysis with two points on which there is general agreement. The first is that individuals vary in the total amount of talent or ability they possess. This simple statement overlooks the whole nature-nurture problem, the effects of education, and all of the difficulties of measuring talent. Moreover, it oversimplifies the whole matter by treating ability as a trait that an individual possesses rather than as an attribute of the behavior he exhibits. Nevertheless, to say that different individuals possess different total amounts of ability is a convenient way of stating an idea that is generally accepted.

The second point is that ability is not a unitary trait but expresses itself in various forms or special abilities. We may side with L. L. Thurstone in believing that a relatively small number of more or less independent primary abilities provide a satisfactory description of human ability, or we may side with Godfrey Thompson in postulating a large number of highly specialized abilities. For our purpose, it makes little difference which of these positions one prefers. All that is essential is that we agree that ability is a many-sided affair and that an individual may be better in one kind of ability than he is in another.

Now let us suppose that an individual could distribute his ability over various kinds of performances in any way he preferred. Within limits, this is a reasonable proposition, for each individual does exercise some control. If a student neglects the academic subjects in order to practice on the piano, he will become a better pianist, and a poorer scholar. Alternatively, he can concentrate on something else and neglect the piano entirely. Students constantly make educational decisions, allocate study time, choose schools, select reading matter, or neglect their studies. All such decisions influence the extent to which one or another ability will be developed.

Now let us move from this realistic situation to its unrealistic limit, and to simplify the task let us arbitrarily assign some numbers to the situation. Suppose that a given individual has 1,000 units of ability—another individual might have more or fewer—and let us suppose that he can distribute these 1,000 units in any way he chooses over 20 different kinds of ability. If he wishes to be a completely well-rounded individual, he would assign 50 units to each of the 20 abilities. Or, he might elect the 10 kinds of ability that he thinks most important and assign 100 units to each, neglecting completely the other 10 kinds of ability because they seem to him to be unimportant. Or, at the extreme, as a kind of talent gambler, he might stake his whole 1,000 units on one kind of ability and neglect the other 19 completely. Which of these ways of distributing his total talent fund would be best for the individual?

A parallel question can be asked from the point of view of

society. Suppose that society rather than the individual decides how the 1,000 units will be distributed. Which would best serve society: to assign 50 units to each of 20 different kinds of ability, 100 units to each of 10 kinds, or the whole 1,000 units to a single ability?

We cannot answer these questions without considering the values involved. In real life, these values are often conflicting. The eminent young mathematician has to help care for the children, occasionally to repair the lawn mower, and take his turn in helping to run the affairs of the local Boy Scout troop. As a mathematician, he might like to concentrate all of his units of ability on mathematics. But as a human being with other interests, he has to save some of those units for other and quite nonmathematical kinds of ability and achievement. In real life, many conflicting value considerations are involved, but let us neglect them for the time being and concentrate on the problem of maximizing the social value of human talents.

The value that society places upon different levels of accomplishment does not vary directly with the amount of achievement or its underlying ability, but increases more rapidly than does the amount. A graph relating amount of talent and its social value would be a curve rather than a straight line—doubling the amount of ability more than doubles its value; doubling again the amount again more than doubles the value. The relationship can be illustrated with some arbitrary numbers: if one unit of ability is worth one dollar to society, 50 units are worth more than $50; perhaps 50 units are worth $100. Similarly for larger amounts, 100 units may be worth $500, and 1,000 units may be so valuable as to be priceless. These particular numbers are arbitrary, but that the relationship is nonlinear is clear. The salaries paid to chemists or engineers or members of other professions are not symmetrically distributed about a mean. The distributions are skewed, with a longer tail above the mean than below it. Moreover, there is general recognition that the salaries paid to the ablest people fall far short of being commensurate with their ability. On the ordinary scale of salaries for writers, physicists, and public servants, we make no effort to pay appropriate salaries to a Shakespeare, an Einstein, or a Winston Churchill.

We use other means to compensate outstanding persons whose salaries are not commensurate with their ability. We award Gold Medals to Olympic winners, Nobel Prizes to great scientists, Pulitzer Prizes to outstanding authors and editors, and we have other honors with which we recognize excellence in other fields. Partly by the amounts of money paid for different levels of ability and partly in other forms of compensation, society demonstrates that the value it places on talent increases more rapidly than does the amount of talent.

Now we can return to the question of the most valuable way of distributing talents. From the standpoint of society, the best way to distribute talent is to take maximum advantage of differences in aptitude, interest, and motivation by having each individual concentrate on the thing he can do best. Instead of having the 1,000-unit man distribute his ability 50 units on each of 20 kinds of ability or 100 units on each of 10, have him concentrate the whole 1,000 units on a single ability. In Harold Benjamin's fable, have the eagle be the best flyer in the world and forget about his ability to swim or climb, have the squirrel be the best climber in the world and stop worrying about his inability to fly. In human affairs, follow the same principle. Have one man be the best he can possibly become in one line and another the best he can possibly become in another line. Thus we would have the best physicist, the best poet, the best mathematician, and the best dramatist possible. The total value of the talents so distributed would be incomparably greater than would be the value of the same number of units of talent spread more uniformly over the different men and the different abilities involved.

Recommending that each person be helped to achieve the highest level he can reach in the area in which he has the greatest talent and interest is not the same as recommending that every scholar be a narrow specialist. Some, however, should be specialists, and some should specialize in relatively narrow fields. Physics is generally recognized as the most highly developed science. Further advances are most likely to be made by physicists who concentrate on a particular area of physics. Thus we want highly specialized physicists. But we also want physicists of wider interest and knowledge: persons who can bridge the gaps between physics and biology or physics and other sciences, persons who are interested in the practical applications of physical principles, and persons who are interested in attempting to translate physics into terms that the rest of us can try to understand. This diversity among physicists is essential if physics itself is to advance and if other fields of intellectual and practical endeavor are to benefit maximally from those advances.

From the standpoint of social value, maximum diversity would be the ideal; but like many another ideal, it is unattainable. In real life we must recognize that the best mathematician in the world must do something besides mathematics and that the best poet cannot spend all his energy on poetry. But the fact that the extreme case is unrealistic does not destroy the principle. The principle is this, and I state it now in realistic rather than imaginary terms: to the extent that we can control the distribution of talent, it is socially desirable to maximize the diversity, both within and among individuals.

This is the ideal. Before we consider methods of reaching toward that ideal, it is worthwhile briefly to look at its opposite, for then we will have set the boundaries within which we can maneuver in our educational and guidance practices.

In *Brave New World*, Aldous Huxley (1932) described a society in which most individuals were born as members of batches. Born, you will remember, is not the right word: old-fashioned human birth had been replaced by a kind of controlled embryology in which any desired number of identical individuals could be developed from a single fertilized egg. The eggs were developed in vitro, and at the proper time babies, instead of being born, were decanted. Through controlled nutrition, and through proper training and education, the members of a batch could be made to have any desired level of ability, and all the members of a batch were as alike as identical twins that had been reared together. We can dismiss *Brave New World* as satirical exaggeration; but we cannot dismiss the kind of society that Huxley was satirizing, for there are forces in society that tend in the direction of homogeneity, and there are cultural values that make homogeneity seem desirable.

Between the unreality of *Brave New World* and the unreality of maximum diversity there is a wide range. Within this range we have considerable room to choose the kind of society we want ours to be. Ultimately the essential choices will be made by the nation as a whole, through the processes of democratic action. But in a more immediate sense, and on the important aspect of talent distribution, choices must be made by those persons who are professionally engaged in the development and handling of talent.

As to how far we should go in the direction of diversity, I have only two suggestions, and both must be stated in general terms. One is that we should go as far as we can. The other is that the greater the ability with which we are dealing, the greater is the amount of idiosyncrasy we can tolerate. The brief and brilliant career of the Indian mathematician Ramanujan (Newman, 1957) illustrates both principles. The name may be strange, for Ramanujan was a mathematicians' mathematician and was little known outside of mathematical circles. Yet he has been described as "quite the most extraordinary mathematician of our time." At the age of 15, he was loaned a copy of Carr's *Synopsis of Pure*

Mathematics. This was all he had, and all he needed, to start him off on a strange, unorthodox, and inspired career of mathematical innovation. Working completely alone, he rediscovered much that had been developed by earlier mathematicians; he followed some false leads and made some mistakes; but in some fields of mathematics his power and originality went beyond any other mathematician in the world.

On the basis of his obvious brilliance, he was given a scholarship; but he lost it at the end of the first term because he failed his examination in English. He never did earn a university degree; but at the age of 25, after working for some years as a clerk, he was given a fellowship at Cambridge where he went to work with G. H. Hardy. Hardy faced the problem of deciding how much he should let Ramanujan go his own way, and how much he should try to correct his mistakes and make him into a more orthodox mathematician. Hardy expressed his dilemma in these words:

> It was impossible to ask such a man to submit to systematic instruction, to try to learn mathematics from the beginning once more. I was afraid too that, if I insisted unduly on matters which Ramanujan found irksome, I might destroy his confidence or break the spell of his inspiration. On the other hand there were things of which it was impossible that he should remain in ignorance. . . . It was impossible to let him go through life supposing that all the zeros of the Zeta-function were real.

The moral of the story is that, if we are dealing with a Ramanujan, we can put up with a great deal of eccentricity; if we are dealing with a lesser mind, we can insist on more conformity. Even with a Ramanujan there is a limit, but let us in all cases push that limit as far out as we can.

Implications

Let me now briefly suggest some of the implications of the principle that it is socially valuable to increase the diversity of talent. Each of these implications relates to practices that are under our professional control.

The first implication is that it is desirable to make wider use of tests of special ability or aptitude to supplement our tests of general ability. De Haan and Havighurst (1957) found, in a survey of 40 school systems, that nearly all used tests of general intellectual ability as a means of appraising the potential of their students, but only 3 used tests of special aptitudes. Failure to use special tests increases the danger of overlooking students with unusually high potential in art, music, creative writing, and other abilities that are not well measured by the usual tests of general intellectual aptitude.

A second implication is that it is desirable to increase the use of separate scores for separate types of ability and to decrease the use of single scores that represent the sum or combination of several part scores. When students are being selected for awards or for admission to the next higher educational level, global measures are the easiest ones to use. Moreover, global measures are the ones that are likely to give the highest validity coefficients. Most of our usual measures of success are factorially complex and can be better predicted by factorially complex tests than by factorially simpler ones.

We pay a price, however, for the ease of use and for the higher validity of general measures of aptitude. The price we pay for using general measures is that we reduce the apparent size of the pool of talent on which we can draw. Relying solely on tests of general intellectual aptitude reduces the size of the talent pool because various kinds of ability, although usually positively correlated with one another, are by no means perfectly correlated.

In the Quincy youth development study, selection of the top 10% of the children in general intellectual ability, the top 10% in leadership, and the top 2% in drawing ability included 16% of the total population. The authors estimate that, had they also included the top 10% each in music, dramatic ability, creative writing, and mechanical ability, they would have brought into their talent development program 20–25% of the total child population (De Haan & Havighurst, 1957).

In Kenneth Little's study (1958) of Wisconsin high school graduates, he used the usual measures of high school grades and general intelligence. But he went beyond these measures by asking the teachers to identify those of their students who were specially gifted in any field. About 20% of the students so identified had not ranked in the upper quarter of their graduating class in either general scholastic achievement or general mental ability. Included were students whom the teachers identified as being specially gifted in art, music, science, and other fields. Clearly the use of tests of special aptitude and the use of individual grades and scores rather than averages identifies a larger number of talented young persons and thus lays the basis for the development of a larger and more diversified talent pool.

An opportunity to use the more detailed information made available by separate scores is found in the award of scholarships and fellowships. The person who is high on every score and thus high on the sum or average of his scores should, of course, be encouraged to continue his education, and such students clearly merit awards, scholarships, and fellowships. But when we drop down a step or two below the generally superior level, we still tend to base awards on the average score instead of looking for evidence of exceptionally high merit in individual fields or abilities. I would suggest that in awarding scholarships when we reach this slightly lower general level, we make some of the awards to students who have earned very high marks on individual tests or measures of ability. We will probably experience some lowering of validity coefficients, we may make awards to a few unproductive eccentrics; but we will enhance our chances of picking up a few persons so highly gifted and so intensely interested along one line that they have neglected, or rebelliously disdained, to keep pace with their fellows in other lines.

A third implication is that the patterning of abilities should be avoided in the selection or guidance of persons entering or contemplating entering a particular occupation. You may recall the long history of unsuccessful efforts to find the optimal pattern of abilities and personality traits that characterize the successful members of an occupational group. No one has stated the hope for such patterns better than Clark Hull (1928) who, thirty years ago, pointed out that vocational guidance would be easy if we had measures of the various kinds of ability and if we had carried out the analyses necessary to determine the weight with which each type of ability enters into the determination of success in each of a variety of occupations. Under the system that Hull anticipated, an applicant for vocational guidance would be given a battery of tests that measured all of the major types of ability. His scores on these tests would be fed into a computer which already contained in its storage unit the regression weights of each ability on each of a variety of occupations. The sum of the products of the ability scores and the corresponding regression weights for a given occupation would then be automatically computed and would represent the applicant's predicted standard score for success in that occupation. With a modern computer, it would be possible to determine very quickly the predicted standard scores for success in each of a large number of occupations.

In the days since Hull wrote this description, the necessary computers have reached a high stage of development; tests of different kinds of ability have been improved, although not nearly so much as the computers. But we have also learned enough about ability, vocations, and the factors that make for success to have concluded that the kind of differential prediction that Hull described is not feasible. A major reason is that relatively diverse patterns of ability are consistent with success in a single vocation. Any professional field includes opportunities for such a variety of persons—persons differing in abilities and differing in personality traits—that there is no simple or single pattern that is either essential or sufficient. Consider engineering, or medicine, or psychology, or any other field of work that demands intellectual ability. Each title covers a wide variety of tasks; each field includes opportunities for a wide variety of persons.

The search for a pattern characteristic of each profession has failed. As I have considered this failure, I have become convinced that we were on the wrong track in looking for distinctive patterns. For law, medicine, engineering, psychology, and other fields are enriched by having within their ranks a wide range of patterns of ability.

Conclusion

It would be possible to present other implications of the values of diversity, implications for the guidance and for the education of talented students. A general discussion of these fields would take far too long, and I will refrain, for now it is time to conclude. The needs of the nation for highly developed talent are growing and will continue to grow. This is an inevitable feature of the kind of complex, industrialized, specialized society in which we live. If we are to make full use of our intellectual resources, the first requisite is that we employ all the means at our command to encourage the development of talent. The second requisite is that they learn more about the social factors that aid or impede the development of talent.

I expect that these two points are noncontroversial. I am not so sure about the third point that I have advanced. Some of you may disagree with part or all of what I have said about the strategy of optimal distribution or deployment of talent. I readily grant the privilege of disagreement, for you have given me the opportunity to argue that we should go beyond personal action and beyond scientific research to consider the question of how our professional activities concerned with talent can be supported and unified by an underlying policy of talent development—a policy that seeks to maximize achievement and thus to maximize the value to society of our resources of talent.

What I have attempted to do is to state the first principles of a strategy of talent development, a strategy that provides a unifying rationale for our efforts to improve the construction and interpretation of tests, and the counseling, guidance, and education of talented young minds. The strategy is one of increasing the diversity of talent, in an individual, within an occupation, and in society. There will always be counterpressures that must be respected; but to the extent that we succeed in increasing the diversity of talent, we will have increased its value to society.

References

Benjamin, H. *The cultivation of idiosyncrasy.* Cambridge, Mass.: Harvard Univer. Press, 1955.

Bridgman, D. S. *Losses of intellectual talent from the educational system prior to graduation from college.* Washington, D.C.: NSF.

Brower, C. H. The year of the rat. Address to Advertising Federation of America, Boston, February 9, 1960.

De Haan, R. F., & Havighurst, R. J. *Educating gifted children.* Chicago: Univer. Chicago Press, 1957.

Gardner, J. W., *et al. The pursuit of excellence: education and the future of America.* (The "Rockefeller" report on education.) Garden City, N.Y.: Doubleday, 1958.

Hull, C. L. *Aptitude testing.* Yonkers-on-Hudson, N.Y.: World Book, 1928.

Huxley, A. *Brave new world.* Garden City, N.Y.: Doubleday, Doran, 1932.

Little, J. K. A state-wide inquiry into decisions of youth about education beyond high school. University of Wisconsin, 1958.

Newman, J. R. Srinivasa Ramanujan. In *Lives in science.* New York: Simon & Schuster, 1957, pp. 257–269.

Strodtbeck, F. L. Family interaction, values, and achievement. In D. C. McClelland *et al., Talent and society.* Princeton, N.J.: Van Nostrand, 1958, pp. 135–194.

Swanson, E. O. Is college education worthwhile? *J. counsel. Psychol.,* 1955, 2, 176–181.

Wolfle, D. *America's resources of specialized talent.* New York: Harper, 1954.

John M. Stalnaker

Recognizing and Encouraging Talent[1]

The National Merit Scholarship Program was created some 5 years ago as a means of arousing the public's awareness of and respect for intellectual talent and in this way to encourage the development of such talent. Ideally, a scholarship program will extend its influence far beyond the small group of students who are actually given scholarships. By helping to foster a climate of opinion favorable to intellectual excellence, it will stimulate latent talent.

One of the popular themes of the day is the need to develop fully our human resources. There is no need to labor the point here, except to say that this need is the reason for the Merit Program. Suffice it to observe that the saying, "Knowledge is power," has never been more true than it is today, and that knowledge has become so complex and extensive that more and higher education are almost absolute requisites for advancing our knowl-

1. This paper is based on the Walter Van Dyke Bingham Memorial Lecture given at Carnegie Institute of Technology, March 23, 1961. It was first published in the *American Psychologist,* 1961, vol. 16, no. 8 (August), pp. 513–522.

edge—and advance it we must on many fronts. Good minds are required even to keep up with the new developments today. Only the most talented minds will make new breakthroughs for us. Higher education is becoming a requirement, not only for individual fulfillment, but also for national survival in this day when man-made weapons are capable of destroying the world.

Moreover, the untrained and the uneducated have greater and greater difficulty in finding a useful place in the modern world. Whitehead's prophecy that there will be no appeal from the judgment which will be pronounced on the uneducated is about to become true.

As a nation we are slowly awakening to our responsibilities in education. To be sure, we have since our founding shown a certain dedication to universal education. In no major country in the world today is education more widely available than in the United States. There are colleges in every state and in every major city, and the number of these institutions is constantly increasing. Today, over half of our secondary school graduates enter college and the proportion is increasing each year.

But until recently we have not been concerned that our youth learn at as fast a pace as their ability permits the basic principles of those subjects without which life in the modern world is inconceivable. While paying lip service to the ideal of universal education, we have neglected our schools (and their teachers). We have asked that teachers instruct our children without demanding effort from the students. The quality of educational opportunity is poor in many places and the educational standards low. Universal availability of high quality education will provide a proving ground for all youth to show their ability.

Now we are faced with a serious international situation which threatens our very existence. The power which recognizes talent and develops it to the productive stage, quickly and in quantity, has the best chance of winning the race.

When the National Merit Scholarship Corporation was created in mid-1955, Sputnik I was not for another 2 years to arouse the American public to a new concern about the nature and quality of its education. The prevailing atmosphere in the schools at that time was a peaceful calm. Adjustment and contentment were the goals. Schools were permissive, relatively noncompetitive, and paid little attention to standards of performance. There were no priorities in subject matter; courses were offered in homemaking, family living, cooking, and the like. Competition was deemphasized. Every child should enjoy success. High school graduates were often not able to read or write at the level required for college work. As a result remedial courses were common in the colleges.

While there was much talk about talent, the temper of the people encouraged competition in the sports rather than the academic arena. Little league ball clubs could count on parental interest, financing, and guidance. As Elmo Roper has observed: "We have no folk tradition that seeks out and trains and sponsors and takes pride in exceptional intellectual talent. There are no little leagues of the mind."

What a nation respects and honors tends to prosper and grow. The star player on the winning basketball team can be assured of great public recognition and acclaim. The entire town will turn out to honor him. Newspapers will devote space to his amazing performance. The school itself may dismiss classes to celebrate the great victory. College scouts and "admission counselors" will visit him. Young children notice what is honored by adults, what adults judge to be important.

The serious, able youngster who devoted himself to scholarly work received no such public acclaim back in the days before 1955. His classmates regarded him as a "brain"—a term of opprobrium at that time—and ignored him. No public recognition stimulated him to greater effort. His juniors did not look up to him with envy in their hearts and a determination to follow in his footsteps.

The National Merit Scholarship Program was created to help to change this dismal, distorted picture. Could some of the elements of the contest be brought into the intellectual field? Conant in his *Citadel of Learning* remarked that the spirit of competition need not be deplored; it might under certain conditions be a healthy motivating force in the academic field. "Local enthusiasm," he said, "needs to be aroused for discovering and adequately educating those who are intellectually gifted."

The problem was to design a contest in the intellectual field suitable for students in the upper years of high school. Scholarships would be the incentive—the motive power—and the program would have several important objectives.

First of all, the Merit Program would be a champion of able and talented youth. Most scholarship money is controlled by a relatively small number of colleges, who use it mostly for institutional promotion and development. Much of it is spent attracting the talented student from one college to another. The Merit Program, on the other hand, finds able students, wherever they may be, and helps them attend any college they select and study any curriculum of interest to them.

Another objective of the Merit Program would be to arouse public interest in intellectual talent. With the help of the secondary schools of the nation—all 25,000 of them—the Merit Program launched a dramatic campaign to find and publicize exceptionally able students. The top performers in such a national contest would receive notice in the local press, and thus the townspeople would become aware of that most precious of all their resources, talented local youngsters.

It was hoped that the Merit Program would be a mechanism to assure—to the extent of its resources—that no unusually talented student was denied a college education because of the economic status of his family. In addition to offering a substantial number of scholarships itself, the Merit Program notifies other scholarship agencies about the students it finds, thus helping exceptional students to obtain financial aid.

The Merit Program had as another objective the prevention of wasteful duplication. Any number of sponsors can utilize without cost the selection mechanism of the Merit Program to locate students having the particular characteristics of interest to them, so that they can support such students in their further education.

The Merit Program was aimed to help create a climate of opinion in which intellectual excellence would be respected and encouraged. "The United States has not achieved the tradition of respect for learning in all fields that is so much a part of the culture of other peoples," writes the Director of the National Science Foundation, Alan T. Waterman. "Above all, we must strive for a climate of opinion that will be favorable to our intellectual as well as creative activities."

Perhaps most important of all, the Merit Program, by gathering data on able students throughout the land, will contribute to our knowledge about the location, background, and development of unusual intellectual talent. Research activities constitute an integral and basic part of the Merit Program operation.

These several hoped-for outcomes are broad as well as deep, and they will not be achieved easily or quickly. Many obstacles were anticipated.

Legally, the National Merit Scholarship Corporation is a nonprofit corporation in the State of Illinois. It restricts its activities to scholarship matters but within that field it handles all phases. An independent corporation not responsible to any other organization or group, it is controlled by a board of 22 Directors drawn from the fields of business, higher education, and secondary education. The board creates the basic policies of the corporation and oversees its general operations.

In addition to this board, there is an advisory council which recommends to the corporation's President procedures which will have the greatest educational values. There is also a research advisory board which reviews research activities and recommends new directions for research.

Conducting a national talent search, informing business organizations and others about how they can help to advance the program (i.e., raising money), selecting able students, aiding them to finance their education, and following them through their college career requires a well-trained staff and a considerable budget.

When the National Merit Scholarship Corporation was established in 1955, the administrative costs of the program had been underwritten for the following 15 years, and at least $1,000,000 had been made available for scholarships each year for the first 10 years. The total amount of money pledged by the Ford Foundation as a part of its broad program for assisting in the development and improvement of formal education was $20,000,000. The Carnegie Corporation of New York also agreed to advance $500,000 for administering the program during its first 5 years of operation; it has given an additional $250,000 to finance research during the second 5 years.

Business organizations were immediately invited to finance additional scholarships. The number of sponsors has increased year by year; by 1961 some 135 different sponsors will be offering a total of over 525 sponsored Merit Scholarships at an estimated cost to them of $2,500,000. This is in addition to the scholarships awarded by the corporation out of its resources provided through the founding grants.

The scholarship competition is conducted in this way: At the beginning of the school year all secondary schools in the United States and its territories are invited to participate in the National

Merit Scholarship Program. Participation is by school, not by individual student.

In 1960 some 15,000 schools took part in the Merit Program. There are in the United States approximately 25,000 secondary schools, but one must remember that less than one-tenth of these schools enroll over half of all students in secondary education. It is estimated that the schools which took part in the Merit Program in 1960 enroll 85% or more of all of the secondary school students in the country.

The school itself selects those of its students who will participate in the first stage of the program, a preliminary selecting test. In some schools a small number are invited to participate; in others the preliminary test is given to the entire class of third year students. Approximately 600,000 students, or about one-third of all the third year students in high school, took part in the program this past year.

The selecting test measures both the aptitude and the attainment of the student. The test is 44 pages in length and requires 3 hours for its administration. The mere act of taking the test is itself of definite educational value to the student, since it gives him the benefit of a concentrated experience in dealing with difficult intellectual tasks.

The test measures in a relatively direct fashion the complex skills required for successful work in virtually any college; it is a test of a student's readiness for high level college work. Since the skills it measures are taught in all secondary schools, the test does not favor any particular high school curriculum. Nor is the content of the test such that the student can raise his grade by frantic last-minute study; it covers too much ground for such an effort to be successful.

The scores are reported to the students by the schools. They can then be used, in conjunction with interpretative material which has been supplied to the schools, as an aid in counseling students about their future academic plans and adult careers. So no one loses by taking part in the Merit Program; there is some value for everyone.

There is considerable debate in our secondary schools about the relative importance of aptitude and achievement. Aptitude, it is supposed, is a characteristic one is born with; the schools are in no way responsible for the aptitudes of their pupils. If a person is low in intelligence or aptitude, nothing can be done for him. But achievement is a different story. Here the schools have some responsibility. The student's achievement depends upon his applying his aptitude to a specific field of endeavor. It is obvious that no one is born educated; no matter how high his intelligence is, he can learn only to the extent that he applies himself. With equal effort the very bright student will learn more than the dull student; but if the person of lesser aptitude works more diligently than the individual with greater intelligence, he may indeed climb higher than his brighter associate who has less ambition and drive.

We psychologists are largely responsible for the overemphasis which the public gives to the IQ. Frankly, the IQ is overrated. Unfortunately, parents and even many teachers regard the IQ as an infallible and crucially significant index. As a result, they ignore the importance of the many other characteristics which contribute to attainment. In the final analysis it is not how bright one is, but what one has accomplished that counts. The IQ is an empirically determined index which has certain practical values when used with appropriate caution. However, it lacks a rigorous theoretical foundation. Actually it is a composite of a number of measures of different abilities. Ability is a many-sided affair, as Dael Wolfle pointed out in the Walter V. Bingham Memorial Lecture given a year ago, and any one person may be much better at some things than at others. The IQ represents an averaging of these abilities, and so it smooths over important peaks and valleys.

The gravest danger of the IQ, however, is that it gives a grossly oversimplified picture of the organization of the mind and encourages parents, teachers, and even the students themselves to underestimate the role of effort. The relationship between the IQ and productivity, even in scholarly fields, is not as high as is generally believed.

The pupil, the teacher, and the parent should put less faith in IQ. Motivation, ambition, the ability to direct one's efforts toward a specific goal, sheer energy level, if there is such a trait—these are the characteristics which, though they are difficult to measure, determine achievement. The burning desire to excel, to be first, to be best can wisely be traded for a dozen IQ points any day.

In every aspect of life it is what one accomplishes that counts, not what his unused intelligence is, or what he might have done under other circumstances. In the Merit Program the effort of the student is considered, and all students are encouraged to apply themselves to attain greater heights in the intellectual realm.

The screening test in the Merit Program is handled by a recognized testing agency, Science Research Associates. The National Merit Scholarship Corporation does not prepare tests, sell tests, or derive any money from test sales. The corporation does specify the nature of the test it wishes and the conditions that the contractor must meet in supplying the test. To meet the heavy costs of testing, each participant pays a fee of $1.00 directly to the testing agency. If a student is unable to pay this fee, the National Merit Scholarship Corporation pays it for him.

On the basis of this screening test, a group of 35,000 students is given some type of recognition each year. Though 35,000 is a large group, it represents less than 3% of the annual crop of high school graduates. In order to have students representative of every section of the United States, the top scoring students, the Semifinalists, are chosen separately for each state. In the United States, it is the state which establishes educational policies and procedures, and consequently states differ in their educational facilities and methods. It is assumed that if we select the very best from each state, the result will be a group of superior quality, with each state contributing its proper share. Geographic representation contributes to the vitality of any national program.

Of the 35,000 students who are given recognition each year, about 10,000 are named Semifinalists. They constitute the top group, with the more populous states having more representatives and the less populous states having fewer, just as in the lower house in our Congress. California, for example, has over 750 Semifinalists while Nevada has under 15.

In addition to the Semifinalists, who constitute less than 1% of the high school graduates, a second group is selected. The 25,000 students in this group are sent Letters of Commendation encouraging them to continue with their education. The number of commended students in each state varies according to the proportion scoring high on the test nationally, without regard to the state-by-state selection of the Semifinalists. In New York, for example, in 1960 there were almost 5,000 Letters of Commendation awarded, while in three of our states, fewer than 25 students won this honor.

The Letters of Commendation were introduced in the third year of the Merit Program. At that time some skepticism was expressed as to the value of a form of recognition which is not accompanied by any financial aid. However, the results of our preliminary studies indicate that such recognition has a stimulating influence on able students. It gives them more self-confidence, it encourages them to apply themselves, and it causes them to set somewhat higher intellectual goals in life. Public recognition by itself can have a beneficial effect. When properly handled, simple means can be effective in encouraging talent.

After the 10,000 Semifinalists have been selected, they are asked to take a second test, the Scholastic Aptitude Test of the College Board. Each Semifinalist is also requested to supply certain information about himself and to have his school submit his academic record and its recommendation. Virtually all of the Semifinalists, over 97%, meet these requirements and confirm their earlier test scores. They thereby become Finalists in the program, and are eligible to receive a Merit Scholarship.

Unfortunately there is not enough money available to award a Merit Scholarship to every Finalist. The field must be narrowed even further. The recipients of the National Merit Scholarships (unsponsored scholarships made possible by the founding grants) are chosen by a committee of people skilled in exercising the kind of judgment required. This committee meets to review the list of Finalists and, on the basis of the school's recommendations, the students' test scores, academic records, and outside activities and work, to select those students from each state whom they believe to be the most highly qualified. The number of scholarships awarded in each state is roughly proportional to the high school graduates in that state in the most recent year for which statistics are available.

In addition to the unsponsored National Merit Scholarships, the corporation distributes scholarships sponsored by corporations, foundations, and individuals. Many of these sponsors leave the selection of the winners of their scholarships to the same committee which selects the winners of National Merit Scholarships. However, a sponsor may, if he wishes to do so, choose from among the Finalist group (all of whom have proved themselves to be academically qualified) those students who meet their special interests. For example, some sponsors prefer students who have an interest in science; while some prefer students residing in certain geographic areas. Many sponsors are interested in helping to finance the education of any employees' children who achieve the high status of Finalist in the Merit Program.

The secondary schools are sent complete reports on every phase of the Merit Program. In addition, the Semifinalists are listed in a book which is distributed to all colleges and other scholarship-granting agencies. Partly as a result of this distribution of names, these students receive many additional scholarship offers. About half of the Semifinalists receive either a Merit Scholarship or some other offer of financial aid.

When the students take the initial selecting test, they are asked to name the two colleges they would prefer to attend. Each college is sent a list of the students who have named that particular institution with the students' scores on the screening test. As a result, each student on the list is likely to be given greater consideration by the college for admission or financial aid than he otherwise might.

The Merit Finalists are selected without regard to their financial need. The selection is based on ability only. Thus the student selected for a Merit Scholarship may be one whose family is able to support him in college, or he may be one who needs outside help in financing his college career. On the basis of this information the amount of money to accompany the scholarship is determined. The amount depends upon the family's ability to support the student at the college of his choice.

In determining the extent of a student's need two factors are considered. The first is the amount of money the family can be expected to contribute, and the second is the cost of attending the college selected by the student. The individual stipends range from a minimum of $100 a year to a maximum of $1,500 a year. Each scholarship covers 4 years of college, assuming that the winner progresses at a normal rate and does satisfactory work.

The need factor is re-evaluated each year. If it is found that the ability of the family to support the student has changed, a new stipend is set. For example, the need of one student, the son of a business executive, was assessed at $100 a year at the time he won his scholarship. During the student's freshman year in college his father suffered a fatal heart attack. The Scholar's situation was then re-evaluated and his stipend was changed from the minimum to the maximum of $1,500 a year. In a sense, a Merit Scholarship is an insurance policy.

About a third of the Merit Scholars currently receive an annual stipend of $250 or less. At the other extreme, about 20% receive the maximum stipend of $1,500. At the present time, the average stipend is around $827 a year. Even when the amount received is only $250 or $300 a year, it can make the difference between the student's attending the college of his choice and his going to an institution which he believes to be less satisfactory. The Merit Scholarship money therefore is of major significance to most of the students.

In addition to the stipend paid to the Merit Scholar, each scholarship is accompanied by a grant to the college to be used in whatever way the college wishes. The purpose of this grant is to call public attention to the importance of assisting privately supported colleges. In 1959–60 over $750,000 was paid to the colleges. During the same year, payments to the students amounted to over $2,200,000.

Obviously, the Merit Scholar has been selected with great care from among hundreds of thousands of participants, and he is an interesting—sometimes an exciting—young person. He has scored in the top fraction, about 1%, of the high school seniors in his state. His high school academic record and recommendations are superior. His activities outside the classroom testify that he is a person of some breadth. He has been chosen as representative of the most intellectually promising of the younger generation.

In selecting scholarship winners, no consideration is given to the student's family background or social and economic status, nor is his being from the city or the country taken into account. The task is to select the most promising young people without regard to their financial need. After this has been done it is possible—as a part of the research activity, not the scholarship program as such—to check into parental occupations. As might be expected, many of the winners have parents who are well educated; the father is a physician, a lawyer, a teacher, or an executive. The interesting fact, however, is that many of the parents have more ordinary occupations.

Among the parents of the group awarded Merit Scholarships in 1959, we find barbers, bookkeepers, butchers, cab drivers, carpenters, cashiers, chauffeurs, clerks, construction workers, electricians, farmers, firemen, glass workers, junk collectors, mail carriers, mechanics, and painters. Of course some of the fathers are accountants, attorneys, business executives, clergymen, college administrators, editors, economists, physicians, and teachers. Clearly, ability is where you find it; one cannot tell from a parent's occupation or social and economic background whether or not the child will have unusual mental ability. That is why equality of educational opportunity is prized in a democracy.

The personalities of Merit Scholars are of particular interest. The public usually thinks of the very bright young student as a rather peculiar, introverted type—smaller in physique than the average, somewhat antisocial, and rather narrow in his interests.

But this image is a false one. The brainy can be brawny too. Research has shown that gifted young people are generally taller, heavier, and physically and mentally healthier than those of average intelligence. From studies of Merit Scholars we know that they have a tendency to be dominant in social situations, or more accurately, not to be submissive. They have a greater interest in people, less tendency to withdraw from social situations, and more sophistication and self-confidence than the average person. They are less tense, less anxious, less given to feelings of insecurity or depression. They show unusual originality, imagination, and resourcefulness. Most important, perhaps, researchers have characterized the Merit Scholars as "risk-takers in the field of ideas."

Where do these Scholars choose to go to college? There are well over a thousand 4-year, degree granting colleges in the United States. Since the Merit Scholars are selected from every state in the Union, it might be expected that they would spread themselves among the colleges more or less evenly. But quite the contrary is the case. A relatively small number of colleges are chosen by this high quality group of students. In the school year 1960–61, Merit Scholars are attending some four hundred different colleges and universities. One institution alone, Harvard College, has attracted almost 10% of the Merit Scholars. The 12 colleges most popular with this group attract about a third of the Merit Scholars. These are, in order: Harvard, Massachusetts Institute of Technology, Stanford, Radcliffe, Princeton, California Institute of Technology, Yale, Rice, University of Michigan, Oberlin, Swarthmore, and Cornell.

In March 1960, the 34,000 highest scoring students (who were then juniors in high school) were asked to name the one college they most wanted to attend. If any bias enters this poll, it is unknown. In this popularity contest, in which only the very brightest students have a vote, we again find a marked preference for a small number of institutions. Over one-third of these very able young men wished to attend the following colleges in the order named: Massachusetts Institute of Technology, Harvard, California Institute of Technology, Stanford, Princeton, Cornell, Yale, University of California at Berkeley, Notre Dame, and University of Michigan. Approximately one-fifth of the girls named as their first choice the following 10 institutions (listed in order of their popularity): Radcliffe, Stanford, Cornell, Wellesley, University of Michigan, University of California at Berkeley, Oberlin, Smith, Swarthmore, and Northwestern.

If we consider the number of these able students who named a particular college as a percentage of the number of students that institution admits, we get a different rank order. For the male students, California Institute of Technology was named by somewhat over four times the number of students it admits into its entering class. Next in order is Massachusetts Institute of Technology named by almost twice the number of students it admits in its freshman class. Following these two institutions come in order: Harvard, Rice, Amherst, Swarthmore, Reed, Stanford, Princeton, University of Chicago, Oberlin, Yale, Columbia, Dartmouth, Carleton, and Wesleyan University—all attracting from this very select group a vote equal to 30% or more of its entering class. If we consider the girls and rank the colleges according to their popularity with this superior group, but relative to the size of the incoming freshman class, we get this order: Swarthmore, Radcliffe, Middlebury, Rice, Stanford, Reed, Oberlin, Cornell, Carleton, Wellesley, Bryn Mawr, Smith, University of Chicago, Barnard, and Mount Holyoke.

These figures may not have any great significance. Because a student named a college as his preference, it does not necessarily follow that he is equipped intellectually, socially, or financially to attend that college, or that he would be accepted by it. We need a good deal more information before we can adequately interpret this popular vote. However, the public's interest in such polls suggests that they are worthy of some consideration. No popularity contest should be allowed to obscure the difficult problem of matching a particular student with the institution which will bring about his maximum development. In the high school-college guidance work to date too frequently the blind have been leading the blind.

One problem encountered by the Merit Program is the tendency of the public and the press to use the results of the program as an index of the value of a particular school or college. The public is apt to conclude quite erroneously that the colleges which are most popular with Merit Scholars are the best colleges for all students. Likewise, secondary schools having a large number of Finalists in the Merit Program are sometimes said to be "better" than other schools having a smaller number of Finalists. But the quality or effectiveness of a school cannot properly be judged by the number of its students who win awards in the Merit Program. All selections are made on an individual basis. The distribution of the population throughout a state, the size of a school, the native intelligence of its top students, the nature of the community where the school is located, and many other factors having nothing to do with the total effectiveness of a school can influence its number of award winners. Although it is recognized that award winners bring honor to their schools and their parents as well as to themselves, the press and the public are encouraged to judge each student individually and to refrain from comparisons of schools and colleges.

What has been the college record of Merit Scholars? The first class of Merit Scholars entered college in the fall of 1956. This initial group numbered 555, 402 (72%) of them boys and 153 (28%) girls. Of the first group, 88% of the girls and 81% of the boys have now graduated.

The outstanding record made by those who have graduated is striking. Over 60% stood in the top 10% of their class; a fifth of the group was in the top 1%. About 80% graduated with some academic honor. A number led their class—like the charming young woman who selected a college of mining and ranked first in her class, composed mainly of men, every 1 of the 4 years, graduating with high honors and incidentally gaining a husband in the process. Both are now in graduate school.

Their records in campus leadership were also outstanding. About 1 in 5 held leadership positions. Many Merit Scholars were editors of major campus publications and presidents of major student government organizations and living groups, and 20 won their letters in varsity sports.

Of these graduates, 18% of the boys and 37% of the girls have married. Slightly over 10% of the original group are still in college, because they are taking 5-year programs or because they took a year out for some reason. It is anticipated that approximately 94% of the original group will receive college degrees within 5 years after entering college.

Up to the present time slightly over 6% of this first group have left the program for one reason or another. Only 17 Merit Scholars had their scholarships terminated because of unsatisfactory work in colleges of their choice, and more than half of these students are back in college today. Fifteen Merit Scholars—eight girls and seven boys—withdrew from college while in good academic standing. Most of the girls withdrew in order to marry, and of these the majority expect to complete their degree requirements eventually.

Most of the first group of Merit Scholars are continuing their formal education beyond the bachelor's degree. Over 80% of the men and almost 60% of the women in this group plan to go on to graduate or professional schools. Eighty percent of them hold fellowships and assistantships, about half from sources outside the college or university.

The Merit Scholars obviously are a distinguished group. But what of those Finalists who did not win scholarships? We have found that over 94% go on to college. About one-half of the group are receiving some type of scholarship aid and we believe we have helped them to do so.

Of the boys who took the screening test and who ranked in the top third of all juniors in the country, about 87% are now full-time students in some college. The same is true of about 77% of the girls. Many of these students have received some scholarship help, and research shows that the higher an individual's test score, the greater the probability that he holds a scholarship.

In a recent study, one of the research staff members examined the nature of academic achievement and creative behavior in the Finalists. He finds support for the idea that the creative person (as opposed to the academic achiever) is one who is independent, intellectual, expressive, asocial, and consciously original. The mothers of creative persons are permissive and ready to accept the ideas and impulses of the young, while their fathers want them to be curious and self-reliant.

Preliminary research results suggest that these creative people are not favored by the groups who select scholarship winners. At present there are no adequate measures of potential creativity, although researchers at Merit and other places are beginning to make progress on this problem.

John Holland, Director of Research for the National Merit Scholarship Program, has written:

> It is imperative that we learn how to identify the creative person so that we can seek out and encourage such students, whatever their application form debits. They should not be penalized for their failure to play the good boy role for their high school teachers, or to satisfy the pointless demand for well-roundedness by dissipating their energies in a frenetic round of extracurricular activities and good works.

This year the Merit Program is testing some preliminary notions about creativity by selecting a small group of students from its Finalists who appear to be particularly creative.

Has the Merit Program succeeded in encouraging the recognition and development of talent? Measurement of impacts of an attack on such a broad front is difficult; we must allow more time for the dust to settle before we can take sightings. The first class of Merit Scholars is just getting under way in graduate school.

The letters of comment which reach us are overwhelmingly favorable. One official from a small college comments on the leavening effect of its six Merit Scholars:

> It is difficult to estimate the impact which these six students are having on the campus, but beyond all doubt it is terrific.

States a college president:

> The program has been successful in influencing the junior and senior high school students to approach their academic programs with seriousness of purpose which was not common a few years ago.

The chancellor of the Telluride Association, who visits many schools each year, attributes much of the high school student's changed attitude toward academic work to the influence of the Merit Program. He goes on to say:

> It is getting so a man may be a first-class scholar in a high school today and not lose social caste.

A high school principal writes:

> The Merit Program is making a critical contribution to educational thought . . . the most wonderful thing about your work is that its influence will be everlasting, for it affects profoundly the lives of boys and girls.

From the students themselves we occasionally receive some heart-warming letters. For example, a young lady from Indiana writes:

> Your program was no small factor in causing me to go to college. You see I am the first person in my family who ever indicated a desire to attend college. My parents did not even attend high school. As a result, it was not easy to convince myself and my family that college was for me. However, when I won a Certificate of Merit I was convinced I should go to college, and it helped me to win my parents over to my view.

The press's coverage of the Merit Program, increasing each year, gives evidence of the public's growing interest. Among the clippings which arrived this month was a letter to an Illinois newspaper from one of the recently graduated Merit Scholars. He says in part:

> The most significant effect of the National Merit Program is not conservation or insurance, but stimulation. National Merit winners and Finalists acquire recognition and self-realization that (1) prompts those to go to college who might not have done so otherwise, whether they received a scholarship or not; (2) encourages them to go to colleges where there is a keener competition and a greater exchange of ideas; (3) produces an incentive to work commensurate with ability. This stimulation is not a short-lived thing; it builds upon itself. The high percentage of Merit Scholars who have gone into graduate study is some evidence of this. In my own case I believe that I can say that my desire for worthwhile achievement is at present stronger than it ever was.

Evidence by testimonial, however interesting, is not convincing to the scientist. After an additional several years have gone by, an attempt will be made to obtain more accurate estimates of the impact of the Merit Program.

Because the data on talented students which have been collected are of an unparalleled quality and magnitude, the research activities of the Merit Program are particularly important and promising. Much of our research is directed toward developing new methods of scholarship selection. Heretofore, the very success of the objective scholastic aptitude and college readiness tests has discouraged experimentation with measures of other significant characteristics. It might be valuable, for example, to study such background factors as the family, the community, and the friends of able students, to ask what cultural elements in the student's background contribute to develop his talent to a productive level. The student's scholarly activity independent of classroom work may also be of greater significance than has been suspected previously.

It is difficult to assess the significance of personal characteristics not measured by the widely used scholarship selection tests, but more thorough measurement in this area may prove to be important in the identification of able persons who will be productive after college.

The Merit Program is conducting research in several other areas. The results of its research are being reported in the professional journals and through technical progress reports. This research activity, a fundamental part of the Merit Program, contributes to the health of the entire program and prevents any of the procedures from becoming frozen.

In many ways the Merit Program is a pilot venture, making explorations in an important but very complex field. By working with schools throughout the entire land, with their ablest pupils, and with the colleges which attract such students, the Merit Program gains experience in recognizing and encouraging talent. We are establishing a few guideposts and a few warning signs.

Consider an example. Talent loss is a concept which we are working to define more meaningfully. For the moment we will take it to refer to those students who are capable of doing superior college work but do not go to college. Many of these students, most of whom are girls, come from lower socioeconomic levels and from areas where college attendance is unusual. Apart from financial need, lack of motivation is the primary cause of their not going on to college. If we are to prevent this talent loss—and prevent it we must—we must identify these students in the seventh or eighth grade, perhaps even earlier.

Such talented young pupils should be introduced early in their lives to the world of ideas, to books, to scientific laboratories, and to the fun of learning. When optional routes are offered in high school, they should be guided down the path of heavy intellectual activity. Only in this way will they be both motivated and prepared to compete in the latter years of high school; only in this way can they win their share of financial help for college. Early stimulation, followed by superior educational opportunities, is the key.

Of the many things we have learned in operating the Merit Program for 5 years, the most significant is how little we know about identifying creative talent, and how much less about its proper development. The extensive folklore about able students and scholarships must be challenged, if more effective procedures are to be developed. Every sizable scholarship program should have a companion research program to find out what effect it is having, and how it can do the job better.

To discover talent we must initiate bold new methods based on sound theory and applied with imagination and practical ingenuity. Private ventures, like the Merit Program, should not be afraid to experiment, to attempt new approaches, to venture beyond established practices.

The Merit Program will continue to experiment and to learn. It will continue to encourage the public to honor intellectual excellence, to excite each community about its own able youth, to make higher education a possible goal for many students of demonstrated promise, and to create a climate favorable to intellectual excellence. It is an action program dedicated to recognizing and encouraging talent, goals which many years ago Bingham knew were among the most important ones toward which citizens of a democracy must strive. In the words of John Gardner: ". . . an undiscovered talent, a wasted skill, a misapplied ability is a threat to the capacity of a free people to survive."

Donald W. MacKinnon

The Nature and Nurture of Creative Talent[1]

Let me say first how deeply appreciative I am of the honor of having been chosen the Walter Van Dyke Bingham Lecturer for 1962. It has for me especial meaning to be provided this opportunity to honor the memory of a man I respected so much and whose work was such a pioneering contribution to that field of psychology to which I have given most of my energies as a psychologist. I am grateful, too, for this opportunity to express to Mrs. Bingham the gratitude of all psychologists for her generosity in establishing this series of annual lectures on the discovery and development of exceptional abilities and capacities. Our literature has been greatly enriched by the lectures which she has made possible.

I should like also to congratulate Yale University for having been chosen this year as the institution to be honored for its contributions to the study of talent, and to thank all those who have made such pleasant arrangements for this occasion.

1. This paper is based on the Walter Van Dyke Bingham Lecture given at Yale University, New Haven, Connecticut, April 11, 1962. It was first published in the *American Psychologist*, 1962, vol. 17, no. 7 (July), pp. 484–495.

There is a story, first told I believe by Mark Twain which, had Dr. Bingham known it, would have been, I am sure, one of his favorites. It is about a man who sought the greatest general who had ever lived. Upon inquiring as to where this individual might be found, he was told that the person he sought had died and gone to Heaven. At the Pearly Gates he informed St. Peter of the purpose of his quest, whereupon St. Peter pointed to a soul nearby. "But that," protested the inquirer, "isn't the greatest of all generals. I knew that person when he lived on earth, and he was only a cobbler." "I know that," replied St. Peter, "but if he had been a general he would have been the greatest of them all."

Dr. Bingham spent his life worrying about cobblers who might have been generals and indeed about all those who fail to become what they are capable of becoming because neither they nor others recognize their potentialities and nourish their realization. Dr. Bingham was one of the first to insist that it is not enough to recognize creative talent after it has come to expression. He reminded us that it is our task as psychologists and as educators either through our insights or through the use of validated predictors to discover talent when it is still potential and to provide that kind of social climate and intellectual environment which will facilitate its development and expression.

Whatever light I shall be able to shed on the nature and nurture of creative talent comes in the main from findings of researches carried on during the last six years in the Institute of Personality Assessment and Research on the Berkeley campus of the University of California, and supported in large part by the Carnegie Corporation of New York.

In undertaking such a study one of our first tasks was to decide what we would consider creativity to be. This was necessary, first, because creativity has been so variously described and defined, and second, because only when we had come to agreement as to how we would conceive creativity would we be in a position to know what kinds of persons we would want to study.

We came easily to agreement that true creativeness fulfills at least three conditions. It involves a response or an idea that is novel or at the very least statistically infrequent. But novelty or originality of thought or action, while a necessary aspect of creativity, is not sufficient. If a response is to lay claim to being a part of the creative process, it must to some extent be adaptive to, or of, reality. It must serve to solve a problem, fit a situation, or accomplish some recognizable goal. And, thirdly, true creativeness involves a sustaining of the original insight, an evaluation and elaboration of it, a developing of it to the full.

Creativity, from this point of view, is a process extended in time and characterized by originality, adaptiveness, and realization. It may be brief, as in a musical improvisation, or it may involve a considerable span of years as was required for Darwin's creation of the theory of evolution.

The acceptance of such a conception of creativity had two important consequences for our researches. It meant that we would not seek to study creativity while it was still potential but only after it had been realized and had found expression in clearly identifiable creative products—buildings designed by architects, mathematical proofs developed by mathematicians, and the published writings of poets and novelists. Our conception of creativity forced us further to reject as indicators or criteria of creativeness the performance of individuals on so-called tests of creativity. While tests of this sort, that require that the subject think, for example, of unusual uses for common objects and the consequences of unusual events, may indeed measure the infrequency or originality of a subject's ideas in response to specific test items, they fail to reveal the extent to which the subject faced with real life problems is likely to come up with solutions that are novel and adaptive and which he will be motivated to apply in all of their ramifications.

Having thus determined that we would limit our researches to the study of persons who had already demonstrated a high level of creative work, we were still confronted with the problem of deciding from which fields of creative endeavor we would seek to recruit our subjects.

The fields which we finally sampled were those of creative writing, architecture, mathematics, industrial research, physical science, and engineering.

If one considers these activities in relation to the distinction often made between artistic and scientific creativity, it may be noted that we have sampled both of these domains as well as overlapping domains of creative striving which require that the practitioner be at one and the same time both artist and scientist.

Artistic creativity, represented in our studies by the work of poets, novelists, and essayists, results in products that are clearly expressions of the creator's inner states, his needs, perceptions, motivations, and the like. In this type of creativity, the creator externalizes something of himself into the public field.

In scientific creativity, the creative product is unrelated to the creator as a person, who in his creative work acts largely as a mediator between externally defined needs and goals. In this kind of creativeness, the creator, represented in our studies by industrial researchers, physical scientists, and engineers, simply operates on some aspect of his environment in such a manner as to produce a novel and appropriate product, but he adds little of himself or of his style as a person to the resultant.

Domains of creative striving in which the practitioner must be both artist and scientist were represented in our researches by mathematicians and architects. Mathematicians contribute to science, yet in a very real sense their important creative efforts are as much as anything else personal cosmologies in which they express themselves as does the artist in his creations. So, too, in architecture, creative products are both an expression of the architect and thus a very personal product, and at the same time an impersonal meeting of the demands of an external problem.

If in reporting the findings of our researches I draw most heavily upon data obtained from our study of architects (MacKinnon, 1962), it is for two reasons. First, it is the study for which, in collaboration with Wallace B. Hall, I have assumed primary responsibility. Second, it is in architects, of all our samples, that we can expect to find what is most generally characteristic of creative persons. Architecture, as a field of creative endeavor, requires that the successful practitioner be both artist and scientist—artist in that his designs must fulfill the demands of "Delight," and scientist in that they must meet the demands of "Firmnesse" and "Commodity," to use the words of Sir Henry Wotton (1624). But surely, one can hardly think that the requirements of effective architecture are limited to these three demands. The successful and effective architect must, with the skill of a juggler, combine, reconcile, and exercise the diverse skills of businessman, lawyer, artist, engineer, and advertising man, as well as those of author and journalist, psychiatrist, educator, and psychologist. In what other profession can one expect better to observe the multifarious expressions of creativity?

It should be clear that any attempt to discover the distinguishing traits of creative persons can succeed only in so far as some group of qualified experts can agree upon who are the more and who are the less creative workers in a given field of endeavor. In our study of architects we began by asking a panel of experts—five professors of architecture, each working independently—to nominate the 40 most creative architects in the United States. All told they supplied us with 86 names instead of the 40 they would have mentioned had there been perfect agreement among them. While 13 of the 86 architects were nominated by all five panel members, and 9 nominated by four, 11 by three, and 13 by two,

40 were individual nominations each proposed by a single panel member.

The agreement among experts is not perfect, yet far greater than one might have expected. Later we asked 11 editors of the American architectural journals, *Architectural Forum*, *Architectural Record*, the *Journal of the American Institute of Architects*, and *Progressive Architecture*, to rate the creativity of the 64 of the nominated architects whom we invited to participate in the study. Still later we asked the 40 nominated creative architects who actually accepted our invitation to be studied to rate the creativity of the invited 64 architects, themselves included. Since the editors' ratings of the creativity of the architects correlated +.88 with the architects' own ratings, it is clear that under certain conditions and for certain groups it is possible to obtain remarkable agreement about the relative creativeness of individual members of a profession and thus meet the first requirement for an effective study of creative persons.

A second requirement for the successful establishment of the traits of creative individuals is their willingness to make themselves available for study. Our hope was to win the cooperation of each person whom we invited to participate in the research, but as I have already indicated in the case of the architects, to obtain 40 acceptances, 64 invitations had to be sent out.

The invitation to this group, as to all the creative groups which we have studied, was to come to Berkeley for a weekend of intensive study in the Institute of Personality Assessment and Research. There, in groups of tens, they have been studied by the variety of means which constitute the assessment method—by problem-solving experiments; by tests designed to discover what a person does not know or is unable or unwilling to reveal about himself; by tests and questionnaires that permit a person to manifest various aspects of his personality and to express his attitudes, interests, and values; by searching interviews that cover the life history and reveal the present structure of the person; and by specially contrived social situations of a stressful character which call for the subject's best behavior in a socially defined role.

The response of creative persons to the invitation to reveal themselves under such trying circumstances has varied considerably. At the one extreme there have been those who replied in anger at what they perceived to be the audacity of psychologists in presuming to study so ineffable and mysterious a thing as the creative process and so sensitive a being as a creative person. At the other extreme were those who replied courteously and warmheartedly, welcoming the invitation to be studied, and manifesting even an eagerness to contribute to a better understanding of the creative person and the creative process.

Here we were face to face with a problem that plagues us in all our researches: Are those who are willing to be assessed different in important ways from those who refuse? With respect to psychological traits and characteristics we can never know. But with respect to differences in creativeness, if any, between the 40 who accepted and the 24 who declined our invitation, we know that the two groups are indistinguishable. When the nominating panel's ratings of creativity were converted to standard scores and the means for the 24 versus the 40 were compared, they were found to be identical. When the editors' ratings were similarly converted to standard scores, the mean for the nonassessed group was slightly higher (51.9) than for the assessed sample (48.7), but the difference is not statistically significant.

Certainly we cannot claim to have assessed the 40 most creative architects in the country, or the most creative of any of the groups we have studied; but it is clear that we have studied a highly creative group of architects indistinguishable in their creativity from the group of 24 who declined to be studied, and so with the other groups too.

A third requirement for the successful determination of the traits of highly creative persons in any field of endeavor is that the profession be widely sampled beyond those nominated as most creative, for the distinguishing characteristics of the restricted sample might well have nothing to do with their creativeness. Instead they might be traits characterizing all members of the profession whether creative or not, distinguishing the professional group as a whole but in no sense limited or peculiar to its highly creative members. In the case of the architects, to use them once again as an example, two additional samples were recruited for study, both of which matched the highly creative sample (whom I shall now call Architects I) with respect to age and geographic location of practice. The first supplementary sample (Architects II) had had at least two years of work experience and association with one of the originally nominated creative architects. The second additional sample (Architects III) was composed of architects who had never worked with any of the nominated creatives.

By selecting three samples in this manner, we hoped to tap a range of talent sufficiently wide to be fairly representative of the profession as a whole; and we appear to have succeeded. The mean rating of creativity for each of the three groups—the ratings having been made on a nine-point scale by six groups of architects and experts on architecture—was for Architects I, 5.46; for Architects II, 4.25; and for Architects III, 3.54, the differences in mean ratings between each group being statistically highly significant.

So much for method and research design. I turn now to a discussion of the nature of creative talent as it has been revealed to us in our researches.

Persons who are highly creative are inclined to have a good opinion of themselves, as evidenced by the large number of favorable adjectives which they use in self-description and by the relatively high scores they earn on a scale which measures basic acceptance of the self. Indeed, there is here a paradox, for in addition to their favorable self-perceptions the very basic self-acceptance of the more creative persons often permits them to speak more frankly and thus more critically and in unusual ways about themselves. It is clear, too, that the self-images of the more creative differ from the self-images of the less creative. For example, Architects I, in contrast to Architects II and III, more often describe themselves as inventive, determined, independent, individualistic, enthusiastic, and industrious. In striking contrast Architects II and III more often than Architects I describe themselves as responsible, sincere, reliable, dependable, clear thinking, tolerant, and understanding. In short, where creative architects more often stress their inventiveness, independence, and individuality, their enthusiasm, determination, and industry, less creative members of the profession are impressed by their virtue and good character and by their rationality and sympathetic concern for others.

The discrepancies between their descriptions of themselves as they are and as they would ideally be are remarkably alike for all architects regardless of their level of creativeness. All three groups reveal themselves as desiring more personal attractiveness, self-confidence, maturity, and intellectual competence, a higher level of energy, and better social relations. As for differences, however, Architects I would ideally be more sensitive, while both Architects II and III wish for opposites if not incompatibles; they would ideally be more original but at the same time more self-controlled and disciplined.

As for the relation between intelligence and creativity, save for the mathematicians where there is a low positive correlation between intelligence and the level of creativeness, we have found within our creative samples essentially zero relationship between the two variables, and this is not due to a narrow restriction in range of intelligence. Among creative architects who have a mean score of 113 on the Terman Concept Mastery Test (1956), individual scores range widely from 39 to 179, yet scores on this measure of intelligence correlate −.08 with rated creativity. Over the whole range of intelligence and creativity there is, of course, a positive relationship between the two variables. No feeble-minded subjects have shown up in any of our creative groups. It is clear, however, that above a certain required minimum level of intelligence which varies from field to field and in some instances may be surprisingly low, being more intelligent does not guarantee a corresponding increase in creativeness. It just is not true that the more intelligent person is necessarily the more creative one.

In view of the often asserted close association of genius with insanity it is also of some interest to inquire into the psychological health of our creative subjects. To this end we can look at their profiles on the Minnesota Multiphasic Personality Inventory (MMPI) (Hathaway & McKinley, 1945), a test originally developed to measure tendencies toward the major psychiatric disturbances that man is heir to: depression, hysteria, paranoia, schizophrenia, and the like. On the eight scales which measure the strength of these dispositions in the person, our creative subjects earn scores which, on the average, are some 5 to 10 points above the general population's average score of 50. It must be noted, however, that elevated scores of this degree on these scales do not have the same meaning for the personality functioning of persons who, like our subjects, are getting along well in their personal lives and professional careers, that they have for hospitalized patients. The manner in which creative subjects describe themselves on this test as well as in the life history psychiatric interview is less suggestive of psychopathology than it is of good intellect, complexity and richness of personality, general lack of defensiveness, and candor in self-description—in other words, an openness to experience and especially to experience of one's inner life. It must also be noted, however, that in the self-reports and in the MMPI profiles of many of our creative subjects, one can find rather clear evidence of psychopathology, but also evidence of adequate control mechanisms, as the success with which they live their productive and creative lives testifies.

However, the most striking aspect of the MMPI profiles of all our male creative groups is an extremely high peak on the *Mf* (femininity) scale. This tendency for creative males to score relatively high on femininity is also demonstrated on the Fe (femininity) scale of the California Psychological Inventory (CPI) (Gough, 1957) and on the masculinity-femininity scale of the Strong Vocational Interest Blank (Strong, 1959). Scores on the latter scale (where high score indicates more masculinity) correlate −.49 with rated creativity.

The evidence is clear: The more creative a person is the more he reveals an openness to his own feelings and emotions, a sensitive intellect and understanding self-awareness, and wide-ranging interests including many which in the American culture are thought of as feminine. In the realm of sexual identification and interests, our creative subjects appear to give more expression to the feminine side of their nature than do less creative persons. In the language of the Swiss psychologist, Carl G. Jung (1956), creative persons are not so completely identified with their masculine *persona* roles as to blind themselves to or to deny expression to the more feminine traits of the *anima*. For some, to be sure, the balance between masculine and feminine traits, interests, and identification, is a precarious one, and for several of our subjects it would appear that their presently achieved reconciliation of these opposites of their nature has been barely effected and only after considerable psychic stress and turmoil.

The perceptiveness of the creative and his openness to richness and complexity of experience is strikingly revealed on the Barron-Welsh Art Scale of the Welsh Figure Preference Test

(Welsh, 1959), which presents to the subject a set of 62 abstract line drawings which range from simple and symmetrical figures to complex and asymmetrical ones. In the original study (Barron & Welsh, 1952) which standardized this scale, some 80 painters from New York, San Francisco, New Orleans, Chicago, and Minneapolis showed a marked preference for the complex and asymmetrical, or, as they often referred to them, the vital and dynamic figures. A contrasting sample of nonartists revealed a marked preference for the simple and symmetrical drawings.

All creative groups we have studied have shown a clear preference for the complex and asymmetrical, and in general the more creative a person is the stronger is this preference. Similarly, in our several samples, scores on an Institute scale which measures the preference for perceptual complexity are significantly correlated with creativity. In the sample of architects the correlation is +.48.

Presented with a large selection of one-inch squares of varicolored poster board and asked to construct within a 30-minute period a pleasing, completely filled-in 8″ × 10″ mosaic (Hall, 1958), some subjects select the fewest colors possible (one used only one color, all white) while others seek to make order out of the largest possible number, using all of the 22 available colors. And, again citing results from the architects, there is a significant though low positive correlation of +.38 between the number of colors a subject chooses and his creativity as rated by the experts.

If one considers for a moment the meaning of these preferences on the art scale, on the mosaic test, and on the scale that measures preference for perceptual complexity, it is clear that creative persons are especially disposed to admit complexity and even disorder into their perceptions without being made anxious by the resulting chaos. It is not so much that they like disorder per se, but that they prefer the richness of the disordered to the stark barrenness of the simple. They appear to be challenged by disordered multiplicity which arouses in them a strong need which in them is serviced by a superior capacity to achieve the most difficult and far-reaching ordering of the richness they are willing to experience.

The creative person's openness to experience is further revealed on the Myers-Briggs Type Indicator (Myers, 1958), a test based largely upon Carl G. Jung's (1923) theory of psychological functions and types.

Employing the language of the test, though in doing so I oversimplify both it and the theory upon which it is based, one might say that whenever a person uses his mind for any purpose, he performs either an act of perception (he becomes aware of something) or an act of judgment (he comes to a conclusion about something). And most persons tend to show a rather consistent preference for and greater pleasure in one or the other of these, preferring either to perceive or to judge, though everyone both perceives and judges.

An habitual preference for the judging attitude may lead to some prejudging and at the very least to the living of a life that is orderly, controlled, and carefully planned. A preference for the perceptive attitude results in a life that is more open to experience both from within and from without, and characterized by flexibility and spontaneity. A judging type places more emphasis upon the control and regulation of experience, while a perceptive type is inclined to be more open and receptive to all experience.

The majority of our creative writers, mathematicians, and architects are perceptive types. Only among research scientists do we find the majority to be judging types, and even in this group it is interesting to note that there is a positive correlation (+.25) between a scientist's preference for perception and his rated creativity as a scientific researcher. For architects, preference for perception correlates +.41 with rated creativity.

The second preference measured by the Type Indicator is for one of two types of perception: sense perception or sensation, which is a direct becoming aware of things by way of the senses versus intuitive perception or intuition, which is an indirect perception of the deeper meanings and possibilities inherent in things and situations. Again, everyone senses and intuits, but preliminary norms for the test suggest that in the United States three out of four persons show a preference for sense perception, concentrating upon immediate sensory experience and centering their attention upon existing facts. The one out of every four who shows a preference for intuitive perception, on the other hand, looks expectantly for a bridge or link between that which is given and present and that which is not yet thought of, focusing habitually upon possibilities.

One would expect creative persons not to be bound to the stimulus and the object but to be ever alert to the as-yet-not-realized. And that is precisely the way they show themselves to be on the Type Indicator. In contrast to an estimated 25% of the general population who are intuitive, 90% of the creative writers, 92% of the mathematicians, 93% of the research scientists, and 100% of the architects are intuitive as measured by this test.

In judging or evaluating experience, according to the underlying Jungian theory of the test, one makes use of thought or of feeling; thinking being a logical process aimed at an impersonal fact-weighing analysis, while feeling is a process of appreciation and evaluation of things that gives them a personal and subjective value. A preference for thinking or for feeling appears to be less related to one's creativity as such than to the type of materials or concepts with which one deals. Of our creative groups, writers prefer feeling, mathematicians, research scientists, and engineers prefer thinking, while architects split fifty-fifty in their preference for one or the other of the two functions.

The final preference in Jungian typology and on the test is the well-known one between introversion and extraversion. Approximately two-thirds of all our creative groups score as introverts, though there is no evidence that introverts as such are more creative than extraverts.

Turning to preferences among interests and values, one would expect the highly creative to be rather different from less creative people, and there is clear evidence that they are.

On the Strong Vocational Interest Blank, which measures the similarity of a person's expressed interests with the known interests of individuals successful in a number of occupations and professions, all of our creative subjects have shown, with only slight variation from group to group, interests similar to those of the psychologist, author-journalist, lawyer, architect, artist, and musician, and interests unlike those of the purchasing agent, office man, banker, farmer, carpenter, veterinarian, and interestingly enough, too, policeman and mortician. Leaving aside any consideration of the specific interests thus revealed we may focus our attention on the inferences that may be drawn from this pattern of scores which suggest that creative persons are relatively uninterested in small details, or in facts for their own sake, and more concerned with their meanings and implications, possessed of considerable cognitive flexibility, verbally skillful, interested in communicating with others and accurate in so doing, intellectually curious, and relatively disinterested in policing either their own impulses and images or those of others.

On the Allport-Vernon-Lindzey Study of Values (1951), a test designed to measure in the individual the relative strength of the six values of men as these values have been conceptualized and described by the German psychologist and educator, Eduard Spranger (1928), namely, the theoretical, economic, esthetic, social, political, and religious values, all of our creative groups have as their highest values the theoretical and the esthetic.

For creative research scientists the theoretical value is the highest, closely followed by the esthetic. For creative architects the highest value is the esthetic, with the theoretical value almost as high. For creative mathematicians, the two values are both high and approximately equally strong.

If, as the authors of the test believe, there is some incompatibility and conflict between the theoretical value with its cognitive and rational concern with truth and the esthetic value with its emotional concern with form and beauty, it would appear that the creative person has the capacity to tolerate the tension that strong opposing values create in him, and in his creative striving he effects some reconciliation of them. For the truly creative person it is not sufficient that problems be solved; there is the further demand that the solutions be elegant. He seeks both truth and beauty.

A summary description of the creative person—especially of the creative architect—as he reveals himself in his profile on the California Psychological Inventory (Gough, 1957) reads as follows:

> He is dominant (Do scale); possessed of those qualities and attributes which underlie and lead to the achievement of social status (Cs); poised, spontaneous, and self-confident in personal and social interaction (Sp); though not of an especially sociable or participative temperament (low Sy); intelligent, outspoken, sharp-witted, demanding, aggressive, and self-centered; persuasive and verbally fluent, self-confident and self-assured (Sa); and relatively uninhibited in expressing his worries and complaints (low Wb).
>
> He is relatively free from conventional restraints and inhibitions (low So and Sc), not preoccupied with the impression which he makes on others and thus perhaps capable of great independence and autonomy (low Gi), and relatively

ready to recognize and admit self-views that are unusual and unconventional (low Cm).

He is strongly motivated to achieve in situations in which independence in thought and action are called for (Ai). But, unlike his less creative colleagues, he is less inclined to strive for achievement in settings where conforming behavior is expected or required (Ac). In efficiency and steadiness of intellectual effort (Ie), however, he does not differ from his fellow workers.

Finally, he is definitely more psychologically minded (Py), more flexible (Fx), and possessed of more femininity of interests (Fe) than architects in general.

There is one last finding that I wish to present, one that was foreshadowed by a discovery of Dr. Bingham in one of his attempts to study creativity. The subject of his study was Amy Lowell, a close friend of his and Mrs. Bingham's, with whom he discussed at length the birth and growth of her poems, seeking insight into the creative processes of her mind. He also administered to her a word association test and "found that she gave a higher proportion of unique responses than those of any one outside a mental institution" (Bingham, Millicent Todd, 1953, p. 11). We, too, administered a word association test to our subjects and found the unusualness of mental associations one of the best predictors of creativity, and especially so when associations given by no more than 1% to 10% of the population, using the Minnesota norms (Russell & Jenkins, 1954), are weighted more heavily than those given by less than 1% of the population. Among architects, for example, this weighted score is for Architects I, 204; Architects II, 128; and Architects III, 114; while for the total sample this measure of unusualness of mental associations correlates +.50 with rated creativity.

And Dr. Bingham, like us, found that there are certain hazards in attempting to study a creative poet. His searchings were rewarded by a poem Amy Lowell later wrote which was first entitled "To the Impudent Psychologist" and published posthumously with the title "To a Gentleman who wanted to see the first drafts of my poems in the interest of psychological research into the workings of the creative mind." We, I must confess, were treated somewhat less kindly by one of our poets who, after assessment, published an article entitled "My Head Gets Tooken Apart" (Rexroth, 1959).

Having described the overall design of our studies, and having presented a selection of our findings which reveal at least some aspects of the nature of creative talent, I turn now, but with considerably less confidence, to the question as to how we can early identify and best encourage the development of creative potential. Our findings concerning the characteristics of highly creative persons are by now reasonably well established, but their implications for the nurture of creative talent are far from clear.

It is one thing to discover the distinguishing characteristics of mature, creative, productive individuals. It is quite another matter to conclude that the traits of creative persons observed several years after school and college characterized these same individuals when they were students. Nor can we be certain that finding these same traits in youngsters today will identify those with creative potential. Only empirical, longitudinal research, which we do not yet have, can settle such issues. Considering, however, the nature of the traits which discriminate creative adults from their noncreative peers, I would venture to guess that most students with creative potential have personality structures congruent with, though possibly less sharply delineated than, those of mature creatives.

Our problem is further complicated by the fact that though

our creative subjects have told us about their experiences at home, in school, and in college, and about the forces and persons and situations which, as they see it, nurtured their creativeness, these are, after all, self-reports subject to the misperceptions and self-deceptions of all self-reports. Even if we were to assume that their testimony is essentially accurate we would still have no assurance that the conditions in the home, in school, and in society, the qualities of interpersonal relations between instructor and student, and the aspects of the teaching-learning process which would appear to have contributed to creative development a generation ago would facilitate rather than inhibit creativity if these same factors were created in today's quite different world and far different educational climate.

In reporting upon events and situations in the life histories of our subjects which appear to have fostered their creative potential and independent spirit, I shall again restrict myself to architects. One finds in their histories a number of circumstances which, in the early years, could well have provided an opportunity as well as the necessity for developing the secure sense of personal autonomy and zestful commitment to their profession which so markedly characterize them.

What appears most often to have characterized the parents of these future creative architects was an extraordinary respect for the child and confidence in his ability to do what was appropriate. Thus they did not hesitate to grant him rather unusual freedom in exploring his universe and in making decisions for himself—and this early as well as late. The expectation of the parent that thc child would act independently but reasonably and responsibly appears to have contributed immensely to the latter's sense of personal autonomy which was to develop to such a marked degree.

The obverse side of this was that there was often a lack of intense closeness with one or both of the parents. Most often this appeared in relation to the father rather than to the mother, but often it characterized the relationship with both parents. There were not strong emotional ties of either a positive or a negative sort between parent and child, but neither was there the type of relationship that fosters overdependency nor the type that results in severe rejection. Thus, if there was a certain distance in the relationship between child and parent, it had a liberating effect so far as the child was concerned. If he lacked something of the emotional closeness which some children experience with their parents, he was also spared that type of psychological exploitation that is so frequently seen in the life histories of clinical patients.

Closely related to this factor of some distance between parent and child were ambiguities in identification with the parents. In place of the more usual clear identification with one parent, there was a tendency for the architects to have identified either with both parents or with neither. It was not that the child's early milieu was a deprived one so far as models for identification and the promotion of ego ideals were concerned. It was rather that the larger familial sphere presented the child with a plentiful supply of diverse and effective models—in addition to the mother and father, grandfathers, uncles, and others who occupied prominent and responsible positions within their community—with whom important identifications could be made. Whatever the emotional interaction between father and son, whether distant, harmonious, or turbulent, the father presented a model of effective and resourceful behavior in an exceptionally demanding career. What is perhaps more significant, though, is the high incidence of distinctly autonomous mothers among families of the creative architects, who led active lives with interests and sometimes careers of their own apart from their husbands'.

Still other factors which would appear to have contributed to the development of the marked personal autonomy of our subjects were the types of discipline and religious training which they received, which suggest that within the family there existed clear standards of conduct and ideas as to what was right and wrong but at the same time an expectation if not requirement of active exploration and internalization of a framework of personal conduct. Discipline was almost always consistent and predictable. In most cases there were rules, family standards, and parental injunctions which were known explicitly by the children and seldom infringed. In nearly half the cases, corporal punishment was not employed and in only a few instances was the punishment harsh or cruel.

As for religious practices, the families of the creative architects showed considerable diversity, but what was most widely emphasized was the development of personal ethical codes rather than formal religious practices. For one-third of the families formal religion was important for one parent or for both, but in two-thirds of the families formal religion was either unimportant or practiced only perfunctorily. For the majority of the families, in which emphasis was placed upon the development of one's own ethical code, it is of interest to inquire into the values that were most stressed. They were most often values related to integrity (e.g., forthrightness, honesty, respect for others), quality (e.g., pride, diligence, joy in work, development of talent), intellectual and cultural endeavor, success and ambition, and being respectable and doing the right thing.

The families of the more creative architects tended to move more frequently, whether within a single community, or from community to community, or even from country to country. This, combined with the fact that the more creative architects as youngsters were given very much more freedom to roam and to explore widely, provided for them an enrichment of experience both cultural and personal which their less creative peers did not have.

But the frequent moving appears also to have resulted frequently in some estrangement of the family from its immediate neighborhood. And it is of interest that in almost every case in which the architect reported that his family differed in its behavior and values from those in the neighborhood, the family was different in showing greater cultural, artistic, and intellectual interests and pursuits.

To what extent this sort of cultural dislocation contributed to the frequently reported experiences of aloneness, shyness, isolation, and solitariness during childhood and adolescence, with little or no dating during adolescence, or to what extent these experiences stemmed from a natural introversion of interests and unusual sensitivity, we cannot say. They were doubtless mutually reinforcing factors in stimulating the young architect's awareness of his own inner life and his growing interest in his artistic skills and his ideational, imaginal, and symbolic processes.

Almost without exception, the creative architects manifested very early considerable interest and skill in drawing and painting. And also, with almost no exception, one or both of the parents were of artistic temperament and considerable skill. Often it was the mother who in the architect's early years fostered his artistic potentialities by her example as well as by her instruction. It is especially interesting to note, however, that while the visual and artistic abilities and interests of the child were encouraged and rewarded, these interests and abilities were, by and large, allowed to develop at their own speed, and this pace varied considerably among the architects. There was not an anxious concern on the part of the parents about the skills and abilities of the child. What is perhaps most significant was the widespread definite lack of strong pressures from the parents toward a particular career. And this was true both for pressures away from architecture as well as for pressures toward architecture by parents who were themselves architects.

The several aspects of the life history which I have described were first noted by Kenneth Craik in the protocols for the highly creative Architects I. Subsequently, in reading the protocols for Architects II and III as well as Architects I, a credit of one point for the presence of each of the factors was assigned and the total for each person taken as a score. The correlation of these life history scores with rated creativity of the architects is +.36, significant beyond the .005 level of confidence.

And now I turn finally to a consideration of the implications of the nature of creative talent for the nurturing of it in school and college through the processes of education.

Our findings concerning the relations of intelligence to creativity suggest that we may have overestimated in our educational system the role of intelligence in creative achievement. If our expectation is that a child of a given intelligence will not respond creatively to a task which confronts him, and especially if we make this expectation known to the child, the probability that he will respond creatively is very much reduced. And later on, such a child, now grown older, may find doors closed to him so that he is definitely excluded from certain domains of learning. There is increasing reason to believe that in selecting students for special training of their talent we may have overweighted the role of intelligence either by setting the cutting point for selection on the intellective dimension too high or by assuming that regardless of other factors the student with the higher IQ is the more promising one and should consequently be chosen. Our data suggest, rather, that if a person has the minimum of intelligence required for mastery of a field of knowledge, whether he performs creatively or banally in that field will be crucially determined by nonintellective factors. We would do well then to pay more attention in the future than we have in the past to the nurturing of those nonintellective traits which in our studies have been shown to be intimately associated with creative talent.

There is the openness of the creative person to experience both from within and from without which suggests that whether we be parent or teacher we should use caution in setting limits upon what those whom we are nurturing experience and express.

Discipline and self-control are necessary. They must be learned if one is ever to be truly creative, but it is important that they not be overlearned. Furthermore, there is a time and place for their learning, and having been learned they should be used flexibly, not rigidly or compulsively.

If we consider this specifically with reference to the attitudes of perceiving and judging, everyone must judge as well as perceive. It is not a matter of using one to the exclusion of the other, but a question of how each is used and which is preferred. The danger for one's creative potential is not the judging or evaluating of one's experience but that one prejudges, thus excluding from perception large areas of experience. The danger in all parental instruction, as in all academic instruction, is that new ideas and new possibilities of action are criticized too soon and too often. Training in criticism is obviously important and so widely recognized that I need not plead its case. Rather I would urge that, if we wish to nurture creative potential, an equal emphasis be placed on perceptiveness, discussing with our students as well as with our children, at least upon occasion, the most fantastic of ideas and possibilities. It is the duty of parents to communicate and of professors to profess what they judge to be true, but it is no less their duty by example to encourage in their children and in their students an openness to all ideas and especially to those which most challenge and threaten their own judgments.

The creative person, as we have seen, is not only open to experience, but intuitive about it. We can train students to be accurate in their perceptions, and this, too, is a characteristic of the creative. But can we train them to be intuitive, and if so how?

I would suggest that rote learning, learning of facts for their own sake, repeated drill of material, too much emphasis upon facts unrelated to other facts, and excessive concern with memorizing, can all strengthen and reinforce sense perception. On the other hand, emphasis upon the transfer of training from one subject to another, the searching for common principles in terms of which facts from quite different domains of knowledge can be related, the stressing of analogies, and similes, and metaphors, a seeking for symbolic equivalents of experience in the widest possible number of sensory and imaginal modalities, exercises in imaginative play, training in retreating from the facts in order to see them in larger perspective and in relation to more aspects of the larger context thus achieved—these and still other emphases in learning would, I believe, strengthen the disposition to intuitive perception as well as intuitive thinking.

If the widest possible relationships among facts are to be established, if the structure of knowledge (Bruner, 1960) is to be grasped, it is necessary that the student have a large body of facts which he has learned as well as a large array of reasoning skills which he has mastered. You will see, then, that what I am proposing is not that in teaching one disdain acute and accurate sense perception, but that one use it to build upon, leading the student always to an intuitive understanding of that which he experiences.

The independence of thought and action which our subjects reveal in the assessment setting appears to have long characterized them. It was already manifest in high school, though, according to their reports, tending to increase in college and thereafter.

In college our creative architects earned about a B average.

In work and courses which caught their interest they could turn in an A performance, but in courses that failed to strike their imagination, they were quite willing to do no work at all. In general, their attitude in college appears to have been one of profound skepticism. They were unwilling to accept anything on the mere say-so of their instructors. Nothing was to be accepted on faith or because it had behind it the voice of authority. Such matters might be accepted, but only after the student on his own had demonstrated their validity to himself. In a sense, they were rebellious, but they did not run counter to the standards out of sheer rebelliousness. Rather, they were spirited in their disagreement and one gets the impression that they learned most from those who were not easy with them. But clearly many of them were not easy to take. One of the most rebellious, but, as it turned out, one of the most creative, was advised by the Dean of his School to quit because he had no talent; and another, having been failed in his design dissertation which attacked the stylism of the faculty, took his degree in the art department.

These and other data should remind all of us who teach that creative students will not always be to our liking. This will be due not only to their independence in situations in which nonconformity may be seriously disruptive of the work of others, but because, as we have seen, more than most they will be experiencing large quantities of tension produced in them by the richness of their experience and the strong opposites of their nature. In struggling to reconcile these opposites and in striving to achieve creative solutions to the difficult problems which they have set themselves they will often show that psychic turbulence which is so characteristic of the creative person. If, however, we can only recognize the sources of their disturbance, which often enough will result in behavior disturbing to us, we may be in a better position to support and encourage them in their creative striving.

References

Allport, G. W., Vernon, P. E., & Lindzey, G. *Study of values: manual of directions.* (Rev. ed.) Boston: Houghton Mifflin, 1951.

Barron, F., & Welsh, G. S. Artistic perception as a possible factor in personality style: its measurement by a figure preference test. *J. Psychol.*, 1952, 33, 199–203.

Bingham, Millicent Todd. Beyond psychology. In *Homo sapiens auduboniensis: a tribute to Walter Van Dyke Bingham.* New York: National Audubon Society, 1953, pp. 5–29.

Bruner, J. S. *The process of education.* Cambridge, Mass.: Harvard Univer. Press, 1960.

Gough, H. G. *California Psychological Inventory manual.* Palo Alto, Calif.: Consulting Psychologists Press, 1957.

Hall, W. B. The development of a technique for assessing aesthetic predispositions and its application to a sample of professional research scientists. Paper read at Western Psychological Association, Monterey, California, April 1958.

Hathaway, S. R., & McKinley, J. C. *Minnesota Multiphasic Personality Inventory.* New York: Psychological Corporation, 1945.

Jung, C. G. *Psychological types.* New York: Harcourt, Brace, 1923.

Jung, C. G. *Two essays on analytical psychology.* New York: Meridian, 1956.

MacKinnon, D. W. The personality correlates of creativity: a study of American architects. In G. S. Nielsen (ed.), *Proceedings of the XIV International Congress of Applied Psychology, Copenhagen 1961.* Vol. 2. Copenhagen: Munksgaard, 1962, pp. 11–39.

Myers, Isabel B. *Some findings with regard to type and manual for Myers-Briggs Type Indicator, Form E.* Swarthmore, Pa.: Author, 1958.

Rexroth, K. My head gets tooken apart. In *Bird in the bush: obvious essays.* New York: New Directions Paperbook, 1959, pp. 65–74.

Russell, W. A., & Jenkins, J. J. The complete Minnesota norms for responses to 100 words from the Kent-Rosanoff Word Association Test. Technical Report No. 11, 1954, University of Minnesota, Contract N8 onr66216, Office of Naval Research.

Spranger, E. *Types of men.* (Trans. by Paul J. W. Pigors). Halle (Saale), Germany: Max Niemeyer, 1928.

Strong, E. K., Jr. *Manual for Strong Vocational Interest Blanks for Men and Women, Revised Blanks (Form M and W)*. Palo Alto, Calif.: Consulting Psychologists Press, 1959.

Terman, L. M. *Concept Mastery Test, Form T manual.* New York: Psychological Corporation, 1956.

Welsh, G. S. *Welsh Figure Preference Test: preliminary manual.* Palo Alto, Calif.: Consulting Psychologists Press, 1959.

Wotton, Henry. *The elements of architecture.* London: John Bill, 1624.

Edwin E. Ghiselli

Managerial Talent[1]

It is, indeed, an honor for me to have been chosen to participate in this series of annual Walter Van Dyke Bingham Memorial Lectures. It permits me publicly to express my thanks to a man who many years ago gave me guidance in my professional career, and who stimulated my thinking and encouraged my work in industrial psychology. With all of the recognitions he received, and so well deserved, for his many contributions to his profession and to his country, he always remained a warm and understanding man, ever ready to hear out the ideas of others and to foster their development. So today I do not so much feel that I am delivering a lecture, but rather as though I were again spelling out ideas as I did in the past to Dr. Bingham so that they thereby become clearer in my mind.

The University of Michigan is to be congratulated for having been chosen as the site of this lecture. Again recognition is given to this institution, which because of the high quality and quantity of its research and human product, has played, and increasingly

1. This paper is based on the Walter Van Dyke Bingham Lecture given at the University of Michigan, April 26, 1963. It was first published in the *American Psychologist,* 1963, vol. 18, no. 10 (October), pp. 631–642.

continues to play, so unique and important a role in the history of psychology. Yet it is difficult for me to think of the University as an institution since it is peopled with so many friends and former colleagues. So for this reason, too, I feel I am not giving a discourse but rather that I am again taking advantage of the tolerance and understanding of colleagues to talk about some ideas of mine.

As a representative of her husband's profession, I should like to express our thanks to Mrs. Bingham for her generosity in establishing this series of lectures. Throughout his life Dr. Bingham directed his efforts to fostering the full utilization of human resources. He not only saw the value to society of the assessment of human talents, but also its importance for the self-actualization of the individual. By these lectures devoted to the identification and nurture of human talent, his goals continue to be pursued.

Before World War II industrial psychologists largely concerned themselves with the men and women who labor in the factory or keep the books in the office. But in the past 15 years there has been a great surge of interest in examining the nature of those who in business and industrial establishments direct, administer, and organize—that is, manage. I am not at all sure what has caused this shift in interest. I think it not impossible that psychologists have stood in awe of those in high places, viewing managers stereotypically as a category apart from ordinary folk. But now for some reason or another managers are seen as human beings, beings who strive, who bleed, who have feelings, needs, and frustrations, and who differ among themselves in abilities, personality traits, and performances in the same way as do other people. The denizens of Olympus, then, are seen as being of the same stuff as those of Attica.

Psychologists who study management stand accused by critics

of the social scene of a score of trespasses, from surreptitiously destroying individuality among managers to trying to raze the very foundation of American business and industry, individual initiative, with precisely the same objective that brought my great-grandfather to the California mother lode in 1849—gold. And certainly there is some substance for these critics' adverse comments since there has been a plethora of pseudoscientific discourses about the nature and nurture of managers together with a variety of unvalidated action programs for their selection and training. However, much serious work is being conducted, and while our knowledge and understanding is still small, progress is being made in the development of a solid body of empirically determined facts and in sharper and more exact theory. The best testimony of this is the significant work of the social-industrial psychologists here at the University of Michigan, the effects of which are seen throughout the social sciences and in the business and industrial community.

In recent years a group of us at the Institute of Industrial Relations of the University of California—Mason Haire, Lyman Porter, and myself—have been studying the nature of organizations and the psychological characteristics of managers. The investigations of my colleague, Mason Haire (1959), have shown that as business and industrial organizations grow and develop, it is in the very nature of the case that their integrative and coordinative activities assume greater and greater importance. This is indicated by the fact that the larger an organization becomes the greater is the proportion of individuals in it whose functions are of an administrative rather than of a directly productive sort. With the increasing sizes of our business and industrial establishments, then, there would appear to be a real need for psychologists as well as other social scientists to examine the nature of those who manage, so that these establishments can operate as effective organizations.

I shall begin my discussion by trying to define the term manager. I fear my definition will not be as tight as one might wish, but perhaps it will suffice to delineate the general realm of occupational activity wherein I wish to examine talent. Then I shall treat briefly with the problem of gauging success in the performance of managerial activities. I believe that success in management must be viewed broadly, and is not yet readily subject to precise and objective measurement. The main body of my presentation will be concerned with an examination of what I believe to be important facets of managerial talent. In this connection I shall present some of my empirical studies of the psychological properties I have termed management traits. Finally, I shall mention briefly some of our findings on the motives and aspirations of managers, since I believe they will cast additional light on the nature of managerial talent.

While management is reasonably distinguishable as a class in the broad spectrum of occupations, it cannot be said that there is any unanimity of opinion on which particular individuals should be included in it. Perhaps a common root to many of the definitions of the term manager is that a manager is any person in an organization who supervises the activities of others. Such a definition not only includes such first line supervisors as industrial foremen, but also leadmen and craftsmen who direct apprentices, neither of whom are considered to be management personnel. Furthermore, there are some individuals whom almost everyone would place in the category of management, such as safety engineers and legal counselors, who may supervise no one but their secretaries. While certainly one element in the decision of whether to classify an individual as a manager, supervision is not the sole criterion.

Another common root in many definitions of management is that which stems from the meaning of the word to manage. Lexicographically, to manage is to direct, to execute, to carry out, to guide, and to administer, and, interestingly enough, to cope with, to bring about by contriving, and to husband. I am sure that there are many in management who would think that the latter are more descriptive of their activities than are the former. In any event, both arm chair analyses of the job of manager and careful systematic studies of what managers actually do, such as those of Shartle (1956) and the Ohio State University group, give support to the use of functions such as these to distinguish the class of managers in the taxonomy of occupations. Certainly the functions of directing, administering, and the like, do not provide precise criteria for differentiating management positions from those of other sorts, but at least they are guideposts. In general they describe the activities of the persons in the upper portions of the organizational hierarchy.

The personnel of a business or industrial establishment can be roughly classified by level. The individuals at the upper levels are concerned with the overall government of the organization and the formulation of broad plans and policies. Here we find the presidents, vice presidents, and, depending upon the size and nature of the enterprise, those who head major operations or geographical areas. The task of those at the next level is to crystallize the general policies and plans developed at the highest level, formulating them into specific and workable procedures. At this second level are included those who operate divisions or departments in an organization, together with staff personnel who are concerned with specialized activities. The next level are the first line supervisors who are charged with putting into effect the specific procedures prepared at the level above, by the immediate direction of the activities of the line workers. Finally, at the lowest level of the organizational hierarchy are the individuals who directly produce goods and services.

A broad distinction can be drawn between those workers whose activities directly result in the production of goods and services, and those whose activities are of a planful, integrative, and directive character. It is the latter, those in the upper three levels of the organization, who typically are termed management and are distinguished from the producers or line workers. So it is common to speak of three managerial levels, upper management, middle management, and lower management.

If I am to discuss managerial talent, I should, I suppose, be prepared to indicate how a more successful manager can be distinguished from a less successful one. The measurement of job success, the so-called criterion problem, has plagued industrial psychology since its birth. It is not a simple task even with simple jobs, and with management jobs their very complexity makes the problem seem almost insurmountable. The subject has been extensively discussed and empirically examined, but certainly the fundamental issues have not been settled.

Psychologists put great value on precisely quantified and objective appraisals of individuals, appraisals based on concrete and objective measures of each of the various specific aspects of the performance under consideration. While it is obviously true that such appraisals do have many desirable features, I nonetheless believe that there is a case to be made for the purely subjective, global, overall assessments, as are given by one person's opinions or ratings of the performance of another person.

Just because they are expressed in quantified terms, objective measures of performance may erroneously convey the impression that the differences among individuals are great, whereas in fact the differences may be quite small and insignificant. Furthermore, as Likert (1961) has pointed out, those aspects of performance which we can measure objectively, often are quite unimportant and irrelevant. The sharpness with which an executive keeps his pencils can be measured with a high degree of reliability but has little bearing on evaluations of his success as a manager. The relevance and importance of the various activities connected with a job are matters apart from their mode of measurement, and, indeed, are purely value judgments. I do not mean to imply that objective measures of managerial behavior are worthless. Quite the contrary. Recent studies of great ingenuity have been most fruitful of ideas, and have given new insights into the nature of managerial functions (Frederiksen, 1962; Tagiuri, 1961). Nevertheless I do not believe that at the present time they are sufficiently well worked out and tested, and do not give the types of evaluations required.

Psychologists have examined extensively the subjective evaluations, or judgments, of one person by another, and invariably find them wanting. It has been endlessly demonstrated that one man's assessment of the performance of another is influenced by all manner of irrelevant matters. A foreman's ratings of the job proficiency of his subordinates may be in part determined by whether the men are Giant or Dodger fans, and the ratings of the vice presidents made by the president of a company may be biased by whether they prefer Brand X or Brand Y political party. Furthermore, two individuals seldom agree perfectly in their opinion of a third, and when they do collusion is suspected.

Yet, the fact that subjective appraisals of performance are not entirely based on irrelevant matters, and there is some and often considerable agreement among different assessors, is too often forgotten. Furthermore, as Bingham (1939b) so clearly pointed out many years ago, subjective appraisals not only permit a meaningful integration of the individual's performance in the various aspects of his job, but also permit an evaluation in terms of the demands of the setting in which the job occurs. For the present, then, I prefer subjective evaluations of managerial performance.

I have been cavalierly speaking of management as if it were a single job. This is, of course, quite incorrect. The managerial occupation includes a wide variety of positions and the differences among them are great. Managerial jobs range from those with considerable personal authority and responsibility to those which are purely advisory. Some are completely enmeshed in a fabric of interpersonal relationships, whereas others are as lonely as the job of lighthouse keeper. While some demand a professional background, others require no special training. In the work of Hemphill (1960) we have the beginning of an empirically based taxonomy of managerial jobs. But we have so few precise descriptions of managerial jobs and the overlap among them is so great that as a group they appear amorphous. They can be classified into some broad categories such as line and staff, or into functional groups such as production, financial, and sales, but such categories are of the grossest sort.

But I do not see this lack of a clearly defined classification of managerial jobs as a serious problem in the study of managerial talent. It seems to me that one of the characteristics of managers is their movement from one position to another. Furthermore, this movement, often but not always in the form of advancement, is especially characteristic of those of superior talent. There is, then, in a successful manager's career a concatenation of transmigrations among managerial posts which are quite different in character. A person manifests managerial talent not just because he performs well in one given type of position, but because he has the capacity to perform a variety of them well, and the adaptability to change from one activity to another quite different activity.

I have so far tried to make two points, first that it is possible through purely subjective judgment to appraise managerial success, and second that in talking about managerial talent and managerial success we should not just consider an individual's performance on a single job but rather his progress through a series of positions, in other words, his career as a manager.

Over the years I have been called on in one connection or another to assess the managerial talent of a number of men. My appraisals were based entirely on an interview with each man, plus his vita, and very occasionally a conversation with his superior or a colleague. I would like to illustrate my points with four short case descriptions. Two of these men I judged to be of superior managerial talent, and two inferior. The careers of two were entirely in one company and the other two made changes from one establishment to another. All four men were college graduates, having majored either in economics or business administration, and all four were in their middle forties when I saw them. From these four cases I think you will be able to see that it is not at all impossible to gauge the career success of a manager without objective and quantitative measures of his performance.

The first man, after a short and unsuccessful 2 years as a college instructor, took a position in the research and development department of a large organization. After 2 years he became the head of a division in the department, and after 2 more the department chief. His outstanding talents as an analyst brought him to the attention of top management, and with increasing frequency his recommendations were incorporated into the organization's policy. At 35 he became assistant vice president for research and development, and the following year vice president. Here he manifested not only executive ability but also the capacity to influence the board of directors whom top management considered to be far too conservative. The vice president for operations retiring, my man was given his position. The interesting thing is that he was placed in this post purely for storage because he was already marked for the presidency. He had no real feel for operations, and both he and his superiors realized it. By 42 he was executive vice president, and by 45 president. Here we have a career which I believe indisputably is a successful one as a manager.

The second man began his career as a salesman for a small instrument manufacturing company. Because of his aggressiveness as a salesman he was made sales manager, and after 5 more years he was made general manager, and finally president and partner. The company had been experiencing lean times, and it was largely as a result of his efforts, both in promotion and in operations, that it became financially strong. Indeed, its position was so good that a larger company made such a handsome offer the partners could not refuse it. His services then were sought and obtained by a firm of underwriters in a policy-making position involving the purchase and reconstruction of small businesses. Again, a career that clearly is a successful one.

The third man began his career with a brokerage house as an analyst. After 8 years he became the head of the bookkeeping division, and by the time he reached his middle thirties he was made supervisor of the office activities. Here he remained until he was 47. Seeing no further possibility of advancement, and none being promised, he left the company and became a real estate salesman. While, to be sure, in this last job he increased his income, the picture of his career as a manager is quite unimpressive, showing a slow rate of advancement with a final plateau at a lowish level of middle management.

The fourth man began his occupational career with an accounting firm. After some 6 years he was "stolen" by one of the company's clients, to head its accounting division. Later he became the comptroller, but after a few years finding himself unhappy with the responsibility, he quit. He then obtained the position of treasurer with a ferry company in San Francisco, even though the salary was substantially less and he knew it was a dying business. In a couple of years the company dissolved when the ferry route was finally bridged. Out of a job he was back where he began more than 20 years before, seeking employment as an accountant. Here is a career with initial growth and promise, but with a later decline; a career one would not term successful. If his success were measured objectively I suppose the trend would be a quadratic with a negative coefficient. But surely with this, as with the other cases, the subjective assessment is sufficiently precise.

There have been many analyses of the psychological traits important in the performance of managerial functions, together with a substantial number of empirical investigations of the measured traits which distinguish management from line workers, and the measured traits which are related to indices of the success of managers (Harrell, 1961). At the University of California we have tried to obtain some notion of the traits which are of prime importance for managers by comparing the self- and role perceptions of managers at different levels, managers and line workers, and successful and unsuccessful managers (Ghiselli & Barthol, 1956; Porter, 1958, 1959; Porter & Ghiselli, 1957). From the constellations of role and self-perceptions which differentiate these various groups, we have endeavored to develop a picture of the significant managerial traits. Material of this sort lends itself to a variety of interpretations, and it is likely others would interpret our findings in ways somewhat differently than we have. Nevertheless, we do believe our interpretations have some validity inasmuch as we have been able to demonstrate that certain of these patterns of self-perception are related in important ways to the manner in which task-oriented groups govern themselves (Ghiselli & Lodahl, 1958a, 1958b).

From these various analyses I have come to the conclusion that important to managerial success are the traits of intelligence, supervisory ability, initiative, self-assurance, and perceived occupational level. I do not mean to imply that success in management is determined solely by these five traits, for certainly there are many others. Nevertheless, it does seem to me that these particular five traits—intelligence, supervisory ability, initiative, self-assurance, and perceived occupational level—play a key role in managerial functions and therefore are major facets of managerial talent. I should, therefore, like to summarize my work on them (Ghiselli, 1955b, 1956a, 1956b, 1959, 1963a, 1963b).

Let me first consider the trait of intelligence. Today we generally accept the proposition that tests of intelligence measure significant psychological properties of the individual. Yet, we do not seem to worry very much any more about what these specific properties are. I suspect there is a certain amount of battle fatigue as a result of the long and indecisive war we psychologists waged among ourselves during the first 4 decades of the century about the nature of intelligence and the validity of tests proclaimed as measuring it. I doubt if there are very many now who consider intelligence as the single all-important ability that Spearman conceived it to be. Rather we tend to think of intelligence tests as measuring a domain of various cognitive abilities more or less related logically if not psychologically. Intelligence we take to be an important determiner of behavior in those situations involving mental power and problem solving, where the individual is called upon to deal with ideas, abstractions, and concepts.

One of the well-popularized results of the first great mass testing of adults, the measurement of the intelligence of soldiers in the American Army in World War I, was the relationship found between level of occupation and intelligence test scores (Bingham, 1937). It was noted that when soldiers were sorted out into groups in terms of their civilian occupations, those in the so-called higher occupations on the average earned higher scores than those in the lower occupations. Since World War I this relationship between level of occupation and intelligence has been demonstrated a number of times. Men in the professions obtain the highest scores, followed in order by those in managerial, supervisory, and clerical jobs, and finally those in the various industrial jobs show average scores in descending order of skilled, semi-skilled, and unskilled workers.

In all of these investigations there is found a substantial amount of variation in scores among individuals in any one occupational group. Thus some factory workers earn higher scores than those earned by some lawyers. Nevertheless, the relationship between level of occupation and measured intelligence is quite substantial.

The intelligence test scores of persons in management positions fall in the higher ranges of the distribution of scores of the general employed population. Furthermore, it appears that by and large those in lower management have the lowest scores and those in upper management the highest ones. There is quite a substantial difference in intelligence between lower and middle management, but the difference between middle and upper management is small. As a matter of fact, lower management and line workers are about the same in measured intelligence. Industrial foremen are about equal to skilled workers, but office supervisors do seem superior to clerical workers. It is probable that among office supervisors are some young people in trainee positions who are slated for higher management positions. The average intelligence test scores of those who hold positions in the upper and middle levels of management is very high, indeed, and is reported to exceed the scores of about 96% of the population (Harrell, 1961). Over the years I have tested several hundred managers at these levels in a variety of different businesses and industries. Interestingly enough their average score, too, happens to fall at the ninety-sixth percentile.

There is a substantial body of evidence which indicates that there is a relationship between level of occupation and the degree to which job success can be predicted by intelligence test scores (Ghiselli, 1955a). As one moves up the scale of occupations from the unskilled to the upper managerial, one finds not only higher and higher average test scores but also higher and higher correlations between intelligence test scores and job success. Nevertheless, even at the upper two levels of management, the relationship between intelligence test scores and job success is by no means high, and while the reported relationships vary in magnitude from one investigation to another, by and large they are perhaps best described as being moderate.

So one might take the position that the greater the measured amount of intelligence an individual possesses the higher he is likely to rise in the organizational hierarchy, and the greater is the probability he will be a successful manager. But I am not sure that the latter part of this generalization can be accepted without question, at least at the higher levels of test scores. There have been suggestions that at the middle and upper managerial levels there is not a simple one-to-one relationship between intelligence and managerial ability. Rather it would appear that the relationship between intelligence and managerial success may be curvilinear, with not only those managers earning low scores being on the average poorer, but also those earning very high scores.

I have found this to be the case with three groups of managers. The average scores of all of these groups were quite high, as I reported earlier they exceeded the scores of about 96% of the general population. In each group I divided the men into those whose scores fell above this point and those whose scores fell below it. In every group, for the men with the lower scores there was a positive relationship between intelligence and success and for the men with the higher scores the relationship was negative. In other words, for individuals of higher and higher intelligence there is a greater and greater probability they will achieve success as managers until a critical intellectual level is reached. This level is quite high, indeed, but above it individuals with higher and higher scores have less and less chance of being successful managers.

For one of these groups, a group of executives in a financial organization, success was gauged by the higher management of the organization. Without in fact knowing what the scores were, it was the men who earned the highest and the lowest scores whom higher management invited to leave. A second group was comprised of individuals the success of whose managerial careers I appraised. I mentioned earlier the nature of these appraisals and gave some examples. These men were employed in a wide variety of different organizations and held a wide variety of different managerial positions. Yet, the careers of those earning the very highest scores were not as successful as the careers of those who earned somewhat lower scores. The measure of success I used with the third group I think is most interesting and significant. For these men success was gauged solely and entirely in terms of how the individual appraised himself. I asked managers to evaluate their own careers, indicating the degree to which they themselves believed they were successful. These reports were, of course, anonymous. It was both the managers who earned very high and low intelligence test scores who viewed their careers with the greatest misgivings. So there does appear to be some substance to the notion that a curvilinear relationship exists between intelligence and managerial success, with the very very bright, as well as those more poorly endowed, being less likely to be successful than those at intermediate levels.

We have seen that the evidence indicates intelligence to be an important factor in managerial success, and therefore it is one of the facets of managerial talent. Individuals of higher and higher intelligence have greater and greater chances of being successful managers. This relationship holds until a very high level of intelligence is reached, and then there appears to be a brief trend in the opposite direction. Individuals who fall among the top 2 or 3% of the population in intelligence are somewhat less likely to be successful managers than those immediately below them. It is possible that those individuals at the very extreme high levels of capacity to deal with abstract ideas and concepts do not find in managerial activities the intellectual challenge they need.

In recent years, discussions of conditions for effective organizations, particularly those discussions with a so-called human relations orientation, have stressed the importance of leadership. Indeed, the naive student might well suspect that the sole function of management is leadership, with top management leading middle management, middle management leading lower management, and lower management leading line personnel who do all the work. The implication seems to be that if management provided proper leadership, both for itself and for line workers, all organization ills would be cured. While it is unquestionably true that one of the functions of managers is to supervise the activities of those lower in the organization, and that the better supervision management provides the better the organization will function, leadership and the supervision of subordinates is only among the many functions that managers perform.

Still, the life of a business or industrial organization lies in the individuals who people it. If the organization is to function as an effective social entity, its human parts must operate in an integrated fashion. As yet, the most effective integrative machinery our species, Homo so-called sapiens, has been able to develop is an authoritarian hierarchy of individuals, a series of superiors and subordinates, ranging in a business or industrial organization from the president at the top to the line workers at the bottom. Except for the individuals at the top and bottom, each person has two roles, one as the supervised and the other as the supervisor. Each has his activities directed by a superior and in turn directs the activities of subordinates. It is not impossible that in the future social science will provide some quite different type of machinery which more fully utilizes the varieties of human talent and increases individual freedom, creativity, and self-fulfillment. In the meantime, we are stuck with a system wherein ability to supervise the activities of others is a primary matter.

I do not think it appropriate here to enter into a discussion of what constitutes effective supervision. Notions about the nature of good supervision vary widely and are likely to be, if I may say so, contaminated by theoretical notions about leadership, and by social views. It does seem clear that what are good supervisory practices in one situation may be poor in another. For my purposes here I shall simply take good supervision to be that behavior which management, in a given situation, says is good supervision as distinguished from that behavior which management says is poor supervision. In other words, I am again taking ratings, or personal and subjective estimates, as an adequate index of success, in this case as a criterion of supervisory ability. The test I use as a measure of supervisory ability I consider to be a valid measure of this trait since, in widely differing organizations, the scores individuals earn on it are related to the ratings of supervisory ability assigned to them. Therefore, I can perhaps say that by superior supervisory ability I am referring to the effective utilization of whatever supervisory practices are indicated by the particular requirements of the situation.

My findings indicate that there is a relationship between supervisory ability and occupational level just as there is with intelligence and occupational level. As one proceeds up the scale of occupations from line workers through lower and middle management to top management there is a progressive increase in capacity to supervise the activities of others. The difference between lower management and line workers surprisingly enough is small. But there is a considerable superiority of middle management over lower management, and an equally great difference between middle and upper management. In capacity for leadership the higher levels of management are quite superior, and the top level of management is outstanding.

As one might expect, with line workers there is little or no relationship between measured capacity for supervision and job performance. But with managers at all organizational levels I find supervisory ability bears quite a substantial relationship to the evaluations of their performance as managers. Indeed, of all of the five traits I have termed management traits, this seems to be of paramount importance. Furthermore, my investigations indicate that supervisory ability is a somewhat more important determiner of success at the upper management levels than it is at the lower levels, though the differences are not great. Ability to direct the activities of others, then, is a significant aspect of managerial talent, and on the average the higher and higher an individual makes his way in the organizational hierarchy the more qualified is he likely to be as a supervisor, and the more important this ability is to his success as a manager.

Many persons in management who possess quite adequate intellectual and social talents and who are highly motivated, nevertheless are sometimes found wanting by their superiors. They do their work carefully, they exercise good judgment, they are zealous, and they are adept at interpersonal relationships. Yet, there is a certain independence and inventiveness which is missing in their performance. Such people are often described as lacking in the quality termed initiative.

At great length managers deplore and bewail the absence of initiative in their subordinates, though they seem less willing to rejoice in its presence. The importance of initiative is stressed at all organizational levels, yet few have addressed it empirically, much less attempted to measure it. Unquestionably initiative is an elusive and vague trait, and is a complex one involving a variety of dimensions of personality. With far less wisdom than I hope is my wont, I have tried both to define and to measure initiative.

It seems to me that initiative has two aspects. One is motivational and involves the beginning of actions, and the other is cognitive and involves the capacity to note and to discover new means of goal achievement. The first aspect involves the ability to act independently and to initiate actions without stimulation and support from others. The second aspect involves the capacity to see courses of action and implementations that are not readily apparent to others. Both aspects have the property of being self-generative. It does not seem to me that initiative implies a capacity to maintain motivation and sustain goal-oriented activity in the face of frustration. Rather a person who possesses initiative is an inaugurator or originator who opens new fields and conceives of novel ways of doing things.

Very likely the test I use to measure initiative is a chancy thing. Even so, I regard it with a certain satisfaction. It is valid in the sense that scores on it are related to superiors' ratings of initiative. But more than that it differentiates those individuals who say they want a job wherein they can use their initiative from those who disclaim any such desire. If I am correct in viewing initiative as being self-generative, then self-reports, such as these reflecting the way an individual proposes to go about things, are of particular importance.

The relationship I find between measured capacity for initiative and age is an interesting one. With line workers there is a progressive decrease in initiative with increasing age, and past the age of 40 initiative shows a sharp and significant drop. On the other hand, with persons in management positions there is a continuous, though small, increase in initiative with age. This suggests the possibility that being in a situation where initiative is not required kills its expression, and being in a job where there are many and continued opportunities to manifest initiative fosters it.

If initiative is an important aspect of managerial talent it should be related to level of occupation; and, indeed, I find this to be the case. Proceeding from line workers through lower and middle management to upper management there is, on the average, an increase in the measured capacity for initiative. Members of upper management appear to be particularly outstanding in this trait. But at all occupational levels there is a wide range of differences among individuals. Even among the laboring groups there is a substantial number of individuals who possess very high levels of capacity for initiative. The supply of people who are outstanding in initiative is substantial. All that is needed is a situation wherein those who possess it can utilize it.

At the upper two levels of management there is a positive relationship between initiative and job performance. The greater the individual's capacity for initiative the more likely he is to be judged as being a good manager. On the other hand, at the lower levels of management and with line jobs, in general I find either no relationship at all between initiative and evaluations of job performance, or a negative relationship. So while initiative might be rewarded at the higher levels of management, at the lower levels it is likely to be punished.

The fourth trait I consider to be an aspect of managerial talent is self-assurance. By self-assurance I mean the extent to which the individual perceives himself to be effective in dealing with the problems which confront him. There are those persons who see themselves as being sound in judgment and able to cope with almost any situation, whereas other people think of themselves as being slow to grasp things, making many mistakes, and being generally inept. The former stand high in self-assurance, and the latter low.

One thinks of the military commander whose utter self-confidence, an almost arrogant self-confidence, permeates his entire troop, reassuring them that all is and will continue to be well, and so impels them to all manner of brave deeds. Undoubtedly the self-assurance of any superior, military or otherwise, often has this sort of effect upon the performance of his subordinates. While certainly self-assurance is often the fool's way, leading him to tread where wiser men will not go, nevertheless it can be the very instrument which enables the individual to deal with his problems and to make decisions about them so that his performance is effective. Because of his confidence in himself he is willing and eager to meet problems head on. Since in many situations any kind of decisive action is better than none at all, the self-confident individual may well achieve the greater success.

Defining self-assurance as I do permits me to demonstrate the validity of my test of the trait in a very simpleminded way. With unbounded self-assurance I simply show that my test differentiates people who believe themselves to be effective individuals from those who believe themselves to be ineffective. I have found that my test differentiates those students who see themselves as scholars from those who see themselves as dunces, those workmen who describe themselves as highly skilled from those who describe themselves as being of lesser proficiency, and those managers who openly admit their performance is excellent from those who confess theirs is lacking.

As with the other managerial traits, as one proceeds from the lower occupational levels to the higher ones there is a greater and greater amount of self-assurance manifested by the personnel at those various levels. There is a substantial distinction between lower and middle management, but also between middle and upper management. Highly placed executives are outstanding in the confidence they have in themselves.

With line workers there is no relationship between their measured self-assurance and their job success. At all three managerial levels there is some, but quite modest, relationship. So while I would consider self-assurance a facet of managerial talent, it, together with initiative, seems to be of lesser importance than intelligence, supervisory ability, and perceived occupational level.

I come now to the fifth and last of the traits I have taken to be aspects of managerial talent, the trait I call perceived occupational level. Whether rightly or wrongly, for good or for evil, we order occupations, as I have done here, from the unskilled through the semiskilled, skilled, clerical, sales, and lower management jobs, to the upper management jobs and professions. The average scores earned by these occupational groups on a variety of psychological traits order them in this manner, or approximately so, and the order reflects their social desirability, their snob appeal, in our society. So in our thinking we have crystallized the notion of a scale of occupations, and we place individuals on that scale in terms of the occupational level of the job they now hold, the job they have the ability to hold, the job they aspire to, and the like.

The monumental work of E. K. Strong (1943) on occupational interests, work stemming from the early research stimulated by Bingham at the Carnegie Institute of Technology, has, among other things, shown that the patterns of interests of persons at different occupational levels are different. Knowing an individual's interest pattern, then, he can be placed on the scale and be described as having the interests of people in the higher occupations, the middle occupations, or the lower occupations.

Just as individuals differ in their patterns of interests so they also differ in their patterns of self-perceptions. Some persons think of themselves as being honest, cautious, and industrious; others think of themselves as being reliable, inventive, and sociable; and so on. Inasmuch as the patterns of interests of workers at different occupational levels differ, we would expect their self-perceptions also to be different. This I have found to be true. I have developed a test wherein the individual describes himself, and these self-perceptions are different for workers at different occupational levels. So I can locate an individual on the occupational scale by ascertaining the level where workers describe themselves in about the same way as he does.

Occupational-level scales based on such matters as interests and self-perceptions generally are considered to measure something akin to level of aspiration. The individual who is placed high on such a scale is regarded as one who wants the responsibility and prestige associated with higher-level jobs, and believes he has the talents required by them. An individual who is placed low on the scale is one who is content with less by way of rewards and status.

By the very nature of my test of perceived occupational level, line workers on the average fall at the lower ranges of the scale and persons holding upper management positions fall at the top, with lower and middle management being intermediately placed. All of the groups are widely differentiated in terms of perceived occupational level, but the largest difference is between lower and middle management. So it would seem that in terms of the way they perceive themselves, line workers and lower management constitute one family, and middle and upper management constitute another family.

I find the same family division in terms of the relationship between perceived occupational level and job proficiency. At the upper two levels of management the relationship between perceived occupational level and job success is positive, and in general at the lower level of management and with line workers it is negative. That is, at the upper levels of management, the more an individual perceives himself in the same way as do those who are in fact high occupationally, the better his performance is judged to be. With lower management and line workers the situation is just the reverse. The more an individual perceives himself in the same way as those who are high occupationally, the poorer his performance is judged to be.

There seems to be adequate justification, then, for considering perceived occupational level as an aspect of managerial talent. Seeing oneself in the same way as those in upper management do would seem to provide the needed stimulation for the individual to perform in ways which insure his moving up the organizational ladder.

I have traced for you my thinking about what I consider to be some of the major facets of managerial talent. Managerial talent has a heavy intellectual component. It perhaps does not represent the very highest levels of abstract thinking, but it does involve the capacity to see and to develop novel solutions to problems. While not synonymous with leadership, managerial talent does manifest itself in the effective direction of others. Finally, managerial talent implies a willingness to depend on oneself coupled with a self-generated impetus to activity and a striving for, and a willingness to accept, the authority and responsibility which goes with high-level positions in organizations. This suggests that the substratum of managerial talent is individuality, and its corollary, the desire for self-realization through creative activity.

Individuality is a term which has very different connotations for different people. Consequently, when one describes a person as being individualistic, some will take him to be a genius and others will take him to be some kind of a nut. If we are to deal with individuality with scientific impartiality we must define it so that the term carries no emotionally loaded meanings. For purposes of examining it empirically, I have defined individuality as the extent to which a person's pattern of traits is unique, that is, the extent to which it is dissimilar from other patterns which are characteristic of many individuals (Ghiselli, 1960).

Therefore, it is possible to conceive of a dimension of individuality. At the one extreme are those persons whose patterns of traits are very different from those of other people, and at the opposite extreme are persons whose patterns are very much like those of a substantial number of people. Furthermore, we can talk about a person's individuality in a variety of domains of behavior. A person might be very individualistic in his behavior which is job connected, doing things in ways which are novel and different, and at the same time he may be quite nonindividualistic in his social behavior, doing just the things that the large proportion of people do in social intercourse.

With a group of men at the level of middle management, I examined individuality in managerial behavior in relationship to job success (Ghiselli, 1960). My results indicated that the men who displayed the greatest individuality in managerial behavior were in general the ones judged to be the best managers. These findings, of course, are counter to the notion so commonly advanced by social critics today that individuality hinders those who aspire to the higher levels of management. Unquestionably there is some substance to the argument that the way to succeed in business is to conform. Indeed, I can give some supporting instances. But I believe the discussions are clouded by poor definitions of the terms "individuality" and "conformity." Furthermore, I am concerned here with managerial talent and individuality in relation to how the individual does his work, and not to how he behaves with respect to the social milieu of his organization.

Haire, Porter, and I are currently engaged in studying the motivations, goals, and attitudes of managers (Haire, Ghiselli, & Porter, 1963; Porter, 1962, 1963). We have questioned several thousand managers not only in the United States but also in a variety of countries throughout the entire world. Not unexpectedly, we find the effects of cultural differences and that the goals of Japanese and Norwegian managers are not precisely the same, nor are those of Indian and Italian managers. Nevertheless, in one respect we find a high degree of unanimity among managers in all countries and at all levels of management. More than anything else, managers want the opportunity to use their talents to the utmost in their work, to act independently, to realize themselves as individuals. Self-realization and autonomy universally are more important to managers than prestige, social satisfactions, and even security.

So I believe there is some substance for my suggestion that the substratum of managerial talent is individuality and the desire for self-realization through creative activity. It seems to me that this gives flavor and meaning to the picture I drew of the talented manager as one who is well endowed intellectually, gifted with the capacity to direct the efforts of others, self-stimulated to action, confident in his abilities, and striving for a position where he can most fully utilize them.

If it seems I am describing a paragon of all the virtues, let me remind you that I am speaking of talent, which, as Bingham (1939a) put it, is exceptional ability. There are managers and managers, and not all of them manifest high levels of managerial talent. Indeed, the proportion of those who do may not be large. Those of greater managerial talent do their work well and advance in their organizations, and those of lesser managerial talent perform in a pedestrian manner, leave management for other employment commensurate with their particular abilities, or at retirement terminate their careers at low or intermediate managerial levels. Furthermore, I would point out that persons with the properties I have called managerial talent might well be ill fitted for other kinds of activities. The picture I have drawn of a person with managerial talent very likely does not well describe the scientist, the physician, nor the politician. So I am not describing that rare individual who could equally well be king, prelate, or general. Nevertheless, the individual with managerial talent is a gifted person, and an unusual one. Proper use of his gifts will give him the rewards and satisfactions he needs and deserves, and at the same time will maintain the wheels turning in industry and the goods moving in business for the benefit of society as a whole.

References

Bingham, W. V. *Aptitudes and aptitude testing.* New York: Harper, 1937.

Bingham, W. V. Administrative ability, its discovery and development. Pamphlet No. 1, 1939, Society for Personnel Administration, Washington, D.C. (a)

Bingham, W. V. Halo, invalid and valid. *J. appl. Psychol.,* 1939, *23,* 221–228. (b)

Frederiksen, N. Factors in in-basket performance. *Psychol. Monogr.,* 1962, *76* (22, Whole No. 541).

Ghiselli, E. E. The measurement of occupational aptitude. *U. Calif. Publ. Psychol.,* 1955, *8,* 101–216. (a)

Ghiselli, E. E. A scale for the measurement of initiative. *Personnel Psychol.,* 1955, *8,* 157–164. (b)

Ghiselli, E. E. Correlates of initiative. *Personnel Psychol.,* 1956, *9,* 311–320. (a)

Ghiselli, E. E. Occupational level measured through self perception. *Personnel Psychol.,* 1956, *9,* 169–176. (b)

Ghiselli, E. E. Traits differentiating management personnel. *Personnel Psychol.,* 1959, *12,* 535–544.

Ghiselli, E. E. Individuality as a factor in the success of management personnel. *Personnel Psychol.,* 1960, *13,* 1–10.

Ghiselli, E. E. Intelligence and managerial success. *Psychol. Rep.,* 1963, *12,* 898. (a)

Ghiselli, E. E. The validity of management traits in relation to occupational level. *Personnel Psychol.,* 1963, *16,* 109–113. (b)

Ghiselli, E. E., & Barthol, R. Role perceptions of successful and unsuccessful supervisors. *J. appl. Psychol.,* 1956, *40,* 241–244.

Ghiselli, E. E., & Lodahl, T. M. The evaluation of foremen's performance in relation to the internal characteristics of their work groups. *Personnel Psychol.*, 1958, *11*, 179–187. (a)

Ghiselli, E. E., & Lodahl, T. M. Patterns of managerial traits and group effectiveness. *J. abnorm. soc. Psychol.*, 1958, *57*, 61–66. (b)

Haire, M. Biological models and empirical histories of growth of organizations. In M. Haire (ed.), *Modern organization theory.* New York: Wiley, 1959, pp. 272–306.

Haire, M., Ghiselli, E. E., & Porter, L. W. Cultural patterns in the role of the manager. *Industr. Relat.*, 1963, *2*, 95–117.

Harrell, T. W. *Manager's performance and personality.* Cincinnati, Ohio: South-Western, 1961.

Hemphill, J. K. Dimensions of executive positions. Columbus: Ohio State Univer. Press, 1960. (Bur. Bus. Res. Monogr. No. 98.)

Likert, R. *New patterns of management.* New York: McGraw-Hill, 1961.

Porter, L. W. Differential self-perceptions of management personnel and line workers. *J. appl. Psychol.*, 1958, *42*, 105–108.

Porter, L. W. Self-perceptions of first-level supervisors compared with upper-management personnel and with operative line workers. *J. appl. Psychol.*, 1959, *43*, 183–186.

Porter, L. W. Job attitudes in management: I. Perceived deficiencies in need fulfillment as a function of job level. *J. appl. Psychol.*, 1962, *46*, 375–384.

Porter, L. W. Job attitudes in management: II: Perceived importance of needs as a function of job level. *J. appl. Psychol.*, 1963, *47*, 141–148.

Porter, L. W., & Ghiselli, E. E. The self perceptions of top and middle management personnel. *Personnel Psychol.*, 1957, *10*, 397–406.

Shartle, C. L. *Executive performance and leadership.* Englewood Cliffs, N.J.: Prentice-Hall, 1956.

Strong, E. K. *Vocational interests of men and women.* Stanford, Calif.: Stanford Univer. Press, 1943.

Tagiuri, R. (ed.). *Research needs in executive selection.* Boston: Harvard Univer. Graduate School Business Administration, Division Research, 1961.

Norman H. Mackworth *Originality*[1]

Great care is needed when one is choosing a title for an address of this kind. I heard, for example, about the tragic fate of someone who gave a talk about computers entitled "Artificial Intelligence." His audience claimed that it was too autobiographical. By calling my paper "Originality," I feel I could be running a different kind of risk. There is only one way in which I can claim first-hand experience of originality. I have had the good fortune to meet and work with some of the most original people in the world—on both sides of the Atlantic. This has been and is so rewarding that it is only fitting that I should try to add something to what has been said on the subject.

My 10 distinguished predecessors, granted this very real honor, have covered the ground most thoroughly. Furthermore, seven excellent books have recently been published on the subject (Coler, 1963; Gruber, Terrell, & Wertheimer, 1962; Harper, Anderson, Christensen, & Hunka, 1964; Koestler, 1964; Miller,

1. This paper is based on the Walter Van Dyke Bingham Lecture given at Pennsylvania State University, May 27, 1964. It was first published in the *American Psychologist*, 1965, vol. 20, no. 1 (January), pp. 51–66.

Galanter, & Pribram, 1960; Sayre & Crosson, 1963; Taylor & Barron, 1963). It would be foolish to try to summarize this wealth of material; as an alternative, I shall present some ways of looking at *scientific originality.* I hope that some of these thoughts are sufficiently explicit that they can be tested by experiment or administrative change.

Problem Solver and Problem Finder

Solving versus Finding Problems

Most people are quite clear by now that there are real differences between scientists who are largely solving problems and those who are mainly raising questions. The novelist C. P. Snow (1960) notes these two worlds even within the scientific community. He speaks from considerable experience since he took a large part in the relocation of senior scientists in wartime Britain. He distinguishes between those who are better at solving given problems and those who can formulate new concepts not previously studied. Much more research should now be aimed at understanding the somewhat mysterious ways of these problem finders, although obviously it will be a very long time before the deep insights of a Rutherford are analyzable to any extent (Eve, 1939). A crude yardstick for the stature of successful prophets is the number of years that others have taken to prove that they were indeed right. A Rutherford would score as much as 10 on this scale, since he was sometimes very far ahead of the evidence on atomic structure. Great achievements were also made by Turing who sketched the essentials of digital computers about 10 years before these were actually in existence (Armer, 1963; Green, 1963; Oettinger, 1964).

Scientific Inflation

There are several reasons why the distinction between the problem solver and the problem finder is vital. First of all, problem finding is more important than problem solving. Indeed the greatest contribution that can be made nowadays is to formulate new and testable ideas; the scientist who does not speculate is no scientist at all (Hebb, 1958).

Second, problem finding is so very different from problem solving that further intensive study of simple problem solving is not going to add much to our understanding of originality. The broader cognitive processes have to be tackled in general experimental studies of people who are doing problem finding since this is a much more complex process.

A third reason for studying problem finders is that they undoubtedly form a scientific bottleneck. Problem finders are already scarce, yet they are going to be even more in demand as the years go by. This is due to a plain but startling fact. The rate at which discoveries are made now depends more than ever on the number of people who can *formulate* important research problems.

Scientific progress is no longer determined by the number of people who are good at solving problems because already the supreme problem solvers of our day are machines (Feigenbaum & Feldman, 1963; Greenberger, 1964; Minsky, 1963; Reitman, 1964). The scientist will eventually be freed of even more drudgery by digital computers (Wang, 1963). It is therefore all the more surprising that every branch of science is now being held back because thoughtless engineering has seriously handicapped the widespread introduction of these remarkable techniques. Digital computers have not yet been planned to receive messages from humans. For example, one small change in a program may take a week to introduce. Far too few designers have tried to make it possible to change computer programs quickly. No other devices in the world are quite so badly designed from the point of view of ease of human use.

The great designers of this century will be those who produce computers that readily respond to man's changing thoughts. The automation of science will start when friendly thinking aids replace the present rather distant oracles. This advance, however, may well lead to a most serious scientific inflation. A superabundance of problem-solving techniques could cause a famine of ideas. Once their programs are written, machines are very impressive at solving problems. More can be done in 1 day than in a lifetime of unaided calculations. For example, a program written by Wang recently enabled a digital computer to solve as many as 350 theorems, taken from the first 13 chapters of *Principia Mathematica,* in just under 8½ minutes (Pierce, 1964). Similarly, a problem has been answered in 8 seconds that took the astronomer, Kepler, nearly 2 years to solve.

Machines may eventually also assist in problem finding. Real pioneers such as Licklider (1960) and Minsky (1963), as well as Yntema and Torgerson (1961) have discussed some of the extraordinary benefits (and difficulties) of making digital computers more approachable in the sense of establishing two-way interplay between man and machine. The real excitement is due to begin when the computer regularly comes in at the level of a coauthor; in other words, computers will soon work with men at formulating problems in a give-and-take manner. This implies that the scientist sits at his own private keyboard and operates the machine himself, feeding in first approximations in data form and watching for the results. Hopefully, he will always have a programmer beside him as a safety pilot, since really large and fast computers need an experienced hand if disaster is to be avoided (Newman, 1962). Already such computers are being designed to be employed by many users at remote stations via telephone wires. Existing computers are already fast enough to handle as many as 3,000 such private consoles (McCarthy, 1964). It is therefore not just science fiction to imagine that in a few years every competent basic research man in the United States could have this remarkable facility with his own keyboard in his office.

At first these investigators might well be in a state of fascinated anguish. All this potential problem-solving power will be at their fingertips. For the first time they will have absolute freedom to think. Plans will be tested quickly, and analyzed data will pour back from the machine. Nothing-to-do-but-think may be a mixed blessing when creative ideas do not come fast enough (Licklider, 1964). Later, however, these new and stimulating arrangements may greatly accelerate the whole pace of research because researchers will learn the results of their labors so quickly. Publication could be remarkably stimulating and different. Keyboards could rattle away during the night hours to print out messages from selected colleagues. Eventually, however, this would reduce the invisible college effect noted by Price (1961), because fine words coming in quickly and easily from the wilds could make a good man more detectable.

But escape into the future solves few problems in the present, so we should resume our central theme of human talent. Consider, for example, how Houssay (1961) phrased his views as he received his Nobel Prize.

> The most remarkable piece of research apparatus is the human brain. Some people want to buy every piece of equipment known to science. They believe that with a beautiful building filled with modern equipment they have a first rate research institute. That is a superstition. The great discoveries have been made by men working alone [p. 36].

Although this is the general pattern for present-day research, most people do not realize that by far the most usual way for an original concept to start is in exactly one brain. The individual inventor is often more important than any corporate research by a team of people. The man who found penicillin felt that a team of people was fine when you had something to go on, but when you had nothing to go on, a team was the worst possible way of starting. Jewkes, Sawers, and Stillerman (1961) also make a strong case for the idea that the day of the individual inventor is by no means over. They reached this conclusion after carefully analyzing more than 60 of the main inventions of the twentieth century. They found a tendency for originality to show up in areas quite different from the inventor's own field. For example, the automatic dial telephone was devised by a mortician. The inventor of xerography was a lawyer. The pneumatic tire came from a veterinary surgeon. There are remarkably few scientists in the ranks of the inventor. Specialization may have so cramped their inventive abilities that they hesitate to put forward their ideas beyond their own subjects. A related matter is that important general problems involving many disciplines are sometimes not undertaken for a rather similar reason. Experts are often reluctant even to start to discuss problems in which they cannot see the whole picture for themselves. This is rather surprising because all would agree with Barzun (1964) that the aims of science are to discover a network of facts and make general statements about them.

Problem finders are scarce because this kind of basic thinking is very difficult to undertake. Indeed a good problem is often half a discovery. But there are several other reasons—relating to the streamlining of college procedures—why there are not enough idea men. Current mental tests are biased against problem finders because they inevitably favor the solver. Quite recently it was again emphasized that educational psychologists use examinations and intelligence tests which pick out the efficient verbal reasoners rather than the intuitive observers or constructive thinkers (Burt, 1964). The problem finders that do reach college probably insist on setting their own goals and then may become so spiritedly rebellious that some authorities like MacKinnon (1963) even wonder whether all colleges should even try to seek out the potentially creative. Then again, there is a high wastage during the PhD years, since the solution of given problems may not suit the abilities of the problem finder and such candidates may get lost in the rush of deadlines so characteristic of this time.

Certain specific problems simply do not permit any originality at all. Guilford (1963) has termed this kind of activity convergent thinking. Here the problem solver is quite goalbound, as in the ubiquitous and iniquitous multiple-choice examination. For about 20 years, would-be researchers have learned that one answer rings the bell. Guilford contrasts this convergent thinking with divergent thinking, a classification which resembles the comparison made by Bartlett (1950, 1958) between closed and adventurous thinking.

The Nature of Problem Finding

In research, however, many bells ring out for one success, especially in general investigations. Yet basic research is so very fundamental and buried that most people have never even heard of it. Somehow it seems strange that this quiet partner should be so little understood. The National Science Foundation has repeatedly drawn attention to the great potential interest for the man in the street of this adventurous thinking quite characteristic of basic research. They have defined this activity as a continuing search for new knowledge—guided primarily by an interest in learning more about the ways of nature (NSF, 1961). A less ambitious view was that of Cannon (1945). He said that what the experimenter is really trying to do is to learn whether facts can be established which will be recognized as facts by others and which will support some idea of his own. Highly important attempts are now being made by the National Science Foundation, and others, to keep alive the early curiosity that children so often lose during their school years. The individual scientist usually enjoys a keen sense of adventure and excitement. Indeed, the creative researcher is just as involved in his work as is the poet or the artist (Roe, 1964). This is partly because he has developed the sustaining habit of truth, a somewhat rare quality. Wiener (1954, 1964) and Bronowski (1956) have stressed these aspects and emphasized that the good research man also has a feeling for human dignity which he shares with the vast majority of investigators throughout the world.

Genuine satisfactions also come from the exquisite elegance with which laws can be seen to be condensed into concepts. This is best described by Bronowski (1956) who indicated that "science takes its intellectual coherence and imaginative strength from the concepts at which its laws cross, like knots in a mesh [p. 67]." Such order must usually be discovered by methods discussed by Beveridge (1950), Moles (1957), and Bernard (1961); it does not often display itself simply. In a sense, it must be created. Several studies have noted that disorder does not too greatly dismay original-minded scientists. They like to be able to resolve it. They definitely prefer complexity in test situations. It forms a challenge, just like a complicated case is exciting for the medical man. But details and facts are not nearly so interesting for their own sake as for their meanings and implications (MacKinnon, 1962). Creative individuals have an exceptionally strong need to find order where none appears on the surface. The apparently unclassifiable gains their fascinated attention (Barron,

1963). They merely wish to understand the natural world, whereas the more practical man wishes to control it (Snow, 1964). In his important book on the way of an investigator, Cannon (1945) describes experiences in medical research; he notes that curiosity is the mainspring of his inventive and persistent industry. It is a prime requisite for a career of exploration because without it the researcher is dead. For those who believe in it, the unexpected can happen from time to time.

The real mark of the basic researcher is that the unforeseen problem is a joy and not a curse. Paradoxically, the basic research man is searching for the unexpected. That is what he is doing down there grubbing around the roots of knowledge. He is looking for the problems, and that is what his working life is for—not just to hit the targets, but to find them. In other words, an uncharted hill is not an obstacle; it is a new height to be scaled because it provides a different viewpoint from which innumerable details can be seen in perspective.

More than ever, men are needed to try to define the unexpected problems, whether these are to be found in basic research, in space research, or in air defense. There are human aspects of intelligence which have not yet been touched upon in information-processing models of thinking, although this approach has already proved of real value. Digital computers are seriously inadequate as problem finders. Their silent majesty has this major flaw in that they cannot process the unexpected by themselves. Quite often they can be seen marching their troops off in the wrong direction during the battle of ideas (Neisser, 1963). People, however, do not usually have to have their whole program laid out in advance. Hebb (1958) has emphasized that "the better the idea, the more likely it is to have been extremely vague, inchoate, when experimentation began, and to have become definite only as a *result* of the experiment [p. 464]."

An activity like problem finding would seem to be close to the heart of originality in creative thinking in science. The person builds up a mental model of the likelihood of events. Bruner (1957a, 1957b) has described how an information-processing approach to cognition can be used to describe complex thought processes. In his papers, "On Perceptual Readiness" and "On Going Beyond the Information Given," he has primarily aimed at an understanding of how people build up coding systems that apply beyond the situation in which they were learned. Not only are the stimuli from the environment summarized, but new information can be generated. Perceiving accurately under substandard conditions consists in being able to refer stimulus inputs to appropriate coding systems. Where the information is fragmentary, one reads the missing properties of the stimulus input from the code to which part of the input has been referred. Another important paper is on "Memory Mechanisms and the Theory of Schemata" by Oldfield (1964). This summarizes the early views of Head and Bartlett (1932) on the survival of fragments of experience in schemata and indicates how recall consists in their reconstruction. Oldfield also describes how incoming messages might be summarized for storage as common patterns. Inputs departing from such schemata are stored unsummarized, and dominant details will then act as labels for storage and starting points for recall.

The hallmark of the creative enterprise is that there should be effective surprise because only minds with structured expectancies and interests can distinguish real trends from trivial improbabilities (Berlyne, 1960; Bruner, 1962). The triumph of such a state is that it takes one beyond common ways of experiencing the world; this is why original scientists so often fairly bubble with excitement most days of the year. Stimulating tensions are created even by differences between expected and actual circumstances which seem unbelievably slight to the man in the street. The inventor is also often stimulated to further efforts by no more than the differences between a strong mental image of the ideal version of his intended device and the actual miserable achievements to be seen in his prototype equipment. The more abstract thinker enjoys a similar spur—but now the intensity comes from a mismatch between a mental model of reality and experimental evidence from the real world. Visual images of expected events may be so strong in some biologists that Roe (1964) found they were practically watching mental movies. The mismatch may often be based on the difference between this expected state and the *apparent* actual facts of reality rather than the actual facts, since these can be either wrong, scanty, or late (Forrester, 1964).

The need to change a conceptual framework of ideas is yet another reason why originality is so rarely found. Few people can tolerate the ultimate dilemma: Good scientists have to be careful conservatives and wild radicals almost at the same time. An intellectual framework must be acquired by reading and experiment, and then prudently followed to give a basis from which to detect any significant variations from normality. The real test comes when this faithful framework has to be discarded rather quickly because another set of ideas fits the actual events more closely (Polyani, 1963). Conformity is then the cardinal sin. Good scientists must not only be willing to take risks but they must in fact positively enjoy doing so; indeed they have been termed intelligent, bold introverts (Cattell, 1963; McClelland, 1963). They have also been described as logical, opinionated, impatient, intense, thorough, meticulous, reserved, and clannish by Orth (1959). Creative scientists are also unusually hard working to the extent of appearing almost obsessed with their job. The *one* characteristic all of them have had without exception is an intense devotion to their work. They work nights, weekends, holidays, all of the time (Roe, 1964). A sidelight on the reasons for this endless activity at the frontier has been given by Land, who invented the Polaroid camera (Bello, 1959).

> I find it important to work intensively for long hours when I am beginning to see solutions to a problem. At such times atavistic competences seem to come welling up. You are handling so many variables at a barely conscious level that you can't afford to be interrupted. If you are, it may take a year to cover the same ground you could otherwise in sixty (60) hours [p. 124].

Short-term aims often kill long-term objectives. For example, with reports and studies and telephones to be dealt with every minute, nothing great is accomplished, only small work is done (Houssay, 1961).

At the other end of the scale is the data gatherer—the gleaner as opposed to the guesser. Apart from a series of work samples, the best way to detect the problem solver is to ask him which of five specific but very dissimilar areas he would like to study. Often he may be right in saying that he has no strong preference for any of these very different proposed investigations; he has not structured his experience enough to give even vague guidelines for his thinking.

The drawback of the absence of any relevent conceptual framework can be found in trained scientists when they are working outside their usual fields. This has been well described by Blade (1963) who was quite unable to classify the various types of spruce trees found during a vacation in Maine. Being an amateur botanist, he had no structured system of categories into which he could place the very large number of variations to name them in some meaningful way. It was only after several days that he began to recognize the presence of rules that had escaped him at first. All the possible categories had to be thought out for use in a program in the same way as all the possible moves on a checkerboard have been narrowed down into the rules for checkers or chess (Koestler, 1964).

The Nature of Problem Solving

Problem solving is more often found in a practical setting just as problem finding can best be studied in the setting of basic research. But basic research and practical research are inseparably intertwined (Naval Research Advisory Committee, 1959). Indeed they help each other just like the two kinds of blood vessels in the body. There are some useful parallels to be drawn between the gathering of information and the circulation of the blood with its system of outgoing arteries and incoming veins. Outward from the heart go these red and practical arteries always subdividing until they end in the diverging capillary tree. Each of these tiny arterial capillaries, therefore, comes to bear on just one small part of the body. This rather resembles the analytic way in which the red-blooded practical answer is found by constantly narrowing down the search to end up with one highly specific choice. For a time the arterial capillaries are indistinguishable from the venous capillaries. But then inward come the blue and abstract veins, always converging and converging to get to the heart of the matter. This merging and synthesizing process broadly includes more and more of the details flowing in the system. The unifying concepts of basic research are therefore found by a grouping together. This entails guiding wider and wider ranges of details into a few deceptively simple pathways, seldom foreseen, and converging into sweeping blue-sky abstractions.

Something of the nature of the early process that takes place at the start of scientific problem solving has been outlined in an exciting manner by Polyani (1963), who made some valuable points by discussing a problem in astronomy. The question was whether the observed deviations from the theoretical path of a planet showed any real regularity against the background of other variations in the same track which arise from observational errors. Were these perturbations quite random, and, therefore, just background noise? Or did they really consist of a definite signal of some significance? Computers already help to a considerable extent in solving such problems. Particularly relevant here are multiple recording techniques to analyze waveforms in electroretinograms; these can average out random effects and detect regularity beneath the disorder. This is a very simple kind of problem-solving behavior. The variations are being detected by a given classification system based on a clear knowledge beforehand of the only way the stimulus can vary.

Much more complex forms of human problem solving have recently been analyzed by some very successful attempts to write programs for digital computers which will simulate human problem solving. For example, Newell, Shaw, and Simon (1958a, 1958b, 1963a, 1963b) have studied the machine solution of chess problems and mathematical theorems by such means. They have found it quite possible to instruct their computers to adopt shortcuts which people often taken in reaching answers (Newell & Simon, 1961, 1963). Their General Problem Solver, for example, is a program which reasons about ends and means. It is capable of defining ends, seeking means to attain them, and, in the process of so doing, defining new subsidiary ends or subgoals to the original end. By breaking down the problem into subproblems, the solution becomes more flexible. Similarly, the problem has sometimes been simplified by omitting certain details. Alternatively, the solution of an apparently related parallel problem is a help. Another favorite shortcut is to work backwards from the end of the problem to the beginning (Simon, 1964). This work has so far been more successful at simulating human intelligence than in replacing it by a more efficient problem-solving machine (Minsky, 1963). The main contribution has been that these authors have given psychologists a language in which they can be both explicit and comprehensive when expressing their theoretical concepts (Miller *et al.*, 1960). This language may sometimes look rather like Braille to the uninitiated, but at least it is clear and definite. The enormous detail in these programs has also made some of their ideas hard to grasp, but in general this simulation approach does enable ideas to be stated quite definitely and their implications to be thoroughly tested. For example, Newell, Shaw, and Simon have already produced programs for their General Problem Solver such that it is quite impossible to tell from step-by-step verbatim records whether the problem was being solved by a man or by a machine. By such methods they have therefore already achieved very considerable advances in the understanding of problem solving by humans (Hovland, 1964; Miller, 1962, 1964; Reitman, 1964).

Some Differences between Problem Solving and Problem Finding

Computer terminology undoubtedly also helps by expressing the relationships between problem solving and problem finding. These two activities look alike at first sight. Indeed it is true that people are in search of a program or an organized set of mental rules whether they are solving problems or finding them. This similarity has rather misled some into believing that problem solving and finding are more closely related than they really are. Newell, Shaw, and Simon (1958b) have even claimed that:

> Creative activity appears simply to be a special class of problem solving activity characterised by novelty, unconventionality, persistence and difficulty in problem formulation [p. 5].

This definition is much too limited in scope compared with the better and more extensive definition by Sprecher (1959); he emphasized the essential fact that a truly creative contribution generates additional creative activity,

> For example, an important scientific theory provides new solutions to problems hitherto unsolved, new perceptions of problems hitherto unperceived, and new discoveries. This characteristic provides a basis for measurement of levels or degree of creativity. At the bottom of the scale, the creative product simply solves the immediate problem to which it was directed. At the top of the scale, the creative product provides the solution not only to the immediate problem, but also to a wide range of related problems, affects broad areas of thought and activity and may even open up new fields of research or technology or other action or progress . . . [p. 155].

Both these definitions, however, lose sight of the main point that there is an all-important qualitative difference between problem solving and finding. It is clear that *problem solving is a choice between existing programs or sets of mental rules—whereas problem finding is the detection of the need for a new program based on a choice between existing and expected future programs.* It is this consideration of possible new plans and their subsequent construction that accounts for the successful additional outburst of related activity that follows a good problem. This can sometimes even come from discarded programs that proved unsuitable for the initial question. The creative scientist often appears to stumble across new problems. To do this he must start by noting the need for looking at data in a fresh way for a given purpose. The alert problem finder must then be able to produce these changes in his mental coding arrangements. In a sense, he can only do this by devising new mental programs or plans and realizing they are more suitable for relating the facts than the existing mental rules. Quite unexpectedly these new programs may also apply to other problems which can now be tackled for the first time.

In comparing problem solving and finding it is sometimes convenient to describe them side by side as in Table 1.

Some Research Possibilities on Problem Finding

Problem finding is difficult for computers because at present they are not self-programed, whereas people can change their own programs completely. Unlike machine programs, people can do this repeatedly without losing valuable experience collected over long periods of time. One of the most fruitful research ideas is believed to be to study how people develop new mental programs or plans without starting afresh each time (Miller *et al.*, 1960). Such investigations would be partly experimental and partly descriptive in nature; they should give some leads on how people grind out general laws from collections of facts, to borrow a gloomy phrase from Charles Darwin, who was himself a champion program changer (Darwin, 1902).

Problem finding in research is essentially the establishment of the need for a new and highly complex mental program. This kind of creative activity is one of the most intricate ways in which humans interact with their environment. Such highly intellectual processes are, therefore, too involved to permit adequate analysis by direct study. Very fortunately, however, it may be feasible to dissect out and follow the formulation of new programs in simpler but related situations. The suggestion is to have experimental studies of the classifying of substandard visual patterns—especially the type of task in which rules would have to be formulated to set up satisfactory coding systems from inputs which are either incomplete or faulty (Bruner, Goodnow, & Austin, 1956).

Table 1. Problem solving and problem finding by humans.

	Problem solving	Problem finding
Definition	Problem solving is the selection and use of an existing program from an existing set of programs.	Problem finding is the detection of the need for a new program by comparing existing and expected future programs.
Objective	To *choose correctly between existing programs*—in order to select the one program that effectively elicits the required actions from a set of possible responses.	To *choose correctly between existing and expected future programs*—in order to devise new programs and to realize that one or more of these would be more suitable than any of the existing programs in eliciting the required actions.
Method	Experiment more than thought minimizes the mismatch between the desired and apparent actual states.	Thought more than experiment minimizes the mismatch between the desired and apparent actual states.
Outcome	Success is the discovery of one specific acceptable answer to one well-defined problem.	Success is the discovery of many general questions from many ill-defined problems.

We need then to know more about simple coding, especially how new coding categories are formulated and selected. This work would resemble the studies on the extent to which, for example, the seven million colors are usually summarized into the usual 20 convenient categories (Bruner, Postman, & Rodrigues, 1951). We also need to learn how input categories can be *changed* to suit the circumstances. The reason is simply that we must understand how the scientist appreciates the need for the formation of a new program. He must obviously do this by relating the customary facts to his existing set of categories; in this way he finds that these are not adequate to cover some new way of looking at the usual evidence. The crux of the experimental approach would therefore be to discover how people set up rules for visual pattern recognition. The more we learn about this rule finding, the closer we shall come to some understanding of the coding procedures and categories involved in research and decision making (Tolcott, Chenzoff, Crittenden, Flores, Frances, Kelley, & Mackworth, 1960).

This new mental program in research thinking is inevitably organized so that the plan forms a related set of instructions arranged in rank order. It would be particularly interesting, therefore, to devise studies in which the test subjects had to develop a filing system for unfamiliar visual shapes without knowing the categories into which these fell. The subjects would, however, know that they were intended to make this into some hierarchical set of categories. Initially, the most suitable test material would be a large unclassified collection of hundreds of individual fingerprints. These would be shown in sets of about 10 prints at a time to ease the burden on immediate memory. The subject would then have to indicate which of these prints seemed to be closely related to one another. The set of 10 prints would then be replaced by another set which would now, however, contain some items previously seen. The fingerprints which were most often linked with others would constantly be fed back by the experimenter and included in the changing sample array so that eventually a row of highly typical fingerprints might be obtained in the display; each such print would be rather unlike the other in some respect. Every subject might well end up with a different row of typical fingerprints because there would clearly be many kinds of rules that could be applied. Note, however, that the subject need not even verbally formulate the rules he was using in building up these groupings by cross-reference. He could point at the items that appeared to belong together without giving any reasons (Fano, 1964). If necessary, however, a stand eye camera could also record the track of his line of sight as it wandered to and fro across the row of prints (Mackworth & Kaplan, 1963). These eye tracks might well be specially interesting since they could automatically register fleeting mismatches eventually corrected on the way to the final decisions (Bartlett, 1958).

By such means (and subsequent verbal report) it would be possible to discover the rules that the subject was developing. This could determine how the decision tree was growing, and how far it resembled various standard classification trees known only to the researcher. The emphasis would be on climbing up the roots of this tree and on working toward a few broad categories away from those early insufferable details. Part of the experimenter's task would be to devise meaningful ways of evaluating the suggested categories. For example, he might try out any such proposed clusters of items by giving the selected typical prints to other subjects to use as group samples: In this way he could find out how effective these were in practice as key items expressing rules for classifying shapes.

A side benefit of this kind of work is that it could help to devise machine pattern-recognition procedures. The limiting factor in the power of machines to recognize patterns is the inability of humans to identify the promising features in patterns that would be indicative in classifying them. Nobody yet really understands how people recognize general visual patterns; therefore, computers still find pattern recognition one of the hardest forms of work because no one knows the instructions that the programs should contain (Neisser, 1963; Sayre & Crosson, 1963).

Ideas for rule-finding studies in humans might well eventually come from machines searching and attempting to discover regularity in data. But computers and their programs are not likely to help very much with this at present. Although computers are usually by no means self-programing, they can already improve an existing program—and it is exciting to see these beginnings of computer learning by experience. For example, the machine recognition of specific hand-printed capital letters has led to programs that found for themselves the features that differentiated the various letters (Selfridge & Neisser, 1963). Computers have also been programed so that the skill with which they played checkers improved more or less continuously, since the machine could learn at each move. Samuel (1963) used a novel approach here in that his program provided two different machine players, Alpha and Beta. In this arrangement, Alpha was the front man who played the humans and Beta was the backroom boy acting as a pacer. Alpha often proposed some improvement after each of these matches. But these suggested changes were only accepted by the program after they had been solemnly checked out during a further intramural game between Alpha and Beta!

We may yet see extensive problem finding by machines. There are some very interesting possibilities that could emerge from this description, by Simon (1960b), of the ideal self-programing form of computer instructions for the next step in this remarkable journey. This would no longer be a highly stereotyped program,

> but a program that makes the system's behavior highly conditional on the task environment, on the task goals and on

> the clues extracted from the environment that indicates whether progress is being made toward these goals. It will be a program that analyzes by some means its own performance, diagnoses its failures and makes changes that enhance its future effectiveness [p. 25].

It is already true that a computer program has conjectured new theorems—or supposed theorems—and set up the subgoal of proving these (Newell, Shaw, & Simon, 1958b). But these new theorems were found by working backward from the goal of proving a related theorem—and how often is an associated goal known? Wang (1963) describes generating 1,000 theorems in 1 hour, and it is also true that IBM computers have formed hypotheses in explicit situations (Kochen, 1961). So far, only people have been able to search amongst poorly defined alternatives for vaguely stated objectives. But we have already learned from Hebb (1958) that this is exactly the kind of situation that leads even experienced research men to some of their best ideas. Nevertheless Simon (1960a) has predicted that, before 1970, computer programs will be able to solve the range of problems that humans can tackle including questions that are not at all well structured. To an increasing extent, computers will write their own programs and they may even be able to formulate some problems. But on the whole, man will still be rather better at undertaking vaguely specified problem finding.

There remains, therefore, only one hope for any androboosters like Neisser (1963), Barzun (1964), and myself. Problem finding will always be difficult for machines (if not downright impossible) when even related end goals or subgoals are absent. Basically it is a rather exacting requirement to have to work back from an unknown point—or to have to simplify the mismatch between present position and an unknown destination. Some might therefore hold the view that problem finding is the last refuge for the unaided brain in science—simply because there are people who have this unusual ability to search for the unexpected. Yet even such problem finders would be wiser to join them (rather than try to beat them). Man remains the senior partner for this purpose even if the association is called man-computer symbiosis.

The Individual and the Institute

Research Setting

But no man is an island, least of all the good investigator. The second part of this talk, therefore, considers the relation between the creative research man and other people. In his youth and later he may well have usually been a minority of one, according to Torrance (1962), Getzels and Jackson (1962), and Hofstadter (1963). Any creative character therefore raises special problems as well as the research questions he asks when he enters the doors of a research organization. It is interesting to try to detect at least some of the essential administrative circumstances that facilitate original ways of thinking. Various long lists of the factors involved have been prepared; the best of these being in Taylor and Barron (1963), and in Coler (1963). But these details may obscure the outstanding fact that, in general, the social and intellectual environment is of much greater importance than the physical surroundings. For example, Orth (1959) has recognized that the optimum climate for industrial research is largely determined by the background of opinion set by the management.

Some architectural design features should be mentioned in passing, however, because these make for an easier relationship with others. The first is a comparatively small matter—simply that good air conditioning may be an essential in certain areas to avoid the disastrous lassitude and irritability so fatal for intellectual activity. The second architectural point is more fundamental. There is a need for accidental discussion and casual communication and this can be contrived by what might be termed arranged meeting spaces. The long row of small separate rooms is great for monks but not for research men. In other words, researchers need togetherness from time to time, almost as much as they need to close the door and spare the mind. When, therefore, six or more such doors open on the same meeting place, it is surprising how much easier it is to have a meeting of the minds that initially results from quite accidental encounters.

Formation and Destruction of Ideas

Now, why should it be important to make such elaborate and somewhat tortuous arrangements to encourage mental encounters between scientists? The answer is simply that original people of this kind have inevitably built up their own very strong framework of ideas which need to be tested (to destruction, if necessary). We have discussed how essential it is to build up such a structure. But these same fixed ideas can be an occupational hazard for even the best of men; they can form a door shut against further thinking rather than a ladder to the stars. Such scientists work from a one-reel program. The near-great develop one unique approach to certain problems and never change that mental program. But the really great are kept genuinely humble; they know they are going to have to change and change and change their approach to almost the same set of ideas over and over again. Perhaps they resemble fine generals who can confidently act on the best guess about an exceedingly chaotic battle. They are able to change the rules of their strategy when suddenly the smoke clears to reveal an apparently slight trend in the tactical situation which makes nonsense of their present approach. What we need from a theory is that it should hold together long enough to lead us to a better one (Hebb, 1958).

Frequent meetings with others are therefore vital, a matter considered by Hughes (1963) in some detail. Original people have inevitably built up such a rigid structure of ideas that it takes a head-on collision with an equally strong (or even more rigid) mental structure of a different kind to have the desired effect. This effect will be to convert that endless journey round one single skull into more than the regular creaking of a mental treadmill. The more eminent the skull, the further it has to travel to find the few people in the world who can put these revered but imprisoned brains into new and better shape. Henle (1962) interestingly discusses the need to consider the death of old ideas as well as the birth of new concepts.

The painless way of altering research assumptions is the well-known working-research fellowship, lasting perhaps a year. This can blur the stored mental patterns sufficiently to permit a recombining of their elements into quite new shapes. I was privileged to help Sir Frederic Bartlett start a series of such visits from the United States to the Medical Research Council's Applied Research Unit in Cambridge, England. My successor there, Donald Broadbent, has done such a fine job that a whole series of National Science Foundation fellowships has been held there in the last few years. The host unit also greatly benefits by such visits, and I believe the advantages of this idea could be extended if in general the host institute in England could provide a nucleus of workers to be associated with the visitor in some new field. They can then continue the good work when the visitor returns to the United States.

There is another administrative experiment which is currently in progress at many universities. This is the establishment of multidisciplinary research centers which are able to provide opportunities to meet specialists from other fields. I believe that such institutes can do a great deal of good to provide stimulating research surroundings in university settings. In the Harvard Center of Aerospace Health and Safety, for example, Ross McFarland has brought together medical men and engineers, psychologists, physiologists, and anthropologists. Similarly in the Harvard Center for Cognitive Studies, Jerome Bruner and George Miller have associated psychologists, sociologists, physiologists, computer experts, mathematicians, linguists, and philosophers. The success of such arrangements undoubtedly depends on the feeling of common purpose that can be developed so that the various individuals work together really effectively. Hebb (1958) mentions the stimulation to new ideas, the criticism and guidance that is possible when workers with different backgrounds and skills effectively understand one another's languages and modes of thought. This genuine cooperation is characterized mainly by people exchanging ideas before and during the experimental phase of their investigations rather than after their work has been completed. A suggestion here is to encourage people to have at least two research problems. One would be their own individual work which would occupy most of their time. The other problem would, however, be a group research study, perhaps 1 day a week. Groups of not more than six scientists would meet on common ground over a shared topic of investigation conducted on the same research subjects or patients.

One of the most successful experiments of this cooperative type is to be found in the University of California's San Francisco Medical Center, where there is the Cardiovascular Research Institute, directed by Julius Comroe, also the Professor of Physiology. It is interesting that this group received a 7-year grant in 1961 from the Public Health Service. They mention in the 1961–62 annual report from the Institute that this long-term support has many advantages (Comroe, 1962).

> It provides stable support for many competent scientists for whom there are no university-supported positions. It permits individual scientists to spend more time in research than in grant administration. It encourages long-term research planning and an attack on difficult, long-term problems rather than on easier problems which provide quick answers [p. 14].

Research Support

It would be logical for this trend towards longer-term grants to continue, as the Government's own Office of Naval Research maintains that basic research is indeed a long-term affair with them since the average length of their projects was 5 years in 1959. The National Science Foundation has also taken the lead by publishing recently a report entitled "Investing in Scientific Progress," which has many useful ideas on the scientific and educational requirements during the present decade (NSF, 1961).

Some outstandingly interesting comments have been made by Roth (1963). He speaks as a Special Assistant to the National Aeronautics and Space Administration; he is able to indicate the general educational reforms required, since he is also Professor of Mathematics at New York University. Then, as Director of the Office of Research Services, he goes on to specify 10 important ideas on educational research. Roth suggests, for example, that bright students (both undergraduate and graduate) who are believed to be potentially creative might be permitted to forgo formal classwork in their major fields to enable them to work under the supervision of a keen faculty member. He favors the use of institutional grants to universities rather than a reliance on grants and contracts awarded to individuals. On the other hand, the National Institutes of Health have found a way of supporting individual scientists by career awards through universities. This arrangement has one great merit for Government and investigator alike; it encourages the open and free discussion of research ideas and plans. Direct support of separate research projects often stifles such discussions before the ideas are sold to the Government.

At the risk of being thought to be against motherhood, I want to mention the hypothetical case of the $30,000 contract for 1 year. Let us suppose that each of 30 groups throughout the country spend $1,000 on proposal writing and travel to meetings to try to win such support. Then, across the country as a whole, the actual cost of writing such proposals would seem to amount to the value of the contract itself. Not all the unsuccessful efforts would be lost by any means, since proposal writing and evaluating are forms of problem finding. But it is hard to follow the economics of it, despite the obvious benefits resulting from competition between groups of people rather than between individuals.

Land (1964) has recently discussed (in one of his all too rare publications) the various dilemmas facing any government that would like to support inventions. He indicates that government support is not likely to be forthcoming for inventions because government funds are liable to be kept for ventures that usually succeed—and most inventions fail financially.

The balance between stability and change has to be held within society as well as within the investigator:

> Invention involves breaking through a series of barriers which are both intellectual and social. . . . Nearly every worthwhile invention will thus seem to be a war comprising many battles, every battle being against fixed attitudes. These fixed attitudes are fundamental human characteristics that are of the very nature of life and society. Our survival from moment to moment depends upon them. . . . The paradoxical problem which society must face is that on the one hand its stability depends on resisting change but its growth, vitality and healthy future depend on the cautious substitution of

> new arrays of order for old arrays of order. . . . How can we protect an individual from the group when an individual is seeking to destroy a sequential array of attitudes and replace them with a new sequence which in his opinion will be better for society? . . . Rigidity is the other name for people in the aggregate. . . . Society cannot know novelty because it is rigid and yet it proposes to protect and affirm the novelty of what the inventor offers. Yet the patent system protects and encourages the inventor and makes possible the long, long investment by his associates in the most exciting and fantastic kind of gamble there is: a gamble not for the victory of a horse but a gamble for the grand victory of some great new contribution to our society [p. 159].

But the fact that perhaps less than 1 invention in 50 makes any money at all is in some ways all to the good. Financial disasters can emphasize the lasting advantages of intellectual activity. In his new book entitled *From Dream to Discovery,* Selye (1964) remarks that his father twice lost all his possessions and then told his son, who eventually achieved fame as a biochemist, that studying and research gave possessions that could never be lost. There are other satisfactions, too. Our century has seen one of the greatest investigators of all time, Sir Alexander Fleming. He once laughed along in a talk to some medical students in Cambridge, England, that he had heard from friends that a certain amount of money was being made out of penicillin. In fact, his achievement was measured in somewhat different terms—because he knew he had saved more lives by this discovery than any one man ever had before in the whole human history (Maurois, 1959). Although Sir Alexander Fleming was also a Scotsman, I must admit that Scotland has had no monopoly on great men.

Only One Brain

Let me mention, for example, one of the finest scientists that the United States has ever had—Robert Goddard. Even he found it difficult to gain a hearing, at first. As early as 1910, he wrote a paper on the "Possibility of Navigating Interplanetary Space." But this was obviously such a wild and really far-out idea that a popular scientific journal turned it down.

Now that the United States has 20-billion-dollar plans to reach the moon, it is interesting to record that these efforts, costing about 10 million dollars a day, started with this very same wild dream. Goddard himself realized it would be the last pioneering expedition to be made by humans (Dewey, 1962). It was exactly 50 years ago this summer that the principles of modern rockets were clearly established when Goddard was granted the first patents on a multistage rocket in 1914. There were all the essential rocket features such as, (*a*) the combustion chamber with its nozzle, (*b*) the system of feeding fuel, and (*c*) the multistage idea. They constituted the fruits of one man's work at research. The discoveries had all been made but were expressed in miniature. Goddard's little rocket was about a foot long and weighed only a few pounds. Then several thousands of men got to work, and 50 years later on January 19, 1964, the Saturn I rocket roared skywards. This successful monster was now more than 200 feet long and many tons in weight. These further changes that produced the largest rocket in the world were the result of development as opposed to research activities. One man did the early research and then tens of thousands of people followed through with the development. These magnificent further technical achievements by Wernher von Braun and his team, among others, led to widespread congratulations for a fine group who had obviously done really important work. But who remembered

Goddard, the man who had sparked off this whole idea? This answer is contained in the following story of the two hats. During the celebrations, President Johnson joked that von Braun might now have some difficulty in fitting on the hat he had recently been given in Texas. But there was no mention of the other hat, that battered, old straw hat Goddard used to wear during all those long years of field trials. For 2 years Goddard had deliberately left this hat gathering dust on the empty laboratory bench when he had to close down his laboratory between the wars due to lack of government funds. This straw hat was a sign that he would return—which he did. But few seem to remember him at all nowadays.

Conclusions

Let me end on a note of cautious optimism. I believe Walter Van Dyke Bingham had a farseeing idea when he proposed these lectures on the "Discovery and Development of Exceptional Abilities and Capabilities." His concern was to help the individual and his feeling for human dignity was what placed Bingham himself in a very special category. Surely we can now look forward with some real hope that talent will not always pass unrecognized. Very many examples could be given, but let me mention only three great Americans whose talents have done so much for psychology. Their achievements have demonstrated that the present situation as regards talent discovery and development can indeed work remarkably well at times. I think of Walter Miles, Henry Imus, and Norbert Wiener—a great research man, a great administrator, and a great thinker, respectively. These three kinds of talents have been brought to bear on some of the hardest problems of our age. Surely no system is too far wrong if such men can reach the top? You all know how Walter Miles has epitomized the ingenuity of the experimentalist. Similarly,

Henry Imus stands as a fine executive with a flair for supporting good research men. Norbert Wiener has demonstrated the deep originality of the thinker. It was a great friend of Wiener's, Sir Frederic Bartlett (1958), who noted in his book on *Thinking, an Experimental and Social Study* that the most important feature of original experimental thinking was the discovery of overlap and agreement where formerly only isolation and difference were recognized. This was certainly characteristic of Wiener who crossed so many boundaries, both national and scientific. As a scientific tribute let me say that the first part of my summary is based on one of his last talks at Massachusetts Institute of Technology (Wiener, 1964).

Summary

1. Originality and individuality are badly needed in science—more than ever before.

2. The current information explosion is not at all what it seems to be; more bad papers only make it harder to find the good ones. "Keep the monkeys away from the typewriters!" (This cogent cry from Wiener ranks with Rutherford's delightful dictum: "Go home, my boy— and think!")

3. Intellectual honesty is also required in the sense of willingness to take a chance on the tougher problems as well as on the easier ones.

4. Make some mistakes and admit them. More promising problems may be found in the ruins of these failures. "It is better to be naive and productive, than sophisticated, hypercritical and sterile [Hebb, 1958, p. 464]."

5. Since unifying statements rather than detailed facts are the ultimate general aim, experimentalists should speculate in print more then they do on the broad implications of their work; this may lead on to even more meaningful questions.

6. There is no more fascinating problem in the world than the study of the kind of people who do scientific research. Take heart, however, if their activities are not yet all quite clear. We are ourselves setting out on the long pilgrimage involved in every creative venture. This has been ably defined (Roe, 1963) as "a way of life which emerges from a background of absorption in a topic and begins in a state of imaginative, muddled suspense [p. 177]."

7. Finally, it was John F. Kennedy who said so briefly that one man can make a difference and that every man should try.

References

Armer, P. Attitudes toward intelligent machines. (Orig. publ. 1960.) In E. A. Feigenbaum & J. Feldman (eds.), *Computers and thought.* New York: McGraw-Hill, 1963.

Barron, F. The needs for order and for disorder as motives in creative activity. In C. W. Taylor & F. Barron (eds.), *Scientific creativity: Its recognition and development.* New York: Wiley, 1963.

Bartlett, F. C. *Remembering.* Cambridge: Cambridge Univer. Press, 1932.

Bartlett, F. C. Programme for experiments on thinking. *Quarterly Journal of Experimental Psychology,* 1950, 145–162.

Bartlett, F. C. *Thinking, an experimental and social study.* London: Allen & Unwin, 1958.

Barzun, J. *Science: the glorious entertainment.* New York: Harper & Row, 1964.

Bello, F. The magic that made Polaroid. *Fortune,* 1959, 59, 124–129.

Berlyne, D. E. *Conflict, arousal, and curiosity.* New York: McGraw-Hill, 1960.

Bernard, Claude. *An introduction to the study of experimental medicine.* (Orig. publ. 1865.) New York: Collier Books, 1961.

Beveridge, W. I. B. *The art of scientific investigation.* London. Heinemann, 1950.

Blade, E. Creative science. In M. A. Coler (ed.), *Essays on creativity in the sciences.* New York: New York Univer. Press, 1963.

Bronowski, J. *Science and human values.* New York: Harper, 1956.

Bruner, J. S. On going beyond the information given. In *Contemporary approaches to cognition.* Cambridge: Harvard Univer. Press, 1957. (Reprinted in R. J. C. Harper, C. C. Anderson, C. M. Christensen, & S. M. Hunka (eds.), *The cognitive processes: readings.* Englewood Cliffs, N.J.: Prentice-Hall, 1964.) (a)

Bruner, J. S. On perceptual readiness. *Psychological Review,* 1957, *64,* 123–152. (Reprinted in R. J. C. Harper, C. C. Anderson, C. M. Christensen, & S. M. Hunka (eds.), *The cognitive processes: readings.* Englewood Cliffs, N.J.: Prentice-Hall, 1964.) (b)

Bruner, J. S. The conditions of creativity. (Orig. publ. 1958.) In H. E. Gruber, G. Terrel, & M. Wertheimer (eds.), *Contemporary approaches to creative thinking,* New York: Atherton Press, 1962.

Bruner, J. S., Goodnow, J. J., & Austin, G. A. *A study of thinking.* New York: Wiley, 1956.

Bruner, J. S., Postman, L., & Rodrigues, J. Expectation and the perception of color. *American Journal of Psychology,* 1951, *64,* 216–227.

Burt, C. Foreword in A. Koestler, *The act of creation.* New York: Macmillan, 1964.

Cannon, W. *The way of an investigator.* New York: Norton, 1945.

Cattell, R. B. The personality and motivation of the researcher from measurements of contemporaries and from biography. In C. W. Taylor & F. Barron (eds.), *Scientific creativity: its recognition and development.* New York: Wiley, 1963.

Coler, M. A. (ed.). *Essays on creativity in the sciences.* New York: New York Univer. Press, 1963.

Comroe, J. The 1961–1962 annual report, 1962, University of California, Cardiovascular Research Institute, San Francisco Medical Center.

Darwin, F. (ed.). *Charles Darwin.* London: Murray, 1902.

Dewey, A. P. *Robert Goddard, space pioneer.* Boston: Little, Brown, 1962.

Eve, A. S. *Rutherford.* New York: Macmillan, 1939.

Fano, R. M. Discussion of a library for 2000 A.D. (Orig. publ. 1961.) In M. Greenberger (ed.), *Computers and the world of the future.* Cambridge: M.I.T. Press, 1964.

Feigenbaum, E. A., & Feldman, J. (eds.). *Computers and thought.* New York: McGraw-Hill, 1963.

Forrester, J. W. Managerial decision making. (Orig. publ. 1961.) In M. Greenberger (ed.), *Computers and the world of the future.* Cambridge: M.I.T. Press, 1964.

Getzels, J. W., & Jackson, P. W. *Creativity and intelligence.* New York: Wiley, 1962.

Green, B. F. *Digital computers in research.* New York: McGraw-Hill, 1963.

Greenberger, M. (ed.). *Computers and the world of the future.* Cambridge: M.I.T. Press, 1964.

Gruber, H. E., Terrell, G., & Wertheimer, M. (eds.). *Contemporary approaches to creative thinking.* New York: Atherton Press, 1962.

Guilford, J. P. Intellectual resources and their values as seen by scientists. In C. W. Taylor & F. Barron (eds.), *Scientific creativity: its recognition and development.* New York: Wiley, 1963.

Harper, R. J. C., Anderson, C. C., Christensen, C. M., & Hunka, S. M. (eds.). *The cognitive processes: readings.* Englewood Cliffs, N. J.: Prentice-Hall, 1964.

Hebb, D. O. Alice in Wonderland or psychology among the biological sciences. In H. F. Harlow & C. N. Woolsey (eds.), *Biological and biochemical bases of behavior.* Madison: Univer. Wisconsin Press, 1958.

Henle, Mary. The birth and death of ideas. In H. E. Gruber, G. Terrell, & M. Wertheimer (eds.), *Contemporary approaches to creative thinking.* New York: Atherton Press, 1962.

Hofstadter, R. *Anti-intellectualism in American life.* New York: Knopf, 1963.

Houssay, B. My struggle for science. *World Health,* 1961, Sept.–Oct., 36.

Hovland, C. I. Computer simulation of thinking. (Orig. publ. 1960.) In R. J. C. Harper, C. C. Anderson, C. M. Christensen, & S. M. Hunka (eds.), *The cognitive processes: readings.* Englewood Cliffs, N. J.: Prentice-Hall, 1964.

Hughes, H. K. Individual and group creativity in science. In M. A. Coler (ed.), *Essays on creativity in the sciences.* New York: New York Univer. Press, 1963.

Jewkes, J., Sawers, D., & Stillerman, R. *The sources of invention.* London: Macmillan, 1961.

Kochen, M. Experimental study of "hypothesis formation" by computer. In C. Cherry (ed.), *Information theory fourth London symposium.* London: Butterworths, 1961.

Koestler, A. *The act of creation.* New York: Macmillan, 1964.

Land, E. The role of invention in organized society. *Product Engineering,* 1964, March 2, 159.

Licklider, J. C. R. Man-computer symbiosis. *IRE Transactions on Human Factors in Electronics,* 1960, *1,* 4–11.

Licklider, J. C. R. Discussion on the computer in the university. (Orig. publ. 1961.) In M. Greenberger (ed.), *Computers and the world of the future.* Cambridge: M.I.T. Press, 1964.

McCarthy, J. Time-sharing computer systems. (Orig. publ. 1961.) In M. Greenberger (ed.), *Computers and the world of the future.* Cambridge: M.I.T. Press, 1964.

McClelland, D. C. The calculated risk: an aspect of scientific performance. In C. W. Taylor & F. Barron (eds.), *Scientific creativity: its recognition and development.* New York: Wiley, 1963.

MacKinnon, D. W. The personality correlates of creativity: a study of American architects. In G. S. Nielsen (ed.), *Proceedings of the XIV International Congress of Applied Psychology, Copenhagen, 1961.* Vol. 2. Copenhagen: Munksgaard, 1962, pp. 11–39.

MacKinnon, D. W. Measurement of creativity. Unpublished manuscript, Harvard College Admissions Institute, July 1963.

Mackworth, N. H., & Kaplan, I. Points of view and lines of sight. *Ikon,* 1963, *13,* 45–60.

Maurois, A. *The life of Sir Alexander Fleming.* New York: Dutton, 1959.

Miller, G. A. The study of intelligent behavior. (Orig. publ. 1961.) In A. Oettinger (ed.), *Proceedings of a Harvard symposium on digital computers and their applications.* Cambridge: Harvard Univer. Press, 1962.

Miller, G. A. (ed.). *Mathematics and psychology.* New York: Wiley, 1964.

Miller, G. A., Galanter, E., & Pribram, K. H. *Plans and the structure of behavior.* New York: Holt, Rinehart & Winston, 1960.

Minsky, M. Steps towards artificial intelligence. (Orig. publ. 1961.) In E. A. Feigenbaum & J. Feldman (eds.), *Computers and thought.* New York: McGraw-Hill, 1963.

Moles, A. A. *La création scientifique.* Genève: René Kister, 1957.

National Science Foundation. *Investing in scientific progress.* Washington, D.C.: NSF, 1961.

Naval Research Advisory Committee. *Basic research in the Navy.* Washington, D.C.: United States Department of Commerce, Office of Technical Services, 1959.

Neisser, U. The imitation of man by machine. *Science,* 1963, *139,* 193–197.

Newell, A., Shaw, J. C., & Simon, H. Elements of a theory of human problem solving. *Psychological Review,* 1958, *65,* 151–166. (a)

Newell, A., Shaw, J. C., & Simon, H. The processes of creative thinking. Report No. P-1320, 1958, Rand Corporation. (b)

Newell, A., Shaw, J. C., & Simon, H. Chess playing programs and the problem of complexity. (Orig. publ. 1958.) In E. A. Feigenbaum & J. Feldman (eds.), *Computers and thought.* New York: McGraw-Hill, 1963. (a)

Newell, A., Shaw, J. C., & Simon, H. Empirical explorations with the logic theory machine: A case study in heuristics. (Orig. publ. 1957.) In E. A. Feigenbaum & J. Feldman (eds.), *Computers and thought.* New York: McGraw-Hill, 1963. (b)

Newell, A., & Simon, H. A. Computer simulation of human thinking: *Science,* 1961, *134,* 2011–2017.

Newell, A., & Simon, H. GPS, a program that simulates human thought. (Orig. publ. 1961.) In E. A. Feigenbaum & J. Feldman (eds.), *Computers and thought.* New York: McGraw-Hill, 1963.

Newman, E. B. Paracomputers in psychological research. (Orig. publ. 1961.) In A. Oettinger (ed.), *Proceedings of a Harvard symposium on digital computers and their applications.* Cambridge: Harvard Univer. Press, 1962.

Oettinger, A. G. Programming the Edsac to go shopping. (Orig. publ. 1952.) In G. A. Miller (ed.), *Mathematics and psychology.* New York: Wiley, 1964.

Oldfield, R. C. Memory mechanisms and the theory of schemata. (Orig. publ. 1954.) In R. J. C. Harper, C. C. Anderson, C. M. Christensen, & S. M. Hunka (eds.), *The cognitive processes: readings.* Englewood Cliffs, N.J.: Prentice-Hall, 1964.

Orth, C. D. The optimum climate for industrial research. *Harvard Business Review,* 1959, *37,* 55–64.

Pierce, J. R. What computers should be doing. (Orig. publ. 1961.) In

M. Greenberger (ed.), *Computers and the world of the future.* Cambridge: M.I.T. Press, 1964.

Polyani, M. Experience and the perception of pattern. In K. M. Sayre & F. J. Crosson, *The modeling of mind: computers and intelligence.* Notre Dame: Univer. Notre Dame Press, 1963.

Price, D. J. de S. *Science since Bablyon.* New Haven: Yale Univer. Press, 1961.

Reitman, W. R. Information-processing models in psychology. *Science,* 1964, *144,* 1192–1198.

Roe, Anne. Psychological approaches to creativity in science. In M. A. Coler (ed.), *Essays on creativity in the sciences.* New York: New York Univer. Press, 1963.

Roe, Anne. *The making of a scientist.* New York: Dodd, Mead, 1964.

Roth, S. G. Creativity in an academic atmosphere. In M. A. Coler (ed.), *Essays on creativity in the sciences.* New York: New York Univer. Press, 1963.

Samuel, A. L. Some studies in machine learning using the game of checkers. (Orig. publ. 1959.) In E. A. Feigenbaum & J. Feldman (eds.), *Computers and thought.* New York: McGraw-Hill, 1963.

Sayre, K. M., & Crosson, F. J. *The modeling of mind: computers and intelligence.* Notre Dame: Univer. Notre Dame Press, 1963.

Selfridge, O., & Neisser, U. Pattern recognition by machine. (Orig. publ. 1960.) In E. A. Feigenbaum & J. Feldman (eds.), *Computers and thought.* New York: McGraw-Hill, 1963.

Selye, Hans. *From dream to discovery.* New York: McGraw-Hill, 1964.

Simon, H. A. The corporation: will it be managed by machines? In M. Anshen & G. L. Bach (eds.), *Management and corporations, 1985.* New York: McGraw-Hill, 1960. (a)

Simon, H. A. *The new science of management decision.* New York: Harper & Row, 1960. (b)

Simon, H. A. Simulation of human thinking. (Orig. publ. 1961.) In M. Greenberger (ed.), *Computers and the world of the future.* Cambridge: M.I.T. Press, 1964.

Snow, C. P. *The search.* New York: Signet, 1960.

Snow, C.P. *The two cultures: and a second look.* New York: Mentor, 1964.

Sprecher, T. B. Chairman's report on criteria of creativity at Third Utah Conference, 1959. Cited by Anne Roe in Psychological approaches to creativity in science, in M. A. Coler (ed.), *Essays on creativity in the sciences.* New York: Univer. Press, 1963, p. 155.

Taylor, C. W., & Barron, F. (eds.). *Scientific creativity: its recognition and development.* (National Science Foundation Utah Conferences, 1955, 1957, 1959) New York: Wiley, 1963.

Tolcott, M., Chenzoff, A. P., Crittenden, R. M., Flores, I., Frances, A. S., Kelley, C. R., & Mackworth, N. H. Human decision making as related to air surveillance systems. *United States Air Force Command and Control Division Technical Report,* 1960, No. 61–9.

Torrance, E. P. *Guiding creative talent.* Englewood Cliffs, N.J.: Prentice-Hall, 1962.

Wang, H. Towards mechanical mathematics. (Orig. publ. 1960.) In K. M. Sayre & F. J. Crosson (eds.), *The modeling of mind: computers and intelligence.* Notre Dame: Univer. Notre Dame Press, 1963.

Wiener, N. *The human use of human beings: cybernetics and society.* Garden City, N.Y.: Doubleday, 1954.

Wiener, N. Intellectual honesty and the contemporary scientist. *M.I.T. Technology Review,* 1964, *66,* 17–18, 44–47.

Yntema, D. B., & Torgerson, W. S. Man-computer cooperation in decisions requiring common sense. *IRE Transactions on Human Factors in Electronics,* 1961, *2,* 20–26.

Philip E. Vernon

Ability Factors and Environmental Influences[1]

I am deeply appreciative of the honor of being invited to give this year's Walter Van Dyke Bingham Lecture, and would especially like to applaud the initiative of Mrs. Bingham and the American Psychological Association Committee in including some psychologists from outside the United States in their scheme. England indeed has been greatly favored by the selection first of Cyril Burt, then of Norman Mackworth and myself; and I think that this is appropriate, because the Binghams had many friends and were widely respected among British applied psychologists. But might I venture to suggest that the Committee will also sometimes look further afield and consider whether other suitable lecturers might not be found, perhaps from France or Scandinavia, perhaps Canada or Australia? I would like also to take this opportunity to express my thanks to the Local Committee, and particularly to Robert Perloff, for the efficiency and the generosity of their arrangements. It is a special pleasure to visit Purdue University, which has long been associated in my

1. This paper is based on the Walter Van Dyke Bingham Lecture given at Purdue University, April 21, 1965. It was first published in the *American Psychologist,* 1965, vol. 20, no. 9 (September), pp. 723–733.

mind with contributions to applied psychology, for example with the work of Joseph Tiffin, Hermann Remmers, and Charles Lawshe.

Although I have not, like some previous lecturers, had the privilege of close professional contacts with Dr. Bingham, apart from friendly meetings at International Congresses, I have always admired *Aptitudes and Aptitude Testing* (Bingham, 1937) as one of the most sound and comprehensive treatments of the topic. During World War II it was a main textbook for the British military psychologists and personnel selection officers whom we trained for allocation of recruits to suitable trades. Bingham and Moore's (1931) *How to Interview* is likewise still a valuable text for occupational psychologists. And on looking up Dr. Bingham's career, I was delighted to find that his first love was the psychology of music and that he eventually came to vocational and military testing via educational psychology, for these are the areas in which I too have chiefly been interested.

In *Aptitudes and Aptitude Testing,* Walter Van Dyke Bingham (1937) clearly attaches major importance to general intelligence, as I wish to do today. But he took no doctrinaire theoretical position on the nature of intelligence, being content to define it as the ability to solve new problems, which he recognized as the product of endowment + growth + opportunity. He admitted, too, that intelligence is complex, that there might be different intelligences for dealing with different kinds of problems, though he did not commit himself as to which main types should be distinguished. He tended rather to classify aptitudes in terms of the main kinds of jobs for which people might be selected.

I want, then, to ask again what are the most useful psychological dimensions or factors under which the vocational psychologist can conceptualize people, and how do these originate? What can research tell us of the environmental influences that chiefly contribute to individual differences in these abilities? I intend to argue the case for a model, or structure, of ability factors which, even 3 years ago, might have been considered by most American psychometrists as hopelessly old-fashioned. This is the model based on g, the general intellectual factor, plus major and minor group factors. Thurstone's scheme of multiple primary abilities is preferred by almost all psychometrists, though apparently it is seldom adopted by counselors or others who use tests for reaching practical decisions. Despite Thurstone's and Guilford's assurance that general intelligence is too vague and heterogeneous a construct to be worth measuring—we should break it down into its components and measure each individual's profile of factors—most practicing psychologists in schools, clinics, and industry happily go on using the familiar group or individual tests of intelligence. The main concessions they make to the factorist are to obtain separate linguistic and quantitative scores in some academic aptitude tests, and separate verbal and performance scores in the Wechsler scales. When I visited some military psychological establishments in 1957, I was told more than once that military psychologists could not ignore g. Try as they would to find differential tests for different army trades, intercorrelations were always so high that recruits appeared to be differentiated more by all-round level of ability than by type of ability, that is to say, by g rather than by factor profile. Table 1 provides another instance, extracted from the Psychological Corporation's follow-up studies of the Differential Aptitude Tests. True, these are not pure factor tests, but their aim is to give differential predictions for different educational courses or jobs. I have underlined the four highest validity coefficients in each column, and you will see that the pattern of coefficients for different school courses is sickeningly similar. Verbal and Reasoning tests, that is those which are most typical of the conventional general intelligence test, together with the Numerical test, tend

Table 1. Differential Aptitude Tests: Median Correlations With School Grades Among Several Classes of Ninth-Twelfth-Grade Boys.

	English	Maths	Science	Social studies
Verbal reasoning	.49	.33	.54	.48
Numerical computation	.48	.47	.52	.46
Abstract reasoning	.32	.32	.42	.32
Space	.26	.26	.34	.24
Mechanical comprehension	.21	.19	.40	.21
Clerical speed and accuracy	.22	.16	.24	.21
Spelling	.44	.28	.36	.36
Sentences (English usage)	.50	.32	.45	.43

Note. Four highest coefficients in each column are underlined.

to give the best correlations throughout, and only to a limited extent do Space and Mechanical tests add something to the prediction of ability in science courses.

Currently there seems to be greater recognition of the failure of multiple-factor profiles to fulfill their promise, and scepticism over the proliferation of factors. In 1962 Lloyd Humphreys came out in favor of something very similar to the British g + group-factor model, and last year Quinn McNemar (1964) trenchantly criticized the American multiple factorist's "fragmentation of ability, into more and more factors of less and less importance . . . [p. 872]." A general intelligence factor seems unavoidable since substantial positive intercorrelations are found when any cognitive tests are applied to a fairly representative population. But at the same time intelligence has many aspects which can usefully be represented, as Thurstone did, in terms of partially distinct though overlapping primary factors. The trouble arises because any one of these major primaries can be endlessly fractionated, depending simply on the number and variety of different tests in that area which the psychometrist can think up and, I would add, on the homogeneity—the restriction in the range of g—in the tested population. I would entirely agree with Humphreys (1962) that it is useful to superimpose on the hierarchical group-factor model Guttman's notion of facets. Test intercorrelations are affected not only by test content but by the form or technique of the test, its speededness, level of difficulty of the items, whether multiple-choice or creative response, whether analogies, series, or classifications, and so forth. These facets, which are seldom of much diagnostic interest, have been variously referred to as method factors (Campbell & Fiske, 1959), formal factors and work attitudes (Vernon, 1958), instrument factors (Cattell, 1961), and response sets (Cronbach, 1950).

Hierarchical Group-Factor Theory

Figure 1 gives the best indication I can manage of the factors that emerge most consistently when large and varied test batteries are applied to representative samples of adolescents or

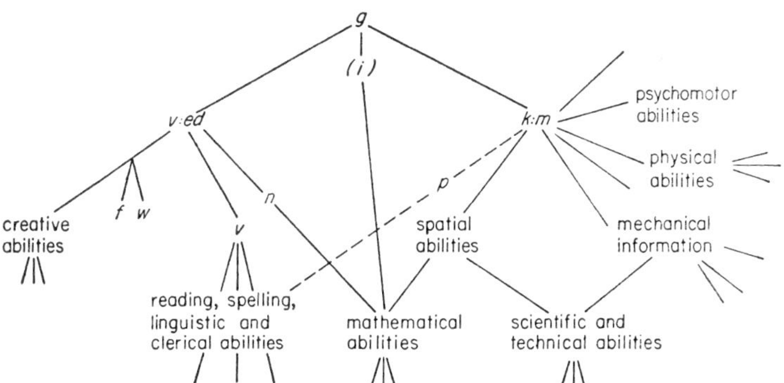

Fig. 1. Diagram of the main general and group factors underlying tests relevant to educational and vocational achievements.

young adults (Vernon, 1961). I admit, of course, that there is no one final structure, since so much depends on the population tested, its heterogeneity and educational background, the particular tests chosen, and the techniques of factorization and rotation employed. I have followed British usage in naming the factors by small letters to differentiate them from the corresponding American primaries from which the *g* element has not been removed.

After removing the general factor (whether by group-factor technique or by rotation of centroid factors), the positive residual correlations always fall into two main groups—the verbal-educational (*v:ed*) group and the spatial-practical-mechanical group. The *v:ed* factor usually yields additional minor fluency and divergent thinking abilities—scholastic and *n* or number subfactors. Likewise the *k:m* complex includes perceptual, physical, and psychomotor, as well as spatial and mechanical factors, which can be further subdivided by more detailed testing. In addition there seem to be various cross-links: For example, clerical tests usually combine verbal ability and perceptual speed, *p;* likewise math and science depend both on number and spatial abilities, *n* and *k*. Sometimes an inductive reasoning ability (also very relevant to science) can be distinguished, though most of the common variance of reasoning tests is apt to be absorbed into *g*. At a still lower level in the hierarchy come what are usually referred to as specific factors, though of course any specific can be turned into an additional narrow group factor by devising additional tests.

Now despite certain differences of analytic technique and interpretation of factors, the hierarchical model and the multiple-factor model are fundamentally in agreement. It is just as legitimate to start, as it were, from the bottom upwards—that is to say, to extract the primaries—and from their intercorrelations calculate the second-order factors, and if need be a third-order factor, corresponding to our major group factors and *g*. Bernyer (1958) has shown that the two approaches can yield almost identical results. In actual practice, however, rather few multiple-factor analysts (R. B. Cattell, 1963, is a notable exception) bother to allow for obliquity or go on to calculate the higher-order factor loadings of their tests; and when they do so the results are apt to be very inconsistent. British *g* factor very regularly shows its largest loadings on tests like Progressive Matrices, Shipley Abstraction and Arithmetic Reasoning, whereas American second-order factors appear to have no stable content. Clearly the main reason why you favor multiple factors is that so much of your work is done with rather homogeneous groups like college students or officers in the armed services, where the range of *g* is so restricted that in effect you only get the group factors which can be rotated to orthogonal simple structure without serious distortion. Several psychometrists, such as Garrett (1946) and Cattell (1963), are inclined to ascribe the lesser prominence of *g* in these older groups to the differentiation of abilities with age, but there is little doubt that in every piece of research claiming to show such differentiation, the older groups are actually more highly selected, less representative. Take, for example, the recent large-scale survey of Grade 9 to 12 students in Project Talent (Flanagan, Davis, Dailey, Shaycoft, Orr, Goldberg, & Neyman, 1964). I picked out seven of the tests which seemed as different as possible from one another, whose intercorrelations would therefore depend mainly on *g*, not on common group factors. These were: Farming Information, Memory for Words, English Expression, Creativity, 3-Dimensional Visualization, Arithmetic Computation, and Clerical Checking. At Grade 9 their average intercorrelation among boys was .280, implying that some 28% of their variance could be ascribed to a general factor. By Grade 12 almost every correlation had decreased and the mean was now .241, i.e., some 24% of general variance. However, one notes that the sample at Grade 9 numbered over 39,000, at Grade 12 only 30,000. Clearly more of the duller students would have dropped out by Grade 12, so that the sample was more homogeneous, and this would more than account for the lowered correlations. In the British Army during World War II, with an almost complete spread of ability, correlations between dissimilar tests were if anything higher than those usually found with fourth- to sixth-grade students (Vernon, 1961).

From the point of view of the practical tester, the hierarchical model seems more logical since, in making educational or vocational decisions, he can cover most of the ground just by applying *g* or *g* + *v* tests, and then supplement by spatial-mechanical, clerical, number, or other group-factor tests where relevant. In other words, measures of factors which are higher in the hierarchy generally have better external validity, or more generalizability (Cronbach, Rajaratnam, & Gleser, 1963) to capacities of everyday life; whereas many of the published primary factors seem to be so narrow, so specific to the particular test material, as to have no practical use. This is true, for example, of Thurstone's and other rote memory factors. The user is tempted, even encouraged, to regard them as measuring memorizing ability which is likely to be highly relevant to school learning. In fact they usually correlate with scholastic achievement only insofar as they have not been purified of *g* and *v*. Similarily a large proportion of Guilford's numerous factors of intellect have failed to show any external validity which could not be accounted for by their *g*, *v*, and space content, though I would agree that some of his originality and creativity factor tests may cover a little fresh ground.

Perhaps the basic source of disagreement is that Thurstone and Guilford regarded primary factors almost as fundamental components or chemical elements of the mind, which in combination go to make up all the important human capacities; whereas

Godfrey Thomson (1939), Cyril Burt (1940), and I have always tried to keep in mind that factors are primarily classifications of similar tests. And just because a lot of tests appear to involve memorizing or whatever, and intercorrelate positively, this does not prove that they are good measures of the memorizing that children do in school.

Psychological Origins of Factors

At the same time *g* theory has its difficulties, in particular that *g* is not, as Spearman believed, determinate—that is to say, one and the same *g* whatever cognitive tests one likes to apply. Psychologically it is the all-round level of our thinking skills; while statistically it is merely the average of a battery of tests of intellectual capacities which are so diverse that the group factors or facets involved in each separate test mostly cancel one another out. Hence although we know what kinds of tests are most saturated with *g*, it can still vary according to the particular measures the psychologist likes to use. Perhaps, though, this is not a serious disadvantage, since it is what one would expect in the light of the psychological contributions of Hebb (1948) and Piaget (1950), Ferguson (1954) and Hunt (1961).

All of these writers point to the need to get away from the notion of intelligence as a definite entity, an autonomous mental faculty, which simply matures as children grow up. Rather we have to think of it in terms of a cumulative formation of more and more complex and flexible schemata (Piaget's term) or phase sequences (Hebb), or what Miller, Galanter, and Pribram (1960) call plans, which develop through interaction between the growing organism and its environment. They depend both upon environmental stimulation and on active exploration and experiment (Piaget's accommodation and assimilation); i.e., they are formed and organized by use. This implies, to a much greater extent than

Piaget seems to have recognized, that they also depend upon personality and motivational factors, organic and social drives, curiosity and interests; and that they are channelled by family, cultural, and educational pressures. Intelligence, then, refers to the totality of concepts and skills, the techniques or plans for coping with problems, which have crystallized out of the child's previous experience. Most representative of these, as Fe guson points out, are the thinking skills which have been overlearned and which are transferable to a wide variety of new situations. Although, of course, each person's accumulation of skills is different, all persons who have been brought up within a fairly homogeneous culture can reasonably be compared at any set of tasks which that culture values and which it likes to include within its conception of intelligence. But obviously, also, the whole structure, from perceptual and linguistic schemata upwards, may differ markedly in other cultures. The group of skills which we refer to as intelligence is a European and American middle-class invention: something which seems to be intimately bound up with puritanical values, with repression of instinctual responses and emphasis on responsibility, initiative, persistence, and efficient workmanship. It is a kind of intelligence which is specially well adapted for scientific analysis, for control and exploitation of the physical world, for large-scale and long-term planning and carrying out of materialistic objectives. It has also led to the growth of complex social institutions such as nations, armies, industrial firms, school systems, and universities, though it has been notably less successful in working out solutions of group rivalries or providing harmonious personal adjustment than have the intelligences of some more primitive cultures. Other cultures have evolved intelligences which are better adapted than ours for coping with problems of agricultural and tribal living. The aboriginal in the Australian desert and the

Eskimo in the Far North have many schemata far more efficient than our own. Again subcultures such as our lower working class, or rural groups, develop rather different intelligence.

How about ability factors other than *g*? It seems entirely plausible that different kinds of skills, or those applied to different kinds of problems, should group together and yield the various group or primary factors that the mental tester discovers. But any reification of such clusters into entities or basic faculties of mind, or what Spearman calls an oligarchic system, is to be deplored. The grouping depends mainly on what cultural and educational pressures dictate. Thus it is very natural, at least in Western cultures, that all the skills bound up with language and school should show a common factor over and above *g*, and that all contrasted skills of a noneducational type should show a different factor. Likewise we can envisage a whole host of minor group factors arising from the overlapping of schemata involved in similar tasks.

Cross-Cultural Testing

Let me now turn to the second half of my title—namely, the environmental influences or other casual agencies that underlie the development of different patterns of abilities. Here, too, the adoption of the hierarchical model simplifies our problem. It would be extraordinarily difficult to inquire into the agencies associated with a large number of Thurstone's primary factors, with Rote Memory, Induction, Fluency, etc., let alone with Guilford's 60 or more factors, since there would be so much overlapping. It seems more feasible to explore the agencies contributing to general intelligence, and those particularly relevant to verbal-educational and to spatial-practical factors—the group factors that carry a lot of everyday-life variance, and to proceed from there to find out what we can about contributory influences to minor factors of, say, creativity, number, art, music, athletic ability, etc., holding intelligence constant.

I would urge that this is a major responsibility of applied psychology in the second half of the twentieth century. If we are to help the newly developing, nontechnological nations of Africa, Asia, South America, and elsewhere, we must know more about the environmental and other handicaps which retard the development of those abilities that are needed for technological advancement (cf. Schwarz, 1961; Vernon, 1962). We want to assist them in selecting children who will make good professionals, teachers, commercial and political leaders, and technicians, and to tell them what factors of diet and health, cultural tradition and family upbringing, and schooling most require attention if they are to produce sufficient highly skilled personnel.

It is in the controversial area of cross-cultural testing that I am at the moment carrying out a series of small-scale researches, supported by the Association for the Aid of Crippled Children. My wife and I have applied a varied battery of tests, mostly individual, to a reference group of 100 11-year-old boys in England, to 50 boys of the same age in Jamaica, and to 90 Canadian Indians and Eskimos; and I hope to sample some African and other cultural groups later. I am confining myself to boys because, as Schaefer and Bayley (1963) point out, the long-term effects of upbringing are more clear-cut than in girls. Also I am working with groups which, by 11 years of age, have acquired enough English to understand oral instructions. Now I am well aware of the difficulties of cross-cultural testing which Anastasi (1958), for example, has discussed; and indeed it follows from what was said earlier that there is no such thing as a culture-free or culture-fair test. But insofar as the developing nations are aiming to achieve viable technological civilizations, they will need Western-type intelligence. Thus it is entirely legitimate to compare their standing with that of Europeans or Americans on tests which are known to sample abilities relevant to Western-type achievements. Moreover, insofar as the contrasted cultures provide a much wider range of environments than commonly occur within Western societies, their test scores should throw a clearer light on the determinants of abilities.

Determinants of Test Performance

Let us broadly distinguish the following classes of determinants:[2]

A. Genetic factors which are nonobservable and nonmeasurable, though we know that they exist since foster children or orphans continue to show some resemblance to their true parents who have had nothing to do with their upbringing. Presumably individuals differ in some quality of the plasticity of the nervous system which makes possible the building up of any schemata or plans; and it may well be that there are genetic differences contributing to linguistic and spatial aptitudes which tend to be sex linked. Certainly there are genetic factors in musical and possibly in mathematical and other talents, however much environment also contributes. One cannot rule out the possibility of genetic differences in aptitudes among ethnic groups or so-called races, but I would agree with the United Nations Educational, Scientific, and Cultural Organization manifesto that we cannot prove them; and they are likely to be small compared with environmentally produced differences.

2. Note the parallel between this classification and Hebb's Intelligence A and B. Elsewhere (Vernon, 1955), I have coined the term "Intelligence C" to refer to actual test results, i.e., to the particular sampling of Intelligence B which an intelligence test provides. Intelligence C also differs from B on account of the facets or instrument factors mentioned above; in other words it is distorted by the C type of determinant.

B. An enormous amount of research, using very varied approaches, has helped to pinpoint the major environmental handicaps to mental development, and I will try to sketch this briefly under nine main headings.

1. Physiological and nutritional factors. These mainly operate during pregnancy and parturition (cf. Stott, 1960); though certain diseases and malnutrition may also be important later insofar as they lower the energy and activity level that the growing child needs to explore his environment and seek out self-stimulating experiences.

2. Perceptual deprivation in the preschool years is suggested by Piaget's and Hebb's work. This may well operate in such situations as Spitz (1945) and Wayne Dennis (1960) describe, but would hardly seem important in most cultural groups where nature provides plenty of sticks, stones, water, and human contacts. I would rather emphasize conceptual deprivation during the school years when parents fail to answer questions, encourage curiosity, and provide books, TV, and other types of experience (cf. Bloom, 1964).

3. Repression of independence and constructive play, either through overprotection, arbitrary subjection, or conformity to tribal traditions. This is very noticeable in West Indian and African societies, and seems to be linked particularly with deficit in spatial abilities, in 3-dimensional perception (cf. Hudson, 1962), and in technical skills. My recent studies with Eskimo boys reveal a strong contrast.

4. Family insecurity and lack of planfulness. In families living at the subsistence level, immediate gratification of hunger and sex needs naturally takes precedence over long-term, purposive planning—the Pleasure Principle over the Reality Principle—and discourages the development of internal controls and rational thinking. In our own culture, Schaefer and Bayley (1963) have

shown the ill effects of parental anxiety, irritability, punitiveness, and rejection on later intellectual as well as social traits.

5. Female dominance. In many cultures, including the West Indian though not the Canadian Indian or Eskimo, the father may take little part in child rearing, and there is a lack of masculine models with whom the boy can identify. According to Witkin's (Witkin, Dyk, Faterson, Goodenough, & Karp, 1962; Witkin, Lewis, Hertzman, Machover, Meissner, & Wapner, 1954) and some other findings, this may favor verbal at the expense of spatial abilities.

6. Education in the underdeveloped countries is often defective, brief or irregular, starved of materials. Teachers may be poorly qualified and they may follow highly formal and mechanical methods, discouraging any intellectual initiative. Yet at the same time even bad education contributes greatly to the development of nonverbal as well as verbal abilities when the average home provides no intellectual stimulation.

7. Linguistic handicaps are almost universal in these societies. There may be a variety of dialects, or a debased and simplified pidgin or Creole; yet English, or sometimes French, is the main medium of instruction, especially for higher education. Unless the child can acquire complete facility in this second language he is likely to be backward in conceptual development and thinking skills, and this too seems to be reflected in nonverbal reasoning as well as in linguistic tests.

8. The conceptual and grammatical structures of the native language may differ markedly from those of English, so that the classifications or relations demanded by a Western-type test may be quite unfamiliar, although the non-Western child can very well classify, relate, and abstract in concrete situations. Again he may never have acquired the ability to interpret pictures as portraying 3-dimensional objects (cf. Biesheuvel, 1952).

9. Adult roles and adolescent aspirations. Here there is little definite evidence. But it is reported of some North American Indian and other cultures that children show fairly normal intellectual development till adolescence, but then, when they realize the depressed status of their minority culture—the absence of opportunity for progress and advancement—apathy sets in. To adapt Gordon Allport's description of personality as "Becoming," intelligence may depend on the future as well as on the past. It is interesting to speculate whether a Western adult does not also cease growing intellectually at 20, 30, 50, or later when he reaches his peak of aspiration and curiosity.

C. This group of determinants obviously overlaps in practice with the B group. But it refers to those characteristics of the test which frequently distort the results of unsophisticated testees, and which could be fairly effectively controlled by appropriate modifications of the form of the test and its administration. Schwarz (1961) has laid down a useful series of principles for getting across Western-type tests to African subjects which, in effect, amounts to teaching them the required mode of response before giving the test. I would still question whether any multiple-choice group test such as Schwarz uses, especially any involving time limits, is suitable for cultures with such different modes of thought and such different attitudes to competition, to working on one's own, or to working at speed.[3] Thus I preferred in my own work to rely more on individual, free-response tests, given like the Terman-Merrill, so that one can expand explanations as necessary and try to ensure that motivation is adequate.

While I hope that this summary of determinants and handi-

3. It is only fair to point out that Schwarz is not concerned with cross-cultural comparisons, but with devising tests which will give useful predictions within African cultures. Thus a speeded test, say, may actually be more predictive of suitability for technical jobs in a culture where speed plays little part in conventional living.

caps provides some clarification, the interpretation of cross-cultural data is still extremely tricky, for test results alone tell us little about what determinants are operating in any particular test. Whiting and Whiting (1960) point out that we may be unaware of the crucial parameters in an unfamiliar culture, and Irvine (1965) argues that different sources of variance may be operating: A particular test may be measuring essentially different things in different cultural contexts. For example, amount and quality of schooling may have very little effect on nonverbal tests like Progressive Matrices, Porteus Mazes, or Draw-a-Man in Western cultures, but may have much greater effects in societies where intellectual stimulation by the home is lacking. However one can hope to make some progress: (*a*) by contrasting a number of different cultures, (*b*) by applying factor analysis within each culture to see how the abilities group and what differences occur in factor patterns, (*c*) by obtaining assessments of major determinants with each culture and observing their correlations with the various test scores or factors.

Some Results Obtained in England and the West Indies

Table 2 indicates the main results of group factor analyses among my English and Jamaican subjects; loadings are shown merely by + or ++ signs, as the detailed figures are available elsewhere (Vernon, 1965). It may be seen that the general pattern is similar in the two groups, though there are some differences in the content of particular tests. In the English group there are a large educational and a subsidiary linguistic factor, a large perceptual-spatial factor, and some separation of the more practical performance tests. With the smaller numbers in the Jamaican sample, these subsidiary factors are less clear-cut, and the only sign of a practical factor is in Porteus Mazes and Formboard. The educational factor is definitely more pervasive,

Table 2. Main Factor Loadings of Tests Given to English and West Indian Eleven-Year Boys.

Tests	Mean West Indian deviation quotient	English factors					West Indian factors			
		g	Educational	Verbal	Perceptual	Practical	*g*	*v:ed*	Perceptual	Practical
Arithmetic Achievement	84	++	+				++	+		
Spelling	94	+	+				+	+		
Memorizing lists of words	91	+	+		+		+	+		
English comprehension, usage, spelling	82	+	+	+			+	+		
Vocabulary, group multiple-choice	83	+	+	+			+	+		
Vocabulary, individual Terman-Merrill	72	+	+	+			+		–	
Memorizing oral information	72	+	+				+	+		
Abstraction, verbal induction	?75	++	+							
Piaget, arithmetic-orientational }	86	++					+	+	+	
Piaget, visualization-conservation }		+			+	+	++			
Matrices, nonverbal induction	75	++					++			
Concept formation, sorting test	90	+		+			++			

Porteus Mazes	91	+			+	+		+
Vernon Formboard	68	+	+	+	+		+	+
Kohs Blocks (WISC-Jahoda)	75	++	+	+	++	+	+	
Goodenough Draw-a-Man	91	+	+	+	+	+	+	
Gottschaldt (Embedded) Figures	88	+	+		+		+	
Reproducing Designs (Bender-Gestalt and Terman-Merrill)	87	+	+		+	+	+	
Picture Recognition, 3-D Perception	?85	+	+		+	+		

Note. + indicates loading of psychological interest, almost all statistically significant; ++ represents loadings of .70 or over. In the second column, certain quotients are preceded by "?" where the identical test was not given to the two groups and an approximate estimate was made.

entering not only into verbal but also most of the paper-and-pencil perceptual tests. Probably it represents general sophistication in understanding instructions and coping with symbolic material, whether verbal or pictorial. The best general factor tests—Piaget, Matrices, and Concept Formation—are those involving the simplest oral instructions and creative responses.

The median Jamaican performance in each test was expressed as a deviation quotient relative to the English distribution, and it will be seen that these figures range from 94 for Spelling down to 68 for Formboard, i.e., from .4 σ to 2.1 σ below the English mean. Performance is generally best on the more mechanical attainments, though very weak on vocabulary and on information learning, which involve verbal comprehension. The quotients for perceptual tests, including Draw-a-Man, are also mainly around 85–90, and the most serious deficits are in verbal and nonverbal induction, Kohs Blocks, and Formboard—that is in *g* and practical-spatial abilities. This bears out my point that no test can be regarded as culture fair. Jamaican boys actually score better on conventional verbal intelligence and achievement tests, despite their linguistic handicap, than they do on tests which would appear to be purer measures of *g*, or of what Cattell (1963) refers to as fluid ability. I suspect that the same result would be found among Negroes in the United States.

Within each group the environmental variables listed in Table 3 were assessed on the basis of semistructured interviews with the boys and reports from the teachers. Time and expense did not permit home interviews, and in any case I was more interested in home and schooling over the past few years than in the kind of details of early upbringing that Sears, Maccoby, and Levin (1957), Prothro (1961), and others have studied. I would certainly not claim high reliability for these assessments, yet they yielded some quite substantial and plausible correlations with the ability factors. The cultural level of the home is clearly

Table 3. Correlations of Ability Factors with Environmental Variables among English and West Indian Eleven-Year Boys.

Environmental assessments	English factors					West Indian factors			
	g	Educational	Verbal	Perceptual	Practical	*g*	*v:ed*	Perceptual	Practical ?
Length and regularity of schooling	−.15	.31		.21		.23	.19	.26	
Family pattern: unbroken versus broken home	−.11	.30			.14	−.17	.24	.15	+
Stable home background versus frequent shifts						.14	.17		+
Economic: parents' job, housing, equipment	.38	.18	.24			.27	.28		+
Cultural stimulus: books in home, education of relatives, parent interest in education	.56	.29	.16			.33	.46	.25	
Male dominance and identification versus female overprotection or dominance					.39	.25		.27	
Initiative and maturity encouraged in play and household activities	.13			.13		.27	.16		+
Planfulness: rational home climate versus impulsive, emotional, arbitrary	.32	.26				.32			
Linguistic background	.49	.31	.24			.47	.41	.28	
Child's health, physical development, and nourishment							.21	.19	

Note. As explained above, no clear practical group factor was established in the West Indian sample. However, Porteus Mazes and Formboard gave substantial positive residual correlations with certain variables, indicated by +.

the most significant single influence—more important than socioeconomic rating; and in the Jamaican group, but not the English, it affects perceptual as well as general and educational abilities. Linguistic background is similar, and the planfulness or rationality of the home is particularly associated with *g* factor. Curiously the unbroken home or nuclear family pattern gives slight negative correlations with *g* in both groups, though positive with other factors.[4] Encouragement of initiative, independence, and maturity seems more important in the Jamaican than the English group though it did not relate, as I had hypothesized, to perceptual-practical abilty. But male dominance definitely linked with some aspect of this factor.

During the past 2 months I have been working with groups of boys in Indian reservations in Southern Alberta and Eskimos in the Mackenzie Delta in Arctic Canada. The results are not yet fully scored, let alone analyzed, but they do already bring out one important point—that different groups at similar levels of acculturation, and with similar language difficulties, may show very different patterns of scores. The Eskimos are just about equal to Jamaican standards in written English, though much behind in arithmetic, probably because less stress is laid in Canadian schools on mechanical drill. The Indian boys do somewhat less well on achievement tests; their linguistic handicap is generally greater since less English is spoken in their homes or at school. Like the Jamaicans they are most retarded in oral understanding and vocabulary.

Both groups score much higher than the Jamaicans on Kohs Blocks and other spatial tests, with a mean quotient of 88 instead of 75; and the Eskimos come up very well also on the inductive reasoning tests—Abstraction and Matrices. Now economic con-

4. No explanation can be offered for the slight negative association of schooling with *g* in the English group. In both groups it appears to contribute to spatial as well as to educational development.

ditions are extremely poor in all three groups, and there is similar family instability and insecurity. Thus it seems reasonable to attribute the better performance of Eskimo and Indian groups to the greater emphasis on resourcefulness in the upbringing of boys, perhaps combined with their strong masculine identification. True, the traditional hunting-trapping life is rapidly disappearing and the majority of parents are wage earning or on relief, but the children are still brought up permissively and encouraged to explore and hunt. Moreover, a subgroup of the Eskimos who came from the most isolated Arctic communities scored better on all three of the tests just mentioned than did those who lived in closer contact with whites and had become more acculturated.

Data such as these do not, of course, necessarily prove causality. Thus the correlation between cultural level of the home and intellectual development in the child might arise because brighter parents, who have brighter children, also provide them with better cultural and educational stimulation. Clearly the cross-sectional survey needs to be complemented by longitudinal and, if possible, direct experimental studies. We are on the verge of extremely exciting advances in the understanding and control of intellectual and personality development through such varied approaches as social learning and reinforcement theory, direct observation and follow-up of children, socioanthropological studies, and work such as I have described with mental tests and factor analysis. But I would not claim to have done more than to have scratched the surface, and to have raised many more problems than I have solved.

References

Anastasi, A. *Differential psychology.* New York: Macmillan, 1958.

Bernyer, G. Second order factors and the organization of cognitive functions. *British Journal of Statistical Psychology,* 1958, *11,* 19–29.

Biesheuvel, S. The study of African ability. *African Studies,* 1952, *11,* 45–58, 105–117.

Bingham, W. VanD. *Aptitudes and aptitude testing.* New York: Harper, 1937.

Bingham, W. VanD., & Moore, B. V. *How to interview.* New York: Harper, 1931.

Bloom, B. S. *Stability and change in human characteristics.* New York: Wiley, 1964.

Burt, C. *The factors of the mind.* London: Univer. London Press, 1940.

Campbell, D. T., & Fiske, D. W. Convergent and discriminant validation by the multitrait-multimethod matrix. *Psychological Bulletin,* 1959, *56,* 81–105.

Cattell, R. B. Theory of situational, instrument, second order, and refraction factors in personality structure research. *Psychological Bulletin,* 1961, *58,* 160–174.

Cattell, R. B. Theory of fluid and crystallized intelligence: A critical experiment. *Journal of Educational Psychology,* 1963, *54,* 1–22.

Cronbach, L. J. Further evidence on response sets and test design. *Educational and Psychological Measurement,* 1950, *10,* 3–31.

Cronbach, L. J., Rajaratnam, N., & Gleser, G. C. Theory of generalizability: A liberalization of reliability theory. *British Journal of Statistical Psychology,* 1963, *16,* 137–163.

Dennis, W. Causes of retardation among institutional children: Iran. *Journal of Genetic Psychology,* 1960, *94,* 47–59.

Ferguson, G. A. On learning and human ability. *Canadian Journal of Psychology,* 1954, *8,* 95–112.

Flanagan, J. C., Davis, F. B., Dailey, J. T., Shaycroft, M. F., Ott, D. B., Goldberg, I., & Neyman, C. A. Project TALENT: The American high-school student. Final report, 1964, University of Pittsburgh, Cooperative Research Project No. 635, United States Office of Education.

Garrett, H. E. A developmental theory of intelligence. *American Psychologist,* 1946, *1,* 372–378.

Hebb, D. O. *The organization of behavior.* New York: Wiley, 1948.

Hudson, W. Pictorial perception and educational adaptation in Africa. *Psychologia Africana*, 1962, *9*, 226–239.

Humphreys, L. G. The organization of human abilities. *American Psychologist*, 1962, *17*, 475–483.

Hunt, J. McV. *Intelligence and experience*. New York: Ronald Press, 1961.

Irvine, S. H. Testing abilities and attainments in Africa. *British Journal of Educational Psychology*, 1966, *35*, 24–32.

McNemar, Q. Lost: Our intelligence? Why? *American Psychologist*, 1964, *19*, 871–882.

Miller, G. A., Galanter, E., & Pribram, K. H. *Plans and the structure of behavior*. New York: Holt, 1960.

Piaget, J. *The psychology of intelligence*. London: Routledge & Kegan Paul, 1950.

Prothro, E. T. *Child-rearing in the Lebanon*. Cambridge: Harvard Univer. Press, 1961.

Schaefer, E. S., & Bayley, N. Maternal behavior, child behavior and their intercorrelations from infancy through adolescence. *Monographs of the Society for Research in Child Development*, 1963, *28*, No. 87.

Schwarz, P. A. *Aptitude tests for use in the developing nations*. Pittsburgh, Pa.: American Institute for Research, 1961.

Sears, R. R., Maccoby, E. E., & Levin, H. *Patterns of child rearing*. Evanston, Ill.: Row, Peterson, 1957.

Spitz, R. A. Hospitalism: An inquiry into the genesis of psychiatric conditions in early childhood. *Psychoanalytic Studies of Children*, 1945, *1*, 55–74.

Stott, D. H. Interaction of heredity and environment in regard to "Measured Intelligence." *British Journal of Educational Psychology*, 1960, *30*, 95–102.

Thomson, G. H. *The factorial analysis of human ability*. London: Univer. London Press, 1939.

Vernon, P. E. The assessment of children. In University of London Institute of Education, *Studies in education*. Vol. 7. London: Evans, 1955. Pp. 189–215.

Vernon, P. E. Educational testing and test-form factors. (Res. Bull. 58–3) Princeton, N. J.: Educational Testing Service, 1958.

Vernon, P. E. *The structure of human abilities*. (2nd ed.) London: Methuen, 1961.

Vernon, P. E. Intellectual development in non-technological societies. In G. Nielsen (Ed.), *Proceedings of the XIV International Congress of Applied Psychology*. Vol. 3. *Child and education*. Copenhagen: Munksgaard, 1962. Pp. 94–105.

Vernon, P. E. Environmental handicaps and intellectual development. *British Journal of Educational Psychology*, 1965, 35, pt. 1, pp. 9–20; pt. 2, pp. 117–126.

Whiting, J. W. M., & Whiting, B. B. Anthropological study of child rearing. In P. H. Mussen, *Handbook of research methods in child development*. New York: Wiley, 1960. Ch. 27.

Witkin, H. A., Dyk, R. B., Faterson, H. F., Goodenough, D. R., & Karp, S. A. *Psychological differentiation: Studies of development*. New York: Wiley, 1962.

Witkin, H. A., Lewis, H. B., Hertzmann, M., Machover, K., Meissner, P. B., & Wapner, S. *Personality through perception*. New York: Harper, 1954.

Index

Index